THE *American* Presidency

THE *American*

Presidency

An Intellectual History

Forrest McDonald

UNIVERSITY PRESS OF KANSAS

Published by the University Press of
Kansas (Lawrence, Kansas 66049),
which was organized by the Kansas
Board of Regents and is operated
and funded by Emporia State
University, Fort Hays State
University, Kansas State University,
Pittsburg State University, the
University of Kansas, and Wichita
State University

Library of Congress
Cataloging-in-Publication Data

McDonald, Forrest.
    The American presidency : an
intellectual history / Forrest
McDonald.
        p.   cm.
    Includes index.
    ISBN 0–7006–0652–1 (alk.
paper)
    1. Presidents—United States—
History.   I. Title.
JK511.M34   1994
353.03'13'09—dc20   93–30235

Printed in the United States
of America

10 9 8 7 6 5 4 3

Contents

Preface

This book originated in a political controversy that I wanted to understand but did not want to become involved in—namely, whether the enormous growth of the responsibilities vested in the American presidency has been necessary, practical, or desirable. The subject intrigued me partly because of the many years I have spent studying the origins and early implementation of the constitutional system but also because of the striking reversal of ideological positions concerning the presidency that has taken place in recent decades.

Beginning with the New Deal, scholars and politicians of a liberal disposition, which usually but not invariably meant Democrats, strongly favored the aggrandizement of the presidency at the expense of the Congress and the Supreme Court. Those who leaned the other way, conservative and/or Republican, favored reducing the power of the executive—by strengthening the Congress and the Court if it could be done in no other way. Both sides adhered to their positions through the Eisenhower years—even though partisan self-interest might have suggested a change of tunes since Eisenhower was, at least in comparison to his immediate predecessors, a conservative—and they continued to hold fast to their positions through Lyndon Johnson's Great Society and until 1968.

Then came the reaction against what was generally perceived as excesses by the Johnson and Nixon administrations, and a crossover began. Epitomizing the liberal change in attitudes was the publication in 1973 of *The Imperial Presidency* by Arthur Schlesinger, Jr., who had long been among the most eloquent champions of an active presidency. Almost simultaneously, the Democratic-controlled Congress began to reassert powers, especially in regard to fiscal policy and the conduct of foreign relations, which had over the course of time gravitated toward the executive branch. Upon the election of Ronald Reagan (together with a continued Democratic monopoly of power in the House of Representatives) almost all Republicans and many conservatives came to believe that presidential power was a pretty good thing after all. Thus, I set out to build upon my earlier research, study the voluminous literature on the presidency, and see if I could resolve the controversy in a reasonably objective fashion that reflected the historical record.

It became evident, however, that the question could not be answered unless I were willing to write a polemic on one side or the other, and that I refused to do. Something else became evident as well: Vast as the body of writing on the presidency is, there has been no satisfactory general history of the office in modern times. Histories of particular presidencies are abundant, and many of them are excellent; studies of aspects of the presidency, from its budgetary and war-making functions to its image making, are plentiful, and again many are of high quality; but of survey histories of the presidency, there are none.

I have attempted here to fill that gap. Perhaps what I have written can best be described as a history of the idea of the presidency—how it was born, how it was initially implemented, how it has evolved, and what it has become through practice. I offer no technical constitutional or theoretical analysis of recent developments in the office; I leave that to political scientists and legal scholars though I believe I have provided them with a good deal to chew on. I have tried to maintain a neutral stance. I admire the presidency as an institution, have the highest esteem for the men who created it, and have great regard for some of those who have personified it. But I am not sanguine about its future and do not see how anyone who lived through the 1992 presidential election could be. I offer, however, no prescriptions for salvaging the office, only an account of how it came to be what it is.

CHAPTER I

Introduction

The presidency of the United States is often described as the most powerful office in the world. In one sense the description is accurate, for even casual decisions made in the White House can affect the lives of millions of people. But power is not merely the capacity to influence the course of events; any madman with a gun can do that. Rather, power is the ability to exert one's will with more or less predictable results, to command action, to cause desired outcomes. In that basic sense, the president has but limited formal power, and what he has is restrained by the countervailing power of Congress, the courts, the bureaucracy, popular opinion, the news media, and state and local governments. What presidents do have is awesome responsibilities combined with unique opportunities to persuade others to do their bidding—opportunities enhanced by the possibility of dispensing favors, by the mystique of presidential power, and by the aura of monarchy that surrounds the president.

In truth, presidential power is complex and ambiguous, traits that stem from the constitutional provisions for the office. Article 2 of the Constitution declares unequivocally that "the executive Power shall be vested in a President of the United States"; but in sharp contrast to Article 1, which specifies in meticulous detail what the legislative powers are to be and how they are to be exercised, the executive article is imprecise, even muddled. To be sure, some of the president's powers are enumerated: He is made commander in chief of the armed forces, and he is authorized to grant pardons and reprieves, to veto legislation, and (with the consent of the Senate) to make treaties and appoint judges and ambassadors. Yet many of the traditional executive powers—or, rather, those of the crowned heads of Europe, which is not entirely the same thing—are shared by the president and one or both houses of Congress. Other historically executive powers, such as the powers to coin money and to declare war, are vested exclusively in Congress.

In construing any law, including an organic law such as the Constitution, the obvious first step is to look at the meaning of the operative words. "Executive" and "execute" derive from the Latin *ex sequor,* meaning variously "to follow out," "to carry out," or "to punish." By implication, if the president's power is executive only, his function is simply to carry out or to execute what someone else wills to be done: The president has no will of his own. Such a construction is implicit in the second earliest (1430) use of the word "execute" cited by the *Oxford English Dictionary:* "to execute the biddying of the Kying."[1] It is also suggested by the language of Article 2, Section 3, charging the president to "take Care that the Laws be faithfully executed." "The Law," like "the Kying," bids; the president carries out that bidding.

There are, however, serious problems with such a strict construction on the interpretation of presidential power. One is that "the Laws" the president is to execute are not only those passed by Congress; in addition to statutes, the Constitution expressly recognizes as law all treaties, the Constitution itself, and the law of nations. Recognition of the law of nations is tantamount to recognition of an unwritten natural law, the execution of which provides considerable room for presidential discretion. Moreover, even the most carefully written laws cannot provide for every contingency, and the executive authority must necessarily extend into the interstices. Most impor-

---

1. *The Compact Edition of the Oxford English Dictionary,* 2 vols. (Oxford, Eng., 1979), 1:921. The president has a negative will, of course, in the veto, but that is a share in the legislative power, not a purely executive power.

tantly, presidential power also arises from what Thomas Jefferson referred to as the law of *salus populi*. "A strict observance of the written laws," he wrote, "is doubtless *one* of the high duties of a good citizen, but it is not *the highest*." The highest is the law of self-preservation, applicable to states as well as to individuals, which sometimes makes it "a duty in officers of high trust, to assume authorities beyond the law." To jeopardize the safety of the "very high interests" of the country "by a scrupulous adherence to written law, would be to lose the law itself . . . thus absurdly sacrificing the end to the means."[2]

Here we approach a central dilemma of constitutional government. It is vital, for the safety and well being of the nation, that there be a chief executive officer who can, when circumstances warrant it, operate outside or above the law. Yet it is dangerous as well, hence the need for restraints and limits on presidential authority. The dilemma is this: Though the restraints and limits are necessary, they are not, in the nature of things, susceptible to delineation and definition.

The eighteenth-century Americans who established the presidency had at least two ways of determining whether a given course of presidential action was acceptable. One was described by James Madison in *Federalist* 51: "Ambition must be made to counteract ambition,"

---

2. Jefferson to John B. Colvin, Sept. 20, 1810, in *Thomas Jefferson: Writings,* ed. Merrill D. Peterson (New York, 1984), 1231–1234. Americans were familiar with this doctrine but skeptical about it. Most were more concerned about the question of who determined the necessity or higher interest that superseded law. James Otis, "The Rights of the British Colonies Asserted and Proved" (Boston, 1764), wrote: "*Salus populi suprema lex esto* is of the law of nature and part of that grand charter given the human race . . . by the only monarch in the universe who has a clear and indisputable right to *absolute* power, because he is the *only* One who is *omniscient*" (in *Pamphlets of the American Revolution 1750–1776,* ed. Bernard Bailyn [Cambridge, MA, 1965], 424). Similarly, Daniel Dulany, "Considerations on the Propriety of Imposing Taxes in the British Colonies" (Annapolis, 1765), wrote: "On some emergencies the King, by the constitution, hath an absolute power to provide for the safety of the state, to take care, like a Roman dictator, *ne quid detrimenti capiat respublica,* and this power is not specifically annexed to the monarchy by any express law; it necessarily results from the end and nature of government. But who would infer from this that the King in every instance or upon every occasion can, upon the principles of the constitution, exercise this supreme power?" (ibid., 620–621). For the Constitution's express recognition of the law of nations, see Article 1, Section 8, para. 10.

which is to say that political institutions must be so arranged as to make it in the self-interest of everyone else to resist encroachments by the executive. If the president cannot overcome such resistance, his proposed actions are ipso facto unacceptable. This realistic—or cynical—reliance upon the baser instincts of humans was reinforced by the second determinant, a force that is less tangible but no less real: the sanction of custom, usage, and history.

It is the aim of this book to explicate what have, over the years, been considered the legitimate perimeters of presidential action. Toward that end, the work is divided into three parts: the roots, the establishment, and the evolution of the office. Part One, "Roots," begins, not with the creation of the presidency, but with what underlay it. The Framers had a conceptual problem. They sought to design a form of government known as "mixed," compounded of the three classical, simple forms—government by the one (monarchy), the few (aristocracy), and the many (democracy). The construction of a genuine mixed system was, according to some eminent political theorists— Jean Bodin, for instance—theoretically impossible, and even if it were theoretically possible another obstacle stood in the way.[3] After 1776 monarchy was anathema to most Americans; thus the Framers had to devise an institutional substitute for the crown. And yet almost everything they knew about government by the one, in a mixed or in a simple polity, was derived from the examples of kings.

Their grasp of that subject, however, was awesome in its range and depth, and if we are to understand how they used it to fashion an institution unprecedented under the sun, we must survey the relevant sources of their learning. Five chapters are devoted to exploring those sources: one concerning the great English commentators on the constitution and laws of England whose works we know the Framers read; another on the political philosophers with whose works they were demonstrably familiar; a third on historians, ancient and contemporary, whose writings were in common circulation in eighteenth-century America; a fourth on the colonial experience with

---

3. Jean Bodin, *The Six Bookes of a Commonweale: A Facsimile Reprint of the English Translation of 1606,* ed. Kenneth Douglas McRae (Cambridge, MA, 1962; orig. 1576), bk. 2, chap. 1, pp. 183–197.

executive power; and a fifth on the Revolutionary experience. It is important to observe that their understanding of these matters might or might not square with that of later scholarship. Their notions about the collapse of the Roman Republic or the English constitutional struggles of the seventeenth century, for example, vary in many ways from what is now known (or thought) about those events. Current knowledge, however, is irrelevant, for the purpose of the exercise is to understand as clearly as possible the ideas the Framers could have derived about executive power from the sources available to them.

Once that terrain has been explored, we turn to Part Two, the establishment of the presidency, which consists of four chapters—one each on the Constitutional Convention, the contests over ratification, the presidency of George Washington, and the presidency of Thomas Jefferson (with a passing review of Jefferson's Republican successors). As we shall see, the establishment of the presidency did not end with the writing and ratification of the Constitution, for the Framers deliberately sketched Article 2 in broad strokes, leaving the early occupants of the executive branch to fill in the details. They hoped, albeit somewhat uneasily, that George Washington (whom everyone expected to be the first president) could establish precedents that would invest the office with sufficient vigor and yet leave it safe to entrust to successors. They were somewhat remiss about providing the president with advisers: No cabinet was established, the president was authorized only to "require the Opinion, in writing, of the principal Officer in each of the executive Departments," and the Senate was vaguely charged with giving the president "advice and consent" in certain matters. Soliciting the opinions of the Supreme Court was not forbidden, and the Court might have evolved into an advisory council. No provision (except impeachment) was made for the removal of presidential appointees; and Alexander Hamilton and others thought that oversight, if it was an oversight, opened the way for the evolution of a ministerial system on the English model with the president serving as a passive, symbolic monarchy. Again it was problematic whether the method of electing the president, adopted at nearly the last minute of the convention as an experimental compromise, would prove workable in practice; even if it did, some method for choosing candidates for the office would have to be devised. It was not for a long time that these and other questions would be answered. Thus, careful attention is paid to the precedents and practices established by the early presidents, especially Washington and Jefferson.

Part Three traces the evolution of the presidency from Andrew Jackson's time to the present. It is organized topically in terms of general clusters of powers and relationships: one chapter on the president and the law, one on the president and administration, two on the relations between president and Congress in regard to legislation and the conduct of foreign affairs, and one on the president as myth and symbol. The work concludes with a brief analysis of the enormous gap between what has come to be expected of presidents and what they can reasonably hope to accomplish.

Such an inquiry will indicate how it happened that, though the presidency has expanded beyond anything imagined by its creators, it—unlike Congress and the judiciary—remains functionally true to the original design. The inquiry may also indicate how it happened that, though the powers of the office have sometimes been grossly abused, though the presidency has become almost impossible to manage, and though the caliber of the people who have served as chief executive has declined erratically but persistently from the day George Washington left office, the presidency has been responsible for less harm and more good, in the nation and in the world, than perhaps any other secular institution in history.

PART One

Roots

The Framers of the Constitution were, for the most part, intensely practical men who were skeptical, even contemptuous, of abstract schemes of political theory. Nonetheless, the invention of the presidency was an idea, a construct of the imagination that—in the absence of a model to copy—was of necessity built of other ideas. Some of these other ideas arose from personal experience in government, business, and military service; most, again of necessity, were derived from the abstract symbols that constitute the printed word.

From a variety of sources, modern scholars have been able to learn what the Framers read, or rather what was available for them to read. Determining the precise content of what any individual did read, and what parts of it stuck in the memory, is considerably less certain. Sometimes speakers in the Constitutional Convention cited historians or philosophers or the Bible as authority for their observations, but that was not the norm. As a rule, they spoke as if every word they uttered was original, and if modern readers of their speeches and arguments have no way of knowing better, they might assume that these utterances were in fact original.

But we do have ways of knowing better. The key is suggested in a delightful but revealing little essay on plagiarism that Henry Fielding wrote as the introduction to one of the books of *Tom Jones*. When one lifted passages from obscure authors, Fielding declared, one was obliged to cite the author, but when one quoted from a source that every educated person knew or was presumed to know, it was a compliment to both the author and the reader not to mention the source. Conversely, to write or say something that was (or should have been) familiar to all and then to add that the words came from Shakespeare or the Bible or whatever was to insult the audience and diminish the author's fame.

Many instances of eighteenth-century Americans' quoting or paraphrasing, without attribution, the various sources summarized in Part One are to be found in the footnotes to both Part One and Part Two. It may be helpful, however, to offer a few examples here. On August 15, 1787, in a debate about the veto power at the Constitutional Convention, Gouverneur Morris made a point by dropping the cryptic line, "The Ephori of Sparta became in the end absolute." He offered not a word of clarification, but we must assume his listeners knew enough Greek history to understand what he meant. A month or so earlier, James Wilson had moved that the president be chosen by electors taken by lot from the members of Congress. Everyone recognized, though no one said, that the idea rather obviously came from the example of ancient Rome. If any purpose could be served by doing so, one could narrow Morris's and Wilson's probable sources to a handful of authors. (Similarly, when Wilson, discussing Shays' Rebellion on the eve of the convention, said, "We walked on ashes concealing fire beneath our feet," his audience understood that the line came from Horace.)

Again, on July 21, concerning a proposal to join the executive and the judiciary in the exercise of the veto, James Madison, Wilson, Nathaniel Gorham, Oliver Ellsworth, George Mason, Caleb Strong, Gouverneur Morris, Luther Martin, Elbridge Gerry, and John Rutledge spoke at length; the entire discussion revolved around the teachings of Montesquieu, but no one mentioned him by name. Yet again, on the numerous occasions on which a delegate made a biblical reference, he might or might not mention the source. On June 28, for example, Benjamin Franklin referred to the fall of a sparrow and to the builders of the Tower of Babel, and he rather condescendingly cited "the sacred writings"; but when Gouverneur Morris spoke of "loaves and fishes" on July 2 and John Dickinson spoke of a "Shibboleth," on August 13, they did not. I am not nearly learned enough to catch all such references. When Madison records John Rutledge as saying on August 13 that a certain proposed restriction was "but a mere tub to the whale," I recognize that the line comes from Jonathan Swift's "A Tale of a Tub"; but the source of the lines quoted by Morris the next day—"talking Lords who dare not face the foe" and "entrenched in parchment to the teeth," which Madison put in quotation marks—are beyond my ken. Even so, I can recognize enough of the references to feel confident that the Framers were thoroughly familiar with the sources discussed in the chapters constituting Part One.

Two more prefatory observations need to be made. One pertains especially to Chapters 2 through 5, on the works of English legal commentators, political philosophers, and historians that were available to the Framers. Sometimes those sources contain inaccuracies (or, in the case of philosophers, poor translations), but I am not concerned with those shortcomings: The object of Part One is not to correct the Framers' understanding but to know as much as possible of what they knew so as to understand what they had to draw upon in creating the executive branch of the American government. The other point is closely related. I have made no effort to summarize or to analyze everything the Framers could learn about English constitutional development or the history of government among the ancient Jews, Greeks, and Romans; rather, I have concentrated only on those aspects of the subjects that directly or tangentially shed light on the question of executive power.

CHAPTER **2**

The Great Legal Commentators

The obvious model available to the creators of the American presidency was that of the crown of England. By the time of the American founding, the English had evolved a form of limited monarchy that was both stable and consistent with ordered liberty. Most members of the Philadelphia convention of 1787 warmly admired the "mixed" English system; Alexander Hamilton went so far as to assert that in regard to executive power, the "English model was the only good one."[1]

It had not always been thus. For many centuries prior to the eighteenth, England's history had been pockmarked by regicides and usurpations, by seasons of tyranny followed by times of virtual anarchy. The one and the few—the king and the barons—were locked in repeated conflicts; later the many—the commons—joined the fray. Within the broadly agreed-upon confines of monarchy, one or another enjoyed a short-lived supremacy. The turbulence was not, however, random. English history moved, albeit erratically, from a medieval kingship to a thoroughly mixed constitution.

The Framers of the United States Constitution were familiar with

---

1. *The Records of the Federal Convention of 1787,* ed. Max Farrand, 4 vols. (New Haven, CT, 1937), 1:289 (Madison's Notes, June 18).

that development, partly from a generalized knowledge of English history but more particularly from the great commentators on English law and constitutional custom. As it happened, most of the commentators whom American lawyers routinely studied—including Henry Bracton of the thirteenth century, Sir John Fortescue of the fifteenth, and Sir Edward Coke and Matthew Hale of the seventeenth, though not Sir William Blackstone of the eighteenth—had penned their works during times of severe constitutional crisis in England. Preparing for the bar in America therefore educated lawyers in the history of the British monarchy, and nearly two-thirds of the delegates to the Philadelphia convention had had such educations.

Formidable obstacles prevented the Framers from following the British model directly, of course. As Charles Pinckney pointed out, unnecessarily, during the convention, Americans had a different history from the English: Britain contained "three orders of people distinct in their situation, their possessions & their principles," namely royalty, peers, and people, whereas "the U. States contain but one order."[2] Yet if the Americans could not copy the English system, they could not entirely escape its influence, either.

———— The oldest treatise on English law still being studied in the eighteenth century, Bracton's *De Legibus et Consuetudinibus Angliae,* had been written during the so-called Baron's War led by Simon de Montfort against Henry III. In 1258 the rebellious barons forced Henry to agree to the Provisions of Oxford, which established an indirectly elected king's council subject to baronial control and compelled him to meet regularly with a Great Council. When that settlement collapsed, civil war broke out. Bracton's work (1259) was written in the midst of all this; his authority was a collection of several thousand court cases that he had gathered in his capacity as a judge on the *coram rege,* predecessor of the privy council and the Court of the King's Bench.[3]

2. Ibid., 1:398–401 (Madison's Notes, June 25).

3. *Bracton on the Laws and Customs of England,* ed. George E. Woodbine, trans. with revisions and notes Samuel E. Thorne, 4 vols. (Cambridge, MA, 1968); vol. 2 contains *De Legibus.* Donald S. Lutz, *A Preface to American Political Theory* (Lawrence,

If Bracton is read selectively, he appears to be self-contradictory; he can seem to be a "blockhead," as Charles McIlwain put it. Indeed, during the constitutional struggle that attended the reigns of James I and Charles I, advocates of absolute monarchy and champions of parliamentary supremacy could and did quote Bracton freely in support of their positions.[4]

On the one hand, Bracton insisted that kings ruled by divine right and were the vicars of God. The king "has no equal within his realm." Since "no writ runs against him," he cannot be commanded to do anything. He can be asked "to correct and amend" his ways, but "if he does not, it is punishment enough for him that he awaits God's vengeance. No one may presume to question his acts, much less contravene them." Elsewhere, Bracton wrote that "neither justices nor private persons ought or can dispute concerning royal charters and royal acts" and that "no one can pass judgment on a charter or an act of the king, so as to make void the king's act." Moreover, he cited the maxim of Ulpian, one of the principal authors of the Justinian Code, *quod principi placet legis habet vigorem*—"whatever pleases the prince has the force of law."[5]

On the opposite hand, Bracton insisted that the king was bound by law, which in England (and, he said, only there) included the unwritten law enshrined in custom. And despite the citation of Ulpian, Bracton declared that the law was not merely the king's will, "but what has been rightly decided with the counsel of his magnates, deliberation and consultation having been had thereon, the king giving it *auctoritas*." The king was also restrained precisely because he was the vicar of God, his power being "that of *jus,* not *injuria*." The power of *injuria* "is from the devil, not from God, and the king will be the minister of him whose work he performs."

KS, 1992), 159–164, does not include Bracton in his list of "European Works Read and Cited by the American Founding Generation," but see *The Law Practice of Alexander Hamilton, Documents and Commentary,* ed. Julius Goebel, Jr., 2 vols. (New York, 1964, 1969), 1:853, for Hamilton's copy of the 1569 edition.

4. Charles H. McIlwain, *Constitutionalism Ancient and Modern* (Ithaca, NY, 1947), 173.

5. Bracton, *De Legibus,* 33, 305; McIlwain, *Constitutionalism,* 70, 72.

Bracton added that law must have "the general agreement of the *res publica*" and that the king "is called *rex* not from reigning but from ruling well, since he is a king as long as he rules well but a tyrant when he oppresses by violent domination the people entrusted to his care." He must therefore "temper his power by law, which is the bridle of power."[6]

The confusion is readily dispelled. As McIlwain pointed out long ago, Bracton depicted royal powers as being of two distinct kinds, those pertaining to the governance (*gubernaculum*) of the realm and those pertaining to jurisdiction (*jurisdictio*). In regard to the former the king's power is absolute and "not fit for the tongue of any lawyer." Comprehended in this power were routine administration, the granting of charters, and most importantly controlling "those who would rise in revolt and disturb the peace of the realm." In the matter of jurisdiction the king meted out justice, attributing to each man what was his own by right, redressing private or public wrongs and protecting private rights. Here, the king was bound entirely by the laws; the fundamental principle, defined classically in the twenty-

6. Bracton, *De Legibus,* 305. This qualification of the absolute or divine right of kings was echoed repeatedly by colonial American writers. See, for example, Jonathan Mayhew, "Concerning Unlimited Submission and Nonresistance to the Higher Powers," in *Pamphlets of the American Revolution,* ed. Bernard Bailyn (Cambridge, MA, 1965), 221–223, 226–227, 232, 239; James Otis, "The Rights of the British Colonies Asserted and Proved" (ibid., 424–425); Abraham Williams, "An Election Sermon, 1762," in *American Political Writing during the Founding Era 1760–1805,* ed. Charles S. Hyneman and Donald S. Lutz, 2 vols. (Indianapolis, IN, 1983), 1:7, 11–12; Daniel Shute, "An Election Sermon, 1768" (ibid., 1:112); John Tucker, "An Election Sermon, 1771" (ibid., 1:161–165); Gad Hitchcock, "An Election Sermon" (ibid., 1:285). Hitchcock's phraseology draws on religion: "The great end of a ruler's exaltation is the happiness of the people over whom he presides; and his promoting it, the sole ground of their submission to him. In this rational point of view, St. Paul, that great patron of liberty, speaking of the design of magistracy, hath thought fit to place it—'he is the minister of God to thee for good' [Rom. 13:4]"; others used Lockean social-contract theory as a base; all regarded the executive as servant, not master, whose powers depend on executing well. "Essays by a Farmer" (probably John Francis Mercer), in *The Complete Anti-Federalist,* ed. Herbert J. Storing, 7 vols. (Chicago, 1981), 5:12, quotes Bracton as "clear and concise . . . all are subject to the King, but the King is subject to the law."

ninth chapter of Magna Carta, was that the king could not arbitrarily abridge the prescriptive rights of any free subject but must proceed in accordance with the law of the land.[7]

The power of *jurisdictio,* though bound by law, was no less fully the king's. But, said Bracton, "since he cannot unaided determine all causes and jurisdictions, that his labour may be lessened, the burden [is] divided among many." That is, the king "must select from his realm wise and God-fearing men . . . to whom there may be referred doubtful questions and complaints of wrongdoing"—in other words, judges. Judges were the king's ministers, acting under the king's authority but not by his will, even though the king appointed and could remove the judges as he pleased.[8]

In sum, the state—if we may use an inapposite modern term in reference to a thirteenth-century set of arrangements—consisted of the king, counseled for certain purposes by his barons, and of the king's law courts. After 1265, it sometimes included counsel by representatives of the burgesses and knights of the shire, again for limited purposes set by the king. In this restricted sense, by the mid-fourteenth century, when the summons of the Commons became usual, the state can be loosely said to have included the Parliament.

———— The next commentator on the English crown whose works were studied in eighteenth-century America was Sir John Fortescue. Fortescue was chief justice of the King's Bench during the reign of Henry VI and was titular chancellor in exile during the 1460s, after Henry had been ousted by the Yorkist Edward IV. During that time he wrote three books. *On the Governance of England* is said to be the first treatise on the subject written in English ("there bith ii kyndes of kyngdomes, of the wich that on is a lordship called in laten dominium regale"). Another was a substantial work about natural law. The third and best known, *De Laudibus Legum Angliae* ("In Praise of the Laws of England"), was written to introduce Henry's son and heir, Prince Edward, to the constitution and laws of the

7. McIlwain, *Constitutionalism,* 83, 85–86, 177, and passim. The flavor of the term *gubernaculum* is conveyed by the fact that it also meant "rudder" or "helm."

8. Bracton, *De Legibus,* 306–307.

kingdom; it is in the form of a dialogue between the chancellor and the prince.[9]

De Laudibus was immensely popular and influential. Between its first publication in 1546 and the appearance of John Selden's edition in 1616, it went through nine printings, seven of them in English. Like Bracton's work, it was extensively cited as authority by both monarchists and parliamentarians during the reigns of James I and Charles I. It continued to be read throughout that century and the next, partly because it seemed to place the roots of the Glorious Revolution and of subsequent constitutional developments in remote antiquity. Significantly, it was reprinted (in English) at the height of the tension between crown and colonies in 1775.[10]

De Laudibus formulated three sets of ideas that, when subsequent writers brought them to maturity, became cardinal tenets of the political credo of late eighteenth-century Americans. The first was the myth of the ancient constitution. Drawing upon the essentially fictitious *Historia Regum Britanniae* of Geoffrey of Monmouth (ca. 1136), Fortescue solemnly assured the prince that the English kingdom had been established in ancient times by Brutus, the great-grandson of Aeneas, founder of Rome. At the outset laws were agreed upon, and even though England was later ruled by the Romans, then the Britons again, then the Saxons, the Danes, again the Saxons, and finally the Normans, "throughout the period of these nations and their kings, the realm has been continually ruled by the same customs, as it is now." The laws of no other kingdom in the world, Fortescue asserted, were "so venerable for their antiquity." When the myth of the ancient constitution was developed more fully by Sir Edward Coke in the seventeenth century and given some twists by Bolingbroke in the eighteenth, it would appeal powerfully to Revolutionary Americans, who saw themselves as the restorers and defenders of that constitution.[11]

9. *Sir John Fortescue on the Governance of England,* ed. Charles Plummer (Oxford, Eng., 1885), 109; Sir John Fortescue, *De Laudibus Legum Angliae,* ed. and trans. S. B. Chrimes (Cambridge, Eng., 1949).

10. See Thomas G. Barnes, *Introduction,* a separate small volume published with the Legal Classics Library edition of *De Laudibus* (Birmingham, AL, 1984), 4 and passim.

11. Chrimes, ed., *De Laudibus,* 33, 39–40, 158n. For an excellent analysis of Ameri-

The second of Fortescue's ideas to take deep root in America was a medieval commonplace, that of the contractual theory of the origin of government and its companion, the idea that every just government derives its legitimacy from the consent of the governed. His was no tentative formulation, based like Bracton's on divine right. Fortescue declared that kingdoms arose in only two ways: through force, in which case they were absolute, as in France, or through compact, in which case they were limited, as in England. In *De Laudibus,* after the chancellor instructs the prince in this matter, the prince recapitulates the lesson, saying that "no people ever formed themselves into a kingdom by their own agreement and thought, unless in order to possess safer than before both themselves and their own [property], which they feared to lose." The king could not deprive the people "of their means," for it was "to avoid the loss" of their property "as well as to protect their bodies" that they submitted "of their own will to the government of a king." The king "is not able himself to change the laws without the assent of his subjects nor to burden an unwilling people with strange imposts, so that, ruled by laws that they themselves desire, they freely enjoy their properties, and are despoiled neither by their own king nor any other."[12]

Fortescue's third message for eighteenth-century American readers was somewhat more involved. In *De Laudibus* he described the kingdom of England with the phrase *dominium politicum et regale.* Even in *The Governance of England* he employed that Latin terminology. On the face of things, it would appear that he meant much the same thing that Bracton had meant by *jurisdictio* and *gubernaculum,* namely that in certain areas the king's power was restricted by law and in others it was absolute, the difference being that according to For-

---

can attitudes toward the English constitution and their rights as Englishmen, see John Phillip Reid, *Constitutional History of the American Revolution: The Authority of Rights* (Madison, WI, 1986).

12. Chrimes, ed., *De Laudibus,* 25, 31–35. See also Quentin Skinner, *The Foundations of Modern Political Thought,* 2 vols. (Cambridge, Eng., 1978), 2:163ff., pointing out that the consensual basis of legitimate policy was "a scholastic commonplace, one which the followers of Ockham no less than Aquinas had always emphasized," and that sixteenth-century Thomists, especially Francesco Suárez, carried it "to a new peak of development."

tescue Parliament, representing both lords and commons and therefore the "whole people," had a more explicit voice in declaring what the law was. This impression is buttressed by the similarity of Fortescue's description of the workings of law courts to Bracton's: "It will not be expedient for you to investigate precise points of the law by the exertion of your own reason, but these should be left to your judges and advocates. . . . In fact, you will render judgements better through others than by yourself, for none of the kings of England is seen to give judgement by his own lips, yet all the judgements of the realm are his, though given through others."[13]

In 1885, however, the editor of the more or less definitive edition of Fortescue's *Governance of England,* the Reverend Charles Plummer, interpreted Fortescue's constitution quite differently in his introduction. Plummer read *politicum* to mean "republican" and saw Fortescue as foreshadowing the kind of government that emerged in the eighteenth century—a mixed government of king-in-parliament that was unlimited, sovereign, able to command anything not physically impossible.[14]

The best of modern scholarship—including the works of McIlwain, S. B. Chrimes, J. G. A. Pocock, and Michael Mendle—rejects Plummer's interpretation decisively. Chrimes says that "Fortescue's theory of regal and political domination is in no sense a theory of constitutional monarchy. It is essentially a theory in line with the typical medieval theory of the kingship which was not tyranny, of the king ruling according to law"; he adds that for Fortescue statutes are "purely declaratory of law which exists already." Pocock finds it inaccurate to call the *dominium politicum et regale* a mixed monarchy; rather, the two "persisted in association but not in admixture." Mendle writes that "while Fortescue is rightfully a source of the idea of limited royal government, he was not a proponent of mixed government properly so called." Rather, his mixture "was of laws, not men; his fundamental distinction was bipartite rather than tripartite."[15]

13. Chrimes, ed., *De Laudibus,* 23.

14. Plummer, ed., *Fortescue on the Governance of England,* introduction.

15. Chrimes is quoted in R. W. K. Hinton, "English Constitutional Theories from Sir John Fortescue to Sir John Eliot," *English Historical Review* 75 (1960):413n.; J. G. A.

But the best modern scholarship was not available to eighteenth-century Americans, and the commentary that was available accorded with Plummer's view. In 1737 an Englishman, Francis Gregor, published a new translation (using John Selden's Latin text, not an original manuscript) that was reprinted in 1741 and again in 1775 and was thus the version that Americans read. Gregor demonstrably took some liberties with the text. Where Fortescue's Latin read *"Hii sunt fructus quos parit regimen politicum et regale"*—clearly "these are the fruits which the political and regal government yields"—Gregor rendered the sentence as "these are the advantages consequent from that *political mixed government* which obtains in *England.*" Elsewhere he had Fortescue referring to a "mixt" constitution although the original said no such thing. And Gregor made clear his meaning of mixt or mixed constitution by having Fortescue say that English statutes are made by the prince *"with the concurrent consent of the whole kingdom, by their Representatives in Parliament."* In sum, the ancient constitution about which Americans read in this bowdlerized Fortesque was a mixed form of government, and had been all along.[16]

Finally, Gregor made Fortescue's compact theory of government more pointedly "Lockean" than the original: The English people "formed themselves into a kingdom by their own compact and consent," appointing their king "to protect his subjects in their lives, properties and laws; for this very end and purpose he has the delegation of power from the people; and he has no just claim to any other power than this."[17]

——— Whatever construction be put on Fortescue, it must be remembered that he no less than Bracton was writing in a medieval con-

———

Pocock, *The Ancient Constitution and the Feudal Law: A Study of English Historical Thought in the Seventeenth Century: A Reissue with a Retrospect* (Cambridge, Eng., 1987), 306–307; Michael Mendle, *Dangerous Positions: Mixed Government, the Estates of the Realm, and the Making of the* Answer to the xix propositions (Tuscaloosa, AL, 1985), 42.

16. Chrimes, ed., *De Laudibus,* xcv, 88–89; Sir John Fortescue, *De Laudibus Legum Angliae,* trans. Francis Gregor, with notes by Andrew Amos (Cambridge, Eng., 1825; repr. of 1737, 1741, and 1775 eds.), 139.

17. Gregor, trans., *De Laudibus,* 38–41.

text in which the great men (barons and others) had powerful claims, and the king, as a practical matter, was sometimes the most potent of them, a *primus inter pares,* and sometimes rather less. Thus Bracton and Fortescue, in saying that the king was absolute in certain areas and bound by law in others, were bolstering as well as limiting the authority of the crown. During the sixteenth century, kings in western Europe, England included, generally broke the powers of the magnates and emerged as embodiments of centralized states. In England, however, the transformation took a distinctive form. The Tudors skillfully strengthened the instruments of central government—common law courts, new prerogative courts, the council—and weakened the bonds between the great men and their underlings. From the ranks of the subvassals came the gentry, to whom the Tudors readily handed control of the counties so long as the gentry followed their lead rather than that of the weakened magnates. At times this arrangement was precarious; in 1569 and in the last years of her reign Elizabeth was threatened by a resurgence of the old politics. Nevertheless, by the accession in 1603 of James I, power had been greatly centralized. But there was a catch: The resentments had been centralized as well. In particular, Parliament and the older common law courts (now the political and ideological haunts of the gentry) had become jealous enough of their roles to bestir themselves upon occasion to resist the rising force of absolutism.[18]

Before considering the writings of Sir Edward Coke, who regularly failed in the short run but in the long run proved to be the most influential of James's juristic adversaries, it is well to put the Stuarts' efforts to establish absolute monarchy in perspective. Though few eighteenth-century Americans uttered such heresies, absolute monarchy was more efficient than English-style constitutional monarchy, was probably as just, and may have been no less compatible with the security of the subjects in their lives and property. Equally important, James was more committed to absolutism in theory than in practice. He did write two books in which he argued that kings were

18. I have generally followed W. S. Holdsworth, *A History of English Law,* 7 vols. (Boston, 1921–1928), 4:200ff., 211. See also *The Tudor Constitution: Documents and Commentary,* ed. Geoffrey Elton, 2d ed. (Cambridge, Eng., 1968).

sent by God to rule and could be judged only by God, the subject being bound to obey even unjust commands "without resistance, but by sobs and tears to God"; a wicked king, he said, must be obeyed because he "is sent by God for a curse to his people, and a plague for their sinnes." Too, in an oft-quoted address to Parliament in 1610 he said that "as to dispute what God may do is blasphemy . . . so it is sedition in subjects to dispute what a king may do." But in the same address he declared that as king he was bound by God's law to protect the people and "the fundamental laws of the kingdom" and was doubly bound by his coronation oath. And though his policies elicited conflict, he was careful at all times to operate within the limits of the common law.[19]

Moreover, though Coke was for centuries lionized in England and in America as a principled champion of law and liberty against a would-be tyrant, his motives were sometimes less than high-minded. He was chief justice of the Court of Common Pleas from 1606 to 1613 and of the King's Bench from 1613 until James dismissed him three years later. The judges on those courts, the highest in the land except for the "High Court of Parliament," were compensated by the fees they collected, which were enormous. Under the Tudors, pre-rogative courts such as Admiralty, Chancery, and the Star Chamber had proved more tractable and were used in increasing numbers and kinds of cases; James I proposed to continue that practice. Thus when Coke and other common lawyers resisted him they were pro-tecting the wealth and power of what they regarded as their private turf. James recognized their motivation, perceived the threat to liberty posed by judges who usurped the law-making function, and set himself against them. The assembled judges were to "remember you are no makers of law, but interpreters of law, according to the true sense thereof; for your office is *ius dicere,* and not *ius dare*" ("to speak the law, not to give the law"). He added that their interpretations

---

19. *The Stuart Constitution, 1603–1688: Documents and Commentary,* ed. J. P. Ken-yon, 2d ed. (Cambridge, Eng., 1986), 8, 11–13 (speech to Parliament, March 21, 1610); Holdsworth, *English Law,* 6:12n.; *The Political Works of James I: Reprinted from the Edition of 1616,* ed. Charles H. McIlwain (Cambridge, MA, 1918), 67. The two books referred to in this paragraph are *The Trew Law of Free Monarchies* and *Basilikon Doron.*

must accord with common sense and reason, not just with the secrets of their craft, for "if your interpretation be such as other men which have logic and common sense understand not the reason, I will never trust such an interpretation."[20] The admonition was justified. The common law was arcane, treacherously complex, arbitrary, and replete with fictions, and its practitioners intended to keep it that way.

But precisely because Coke had the reputation he did among Americans, his views on the powers of the crown carried weight when Americans came to constitute their own executive. Coke published four volumes of *Institutes of the Lawes of England* and thirteen volumes of *Reports,* in which he systematized the principles of English law by reporting (and sometimes all but making up) precedents and cases; the last two volumes of *Reports* largely concern the prerogatives of the crown. The material is diffuse, often obscure, and regularly concerned with minutiae, but taken as a whole Coke's work can be fairly said to have been the front line in a battle to save the common law from extinction. Its guiding principle was that the king is under the law, bound by the interpretations of the common law judges, since only they could comprehend the mysteries of the immutable ancient constitution.[21]

Three sets of Coke's pronouncements in particular bore upon the creation and implementation of the American presidency. The first involved the king's relationship with the law courts. It was accepted that no writ could be served against the king, but James went further, declaring that he himself was the supreme judge, the appointed judges being his "shadows and ministers," and that "the King may, if he please, sit and judge in Westminster Hall in any Court there, and call

20. Holdsworth, *English Law,* 5:413, 524; Kenyon, ed., *Stuart Constitution,* 74ff., 84–85.

21. Kenyon, ed., *Stuart Constitution,* 86; Holdsworth, *English Law,* 5:430n. For Coke, I have used the William S. Hein 1986 facsimile reprint (Buffalo, NY, 1986) of the 1797 London printing of the second, third, and fourth parts of the *Institutes.* It should be noted that several eminent jurists, including Thomas Egerton, Viscount Ellesmere, stoutly opposed Coke in some of his attempts to curtail royal power; see *Law and Politics in Jacobean England: The Tracts of Lord Chancellor Ellesmere,* ed. Louis A. Knafla (Cambridge, Eng., 1977). Christopher Hill, *Intellectual Origins of the English Revolution* (Oxford, Eng., 1965), 250–254, contains a summary of Coke's pronouncements.

their judgment in question." Coke held to the contrary, ruling (consistently with Bracton and Fortescue) that the "king in his own person cannot judge any case, either criminal . . . or betwixt party and party." James was extremely angry and severely rebuked Coke, but in time Coke's view, the older view, prevailed. In a related matter a few years later, Coke and his fellow judges on the King's Bench set a precedent that Americans would regard as important when the bench refused (in violation of established custom and ongoing usage) to honor James's request for what amounted to an advisory opinion.[22]

A second judgment concerned the king's power to grant dispensations. It was an established principle that the crown could exempt individuals from the obligations or penalties of a law. (Lest it be thought that "the executive power of the United States" contemplated no such authority, consider that presidents have granted amnesty—immunity from prosecution—from the very beginning and have granted pardons before as well as after the judgment.) But the Tudors had overused and misused the power, particularly by granting monopolies to conduct trade that was prohibited by statute. The year before James ascended the English throne, Coke and the other judges on the Court of Common Pleas declared one such use of the dispensing power "utterly against law." Three years later the court limited the dispensing power differently, declaring it unlawful for the king to confer it on others. Significantly, that prevented the conversion of local officials (such as wool inspectors or supervisors of weights and measures) into royal officials and thereby precluded the development of a nationwide bureaucracy to regulate trade. In short, it left the portion of the executive power that was outside Westminster in the hands of the sheriffs, the local justices of the peace, and the judges of Common Pleas and King's Bench when they sat on the assize courts in the provinces.[23]

22. Prohibitions del Roy (1607), Peacham's Case (1615), *The Reports of Sir Edward Coke,* 13 parts (London, 1776), 12:63–65; Kenyon, ed., *Stuart Constitution,* 76, 80–81; Holdsworth, *English Law,* 5:430–431. James I sometimes appointed special commissions of inquiry to circumvent normal court procedures—commissions that bear a resemblance to modern special prosecutors. Charles I later extracted an advisory opinion in the Ship Money case.

23. Holdsworth, *English Law,* 4:205, 349, 358–359.

A third of Coke's pronouncements that became relevant to American president-makers pertained to royal proclamations. The extent of the prerogative power to issue proclamations having the force of law was unclear. It was generally accepted that the king could proclaim martial law or issue proclamations regarding coinage, foreign affairs, and the governance of the army and navy. But kings had used proclamations in other ways since the fifteenth century. In 1539 Parliament enacted the Statute of Proclamations, giving proclamations the force of law except in regard to life or limb and the forfeiture of property. That statute did not work well because it was to be enforced by the king's council, which was ineffective, and it was repealed during the first year of the reign of Edward VI. Though repeal was intended to curtail proclamations, it may in practice have abolished the limitations on them instead, and some proclamations were subsequently used to impinge upon property and personal liberty. When James I ascended the throne, he began to issue them to regulate an enlarged range of economic activity, such as fixing the prices of commodities not previously controlled, licensing ale houses, and prohibiting various marketing practices—much in the fashion of modern administrative law made by federal regulatory agencies. In 1610 the House of Commons complained of James's use of proclamations. The next year, in the *Case of Proclamations* Coke declared the limits upon the proclamation power: "The King cannot change any part of the common law nor create any offence by his proclamation which was not an offence before, without Parliament." It was not until after the Restoration that this principle would become generally accepted, however.[24]

———— There were observers who thought, when Coke died in 1634, that the constitutional order was already coming apart, and soon it did: civil war, the execution of the king in 1649, the commonwealth, the Protectorate of Oliver Cromwell. No model there for American president-makers, only a caution.

24. Frederic W. Maitland, *The Constitutional History of England* (Cambridge, Eng., 1926), 253–254, 256–258; *Coke Reports*, 12:74 (1611); Holdsworth, *English Law*, 4: 100–101, 296–307.

One great common lawyer lived, even thrived, through it all. Sir Matthew Hale was a man of such learning and integrity that he could defend royalists in the 1640s and then be appointed a high court judge by Cromwell and yet later be appointed lord chief justice by Charles II. He wrote voluminously, much of his writing being addressed to reconciling the changes that had taken place during his lifetime in the law as received from Coke and earlier common lawyers. His most interesting work, on the prerogatives of the king, was neither published nor circulated at the time (it was first published in 1976) and therefore is irrelevant to the study at hand. Two things may be said about it, however. Hale repeated his predecessors' view that the king's power was exercised through two different channels, which he called "jurisdiction" and "empire or command," suggesting that such duality inheres in executive authority. Moreover, Hale mentions these areas of "command" in a published treatise that became a standard manual for American lawyers, *The History of the Pleas of the Crown*, as well as in his *History of the Common Law*. The areas of command included the powers to conduct foreign relations, make war or peace, suppress insurrections, coin money, punish counterfeiters, establish weights and measures, and regulate domestic trade.[25]

Hale's important contribution to Americans' understanding of the constitutional monarchy of England lay in his reformulation of the myth of the immutable ancient constitution. Hale was at great pains to disprove (what almost no one except Thomas Hobbes asserted) the proposition that the Norman Conquest had negated the existing laws and constitution, but he admitted that changes had been numerous. It was not possible, he wrote, to know what the law was originally, but he devoted two full chapters to tracing the changes that had taken place since 1216. In "a very great measure," however,

25. Matthew Hale, *The History of the Pleas of the Crown*, 2 vols. (London, 1778 ed.); Matthew Hale, *The History of the Common Law of England* (London, 1739 ed.); *Sir Matthew Hale's The Prerogatives of the King*, ed. D. E. C. Yale (London, 1976). The powers are treated in volume 2 of *Pleas of the Crown*, chapters 10–23, all having to do with the heading "treason." See also Pocock, *Ancient Constitution*, chap. 7, and D. E. C. Yale, "Hobbes and Hale on Law, Legislation and the Sovereign," *Cambridge Law Journal* 31 (1972):121–156.

he found that since the "perfections" instituted by Edward I (1272–1307), the law "has continued the same in all succeeding Ages to this Day." (Later, he was substantially confirmed in this judgment by no less a scholar than Frederic W. Maitland.)[26]

Hale formulated an explanation of the process of change that would later win the heart of Edmund Burke. New laws and customs and usages, Hale said, were accrued "secretly and insensibly" over time so that "the Body and Gross of the Law might continue the same, and so continue the ancient Denomination that it first had." He likened the process to the flow of rivers, which, "tho they continued the same Denomination which their first stream had, yet have the Accession of divers other Streams added to them in the Tracts of their Passage which enlarge and augment them." Thus, although use and custom and judicial decisions and acts of Parliament introduced changes, "yet they being only partial and successive, we may with just Reason say, they are the same *English* Laws now, that they were 600 Years since in the general."[27]

That description had to do conceptually with the creation of the American presidency: To a people conditioned to believe that innovation in government was inherently pernicious, Hale's concept of the immutable that changes provided a rationale for changing things as a way of preserving the traditional.

————— The most influential of the great commentators—because he was studied by a large number of American public men, not just the lawyers—was Sir William Blackstone, who took Hale's formulation a step further and provided a history as well as an analysis of the British monarchy. In the concluding chapter of his magisterial four-volume *Commentaries on the Laws of England,* Blackstone provided Americans a survey of England's experience in what Harvey Mansfield has called the process of "taming the prince." In the doing, he employed a dialectical model of history according to which the ancient constitution was repeatedly overturned and as often restored,

26. Hale, *History of the Common Law,* 133–175 (quote at 163); Maitland, *Constitutional History,* 18–23.

27. Hale, *History of the Common Law,* 62. See also Pocock, *Ancient Constitution,* 148–175.

each time with a few improvements that made it "more perfect" than before, until it reached the state of perfection it had achieved when Blackstone wrote in the 1760s.[28]

Blackstone shared Hale's view that it was impossible to know what the constitution had been in remote antiquity, but he was willing to assign a time to its organization, namely the reign of Alfred the Great (871–899). Alfred, he said, undertook "a most great and necessary work, . . . no less than to new model the constitution." Even that beginning was a restoration of sorts, for Alfred had set out to and did "rebuild it on a plan that should endure for ages; and, out of it's old discordant materials, which were heaped upon each other in a vast and rude irregularity, to form one uniform and well-connected whole." He centralized administration under a "supreme magistrate, the king," in whom "all the executive authority of the law was lodged" and who dispersed justice "by distinct, yet communicating, ducts and channels." That arrangement, Blackstone wrote, lasted "for near a thousand years unchanged, from Alfred's to the present time."[29]

Then came the "Danish invasion and conquest, which introduced new foreign customs." Yet the "noble fabric" could never be permanently cast aside, and so, when the Danes were finally expelled, "the English returned to their ancient law; retaining however some few of the customs of their late visitants." It was Edward the Confessor (1042–1066) who completed the work of compiling a "uniform digest or body of laws" for the whole kingdom, "which is now known by the name of the common law." This was but "a revival of king Alfred's code, with some improvements suggested by necessity and experience." All the laws mentioned so far were the work of kings though Blackstone listed first among "the most remarkable" of these "Saxon"

28. My copy of Blackstone was published in London in 1791. Pagination in eighteenth-century editions retained in the margins the original pagination. See Jerrilyn Greene Marston, *King and Congress: The Transfer of Political Legitimacy, 1774–1776* (Princeton, NJ, 1987), 327 n.16: "The first American edition of Blackstone's *Commentaries,* in 1771–1772, had an advance subscription of 1,587 sets, a truly astonishing number." The Mansfield reference is to *Taming the Prince: The Ambivalence of Modern Executive Power* (New York, 1989).

29. Blackstone, *Commentaries,* 4:410–411.

laws the "constitution of parliaments, or rather, general assemblies of the principal and wisest men in the nation."[30]

Unlike most of his predecessors, Blackstone was not loath to describe the Norman invasion as a conquest. Indeed, he wrote that England after 1066 "groaned under as absolute a slavery, as was in the power of a warlike, an ambitious, and a politic prince to create." Moreover, it took many generations for the English "to redeem themselves and their posterity into that state of liberty, which we now enjoy." Nor was this recovery to be considered "as encroachments on the crown, and infringements on the prerogative, as some slavish and narrow-minded writers in the last century endeavoured to maintain." Rather, it was "a gradual restoration of that antient constitution, whereof our Saxon forefathers had been unjustly deprived."[31]

The restoration was completed with Magna Carta, after which, during the reign of the "English Justinian," Edward I, the law received a "sudden" new "perfection." Yet it was not long before more civil wars and usurpations followed, reminding one of David Hume's question: If the constitution were so excellent, how could it be so frequently and easily overthrown or perverted?[32]

When Blackstone dealt with the Tudor and Stuart monarchs he became most instructive for American president-makers. He praised Henry VIII for the Reformation and other achievements but deplored that "the royal prerogative was then strained to a very tyrannical and oppressive height" and that Parliament had at his bidding enacted the short-lived Statute of Proclamations. As for Elizabeth, "she was a wise and excellent princess, and loved her people," yet she increased the power of the Star Chamber, "kept her parliaments at a very awful distance," and carried the prerogative "as high as her most arbitrary predecessors." And though she refrained from abusing her

30. Ibid., 4:411–412. Jefferson records that in revising the law code of Virginia "I had only to reduce the law to its ancient Saxon condition, stripping it of all the innovations and rigorisms of subsequent times, to make it what it should be" (*The Writings of Thomas Jefferson*, vol. 5, ed. H. A. Washington [New York, 1854], 461).

31. Blackstone, *Commentaries*, 4:418–420.

32. Ibid., 4:423–425; David Hume, *Essays Moral, Political, and Literary*, ed. Thomas Hill Green and Thomas Hodge Grose, 2 vols. (1964; repr. of London, 1882 ed.), 1:108.

power, her reign was not the golden age of liberty "that we were formerly taught to believe: for, surely, the true liberty of the subject consists not so much in the gracious behaviour, as in the limited power, of the sovereign."[33]

As for the Stuarts, Blackstone's treatment was more nearly in accordance with David Hume's than with the Whig version fashionable in America. He depicted James as having used the prerogative in an "unreasonable and imprudent" fashion and having claimed "a more absolute power inherent in the kingly office than had ever been carried into practice," but he also saw James as being so "pusillanimous" that he was unable to cause much mischief. Blackstone recited the "enormities" perpetuated by Charles I, including the extortion of forced loans, arbitrary imprisonments, collecting revenues and ruling without Parliament, and otherwise straining the prerogative "not only beyond what the genius of the present times would bear, but also beyond the examples of former ages." Yet most of his actions were constitutional, despite the complaints, and besides, most of the injuries were redressed by the king in Parliament before the civil war broke out. This capitulation, however, cost Charles "the reputation of sincerity; which is the greatest unhappiness that can befal a prince." In the circumstances "popular leaders (who in all ages have called themselves the *people*)" rose to overthrow everything and "murder their sovereign."[34]

In dealing with the reign of Charles II, in which "the true balance between liberty and prerogative was happily established by law," Blackstone recited a number of instances in which "branches of the prerogative" had been "lopped off" and others "more clearly defined." The habeas corpus act, for example, limited the prerogative, as did acts restricting the pardoning power and regulating the civil list (administrative personnel). That brought Blackstone to an apparent contradiction, for if Parliament could define and even abolish

33. Blackstone, *Commentaries*, 4:433. It is not in fact true that Elizabeth increased the power of the Star Chamber, but few American readers had any way of knowing that.

34. Ibid., 4:436–438; David Hume, *The History of England*, 6 vols. (Indianapolis, IN, 1983). See also, generally, H. Trevor Colbourn, *The Lamp of Experience: Whig History and the Intellectual Origins of the American Revolution* (Chapel Hill, NC, 1965).

any given prerogative, the prerogative as such had disappeared.[35] But the contradiction was merely apparent, not real. It was true that sovereignty—which Blackstone defined as the supreme law-making power—resided in Parliament and was unlimited. Parliament could, as he put it, "do everything that is not naturally impossible." But the Parliament consisted of the king and the three estates of the realm, the lords spiritual, the lords temporal, and the commons. The king could not directly and personally initiate legislation, but no parliamentary act could become law without his approval: "The crown has not any power of *doing* wrong, but merely of *preventing* wrong from being done." Thus when the prerogative was pruned or clarified, it was with the consent of the king. (Two important remaining prerogatives included the power to "prorogue" Parliament, which adjourned a session, and the power to dissolve it, which necessitated new elections. Moreover, only the king could call Parliament into session though that power was limited by statute.)[36]

Blackstone waxed fanciful in describing the "mixed" or "balanced" constitution that established these arrangements. The "three principal ingredients of good polity," he wrote, were virtue, wisdom, and power. The commons provided the virtue, the lords the wisdom, the king the power. If sovereignty resided in any one or two of the branches (the lords spiritual and temporal sitting as a single body), the polity would lack at least one of the essential ingredients and therefore be dangerous. But since each branch could act as a negative on the other two, the state posed no threat to liberty or property even though its power was unlimited. The constitution was "so admirably tempered and compounded, that nothing can endanger or hurt it, but destroying the equilibrium of power between one branch of the legislature and the rest."[37]

35. Blackstone, *Commentaries*, 4:439.

36. Ibid., 1:150, 153, 154, 161–162, 186–188.

37. Ibid., 1:50–51. Compare the king's "Answer to the xix propositions," June 18, 1642, in Kenyon, ed., *Stuart Constitution*, 18–20. John Adams wrote in February 1773: "Many people receive different ideas from the words *legally and constitutionally*. The law has certainly established in the crown many prerogatives, by the bare exertion of which, in their utmost extent, the nation might be undone. The prerogatives of war and peace, and of pardon, for examples, among many others. Yet it would be

———— The royal prerogative, "in the exertion whereof consists the executive part of the government," was bound by law, but within that limit it was absolute. The king exercised will and discretion, and in the nature of things he must be permitted to do so, for it is impossible, "in any practical system of laws, to point out beforehand those eccentrical remedies, which the sudden emergence of national distress may dictate, and which that alone can justify." The king's "irresistible and absolute" prerogative consisted "(as Mr. Locke has well defined it) in the discretionary power of acting for the public good, where the positive laws are silent." If this power was abused, Parliament would call the king's advisers (but never the king himself) "to a just and severe account" through impeachments or prosecutions.[38]

————

absurd to say that the crown can constitutionally ruin the nation, and overturn the constitution. The British constitution is a fine, a nice, a delicate machine; and the perfection of it depends upon such complicated movements, that it is as easily disordered as the human body; and in order to act constitutionally, every one must do his duty. If the king should suffer no parliament to sit for twelve years, by reason of continual prorogations, this would be an unconstitutional exercise of prerogative. If the commons should grant no supplies for twelve years, this would be an unconstitutional exertion of their privilege. Yet the king has power legally to do one, and the commons to do the other" (*The Works of John Adams, Second President of the United States,* ed. Charles Francis Adams, 10 vols. [Freeport, NY, 1969], 3:556).

38. Blackstone, *Commentaries,* 1:243, 251–252. Blackstone defines the prerogative as "that special pre-eminence, which the king hath, over and above all other persons, and out of the ordinary course of the common law, in right of his regal dignity. It signifies, in it's etymology, (from *prae* and *rogo*) something that is required or demanded before, or in preference to, all others. And hence it follows, that it must be in it's nature singular and eccentrical; that it can only be applied to those rights and capacities which the king enjoys alone" (ibid., 1:239). *The Oxford English Dictionary,* 2 vols. (Oxford, Eng., 1979), 2:1293, lists the word as coming from the Latin *praerogativa,* "a previous choice or election; a fore-token, prognostic," deriving from the voting practice in ancient Rome. The *praerogativa* was the tribe or century that was privileged to cast its vote first in the comitia, thus presaging (and influencing) the rest of the voting. The OED notes its development in constitutional history as it came to mean "a prior, exclusive, or peculiar right or privilege," more specifically in Great Britain "the *royal prerogative,* a sovereign right (in theory) subject to no restriction." It lists the present prerogative as including "the right of sending and receiving ambassadors, of making treaties, and (theoretically) of making war and concluding peace, of conferring honours, nominating to bishoprics, and giving all commissions in the army and navy, of

Blackstone sketched out, in the space of twenty-nine pages, a description of the prerogative powers as they stood in his time. One broad set of powers had to do with the conduct of foreign relations. The king had sole power to send and receive ambassadors, to make treaties, leagues, and alliances, and to declare war and make peace. By law, his ministers were required to issue letters of marque and reprisal (permits allowing private citizens to levy war on the high seas) upon "due demand." The prerogative also included granting safe conduct to foreigners.[39]

In domestic affairs, the king's prerogative was a shadow of what it had been, but it was still formidable. Most importantly the king was commander in chief of all the armed forces, he enlisted and provided for the governance of army and navy personnel, and he had the sole power to erect forts and other defense facilities. Next came a number of powers over domestic commerce: The king designated ports of entry and export though he could not confine the limits of a port once it was established. He erected beacons, lighthouses, and sea markers. He was authorized by statute to prohibit the exportation of arms and ammunition and to prohibit people from leaving the kingdom. He could erect corporations for commercial or other purposes. He coined money and regulated its value. He established markets and fairs and had the authority to fix standards of weights and measures, though in practice Parliament set those standards.[40]

The king was the prosecutor of the law and had the power to pardon those who violated it. Blackstone's account of the origin of the pardoning power is interesting. Under "the old Gothic constitution," he wrote, the king was bound by his coronation oath to conserve the peace, and if a subject injured the person of another, the offender thereby accused the king of a species of perjury. The king, being the offended party, thus had the power not to punish. Histori-

---

choosing ministers of state, summoning Parliament, and refusing assent to a bill, of pardoning those under legal sentence," the exercise of which is limited by the rights of Parliament, the constitution, and the "general approval and support of the nation."

39. Blackstone, *Commentaries,* 1:253–259.

40. Ibid., 1:262–265, 272–279.

cally, the king also had the power to dispense with or to suspend criminal laws, a dispensing being a pardon issued before trial and conviction, a suspension being a blanket dispensing. James II had greatly offended English Protestants by using these powers for the benefit of Catholics, and though his actions were upheld in the courts, Parliament abolished the suspending power absolutely after the arrival of William and Mary. The matter did not end there, however. Because the king was legally ubiquitous—that is, ever present to prosecute lawbreakers in every part of the kingdom—he could not "nonsuit, for a nonsuit is the desertion of the suit or action by the non-appearance of the plaintiff in court." And yet the attorney general could enter a *non vult prosequi* ("he does not wish to go on"), which was in effect a nonsuit. It also amounted to a dispensing.[41]

There was likewise ambiguity about the status of proclamations. Blackstone, following Coke, declared that the power to issue proclamations depended upon whether "they are grounded upon and enforce the laws of the realm." This was actually the power of determining "the manner, time, and circumstances of putting those laws in execution," which "must frequently be left to the discretion of the executive magistrate." Proclamations could neither make new laws nor repeal existing laws. Blackstone offered several examples. The king could proclaim an embargo in time of war but not in peacetime. He could issue a proclamation to disarm Roman Catholics, that being consonant with a parliamentary act, but he could not issue one to disarm Protestants. The king could, however, proclaim that a state of rebellion existed, which, since he was commander in chief, would activate a host of discretionary powers.[42]

As for courts of justice, these were still acting in the name of the king, but the king's influence over them had been greatly reduced. He appointed the judges (as he did all public officials) without need for confirmation, but since 1702 judges had served during good behavior, not at the pleasure of the prince. They were removable "on

41. Ibid., 1:186, 268–270, and editor's note, citing Coke on Littleton (vol. 1 of *Institutes*), 139. Blackstone mistakenly says that the dispensing power was also abolished; it was merely limited.

42. Coke, *Institutes*, 3:162; Blackstone, *Commentaries*, 1:270–271.

the address of both houses of parliament." The same act that secured the judges' tenure also provided for ample lifetime salaries, thus establishing the "independence" of the judiciary and enabling Blackstone to pay lip service to the doctrine of the separation of powers.[43]

———— Finally, a different set of legal commentators requires attention. Whatever the understanding of executive authority, a major part of it concerned the conduct of relations with foreign states or sovereigns, including the conduct of war; in the western world during the eighteenth century that activity entailed knowledge of the principles of the law of nations, as enunciated by a handful of writers. It was perhaps unnecessary to know much about the subject in making constitutional provision for an executive branch, but access to such knowledge was indispensable to the actual wielding of executive power.

The concept of a natural law (jus naturale) that provided a basis for the law of nations (jus gentium) was rooted in ideas developed by the ancient Stoics and kept alive by Scholastic theorists and jurists. The modern formulation owed much to Hugo Grotius, a professor of law at the University of Groningen when his pioneering work *The Rights of War and Peace* was published in 1625. The next major work, Samuel Pufendorf's *Law of Nature and Nations,* followed in the 1670s. In the eighteenth century the Saxon philosopher Christian Wolff attempted to clarify the relationship between natural and civil law (in a ponderous tome that few could have read), and the Genevan Jean-Jacques Burlamaqui tried the same thing in *Principles of Natural and Politic Law* (1747–1751). Burlamaqui is known to have had a powerful influence upon at least one of the Framers of the Constitution, James Wilson. The generally recognized leading authority, however, was a student of Burlamaqui's, Emmerich de Vattel, whose masterwork, *The Law of Nations, or, Principles of the Law of Nature, Applied to the Conduct and Affairs of Nations and Sovereigns,* first appeared in 1758.[44]

Natural law theory is not to be confused with its cousin, natural

43. Blackstone, *Commentaries,* 1:267–269.

44. This description follows that of Judge James Duane in *Rutgers* v. *Waddington* (1784) as reported in Goebel, ed., *Law Practice of Hamilton,* 1:400–401.

rights theory; Vattel declared that rights were "nothing more than the power of doing what is morally possible, that is to say, what is proper and consistent with duty." Natural law was an elaborate codification of custom, convention, and "right reason," designed to regularize and humanize relations among nations—which, having no common sovereign, as individuals had in a state, were in a "state of nature" with each other. Unscrupulous players sometimes bent, broke, or winked at the rules, but there were rules, covering war as well as diplomacy, and most states adhered to them most of the time. Any executive created by the American Framers would be bound by the law of nations just as the king of England was.[45]

——— To discerning and informed readers, there was more about monarchy than any commentator's summary revealed. Toward the end of his work Blackstone pointed out that the "immoderate reduction of the antient prerogative" diminished executive power "in appearance and nominally." But if "we throw into the opposite scale" the vast amount of force that arose from the passage of the riot act, the establishment of a standing army, and the weight "of personal attachment, arising from the magnitude of the national debt" and the millions appropriated to pay the interest on it, "we shall find that the crown has, gradually and imperceptibly, gained almost as much in influence, as it has apparently lost in prerogative."[46]

That influence was powerfully augmented, though Blackstone did not say so, by an almost mystical quality that inheres in kingship and to some extent in any chief executive office. John Adams referred to it when he wrote that "there never was yet a people who must not have somebody or something to represent the dignity of the state—a doge, an avoyer, an archon, a president, a consul, a syn-

45. There are many editions of Vattel's work. I have used the 1817 Philadelphia edition, which is reprinted from the 1797 London edition. Since pagination varies, Vattel is customarily cited by book, chapter, and paragraph numbers; the quotation is from Preliminaries, para. 3, xli–xlii of my edition. The comments regarding warfare are developed at some length in "Eighteenth-Century Warfare as a Cultural Ritual," in Forrest McDonald and Ellen Shapiro McDonald, *Requiem: Variations on Eighteenth-Century Themes* (Lawrence, KS, 1988), 39–58.

46. Blackstone, *Commentaries,* 4:440–441.

dic."[47] The king, the executive, whatever else he may be, is the symbolic embodiment of the community over which he holds sway, and much of what he does is ritualistic and ceremonial. This part of the executive function is different from yet quite as important as the actual business of running government, for it fulfills a powerful human need.

Thus the English monarchy was vexingly dual in a sense other than that described by Bracton and Fortescue. Part of the problem was that the symbolic role required a regal dignity, a charisma, which was not necessarily to be found in a person gifted in statecraft. And when both sets of qualities were joined in a single person, the office was potentially dangerous. Elizabeth, combining the two, became so powerful, according to Blackstone, as to jeopardize the liberty of her subjects. James I failed despite his many gifts, not least among the reasons being that he did not look like a king.

Upon the ascent of George I the English stumbled onto a solution. He and his successor, who together reigned from 1714 until 1760, had little interest in or understanding of the government. The actual business of governing devolved upon their ministers, who were in practice responsible to the Parliament, which they in turn controlled through patronage, royal favor, and other forms of "corruption." The first "prime minister," Sir Robert Walpole, ran the government from 1721, while George I was king, until 1742, nearly halfway through the reign of George II. Freed from the messy business of governing, those monarchs could perform their symbolic roles without inciting rancor, and a people accustomed to resisting and overthrowing their kings could (and ultimately did) safely idolize them.

George III was a temporary aberration, for he used the machinery that Walpole had built and personally directed policy through his ministers—until he went mad. His long subsequent incapacity completed the process of divorcing the symbolic from the gubernatorial. Thenceforth, the king would be the symbol and his ministers—who were "his" only in the sense that the courts were "his"—would do the governing. He reigned; others ruled.

47. John Adams, *A Defence of the Constitutions of Government of the United States of America,* in Adams, ed., *Works of Adams,* 4:375. The mystical and symbolic quality of the presidency is treated at length in chapter 15 of this book.

CHAPTER 3

Political Philosophers

A second potentially useful body of thought that was available to the creators of the presidency was the work of political theorists. As practical men, most of the Framers were disdainful of abstract theoreticians, system-builders, "political projectors," "learned doctors." John Dickinson expressed a prevailing sentiment when he said that "Experience must be our only guide," for "Reason may mislead us."[1] Nonetheless, the Framers were familiar with a large body of political theory—even if only at second-hand—and they readily conceded the influence of a number of theorists, such as Hume and Montesquieu, upon their ideas.

Moreover, virtually every major political thinker from Machiavelli onward had based his work at least in part upon observation rather than upon theorems and speculative calculations. To be sure, the movement toward a "science of politics" was, as David Hume wrote, based upon inadequate observation. Hume opined that Machiavelli, though "certainly a great genius," was led into "extremely defective" reasonings because his study was limited to "the furious and tyrannical governments of ancient times" and the "little disorderly princi-

1. *The Records of the Federal Convention of 1787,* ed. Max Farrand, 4 vols. (New Haven, CT, 1937), 2:278 (Madison's Notes, August 13).

palities" in Italy. Hume also questioned whether any man was "sufficiently qualified for such an undertaking." Vast changes had happened in human affairs, "contrary to the expectation of the ancients,"
and further changes could be expected.[2]

Even so, the general understanding of politics by the late eighteenth century was sophisticated and had been particularly broadened in respect to problems attending the need for and the dangers of
executive power. Thus it seems fair to say that the Framers could not
have accomplished what they did without the political philosophies
of Machiavelli, Hobbes, Locke, Bolingbroke, Hume, De Lolme, and
a few others.

———— Accounts of the evolution of political thought customarily
begin with the ancient Greeks, but in regard to the American presidency the ancient philosophers were not relevant. Polybius built upon
Aristotle's concept of the three primary forms of government (monarchy, aristocracy, and democracy), declaring that they regularly degenerated into evil opposites (tyranny, oligarchy, and ochlocracy)
unless degeneration were checked by a mixed regime that combined
the best of the three primary forms. Nowhere in their constructs,
however, was there an institution resembling the modern chief executive. The actual execution of the laws was briefly mentioned by
Aristotle in a passage referring to the need to enforce punishments
and guard prisoners, odious tasks that were best divided "so that no
one person takes all the discredit."[3]

Constitution-makers could, therefore, look no further back than
1513, when Machiavelli wrote *The Prince.* The work was of a genre,
manuals for rulers, that had begun mainly with Xenophon and had
found considerable popularity in the late fourteenth and early fif-

2. David Hume, *Essays Moral, Political, and Literary,* ed. Thomas Hill Green and
Thomas Hodge Grose, 2 vols. (1964; repr. of London, 1882 ed.), 1:156, 157.

3. Harvey Mansfield, *Taming the Prince* (New York, 1989), 24 and passim. I have
relied upon this excellent work for guidance with regard to writers before Machiavelli
and have found it helpful regarding those who followed. Mansfield points out, at 47
and 69, that Aristotle does make passing reference to the separation of powers but
without considering the modern conception of an executive branch. Such executive
power as did exist in ancient times will be considered in chapter four of this book.

teenth centuries. The later writers adhered to a Christian cosmology which taught that rulers must shun worldly glory, that they must act morally, that their power derived from God's will, and that they would be punished in the hereafter for wickedness in this life. Machiavelli disregarded considerations of the hereafter and disdained morality, religion, or law except insofar as the manipulation of these secured the prince's first goal, retaining power, and advanced his second, winning secular glory. Thus *The Prince* was the modern exemplar of the genre.[4]

Machiavelli's prince was an executive, not a monarch. In part this was because a monarch was inherently above ordinary mortals and was bound only by God's law; Machiavelli's prince was a mortal, concerned solely with the temporal. He was more particularly an executive, however, because the prince was ever concerned with expediency, with resiliency, with improvisation and adaptation. If he was by nature cautious, he must act boldly when circumstances required boldness; if he was impetuous, then he must rein in his nature and act cautiously. He had to deceive and dissimulate and appear to be whatever was advantageous, and he had to be willing to do great wrongs when expedience dictated. He could seduce Fortune and escape her destructive and fickle influence only if he could "change his nature with times and affairs."[5]

The message of *The Prince* shocked general readers and titillated the cognoscenti, but in some ways Machiavelli's other major work, *Discourses on the First Decade of Titus Livius,* shocked even more. The Florentine revealed in that work that he was warm in his admiration of republicanism, but he thought the degeneracy of his own times prevented the development of an adequate store of virtue, in the Roman sense of the term, in either the citizenry or its leaders. Not least among the reasons, in his view, was the weakness engendered by the Christian religion as compared to the Roman. "Ancient religion," he wrote, "attributed blessedness only to men abounding in worldly

4. *Machiavelli: The Chief Works and Others,* trans. Allan Gilbert, 3 vols. (Durham, NC, 1965). For an essay on the background, see Quentin Skinner, *Machiavelli* (New York, 1981), especially at 24–31.

5. *Machiavelli: Chief Works;* the quoted passage is from *The Prince,* chap. 25, 1:91.

glory, such as generals of armies and princes of states. Our religion has glorified humble and contemplative men rather than active ones. It has, then, set up as the greatest good humility, abjectness and contempt for human things; the other put it in grandeur of mind, in strength of body, and in all the other things apt to make men exceedingly vigorous." The Christian way "has made the world weak and turned it over as prey to wicked men, who can in security control it, since the generality of men, in order to go to Heaven, think more about enduring their injuries than about avenging them."[6]

Though *The Discourses* and *The Prince* were not published in English until 1636 and 1640, a goodly number of English readers knew them, and by the end of the sixteenth century even the vulgar were aware of their messages. Their popularization was mainly the work of dramatists, who uniformly viewed them with horror. Shakespeare's Iago is archetypically Machiavellian, and Richard III says that he would

> Torment myself to catch the English crown:
> And from that torment I will free myself,
> Or hew my way out with a bloody axe.
> Why, I can smile, and murder whiles I smile,
> And cry "Content" to that which grieves my heart, . . .
> I can add colours to the chameleon,
> Change shapes with Proteus for advantages,
> And set the murderous Machiavel to school.[7]

It is small wonder, then, that Americans of the founding generation rarely cited Machiavelli or that when they did the reference was usually made in derogation. The most thorough student of the citations to European thinkers by American political writers between 1760 and 1805, Donald Lutz, surveyed a huge body of political literature containing 3,154 citations to Europeans; Machiavelli was mentioned sixteen times as compared, for example, to 265 references to Montesquieu and 249 to Blackstone. Only on rare occasions was the

6. Ibid., *The Discourses,* bk. 2, chap. 2, 1:331.

7. Felix Raab, *The English Face of Machiavelli: A Changing Interpretation, 1500–1700* (London and Toronto, 1964), 30–58 and passim; Edward Meyer, *Machiavelli and the Elizabethan Drama* (Weimar, 1897); Henry VI, pt. 3, act 3, sc. 2, in *The Complete Works of William Shakespeare,* ed. William Aldis Wright (Philadelphia, 1936), 93.

reference to Machiavelli favorable, as when "A Farmer" (probably John Francis Mercer) said that he was a man of great discernment who was abused by tyrants "because he told the truth" and by others "because he was a republican" or because "they have never read or do not understand his works."[8]

But Machiavelli's effect on eighteenth-century Americans does not end with his negative image. He was studied by most of the political thinkers whom Americans read, and thus they felt his influence indirectly. Sir Walter Ralegh, whose *Universal History* was widely read, was more or less a disciple of Machiavelli as was Francis Bacon, whom Thomas Jefferson reckoned to be one of the three greatest men who ever lived. In *The Discourses* Machiavelli developed the idea that "in every republic there are two opposed factions, that of the people and that of the rich" and that a constitutional balance must be struck between them, in which "one keeps watch over the other." At the Constitutional Convention Gouverneur Morris expressed that idea precisely in proposing that the rich and the poor each be given a branch of Congress. Yet again, Americans recited with approval Machiavelli's maxim that every republic, from time to time, must purge itself of inevitable corruption by making a revolutionary return to its founding principles.[9]

Machiavelli was relevant to the creation of the presidency because he showed how and why the prince or the governor of a republic must go where the law cannot go. In the way in which he formulated it, his prescription was too strong for most Americans' palates; before it could be used others needed to dilute the mix.

8. Donald S. Lutz, "The Relative Influence of European Writers on Late Eighteenth-Century American Political Thought," *American Political Science Review* 78 (1984):189–197; Donald S. Lutz, *The Origins of American Constitutionalism* (Baton Rouge, LA, 1988), 139–147; "Essays by a Farmer," Annapolis *Maryland Gazette,* Feb.–April 1788, in *The Complete Anti-Federalist,* ed. Herbert J. Storing, 7 vols. (Chicago, 1981), 5:49; Hamilton to ———, Dec. 1779–March 1780, in *The Papers of Alexander Hamilton,* ed. Harold C. Syrett et al., 26 vols. (New York, 1961–1979), 2:242. Storing mistakenly identifies the *Maryland Gazette* as a Baltimore paper; the Baltimore paper was the *Maryland Journal.*

9. Raab, *English Face,* 70–76; *Machiavelli: Chief Works, Discourses,* bk. 1, chaps. 2–3, 1:199, 203; Farrand, ed., *Records,* 1:512 (Madison's Notes, July 2).

———— The publication of *The Prince* in English in 1640 was not an event in a vacuum: England just then was being inundated with political tracts, reflective of the constitutional crisis that would lead to civil war and to the commonwealth. Indeed, much of the political theory that the American Framers knew was written during that epoch.

Many of the English writers were "Commonwealthmen," or republicans—Marchamont Nedham, John Milton, James Harrington. There were, of course, differences among them. Nedham notoriously shifted positions with changing political currents and the market for hired pens; Milton thought no political arrangements would work well in the absence of an adequate store of virtuous leaders, Harrington thought that such an absence could be largely offset by agrarian laws (providing relatively equal distribution of land), the secret ballot, and frequent rotation of officeholders. But they uniformly espoused a dual sort of mixed government, compounded not only of the one, the few, and the many but also of a rudimentary separation of powers and a system of checks and balances. The powers were those of a senate or a "natural aristocracy," which was to provide wisdom; a body representative of the people, which was necessary to check the depravity of even the wisest of men; and a magistracy, which merely carried into execution the will of the sovereign bicameral legislative assembly.[10]

Two special features of such systems want notice. They contained no provision for a judiciary as a branch of government separate from the executive; Milton, indeed, wrote of "the judicial execution" of the legislative power. And they normally provided for an elected,

10. James Harrington, *Oceana*, ed. S. B. Liljegren (Westport, CT, 1979), 23, 25, 37, 111–114; Marchamont Nedham, *The Excellencie of a Free State* (London, 1656, repub. 1767 and 1774); Marchamont Nedham, *The Case of the Commonwealth of England, Stated* (Charlottesville, VA, 1969, repr. of London, 1650 ed.); John Milton, "Eikonoklastes," in *The Complete Prose Works of John Milton*, volume 3, ed. Don M. Wolfe (New Haven, CT, 1962), 413; Zera S. Fink, *The Classical Republicans: An Essay in the Recovery of a Pattern of Thought in Seventeenth Century England* (Evanston, IL, 1945), 55–68; Mansfield, *Taming the Prince*, 161–162. John Adams's *Defence of the Constitutions* contains much analysis of the Commonwealthmen, and though it was available to the Framers, we do not know whether any of them had read it.

temporary dictatorship of one person or several, after the Roman model. Milton thought that a dictatorship was necessary only in times of transition from one kind of regime to another. The others commonly held the view that permanent provisions should be made for dictatorships in times of crisis. Nedham went so far as to suggest that executives or kings were necessary only in abnormal times and that before the arrival of the Romans in western Europe and Britain, no indigenous peoples had had them; leaders called kings had been merely commanders in chief, elected in times of "common peril by invasion, &c." That, he said, was the natural order.[11]

Writing on the monarchical side, Thomas Hobbes and Sir Robert Filmer were more interesting and more influential in shaping Americans' ideas about executive power, partly in their own right and partly because of the opposition writing they inspired. Both men were anathema to American republicans, their names (like Machiavelli's) being invoked to discredit an opponent by association.[12] But the thinking of Hobbes and Filmer had penetrated the minds of Americans more pervasively than Americans knew or would have found it politic to admit.

Hobbes began his 1651 classic, *Leviathan,* with an analysis of the nature of man and the human predicament. Man, to Hobbes, had nothing in his brain except impressions originally received through the five senses, though imagination and memory stored and ordered them in various ways. These impressions gave rise to appetites and aversions, and man sought to learn from experience how to obtain the pleasurable and to avoid the unpleasant. Hobbes denied the existence of intrinsic good or evil. Different men, he said, had different appetites and aversions and regarded as good whatever they desired and as evil whatever they hated. Nor were there specific natural

11. Nedham, *Case of the Commonwealth,* 115–116; Nedham, *Excellencie of a Free State,* 60–61, 147–148; Harrington, *Oceana,* 111–112; Fink, *Classical Republicans,* 105, 108; Mansfield, *Taming the Prince,* 161.

12. See, for example, Hamilton's use of Hobbes in "The Farmer Refuted," February 23, 1775, in Syrett, ed., *Hamilton Papers,* 86–87, and James Otis's references to Filmer in "A Vindication of the British Colonies," in *Pamphlets of the American Revolution,* ed. Bernard Bailyn (Cambridge, MA, 1965), 554, 560, or Richard Bland, "The Colonel Dismounted," ibid., 321.

rights, in any meaningful sense of the term. Man could rightfully do anything he willed to obtain what Hobbes called Felicity (and what Thomas Jefferson called the pursuit of happiness). Man's capacity to obtain felicity was power.[13]

That, according to Hobbes, was the nature of man, considered as a solitary individual. The human predicament was that man did not and could not exist except in the company of others, each of whom was likewise a lonely autonomous individual. Moreover, nature made individuals so nearly equal, "in the faculties of the body, and mind," that "the weakest has strength enough to kill the strongest" either by "machination, or by confederacy with others." From that equality arose equality of hope for attaining what one desired, and thus "if any two men desire the same thing, which nevertheless they cannot both enjoy, they become enemies."[14]

Therefore, in a state of nature—"during the time that men live without a common power to keep them all in awe"—competition, distrust, and the desire for safety and dominion marked all human relationships, and men were "in that condition which is called war; and such a war, as is of every man, against every man." There was no law, hence no justice. There was "no place for industry; because the fruit thereof is uncertain: and consequently no culture of the earth; no navigation, . . . no knowledge of the face of the earth"; no arts, letters, society; and "worst of all, continual fear, and danger of violent death; and the life of man, solitary, poor, nasty, brutish, and short." (Compare the comment of the Massachusetts Federalist, Fisher Ames, that liberty in a state of nature was liberty to be "exposed to the danger of being knocked on the head for an handful of acorns.")[15]

If men (or Christians, at any rate) followed the dictates of their religion, this sorry state of things did not need to be. On numerous occasions Hobbes cited the Gospel's Golden Rule, *"whatsoever you require that others should do to you, that do ye to them."* He also offered a

13. Thomas Hobbes, *LEVIATHAN: Or the Matter, Forme, and Power of a COMMON-WEALTH, Ecclesiastical and Civil,* ed. Michael Oakeshott (Oxford, Eng., n.d.), 1–39, 85.

14. Ibid., 80–81.

15. Ibid., 82–83; *The Works of Fisher Ames,* ed. William B. Allen, 2 vols. (Indianapolis, IN, 1983), 64.

negative formulation, "that law of all men, *quod tibi fieri non vis, alteri ne feceris.*" But that law, said he, though always binding in conscience, was not binding in practice where there was no security, for no one could be required to "make himself a prey to others, and procure his own certain ruin, contrary to the ground of all laws of nature, which tend to nature's preservation."[16]

The essence of the human predicament, as Hobbes saw it, was the clash between the will of every man and that of every other man. The solution—the way to obtain peace and security—was for all men to enter a compact surrendering their wills to the will of a sovereign. The sovereign could be one man or an assembly of men (Hobbes preferred a monarchy), but whatever the form of the constitution, the sovereign's will had to be absolute. His power could not be mixed, divided, or limited. He made and enforced the law, and though he could change it, he was bound to rule in accordance with it until he did change it. His task was to establish justice and to keep the peace, and without law there could be neither justice nor peace. Once the compact with the sovereign had been made, it could not be altered by either party.[17]

Though the power of the sovereign was unrestrained, the subjects were not deprived of liberty: Hobbes did not conflate liberty with a share in governance, as later Americans would do. In Hobbes's *Leviathan,* subjects retained liberties for three reasons. One was natural, inherent in the original compact: the "liberty of the subject, is to be derived . . . from the end of the institution of sovereignty, namely, the peace of the subjects within themselves, and their defence against a common enemy." Accordingly, there were some things that the sovereign could not command subjects to do, such as kill themselves or make war against one another; rather, he could so command, but the subjects were not bound to obey. Another reason derived from interest. If the public interest conflicted with private interests, men in government would generally prefer the private. It followed that "where the public and private interest are most closely united, there is the public most advanced," and thus liberty was safest if it was in

16. Hobbes, *LEVIATHAN,* 85, 103, 177.
17. Ibid., 83, 112, 123.

the interest of the sovereign to protect it. Protection was more easily facilitated in a monarchy since the "riches, power, and honour of a monarch arise only from the riches, strength, and reputation of his subjects"—a sentiment Alexander Hamilton and other advocates of a strong presidency would echo.[18]

What was more important, subjects retained their liberty because it was inconceivable (at least Hobbes could not imagine it) that there could be "rules enough set down, for the regulating of all the actions, and words of men." The liberty of the subject lay in those areas where the sovereign refrained from instituting regulations he could not effectively enforce, such as "the liberty to buy, and sell, and otherwise, contract with one another; to choose their own abode, their own diet, their own trade of life, and institute their children as they themselves think fit."[19] (Whatever else Hobbes may have been, he was clearly no prophet.)

The preeminent English theorist of absolutism, Sir Robert Filmer, arrived at his position differently from Hobbes. Filmer wrote *Patriarcha* during the 1620s or 1630s and revised it in later years. He intended it for private circulation, and it was not published during his lifetime. It suddenly became relevant to contemporary politics during the Exclusion Crisis—the struggle to prevent James, a Catholic, from succeeding his brother Charles II—and it was published in 1680 and reprinted in 1685. Among the consequences of its publication was that it stimulated John Locke to essay a rebuttal, *Two Treatises of Government*.[20] The power (and to Locke and like-minded souls, the danger) of *Patriarcha* did not stem from the brilliance of its arguments. The work was derivative, pedantic, repetitive, dogmatic, and turgid. Its strength came instead from its commonsense rejection of the idea of the social compact and its base of almost universally held assumptions about nature, paternal authority, and divine revelation.[21]

18. Ibid., 122–123, 141–143.

19. Ibid., 138–139.

20. Robert Filmer, *Patriarcha and Other Political Works,* ed. Peter Laslett (Oxford, Eng., 1949). For a new edition, see Filmer's *Patriarcha and Other Writings,* ed. J. P. Sommerville (Cambridge, Eng., 1990).

21. The summary in the next four paragraphs is different from but owes much to Laslett's introductory essay in Filmer, *Patriarcha.*

Filmer regarded as absurd the idea that humans had ever lived as equals in a presocial world or that such an imaginary state of nature had been terminated by a rational and voluntary agreement upon a compact with a ruler. The notion, he declared with some accuracy, had been hatched by Scholastics a few centuries earlier to undermine the power of kings and to justify papal authority over them. (If kings ruled by divine right, they were beholden only to God, not the pope; but if they ruled merely on the authority of their subjects, they fell under the intermediate authority of God's vicar on earth.) It was obvious to Filmer that people could never have been equals in a state of nature, for their procreation and survival depended upon the presence of a father. The father's authority was absolute, even as the authority of a captor who spares a victim's life was absolute, and essentially for the same reason: Children, like slaves, owed their existence to their master. No matter how primitive circumstances may once have been, authority and the duty to obey were there from the beginning.

Two premises underlay Filmer's development of that concept of paternal authority into one of patriarchical authority, the idea of the king as father of his people. One derived from the institution of the extended family, the other from the rule of primogeniture, the first being pervasive throughout western culture, the other fairly common. The family comprehended not only all living descendants of the eldest living male but all servants, tenants, and other dependents as well. Authority normally descended to males over females and to first-born males over later-born males. Since (it was assumed) all people ultimately had a common ancestry, some male necessarily was in the direct line of descent of eldest sons from the original father. That someone was the rightful king, whose authority over his extended family—his kingdom—was analogous to that of fathers in the narrower sense.

The common ancestor of all humankind was, of course, Adam. Like most Englishmen of his time, Filmer believed that every word of the Bible was literally true, divinely inspired, and an accurate account of the largest portion of human history. Adam was originally both master and owner of the whole world, responsible solely to God;

even when He created Eve from Adam's rib, Adam continued to be master and owner. When they begat offspring, Adam could and did bequeath parts of his dominion to his sons, and patriarchies began to proliferate. In Noah's time they were reunited, for none but Noah and his family survived the Flood, but Noah also bequeathed portions of his dominions. The diversity of kingdoms was accelerated after God introduced a multiplicity of languages to end the building of the tower of Babel. All legitimate rulers in Filmer's own time were (or were reputed to be) direct descendants of rulers in biblical times, and they ruled as Adam had ruled—by divine right, being answerable only to God.

This line of reasoning had its flaws, but they did not upset people who read *Patriarcha* sympathetically. Admittedly, no living ruler could trace his genealogy to Adam or Noah, but that did not matter. Admittedly, many crowns had been usurped over the centuries, but the usurpers and their descendants were illegitimate, and God would presumably, though not necessarily, restore the rightful rulers and punish the usurpers in His own way and time. Admittedly, there had been and were various nonmonarchical governments, but these too were illegitimate: There was a lawful king for them even if he could not be found. Finally, many philosophers had written of mixed regimes, in which kings shared power with barons and commons; Filmer followed Bodin, and preceded Hobbes, in asserting that no such regime was possible. He went to considerable lengths to demonstrate that the regime in England, reckoned by many to be the mixed regime par excellence, was in actuality an absolute monarchy.

Filmer's argument was totally discredited by Locke and by William Tyrrell; at the time of the American founding claims that kings ruled by divine right were generally out of fashion. But the habits of thinking or, more properly, the unarticulated assumptions upon which *Patriarcha* was based proved resistant to change. In 1763, for example, Patrick Henry argued in the Parson's Cause that a Virginia act of general utility could not be annulled by royal authority, for "a King, by annuling or disallowing Acts of so salutary a nature, from being the Father of his people degenerates into a Tyrant, and forfeits all right to his subjects' Obedience"; Henry was answered with cries of

"Treason, Treason!" On the eve of independence the Tory minister Jonathan Boucher delivered to his Maryland parishioners a set of sermons based directly upon *Patriarcha.* During the war for independence George Washington referred to his immediate subordinates as his family, and Americans later fell into the habit of referring to Washington as the Father of his Country.[22]

———— John Locke's *Two Treatises of Government,* written for the most part between 1679 and 1681 as a refutation of Filmer's *Patriarcha* and first published in 1690 as a justification of England's Glorious Revolution, gained general currency in America during the 1770s by virtue of offering a rationalization for declaring independence. Because of that currency and because Locke's version of the compact theory of the origin of legitimate government became a fundamental part of Americans' thinking about constitutional authority, everything Locke said about government was important to the founding.

To Locke there were three species of power: legislative, executive, and what he called federative, meaning the conduct of foreign relations including war and peace. (He did not allow for judicial power, regarding judging as a passive, albeit essential, function to be performed either by the legislature or by independent judges appointed by the legislature.) The legislative power was *"the supream power,"* the executive subordinate to it. These powers were to be lodged in separate bodies, inasmuch as it might "be too great a temptation to humane frailty apt to grasp at Power, for the same Persons who have the Power of making Laws, to have also in their hands the power to execute them."[23]

Having said that, however, Locke promptly painted himself into a

22. Henry quoted in Lawrence Henry Gipson, *The Coming of the American Revolution* (New York, 1954), 53; for Boucher, see Laslett's introduction, *Patriarcha,* 41.

23. John Locke, *Two Treatises of Government,* ed. Peter Laslett (Cambridge, Eng., 1988), paras. 88–89, 134, 143–148, pp. 324–325, 356, 364–366. All references here and following are to book 2. Many more Americans were familiar with Locke's work than had actually read it. As Donald Lutz has pointed out, "the primary avenue for the introduction of Locke's thinking . . . was through election-day sermons" (Lutz, *American Constitutionalism,* 68 n.16).

corner, for though he pretended to be picturing an abstract and theoretical, well-ordered commonwealth, he was sketching the English constitution as he thought it worked in practice—and that constitution did not readily display a separation of powers. He had to admit that though the executive and federative powers were distinct they both involved command of the armed forces and therefore should be in the same hands. Rival or different commanders of the same force "would be apt sometime or other to cause disorder and ruine." Then Locke had to allow that the executive might legitimately be a member of the legislature. Moreover, the executive had the power as a "Fiduciary Trust" to assemble or dismiss the legislative, since the occasions when legislation was necessary were limited and "Constant *frequent meetings of the Legislative . . .* could not but be burthensome to the People," whereas the need for the executive was continuous.[24]

Locke conceded more to the executive when he treated the prerogative, which he defined as "the Power to act according to discretion, for the publick good, without the prescription of the Law, and sometimes even against it." It was needed because legislatures were "too slow, for the dispatch requisite to Execution," because the law could not foresee and provide for "all Accidents and Necessities, that may concern the publick," and because it was impossible to make laws that would do no harm if executed "with inflexible rigour." The same was true of the federative power.[25]

Locke was aware of the dangers inherent in the prerogative. He could scarcely have failed to be, in light of the rather flagrant abuses committed by Charles II and James II. He recognized, however, that it could be a greater threat in the hands of "a good Prince," for such "cannot have too much *Prerogative,* that is, Power to do good." Thus it was in England that "Prerogative was always *largest* in the hands of our wisest and best Princes: because the People observing the whole tendency of their Actions to be the publick good, contested not what was done without Law to that end." On that tendency rested the observation that "the Reigns of good Princes have been always most

24. Locke, *Two Treatises,* paras. 148, 150–157, pp. 366, 367–373. The final quotation is from para. 156, p. 371.

25. Ibid., paras. 147, 160, pp. 365, 375.

dangerous to the Liberties of their People," for wicked successors could cite their extralegal doings as precedents for the execution of more sinister designs.[26]

There were, however, prospective checks upon excess in the employment of the prerogative. The power could be limited by the legislative. If the legislative and executive disagreed as to the proper exercise of the power, there could "be no *Judge on Earth*," and the people had to resort to another check upon the executive, an *"appeal to Heaven."* Locke made it clear that this check meant resisting tyranny by force—an appeal to heaven being a state of war—and, if necessary, included dissolving the government. Strong medicine that, and just the prescription American patriots needed in 1776. Afterward, when they set about the nicer business of erecting durable and stable governmental institutions, it was hardly a useful recourse.[27]

A third source of safety was more subtle. For Locke, the relationship between governors and the governed was less a matter of contract or compact (though he used both terms with some frequency) than it was a matter of trust. People cannot do without government for long in any state except the most primitive. Lacking government, "the People become a confused Multitude, without Order or Connexion." They must therefore entrust power once again "by erecting a new Legislative, differing from the other, by the change of Persons, or Form, or both as they shall find it most for their safety and good" and by putting "the rule into such hands, which may secure to them the ends for which Government was at first erected."[28]

Libertarians and Machiavels alike may find mutual trust an unacceptable foundation for government. But compare the words of Thomas Jefferson: "Whenever any Form of Government becomes destructive of [the ends for which it was established], it is the Right of the People to alter or to abolish it, *and to institute new Government,* laying its foundations on such principles and organizing its powers in such form, as to them shall seem most likely to effect their Safety and Happiness." Compare also Alexander Hamilton: "Sir, when you have

26. Ibid., paras. 164–166, pp. 377–378.
27. Ibid., paras. 168, 242, pp. 379, 445, and chaps. 28–29 passim.
28. Ibid., paras. 219, 220, 225, pp. 411, 415, and Laslett's introduction, 113–115.

divided and nicely balanced the departments of government; When you have strongly connected the virtue of your rulers with their interest; when, in short, you have rendered your system as perfect as human forms can be; *you must place confidence;* you must give power."[29]

———— A contemporary of Locke's, Sir William Temple, drew the particular attention of Americans because he wrote about a confederation government, the United Provinces of the Netherlands. Temple did not describe an especially happy situation: The Dutch government was extremely clumsy. The consent of all seven provinces was required for making war, establishing alliances, and levying taxes. Each province had a prince who chose deputies to the three "colleges" that constituted the state—the Chamber of Accounts, the Council of State, and the States General. Sovereignty nominally resided in the States General, which had more than 800 members, but was wielded in practice by an "ordinary Council."[30]

The government was free in the sense of being popularly based, albeit by estates, but in no other sense. The people, Temple wrote, were "bridled with hard Laws, terrified with severe Executions, environed with Foreign Forces; and oppress'd with the most cruel Hardship and Variety of Taxes, that was ever known under any Government."[31]

The treatise on the Netherlands was Temple's best-known work but not his only writing. After Temple's death in 1699, Jonathan Swift, who had been his secretary for a decade, gathered the miscellaneous writings and saw to their publication in two large volumes; in that form his work was known to Americans. One of Temple's lengthy essays, "Upon the Original and Nature of Government," contained a number of insights that were of value to the Framers. He opined that

29. Declaration of Independence (italics added); Hamilton's remarks in the New York Ratifying Convention, June 27, 1788, in Syrett, ed., *Hamilton Papers,* 5:95 (italics added).

30. William Temple, "Observations upon the United Provinces of the Netherlands," in *The Works of Sir William Temple, Bart.,* 2 vols. (London, 1740), 1:30–34. G. Morris (July 17) and Butler (Aug. 7) echo Temple at the Constitutional Convention; Farrand, ed., *Records,* 2:31, 202.

31. Temple, *Works,* 1:40.

government was soundest and least oppressive when it was built like a pyramid, on the broadest possible base—a notion repeatedly echoed by James Wilson. He rejected the compact theory of the origins of government, suggesting that by and large governments probably evolved as patriarchies, but he argued more effectively than Filmer had by allowing for the legitimacy of conquests and by rejecting Filmer's absolutist conclusions.[32]

Temple's most profound observation had to do with the nature of power, executive or otherwise. Power, he wrote, *"arising from Strength, is always in those that are governed, who are many."* Authority, on the other hand, *"arising from Opinion, is in those that govern, who are few."* Opinion, he explained, was the belief that those who govern are wise, good, and valorous; if the governed do not believe that their governors are virtuous, government is impossible. Temple offered several historical examples to buttress his point, the most potent being the restoration of Charles II to the English throne in 1660. The Roundheads, he reminded his readers, still had a 60,000-man army and ample revenues, but they no longer had opinion on their side.[33]

——— The next group of political writers who influenced Americans, the eighteenth-century country or opposition party, were far from eager to "place confidence," to trust government without leashing it tightly. A succession of polemicists took up pens against what they regarded as the betrayal of the principles of the Glorious Revolution. They saw threats to liberty and the Revolution everywhere, beginning with fears of Stuart-style standing armies at the turn of the century. The Septennial Act of 1716 seemed to betray the promise of frequent elections; the bursting of the South Sea Bubble in 1720 dramatized the dangers inherent in the public debt and its companion, the Bank of England; the ministry of Sir Robert Walpole (1721–1742), actuated by "corruption," appeared to infect the constitution and English society with moral rot.

The opposition writers were intellectual descendants of the seven-

32. Ibid., 1:99–105.

33. Ibid., 1:97, 105, 107. Hamilton made telling use of this observation and a similar one by Hume in his "First Report on Public Credit," 1790.

teenth-century Commonwealthmen and of Locke as well, except that they were prone to wax almost hysterical in their fear of power. Colonial Americans absorbed all or parts of this ideology, if it can be called that, from a variety of sources—including the poet Alexander Pope, the satirist Jonathan Swift, the playwright John Gay, the novelist Henry Fielding, and the political controversialists John Trenchard and Thomas Gordon (writing as Cato) and Henry St. John, first Viscount Bolingbroke. They absorbed it so thoroughly that "the paranoid style" was episodically to characterize American politics ever after. It would figure especially prominently in the coming of independence and in the establishing of the presidency.[34]

Bolingbroke was the most widely read of the oppositionists in America, and his works formed something of a codification of the litany. Of his voluminous writings two books were particularly influential. *A Dissertation upon Parties* was published first as articles in the weekly newspaper *The Craftsman* in 1733–1734 and then as a book a year later. In it, Bolingbroke declared that the traditional threat to English liberty, the abuse of the prerogative, had been rendered defunct for all time but that an insidious and deadly instrument of tyranny had been erected in its place. Walpole (whom Bolingbroke was careful not to name lest he be jailed for seditious libel) had taken advantage of the naive trust of the inept Hanoverian kings, George I and II (whom he was careful to praise), and had undermined liberty through corruption. By multiplying and manipulating the public debt and the bank paper that was based upon it, Walpole had introduced a spirit of gambling, stockjobbing, moneygrubbing, and paper

34. The best works on the oppositionists include J. G. A. Pocock, *The Machiavellian Moment: Florentine Political Thought and the Atlantic Republican Tradition* (Princeton, NJ, 1975); Isaac Kramnick, *Bolingbroke and His Circle: The Politics of Nostalgia in the Age of Walpole* (Cambridge, MA, 1968); Caroline Robbins, *The Eighteenth-Century Commonwealthman: Studies in the Transmission, Development, and Circumstance of English Liberal Thought from the Restoration of Charles II until the War with the Thirteen Colonies* (Cambridge, MA, 1959); H. Trevor Colbourn, *The Lamp of Experience* (Chapel Hill, NC, 1965); Bernard Bailyn, *The Ideological Origins of the American Revolution* (Cambridge, MA, 1967); and Rodger D. Parker, "The Gospel of Opposition: A Study in Eighteenth-Century Anglo-American Ideology," Ph.D. diss., Wayne State University, 1975.

shuffling; he had used the enormous financial resources at his disposal to buy elections; he had bribed and manipulated members of Parliament with money and the distribution of lucrative appointments. The people themselves were in process of being corrupted by similar means. Thus this minister of the crown brought "as great power to the crown indirectly, as the prerogative, which [people] had formerly dreaded so much, could give directly" and established "universal corruption."[35]

In these circumstances, the old party division between Whigs and Tories had ceased to have any meaning. Instead, there were three "parties." The Jacobites were adherents to the discredited Stuarts and therefore enemies of the constitution as altered by the Revolution; they were impotent and insignificant. The court party included Walpole and the sycophants and toadies who profited from his evil doings and who (Bolingbroke asserted) were professed enemies of the constitution. The country party was country not just in the sense of rural but also in the sense of the people as a whole. The only hope for the restoration of English liberty was for the country party to rally together, gain control of the Commons, and regain the "independency" of that body from the king's ministers. American colonial politicians opposed to policies of royal governors appreciated this political dissertation and commonly referred to themselves as the country party in their struggles.[36]

Bolingbroke himself soon despaired of salvation through the country party, but he found hope in the person of the crown prince, Frederick. For the prince's instruction Bolingbroke wrote late in 1738 a classic work, *The Idea of a Patriot King* (published in 1749). He recapitulated his diagnosis of the corruption of the nation through money and patronage and said that "salvation will not be opened to us, without the concurrence, and the influence, of a Patriot King, the

35. "A Dissertation upon Parties," in *The Works of Lord Bolingbroke,* 4 vols. (London, 1844), 2:123–128, 156, 160–172. It is to be observed that Bolingbroke's diagnosis is essentially the same as Blackstone's except that Blackstone welcomed the change. It is interesting to note that the first edition of Bolingbroke's collected essays, including "The Idea of a Patriot King," was published in America by Benjamin Franklin and David Hull in 1749, the year it was first published in England.

36. Ibid., 2:20–29 and passim.

most uncommon of all phenomena in the physical or moral world." Bolingbroke drew upon Machiavelli in support of his proposition that a "free monarch" could restore the nation by purging its corrupters, abjuring corruption as an instrument, and returning each of the three branches of government to its proper sphere.[37]

Bolingbroke understood perfectly well that the legislative power was by crown in Parliament, but he also believed in a division of functions, which made possible a system of checks and balances that would divide the branches and limit them properly. To Bolingbroke the power of the executive had to be returned to its legitimate, historic function: The crown had the power of the sword in matters foreign and domestic, including the power to declare war; the crown had a general supervision of civil administration, including the appointment of the civil list; and the crown conducted diplomatic relations. Lest these great powers be abused, the Commons had exclusive power of the purse. It alone could vote taxes. (The Lords could only approve or disapprove.) The power of the sword was thus dependent upon that of the purse; therefore the "independency" of the Commons from the crown was essential. The role of the Lords was to serve as "mediators" between the other two branches.[38]

It was largely from a misunderstanding of that description of the English constitution that Montesquieu—a friend and admirer of Bolingbroke—formulated his doctrine of the separation of powers in *The Spirit of the Laws*.[39] In the chapter "Of the Constitution of England," Montesquieu wrote, "When the legislative and executive powers are united in the same person, or in the same body of magistrates, there can be no liberty." Nor could there be liberty "if the judiciary power be not separated from the legislative and executive." (He, like Locke, regarded the judiciary as an essentially passive body, and he believed that the judicial power should not be entrusted to permanent courts.) The legislature was properly divided into two

37. "Idea of a Patriot King," ibid., 2:372–429; the quotation is at 375.

38. "Dissertation upon Parties," ibid., 2:116–123, 130.

39. Robert Shackleton, "Montesquieu, Bolingbroke, and the Separation of Powers," *French Studies* 3 (1949):25–38. Kramnick, *Bolingbroke and His Circle*, demurs from this judgment.

houses: One represented wealth, birth, and station; the other represented the people. The executive power arose not from legislative enactments but from the law of nations, and Montesquieu described it as comprehending making peace or war, sending and receiving ambassadors, preserving public security, and providing against invasion. The executive had a veto power but otherwise had no part in legislation. The legislature had no right to interfere in the exercise of executive authority, but it had the power to impeach royal ministers and the ultimate restraint on the war power of withholding appropriations or dissolving the army.[40]

That was far from an accurate description of the English constitution. Indeed, *The Spirit of the Laws* teemed with inaccuracies. But it was embraced warmly by American colonials, especially those who also embraced Bolingbroke—and for the same reason: a widespread and deep-seated distrust of power.[41]

———— Considerably more positive and accurate was the work of David Hume. That Hume could have been a positive influence might seem strange since he was notoriously skeptical. Besides, in a utopian essay called "Idea of a Perfect Commonwealth," he proposed that a senate "be endowed with the whole executive power of the commonwealth; the power of peace and war, of giving orders to generals, admirals, and ambassadors, and, in short, all the prerogatives of a BRITISH King, except his negative." There would be no chief executive. The executive powers would instead be exercised through a protector, two secretaries of state, six councils, and six commissioners. Hume would provide for a six-month dictatorship during

40. Baron de Montesquieu, *The Spirit of the Laws,* trans. Thomas Nugent (New York, 1949), bk. 11, chap. 6, pp. 151–162. For a serious discussion of Montesquieu's separation-of-powers dictum as applied in Massachusetts, April 1763, to the possibility of the lieutenant governor's being elected councillor, see the exchange of letters T. Q. and J. in the *Boston Gazette and Country Journal,* in *American Political Writing during the Founding Era 1760–1805,* ed. Charles S. Hyneman and Donald S. Lutz, 2 vols. (Indianapolis, IN, 1983), 1:20.

41. Paul M. Spurlin, *Montesquieu in America* (Baton Rouge, LA, 1940). Regarding the inaccuracies, see David Hume to Montesquieu, April 10, 1749, in *The Letters of David Hume,* ed. J. Y. T. Greig, 2 vols. (Oxford, Eng., 1932), 1:133–138, for one example. Hume greatly admired Montesquieu, but he felt it necessary to correct a number of his errors.

extraordinary emergencies, but even then the executive would be plural. In his system, therefore, the legislative power would be "always superior to the executive."[42]

But Hume was too practical a thinker to believe that "experiments merely upon the credit of supposed argument and philosophy" were likely to be adopted or to succeed. Accordingly, he formulated a way, based upon experience, to view the problem of attaining a balance between legislative and executive power—a way that would be useful to those Founders who established the American presidency. Two general propositions preceded his analysis. The first was a definition of free government as one that "admits of a partition of power among several members," whose combined authority might be as great as that of any monarch, "but who, in the usual course of administration, must act by general and equal laws, that are previously known to all members and to all their subjects." The second was a maxim that "in contriving any system of government, and fixing the several checks and controuls of the constitution, every man ought to be supposed a *knave,* and to have no other end, in all his actions, than private interest." Even though that Machiavellian supposition was not true in fact, Hume added, it was by private interest that one must govern the governor and "by means of it, make him, notwithstanding his insatiable avarice and ambition, co-operate to public good." Otherwise, "we shall in vain boast of the advantages of any constitution, and shall find, in the end, that we have no security for our liberties or possessions." In one way and another, large numbers of the American Founders echoed those ideas.[43]

Having laid down his hard-nosed premises, Hume made an extremely perceptive observation. When Hume wrote in the 1740s it was established wisdom that the Glorious Revolution had ensured English liberty through the triumph of the principle of government by crown in Parliament. No such thing had happened, he declared. Indeed, the Revolution Settlement had resulted in legislative absolutism. The crown had no real share in legislation: It theoretically retained a negative, or veto, but that had not been exercised in nearly two generations,

42. Hume, "Idea of a Perfect Commonwealth," in *Essays,* 3:482–486, 489.
43. Ibid., 3:480; "Of the Origin of Government," ibid., 3:116, 117–118.

and no king would dare try to use it again. Moreover, the Lords had "no force or authority sufficient to maintain themselves" without the reciprocal support of the crown. The power of the House of Commons was "so great, that it absolutely commands all the other parts of the government." Even the crown's nominal power of the sword was subordinate to the Commons' control of the purse.[44]

In the circumstances, the only way the crown had of preserving itself, and incidentally the Lords and the balance of the constitution, was through what Bolingbroke and the country party called corruption and dependence. Hume did not endorse "private *bribery*" either of members of the Commons in exchange for their votes, though Walpole probably had not scrupled against it, or of the voters, though the practice was overt and widespread. But he did endorse the use of "the offices and honours which are at the disposal of the crown" to sway the votes of individual members of the Commons. Further, the king could win votes by skillful exploitation of the mystique of the royal presence, which, though far less potent than it had been in times of divine right, continued to inhere in the office even as it would continue with the chief executive in a republic. These influences upon individual legislators, "when assisted by the honest and disinterested part of the house" (and Hume tempered his skepticism by the fundamental assumption that such a bloc existed), would always be enough to "command the resolutions of the whole so far, at least, to preserve the antient constitution from danger."[45]

Hume's ideas on the subject were not entirely original. Hired scribblers in both court-party and country-party camps had been saying much the same thing. But Hume had a respectability most of them lacked, and he made his points in an eminently moderate and sensible way. It is true that Americans found his analysis wanting during the

---

44. "On the Independency of Parliament," ibid., 3:120. William III exercised the veto six times during the early 1690s. The only subsequent use was by Queen Anne on March 11, 1707.

45. Ibid., 3:120, 121n. Americans studying in England were appalled by the corruption. John Dickinson wrote to his father in 1754: "There has been above £1,000,000 drawn out of this city already 'for useful purposes at elections.' . . . It is astonishing to think what impudence & villany are practizd on this occasion" (quoted in Forrest McDonald and Ellen Shapiro McDonald, *Requiem* [Lawrence, KS, 1988], 94).

imperial crisis of the 1760s and 1770s, when the ideas of the opposition writers seemed more germane, and in 1776, when Locke's revolutionary doctrines were to the purpose. But after independence was won and the season for the establishment of durable governmental institutions arrived, a goodly number of Americans turned to Hume for guidance, among them Alexander Hamilton and James Madison.

———— The most recent political writer who was prospectively useful for the creators of the presidency was the Genevan Jean-Louis De Lolme, whose pellucid book, *The Constitution of England; Or, An Account of the English Government,* was published in several editions during the 1780s. Its value arose partly from its comprehensiveness and detail, in contrast to the other writers considered here, who had dealt largely in generalities. (In *Federalist* 70 Hamilton quoted with approval a pronouncement that De Lolme was "deep, solid, and ingenious.") Moreover, the book was palatable to American friends of executive power because De Lolme was as ardent in his republicanism as he was in his enthusiasm for the English constitution.[46]

To De Lolme, balance was the crucial feature in guaranteeing that the English government preserved the liberties of the subject. He employed the approach that, since Montesquieu, had become the convention—the three powers in any government were legislative, executive, and judicial. But he perceived, as Montesquieu had not, that the English government was actually a government of separate institutions sharing various powers. The "executive" (a word De Lolme used interchangeably with "crown") derived sufficient strength from its unity to check the legislative, but its unity made it easier to restrain. Contrary to the opinion of many Americans that a plural executive was safer, De Lolme believed that dividing the executive would put its members into a perpetual turmoil of rivalry for ascendancy. The legislative, on the other hand, was properly divided into two institutions (or three, counting the crown in its capacity as part of Parliament), each of which restrained the others. The judiciary, though independent by virtue of fixed income and lifetime tenure,

46. Jean-Louis De Lolme, *The Constitution of England,* 10 and passim; I used the 1853 London edition, edited by John Macgregor.

was neither an institution nor a "branch" of government, and besides, Parliament was the court of last resort. Parliament also had a power that was both judicial and executive, the power to pass bills of attainder—in which action, in point of strict theory, the king was a part of Parliament. This system of checks and balances was effective, according to De Lolme, because it was in the interest of all concerned to perform their proper constitutional functions.[47]

Before considering the ways in which the royal prerogative was restrained, De Lolme itemized the prerogative powers much in the way Blackstone had done. The first had to do with the administration of justice: the appointment of judges and prosecutors and the pardoning of offenses. Second, the king was "the *fountain of honour*," distributing titles and honors and appointing the civil list, which De Lolme recognized (as Hume had) as being important to exerting adequate influence with Parliament, despite various acts that had limited the ability of members to hold administrative offices. Third was the king's authority to superintend commerce, regulate weights and measures, and coin money. Fourth was his position as "supreme governor" of the established church. Next was the royal position as "generalissimo" of the armed forces and as "the representative and the depository of all the power and collective majesty of the nation" in dealing with foreign states: The king "sends and receives ambassadors; he contracts alliances; and has the prerogative of declaring war, and of making peace, on whatever conditions he thinks proper." In addition, he had the authority to call and dissolve Parliaments. All these powers, of course, were subject to law.[48]

Making sure that they remained under the control of law was a delicate matter, precisely because the instruments at Parliament's dis-

47. Ibid., 10, 143–157, 192–197, 239–241. De Lolme's attitude toward a single executive and the necessity of tying his interests to those of his office had by now become a commonplace; compare Bolingbroke, in the "Dissertation on Parties" (*Works,* 2:127): "A king cannot be tempted to give up the interest of the crown, because he cannot give up this public interest, without giving up his private interest; whereas the members of such assemblies may promote their private interest, by sacrificing to it that of the public." Compare also Hamilton's speech to the same effect in Farrand, ed., *Records,* 1:289 (Madison's Notes, June 18, 1787).

48. De Lolme, *Constitution of England,* 60–63, 71, 73, 259.

posal were so draconian. The king personally was beyond the reach of the law, but his ministers were subject to attainder and to impeachment, and his armies were at the mercy of the Commons' control of the purse. The temptation to abuse power, especially on the part of the Commons, was doubtless strong, but several restraints effectively curbed the temptation. One was self-imposed: The memory of the horrors of confrontational politics under the Stuarts was vivid and painful. (De Lolme was mistaken, however, in believing that Parliament would never aspire to a stronger voice in conducting the executive than it had when he wrote; within a generation, a majority vote in the House of Commons would be necessary for appointing or removing a ministry.)[49]

The rivalry between the Lords and the Commons imposed another restraint. The Commons jealously guarded its exclusive power to originate bills levying taxes and appropriating money, and it always held firm when the Lords attempted to go beyond their authority to reject or accept money bills and instead tried to alter them. The Lords were equally firm in resisting efforts by the Commons to tack regular legislation onto a money bill to ensure its passage. Indeed, blocking such legislation became a standing order in the House of Lords, thereby further protecting the crown against the Commons.[50]

Still another protection of the crown derived from an institutional mechanism that had evolved since the Revolution. De Lolme cited with approval (as had Bolingbroke and others) Machiavelli's famous dictum that governments must periodically be reformed by a return to the original principles upon which they were established. It was generally, though not universally, accepted that the Revolution had been a return to first principles—*revolvere,* the Latin root of "revolution," means "to roll back"—and William III had expressly agreed to restrictive terms when the Convention Parliament invited him to accept the crown in 1688. De Lolme went further, insisting that the death of every king involved the nation in a new reformation through the coronation oath.[51]

49. Ibid., 265–267 and editor's note, 269.
50. Ibid., 67–68 and note.
51. Ibid., 68–71.

Another protection of the crown was that the Commons, at the beginning of every reign, voted the king adequate revenue for life, to support a generous civil list and to provide for the interest on the public debt. Bolingbroke had seen this practice as a source of great evil, but it blunted the severity of the Commons' money power, minimized the need for confrontations, and, as Hume had indicated, provided the king with means to defend himself. Toward the end that the king's ability to defend himself not be excessive, it was provided that no civil officer directly involved in collecting or expending the king's revenues could be a member of Parliament.[52]

Toward the same end, it became customary that contingent appropriations, including those for the support of the army, were made for one year at a time. Moreover, though the king had the command of a standing army, that army was authorized by Parliament to exist for one year at a time; "at the end of that term it is (unless re-established) to be *ipso facto* disbanded; and as the question, which then lies before parliament, is not, whether the army *shall be dissolved,* but whether it shall be *established anew,*" any of the three branches could prevent its continuation. In a quite real sense, that struck to the heart of the problem of executive power. The army was necessary for the defense of the nation—simply because every major European prince had a standing army—but in England it was "joined to the state by only a slender thread, the knot of which may be slipped on the first appearance of danger." That institutional arrangement, together with tradition, ensured that civil authority in England would ever be superior to the military, an indisputable precondition of liberty.[53]

De Lolme made other observations that were particularly relevant to the American founding. One concerned the power to initiate legislation. The king of England, he pointed out, had no such power. He could send messages or suggest that various subjects be considered, but every bill had to be drafted and proposed exclusively by the members of Parliament. (De Lolme seems not to have noticed that the king had always had agents in both houses and that his "prime

52. Ibid., 68, 78–79, 193n., 193–194; Bolingbroke, "Dissertation upon Parties," in *Works*, 2:153–172.

53. De Lolme, *Constitution of England,* 74–75, 295–298.

minister"—a term coined by Bolingbroke in derision of Walpole—
was a member of Parliament and could draft legislation on behalf of
the administration.) At that point, De Lolme digressed to observe
that it was entirely proper for the chief executive in a republic to
initiate legislation. He indicated, however, that dangers inhered in
giving republican executives such authority. At first, those executives
would call on the legislative frequently as a means of enhancing their
power without appearing to usurp it. But the time would ultimately
arrive when executives in a republic had sufficient power that "far-
ther manifestations of the will of the legislature could then only
create obstructions to the exercise of their power," whereupon they
would "begin to consider the legislature as an enemy whom they
must take great care never to rouse."[54]

The second set of observations concerned the relative merits and
dangers of prolonged administrations. It would seem natural, De
Lolme said, to entrust public affairs "to those persons who may be
supposed to have before acquired experience and wisdom" in their
management. Yet history had shown "that public employments and
power improve the understanding of men in a less degree than they
pervert their views." Thus what seemed to be prudence confined the
people in the long run to a passive role and delivered "them up to the
continual enterprises of those, who, at the same time that they are
under the greatest temptations to deceive them, possess the most
powerful means of effecting it." To a generation of Americans conditioned to believe in the validity of Harrington's principle of rotation
in office, that was a stirring admonition.[55]

The third proposition was that, despite De Lolme's cautions, "it
may be laid down as a maxim, that power under any form of government must exist, and be intrusted somewhere." Power simply is; and
one might add a corollary that if it is not exercised responsibly, it will
be exercised irresponsibly.[56]

54. Ibid., 163–164, 165–167.
55. Ibid., 167–168. Rotation was considered equally important in elected offices; a
commonplace of the age was that "where annual elections end, tyranny begins." See
chapter 4, n. 25, of this book.
56. De Lolme, *Constitution of England*, 318.

———— Political writers had gone a long way toward devising an executive that would be both efficacious and safe. Whether the American Founders could go the rest of the way would depend in large measure on their willingness to trust the experiment—in Hobbes's, Locke's, or De Lolme's sense of trust. That, in turn, would depend less upon political theory than upon history.

CHAPTER 4

The Lessons of History

History, to most of the authors of the Constitution, was more valuable than political theory because it was more real; as Bolingbroke put it, history was philosophy teaching by example. Eighteenth-century Americans read widely in history, thought historically, and cited history as authority. During the first three weeks of the Philadelphia convention, for instance, delegates buttressed their positions with historical references at least twenty-three times, not counting references drawn from British, colonial, or recent American history, inclusion of which would treble the total. A number of delegates delivered lengthy addresses on the lessons to be learned from ancient or modern history. During the same period only one political philosopher was mentioned by name.[1]

1. These references are documented in Forrest McDonald, *Novus Ordo Seclorum: The Intellectual Origins of the Constitution* (Lawrence, KS, 1985), 5, n. 13. See also Peter C. Hoffer, "The Constitutional Crisis and the Rise of a Nationalistic View of History in America, 1786–1788," *New York History* 52 (1971):305–323. Milton M. Klein, "Clio Ascendant: The Writing of American History in the Eighteenth Century," *New York History* 68 (1987):23, observes that "history in Europe was as much in vogue in 1750 as poetry had been in the Age of Shakespeare and the novel was to be in the Age of Sir Walter Scott." The same could be said of America. For example, in 1774 Abigail Adams described to her absent husband a "charming" picture of young Johnny's reading to her

Though none but the British had worked out a system of executive authority that combined adequate energy with public safety, history was teeming with examples of experiments in executive power, and from these many principles were to be derived.

Let me emphasize again that the history surveyed here is obviously selective, covering that portion of the past which bore on the task of creating viable executives. Furthermore, the version of the past presented here is not necessarily accurate as measured by modern scholarship; indeed it is often legendary or downright mistaken. The inaccuracies, however, are of no consequence to the task at hand—to reconstruct the relevant portion of the past as the Framers understood it, from the works they read and from none other.

———— The history with which the largest number of Americans were familiar was that recounted in the Bible. Orators and political writers cited and quoted from the Bible more frequently than they referred to Blackstone, Montesquieu, Bolingbroke, and Hume combined. Several of the creators of the presidency, including Gouverneur Morris and John Dickinson, could lay claim to expertise as biblical scholars, and almost every literate American (and many illiterates as well) could follow and understand biblical references when applied in a political context. Moreover, though the Bible is concerned primarily with the relationships between God and the Jewish people, it contains a great deal about the evolution of executive power.

In the earliest part of the story, other nations, notably the Egyptians, had kingships with fairly elaborate administrative machinery, but little was offered regarding governance among the Hebrews. The patriarchs Abraham, Isaac, and Jacob communed directly with God

---

Charles Rollin's *Ancient History,* an activity that also instructed her in the rises and falls of ancient governments (Phyllis Lee Levin, *Abagail Adams: A Biography* [New York, 1987], 39). "The Essex Result," a summary of the views expressed by towns in Essex concerning a constitution for Massachusetts in 1778, advised one who "undertakes to form a constitution . . . to be master of the histories of all the empires and states which are now existing, and all those which have figured in antiquity, and thereby able to collect and blend their respective excellencies, and avoid those defects which experience hath pointed out" (*American Political Writing during the Founding Era 1760–1805,* ed. Charles S. Hyneman and Donald S. Lutz, 2 vols. [Indianapolis, IN, 1983], 1:485).

and attempted to carry out His commands, but their temporal authority rested upon a combination of persuasiveness and positions as heads of tribes or extended families.

Shortly after God delivered the children of Israel from bondage in Egypt ("that they may serve me"), we learn that Moses had been acting as judge in personal disputes as well as being the leader and commander in chief of his people. At that point Moses' father-in-law suggested that the burden was too heavy and that he delegate law enforcement to carefully chosen men, "captains" or "judges," who would constitute a permanent court. The need to instruct these men in the law occasioned Moses' trip to the top of Mount Sinai to receive the Ten Commandments. Moses also received a rudimentary civil and criminal code, complete with punishments, but no further information was provided regarding the execution of the laws. That the captains or judges were also magistrates—and that Moses was the chief magistrate—became clear later, when Moses ordered certain idolators put to death. The priests too had the authority to execute Israelites for disobeying the law.[2]

The next step in the evolution of government came just before the Israelites entered the Promised Land. God told them, through Moses, to govern themselves: "Judges and officers" were to be elected by the men of the several tribes (or the elders) to "judge the people with just judgment." But almost immediately afterward, knowing that the Israelites would shrink from the burdens of self-government (or from obedience to God as king), He instructed them as to what would happen when they asked for an earthly king. God would permit it, but He must choose the king, and the king would have limited powers and would rule according to law.[3]

2. Exod. 9:1, 18:13–27, chaps. 20–23; Num. 11:14–17, 25:4–8; Deut. 1:12–18. I have used the King James version, on the ground that the Framers were likely to have used it. But also extremely helpful are *The New English Bible with the Apocrypha*, ed. Samuel Sandmel (New York, 1976), and *The Cambridge Bible Commentary on the New English Bible: The First Book of Samuel* and *The Second Book of Samuel*, ed. Peter R. Ackroyd (Cambridge, Eng., 1971, 1977).

3. Deut. 16:18, 17:14–20, 21:2. Jonathan Mayhew was "initiated" into the doctrines of civil liberty by "such men as Plato, Demosthenes, Cicero," and other ancients and by "Sidney and Milton, Locke and Hoadley" among the moderns, but he

The experiment in self-government was successful as long as Joshua, Moses' successor, was around. Joshua served as commander of the Israelite armies as they entered and conquered the Promised Land; as soon as he died, the Israelites lapsed into idolatry, and God punished them by allowing their enemies to defeat them. Thereafter, for more than two centuries, God periodically set "judges" over them, whose concern was less with the meting of justice and the enforcement of the law than with commanding them in warfare and delivering them from their enemies and from their own sinfulness. A cycle of prosperity, apostasy, punishment, repentance, and delivery recurred under a succession of judges, from Othniel through Deborah and Gideon to Samson. During that period the people sought to make Gideon king, but he refused; one of his sons, Abimelech, usurped power and made himself king for three years. The Lord clearly opposed monarchy, but the clamor for a king did not abate. In the absence of a king Israel drifted toward anarchy. Repeatedly, we are told, "In those days there was no king in Israel, but every man did that which was right in his own eyes."4

It was the last of the judges, Samuel, who finally gave the Israelites a king. When Samuel grew old, he appointed his two sons as judges to succeed him, but they were corrupt, taking bribes and perverting justice. The elders therefore met and agreed to ask him to "make us a king to judge us like all the nations." Samuel was displeased, and he prayed to the Lord, Who answered that the people were not rejecting

---

"earlier still learn't from the holy scriptures . . . that God gave the Israelites a king [or absolute monarch] in his anger, because they had not sense and virtue enough to like a free commonwealth" ("The Snare Broken," 1766, in *Political Sermons of the American Founding Era 1730–1805,* ed. Ellis Sandoz [Indianapolis, IN, 1991], 258).

4. Josh. passim; Judg. 2:6–15, 17:6, 21:25, and passim. Flavius Josephus, *Antiquities of the Jews,* in *The Genuine Works of Flavius Josephus,* trans. William Whiston, 2 vols. (Boston, 1823), says that "aristocracy . . . is the best constitution" and later notes that Samuel hated "royal government, for he was very fond of an aristocracy," bk. 4, chap. 8, 112, bk. 6, chap. 3, 160. During the contest for ratification in 1788, Samuel Langdon preached a sermon, "The Republic of the Israelites an Example to the American States," in which he traced the biblical history contained in these paragraphs as "the best instructor both in polity and morals," substituting the thirteen American states for the twelve tribes of Israel (Sandoz, ed., *Political Sermons,* 945–957).

Samuel but God Himself. God told Samuel to warn the people about the sort of king who would reign over them: He will draft their sons into military or personal service, he will take their daughters for service in his household, he will tax them unmercifully and reduce them to slavery. Still, the people persisted in their demands to have a king, and the Lord relented.⁵

Despite God's displeasure, the Israelite monarchy (later divided into the separate kingdoms of Judah and Israel) turned out for the most part to be a reasonably happy institution—at least for a time. It helped, of course, that God selected the kings. Though the first choice, Saul, ultimately disobeyed and lost favor with the Lord, Saul ruled well, and the people prospered during most of his twenty-two-year reign. His successor, David, reigned for forty years; David aroused the wrath of God by his adulterous relationship with Bathsheba, his son Absalom led an abortive revolt, and late in his reign the people suffered a three-year famine as punishment; but overall David's kingship was heroic. The next king, Solomon, prayed for wisdom, received it, and ruled wisely and splendidly for forty more years. After that the kingship was a mixed bag; Solomon's son Rehoboam was a wicked tyrant, some successors were genuine monsters, only two (Hezekiah and Josiah, who ruled sixty years between them) were fully approved by the Lord. At last, after nearly half a millennium, both kingdoms collapsed.⁶

---

5. 1 Sam. 8:1–5, 8–15. That "the sons of Samuel . . . walked not in his ways" proved the truth of Prov. 29:2; see Gad Hitchcock, "An Election Sermon," Boston, 1774, in Hyneman and Lutz, ed., *American Political Writing*, 1:282–284. The meaning of 1 Sam. 8 for many Americans was that *"absolute monarchy"* was the least likely form of government to accomplish the desired ends of government, "nor is there any one that has so little pretence to a *divine original,* unless it be in this sense, that God *first* introduced it into, and thereby overturned, the common wealth of *Israel,* as a *curse* upon that people for their *folly* and *wickedness,* particularly in *desiring* such a government" (Jonathan Mayhew, "A Discourse concerning unlimited Submission," in *Puritan Political Ideas 1558–1794,* ed. Edmund S. Morgan [Indianapolis, IN, 1965], 311n). Mercy Warren quotes 1 Sam. 8 in commending Americans for not acting like "the ungrateful Israelites" when considering the presidency (*History of the Rise, Progress and Termination of the American Revolution,* ed. Lester H. Cohen, 2 vols. [Indianapolis, IN, 1988, first ed. Boston, 1805], 2:664).

6. 1 Sam. chaps. 13–15; 2 Sam. chaps. 13–16, 21:1–5; 1 Kings and 2 Kings passim.

Though this "Deuteronomic history"—from Deuteronomy through Second Kings—was not directly useful to the makers of the presidency, it was valuable for the principles it taught. For example, in warning of the probable infidelity of presidents to the policies of their predecessors, Gouverneur Morris remarked that "Rehoboam will not imitate Solomon" and urged that appropriate precautions be devised. And the biblical accounts of the kings after Solomon gave the Framers a chilling message: It is virtually impossible to confine the chief magistrate within the bounds of the law, even if that law be divinely ordained.7

——— Quite as daunting in general was the example of the ancient Greeks. Alexander Hamilton bespoke a common American attitude when he wrote that it was impossible to read of the ancients "without feeling sensations of horror and disgust at the distractions with which they were continually agitated" and at their "perpetual vibration between the extremes of tyranny and anarchy."8

Americans took their Greek history from a variety of sources. Herodotus on the Persian Wars, Thucydides on the Peloponnesian War (in the Hobbes translation), Xenophon (who picked up where Thucydides left off) and Arrian on Alexander the Great were readily available in public and private libraries. Most commonly, Americans read Plutarch's *Lives*, which covered the whole range of Greek and

7. *The Records of the Federal Convention of 1787*, ed. Max Farrand, 4 vols. (New Haven, CT, 1937), 2:113 (Madison's notes, July 25); Josephus, in *Antiquities of the Jews*, bks. 4, 6–8, makes the story quite accessible and points out the message dramatically: See especially bk. 6, chap. 12, on the "wickedness" of kings and the corrupting impact of power. See also Ellis Sandoz, *A Government of Laws: Political Theory, Religion, and the American Founding* (Baton Rouge, LA, 1991), 98–101. For examples of the biblical lesson applied specifically to the presidency, see *The Complete Anti-Federalist,* ed. Herbert J. Storing, 7 vols. (Chicago, 1981), 2:387, 3:29, 112, 4:107–108, 195, 236, 5:59, 6:82–83, 95, 152, 216.

8. *Federalist* 9. Madison in *Federalist* 18 introduces a rehearsal of Greek history: "Among the confederacies of antiquity, the most considerable was that of the Grecian Republics associated under the Amphyctionic Council. From the best accounts transmitted of this celebrated institution, it bore a very instructive analogy to the present confederation of the American States." See also Gilbert Chinard, "Polybius and the American Constitution," *Journal of the History of Ideas* 1 (1940):38–58.

Roman history up to the first century A.D. A large number of modern historians whom Americans read, beginning with Sir Walter Ralegh, had written world histories in which they quoted at length from ancient sources. Possibly the most widely read was Charles Rollin's *The Ancient History,* published in two volumes in 1738. Thomas Jefferson thought the best "digested view" of the history of Greece was Oliver Goldsmith's. James Madison apparently preferred John Gillies' recently published *History of Ancient Greece.* Other readers mentioned John Potter's *Antiquities of Greece.* And John Adams, in his *Defence of the Constitutions,* published shortly before the Philadelphia convention met, devoted a large portion of his work to descriptions of ancient republican governments.[9]

Three chapters of Greek history particularly interested Americans of the founding generation. One concerned Lacedaemonia and its principal city of Sparta, which ardent American republicans in the 1770s professed to admire more than any other Greek city-state. According to legend, Lacedaemonia was given its constitution and laws by a "semi-divine" figure named Lycurgus some time between 1000 and 700 B.C. Lacedaemonia was a communitarian military state in which all male citizens were trained from childhood as disciplined soldiers; they had no other occupations, ordinary labor being done by a slave population four times as numerous as the citizen-soldiers.

9. *The Persian Wars by Herodotus,* trans. George Rawlinson, intro. Francis R. B. Godolphin (New York, 1942); Thucydides, *The Peloponnesian War,* trans. Thomas Hobbes, ed. David Grene (Chicago, 1989); *The Greek Historians: The Complete and Unabridged Works of Herodotus, Thucydides, Xenophon, Arrian,* ed. Francis R. B. Godolphin, 2 vols. (New York, 1942); *Plutarch: The Lives of the Noble Grecians and Romans,* trans. John Dryden, rev. Arthur Hugh Clough (New York, n.d.); Sir Walter Ralegh, *The History of the World,* ed. C. A. Patrides (Philadelphia, 1971); Charles Rollin, *The Ancient History,* 2 vols. (New York, 1841; first English ed., London, 1738); Oliver Goldsmith, *The Grecian History, from the Earliest State to the Death of Alexander the Great,* 2 vols., 8th Amer. ed. (New York, 1816); Jefferson to Peter Carr, Aug. 19, 1785, in *Thomas Jefferson: Writings,* ed. Merrill D. Peterson (New York, 1984), 816; *The Papers of James Madison,* ed. William T. Hutchinson, Robert Allen Rutland et al., 10 vols. (Chicago, 1962–1970), 9:7, 22, 23, 4:169; John Gillies, *The History of Ancient Greece* (Philadelphia, 1831; repr. 1786 London ed.); H. Trevor Colbourn, *The Lamp of Experience* (Chapel Hill, NC, 1965); *The Works of John Adams,* ed. Charles Francis Adams, 10 vols. (Freeport, NY, 1969), especially vol. 4.

To avoid the corrupting influences of luxury and contact with foreigners, trade was severely restricted, and the private possession of gold and silver was forbidden.[10]

The Lacedaemonians had a mixed system of government long before the concept of mixed government had been formulated. Two hereditary monarchs served as ministers of religion, judges in peacetime, and commanders in war. These two kings belonged to and jointly presided over the *gerousia* or senate, which consisted of twenty-eight chiefs of the several tribes, who served for life. The senate had an advance veto on proposed legislation, determining what the legislative assembly could deliberate upon. The latter, the *appella,* was actually two bodies: the greater assembly, composed of 9,000 Spartans, and the lesser assembly, composed of 30,000 Lacedaemonians. To supervise and administer the whole, five magistrates, the "ephori," were elected annually. Once a month the ephori and the kings took mutually supporting oaths that the constitution and laws be kept inviolate and the senate be restrained from usurping power. Lest inordinate power follow from an accumulation of property, as happened elsewhere throughout the ancient world, Lycurgus effected an equal distribution of property.[11]

10. Herodotus, *Persian Wars,* bk. 1, chaps. 65–66; Plutarch, *Lives,* 49–74; Gillies, *Ancient Greece,* 40–47; Goldsmith, *Grecian History,* 1:15–19; Rollin, *Ancient History,* 1:173–178, 2:425. Rollin, at 1:315, points out that gold and silver were introduced, but after heated disagreement, it was decided that only the state could possess such metals; the circulating medium of the citizens was made of iron. "The Essex Result" expressed a common American attitude toward the great lawgivers: "To determine what form of government, in any given case, will produce the greatest possible happiness to the subject, is an arduous task, not to be compassed perhaps by any human powers. Some of the greatest geniuses and most learned philosophers of all ages, impelled by their solicitude to promote the happiness of mankind, have nobly dared to attempt it: and their labours have crowned them with immortality. A Solon, a Lycurgus of Greece, a Numa of Rome are remembered with honor" (Hyneman and Lutz, ed., *American Political Writing,* 1:485).

11. Xenophon, "The Constitution of the Spartans," in Godolphin, ed., *Greek Historians,* 2:658–675; Rollin, *Ancient History,* 1:174; Goldsmith, *Grecian History,* 1:10–14; Gillies, *Ancient Greece,* 41–42; Adams, ed., *Works of Adams,* 4:549–560; *Polybius on Roman Imperialism: The Histories of Polybius,* trans. Evelyn S. Shuckburgh, abr. by Alvin H. Bernstein (New York, 1980), bk. 6, chaps. 10, 48–50, pp. 185–186, 211–213. Plutarch, in his life of Lycurgus, says, at p. 54, that the ephori were added to the

It is easy to be appalled by the rigor and brutality of Lacedaemonian life. The Athenian Alcibiades said, "No wonder the Spartans cheerfully encounter death; it is a welcome relief to them from such a life as they are obliged to lead." And yet, though John Adams described Lycurgus' handiwork as the most nearly balanced constitution in the ancient world, he thought it would have degenerated into an oligarchy but for the suppression of "every other appetite, passion, and affection in human nature" except the love of glory. For whatever reasons, the Lacedaemonian regime survived unchanged for at least four centuries, during most of which it was the dominant power in the region. According to Xenophon, who fought both with and against the Spartans, they had weakened somewhat by the fifth century B.C., but even so they were able to inflict a total defeat upon Athens in 404.[12]

The second event in Greek history that was of special interest to the Founders was Solon's new modeling of the Athenian constitution, traditionally dated in 594 B.C. Athens under Draco—whose code prescribed the death penalty for every imaginable offense—had degenerated into a combination of anarchy and oppression. Corruption plagued the public councils, and the rich were merciless in exploiting the poor, many of whom were forced to sell their children into slavery to pay their debts. The impoverished many were de-

---

constitution 130 years later; but Herodotus, *Persian Wars,* bk. 1, chap. 65, and Xenophon, "Spartan Constitution," include the ephors in Lycurgus' original order. See also Gillies, *Ancient History,* 42, n.5, which points out that Plutarch was mistakenly following Aristotle.

12. Thucydides, *Peloponnesian War,* 11 and passim; Xenophon, "Hellenica," in Godolphin, ed., *Greek Historians,* bks. 1–2, pp. 3–55; Rollin, *Ancient History,* 1:177–180; Adams, ed., *Works of Adams,* 4:553. Alcibiades' quotation is from *The Works of Fisher Ames,* ed. William B. Allen, 2 vols. (Indianapolis, IN, 1983), 1:97. Interestingly, when Alcibiades was forced to flee Athens for Sparta he "won over everybody by his conformity to Spartan habits. People who saw him wearing his hair close cut, bathing in cold water, eating coarse meal, and dining on black broth, doubted, or rather could not believe, that he ever had a cook in his house, or had ever seen a perfumer, or had worn a mantle of Milesian purple" (Plutarch, *Lives,* 249). During the ratification debates "A Briton" in the *Gazette of the State of Georgia,* Dec. 13, 1787, satirically asked why the president should be paid so lavish a salary given Americans' admiration of Spartan society in which "all ranks lived on broth made of beans."

manding a redistribution of all property as well as a cancellation of debts, and they were threatening to take up arms. The rich few had large numbers of clients and other dependents, however, and could have resisted so that wholesale casualties would have resulted on both sides. Solon, a wise and learned man, was wealthy but was trusted by the poor, and he was asked and then authorized to draft a constitution and code of laws. Unlike Lycurgus, he was unable to institute the best constitution he could devise: Instead of leaving the Athenians "the best laws that could be given," as Plutarch has him saying, he gave them "the best they could receive."[13]

Solon sought to establish a system of compromises, checks, and balances. In dealing with the most explosive problem, the extremes of wealth, he struck a middle ground: a general cancellation of debts but no redistribution of property. (Some of his friends capitalized upon foreknowledge of his intentions, going deeply into debt to buy land that they were able to retain after the debts were annulled.) As for governmental reforms, Solon vested in the collective body of citizens, convened in a general assembly, the powers to decide on war or peace, to make or dissolve foreign alliances, to enact all laws, and to elect, approve, and judge the magistrates entrusted temporarily with executive authority. He divided the people into four classes, based upon income. All four could vote in the assembly and serve as jurors in both criminal and civil trials, but only the first three could sit in the senate, hold seats in a sort of super senate called the areopagus, or be elected magistrates. The senate, consisting of 400 members, had the power to convoke the assembly, to veto proposed legislation in advance (as in Sparta), and to make laws that were in force as long as a year. It also had much of the executive authority, including custody of the public treasury and the power to build ships, raise armies and navies, and punish certain crimes. The principal magistrates were nine archons, who were elected indirectly by the people for one-year terms. The first archon was the chief justice, presiding over the civil law courts; the second, who was called king, presided over religious matters; the third, the polemarch, with ten

13. Plutarch, *Lives,* 104–105; Rollin, *Ancient History,* 1:180–185; Gillies, *Ancient Greece,* 162–163; Goldsmith, *Grecian History,* 1:25–29.

elected generals, presided over military matters; the remaining six directed criminal courts and meted justice. At the end of their terms, the archons were reviewed by the people, and if their services were deemed satisfactory they were made life members of the areopagus—which was "the supreme court of judicature" and exercised a general superintendancy over the laws and the lives, religion, and manners of the citizens—and had power in emergencies to assume dictatorial authority.[14]

Plutarch records that as Solon was preparing his reforms, Anacharsis chided him for imagining that the dishonest and covetous Athenians "could be restrained by written laws, which were like spiders' webs," able to catch "the weak and poor, but easily . . . broken by the mighty and rich." Solon replied "that men keep their promises when neither side can get anything by the breaking of them" and that he would arrange his laws so all understood it to be more advantageous "to be just than to break the laws." As Plutarch added, Solon's hopes proved less realistic than his friend's expectations.[15]

Scarcely a generation passed before power was usurped by Pisistratus, who took over "the royal dignities of priest and general" and placed the lesser magistracies in the hands of his partisans. He did "give stability to most of the laws and forms introduced by Solon" but without restoring any power to the demos. He and his sons ruled for sixty-eight years, until some measure of popular participation was restored. Thereafter, Athens grew progressively more democratic as its citizens won victories and booty during the Persian Wars, and in 479 members of the fourth class were made eligible for the magis-

14. Gillies, *Ancient Greece*, 162–164; Plutarch, *Lives*, 106–109; Rollin, *Ancient History*, 1:182, 248 n.7; Goldsmith, *Grecian History*, 1:30–32; Aristotle, "The Constitution of Athens," in Godolphin, ed., *Greek Historians*, 2:681. At 1:171, 180, Rollin records that Athens had become a "commonwealth" in 1070 B.C.: Medon, the first archon—"that is to say, president or governor"—was chosen for life, but that being too monarchical, the term was reduced to ten years and later to one year. During the ratification debate Alexander White presented a rather garbled account of the archons to justify a single executive; see *The Documentary History of the Ratification of the Constitution*, ed. Merrill Jensen and John P. Kaminski et al., 8 vols. to date (Madison, WI, 1976–1988), 8:442.

15. Plutarch, *Lives*, 100; Rollin, *Ancient History*, 1:182; Goldsmith, *Grecian History*, 1:27, 29, 32.

tracies. Democratization was attended by heroic military feats and by corrupt and disastrously unstable domestic politics. As Polybius observed in passing, "the Athenian demus is always in the position of a ship without a commander"; Athens could repel "the greatest and most formidable dangers by the valour of its people and their leaders," but then "in periods of secure tranquillity" they would "gratuitously and recklessly" court disaster. Clearly, the American Framers would have to come up with something better than Solon had.[16]

A third lesson in government from Greek history came not from an event but from a discussion, and a fictitious one at that. Herodotus, who more or less invented written history, sprinkled his *Persian Wars* with imaginary conversations and orations—a convention adhered to by most of the historians who succeeded him in the ancient world. At one point Herodotus describes a group of Persian conspirators discussing the form of government they will impose on their compatriots. One proposes democracy, saying that it had "the fairest of names, equality before the law; and further it is free from all those outrages which a king is wont to commit," as "the magistrate is answerable for what he does." The others reject the rule of the many on the ground that "there is nothing so void of understanding, nothing so full of wantonness as the unwieldy rabble." Another suggests oligarchy, but that too is rejected. In oligarchies, men vie with one another for power and influence, even as in democracies they plot against the public interest; and both forms end in monarchy. The conspirators decide to opt for monarchy at the outset: "What government can possibly be better than that of the very best man in the whole state?"[17]

16. *Polybius on Roman Imperialism,* bk. 1, chap. 44, p. 209; Plutarch, *Lives,* 115–117; Gillies, *Ancient Greece,* 165–167; Rollin, *Ancient History,* 1:184–185, 248, 315, 318–320. Plutarch, in his life of Alcibiades (*Lives,* 261–262), describes how Lysander, after defeating Athens, set up a dictatorship of thirty tyrants. Though the Thirty were soon overthrown, the degeneracy of democracy into despotism was another lesson for Americans. As James Wilson said during the Federal Convention (June 1), "A plurality in the Executive of Government would probably produce a tyranny as bad as the thirty Tyrants of Athens, or as the Decemvirs of Rome" (Farrand, ed., *Records,* 1:74). See also *Federalist* 70.

17. Herodotus, *Persian Wars,* bk. 3, chaps. 80–82. William Pierce, a delegate to the Constitutional Convention, related this discussion to St. George Tucker, June 27, 1787, but he got the story secondhand from Burlamaqui (Jensen and Kaminski, ed.,

In 1776, almost no American patriot shared that line of reasoning. By 1787, no small number had come to appreciate it.

———— Roman history was both more familiar and more instructive to Americans. Titus Livius observed early in his *History of Rome* that "there has never been any commonwealth grander or purer or richer in good examples." Readers of Sallust—the first of the ancients whom schoolboys encountered after memorizing the rudiments of Latin grammar—could have added that there had never been a commonwealth richer in horrible examples.[18]

In addition to Livy and Sallust, American readers had available adequate translations of Dionysius of Halicarnassus, Polybius, and Plutarch among ancient chroniclers of the Roman republic and popular eighteenth-century accounts by Adam Ferguson, the Abbot de Vertot, Oliver Goldsmith, and Charles Rollin. Montesquieu, Walter Moyle, John Adams, and other thinkers wrote essays analyzing the evolution of the republican constitution but assumed that their readers knew the history in general. (The history of imperial Rome was

————

Documentary History of Ratification, 16:446). Pierce added, "I pray you not from this story to conclude that we are to have a Monarchy,—I relate it merely to give you some idea of the various opinions which we have sometimes started."

18. *Livy: A History of Rome: Selections,* trans. and intro. Moses Hadas and Joe P. Poe (New York, 1962), bk. 1; Sallust, *The Jugurthine War: The Conspiracy of Cataline,* trans. and intro. S. A. Handford (London, 1963). Richard M. Gummere, *The American Colonial Mind and the Classical Tradition: Essays in Comparative Culture* (Cambridge, MA, 1963), 174, says that "the delegates to the Constitutional Convention assembled at a time when the influence of the classics was at its height. They were not interested in mere window dressing or in popular slogans. . . . They dealt with fundamental ideas and considered them in the light of their applicability." For examples during the convention when the ancients were directly cited in regard to the executive, see remarks by Wilson (June 1, 16), Butler (June 4), Mason (June 4), Madison (June 7, 19, 29), Hamilton (June 18, 19), Gerry (June 23), and G. Morris (August 15), in Farrand, ed., *Records,* 1:74, 254, 100, 112, 151–152, 319, 465, 290 (307), 329, 393, 2:299–300. See also Gummere, *American Colonial Mind,* 174–190, and Paul A. Rahe, *Republics Ancient and Modern: Classical Republicanism and the American Revolution* (Chapel Hill, NC, 1992), 9–13. For examples of anti-Federalist uses of the ancients to criticize the proposed executive, see Storing, ed., *Complete Anti-Federalist,* 2:311, 313, 414, 3:38, 48, 4:38, 153, 237, 277, 5:17, 139–140, 158–159, 190, 230, 266, 6:19, 94, 103.

less relevant to Americans than treatises on the republic, though they read it anyway, mainly in Suetonius and Tacitus among the ancients and in Edward Gibbon's masterful *Decline and Fall of the Roman Empire*, three volumes of which had appeared before 1787.)[19]

The domestic history of Rome—as opposed to its rise to domination of the known world—was generally understood in terms of cycles of decay. Indeed, Roman history was the history of public morality. According to legend, in 753 B.C. Romulus established a monarchy that ultimately deteriorated into a despotism; in 509 it was overthrown by the patricians, who established an aristocracy; the plebeians soon began to clamor for a share in power and gradually won it over the course of the next two centuries, establishing something of a democracy dominated by a virtuous Senate; the three Punic Wars (264–241, 218–202, 151–146) and conquests in the east introduced great wealth and corruption; the Gracchan reforms failed, venality permeated public life, and democracy degenerated into virtual anarchy; from Marius and Sulla through Julius Caesar sheer force replaced the constitution and laws; and at last in 27, stability was restored by the establishment of the Augustan principate. Vertot closed

19. Dionysius of Halicarnassus, *The Roman Antiquities,* trans. Earnest Cary, 7 vols. (Cambridge, MA, 1932–1950); this translation is based on that of Edward Spelman; some library catalogs listed Dionysius as Spelman: See Colbourn, *Lamp of Experience,* 212. *Polybius on Roman Imperialism;* Plutarch, *Lives;* Adam Ferguson, *The History of the Progress and Termination of the Roman Republic,* 3 vols. (Philadelphia, 1811); Rene Aubert, Abbot de Vertot, *The History of the Revolutions that Happened in the Government of the Roman Republic,* trans. Mr. Ozell, 2 vols., 5th ed. (London, 1740); Oliver Goldsmith, *Pinnock's Improved Edition of Dr. Goldsmith's History of Rome,* 35th ed. (Philadelphia, 1848); Charles Rollin, *The Roman History from the Foundation of Rome to the Battle of Actium,* 16 vols. (London, 1739–1750); Montesquieu, *Considerations on the Causes of the Grandeur and Decadence of the Romans,* trans. Jehu Baker (New York, 1882); *Two English Republican Tracts: Plato Redivivus, or A Dialogue Concerning Government (c. 1681) by Henry Neville; An Essay upon the Constitution of the Roman Government (c. 1699) by Walter Moyle,* ed. Caroline Robbins (Cambridge, MA, 1969); Adams, ed., *Works of Adams,* vol. 4; Gaius Suetonius Tranquillus, *The Twelve Caesars,* trans. Robert Graves, rev. Michael Grant (New York, 1987); Tacitus, *Complete Works of Tacitus,* trans. Alfred John Church and William Jackson Brodribb, ed. and intro. Moses Hadas (New York, 1942). The first volume of Gibbon's *Decline and Fall* was published in 1776, the second and third in 1781, the last three in 1788; I used the three-volume abridgment by D. M. Low (New York, 1962).

his history by saying that the emperor Augustus, by artful conduct, did "insensibly accustom Men free-born and of free condition, to bear with Slavery, and made a new Monarchy supportable to ancient Common-wealths-men."[20]

The example of Rome was valuable to the American Framers partly as a caution and partly for its many permutations in the relationship between executive power and the other branches of government. During the reign of the founding king, Romulus, the crown had limited powers at first: He summoned armies and served as commander in chief, directed the disposition of public moneys, served as religious leader, called the Senate and the popular assemblies into session, presided over the Senate, proposed legislation, and judged serious crimes. But questions relating to peace or war, the election of magistrates, and the dispensing of justice were settled by the assemblies, again subject only to approval of the Senate. As time went on, however, Romulus took on increased power, especially through distributing land and other spoils of war. The upper classes grew restive, and one day Romulus, at the age of fifty-five and after thirty-seven years as king, simply disappeared. The senators were at pains to deny having killed him.[21]

Despite Romulus' demise, the monarchy continued to be tolerably stable for more than a century and a quarter. Romulus left no heirs, and after a year's interregnum in which senators rotated the royal duties and powers among themselves, five days each, a king was elected. Numa (715–673) concerned himself mainly with religious affairs, and his reign was marked by peace and prosperity. The next three kings—Tullius Hostilius, Ancus Marcius, and Lucius Tarquinius Priscus—were likewise elected; they reigned from 673 to 579, and Rome continued to thrive and expand.[22]

20. Vertot, *Revolutions of the Roman Republic,* 2:351 and passim; Gibbon, *Decline and Fall,* 1:46–48; Rollin, *Roman History,* passim.

21. Vertot, *Revolutions of the Roman Republic,* 1:intro. and 1–14; Dionysius, *Roman Antiquities,* bk. 2, chaps. 3, 7, 9–14; Livy, *History of Rome,* bk. 1, chap. 8; Plutarch, "Romulus," in *Lives,* 24–46; Robbins, ed., *Moyle's Constitution of the Roman Government,* 207–208; Rollin, *Roman History,* 1:17–31, 60–62; Goldsmith, *History of Rome,* 66–68, 70.

22. Plutarch, "Numa Pomilius," in *Lives,* 74–92; Vertot, *Revolutions of the Roman Republic,* 1:15–21; Livy, *History of Rome,* bk. 1, chaps. 19, 20, 34; Dionysius, *Roman Antiquities,* bk. 2, chaps. 58–76, bk. 3 passim.

Then troubles set in. The sons of Ancus Marcius, considering Tarquinius Priscus a usurper and thinking one of them should have succeeded their father, assassinated that king. Tarquinius' daughter, however, kept the death a secret and announced that her father had chosen her husband, Servius Tullius, to manage affairs of state until the king recovered. Tullius then played strongly to the poor, canceling debts, distributing land, instituting progressive taxation, exempting the very poorest from both taxes and military service, and promising equal justice before the law. Thus wooed, the people elected Tullius king upon being told of Tarquinius' death, whereupon he ingratiated himself with the rich by dividing the propertied into five classes, based upon wealth, and by instituting a rigged system of voting to ensure that the rich would dominate every popular assembly. These various reforms strengthened Rome militarily and might have stabilized the regime by allying the monarch with the aristocracy but for the murder of Servius Tullius by his son-in-law, Tarquinius Superbus, who seized the kingship without election by the Senate or people.[23]

Tarquin retreated from the public forum and ruled through a personal army of thugs, contemptuous of patricians and plebeians alike. He had most of the senators killed on one pretext or another, which was acceptable to the plebes until he turned on them, abolishing Tullius' laws for equal justice, returning to equal taxation, and conscripting labor for public works. Finally, at the hands of Lucius Junius Brutus, Tarquin was forced from power, and in 509 the commonwealth or republican era began.[24]

23. Dionysius, *Roman Antiquities,* bk. 3, chap. 68, bk. 4, chaps. 1–39; Livy, *History of Rome,* bk. 1, chaps. 34–43; Vertot, *Revolutions of the Roman Republic,* 1: 21–25; Robbins, ed., *Moyle's Constitution of the Roman Government,* 224, 230, 232–233, 243, 245; Rollin, *Roman History,* 1:143–145, 146–171; Goldsmith, *History of Rome,* 80–82.

24. Vertot, *Revolutions of the Roman Republic,* 1:25–30; Rollin, *Roman History,* 1:172–197; Livy, *History of Rome,* bk. 1, chaps. 48–60; Dionysius, *Roman Antiquities,* bk. 4, chaps. 41–72; Plutarch, "Poplicola," in *Lives,* 118–123. Dionysius begins bk. 5, chap. 1, "An aristocracy being now established." Livy begins his bk. 2 (509–468 B.C.), "From this point on my subject will be the history of a free people—its deeds in peace and war, its magistrates now elected annually, and the rule of laws more powerful than men." Among the charges of tyranny levied by Livy against Tarquin are that "he took into his own hands trials in capital cases," that he "abandoned the traditional

The establishment of aristocratic republican institutions, largely the work of Publius Valerius Publicola, entailed several innovations. The first was the replacement of the king with two consuls, patricians annually elected by the people assembled and voting by tribes. The consuls had the same powers the kings had had, but which consul was to exercise which powers was not specified. Sometimes functions were divided by lot, sometimes they were shared, and sometimes a division was agreed to; legally both had full power. The consuls were checked by the need to consult the Senate in matters of peace and war as well as in more routine affairs. Publius Valerius strengthened the Senate (depleted as it had been by Tarquin) by appointing 164 new members, many of them plebeians. Thus began a long process by which wealthy plebeians were merged with patricians to form a new and more viable aristocracy. The consuls could propose legislation to the popular assemblies only after obtaining approval from the Senate, and when laws were passed they required ratification by the Senate. Consuls, upon finishing their terms of service, automatically took seats in the Senate if they were not already members. Plebeians were legally eligible for consulships, but not until the middle of the fourth century did they get a guaranteed place.[25]

---

practice of consulting the senate in all matters," and that he "made war, peace, treaties, alliances" on his own authority (bk. 1, chap. 49).

25. Plutarch, "Poplicola," in *Lives*, 117–130; Vertot, *Revolutions of the Roman Republic*, 1:30–35; Dionysius, *Roman Antiquities*, bk. 5, chaps. 1–59; Livy, *History of Rome*, bk. 2, chaps. 1–2, bk. 4, chap. 5, bk. 6, chaps. 35–37, 42; Adams, ed., *Works of Adams*, 4:520–523; Goldsmith, *History of Rome*, 88; Gibbon, *Decline and Fall*, 1:46–47. Brutus in addressing the Senate specified that the new magistrates, the consuls, "ought to consult with the senate in everything, as the kings formerly did, and to do nothing without your advice, and that they ought to lay before the people the decrees of the senate" (Dionysius, *Roman Antiquities*, bk. 4, chap. 75). Ferguson, *History of the Roman Republic*, 1:16, describes the government as "entirely aristocratical" but says that the consuls "were the sole executive magistrates . . . in place of the king; performed all the functions of royalty . . . united in their own persons all the dignities of the state, those of *Judge, Magistrate,* and *Military Leader.*" Livy makes clear (bk. 2, chap. 1) that liberty under the republic "should not be attributed to any reduction in the authority possessed by the kings but to the limitation of the consular term of office to a single year." John Adams turned this point into the most "infallible" maxim, "where annual elections end, there slavery begins"

Other innovations in the executive authority were soon forthcoming. Though consuls nominally still directed public expenditures, as the kings had, the actual administration of the public finances was now entrusted to two treasurers called quaestors, who doubled as judges and prosecutors in criminal cases. The office of tribune was established. Tribunes were annually elected from the ranks of the people and vested with two important powers, that of the veto ("I forbid") of decrees of the Senate and that of calling the popular assemblies. The function of the tribunes was "to interpose in the Defence of the Plebeians. . . . Such Magistrates seemed designed only to prevent the Oppression of the Distressed; but they did not long contain themselves within the Bounds." From the senatorial point of view, giving tribunes portions of the executive authority was a nuisance. They were forever stirring up trouble. The senators ultimately learned to neutralize them by expanding their number from the original two to ten; any one tribune could veto the proposals of the others, and the Senate could usually find one who would do its bidding.[26]

In the meantime, domestic turbulence was so great except during wars (and sometimes even then) that the Senate resorted to an innovation, the dictatorship. In emergencies, the laws were suspended and one of the consuls, on authorization by the Senate, was appointed dictator with plenary power to last no more than six months. Dic-

---

(*Thoughts on Government* [1776], in Hyneman and Lutz, ed., *American Political Writing,* 1:406); and a rotation was "earnestly recommended" by the town of Lexington in 1778, citing as a "striking Instance" the "Commonwealth of Rome" in which no one could be elected consul, "the Supreme Magistrate," but "once in Ten Years" (*The Popular Sources of Political Authority,* ed. Oscar Handlin and Mary Handlin [Cambridge, MA, 1966], 319).

26. *Polybius on Roman Imperialism,* 187–192; Livy, *History of Rome,* bk. 2, chap. 8; Dionysius, *Roman Antiquities,* bk. 6, chaps. 61, 89–90, bk. 8, chap. 87; Goldsmith, *History of Rome,* 95; Ferguson, *History of the Roman Republic,* 1:21–24; Vertot, *Revolutions of the Roman Republic,* 1:75–79, 308, 413–415 (quote at 78–79). These developments had to be considered in light of Cicero's dictum, "The whole character of a republic is determined by its arrangements in regard to magistrates" (Cicero, *De Re Publica; De Legibus,* trans. Clinton Walker Keyes [London, 1928], in *De Legibus,* bk. 3, chap. 2).

tatorships were not uncommon up to the end of the second Punic War, and Dionysius said that none of the dictators ever abused his power until the institution was revitalized by Sulla in the first century B.C.[27]

Despite these changes, social unrest and discontent with executive authority continued. In 451 ambassadors were sent to Athens to find a good system of laws, and then decemvirs ("ten men") were chosen to draw up a code blending the best of Greek and Roman law for senatorial approval and popular confirmation. The decemvirs did so (the Twelve Tables), but decided also to usurp power for themselves. After a time they were overthrown, but instead of returning to the consular system, the people chose six military tribunes to exert the executive power. After seventy-three days, Rome reverted to having consuls, but during the next century the power of the consuls was gradually weakened, partly by the periodic replacement of consuls and tribunes by military tribunes, partly by an increase in tribunician power when the office existed, and partly by a proliferation of new, specialized executive offices that assumed most executive functions except military command. The routine administration of justice, for example, devolved upon praetors, and the supervision of the market and public entertainments was turned over to curule aediles. In 310 "the Censorship was erected; a new Office, or rather only a Portion taken out of the Consulship," which "became in time, by the Power annexed to it," the power of assigning people to classes, "the most formidable Magistracy in the Republic." The censors "took Cognizance of the Behaviour of every Citizen; the Senators and Knights were subject to their Censors as much as the meanest of the People; they had Power to expel out of those Bodies such as they thought unworthy."[28]

27. Dionysius, *Roman Antiquities,* bk. 5, chaps. 70, 73, 77; Ferguson, *History of the Roman Republic,* 1:17–18; Vertot, *Revolutions of the Roman Republic,* 1:42–44, 2:186–187. One dictator, famous among Americans, was Lucius Quintus Cincinnatus, who during his first dictatorship served sixteen days, defeated the Aequians, abdicated, and returned to his farm (Dionysius, *Roman Antiquities,* bk. 10, chap. 24); Livy, *History of Rome,* bk. 3, chap. 26, reports this as a minor incident later enlarged into a heroic story. See *Federalist* 70, for an American understanding of the institution.

28. Vertot, *Revolutions of the Roman Government,* 1:79, 253–308, 320–340, 421–

It was the consensus among eighteenth-century students of Rome
that the period from roughly 350 to 200 B.C. was the golden age of
the republic. During this time executive power was sufficiently diffused so as to pose no serious danger to liberty but sufficiently specialized so as to provide effective administration. Moreover, because
it became a routine practice for magistrates to take seats in the Senate
upon honorable completion of office, that body was regularly composed of the best of Roman citizens.[29]

Eighteenth-century commentators were likewise agreed as to the
cause of the decline of the republic: corruption of Roman morality by
the accession of great wealth from plunder and tribute, beginning
with the second defeat of Carthage. Throughout the second century
the love of wealth, luxury, and every known form of vice was rampant; the Senate became a closed corporation, taking power to itself
and emasculating the popular assemblies, bribing the tribunes and
the people, the one with cash and the other with free grain and
spectacular entertainments. A mediocracy was studiously promoted
by discouraging its opposite. Cato the Elder set a precedent that
would be repeatedly followed when, in 187 B.C., by a process that
amounted to impeachment, he forced into retirement and exile the
hero of the second Punic War, Scipio Africanus. Not long afterward,

---

422, quotes at 1:330–331; Ferguson, *History of the Roman Republic,* 1:33–34, 42–44;
Goldsmith, *History of Rome,* 106–109; Dionysius, *Roman Antiquities,* bk. 10, chaps.
50–59, bk. 11, chaps. 1–62; Livy, *History of Rome,* bk. 3, chaps. 33–55, bk. 7, chap. 1,
bk. 39, chaps. 40, 41, 44. Montesquieu, *Considerations on the Romans,* 170, calls the
censorship "a very wise institution"; Thomas Tudor Tucker, "Conciliatory Hints,"
Charleston, 1784, links the Decemviri to Cromwell as establishing "themselves more
arbitrary tyrants than those they had contributed to overthrow" (Hyneman and
Lutz, ed., *American Political Writing,* 1:612). Hamilton used the example of the
Decemvirs to show that a plural executive was "more to be dreaded in their usurpation than any *one* of them would have been" (*Federalist* 70).

29. See the works of Vertot, Adams, Ferguson, Montesquieu, Moyle, Rollin, Gibbon, and Goldsmith cited in n. 18 of this chapter. As Ferguson, *History of the Roman
Republic,* said, "If ever there was a body of men fit to govern the world, it was the
Roman senate" (3:243). Cicero, *De Legibus,* bk. 2, chap. 9, p. 381, described the early
state as "the best in the world," and Rollin, *Roman History,* opened book 2 by
quoting Cicero that the commonwealth "rose in all respects to perfection and excellence hardly to be conceived" (1:201).

laws were enacted restricting the various magistracies through higher age requirements and by making reelection of consuls illegal. Such measures kept the best people from serving the republic, but they did not deter competition among corrupt politicians to spend enormous sums to be elected to office, for possession of office now yielded opportunities to plunder great sums.[30]

Constitutional collapse followed the collapse of public and private morality. The beginning of the long crisis was generally dated in 133 B.C., when Tiberius Gracchus, as tribune, proposed a land reform that would have drastically reduced and redistributed the holdings of the greatest landowners. The Senate, whose members were among that wealthy group, suborned Marcus Octavius, the other tribune elected that year, to veto the measure. Tiberius induced the assembly to remove Octavius, and passage of the land reform followed. Before it could be implemented, however, a mob of senators murdered Ti-

---

30. As generalization about a consensus of eighteenth-century historians, the comments in this and the next two paragraphs are derived from the sources in note 19 of this chapter. See, for example, Rollin, *Ancient History,* 2:242: The Romans "immediately after their conquests, suffered themselves to be corrupted by pride and luxury. After Antiochus had submitted to the Roman yoke, Asia, subdued by their victorious arms, conquered in turn its conquerors, by its riches and voluptuousness; and that change of manners was very sudden and rapid, especially after Carthage, the haughty rival of Rome was destroyed." Rollin, in *Roman History,* cites Cicero's *De Legibus* on the change caused by "this unlimited license of inriching themselves" and "the introduction of luxury" and quotes Sallust's *Cataline Conspiracy* on the "*quasi pestilentia*" invasive wealth, 7:370–371; Ferguson, *History of the Roman Republic,* 1:265, cites Livy and Cato on the "ruinous corruption" as "the wealth of the provinces began to flow into the city." American writers echoed this: The republic "at last dissolved in luxury" ("The Essex Result" [1778], Hyneman and Lutz, ed., *American Political Writing,* 1:499); "the luxuries of the east entered Rome in triumph" and "produced an entire change in the public state and manners" so that the Romans "became effeminate and luxurious, and sold their birth-right for a mess of potage" (Samuel McClintock, "A Sermon " [1784]), and "by adopting the luxuries of Asia," Rome "prepared the way for her own ruin" (Samuel Wales, "A Sermon " [1785], both in Sandoz, ed., *Political Sermons,* 804–805, 853). Montesquieu alone, in *Considerations on the Romans,* offered a different explanation: "The magnitude of the republic was fatal to republican government" (300); "the grandeur of empire ruined the Roman republic" (182); "the magnitude of the republic . . . produced the evil, by changing popular tumults into civil wars" (184).

berius and several hundred of his followers. In 123 his brother Gaius Gracchus became tribune, introduced additional reforms, and eventually met the same fate as Tiberius. Henceforth, armed might, not law, determined the course of government.[31] That development was institutionalized in 105 when Gaius Marius, the consul in command of the army that was destroying the wily and treacherous African Jugurtha, formally abandoned the traditional conscription of property holders—the citizen soldiers who had made Rome great—and openly recruited volunteers from the rabble (which had been done sub rosa for some time). Thereafter the troops owed allegiance to their commanders, not to the Roman state, and Rome was for practical purposes ruled by rival military despots. When Augustus Caesar finally prevailed, military rule continued though Augustus was shrewd enough to pretend to restore the ancient constitution.

Different explanations were offered for the death of the republic, each with different implications for American constitution-makers. If the decline in morality resulting from the influx of foreign money were the true cause, America's prospects were all but hopeless; though the United States was not yet a nation unreservedly committed to the pursuit of wealth, it was decidedly commercial. An alternate explanation, elaborated by Polybius in his history of the Punic Wars, was little more heartening. Polybius declared that all forms of government naturally and inevitably mature, age, and die. Though he finished his work before Tiberius Gracchus appeared upon the scene, when Rome might have seemed to be at the height of its power and glory, Rome's subsequent fate followed the pattern that Polybius had described.[32]

A third explanation for the demise of the republic found favor with some Americans, and it alone carried the prospect of success. The key was balance. James Otis and John Adams argued that had the Roman constitution of the fourth and third centuries been fortified by a

---

31. All the sources describe the situation in similar terms, but Vertot's *Revolutions of the Roman Government,* vol. 2, bk. 10, is particularly distressing; one sentence is repeated throughout the book as a kind of knell: "Everything at *Rome* was carried by mere Force and Violence"; see, e.g., 2:123.

32. *Polybius on Roman Imperialism,* the famous bk. 6, 179–220. Ferguson, *History of the Roman Republic,* 3:242, calls the changes "seasonable."

more careful separation of powers and with a provision that each of the branches have an absolute veto, the republic might have lasted indefinitely.[33]

Yet the republic did last nearly four centuries before it began to disintegrate. No small number of Americans would have been content to devise an instrument that would endure as long.

———— Then there was the history of England. English history from the decline of imperial Rome to the Norman Conquest, though shrouded in mystery, was of special interest to Americans, for it was bound up in the cherished myth of the Anglo-Saxon origins of free institutions. A host of seventeenth- and eighteenth-century English historians sang the praises of their forebears, though they had little source material except the writings of some questionable chroniclers and a widely read tract by Tacitus (translated by Thomas Gordon) describing the ancient Germanic peoples as they had lived more than three centuries before the Saxon invasions of Britain began. Thomas Jefferson expressed a sentiment common to many American republicans when he declared that Tacitus was "the first writer in the world without a single exception" and characterized the Saxon period of English history as showing "the genuine form and political principles of the people constituting the nation, and founded on the rights of man."[34]

Those who idealized the Anglo-Saxons on the basis of a reading of Tacitus, however, could not have been reading carefully. The Ger-

33. James Otis, "Rights of the British Colonies Asserted and Proved" (1764), 14, in *Pamphlets of the American Revolution,* ed. Bernard Bailyn (Cambridge, MA, 1965), 428, and Adams, ed., *Works of Adams,* 4:542–549.

34. Colbourn, *Lamp of Experience,* 26–32, 177; Carl J. Richard, "A Dialogue with the Ancients? Thomas Jefferson and Classical Philosophy and History," *Journal of the Early Republic* 9 (1989):433–434. I used a different translation of Tacitus, that of Alfred John Church and William Jackson Brodribb, *Complete Works of Tacitus,* ed. Moses Hadas (New York, 1942). For a description based on Tacitus of the Saxon government from which "the present civil Constitution of England derives its Original," see Richard Bland, "An Inquiry into the Rights of the British Colonies" (1766), in Hyneman and Lutz, eds., *American Political Writing,* 1:70–71; see also Demophilus (George Bryan?), "The Genuine Principles of the Ancient Saxon, or English, Constitution," Philadelphia, 1776, ibid., 340ff.; or Jonathan Mayhew, "A Discourse concerning Unlimited Submission," in Morgan, ed., *Puritan Political Ideas,* 322n.

mans, as he described them, were extremely valorous warriors, and they practiced neither adultery nor polygamy; but they were rapacious, bloodthirsty, drunken, and lazy. When they were not fighting or hunting—killing men or beasts—they lay "buried in sloth" and drunkenness for days on end. They cultivated no crops, that being slaves' work. All in all, Tacitus depicted their society as tribally oriented and nearly anarchic.[35]

Their appeal lay in their form of government, to the extent that they had a government. They had kings, sometimes hereditary and sometimes elective, but the "kings have not unlimited or arbitrary power." Indeed, killing a king was not even treason; murder was punishable by a fine, and that for killing a king was merely a deal stiffer than that for killing other freemen. Nor was the king necessarily commander in chief, for generals were chosen by "merit." The Germans had a council of chiefs who more or less declared the laws, except in important matters, wherein the whole tribe deliberated. Administrative magistrates were elected by the freemen. At least one tribe conducted its religious rites through an assembly of representatives, and trials of criminal cases were conducted by rudimentary juries. It took little imagination for historians and readers to see in these practices a primitive version of a mixed regime of king, lords, and commons and to see its arrangements as embodying a Montesquieuan separation of powers. Moreover, inasmuch as the functions of the Anglo-Saxons' "government" were minimal, it was easy enough to believe that they had been the freest of free peoples.[36]

The Saxon myth was meaningful to Americans of the revolutionary generation because it reinforced their conviction that, in rebelling against the mother country, they were seeking only to regain the ancient liberties that were their birthright as Englishmen and also because of a larger perspective on history of which the myth was a

35. Tacitus, "Germany and Its Tribes" (usually known as *Germania*), chaps. 15, 23, 25, in Hadas, ed., *Works of Tacitus,* 716–717, 720–721.

36. Ibid., chaps. 7, 11, 12, 39, pp. 712, 714–715, 727–728; Colbourn, *Lamp of Experience,* 26–32, 36–37. Pierce Butler to Weedon Butler, May 5, 1788, "We had before us all the Ancient and modern Constitutions on record, and none of them was more influential on Our Judgements than the British *in Its Original* purity" (italics added) (Farrand, ed., *Records,* 3:301).

part. The so-called Whig interpretation of history depicted the Norman Conquest as the destruction of a Saxon Eden—engineered by treachery, not by the force of manly arms—and portrayed English history since then as alternations between liberty and tyranny. Liberty, in this view, meant government mainly by the people, which is to say the commons; tyranny meant government by unrestrained royal prerogative. The climax of this ongoing struggle came during the reign of the Stuarts, beginning in 1603 and ending with the triumph of "the people" and "liberty" in the Glorious Revolution of 1688–1689.[37]

A number of eighteenth-century Whig historians wrote of the Stuart epoch, the most popular being the Frenchman Paul de Rapin-Thoyras (usually cited as Rapin), whose *History of England* was first translated into English in the late 1720s. The Whig historians insisted that the ancient constitution was decidedly in place during the reign of Queen Elizabeth and that James I upset the balance by insisting on the newfangled doctrines of divine right and absolute monarchical authority. His son Charles I carried those unconstitutional doctrines further, provoking the extremism of parliamentary resistance that led to the horrors of civil war, regicide, the commonwealth, and the Protectorate of Oliver Cromwell. Upon the restoration of Charles II in 1660 that dissolute monarch, a secret Roman Catholic, sought to establish in England the kind of absolutism that Louis XIV had effected in France, but he was frustrated by militant Whig members of Parliament whose control of the power of the purse stymied the power of the sword. During the late 1670s and early 1680s, facing the prospect that the childless Charles would die and be succeeded by his brother James, Duke of York, an openly declared Catholic, militant Whigs attempted in vain to enact an Exclusion Bill that would bar Catholics from the throne; Charles blocked them. James did come to the throne in 1685, but he forfeited

---

37. Colbourn, *Lamp of Experience,* passim; Demophilus, "The Genuine Principles of the Ancient Saxon, or English Constitution," in Hyneman and Lutz, ed., *American Political Writing,* 1:340–360; for a recounting of the Saxon myth during the Constitutional Convention, see Pinckney's speech of June 25 in Farrand, ed., *Records,* 1:399; see also John Francis Mercer, a nonsigning member of the convention, in *Essays by A Farmer,* Feb.–April 1788, in Storing, ed., *Complete Anti-Federalist,* 5:38.

his right to the crown by trampling on the constitution and laws and by fleeing the kingdom in the face of an invasion by his son-in-law, William of Orange. In the subsequent Revolution Settlement, the ancient constitution of government by crown in parliament was firmly and finally restored.[38]

Or so the Whigs thought at the time. Writers who came after Rapin, most notably John Trenchard and Thomas Gordon (Cato) and Bolingbroke and his circle (who were in fact Tories, not Whigs), were convinced that the Glorious Revolution had been betrayed by the Financial Revolution and by the rise of a system whereby the king's ministers ruled, not through the exercise of the prerogative but by employing corrupt devices that were alien to the constitution.[39]

For independence-minded American radicals in the 1770s, this interpretation of history could not justify entrusting power to an executive: It taught the opposite. Moreover, few individuals of that description had changed their minds by 1787. Roger Sherman of Connecticut, for example, said at the Constitutional Convention that "he considered the Executive magistracy as nothing more than an institution for carrying the will of the Legislature into effect," the legislature being "the depositary of the supreme will of the Society."[40]

For those Americans who believed in the necessity of executive power, however, there was a different version of the English past that provided ample and persuasive justification for their position. Two of the best (and most readable) sources were written by men who had participated at the highest levels in the events they described—the

38. A good summary of Rapin's version of the Whig interpretation is in Duncan Forbes's editorial introduction to David Hume, *The History of Great Britain: The Reigns of James I and Charles I* (New York, 1970), 25–27. See also Colbourn, *Lamp of Experience,* 42–50, and Henry St. John, first Viscount Bolingbroke, *The Works of Lord Bolingbroke,* 4 vols. (London, 1844), 2:28–123.

39. *The English Libertarian Heritage: From the Writings of John Trenchard and Thomas Gordon,* ed. David L. Jacobson (Indianapolis, IN, 1965), letters 16–18; Bolingbroke, *Works,* 2:5–36, 430–461, and passim. See also Isaac Kramnick, *Bolingbroke and His Circle* (Cambridge, MA, 1968). Benjamin Franklin spread the "New Whig" ideology widely in the colonies; William Pencak, "*Politics and Ideology in Poor Richard's Almanack,*" *Pennsylvania Magazine of History and Biography* 116 (April 1992):193–194.

40. Farrand, ed., *Records,* 1:65 (Madison's notes, June 1).

Earl of Clarendon and Bishop Burnet. Clarendon served Charles I during most of the civil war period, served Charles II during most of that prince's exile, and was his principal minister for seven years after the Restoration. Clarendon wrote harshly of the puritan/parliamentary leaders and favorably of his martyred master, but his narrative of events was, as most people admitted, the best available. Bishop Gilbert Burnet in his *History of My Own Time* depicted James I as pathetic, irresolute, pedantic, and generally disgusting but not as a would-be tyrant. As for Charles I, Burnet opined that that reign "was a continued series of errors" and that Charles "had too high a notion of the regal power, and thought that every opposition to it was rebellion." Yet Charles, too, was far from tyrannical. His parliamentary enemies, on the other hand, were tyrants, because "they believed there were great occasions in which some men were called to great services, in the doing of which they were excused from the common rules of morality"—the attitude of both True Believers and proponents of "reason of state" at all times. Burnet saw Cromwell as a shrewd military dictator and fanatic who believed himself the instrument of God, though he conceded that Cromwell established order in Burnet's native Scotland for the first time in its history.[41]

Those judgments were preliminary to Burnet's story. His "own time" ran from the Restoration until 1685, and especially during the dozen years after 1673, when Burnet took up residence in London. Burnet saw a great deal of Charles II and had no illusions about the king: He was lewd, lascivious, deceitful, lazy, and a secret Catholic in the pay of Louis XIV. Even so, he was no genuine threat to English liberty, for "though he desired to become absolute, and to overturn both our religion and our laws, yet he would neither run the risk, nor give himself the trouble, which so great a design required." Burnet also had no illusions about most of the Whigs in Parliament even though his patron was one of them. The Whigs talked much about liberty and rights, but they were by and large as corrupt and desirous

41. Edward Hyde, Lord Clarendon, *The History of the Rebellion,* 6 vols. (Oxford, Eng., 1731–1732); Bishop Gilbert Burnet, *History of My Own Time,* ed. Osmund Airy, 2 vols. (Oxford, Eng., 1900), 1:3–88. A good summary of Clarendon's work in brief compass is *Characters and Episodes of the Great Rebellion Selected from the History and Autobiography of Edward, Earl of Clarendon,* ed. G. D. Boyle (Oxford, Eng., 1889).

of power as their royal master, and several were quite as treacherous and far more energetic. One measure of their corruption was that the king's ministers began in the 1670s—not later under Walpole, as radical Whig historians supposed—systematic bribery of members of Parliament.[42]

Burnet's account of the squabbling between Charles and the Commons would have been instructive for American executive-makers. The Whigs wanted power: to curtail the prerogative or to share in its use, especially regarding the conduct of foreign relations, the pardoning power, and the spending (as opposed to the appropriating) of public funds. The king wanted money: His expenses were enormous and the Commons never appropriated as much as he needed. Burnet was convinced that given proper leadership the Commons could have obtained everything it desired had it been more generous and less confrontational. The lesson for American Framers, were they disposed to heed it, was that the formal distribution of powers between legislative and executive is not so important as institutionalized means of cooperation.[43]

By far the most popular Tory history of England was David Hume's, published in six volumes between 1754 and 1762. Hume described Rapin's Whig history as "totally despicable"; his own *History* shocked devotees of the Whig interpretation with heresy after heresy. The reign of the sainted Elizabeth, far from being benign and moderate, had been absolutely arbitrary. James I had been foolish and weak, but he had ruled within the confines of the constitution; he and his councils were "more wise and equitable, in their end, than prudent and political, in the means." James's Puritan opponents were devious and hypocritical republicans and fanatics, and their efforts to increase the power of the Commons at the expense of the crown constituted a sharp break with tradition. The 1628 Petition of Right, acceded to by Charles I, was by no means an accurate description of ancient usage, but "such a change in the government, as was almost equivalent to a revolution." The 1630s, during which Charles engaged in personal rule after dissolving Parliament, were by no means

42. Airy, ed., *Burnet's History,* 2:79 and n. 1, 468, and passim.
43. Ibid., 2:211–286.

detrimental to his subjects: "The grievances, under which the English laboured . . . scarcely deserve the name; nor were they either burthensome on the people's properties, or anywise shocking to the natural humanity of mankind." In the constitutional debates of 1641–1642, Charles's position was historically sound; his enemies were radical innovators; the very abolition of the Star Chamber was a mistake; the triumph of the Roundheads, even before the rise of Cromwell (to which it inevitably led), was the triumph of unrestrained government on a magnitude England had never before known. And so on, through the Restoration and the Glorious Revolution. Where Hume did not favor the Stuarts, he offered accounts that Whigs would have regarded as inappropriately balanced descriptions of every dispute between the Stuarts and their foes.[44]

The great value of Hume's history lay not in its shocking effect upon Whig sensibilities but in its crisp analysis of the need for and nature of executive power. In the passage in which Hume defended the Star Chamber, for instance, he pointed out that it had been the only judicial body that could enforce royal proclamations, the jurisdiction of other courts being limited to common law and statutes. Thus "the king may thenceforth issue proclamations, but no man is bound to obey them." The trouble was that the workings of the law were too general and too rigid to apply with dispatch in all circumstances, and in a nation as turbulent and as rife with seditions and conspiracies as England had been—and as the United States was during its infancy—a more flexible system was necessary to preserve

44. David Hume, *The History of England*, 6 vols. (Indianapolis, IN, 1983), 5:11, 13–14, 200, 249, 329, 370–371, and passim. I have used the Liberty Classics edition, which is based on the 1778 edition. In the original, vols. 1 and 2 covered the Stuart period; Hume wrote the earlier history after covering the Stuarts. In the Liberty Classics edition, the volumes are arranged in chronological order so that volumes 5 and 6 are the original volumes 1 and 2. One can get Hume's history from Oliver Goldsmith's *History of England*, a one-volume "condensation" that went through dozens of editions in England and America. Hume admired Rapin until he began the research for his own history. When one of his books of essays was being translated in 1757, he changed his description of Rapin from "the most judicious of our historians" to "Rapin, suitable to his usual Partiality & Malignity." See Hume to James Oswald, June 28, 1753, and to the Abbe Le Blanc, July 22, 1757, in *The Letters of David Hume*, ed. J. Y. T. Greig, 2 vols. (Oxford, Eng., 1932), 1:179, 258.

the public order and to give meaning to public liberty. "No government, at that time," Hume wrote, "appeared in the world, nor is perhaps to be found in the records of any history, which subsisted without the mixture of some arbitrary authority, committed to some magistrate." At most, Hume was willing to concede that possibly "the king was too eminent a magistrate to be trusted with discretionary power"; but he perceived that someone must be.[45]

He also perceived that the Stuarts ultimately failed, not because they sought to transform a historically mixed regime into an absolute one but because their methods were too crude. They attempted to rule by giving commands and expecting to be obeyed, as monarchs on the Continent appeared to do. But continental princes had standing armies to enforce their bidding; England, because of its insularity, depended on fleets instead and had not yet developed large permanent armies. Another crucial condition was that English subjects were different from continental ones. Over the course of the preceding century property holding had become widespread, at least compared to what it had been when barons were the crown's rivals, and what was just as important, information and knowledge had been widely diffused. The English people, in sum, were an intractable lot. Eighteenth-century Americans clearly recognized that the barriers to arbitrary rule that Hume delineated also existed in their society.[46]

At the Constitutional Convention Alexander Hamilton would paraphrase, without attribution, a passage in which Hume summarized the techniques the Stuart kings should have employed instead of naked command or bribery. "Pensions and bribes," Hume wrote, "though it be difficult entirely to exclude them, are dangerous expe-

---

45. Hume, *History of England,* 5:329. As for seditions and other turbulence in the early republic, eruptions occurred in New Hampshire, Massachusetts, Maryland, Delaware, Virginia, and North Carolina during the 1780s and in Pennsylvania and along the frontier in the 1790s. See also chap. 6, n. 41, chap. 8, n. 9, and chap. 9, nn. 54–56 of this book.

46. Hume, *History of England,* 5:12, 18–19, 40–43, 59, 121, 134, and passim. Regarding monarchy in general, Voltaire is to the point: "For a state to be powerful, the people must either enjoy a liberty founded upon laws, or the royal authority must be fixed beyond all opposition" (*The Works of Voltaire, The Age of Louis XIV,* ed. Tobias Smollett, rev. and trans. William Fleming [New York, 1901], 9).

dients for government" and should be avoided as much as possible out of "regard to the virtue and liberty of a nation." But, he added, the influence "which the crown acquires from the disposal of places, honours, and preferments, is to be esteemed of a different nature. This engine of power may become too forcible, but it cannot altogether be abolished, without the total destruction of monarchy, and even of all regular authority."[47]

It is scarcely a source of wonder that Hamilton, an arch champion of executive power, should admire "the cautious and accurate *Hume*," "the Judicious *Hume*." Nor is it surprising that Thomas Jefferson, for most of his life an avowed enemy of executive power, should try for a number of years to get a bowdlerized edition of Hume's history—one with the "heresies" removed—published in America. Even so, when Jefferson took on the mantle of presidential power himself, he would find Hume's maxims—heresies and all—as valuable as Hamilton had.[48]

---

47. Hume, *History of England,* 6:366; Farrand, ed., *Records,* 1:285 (Madison's notes, June 18).

48. Hamilton quotes from *The Law Practice of Alexander Hamilton,* ed. Julius Goebel, Jr., 2 vols. (New York, 1964), 1:616–617; on Jefferson and Hume, see Colbourn, *Lamp of Experience,* 177–180. On Jefferson's presidency, see chapter 10 of this book.

5

The Colonial Experience

In addition to their readings, the authors of the presidency had another large source of information about executive power, namely the experience in government of their several colonies and states. There was a small body of literature on that subject in the form of histories of particular colonies and, most notably, a treatise on colonial administration published by Thomas Pownall, erstwhile lieutenant governor of New Jersey and governor of Massachusetts.[1] Mainly, however, knowledge of executive authority in colonial times was simply "in the air," common currency among public men. There had been considerable variation from colony to colony: New Hampshire had been ruled for years by a family dynasty; North Carolina had undergone a long period of virtual anarchy during the middle years of the eighteenth century; Georgia, the newest colony, relied upon arrangements not duplicated elsewhere; and the provinces ex-

---

1. William Smith, Jr., *The History of the Province of New-York,* ed. Michael Kammen, 2 vols. (Cambridge, MA, 1972; orig. London, 1757); Thomas Hutchinson, *History of Massachusetts-Bay,* 2 vols. (Boston, 1768); Thomas Pownall, *The Administration of the Colonies: Wherein Their Rights and Constitution are Discussed and Stated* (New York, 1971 facs. ed. of London, 1768, 4th ed.). For Pownall, see John A. Schutz, *Thomas Pownall: British Defender of American Liberty* (Glendale, CA, 1951).

isted on a variety of institutional and constitutional bases. But similar patterns of evolution characterized almost all the colonies.

In its broad outlines, and allowing for exceptions, the constitutional history of the mainland American colonies from the late seventeenth century until independence recapitulated the constitutional history of England between the reign of Queen Elizabeth and the reign of Queen Anne. Colonial governors began with the full panoply of prerogative powers—which, as we have seen, extended to legislative and judicial as well as to executive functions. But by little and little, in confrontation after confrontation, the colonial legislatures nibbled away at gubernatorial authority. Their most effective instrument was control over money bills, just as Parliament's had been against the Stuart monarchs. By 1776 they had taken the whole prerogative unto themselves, again as Parliament had done before them.

The experience was not calculated to endow Americans with trust of executive power. And yet there was a strange ambiguity about it: Until the very eve of independence, the vast majority of colonials professed and genuinely felt loyalty and affection for King George III. When he refused to do their bidding and instead sent troops to suppress them, their sense of betrayal was almost total. So was their rejection of executive power.

————— During the seventeenth century, the English empire in America was in a chaotic state. Most of the colonies originated as private business enterprises or as feudal domains, operating in assigned territories under charters granted by the crown. The two earliest, Virginia and Plymouth, lost their charters in 1624 and 1635 and became royal colonies—that is, their governors and councils came to be appointed directly by the crown. The others remained private for varying periods. Charles I chartered two colonies, Massachusetts and Maryland, early in his reign, and Charles II chartered several more, all but one during the early years of the Restoration (Pennsylvania's charter was granted in 1681).[2]

2. The major institutional studies of colonial governors and imperial administration were done long ago: Evarts B. Greene, *The Provincial Governor in the English*

Thereafter the tendency was toward direct royal rule. New York, granted to James, Duke of York, in 1664, automatically became a royal colony upon James's accession to the throne in 1685. Massachusetts, having lost its original charter, got a new one in 1691, but under it the king appointed the governor. The Carolinas, New Jersey, and ultimately Georgia also forfeited their charters and came under royal rule. When everything had shaken down, two colonies, Rhode Island and Connecticut, were self-governing corporate colonies; Maryland, Pennsylvania, and Delaware (the last two had the same governor but separate legislatures) were proprietary colonies in which the Calvert and Penn families stood in place of the crown. The eight others were royal colonies.3

Varied as the arrangements were, all the colonies can be said to have had constitutions, which is to say written documents authorizing and specifying the makeup of government. In the cases of the corporate and proprietary colonies and of Massachusetts, the charters were the constitutions. Among the unchartered royal colonies the constitutions were the commissions to the governors, which scarcely changed from colony to colony or from year to year. The instructions to the governors, unlike the commissions, were not made public, but they too were in some senses also part of the constitutions. It is to be observed that all colonial government derived from the gift of the

Colonies of North America (1898; repr., New York, 1907); Oliver Morton Dickerson, *American Colonial Government, 1696–1765; A Study of the British Board of Trade in Relation to the American Colonies, Political, Industrial, Administrative* (1912; repr., New York, 1962); Elmer Beecher Russell, *The Review of American Colonial Legislation by the King in Council* (New York, 1915); John F. Burns, *Controversies between Royal Governors and their Assemblies in the Northern American Colonies* (Boston, 1923); and Leonard Woods Labaree, *Royal Government in America: A Study of the British Colonial System before 1783* (1936; repr., New York, 1964). Two works of more recent vintage add appreciably to our knowledge of the subject: Jack P. Greene, *The Quest for Power: The Lower Houses of Assembly in the Southern Royal Colonies, 1689–1776* (Chapel Hill, NC, 1963), and Jackson Turner Main, *The Upper House in Revolutionary America, 1763–1788* (Madison, WI, 1967). See also John M. Murrin, "Colonial Government," *Encyclopedia of American Political History,* ed. Jack P. Greene, 2 vols. (New York, 1984), 1:293–315.

3. The evolution is well outlined in Greene, *Provincial Governor,* 1–22.

crown, in keeping with the way things had historically been in England and continued to be in legal fiction.[4]

The colonial governments, whatever their bases, were remarkably similar to one another at least in form. Each had a governor and a council that was part of the executive branch but was also (except in Pennsylvania and Delaware) the upper house of the legislature and at least nominally the supreme court of appeals. In addition, each had a popularly elected representative assembly and a judicial system.

Prior to 1675 the government in London exercised minimal supervision over the colonies. In that year a general supervisory power was vested in the Lords of Trade, a committee of the king's privy council. In 1696, in connection with a navigation act regulating trade within the empire, the Lords of Trade were superseded by the Board of Trade, likewise a committee of the privy council. The Board of Trade reviewed the actions of the colonial governments, whether legislative, executive, or judicial, until the end of the colonial period. Pivotal as the board was, however, in administering colonial affairs, it was not powerful, for it had authority merely to make recommendations. Actual decisions were made by the whole privy council or by the appropriate secretary of state.[5]

That the executive arm of the empire came to be so constituted was a product of changes in the British government and in turn had a considerable impact upon the development of government in the colonies. The privy council had been an outgrowth of the medieval *curia regis,* consisting of the king's household, his tenants-in-chief, and anyone else he chose to invite. For centuries the council had been the main instrumentality through which English monarchs wielded power. After the Glorious Revolution and especially after the accession of George I, it was displaced by the cabinet, consisting of heads of departments (especially the chancellor of the exchequer) who were also members of Parliament, thus effectively merging the executive and legislative branches of government. Meanwhile the privy council degenerated into little more than a formal and ritualistic appendage

4. Ibid., 93–96; Labaree, *Royal Government,* 26–36. Greene reproduces samples of commissions and instructions. Pownall, *Administration,* 56, 62, 68, 83–84.

5. Russell, *Review of Colonial Legislation,* 21; Dickerson, *American Colonial Government,* 17–26; Greene, *Provincial Governor,* 69–71.

of the state—except that the colonies were under its care. Consequently, the grip of the British government on its colonies was relatively feeble.[6]

Historians of the Board of Trade divide its work into four periods. The first, which lasted until 1714 or so, was the best. The personnel was of high quality (John Locke being among the working members), and apparently the agency was efficient and effective. There followed, until mid-century, a time of neglect intermixed with bungling and corruption. The board began to be revitalized in 1748 with the appointment of George Dunk, Earl of Halifax, as president; until 1766 Halifax tried diligently to make the board function effectively. He insisted on having control of the power of appointment, which had previously been the province of the secretary of state for the southern department. As a result the patronage was in the hands of the Board of Trade from 1752 until 1761. Then in 1766 the office of secretary of state for the colonies was created and combined with the presidency of the board. By that time, however, the hour was growing late for imperial governance of the colonies.[7]

The most important task of the board was to review colonial legislation: On its recommendation the privy council approved, suspended, or disallowed all or any part of provincial laws, thus exercising an absolute imperial veto power. Connecticut and Rhode Island were

6. See Edward Raymond Turner, "The Development of the Cabinet, 1688–1760," *American Historical Review* 18 (1913):751–768 and 19 (1914):27–43.

7. Dickerson, *American Colonial Government,* 31–39; Russell, *Review of Colonial Legislation,* 44–48; Ian K. Steele, *Politics of Colonial Policy: The Board of Trade in Colonial Administration, 1696–1720* (Oxford, Eng., 1968), passim; James A. Henretta, *"Salutary Neglect": Colonial Administration under the Duke of Newcastle* (Princeton, NJ, 1972), passim. Suspicion, however, might be cast on Locke's effectiveness as a member of the Board of Trade and even on the board's competence in administration if one reads Locke's *Fundamental Constitutions of Carolina* (1669), a bizarre document, only partially put into effect and entirely abrogated in 1693. In it power was divided and redivided and subdivided; all proprietors, landgraves, caziques, and lords of signiory, barony, and manor were to have powers; scores of offices and suboffices were outlined; there were to be eight supreme courts. The only appealing section was the seventieth, which in effect forbade lawyers from charging fees. *The Federal and State Constitutions, Colonial Charters, and Other Organic Laws,* comp. and ed. Francis Newton Thorpe, 7 vols. (Washington, DC, 1909), 5:2772–2786.

not ordinarily subject to the review, but the proprietary colonies were. Pennsylvania was required to send its statutes for review within five years of enactment, and action was required within six months of receipt. Massachusetts had one year to submit statutes; if no action was taken within three years they became law.[8]

Otherwise there were no time limits, which led to peculiar and capricious results. In regard to about a quarter of the statutes under review at any given time, the board took no action. It was difficult to repeal an act that the privy council (legally, the king) had approved; thus when in doubt the board simply allowed legislation to "lye by probationary," from which limbo it was lawfully binding unless some positive action was taken. The average amount of time that elapsed before colonial statutes were disallowed was three-and-a-half years. One Virginia statute enacted in 1705 was disallowed in 1731. The most exaggerated case of delay concerned North Carolina, which had twenty-six acts disallowed in 1754, five of them thirty-eight years old, the others ranging from three to twenty-four years old. The board could, however, act swiftly in approving a colonial act that it regarded as highly expedient and just as swiftly when colonial legislation was strongly protested by London merchants, as it did in striking down a 1723 New York duty on imports. All told, the board reviewed 8,563 acts submitted by the mainland American colonies, and on its recommendation 469 were disallowed.[9]

Other functions of the board had to do largely with coordination and communication. It drafted instructions to the royal governors and required frequent reports from them. It corresponded with imperial customs officers, who were royal officials working in the colonies but outside the framework of the colonial governments. It tried, sometimes successfully, to induce the governors to hire agents in London for the facilitating of business.

Such efforts were hampered by difficulties of communication. There was no regular mail service until 1755, when fairly regular communication was established with Boston, New York, Philadelphia, Virginia,

8. Russell, *Review of Colonial Legislation*, 37–41 and passim; Labaree, *Royal Government*, 223–226; Dickerson, *American Colonial Government*, 226–283.

9. Labaree, *Royal Government*, 223–224n., 232–233; Russell, *Review of Colonial Legislation*, 221–222.

and (later) Charleston. Boston's port froze in the winter, however, and few transatlantic ships entered New Jersey, Connecticut, or North Carolina. North Carolina was the most isolated from London: In 1745 the board wrote Gov. Gabriel Johnston that it had not received a letter from him for three years though he had in fact been writing regularly; in 1747 he reported that he had just received a letter from the board written in 1744. In wartime (1689–1697, 1702–1713, 1739–1748, 1754–1762) when communication took on an added importance, it was often disrupted by the French navy and by privateers.[10]

———— Given the laxity of the imperial bands, any control England could exercise over the colonies depended mainly upon the governors and their London-appointed executive councils. In Rhode Island and Connecticut the control was all but nonexistent, for governors and councils were locally elected. Nominally, imperial customs officers had jurisdiction there, but geography was a serious deterrent to the successful operation of revenue cutters. One tenuous thread connected the two colonies to the home government: Their charters required that local law conform to the laws of England.[11]

Elsewhere, governors were endowed with prerogatives that were, on paper and for a time in reality, almost on a par with the royal prerogative of earlier times. The governor was the commander in chief; the commissions authorized the governor to appoint officers and either directly or through them to arm, muster, and command the men in the province, to order their movements even to other provinces to pursue enemies, and otherwise to combat enemies, rebels, or pirates. With the advice and consent of the council, the gov-

10. Dickerson, *American Colonial Government*, 133–141. For Gabriel Johnston, see Blackwell P. Robinson, *The Five Royal Governors of North Carolina: 1729–1775* (Raleigh, NC, 1963), 12–26.

11. Dickerson, *American Colonial Government*, 235–238. For Rhode Island generally, see Sydney V. James, *Colonial Rhode Island: A History* (New York, 1975), and his "Rhode Island: From Classical Democracy to British Province," *Rhode Island History* 43 (1984):119–135; for Connecticut, see Richard L. Bushman, *From Puritan to Yankee: Character and the Social Order in Connecticut, 1690–1765* (Cambridge, MA, 1967); Oscar Zeichner, *Connecticut's Years of Controversy, 1750–1776* (Chapel Hill, NC, 1949); and Bruce P. Stark, " 'A Factious Spirit': Constitutional Theory and Political Practice in Connecticut, c. 1740," *William and Mary Quarterly* 47 (1990):391–410.

ernor could also establish fortifications and execute martial law. The Massachusetts charter of 1691 curtailed these powers slightly: Approval of the General Court (legislature) was necessary for ordering men out of the colony without their consent.[12]

In the conduct of "foreign relations" the power of the governors was of limited scope but plenary in matters to which it applied. Governors were not authorized to declare war against sovereign powers, but they could and sometimes did declare war against Indians during emergencies, and actions against rebels and pirates required no declaration. Negotiating treaties with Indians was not expressly authorized, but governors repeatedly did so with advice and consent of the council until the 1760s. Afterward, Indian relations were entrusted to special royal agents. Finally, under the heading of external relations, the governor was the representative of the colony in dealing with other colonies, in such matters as boundary disputes, though as time passed it became customary to refer these to commissioners.[13]

As to internal affairs, the powers of the governors were more formidable. In addition to the powers to grant pardons, censor the press, grant charters of incorporation, and appoint and remove judges, justices of the peace, sheriffs, "and other necessary Officers and Ministers . . . for the better Administration of Justice and putting the Laws in Execution," the governors had powers in three general areas: legislative, fiscal, and judicial.[14]

The legislative powers were varied and broad. Governors had an absolute veto, not subject to being overridden. They sat in the legislature, at least in the early days, by virtue of presiding over the executive council in its capacity as upper legislative house. Later this was objected to and the practice was abandoned, but the governors' in-

12. Greene, *Provincial Governor*, 98–99; Thorpe, ed., *Federal and State Constitutions*, 3:1884.

13. Greene, *Provincial Governor*, 107–110. In Benjamin Franklin's proposed Albany Plan of Union (1754) the "President-General" with the advice of the Grand Council could "hold or direct all Indian treaties . . . and make peace or declare war with Indian nations" (Thorpe, ed., *Federal and State Constitutions*, 1:84). See also James Thomas Flexner, *Lord of the Mohawks: A Biography of Sir William Johnson* (Syracuse, NY, 1989).

14. Greene, *Provincial Governor*, 111, 124–128.

fluence continued to be felt among the councillors. Most importantly, governors had the power to call the legislatures into session, to prorogue them indefinitely, and to dissolve them entirely. They could also designate any place they pleased for the sitting of the legislature.[15]

The governors' fiscal powers were considerable even though the representative assemblies had the exclusive power to originate bills levying taxes or appropriating funds. The assemblies' clout was reduced by a requirement that bills had to be on one subject and "contain no clause foreign to their title." This was designed to keep assemblies from tacking riders onto appropriations bills to ensure approval of legislation that might otherwise be vetoed. When the legislature violated the ban the requirement enabled governors to exercise what would come to be called a "line-item" veto, as for example, when Gov. Francis Bernard of Massachusetts vetoed an appropriation for one of the two military fortifications in a bill passed by the House of Representatives. Once appropriations were passed, it was required that no public funds be spent except under the governor's warrant, and this power to disburse money extended to refusing to disburse if he chose. The governor had, in modern terminology, the power to impound appropriations. Two other limitations on the assemblies' money powers were exercised early in the eighteenth century but soon passed into disuse: The executive council could amend money bills passed by the assembly, and the governor was empowered to fix the salaries and fees of public officials.[16]

The judicial powers of the governors were likewise extensive and diverse. The governor, sometimes with the council and sometimes alone, was chancellor with jurisdiction over cases in equity, and he (or they) constituted the highest American appellate court in cases involving stipulated minimum sums. In criminal cases, actions were brought by attorneys general on orders from the governors. Governors appointed judges and were authorized to create courts, though that right, according to Thomas Pownall, was "universally disputed."

15. Ibid., 145–147.

16. Russell, *Review of Colonial Legislation*, 87; Dickerson, *American Colonial Government*, 159ff.; Burns, *Controversies between Royal Governors and their Assemblies*, 174, 325.

Some governors attempted to extend their judicial authority beyond the broad limits of their commissions and instructions; in the 1760s Gov. Cadwallader Colden of New York insisted that it was legal for jury verdicts to be appealed to the governor and council on matters both of fact and of law.[17] Constitutionally, then, the royal and proprietary governments had quite ample official authorization to carry out the bidding of their masters in the parent country.

———— Yet official authorization is not necessarily the same thing as either authority or power, and a number of conditions ensured that the governors would have difficulties. One problem was personal: Though most governors were honest and able men, some were glaring exceptions. During its early years, for example, New York had a succession of corrupt governors who embezzled public funds and took bribes for winking at piracy. Other governors held office as absentees. In Virginia, for instance, the governor's salary was lucrative and was guaranteed by a provision for permanent revenues; the office was a sinecure. From 1704 until 1768, Virginia governors remained in England collecting their salaries and entrusting the duties of office to resident lieutenant governors who served for relative pittances. In Pennsylvania the proprietor was governor in chief and remained in England, allowing a deputy to fill the actual office, and New York lacked a resident governor much of the time during the 1760s and 1770s. More commonly governors resided in the colonies, but there were complications when they did. They were subordinates of people in London whose perception of what was desirable often conflicted with the perceived interests of the people in the provinces; moreover, for much of the century individuals were assigned governorships of more than one province. Thus from 1702 until 1741 Massachusetts and New Hampshire shared a common governor, as did New York and New Jersey from 1702 until 1738 and Pennsylvania and Delaware until independence.[18]

17. Greene, *Provincial Governor,* 138–139; Pownall, *Administration,* 105; *Pamphlets of the American Revolution,* ed. Bernard Bailyn (Cambridge, MA, 1965), 68; Milton M. Klein, "Prelude to Revolution in New York: Jury Trials and Judicial Tenure," *William and Mary Quarterly* 17 (1960):439–462.

18. Labaree, *Royal Government,* 127n.; Greene, *Provincial Governor,* 57–58; Burns,

Other flaws in the gubernatorial arrangements were institutional. The difficulties imposed by poor communication were compounded by the rigidity of government-by-instruction. Instructions written by the Board of Trade were sometimes drawn with skill and with an understanding of the needs of the colonies, for the board had access to detailed information, but the system was inherently inflexible: It did not allow for the essential element in executive power, discretionary action when circumstances require a departure from written laws or written orders. Whenever colonial governors found it expedient or imperative to violate their instructions, as they frequently did, they faced the prospect of being chastised or recalled.[19]

Another structural weakness involved patronage. Lacking armies that would have made possible the imposition of will by force, the governors could still have their way with the councils and assemblies if they were adroit politicians, but to function successfully, politicians need something to trade. The best counter is remunerative or prestigious office. Militia commissions, which governors had at their disposal, sometimes fit that description; a recalcitrant legislator might be made pliable by the offer of a colonelcy. The trouble with militia commissions as sops was that politicians who were bought with them would not stay bought—as Gov. Francis Bernard learned when he commissioned Col. James Otis—because in America once one held a military rank, even if tentatively or briefly, one was allowed to use its title for life.[20]

Additional forms of patronage were thus necessary. Some governors had patronage in adequate supply, and some did not. The diversity can be seen by considering three colonies. Before South Carolina became a royal colony in 1721, the assembly had taken advantage of

---

Controversies between Royal Governors and their Assemblies, 117n., 225, 267–268, 291–304, 390. See also Paul David Nelson, *William Tryon and the Course of Empire: A Life in British Imperial Service* (Chapel Hill, NC, 1990).

19. Labaree, *Royal Government,* 396, 420–448; Dickerson, *American Colonial Government,* 154–158.

20. Dickerson, *American Colonial Government,* 142–148; Labaree, *Royal Government,* 105–108; Greene, *Provincial Governor,* 187; Ellen E. Brennan, *Plural Office-Holding in Massachusetts, 1760–1780: Its Relation to the "Separation" of Departments of Government* (Chapel Hill, NC, 1945), 67–68.

the proprietors' disarray and assumed the appointment power itself. Royal governors proved unable to change things despite orders from the privy council. Gov. James Glen complained in 1748, "Almost all the places of profit or of trust are disposed of by the General Assembly" and thus "the people have the whole of the administration in their hands," leaving the governor politically impotent. A similar situation obtained in Maryland for opposite reasons; the proprietors made a corrupt business of selling offices to British placemen. By contrast, the Wentworths of New Hampshire, who held the provincial governorship from 1741 to 1775, were able to build a complex network of patronage, and they governed skillfully enough to please both royal officials and the dominant clan in the colony.[21]

The governors' councils, instituted to shore up gubernatorial power against the assemblies, likewise turned out to be a mixed bag. They failed entirely to serve the purpose in the three chartered New England provinces—except, as will be seen, in Massachusetts during the early 1760s. In Virginia and New Jersey the assemblies were moderate most of the time, and thus defense of the governors by the councils was usually unnecessary; when friction did arise, the councils generally followed a conciliatory course. In the other five colonies that had councils, as assemblies grew more radical through the 1760s and 1770s, the councils supported the governors.[22]

Circumstances, however, favored the assemblies over the governors when the two collided—provided the assemblies were organized under determined leadership. The governors' legislative power was essentially negative: They could restrain the assemblies and prevent them from acting, but they had no institutional means for requiring an assembly to act. An artful governor, backed by a popular council,

21. Greene, *Provincial Governor*, 114n., 187; Jere R. Daniell, *Colonial New Hampshire: A History* (Millwood, NY, 1981), 191–237; Charles Albro Barker, *The Background of the Revolution in Maryland* (New Haven, CT, 1940), 147–153; Aubrey C. Land, *Colonial Maryland: A History* (Millwood, NY, 1981), 222–224; M. Eugene Sirmans, *Colonial South Carolina: A Political History, 1663–1763* (Chapel Hill, NC, 1966).

22. For the view of the leading student of the subject, Jackson T. Main, see *Upper House*, 232–233 and passim. See also Labaree, *Royal Government*, 134–171; Greene, *Provincial Governor*, 72–90; Richard L. Bushman, *King and People in Provincial Massachusetts* (Chapel Hill, NC, 1985).

could persuade an assembly to support a measure by blocking another measure that the assembly desired, and such trading was not uncommon in the early days. As the colonials gained political experience, they learned to get their way by withholding the passage of militia bills, sometimes for years on end, thus rendering the governors' military authority meaningless. They proved willing even to jeopardize the public safety to gain desired political ends—a practice still known to legislators more than 200 years after the colonies became a nation.[23]

Above all, the legislatures grew steadily more bold in using their power over money bills to bend the governors to their will. This weapon might have been blunted, if not removed altogether, had Parliament opted to bear the costs of colonial government. Parliament could easily have done so, and on several occasions various people proposed that it should. Yet except for the infant Georgia colony, which Parliament did fund, there was no serious support for assuming the burden. Parliamentary funding would have radically altered the nature of the empire in the direction of the centralized French and Spanish systems. Instead, colonial officials in England urged the colonies to establish permanent revenues for local administration. Only Virginia and Maryland complied, and even they retained the power of the purse in regard to the extraordinary expenditures necessary in wartime.[24]

Underlying the friction between governors and the home government on the one side and the colonials on the other, besides conflicts of interest, was a matter of profoundly felt principle. Royal officials and Britons generally insisted that the colonial governments, including the assemblies, existed by "royal grace and favor" as granted through the commissions and instructions to the governors. Fact and law supported this view. Obviously the assembly could not create

23. Labaree, *Royal Government*, 218–268; Greene, *Provincial Governor*, 188–192; John E. Pomfret, *Colonial New Jersey: A History* (New York, 1973), 151–152, 170–172; Theodore Thayer, *Pennsylvania Politics and the Growth of Democracy, 1740–1776* (Harrisburg, PA, 1953), 42–46, 54–56, 85; Greene, *Quest for Power*, 299–300.

24. Dickerson, *American Colonial Government*, 181–194; Greene, *Provincial Governor*, 59, 177–188. See also the various histories of individual colonies cited in notes 11, 21, and 23 of this chapter. Pownall, *Administration*, 67, 76ff.

itself, and the position accorded with the principle in English law that all rights derived from royal grants. The Americans contended that, whatever the source of their right to have elective assemblies, it was a right the king could not alter or destroy but could merely restrain through the constitutional veto or disallowance. In a vague way at first, then more clearly and firmly as the century wore on, spokesmen for colonial rights assumed that the assemblies were analogous to the House of Commons and that rights to representation and control over money bills were inherently theirs as part of their legacy as Englishmen.[25] It was simply a difference of opinion; but as Americans learned from Sir William Temple and David Hume, opinion is the soul of authority.

———— The struggle between governors and assemblies can be illustrated by the course of events in New York. New York's constitutional development may be said to have begun in 1693, after the attempt of James II to merge the colony into a monolithic New England confederation had miscarried and after some stability had

25. For an explication of the position of the British and the royal governors, see Dickerson, *Royal Government,* 177–178; see also chapter 2 of this book. Statements of American positions can be found in many of the tracts in Bailyn, ed., *Pamphlets of the American Revolution.* For example, Richard Bland, in "The Colonel Dismounted" (1764), justified Virginians' rights as the "birthright of every Englishman," but he also turned the British argument on its head by saying that the rights of Virginians were confirmed in the original charter from James I (Bland cited Coke to the effect that rights once granted cannot be revoked). See also Thomas Fitch, "Reasons Why the British Colonies Should Not Be Charged with Internal Taxes" (New Haven, 1764); James Otis, "Rights of the British Colonies" (Boston, 1764); Oxenbridge Thatcher, "Sentiments of a British American" (Boston, 1764); Stephen Hopkins, "Rights of Colonies" (Providence, 1765); and Daniel Dulany, "Considerations" (Annapolis, 1765), in Bailyn, ed., *Pamphlets of the American Revolution,* 320–321, 323, 387–388, 444, 490, 508–511, 633–634. In *American Political Writing during the Founding Era 1760–1805,* ed. Charles S. Hyneman and Donald S. Lutz, 2 vols. (Indianapolis, IN, 1983), see for example "Brittanus Americanus" (Boston, 1766) and Silas Downer (Providence, 1768), 89, 98. Jack P. Greene, in *Peripheries and Center: Constitutional Development in the Extended Polities of the British Empire and the United States, 1607–1788* (Athens, GA, 1986), 31–32, perceptively observes that the very fact of the governors' claims to an outsized prerogative stimulated the assemblies to claim by analogy a right to powers like those of Parliament.

been restored following Leisler's Rebellion. In that year a newly arrived governor, Benjamin Fletcher, set about aiding and abetting pirates, embezzling royal revenues, and selling crown lands for his own profit. In accordance with his instructions, Fletcher sought from the assembly taxes and appropriations adequate to support his administration for life. The assembly, concerned about possible irregularities in earlier appropriations, was willing to grant the sums for only five years. Soon large amounts of public funds seemed to have disappeared, and the assembly requested an accounting. The governor curtly replied that it was the duty of the assembly to raise the money and the prerogative of the governor and council to spend it. For the assembly's impertinence in making the request, Fletcher prorogued it. After more minor confrontations, Fletcher hit upon the expedient of controlling the assembly by bribing an adequate number of its members with large grants of crown lands—or so his successor informed the Board of Trade.[26]

That successor died after three untroubled years in office, to be replaced in 1701 by a governor who was "one of the very worst that ever held office in the American colonies": Edward Hyde, Lord Cornbury, grandson of the great earl of Clarendon. For eight years Cornbury repeatedly clashed with the assembly in much the way Fletcher had and just as adamantly refused to give the assembly an accounting. Meanwhile, the assembly petitioned Queen Anne to be allowed to appoint its own treasurer; permission was granted, and though the treasurer was authorized to supervise only extraordinary appropriations that were not a part of the standing cost of government, the concession provided a wedge for gaining more. At the same time, Cornbury was having money problems with New Jersey, of which he was also governor. Strains in both colonies steadily in-

---

26. Burns, *Controversies between Royal Governors and their Assemblies,* 291–296, 298–299; Labaree, *Royal Government,* 283–284. J. M. Sosin, *English America and Imperial Inconstancy: The Rise of Provincial Autonomy, 1696–1715* (Lincoln, NE, 1985), 155–160; Jerome R. Reich, *Leisler's Rebellion: A Study of Democracy in New York, 1664–1720* (Chicago, 1953); John C. Rainbolt, "The Creation of a Governor and Captain General for the Northern Colonies," *New York Historical Society Quarterly* 57(1973):101–120; John D. Runcie, "The Problem of Anglo-American Politics in Bellomount's New York," *William and Mary Quarterly* 26(1969):191–217.

tensified, and in 1708 the New York assembly drafted resolutions condemning the governor. In response Cornbury was recalled, even though he was a cousin-german to the queen and had been led to believe that his appointment was "intended for my benefit," not that of the colonies.[27]

Then in 1710 the grounds began to shift. For nearly two decades assemblies had based their position on the commonsense claim that legislative oversight was justified by the evidence of fraud on the part of governors and councils. The new governor, Robert Hunter, who served from 1710 until 1720, was both honest and able; no one accused him of irregularities in managing public funds. But he was greeted by the assembly's assertion that it had the right to determine not only the amounts of appropriations but also their specific application and their time limits. Not even the House of Commons had gone so far. Hunter promptly prorogued the assembly, but he was forced to call it back into session the next spring because the second of the Anglo-French intercolonial wars was moving toward its climax, and New York was in danger of invasion from Canada. No agreement was reached, and Hunter dissolved the assembly. Elections were held, but the membership changed little, and when the assembly met in the summer of 1711 there was a showdown.[28]

The new assembly passed various appropriations measures, the council voted several amendments, and the assembly rejected the amendments with a remarkable manifesto. It was true, the assembly declared, that such legislative power as the council might have came "only from the meer Pleasure of the Prince," but the assembly's power of the purse was an "inherent Right." It did not "proceed from any Commission, Letters Patent or other Grant from the Crown, but from the free Choice and Election of the People; who ought not to be divested of their Property (nor justly can) without their consent." The last clause echoed the principles contained in chapters 12 and 14

27. Burns, *Controversies between Royal Governors and their Assemblies,* 299–303; Beverly McAnear, *The Income of the Colonial Governors of British North America* (New York, 1967), 11–14; Sosin, *English America and Imperial Inconstancy,* 216–220.

28. Sosin, *English America and Imperial Inconstancy,* 222–224; Burns, *Controversies between Royal Governors and their Assemblies,* 304–305; Mary Lou Lustig, *Robert Hunter, 1666–1734: New York's Augustan Statesman* (Syracuse, NY, 1983).

of Magna Carta as well as the words of the "famous statute," *de tallagio non concedendo,* and the drift of the whole declaration was toward a claim that the assembly was on a par with the House of Commons.[29]

The impasse continued for four years, and then Hunter and the council surrendered. The assembly agreed that expenditures be nominally made by warrant of the governor and council, in keeping with Hunter's instructions, but he was forced to agree that the assembly would have exclusive power over the amounts, the duration, the application, the method of disbursement, and the auditing of public accounts. Moreover, the assembly-appointed treasurer became the sole custodian of public funds.[30]

These arrangements held for about twenty years, during which appropriations were made for five-year periods, and relative harmony prevailed in regard to money matters. On a few occasions the assembly tried to parlay its fiscal power into concessions from the governors regarding the chancery court and the frequency of elections. During the governorship of William Cosby, 1732–1736, intense animosities arose over those issues and the question of the governor's sitting in the council. So bitter were feelings that when Cosby died and Lt. Gov. George Clarke became acting governor, the assembly refused for two years to vote appropriations. Finally in 1739 it passed a one-year appropriations bill in which salaries of officers were made payable in the name of the officeholder, not the office. That became the permanent method in the colony, and for practical purposes it gave the assembly control over appointments since the legislators could reject any nominee by refusing to vote him a salary.[31]

29. Burns, *Controversies between Royal Governors and their Assemblies,* 306–307; Sir Edward Coke, *Institutes of the Lawes of England,* ed. William S. Hein (Buffalo, NY, 1986 facs. repr. of London, 1797), 2d series, 532; John Dickinson, "Letters from a Farmer in Pennsylvania," Letter 4, in Forrest McDonald, *Empire and Nation* (Englewood Cliffs, NJ, 1962), 22 and n.

30. Burns, *Controversies between Royal Governors and their Assemblies,* 308–312; Sosin, *English America and Imperial Inconstancy,* 227–230.

31. Burns, *Controversies between Royal Governors and their Assemblies,* 317–327; Labaree, *Royal Government,* 285–287; Dickerson, *American Colonial Government,* 162–163.

By 1748 the assembly had won virtually total control of every important administrative department of the government, including the military. Moreover, the pattern of events in New York had been repeated in most of the other colonies; the assemblies in three more colonies would soon triumph as well. Indeed, at a conference of governors held in Albany in 1748 to discuss Indian relations, the attendees spent a large portion of their time discussing ways they might regain control of the prerogative from the assemblies. Nothing came of their talk.[32]

Were these developments seen in the light of the Whig interpretation of history, it could be concluded that the liberties of the people had triumphed over arbitrary executive authority. But it is worth quoting the sermon preached by Charles Chauncey before the governor and the General Court of Massachusetts in 1749: "Men who strike in with the popular cry of liberty and priviledge . . . may, all the while, be aiming only at power."[33]

———— The ascendancy of the assemblies had been facilitated by the loose administration—"salutary neglect," it has been called—of colonial affairs under Thomas Pelham-Holles, Duke of Newcastle, who served as Britain's secretary of state for the southern department from 1724 until 1748. Newcastle began with enthusiastic hopes for strengthening and rationalizing royal authority in America, and the completion of the transition of the Carolinas from proprietary to royal colonies was part of the fruit of his efforts. He ran into an insurmountable object, however, in Massachusetts. The House of Representatives in that colony had been encroaching on the prerogative for years, one of its most potent weapons against the governors being its practice of voting their salaries on a year-to-year basis. In 1727 Newcastle transferred William Burnet from New York to Massachusetts and instructed him to obtain permanent funding for the salaries of royal governors. The House stubbornly refused and voted

32. Burns, *Controversies between Royal Governors and their Assemblies,* 338ff.; Pownall, *Administration,* 79–80.

33. Charles Chauncy, "Civil Magistrates Must be Just, Ruling in the Fear of God," 1747, in *Political Sermons of the American Founding Era 1730–1805,* ed. Ellis Sandoz (Indianapolis, IN, 1991), 157–158.

Burnet his salary one year at a time. He, too, was stubborn, refusing the salary. The deadlock continued until September of 1729, when Burnet suddenly and unexpectedly died. As Burnet's successor, Newcastle appointed Jonathan Belcher, a Massachusetts native who, Newcastle mistakenly thought, might be able to succeed by entreaty where Burnet had failed. The House continued to vote annual stipends; for two years Belcher refused them, but in 1733 he appealed through his son, asking Newcastle to allow him to accept the assembly's offer. Newcastle capitulated and subsequently lost interest in making appointments with a view toward directing colonial policy. Instead, during the remaining fifteen years of his tenure he was guided, in distributing the American patronage, by concern for building the political strength of the Pelham family connection in Britain. Jockeying for power in England undercut the strength of the royal governors even further; at one point in 1737 five governorships were vacant because of divisions in the ministry.[34]

Reform of the colonial administrative machinery began in 1748, when Newcastle resigned to take up the more prestigious position of secretary of state for the northern department. As indicated earlier, Newcastle's replacement, the Duke of Bedford, induced Halifax to become head of the Board of Trade and in 1752 vested Halifax with powers, including the patronage, that made him a veritable secretary of state for the colonies. Bedford also appointed a number of able and dedicated men to serve on the board, and by 1753 the means for restoring the power of the colonial governors were firmly established.[35]

The timing, however, was spectacularly bad. In 1754 the French and Indian War began, and for the next six years fighting was widespread and intense throughout French and British America. In the circumstances, the British government sorely needed the help of the colonial governments, which meant that cracking down on assemblies was unseasonable. In fact, during the 1750s three additional royal colonies came under the domination of their assemblies.

34. Henretta, *"Salutary Neglect,"* 61–82, 165, 166, 244–245, 259, and passim; Greene, *Provincial Governor,* 171–172.

35. Dickerson, *American Colonial Government,* 39–54; Henretta, *"Salutary Neglect,"* 282–300. The northern secretary handled Britain's relations with northern Europe, the southern those with the Mediterranean countries and the American colonies.

One was New Jersey. When the governorships of New York and New Jersey were separated in 1738, the first governor of the latter colony was Lewis Morris, who had been chief justice of the former. Champions of legislative supremacy employed the usual array of techniques to take over his powers, but they were divided into regional factions. Morris, who had originated many of those methods while serving in the New York assembly, was able to frustrate them until he died in 1746. His successor, Jonathan Belcher, had no more stomach for fighting the New Jersey assembly than he had had for that of Massachusetts; after 1754, when the assembly was frequently called upon to help the war effort, it extracted the full range of concessions. It was able to solidify its gains because New Jersey had three different governors in the four years after Belcher died in 1757.[36]

In Virginia relations between royal executives and the assembly had been relatively pacific during most of the eighteenth century, partly because lieutenant governors served as executives in residence and partly because the ordinary costs of government had been funded on a permanent basis. But when a new lieutenant governor, Robert Dinwiddie, arrived in 1752 he aroused considerable animosity by imposing a sizable fee, payable to himself, for attaching the royal seal to land patents. Accordingly, when he asked for military appropriations in 1754 the assembly did not trust him, and it began micromanaging the war effort by appropriating funds in detail. After the war it lost ground, but the taste of power was addictive. Harmony between royal officials and the assembly was never restored.[37]

In North Carolina the lower house was slow in asserting itself, largely because of the skill with which Gabriel Johnston, royal governor from 1734 to 1752, played off the bitter hostility between representatives from the Cape Fear region and those from the Albemarle Sound area. So intense were feelings that from 1747 to 1754 Albe-

36. Richard P. McCormick, *New Jersey from Colony to State, 1609–1789* (Princeton, NJ, 1964), 69–71; Pomfret, *Colonial New Jersey,* 147–173; Steven G. Greiert, "The Earl of Halifax and the Land Riots in New Jersey," *New Jersey History* 99 (1981):13–31; Eugene R. Sheridan, *Lewis Morris, 1671–1746: A Study in Early American Politics* (Syracuse, NY, 1981).

37. Greene, *Quest for Power,* 6, 158–165, 304–306; John Richard Alden, *Robert Dinwiddie: Servant of the Crown* (Williamsburg, VA, 1973).

marle delegates refused to attend the legislative sessions, and since they were a majority, legislation enacted during those years was of doubtful legality. The factions came together to combat Johnston's successor, Arthur Dobbs, in the late 1750s and early 1760s, and they met with considerable success. It is the consensus among students of the subject that this situation reflected the same kind of constitutional power struggle that had taken place elsewhere, but recent scholarship suggests that the underlying bases of the challenges to Dobbs were less a matter of power than of personalities, land grabs, and embezzlement. Politics was also more violent in North Carolina than in the other colonies. As a longtime veteran of North Carolina politics wrote in 1768, three years after he had moved to Boston, "We have our disturbances as well as you have yours with this Difference—that our People are more Civilized."[38]

Despite these developments and despite gains by other assemblies—in 1756 even the assembly of Maryland was able to extract some concessions from the governor—officials in England remained determined to restore the prerogative in the colonies. Their chances of succeeding were dramatized, just as the war in America was ending, by a series of confrontations over colonial law courts. The one part of the prerogative no assembly had been able to encroach upon was the appointment of judges during the pleasure of the crown or proprietors, rather than during good behavior, as had long been established in England. In 1751 the assembly in Jamaica passed a law establishing judicial tenure during good behavior, only to see the act disallowed two years later. Disregarding that disallowance, in 1759 the antiproprietary party in Pennsylvania (which was dominated by Benjamin Franklin and Joseph Galloway) steered through the assembly a similar act and won the approval of the governor by corrupt means. That act, too, was disallowed. The next year King George II died, and by law all the colonial judgeships became vacant. New York, New Jersey, North Carolina, and South Carolina promptly passed

38. A. Roger Ekirch, *"Poor Carolina": Politics and Society in Colonial North Carolina, 1729–1776* (Chapel Hill, NC, 1981), chap. 5 and passim; Hugh T. Lefler and William S. Powell, *Colonial North Carolina: A History* (New York, 1973), 119–128; for Dobbs, see Desmond Clarke, *Arthur Dobbs, Esquire, 1689–1765* (Chapel Hill, NC, 1957).

laws providing that when the vacancies were filled, the judges would serve during good behavior. These laws were disallowed, but before that happened Gov. Josiah Hardy of New Jersey violated his instructions and appointed judges to the supreme court during good behavior. Not to be trifled with, the Board of Trade summarily recalled him and replaced him with William Franklin.[39]

The effort to restore the prerogative and its ultimate failure are best illustrated by reference to Massachusetts. The country party in the House of Representatives had long dominated the government of the colony, and through the 1750s it was riding high. William Shirley and Thomas Pownall, Massachusetts' governors from 1741 to 1760, preferred cooperation to confrontation, even when that meant sacrificing the prerogative. Then Halifax appointed Sir Francis Bernard, who served throughout the turbulent next decade.[40]

Willy-nilly, for five years Bernard did something that no one had accomplished in living memory: Without intending to do so he established the hegemony of the court party in Massachusetts' government. He was a professional placeman who sought a "quiet and easy administration" from which he could obtain a maximum of legitimate profits by employing "management and intrigue" and by es-

39. Dickerson, *American Colonial Government,* 152–153, 199–207; Russell, *Review of Colonial Legislation,* 190; Labaree, *Royal Government,* 390–396; James Haw, "Patronage, Politics, and Ideology, 1753–1762: A Prelude to Revolution in Maryland," *Maryland Historical Magazine* 85 (1990):236–255. William Franklin was the illegitimate son of Benjamin Franklin; see Willard Sterne Randall, *A Little Revenge: Benjamin Franklin and His Son* (Boston, 1984), and Sheila L. Skemp, *William Franklin: Son of a Patriot, Servant of a King* (New York, 1990). In "A Letter to the People of Pennsylvania," probably written by Joseph Galloway in defense of the Pennsylvania law concerning tenure of judges, the author says that tenure during good behavior was the "policy" in England since "the latter end of the eighth century," a deliberate overstatement; the "final establishment," in the words of John Adams, was clearly the 1701 Act of Settlement, 12 and 13 of Wm. III, c. 2, secs. 3 and 4 (see James Otis, "Rights of the British Colonies" for a complete transcription of the act); see Bailyn, ed., *Pamphlets of the American Revolution,* 264, 430–434, and John Adams, "Independence of the Judiciary," in *The Works of John Adams,* ed. Charles Francis Adams, 10 vols. (Freeport, NY, 1969), 3:530.

40. Burns, *Controversies between Royal Governors and their Assemblies,* 121–147. George Arthur Wood, *William Shirley, Governor of Massachusetts, 1741–1756: A History* (New York, 1920).

chewing partisan conflict.[41] He was assisted by a general euphoria
that prevailed in the colony due to extraordinary prosperity and the
tonic of Britain's successful war for world empire.

Most importantly, he manipulated the patronage in a way that
temporarily cemented his power. His first appointment was key, that
of Lt. Gov. Thomas Hutchinson, who would serve also as chief justice of the superior court. In addition Hutchinson was a member of
the council, judge of probate for Suffolk County, and commander of
the castle (the royal fort on Castle Island)—in other words, he held
offices in the legislative, executive, and judicial branches. Bernard
picked Hutchinson in the expectation that he would join others on
the bench who were inclined to assign customs cases to admiralty
courts, where the judges were likely to convict and thus earn the
governor the lawful one-third of the proceeds, instead of to common
law courts, where juries were prone to acquit. (Inadvertently, the
superior court appointment won Bernard the enmity of James Otis, a
brilliant but unstable lawyer whose father had been promised the
job.)[42]

Hutchinson was only one of many plural officeholders who reigned
as a powerful oligarchy during the first half of Bernard's tenure.
Andrew Oliver, Hutchinson's brother-in-law, was secretary of the
province (an executive office), a member of the council (legislative),
and judge of the inferior court of common pleas of Essex County.
Oliver's brother and son held offices, as did another in-law and a half-
brother of Hutchinson's. Every member of the council held a judicial
seat, and most held executive posts as well.[43]

41. Bernard Bailyn, *The Ordeal of Thomas Hutchinson* (Cambridge, MA, 1974), 46–
47; William Pencak, "The Martyrology of Thomas Hutchinson: Family and Public
Life," *New England Historical and Genealogical Register* 136 (1982):279–293.

42. Bailyn, *Ordeal of Thomas Hutchinson,* 48–49; Brennan, *Plural Office-Holding in
Massachusetts,* 32–33; William Tudor, *The Life of James Otis of Massachusetts* (repr., New
York, 1970).

43. Brennan, *Plural Office-Holding in Massachusetts,* 33–35. Mercy Otis Warren described Hutchinson's education in government: "He had acquired some knowledge
of the *common law* of England, diligently studied the intricacies of *Machiavelian*
policy, and never failed to recommend the Italian master as a model to his adherents"
(*History of the Rise, Progress and Termination of the American Revolution,* ed. Lester H.
Cohen, 2 vols. [Indianapolis, IN, 1988], 1:46).

Repeatedly, stridently, and in vain the leaders of the country party—James Otis, Samuel Adams, Oxenbridge Thatcher—invoked the doctrines of Montesquieu to rally the voters to break up the oligarchy by electing representatives who would oust the councillors. In the long range the arguments took deep root, and people in Massachusetts would become ardent devotees of Montesquieu, understood as an advocate of separation of powers, not by abstract types of authority but by nonoverlapping of personnel. But in the early 1760s the pleas were to no avail. In 1762 Bernard could write to his superiors that "there never was a greater Harmony in the Government than at present," and in the next three annual elections court party adherents won whopping majorities both in the House and in the council.[44]

The undoing of Bernard and his oligarchy was brought about not by what they did but by what the government in London did. The passage of the Stamp Act in 1765 triggered a fiercely hostile reaction in Massachusetts, and the Adams-Otis-Thatcher "popular" party was swept back into power. They did not lose it again, for as Parliament passed the Declaratory Act and the Townshend Duties and as the ministry sent troops to occupy Boston, the country party resumed its customary role as the champion of the rights of the people. The difference was that now the perceived enemy was not the royal governor but the royal government in London.[45]

It had long been the practice among advocates of the assemblies, in Massachusetts and elsewhere, to employ a rhetoric of hyperbole, to talk of tyranny and slavery in describing the pettiest of supposed encroachments. These people continued to speak out as the imperial crisis took shape, and the result was total misunderstanding on both sides of the Atlantic. As Edmund Burke said in Parliament in 1769, "The Americans have made a discovery, or think they have made one, that we mean to oppress them; we have made a discovery, or think

---

44. Brennan, *Plural Office-Holding in Massachusetts,* 54–73. John C. Miller, *Sam Adams: Pioneer in Propaganda* (Boston, 1936); Pauline Maier, *The Old Revolutionaries: Political Lives in the Age of Samuel Adams* (New York, 1980).

45. The classic work on the Stamp Act and its impact in America is Edmund S. Morgan and Helen M. Morgan, *The Stamp Act Crisis: Prologue to Revolution* (Chapel Hill, NC, 1953). For another account, see Lawrence Henry Gipson, *The Triumphant Empire: Thunder-Clouds Gather in the West, 1763–1766* (New York, 1961), 282–366.

we have made one, that they intend to rise in rebellion against us. . . .
We know not how to advance; they know not how to retreat. . . .
Some party must give way."[46]

Neither party gave way, of course, and thus was born the United
States of America. The way the break came had a powerful influence
on the creation of the presidency; but before that proposition can be
examined, one more aspect of the colonial experience wants notice.

———— For all their resistance to royal officials, Americans professed and felt loyalty, veneration, awe, and love for their kings, and
none was esteemed more highly than George III. They thrilled when
they read that in his first major address as sovereign George had said,
"Born and educated in this Country, I glory in the Name of Briton."
They delighted in his first royal proclamation, "For the Encouragement of PIETY and VIRTUE, and for preventing and punishing of
Vice, Profaneness, and Immorality." That cemented an impression
that George III, like his deceased father Frederick, had been educated
to be a Patriot King by disciples of Bolingbroke. Inasmuch as the
general American view of ministerial government and of London
society was that both were almost terminally corrupt, riddled with
love of luxury, venality, and vice, such a pronouncement filled Americans—and not just the pious—with hopes for reforms that would
remove the strains between popular leaders and royal officials in the
colonies.[47]

What is surprising, and what is relevant, is not that Americans held
that illusion, but that they clung to it so long in the face of evidence
to the contrary. One reason was the widespread understanding, as
well as the legal fiction, that "the king can do no wrong" and that if
he appeared to do wrong it must be assumed (as the law assumed)
that the dirty deed was the work of deceitful ministers. But the

46. *Edmund Burke on the American Revolution: Selected Speeches and Letters,* ed.
Elliott Robert Barkan (New York, 1966), 5–6.

47. William David Liddle, "A Patriot King, or None: American Public Attitudes
toward George III and the British Monarchy, 1754–1776," Ph.D. diss., Claremont,
1970, 133; Robert D. Fiala, "George III in the Pennsylvania Press: A Study in Changing Opinions, 1760–1776," Ph.D. diss., Wayne State University, 1967, 54, 55. The
remaining three paragraphs of this chapter are derived from these excellent studies.

feeling ran deeper than that, as is exemplified by the experiences of two young Americans, both of them staunch antiprerogative men, upon traveling in London. Benjamin Rush, a Pennsylvanian, went in 1769 into the House of Lords and "gazed for some time at the throne with emotions that I cannot describe." He persuaded a guard to let him sit on the throne, which he did "for a considerable time" until he was suddenly overcome by "a kind of horror" at the trespass he was committing. Josiah Quincy, Jr., who in the summer of 1774 published a scathing attack on British policy and on the king in particular, in November of the same year saw George III opening a new session of Parliament and was overwhelmed by the same kind of emotions that had flooded over Rush.[48]

Thus it was that, as the imperial crises unfolded between 1765 and 1776, Americans could repeatedly turn to the king for support against Parliament and the ministers and expect to get it. When the hated Stamp Act was repealed in 1766, the widespread rejoicing was accompanied by a general belief that the king had responded to American petitions, sacked the prime minister, and ordered the repeal. When the Townshend Duties were enacted in 1767, there was some confusion as to why the king was so slow in undoing that wicked parliamentary/ministerial usurpation, but no one blamed him. When the duties (except that on tea) were repealed in 1770 it was again assumed that the king had straightened the matter out. Even in 1774, after Massachusetts' government was substantially replaced by military rule as punishment for the Boston Tea Party, almost no one faulted the king. That year James Wilson of Pennsylvania and Thomas Jefferson of Virginia published lengthy pamphlets advancing the radical proposition that Parliament had no authority over the colonies whatsoever and stood in the same relationship to the crown as each of the colonial legislatures did. Indeed, both pamphlets called upon the king to exert his prerogative and to intervene in the colonials' behalf against Parliament. In 1775, while he commanded American troops against

48. The Rush and Quincy experiences are from Liddle, "Patriot King," 255, 275, 316. See also Jerrilyn Greene Marston, *King and Congress* (Princeton, NJ, 1987), 13–14, 35–39, 338 nn. 3, 4. For Rush, see Carl Binger, *Revolutionary Doctor: Benjamin Rush, 1746–1813* (New York, 1966), and for Quincy, see Josiah Quincy, *Memoir of the Life of Josiah Quincy, Jun., of Massachusetts* (Boston, 1825).

the redcoats in Boston, George Washington could not bring himself to refer to the enemy as "the king's troops"; he wrote "the ministers' troops" instead. As late as the fall of 1775 the Continental Congress was petitioning the king for redress of grievances, still hoping that he would save them.[49]

Then the news came from London that the king had personally denounced the American "rebels," personally ordered their repression by force, personally arranged for German mercenaries to be hired to force the Americans into submission. The news was utterly shattering precisely because belief in the virtue of this Patriot King had been intense. No people could have felt more betrayed.[50] It seemed unlikely that Americans would ever believe in executive authority again—except that in their hearts they yearned to believe.

49. The works of Liddle and Fiala, passim. The Washington quote is from Liddle, 376. Wilson's pamphlet was *Considerations on the . . . Legislative Authority of the British Parliament* (Philadelphia, 1774); Jefferson's was *Summary View of the Rights of British America* (Williamsburg, 1774).

50. See, for example, Jerrilyn Greene Marston, "The Abdication of George III," *New England Historical and Genealogical Register* 129 (1975):133–149.

6

The Revolutionary Experience,

1776–1787

The closing of the Declaration of Independence professes "a firm reliance on the Protection of Divine Providence." That was no idle assertion. Given the audacity, nay foolhardiness, of the earthly task the Americans were undertaking, they sorely needed heavenly assistance. They had set out to win a war against a great world power and to do so with only a shadow of a national government that had no administrative apparatus, no capacity to tax, and no authority to command anyone to do anything.[1]

Even worse, they were undertaking a quintessentially executive function without the benefit of an executive. Rather, they had a multiplicity of executives working at cross-purposes, albeit toward the same end. There was the Continental Congress, consisting usually of thirty-odd bickering, sometimes corrupt, more often incompetent delegates from thirteen states, attempting to supervise and pay for the war; there were the state governments, all but one of

---

1. The profession was an appropriate piety, but it was also a clever turn on Jefferson's part: It was a subtle reminder that declaring independence was, in Locke's sense of the phrase, "an appeal to heaven."

which had emasculated their executive branches; and there was the Continental army and its commander in chief, George Washington.

Crisis after crisis arose during the war, and as the United States managed to survive and ultimately win the decisive battle at York-town in 1781, no small number of Americans believed that God had indeed protected them. But some also believed that American security and liberty could not last long unless a stronger central government, complete with a powerful chief executive, was created. After the war, when half-hearted civil wars and rebellions began to erupt, that conviction became more widespread, and the establishment of the Constitution became possible.

To put it differently, experience taught Americans that safety and ordered liberty cannot exist without competent government and that government without executive authority is no government at all. To put it differently still, they learned that prudence dictated that they not count exclusively on divine protection in future, for as Daniel Webster said many years later, miracles do not cluster.

———— The person who did most to spark the reaction against monarchy, apart from George III himself, was Thomas Paine. Paine's pamphlet *Common Sense* was the first major American attack on monarchy as such, and its impact was astounding. A hundred and twenty thousand copies were sold in the first three months after publication in January, 1776, and sales ultimately reached a half million—almost a copy for every free adult male in America. Its effect upon George Washington was typical; Washington wrote that its "sound doctrine and unanswerable reasoning" would leave no one "at a loss to decide upon the propriety of separation" from the British empire.[2]

2. *Selections from the Works of Thomas Paine: The American Crisis, The Age of Reason, Common Sense,* ed. Arthur Wallace Peach (New York, 1928), xviii. For a recent biography, see A. J. Ayer, *Thomas Paine* (New York, 1988). David Ramsay described Paine's "operating on the sentiments of a religious people, scripture was pressed into his service, and the powers, and even the name of a king was rendered odious in the eyes of the numerous colonists who had read and studied the history of the Jews . . . [thereby] prepossessing the colonists in favour of republican institutions, and prejudicing them against kingly government" (*The History of the American Revolution,* ed. Lester H. Cohen, 2 vols. [1789; repr., Indianapolis, IN, 1990], 1:315).

Mixing broad and daring irony, cleverly turned aphorisms, and sledgehammer logic, Paine began the tract with a simplified Lockean account of the origins of government. Society, he wrote, was natural and beneficial, government an invention necessitated by the "defect of moral virtue" in imperfect mankind. "Society in every state is a blessing, but government, even in its best state, is but a necessary evil. . . . Government, like dress, is the badge of lost innocence."[3]

Shifting to the "so much boasted Constitution of England," Paine prefaced his transition by observing that "the more simple anything is, the less liable it is to be disordered, and the easier repaired when disordered." According to that criterion, the English government was hopelessly bad. It was "so exceedingly complex, that the nation may suffer for years together without being able to discover in which part the fault lies." Then Paine turned to the generally accepted notion that the constitution consisted of a union of crown, Lords, and Commons, "reciprocally *checking* each other." That conception was "farcical; either the words have no meaning, or they are flat contradictions." To say that the Commons is a check upon kings presupposes that kings are "not to be trusted" and that the Commons is "either wiser or more worthy of confidence than the crown." But the same constitution vests the king with a veto, which "supposes that the king is wiser than those whom it has already supposed to be wiser than him."[4]

Paine next described the institution of monarchy as "exceedingly ridiculous." He rehearsed the biblical experience with monarchy, "the most prosperous invention the Devil ever set on foot for the promotion of idolatry." As for hereditary succession, it could not be founded upon anything except usurpation, and a continuance of it was pure folly. The strongest proof of its folly was that nature obviously disapproved it; "otherwise she would not so frequently turn it into ridicule, by giving mankind an *ass for a lion*."[5]

3. Peach, ed., *Works of Paine*, 4–5.
4. Ibid., 6–7.
5. Ibid., 10–13. The biblical lesson had been clearly and frequently preached many times before. For example, "that the only form of government which had a proper claim to a divine establishment was so far from including the idea of a King, that it was a high crime for Israel to ask to be in this respect like other nations; and when they were gratified, it was rather as a just punishment of their folly, that they might

He went on to contend that it was "not so much the absurdity as the evil of hereditary succession which concerns mankind." If it ensured "a race of good and wise men it would have the seal of divine authority"; instead it opened the door to fools and the wicked and thus "hath in it the nature of oppression." Many had argued that monarchy provided stability and security, and if this were true, Paine said, it would be a weighty consideration. But the claim was "the most barefaced falsity ever imposed upon mankind," disowned by "the whole history of England." Thirty kings and two minors had reigned in England since the conquest, and in that time there had been "no less than eight civil wars and nineteen Rebellions." The only good part of the English constitution, he adjudged, was the republican part, the Commons, and by corrupt means the crown had "swallowed up the power, and eaten out the virtue" of that body.[6]

Then Paine issued a ringing call for independence and captured the significance of the moment. "The Sun never shined," he wrote, "on a cause of greater worth. 'Tis not the affair of a City, a County, a Province, or a Kingdom; but of a Continent—of at least one eighth part of the habitable globe. 'Tis not the concern of a day, a year, or an age; posterity are virtually involved in the contest, and will be more or less affected even to the end of time by the proceedings now."[7]

These arguments constituted about half of *Common Sense*. The remainder was devoted to an analysis of the war and to a call for a permanent constitutional union. In the scheme of government that

---

feel the burdens of court pageantry, of which they were warned by a very striking description," Samuel Langdon, "A Sermon," 1775, in *Puritan Political Ideas,* ed. Edmund S. Morgan, (Indianapolis, IN, 1965), 358.

6. Peach, ed., *Works of Paine,* 14–15, 16.

7. Ibid., 17–18. Abigail Adams wrote her husband John that she was "Charmed" by *Common Sense* and wondered how an honest person who cared about his country "and the happiness of posterity can hesitate one moment" in adopting its sentiments. "I want to know how those Sentiments are received in Congress?" Adams replied that "Sensible Men" thought the pamphlet contained some sophistries, but "all agree there is a great deal of good sense, delivered in a clear, simple, concise and nervous [vigorous] Style. . . . But his Notions, and Plans of Continental Government are not much applauded. Indeed this writer has a better Hand at pulling down than building." Quoted in Phyllis Lee Levin, *Abigail Adams* (New York, 1987), 77.

Paine put forth, power would be vested in a representative Congress; there was no place for an executive.

————— The Declaration of Independence, like *Common Sense,* employed the Lockean theory of the origin and nature of government, albeit in rather more elegant phraseology.[8] But the most memorable— and most debated and least understood—part of the document is only a preamble. "We hold these truths to be self-evident" and the stirring assertions that follow have inspired countless millions of people the world over for more than two centuries, but to revolutionary Americans the preamble was less meaningful than the allegations that constituted the body of the document: a recitation, three times as long as the preamble, of charges against George III for abuses of his executive authority.

The alleged misdeeds are indicative of the nearly hysterical revulsion Americans felt toward their king; together, the Declaration asserts, they constituted proof of a design to impose "an absolute Tyranny over these States." Some, to be sure, were rather tame and old hat: "He has [through the Board of Trade or royal governors] refused his Assent to Laws, the most wholesome and necessary for the public good." Others concerned Parliament: "He has combined with others to subject us to a jurisdiction foreign to our constitution, . . . giving his Assent to their Acts of pretended Legislation." At the heart of the list, however, is a catalog of genuine horrors:

> He has abdicated Government here, by declaring us out of his Protection and waging War against us.
>
> He has plundered our seas, ravaged our Coasts, burnt our towns, and destroyed the lives of our people.

8. Forrest McDonald, *Novus Ordo Seclorum* (Lawrence, KS, 1985), 58–60, 145–146; Paul A. Rahe, *Republics Ancient & Modern* (Chapel Hill, NC, 1992), 551–553, 557–560, 569, 572, 709; Carl Becker, *The Declaration of Independence: A Study in the History of Political Ideas* (New York, 1922); Garry Wills, *Inventing America: Jefferson's Declaration of Independence* (Garden City, NY, 1978); Ronald Hamowy, "Jefferson and the Scottish Enlightenment: A Critique of Garry Wills's *Inventing America: Jefferson's Declaration of Independence,*" *William and Mary Quarterly* 32 (1975):475–480; and Harry V. Jaffa, "Inventing the Past: Garry Wills's *Inventing America* and the Pathology of Ideological Scholarship," *St. John Review* 33 (1981):3–19.

He is at this time transporting large Armies of foreign Mercenaries to compleat the works of death, desolation and tyranny, already begun with circumstances of Cruelty & Perfidy scarcely paralleled in the most barbarous ages, and totally unworthy the Head of a civilized nation.

He has constrained our fellow Citizens taken Captive on the high Seas to bear Arms against their Country, to become the executioners of their friends and Brethren, or to fall themselves by their Hands.

He has excited domestic insurrections amongst us, and has endeavoured to bring on the inhabitants of our frontiers, the merciless Indian Savages, whose known rule of warfare, is an undistinguished destruction of all ages, sexes and conditions.

The anger and disillusionment thus expressed in the Declaration were echoed in the revolutionary state constitutions.[9] Indeed, New York and Virginia incorporated the entire list of charges against the king into their constitutions, and five other states included the more serious charges in theirs. All the states designed features to prevent executive abuse in future. In doing so, however, they erred on the side of legislative excess. As Jefferson said of the Virginia Constitution, "173 despots"—the number of members of the legislature—"would surely be as oppressive as one."[10]

——— Seven weeks before the Declaration the Continental Congress had recommended that the several colonies/states adopt new constitutions, but it had earlier made special recommendations in response to the particular circumstances of three of the colonies. The first concerned Massachusetts, where fighting between rebels and

9. *The Federal and State Constitutions,* ed. Francis Newton Thorpe, 7 vols. (Washington, DC, 1909), 3:1685ff., 5:259ff., 2787ff., 3081ff., 6:3241ff., 7:3812ff. For some particularly colorful examples of continuing expressions of hostility toward George III, see "A Dialogue between the Devil, and George III, Tyrant of Britain" (Boston, 1782) and "A Sermon Preached on a Day of Thanksgiving" (Philadelphia, 1783), in *Political Sermons of the American Founding Era 1730–1805,* ed. Ellis Sandoz (Indianapolis, IN, 1991), 691ff., 771ff.

10. *Thomas Jefferson: Writings,* ed. Merrill D. Peterson (New York, 1984), 245 (Notes on Virginia, Query 13). Rahe, *Republics,* 558–560, 567–568.

redcoats had begun in the spring of 1775 and where the regularly elected legislature had been suspended. The members of that body, calling themselves a provincial congress, met anyway and requested the permission of the Continental Congress to form a government. The Congress was not yet willing to go so far, and instead it suggested that Massachusetts take the position that its 1691 charter was still in force, that the governor and lieutenant governor were absent from the province and their offices vacant, and that the twenty-eight-man council, elected by the assembly, should act as the executive branch until other arrangements could be made. The council continued to serve as Massachusetts' executive arm until 1780, when the state adopted a permanent constitution.[11]

The second special case was that of New Hampshire, whose royal governor, Sir John Wentworth, fled the colony in June, 1775. The provincial congress there, on recommendation of the Continental Congress, proclaimed a constitution early in 1776. The new government, intended to exist only until pending differences with the mother country could be reconciled (but actually in operation until 1784), had no executive branch; it consisted of a popularly elected house of representatives and a twelve-member upper house or council elected by the lower house. The constitution, which was obviously drawn in haste (and ran only to two pages), apparently contemplated that the laws be executed by county and town officials. In the event, however, something like a de facto chief executive evolved. Meshech Weare was named "first councillor" by the lower house and elected president of the council when that body was organized; then, as the business of the state was entrusted to a committee of safety during legislative recesses, Weare was elected president of that committee, too. By virtue of his combined positions Weare was sometimes able to wield executive power effectively despite the lack of a constitutional mandate.[12]

11. *Letters of Members of the Continental Congress,* ed. Edmund C. Burnett, 8 vols. (Washington, DC, 1921–1936), 1:106–109 and notes; Willi Paul Adams, *The First American Constitutions: Republican Ideology and the Making of the State Constitutions in the Revolutionary Era* (Chapel Hill, NC, 1980).

12. Adams, *First American Constitutions,* 68–70; Edmund Cody Burnett, *The Continental Congress* (New York, 1941), 122–123; Josiah Bartlett and John Langdon to

The third exceptional case was that of South Carolina, where events took a strange turn. In March of 1776, on the suggestion of the Continental Congress, the legislature-turned-provincial congress promulgated a temporary constitution that provided for a "president and commander-in-chief" to be elected by the legislature. Almost all the traditional executive powers were retained by the legislature, but there was one anachronism: The president was given an absolute veto over legislation. After independence was declared, the legislators considered amendments intermittently until March of 1778, when they presented a new constitutional draft to John Rutledge, the state's president, for his approval. Rutledge refused to sign on the ground that the oath of office required him to support the constitution of 1776 and also because the new document deprived the governor—as the executive was now to be called—of the veto. He was overwhelmingly opposed in the legislature, however, and he resigned.[13]

Eight of the ten remaining states—the exceptions being Connecticut and Rhode Island, which continued to operate under their colonial charters—adopted constitutions in response to Congress' general recommendation. All the documents provided for legislative supremacy, and only New York's established a chief executive office that was vested with any significant power.

The extreme was Pennsylvania, whose 1776 constitution, authored mainly by Benjamin Franklin, established a unicameral legislature and no chief executive. Such executive power as it provided was

the Committee of Safety, Oct. 26, 1775, Samuel Adams to Elbridge Gerry, Oct. 29, 1775, Bartlett and Langdon to Matthew Thornton, Nov. 3, 1775, in Burnett, ed., *Letters,* 1:241–242, 244–245, 246–247; Thorpe, ed., *Federal and State Constitutions,* 4:2451–2453; Margaret Burnham Macmillan, *The War Governors in the American Revolution* (New York, 1943), 70. In July 1780, President Weare advised the Committee at Headquarters that he was *"fully* empowered . . . with the committee of safety to call forth *all* and *every* resource of the state when wanted, on the recess of the general court" (Burnett, ed., *Letters,* 5:289); for fulsome praise of Weare, see Samuel McClintock, "A Sermon . . . on the Occasion . . . of the New Constitution," in Sandoz, ed., *Political Sermons,* 802–803.

13. Adams, *First American Constitutions,* 70–72; Thorpe, ed., *Federal and State Constitutions,* 6:3241–3257; David Ramsay, *The History of the Revolution of South-Carolina, from a British Province to an Independent State,* 2 vols. (Trenton, 1785).

placed in a council, whose twelve members were popularly elected by districts for terms up to three years; one-third of the members were rotated out each year. The council had power to appoint judges, naval officers, and the attorney general; it had power to grant pardons and reprieves except in cases of murder, treason, and impeachment; it sat as the court in impeachment trials; the members were ex officio justices of the peace for the whole state. The president of the council was commander in chief of the armed forces of the state, but that power was hedged with restrictions. Just how minimal the council's functions were to be is indicated by the provision that its only employee was to be one secretary.[14]

Other states provided for nominal chief executives, but all were subordinate to the legislatures. They were elected by the legislatures, were restricted by executive councils also elected by the legislatures, and (except in Delaware, where the governor was chosen for three years) served one-year terms. Most executives were limited in the number of terms they could serve. (David Ramsay, in his 1789 history of the Revolution, wrote that "the principle of rotation was carried so far, that in some of the states, public officers in several departments scarcely knew their official duty, till they were obliged to retire and give place to others, as ignorant as they had been on their first appointment.") None of the governors had a veto power. Maryland's alone was given an appointment power that carried some weight, but he, like Virginia's governor, was expressly forbidden to exercise any prerogative power. Only the governors of Delaware and North Carolina had the powers of pardon and reprieve; Virginia's could grant reprieves but not pardons. The executives were nominally commanders in chief of the state armed forces, but their actual

14. Thorpe, ed., *Federal and State Constitutions*, 5:3081–3092 (see especially sections 19 and 20). In 1780 affairs in Pennsylvania became so desperate that the legislature temporarily vested the president of the council with dictatorial power, from which only the lives of the citizens were exempted—though the legislature had no constitutional authority to do such a thing. See Madison to Jefferson, June 2, 1780, and Committee at Headquarters to Joseph Reed, June 12, 1780, in Burnett, ed., *Letters*, 5:182, 211. See also Robert F. Williams, "The Influences of Pennsylvania's 1776 Constitution on American Constitutionalism During the Founding Decade," *Pennsylvania Magazine of History and Biography* 112 (1988):25–48.

powers were restricted by the constitutions and the laws. One governor was given important judicial powers: New Jersey, continuing colonial tradition, named its governor chancellor as well and made him and his council the state's highest appellate court.[15]

As indicated, New York did not conform to the pattern. It provided for a governor to be popularly elected (by ballot, as opposed to the viva voce method that had been used in colonial times) for a term of three years, no limits being placed upon reelection. He exercised a veto through a "council of revision," consisting of himself, the chancellor, and the judges of the supreme court, "or any two of them, together with the governor"; the veto was subject to an override by two-thirds majorities in both houses of the legislature. The governor was empowered to call the legislature into session and prorogue it up to sixty days; he was charged with giving the legislature an annual "condition of the State" report and with recommending such legislation "as shall appear to him to concern its good government, welfare, and prosperity." The governor could grant pardons and reprieves except in cases of treason and murder, transact administrative business, "expedite all such matters as shall be resolved upon by the legislature," execute the laws, "correspond with the Continental Congress, and the other states," and command the armed forces. The state treasurer was appointed by the legislature, but the other high-level appointments were made by a council of appointment, consisting of the governor and four designated senators.[16]

Subsequently Massachusetts adopted a constitution in which the executive had some measure of power, but only with difficulty. Massachusetts was the first state to submit its constitution to the voters for ratification (the rest had simply been proclaimed by the legisla-

15. All the constitutions referred to are in Thorpe, ed., *Federal and State Constitutions,* passim. Ramsay's quotation is from his *History of the American Revolution,* 1:329–330.

16. Thorpe, ed., *Federal and State Constitutions,* 5:2623ff.; the relevant sections are 17 and 24. The first governor, George Clinton, was reelected for six consecutive three-year terms. He was immensely effective in mobilizing cooperation with Washington. Later he became an ardent state particularist and anti-Federalist. See E. Wilder Spaulding, *His Excellency George Clinton, Critic of the Constitution* (New York, 1938), passim.

tures or provincial congresses), and the voters overwhelmingly rejected the one the legislature had written. Sentiment against executive power was so strong that it was seriously proposed that the state
government consist only of a legislature, the laws to be enforced by
officials elected at the county level. In 1779, however, the state held a
constitutional convention (the first) of delegates popularly elected
for the purpose, and that convention turned over its work to John
Adams, who was by then a firm adherent of executive authority. The
convention rejected his proposal to give the governor an absolute
veto, but it accepted provisions for popular annual election of the
governor, a qualified veto, powers of appointment and pardon, and
independence of the governor from the legislature though not from
an executive council. This constitution was finally approved in June
of 1780.[17]

———— What Locke had called the federative powers of the crown—
the conduct of foreign relations including war—devolved not upon
the states but upon the Continental Congress. In attempting to carry
out its functions, Congress was handicapped by lacking two crucial
powers that in the nature of things it could not have. In regard to the
imperial constitution, revolutionary Americans had taken the position that Parliament could neither tax nor legislate for the colonies
because those powers could be exercised only by representatives of
the people affected by them, and Americans were not represented in
Parliament. Similarly, the people were not represented in Congress—
the states were—and thus Congress could not have the power to tax
or the power to coerce individuals. Inasmuch as coercion of states
was impracticable, Congress had to rely upon the voluntary cooperation of the states in executing its decisions. And willingness to cooperate varied with the proximity of the enemy: By and large, where the
redcoats were, the cooperative spirit was, and where they were not, it
was not.[18]

17. Adams, *First American Constitutions,* 86–93, 271–272; for full details of the
Massachusetts Constitution of 1780, see *The Popular Sources of Political Authority,* ed.
Oscar Handlin and Mary Handlin (Cambridge, MA, 1966).
18. The standard general account of the Congress is Burnett, *Continental Congress.*
See also Louis Clinton Hatch, *The Administration of the American Revolutionary Army*

Problems were compounded by the structure and personnel of the Congress. The body was organized as a legislative assembly and voted by states, each state having one vote. Every trifling matter was subject to endless debate and backstage maneuvering. The members were loath to establish executive departments, instead setting up permanent committees—commerce, foreign affairs, marine, treasury, and war—that operated under the direct supervision and control of the whole Congress. The caliber of the membership declined sharply after 1776, and bungling, incompetence, corruption, mutual suspicions, factions, and outright peculation repeatedly marked everything that Congress did or tried to do.[19]

Efforts to finance the war began promisingly but degenerated into chaos. During the first eighteen months after independence was declared, Congress issued $25 million in paper money that the states were supposed to retire over time; the paper bought roughly $23 million in goods and services. Then Congress turned to selling bonds called loan office certificates, taking on by the end of 1778 a public debt of $20 million for which it received about $5 million in cash. Between the fall of 1778 and the end of 1780 it printed another $175 million in paper money, but the bills depreciated so fast that they yielded about $6 million. All the money was then devalued at forty to one, and soon it depreciated out of existence. In 1780 the states took on public debts of their own to help keep the army in the field for a bit longer and also levied taxes payable in specific supplies. Mean-

---

(New York, 1904); Jack N. Rakove, *The Beginnings of National Politics: An Interpretive History of the Continental Congress* (New York, 1979); Forrest McDonald, *E Pluribus Unum: The Formation of the American Republic, 1776–1790* (Indianapolis, IN, 1979), chap. 1.

19. These matters can be traced in Burnett, ed., *Letters; Journals of the Continental Congress,* ed. Worthington C. Ford et al., 34 vols. (Washington, DC, 1904–1937); and Burnett, *Continental Congress.* For example, Henry Laurens in 1778 wrote to Washington, "Virtue and patriotism were the Motto of our Banners when we entered this Contest. where is virtue, where is Patriotism now? when almost every Man has turned his thoughts and attention to gain and pleasures"; and James Mercer, leaving Congress in disgust after only three weeks' service, recommended to the Virginia House of Delegates that in future they choose delegates who were "men of *Integrity* and *Diligence,* and abilities too if to be had," in Burnett, ed., *Letters,* 3:500, 4:464.

while Congress had ordered the army to commandeer the supplies it needed from the inhabitants.[20]

Despite the money and supplies that were raised, the army was in want much of the time, for money and supplies were siphoned off by people in the quartermaster general's and commissary general's departments. In 1778 and 1779 those departments reeked with scandals, and Congress repeatedly attempted to reorganize and police them, but in vain. What was needed, as was pointed out by the Philadelphia merchant and sometime congressman Robert Morris, by Washington's aide-de-camp Alexander Hamilton, and by many another patriot, was for Congress to create independent executive departments, each directed by a single responsible individual. Until the end of 1780, however, Congress was dominated by the "Adams-Lee junto"—a coalition of arch-republican states' righters from New England and Virginia—who ranted and raged against the idea.[21]

Then, early in 1781, just after the belated adoption of the first national "constitution," the Articles of Confederation, a turnover in the membership occurred. A group of ardent nationalists came into control, and an organization of executive departments was effected. Four departments were authorized, each to be headed by a single man with direct and full control over his subordinates. The depart-

20. The indispensable work on wartime finance is E. James Ferguson, *The Power of the Purse: A History of American Public Finance, 1776–1790* (Chapel Hill, NC, 1961). For the information in this paragraph, see pp. 25–69.

21. Ibid., 70–105; Clarence L. Ver Steeg, *Robert Morris: Revolutionary Financier* (Philadelphia, 1954), 24–25; Morris to Horatio Gates, Oct. 27, to the Committee of Secret Correspondence, Dec. 16, to the Commissioners at Paris, Dec. 21, 1776, in Burnett, ed., *Letters*, 2:136, 178, 184; Rakove, *Beginnings of National Politics*, 42, 101–103, 252, 266–267, and passim; Ferguson, *Power of the Purse*, 93–94, 110–111, 113; John Jay to Hamilton, Sept. 18, 1779, Hamilton to James Duane, Sept. 3, 1780, and Robert Hanson Harrison to Hamilton, Oct. 27, 1780, in *The Papers of Alexander Hamilton*, ed. Harold C. Syrett et al., 26 vols. (New York, 1961–1979), 2:183 (at n. 3), 404–405, 490–491 (at nn. 3, 4).

Oliver Ellsworth of Connecticut, whom Nehemiah Hubbard described as a member of the junto, published in the *Connecticut Courant* of Sept. 7, 1779, a vigorous denial that the junto existed—to which another writer responded, "he will never persuade the honest part of the community that there is not a junto in Congress, until he can persuade them not to see with their eyes, and hear with their ears" (Burnett, ed., *Letters*, 4:408–412 and n. 4).

ments were foreign affairs, of which Robert R. Livingston of New York was appointed secretary; finance, of which Robert Morris became superintendent; war, headed by Gen. Benjamin Lincoln of Massachusetts; and marine, which, when the appointed person declined to serve, was assigned temporarily to the department of finance.[22]

The crucial appointment was that of Morris. When he took office on May 14, Morris announced that he did not intend to supply the army. He meant to establish public credit by reorganizing the national finances on a businesslike basis; the Confederation Congress would then be able to supply the troops as it saw fit. But Washington's earnest pleas, the army's exigencies, and the impending climax of the war induced him to change his mind. From May until October Morris worked frantically and ingeniously to stretch the meager resources at his command. His efforts saw the troops through until the battle of Yorktown had been won and independence was assured.[23]

———— What made the American victory possible in the absence of effectual executive institutions was the strength of character of the indispensable man, George Washington. Washington had been appointed commander in chief in June, 1775, partly because he had a reputation as a good soldier earned during the French and Indian War, partly for the political reason that placing a southerner in command of what was then essentially a New England army would dramatize the continentwide nature of the American resistance, and partly because his great dignity of mien and bearing inspired confidence in all who encountered him. Moreover, his integrity, courage, and dedication to the revolutionary cause were unquestionable.[24]

He was not, however, without critics and enemies, especially dur-

22. Ferguson, *Power of the Purse*, 113–114; Burnett, *Continental Congress*, 490–493; Ford, ed., *Journals of Congress*, 19:102–103, 110, 112–113, 290–299, 432–433, 20:545–548, 597–598 (Feb., March, May, 1781), Burnett, ed., *Letters*, 2:210–211, n. 7; George Dangerfield, *Chancellor Robert R. Livingston of New York, 1756–1813* (New York, 1960).

23. Ver Steeg, *Robert Morris*, 58–64, 72–77; William Graham Sumner, *The Financier and the Finances of the American Revolution*, 2 vols. (New York, 1892), 1:261–309.

24. Two exhaustive biographies of Washington are Douglas Southall Freeman's *George Washington: A Biography*, 7 vols. (New York, 1948–1957) and James T. Flexner's *George Washington*, 4 vols. (Boston, 1965–1972). Flexner's one-volume condensation, *Washington: The Indispensable Man* (Boston, 1974), is useful.

ing the early phases of the war. In the fall of 1776 his army was routed in New York, though he managed to hold it together in a retreat to Pennsylvania. Mutterings about his competence were heard in and out of Congress until December 26, when he won a victory over Hessian mercenaries at the battle of Trenton, whereupon Congress adopted a resolution giving him virtually dictatorial powers, after the Roman fashion, for a period of six months. But then members of the Adams-Lee connection, moved by fears of a Cromwell-style "standing army" and by jealousy of Washington's popularity, had second thoughts. Animosity toward military power erupted early in 1777, when Congress debated whether promotion of officers should be made on Washington's recommendation or, as John Adams put it, by Congress "upon the genuine principles of a republic for a new election of general officers annually." A few days earlier Adams had expressed the views of his clique when he belittled "the superstitious veneration which is sometimes paid to General Washington" and said he was "distressed to see some members of this house disposed to idolise an image which their own hands have molten." Such resentment smoldered throughout most of the year, and a desire to oust Washington became common in the junto; but it came to naught, among other reasons because the faction had no plausible candidate as a replacement.[25]

Such a candidate appeared in October in the person of Horatio Gates, a former British officer who commanded the American troops in the stunning triumph over "Gentleman Johnny" Burgoyne at the battle of Saratoga. Burgoyne surrendered with 5,700 men—by far the most significant American success to date—and though the victory was due less to Gates's generalship than to superior numbers and Benedict Arnold's battlefield heroics, Gates was lionized. Washington, for his part, saw an opportunity to bring the war to a rapid

25. Burnett, *Continental Congress,* 233, 268–270; Benjamin Rush diary, Feb. 19, 1777, Samuel Adams to Richard Henry Lee, July 15, 1777, Henry Laurens to John Laurens, Oct. 16, 1777, in Burnett, ed., *Letters,* 2:262–263, 413, 521–522; Flexner, *George Washington, In the American Revolution* (Boston, 1967), 229–230, 238. Oliver Perry Chitwood, *Richard Henry Lee: Statesman of the Revolution* (Morgantown, WV, 1967); Louis W. Potts, *Arthur Lee: A Virtuous Revolutionary* (Baton Rouge, LA, 1981).

conclusion and dispatched Hamilton to Gates's headquarters to borrow enough troops to join with his own for a decisive attack on the British forces in New York or Philadelphia. Gates refused to cooperate, for he coveted the job as commander in chief.[26]

He failed to obtain it, but not for want of effort. On the very day that Burgoyne was surrendering, Congress was voting to establish a three-man board of war, the single executive agency of nonmembers it created before 1781, and late the next month it appointed Gates to the presidency of the board. The others on the board ranged from lukewarm to hostile in their feelings about Washington, and several members of the junto told Gates that the next step was to make Gates commander in chief. As fate would have it, an Irish adventurer who had wrangled a generalship in the American army, Thomas Conway, just then wrote a letter to Gates in which he spoke disparagingly and insultingly of Washington's abilities and called for his ouster. Word of the letter reached Washington at his winter headquarters at Valley Forge; he had known of plotting against him but had had no evidence. Now he confronted Gates. Gates dissimulated, denied knowing of such a letter, admitted it and flew into a rage at Washington's knowing of it, and then abjectly apologized. When congressmen learned of the affair they scurried to dissociate themselves from it. The board of war also discredited itself almost immediately by announcing a grandiose plan for an "irruption" into Canada, which it proved entirely incompetent to launch.[27]

Given the suffering that the army was enduring that winter, the congressmen who had sought to get rid of Washington were in disgrace, and Washington's command was never challenged again. Indeed, in the eyes of the people his stature continued to grow until, as

26. Flexner, *Washington: In the Revolution,* 245–249; Washington to Hamilton, Oct. 30, Hamilton to Washington, Nov. 2, to Gates, Nov. 5, to Washington, Nov. 6, 10, 12, 15, 1777, in Syrett, ed., *Hamilton Papers, 1*:347, 349, 351, 353, 360, 363; Max M. Mintz, *The Generals of Saratoga: John Burgoyne and Horatio Gates* (New Haven, CT, 1990); Paul David Nelson, *General Horatio Gates: A Biography* (Baton Rouge, LA, 1976).

27. Burnett, *Continental Congress,* 281–297; Flexner's *Washington: In the Revolution,* 251, 253–270 is a good account of this so-called Conway Cabal. See also Freeman, *Washington,* 4:586–612.

John Adams had complained, he became an object of adulation. During the summer of 1780, when the American cause appeared doomed, some congressmen were saying that making Washington "sole dictator of America" was "the only means under God by which we can be saved from destruction."[28]

Part of Washington's greatness, and one reason that people trusted him so completely, was that he would never have accepted such a charge. Moreover, though his military "family" was outspokenly disdainful of Congress in private—Hamilton declared that three-fourths of the members were mortal enemies to talent and that three-fourths of the remainder were contemptuous of integrity—Washington never showed the faintest hint of insubordination.[29]

His greatest actions, at least in the eyes of his worldwide audience of admirers, took place after the fighting was over. The first concerned another plot involving Gates. Early in 1783 the army was encamped at Newburgh, New York, waiting for news of the peace treaty and keeping watch over the British troops in New York City lest the peace negotiations fail and fighting begin anew. The soldiers had received almost no pay in hard currency in years, and they faced the prospect of returning home and losing their relative immunity from accumulated private obligations. The officers, especially, had allowed personal affairs to fall into disarray, and unless they received a mustering-out bonus that had been promised them or sizable payments of back wages, many of them had little to look forward to except debtor's prison.[30]

In this circumstance Robert Morris and the nationalists who now dominated Congress thought they saw an opportunity. They combined a threat of a military coup with lobbying by civilian public creditors to pressure Congress and the states to amend the Articles of

28. Ezekial Cornell to the governor of Rhode Island, Aug. 1, James Lovell to Elbridge Gerry, Nov. 20, Thomas McKean to John Adams, Dec. 18, 1780, in Burnett, ed., *Letters,* 5:305, 451–453, 488 n. 3; Freeman, *Washington,* 4:564–586; and Flexner, *Washington: In the Revolution,* 260ff.

29. Hamilton to John Laurens, Jan. 8, 1780, in Syrett, ed., *Hamilton Papers,* 2:254–255.

30. For a fuller account of the incident at Newburgh, see McDonald, *E Pluribus Unum,* 57–67.

Confederation to give Congress an independent revenue and augmented power. Several nationalists wrote to friends among high-ranking army officers urging firmness in demanding their due. As Arthur Lee, one of the few junto men still in Congress, wrote to Samuel Adams, "The terror of a mutinying Army" was being "played off with considerable efficacy."[31]

A number of the officers entertained notions of going beyond making threats. From the tent of Horatio Gates rumors of drastic possibilities began to circulate. From the tent also came two unsigned pamphlets written by Gates's aide-de-camp, John Armstrong, Jr. One proposed that, should the fighting resume, the army head for the wilderness and abandon the nation; should peace be forthcoming, "You have arms in your hands, . . . never sheath the sword, until you have obtained full and ample justice." The second pamphlet called for a meeting at which plans would be considered for overpowering Congress by force.[32]

By a bold and decisive stroke that belied his underlying fear and horror, Washington was able to quell the threat of insurrection. To the surprise of everyone, he attended the meeting in person, and by virtue of rank he presided over it. By the score, officers came in, tempers blazing, only to sit in embarrassed silence as Washington rose. He had written a short speech, and as he took it from his coat pocket he reached with his other hand and extracted a pair of eyeglasses, which only a few intimates knew he needed. "Gentlemen," he began, "you will permit me to put on my spectacles, for I have not only grown gray, but almost blind, in the service of my country. . . . This dreadful alternative, of either deserting our Country in the extremest hour of her distress, or turning our arms against it, . . . has something so shocking in it, that humanity revolts at the idea. . . . I spurn it," he added, as must every man "who regards that liberty, and reveres that justice for which we contend." The officers wept tears of shame, and the mutiny dissolved. As Thomas Jefferson said later,

31. Arthur Lee to Samuel Adams, Jan. 29, 1783, in Burnett, ed., *Letters*, 7:27–28.

32. Freeman, *Washington*, 5:429–431, 436 n. 48; Flexner, *Washington: In the Revolution*, 500–503; C. Edward Skeen, *John Armstrong, Jr., 1758–1843: A Biography* (Syracuse, NY, 1981).

"The moderation and virtue of one man probably prevented this Revolution from being closed by a subversion of the liberty it was intended to establish."[33]

Washington's other great postfighting deed occurred after the British had evacuated New York in December, 1783: He bade farewell to his officers and men and handed his resignation to Congress, vowing never again to enter public life. To a western world steeped in the history of usurpations by commanders of popular armies—from Marius and Sulla and Caesar to Cromwell—this was an awesome display of disinterested love of country. The significance of Washington's act to the establishment of the presidency was that it made the office thinkable.

——— But not many Americans were willing, just yet, to take that step. The continental Union had in fact begun to disintegrate by the time Washington retired, and few people seemed to care.

Attendance in Congress, or the lack of attendance, illustrated a widespread attitude. On June 19, 1783, three months after the climax of the mutinous episode in Newburgh, Congress received word that a band of about eighty soldiers from the Pennsylvania line had left their officers and were heading for Philadelphia, where Congress was meeting, to commit unspecified mayhem and mischief. Congress demanded that the executive council of Pennsylvania order out the local militia for protection, but the council refused on the ground that the militia could not be relied upon. The next day the mutineers arrived and took over a barracks occupied by about 400 troops. On the weekend 400 to 500 soldiers surrounded the statehouse, where Congress and the executive council were in session, and milled around, bayonets fixed, swearing and threatening. Finally the congressmen mustered enough courage to adjourn and file out through the mob. No one was hurt, but Congress decided to abandon Philadelphia and to reconvene in Princeton. Most of the members decided to go home instead,

33. *George Washington: A Collection,* ed. W. B. Allen (Indianapolis, IN, 1988), 210, 214, 217–221; Flexner, *Washington: In the Revolution,* 503–508; Freeman, *Washington,* 5:433–435. Freeman says that Washington read the speech without glasses but used them to read a letter aloud at the end; either way, the effect was electrifying.

and during the next six months there was rarely a quorum of seven states to do business—a problem that would plague the Confederation Congress for the rest of its existence.[34]

And yet, though congressmen strongly denounced the executive council of Pennsylvania, even condemning the state constitution for not providing a vigorous executive, they saw no reason for strengthening their own executive departments. Instead they retreated from the position they had already taken. Late in 1784, when Robert Morris resigned as superintendent of finance, Congress had once more come under the control of men who dreaded central power and feared that the office would evolve into a Walpolean prime ministership—or, more irrationally, that it would come under the control of the French ministry. They accordingly abolished the position and set up a three-man board of treasury in its place.[35]

Moreover, that Congress proved largely ineffectual in handling its

34. The president of Congress to Washington, June 21, 1783, Elias Boudinot to Elisha Boudinot, June 23, 1783, president of Congress, "Proclamation," June 24, 1783, Virginia delegates to the governor of Virginia, June 24, 1783, Benjamin Hawkins to Alexander Martin, June 24, 1783, Elias Boudinot to Washington, June 26, 1783, the president of Congress to the ministers plenipotentiary at Paris, July 15, 1783, in Burnett, ed., *Letters*, 7:193–199, 221–224; Burnett, *Continental Congress*, 575–580. There had long been bad blood between Congress and the Pennsylvania executive council and criticism of the Pennsylvania constitution. See, for example, William Duer, "Statement," March 9, 1779, and Henry Laurens, notes of debates, March 26, 1779, in Burnett, ed., *Letters*, 4:97–103, 119–120. In 1783 the condemnation was stronger: Eleazer McComb referred to "the scandalous neglect of the Executive of Pennsylvania," Alexander Hamilton called the executive "to the last degree weak and disgusting," James Madison saw it as a "disgrace," and Madison, in a letter to Edmund Randolph, Sept. 8, 1783, reported the aftermath: "The Legislature of Pa. have taken every possible step to expiate the default of the Executive short of an impeachment of its members, which the rigor of some members of Cong's included among the terms of reconciliation" (Burnett, ed., *Letters*, 7:202, 203, 208, 290).

35. Burnett, *Continental Congress*, 601–603; the attitude toward Morris was voiced explicitly in a letter from Samuel Osgood to John Adams, Dec. 7, 1783, in which he wrote that Morris "has many excellent Qualities for a Financier, which however do not comport so well with Republicanism, as Monarchy. Ambitious of becoming the first Man in the united States, he was not so delicate in the Choice of Means, and Men for his Purpose, as is indispensably necessary in a free Government" (Burnett, ed., *Letters*, 7:379).

federative powers in peacetime did not convince its members to make institutional changes. As congressman James Madison wrote, it did not dare establish an adequate defensive force because of the old fear of standing armies. Britain and France imposed severe commercial restrictions against American goods and shipping, but the diplomatic corps in Europe (consisting of John Adams, based in London, and Thomas Jefferson, based in Paris) negotiated only two treaties, a meaningless one with Prussia and a treaty of amity and commerce with the Netherlands. Britain and France refused to budge. Spain closed New Orleans to American shipping, thus effectively cutting off navigation of the Mississippi, but when Secretary for Foreign Affairs John Jay negotiated with the Spanish minister about the subject, the negotiations aroused such animosities between northern and southern states that talk of breaking the union into regional confederations began to be heard. North African pirates plundered American shipping in the Mediterranean; Congress sent a commission that accomplished nothing.[36] Meanwhile, in their correspondence congressmen repeatedly bewailed the frequent lack of quorums but insisted that if enough members regularly attended and if Congress obtained an independent source of revenue and one or two additional powers, such as the regulation of interstate and foreign commerce, all would be well.[37]

36. Madison to Edmund Randolph, June 17, 1783, Pierse Long to John Langdon, Aug. 6, 1786, to John Sullivan, Aug. 6, 1786, Theodore Sedgwick to Caleb Strong, Aug. 6, 1786, in Burnett, ed., *Letters,* 7:189–190, 8:413–416; Samuel Flagg Bemis, *Pinckney's Treaty: A Study of America's Advantage from Europe's Distress, 1783–1800* (Baltimore, 1926), 78–90; Burnett, *Continental Congress,* 654–659; Merrill Jensen, *The New Nation: A History of the United States during the Confederation, 1781–1789* (New York, 1950), 169–176, 195–204. Jensen believed that Congress' record in foreign affairs was not as bad as had previously been supposed.

It should be noted that in dealing with domestic matters, particularly western lands, interstate boundaries, and the auditing of Revolutionary War accounts, the record of the Congress was positive. Jensen, *New Nation,* passim; Peter S. Onuf, *The Origins of the Federal Republic: Jurisdictional Controversies in the United States, 1775–1787* (Philadelphia, 1983); and Ferguson, *Power of the Purse.* Interestingly, the celebrated Northwest Ordinance of 1787, unlike its 1784 predecessor, provided for a strong governor and an executive council.

37. See, for example, Abiel Foster to the president of New Hampshire, Dec. 6,

The general complacency—as well as the persistence of fears of conspiracies against American liberty—is illustrated by an episode that took place during the summer of 1785. In Massachusetts, which was suffering more from the British commercial restrictions than the other states, the legislature instructed its congressional delegation to present Congress with a resolution calling for a general convention to revise the Articles of Confederation. The delegates flatly refused, saying that "the great object of the Revolution, was the Establishment of good Government, and each of the States, in forming their own, as well as the federal Constitution, have adopted republican principles." Those arrangements were entirely adequate, but a convention to enlarge the powers of Congress might lead to substantive change in the "federal Constitution." "Plans have been artfully laid, and vigorously pursued," the delegates went on, "to change our republican Governments, into baleful Aristocracies."[38]

Frustrations did begin to mount in 1786, particularly in regard to the failure of diplomatic negotiations and the continuing lack of money. A few proposals for changes were introduced in Congress. Some people believed that Congress must be empowered to enact a uniform system of commercial regulations as a tool for prying loose Britain's and France's trade restrictions. On August 7 Charles Pinckney of South Carolina proposed seven additional articles to the Articles of Confederation, designed to improve the revenues, regulate commerce, and create a seven-judge court that would have been necessary to enforce the commercial regulations; there was no mention of establishing an executive. The proposals got nowhere.[39]

1784, William Ellery to the governor of Rhode Island, Jan. 28, 1785, Massachusetts delegates to the governor of Massachusetts, Sept. 3, 1785, David Howell to William Greene, Oct. 29, 1785, William Grayson to James Madison, March 22, 1786, Thomas Rodney diary, May 3, 1786, in Burnett, ed., *Letters,* 7:621, 8:15–16, 206–210, 243–244, 332–333, 350–351.

38. Elbridge Gerry, Samuel Holton, and Rufus King to Gov. James Bowdoin, Sept. 3, 1785, ibid., 8:206–210. For other examples of the fear of conspiracies against liberty, see ibid., 6:41, 7:378–381, 414–416.

39. Burnett, *Continental Congress,* 663–665; Burnett, ed., *Letters,* 8:350–351. See,

Already, however, the Virginia legislature had issued a call, neither approved nor disapproved by Congress, for a commercial convention to meet in Annapolis in September, 1786. Nine state legislatures voted to send delegates. When a few had arrived, a handful of arch-nationalists (and friends of centralized executive power) decided to declare that efforts to patch together a commercial agreement were hopeless and to request Congress and the several states to call a full-fledged constitutional convention to gather in Philadelphia the following May. This request met as cold a welcome in Congress—at first—as the call from Massachusetts had received. Congress referred the proposal to a committee of three, which referred it to a committee of thirteen, which Congress never appointed.[40]

Then came an explosion. Throughout 1786 there were reports of legislative excesses, particularly in the form of debtor-relief laws and new issues of paper money (the doings in Rhode Island, which issued paper money that rapidly depreciated to one-fifteenth of its face value, were later described in a New York newspaper as "the Quintessence of Villainy; or, Proceedings of the Legislature of the State of Rhode Island"). What was more disturbing to friends of order and government, reports of rioting and mob actions came from Virginia, Maryland, and New Hampshire, a minor civil war broke out in western North Carolina when the locals seceded as the state of Franklin, and a small rebellion erupted in Delaware. And on August 29, just before the meeting of the Annapolis convention, the Hampshire County Court attempted to convene for its fall session in Northampton,

---

for example, David Howell to the governor of Rhode Island, Oct. 29, 1785; Howell, though he recognized that "our Ministers abroad will not be able to obtain very beneficial Treaties of commerce 'till Congress shall be armed with more efficient powers on this subject," was nonetheless reluctant to give substantial powers (Burnett, ed., *Letters*, 8:244).

40. "Annapolis Convention. Address of the Annapolis Convention," Sept. 14, 1786, in Syrett, ed., *Hamilton Papers*, 3:686–690; Thomas A. Emmet, *Annapolis Convention Held in 1786 with the Report of the Proceedings Represented to the States by President John Dickinson* (New York, 1891); Ford, ed., *Journals of Congress*, Sept. 20, 1786; Rufus King to Bowdoin, Sept. 17, King to John Adams, Oct. 2, and Henry Lee to St. George Tucker, Oct. 20, 1786, in Burnett, ed., *Letters*, 8:468–469, 475, 489–490; Burnett, *Continental Congress*, 668–671, 673.

Massachusetts, and found the way blocked by a mob of 1,500 men, one-third of them armed. During the next two weeks armed bands prevented the sitting of the courts in counties in southeastern, central, and western Massachusetts.[41]

Subsequently, 2,000–3,000 malcontents were organized into military companies, officers were appointed—one of whom, Capt. Daniel Shays, was to have the rebellion named for him—and the men began regular drilling. Precisely what they intended to do has not been determined; whatever it was, they never did it. Governor and commander-in-chief James Bowdoin proved no more able to mobilize a reliable militia force than the Pennsylvania executive council had been, but he did not need to: A volunteer army of 4,400 men was raised and financed by Boston merchants. Late in January, 1787, after a brief exchange of fire, the rebels scattered.[42]

The general understanding of what Shays' Rebellion had been about was created from the whole cloth by Henry Knox, a former artillery general who was then serving as the confederation's secretary of war. The previous October, Knox had written Washington that the Shaysites had 12,000 to 15,000 disciplined men under arms and that they intended to march on Boston, rob the Bank of Massachusetts, draw additional troops from New Hampshire and Rhode Island, and march southward with a view toward effecting a general redistribution of

41. McDonald, *E Pluribus Unum*, 208–216; New York *Daily Advertiser*, April 6, 1787; John A. Munroe, *Federalist Delaware* (New Brunswick, NJ, 1954); Jensen, *New Nation*, 332–335; Jeremy Belknap, *The History of New Hampshire*, 3 vols. (Boston, 1792), 3:210ff., 261; Portsmouth *New Hampshire Spy,* Oct. 24, 1786, Jan. 5, 1787; Portsmouth *New Hampshire Mercury,* Oct. 4, 1786; William Plumer to Samuel Plumer, Jr., July 22, 1786, and to John Hale, Aug. 13, Sept. 18, 20, 21, 26, Oct. 6, 1786, in Colonial Society of Massachusetts *Collections* 11 (1906–1907):385–398; Shays' Rebellion Papers, Massachusetts Archives, Boston, 190:226, 231–239, 249–261, 267–274; Boston *Massachusetts Centinel* and *Boston Gazette,* Sept., 1786; John L. Brooke, "To the Quiet of the People: Revolutionary Settlements and Civil Unrest in Western Massachusetts, 1774–1789," *William and Mary Quarterly* 46 (1989):425–462.

42. This brief summary is based upon study of the manuscript collections concerning Shays' Rebellion in the Massachusetts Archives, the American Antiquarian Society, and the Massachusetts Historical Society, especially the Henry Knox Papers. See also "On the Late Disturbances in Massachusetts," Forrest McDonald and Ellen Shapiro McDonald, *Requiem* (Lawrence, KS, 1988), 59–83.

property. Horrified, Washington repeated Knox's report to several correspondents, they spread the word to others, and in one form and another the account found its way into most American newspapers.[43]

The reaction was as strong as the reaction to George III had been eleven years earlier—but with the opposite effect. Seven state legislatures voted to send delegates to the proposed Philadelphia convention despite the lack of sanction by the Congress. On February 21, Congress finally voted to endorse the convention, and five more state legislatures voted to send delegates. Equally portentious, no small number of people began to say that the experiment in republicanism had failed, that Americans needed a king.[44]

———— It had been one thing to reject monarchy and quite another to shed the rituals and symbols and habits that were its comforting, familiar trappings. That a taste for monarchy abided in postwar America was shown in a number of ways. After the Franco-American alliance was signed in 1778, American republicans ritually celebrated the birthday of Louis XVI as they had once celebrated that of George III, and they named counties Bourbon. Congress requested and ultimately received a portrait of Louis and Marie Antoinette to hang in its meeting hall. When the dauphin was born, Americans congratulated one another with festivities. On another level, the sessions of every state legislature except Pennsylvania's began with a ritual exchange between governors and legislators, in solemn reenactment of colonial and British practice.[45]

43. Knox's letter, dated Oct. 23, 1786, is in the Knox Papers; variations of it are to be seen in the various newspapers during the next two months. Regarding circulation of the message in private correspondence, see Henry Lee to Washington, Nov. 11, 1786, and the other letters quoted in the editor's note 2, in Burnett, ed., *Letters*, 8:505.

44. Madison to Washington, Feb. 21, 1787, ibid., 8:545–546. Some congressmen were loath to endorse the convention lest doing so elicit opposition to it. Another consideration was that the New York legislature had recently put "a definitive veto" on the proposed amendment to the Articles of Confederation that would have given Congress power to collect a duty on imports.

45. I have observed the continuation of monarchical rituals in the records of the several legislatures (the rituals were continued at the national level under Washington and Adams but discontinued by Jefferson). Regarding the portrait, see Burnett,

Such lingering symptoms of a mind-set indicate that Americans had a stronger nostalgia for monarchy than they realized or would admit. Some, in fact, had begun to say so, albeit surreptitiously, in the summer before Shays' Rebellion. On this score, congressman Rufus King of Massachusetts wrote a revealing account of attitudes in high-toned circles in New York, where Congress had finally settled. People in those circles were saying that the states must be reduced in number and made more nearly equal in size and that their governments must be made energetic by giving their "magistrates greater authority and responsibility." On the continental stage, they said, "Let there be a federal Government with a vigorous Executive, wise Legislative, and independent Judicial." They declared that a "confederation between so many small, and unequal, Sovereignties never did, or can, answer the views of its Patrons." They pointed to the Greek republics, to France and Spain, to the early medieval English heptarchy—the seven Saxon kingdoms that were plagued by "treasons, insurrection, and wars" until the kingdoms were united by Egbert, bringing "peace and happiness."[46]

King denied that the people so speaking were advocating an American monarchy, but he was aware that some influential people were making moves in that direction. In November, after the Knox version of the rebellion became public, Baron von Steuben—the European

---

Continental Congress, 435, 604; as to the dauphin, see Burnett, ed., *Letters,* 6:343, and various newspapers in the spring of 1785. George Duffield in "A Sermon," Dec. 11, 1783, encouraged "every American lip [to] pronounce a *'Vive le Roi,'* and every heart [to] conspire, 'long may his most Christian majesty, Lewis the Sixteenth,' long may he live, a blessing, and blessed, on earth," in Sandoz, ed., *Political Sermons,* 785. Louis's health was drunk by toasts ranked high in order: In 1778 in Boston he was toasted second, Congress third, and Washington and the army fifth; in 1778 in Philadelphia he was second, Washington fifth, and the army sixth; in 1779 in Philadelphia he was third, Washington and the army eighth; on another occasion he was second, Washington fifth (Burnett, ed., *Letters,* 3:457n., 320n., 4:57n., 300n.). See also William Fowler, "John Hancock: The Paradoxical President," *New England Historical and Genealogical Register* 130(1976):164–177, for monarchical hangovers, particularly Hancock's insistence upon making a farewell speech when he stepped down as president of Congress.

46. King to Jonathan Jackson, Sept. 3, 1786, in Burnett, ed., *Letters,* 8:458–460; Robert Ernst, *Rufus King: American Federalist* (Chapel Hill, NC, 1968).

soldier of fortune whose main contribution to independence had been instilling Washington's army with discipline—took it upon himself to write to Prince Henry of Prussia inviting him to consider becoming regent of America. Steuben claimed that he enclosed an endorsement from Nathaniel Gorham, president of the Congress. Many years later James Monroe, who had been a member of Congress in 1786, asserted that Gorham had written such a letter, expressing "his fears that America could not sustain her independence, and asked the prince if he could be induced to accept regal power on the failure of our free institutions." By the time Monroe made that statement, Gorham was long dead. Whether he had or had not written such a letter, Gorham had expressed great pessimism during the Constitutional Convention about the future of republican institutions and had supported a strong executive.47

In any event, Shays' Rebellion stimulated many Americans, especially in New England, to talk openly of monarchy as a safer guardian of liberty and property than republican institutions could be, particularly in a country as large as the United States. Hector St. John Crèvecoeur, a perceptive French-born observer of the American scene, wrote to a friend that "in the 4 Provinces of New England they Are So weary of the Govt . . . that they Sigh for Monarchy." George Richards Minot, clerk of the Massachusetts House of Representatives and the first historian of the rebellion, recorded that "persons respectable for their literature and their wealth" formed the "seeds of a party favoring monarchy," thus inspiring "very serious apprehensions" among champions of republicanism. Knox wrote to Washington that "three-sevenths" of the people of Massachusetts favored the reconstitution of the continental authority to make it "analogous to the British Constitution."48

47. Burnett, ed., *Letters,* 8:459 n. 3, 497 n. 4; Louise Burnham Dunbar, *A Study of "Monarchical" Tendencies in the United States from 1776 to 1801* (New York and London, 1970), 60, 91, and passim; Richard Krauel, "Prince Henry of Prussia and the Regency of the United States, 1786," *American Historical Review* 17(1911):44–51.

48. Dunbar, *"Monarchical" Tendencies,* 55, 71, 72; George Richards Minot, *The History of the Insurrections, in Massachusetts* (Worcester, 1788), 61–62; Madison to Edmund Randolph, Feb. 25, 1787, in *The Papers of James Madison,* volume 9, ed. Robert A. Rutland et al. (Chicago, 1977), 299; Madison to Washington, Feb. 21, to

Among the delegates to the forthcoming convention, attitudes were mixed. John Dickinson spoke warmly of the British constitution and said that "a firm Executive could exist only in a limited monarchy," that limited monarchy was among the best kinds of government, and that "equal blessings had never yet been derived from any of the republican form." Alexander Hamilton was outspoken in his admiration of the British system and "doubted much whether anything short of it would do in America," but he believed it would be impractical to propose a monarchy because most Americans were not yet ready to accept one. Even so, he thought "we ought to go as far in order to attain stability and permanency as republican principles will admit." One delegate, John Francis Mercer, claimed that he could identify more than twenty monarchists at the convention.49

The more common attitude, however, was that expressed by Washington. Though he had long resisted monarchy, by early 1787 he admitted that "the utility;—nay necessity of the form" might become evident in time. But he did not think the time had come, and he shared a belief with many that it could be deferred indefinitely if the convention acted swiftly to create a strong and stable government with an executive powerful enough to restrain the legislative. James Madison endorsed that view and added that "if no effectual check be devised" to curb legislative excesses, "a revolution of some kind or other would be inevitable." Gouverneur Morris put the same sentiment differently: "If a good government should not now be formed, if a good organization of the [executive] should not be provided, he doubted whether we should not have something worse than a limited Monarchy."50

Edmund Pendleton, Feb. 24, 1787, in Burnett, ed., *Letters*, 8:546, 547; Edward Carrington to Jefferson, June 9, 1787, in *The Papers of Thomas Jefferson*, ed. Julian P. Boyd et al., 24 vols. to date (Princeton, NJ, 1950–1990), 11:407–410.

49. *The Records of the Federal Convention of 1787*, ed. Max Farrand, 4 vols. (New Haven, CT, 1937), June 1, 2, 18, 26, July 6, 17, Aug. 6, 1:66, 86–89, 282–311, 424, 545, 2:34–36, 191–192, and appendixes, 3:66, 319–324.

50. Ibid., June 26, July 24, 1:424, 2:104; Madison to Washington, Feb. 21 and to Edmund Pendleton, Feb. 24, 1787, in Burnett, ed., *Letters*, 8:545–548; Dunbar, *"Monarchical" Tendencies*, 58; Washington to Madison, March 31, 1787, in Rutland, ed., *Papers of Madison*, 9:342–343.

Rufus King had written to a friend the previous summer that, though "the situation of the federal Government is now critical," individual differences of opinion and the states' opposing perceptions of their interests were so potent that there was no reasonable hope for reform—unless there should arise a "Danger of some Evil that will affect each member of the Confederacy." The belief was widespread, though by no means universal, that in Shays' Rebellion such a danger had arisen. Similarly, it was widely but not uniformly believed that the fate of republican government, with a viable chief executive in charge, was about to be determined for all time.[51]

51. King to Jonathan Jackson, June 11, 1786, in Burnett, ed., *Letters,* 8:389.

PART Two

Establishment

Creating the presidency was a bold thing to do, but it was not undertaken boldly. Many of the delegates to the Philadelphia convention remained wary of executive power, and even those who believed the establishment of an energetic executive was imperative understood that it was necessary to proceed cautiously. Not only was care necessary lest members of the convention be offended, it was doubly necessary to avoid arousing the fears of the voters who would be called upon to ratify any constitution the delegates could agree upon. As Pierce Butler of South Carolina put it (in a sentiment that Gunning Bedford of Delaware and others would echo), the delegates "must follow the example of Solon who gave the Athenians not the best Govt. he could devise; but the best they wd. receive."

Circumspection was evident in the very choice of a title for the chief executive. During most of the convention, no title was used; delegates referred to the office simply as "the Executive." Then a committee, assigned the task of arranging the various resolutions that had been adopted into a rough draft of a constitution, employed the word "president." At one point in the committee's deliberations John Rutledge of South Carolina replaced "president" with "governor of the united People & States of America," but that designation was soon dropped. "Governor" smacked too much of *gubernaculum;* it also brought to mind the hated royal and proprietary governors of colonial times and was therefore unacceptable.

"President," by contrast, suggested passivity. The word derives from the Latin *praesidere,* "to sit in front of or at the head of" and, secondarily, "to defend." Variants of the word had been used by the ancient Romans to denote an office in reference to the guardianship of a minor provincial outpost. The executive of New Hampshire was called the president as for a time was that of South Carolina, and the executive council of Pennsylvania was chaired by a president. The presiding officer of the Confederation Congress, who had only the faintest glimmerings of executive authority, was called the president. George Washington was elected president of the Constitutional Convention. And minor social clubs and fraternal organizations had presidents. In sum, the name was familiar and innocuous.

Despite the neutrality of the designation, however, the convention almost went too far toward monarchy in its phraseology. The clause providing for the presidency, when the proceedings were turned over to a drafting committee to give the Constitution its final form, read: "The Executive power of the United States shall be vested in a single person. His stile shall be, 'The President of the United States of America;' and his title shall be, 'His Excellency.'" That title might have been unacceptable to many Americans, and so the drafting committee dropped it and substituted the simple words, "The executive power shall be vested in a president of the United States of America."

Caution was necessary in establishing as well as in crafting the presidency. Pierce Butler wrote shortly after the convention, "We tried to avoid what appeared to Us the weak parts of Antient as well as Modern Republicks." It was a safe assumption that critics of the Constitution and of the early presidents would be acutely sensitive in looking for "weak parts," real and imaginary, that the Framers had incorporated in the instrument. As things worked out, in the contests during ratification, concern about the dangerousness of the presidency was considerably milder than one might have expected—no doubt in part because everyone expected Washington to be the first president and everyone trusted him. From 1792 onward, however, debate about the presidency intensified. The powers and duties of the office had by that time proven to be more ambiguous than they had seemed during the ratification struggle; specifically, many people thought that Alexander Hamilton, as secretary of the treasury, had administered the executive branch in a way that turned it into an office approximating the British monarchy. Furthermore, for nearly a quarter of a century after 1792 the nation was continuously on the brink (and often over the brink) of becoming embroiled in the French revolutionary and Napoleonic wars, and in those circumstances the presidency occupied center stage.

As with Part One, no effort is made in Part Two to present a general history. Chapter 7 treats the drafting of the Constitution, Chapter 8 the ratification, Chapter 9 the presidency of Washington, and Chapter 10 the presidency of Jefferson. Again the principle of selection is relevant to perceptions of the presidency and the institution as an idea. There is therefore virtually no reference to John Adams's presidency; except for stimulating extravagant charges that he was a monarchist, his tenure did almost nothing to shape the office. There is but little mention of the presidencies of Jefferson's three successors. He changed the office and the popular understanding of it; they merely followed in his footsteps.

CHAPTER 7

The Convention

The various delegates to the Philadelphia convention took with them conceptions of executive power derived from a commonly shared general corpus of commentators, historians, political theorists, and colonial and revolutionary experience, but they did not by any means view the subject in identical ways. Diversity could arise partly because of the discrete sources of their ideas: The messages were not entirely compatible, one with another. But the most important reasons that the delegates thought differently about executive power were their individual temperaments and their personal experiences in government.[1]

Neither of the Adamses and none of the Lees had been chosen as delegates to the convention, but the junto's viewpoint—including intense jealousy of central power and fear of executive authority—was represented by a number of delegates. Sam Adams's protégé, Elbridge Gerry, was there from Massachusetts, and Gerry's colleague Rufus King had been something of an ideological soulmate. Roger

1. For group biographies, see M. E. Bradford, *Founding Fathers: Brief Lives of the Framers of the United States Constitution* (Lawrence, KS, 1994), and *Signers of the Constitution,* ed. Robert G. Ferris (Washington, DC, 1976); for economic biographies, see Forrest McDonald, *We The People: The Economic Origins of the Constitution,* new ed. (New Brunswick, NJ, 1992).

Sherman and Oliver Ellsworth of Connecticut had been in the Adams-Lee camp, and two of the three delegates from New York were devout defenders of the rights of the states as were two from Maryland. Three of the Virginians—Gov. Edmund Randolph, George Mason, and James Blair—had views entirely compatible with those of the Lees. Richard Dobbs Spaight of North Carolina was a protégé of Jefferson's; only one delegate from that state was noted for the ardor of his nationalism. All these men had been moved by the recent drift of events to abandon their extreme insularity, but it became clear during the first week of the convention that they had not been sufficiently affected to convince them that a vigorous chief executive was needed.[2]

Two groups had been convinced by experience. The first included men who had been in the army, especially during the darkest hours, and particularly if they had served in proximity to the commander in chief. Among these (besides Washington himself) were Col. Alexander Hamilton, Capt. Nicholas Gilman of New Hampshire, Capt. Jonathan Dayton of New Jersey, Maj. James McHenry of Maryland, Col. William R. Davie of North Carolina, Gen. Charles Cotesworth Pinckney of South Carolina, and Maj. William Pierce of Georgia. The other experience that bred champions of executive power was service in the Congress or in its administrative arms, especially during the period 1779 to 1782 and particularly if the service involved extensive contact with Robert Morris. The prominent delegates of this description, besides Morris himself, were James Wilson, Gouverneur Morris, and George Clymer of Pennsylvania and James Madison. Two more staunch advocates of a strong executive, John Rutledge of South Carolina and William Livingston of New Jersey, were doubtless influ-

---

2. George A. Billias, *Elbridge Gerry: Founding Father and Republican Statesman* (New York, 1976); Robert Ernst, *Rufus King: American Federalist* (Chapel Hill, NC, 1968); Roger Sherman Boardman, *Roger Sherman: Signer and Statesman* (New York, 1971), John G. Rommel, *Connecticut's Yankee Patriot: Roger Sherman* (Hartford, CT, 1979), Christopher Collier, *Roger Sherman's Connecticut: Yankee Politics and the American Revolution* (Middletown, CT, 1971), and Richard J. Purcell, *Connecticut in Transition, 1775–1818* (Middletown, CT, 1963); John J. Reardon, *Edmund Randolph: A Biography* (New York, 1975); Robert A. Rutland, *George Mason: Reluctant Statesman* (New York, 1961), and Helen Hill Miller, *George Mason: Gentleman Revolutionary* (Chapel Hill, NC, 1975).

enced by their experiences as governors of war-ravaged states during the Revolution.[3]

On the whole, advocates of a strong executive were more prestigious, more able, and more numerous than their opposite numbers, but they faced formidable obstacles to having their way. The convention voted by state delegations, each having one vote, and as the convention opened just three—Massachusetts, Pennsylvania, and South Carolina—were clearly dominated by friends of executive power (Virginia was evenly divided). Another problem was that people

3. James T. Flexner, *George Washington,* 4 vols. (Boston, 1965–1972), Douglas Southall Freeman, *George Washington, A Biography,* 7 vols. (New York, 1948–1957), and W. B. Allen, "Washington and Franklin: Symbols or Lawmakers?" *Political Science Reviewer* 17 (1987):109–138; Forrest McDonald, *Alexander Hamilton: A Biography* (New York, 1979); Rudolph J. Pasler and Margaret C. Pasler, *The New Jersey Federalists* (Rutherford, NJ, 1975); Bernard C. Steiner, *The Life and Correspondence of James McHenry* (Cleveland, OH, 1907), and Gary Browne, "Federalism in Baltimore," *Maryland Historical Magazine* 83 (1988):50–57; Blackwell P. Robinson, *William R. Davie* (Chapel Hill, NC, 1957); Marvin R. Zahniser, *Charles Cotesworth Pinckney: Founding Father* (Chapel Hill, NC, 1967); Clarence L. Ver Steeg, *Robert Morris: Revolutionary Financier* (Philadelphia, 1954), Eleanor Young, *Forgotten Patriot: Robert Morris* (New York, 1950), and Ellis Paxson Oberholtzer, *Robert Morris, Patriot and Financier* (New York, 1969); C. Page Smith, *James Wilson: Founding Father, 1742–1798* (Chapel Hill, NC, 1956), Geoffrey Seed, *James Wilson* (Millwood, NY, 1978), Ralph Rossum, "James Wilson and the 'Pyramid of Government,'" *Political Science Reviewer* 6 (1976):113–142, and George W. Carey, "James Wilson's Political Thought and the Constitutional Convention," *Political Science Reviewer* 17 (1987):49–107; Howard Swiggett, *The Extraordinary Mr. Morris* (Garden City, NJ, 1952); Jerry Grundfest, *George Clymer: Philadelphia Revolutionary, 1739–1813* (New York, 1982); Richard Barry, *Mr. Rutledge of South Carolina* (New York, 1971); Theodore Sedgwick, Jr., *A Memoir of the Life of William Livingston* (New York, 1833); *The Papers of William Livingston,* ed. Carl E. Prince et al., 5 vols. (New Brunswick, NJ, 1979–1990).

The bibliography on Madison is enormous. See Jack N. Rakove, *James Madison and the Creation of the American Republic* (Glenview, IL, 1990), Irving Brant, *James Madison,* 6 vols. (Indianapolis, IN, 1941–1961), Ralph Ketcham, *James Madison: A Biography* (New York, 1971), Robert A. Rutland, *James Madison: The Founding Father* (New York, 1987), Drew McCoy, *The Last of the Fathers: James Madison and the Republican Legacy* (New York, 1989), 39–64, Alexander Landi, "Madison's Political Theory," *Political Science Reviewer* 6 (1976):73–112, Harold S. Schultz, *James Madison* (New York, 1970); Lance Banning, "James Madison and the Dynamics of the Constitutional Convention," *Political Science Reviewer* 17 (1987):5–48; William Lee Miller, *The Business of May Next: James Madison and the Founding* (Charlottesville, VA, 1992).

taking a reserved, middle position outnumbered the delegates on both extremes combined. They were amenable to persuasion but only if the advocates could overcome the largest barrier, the lack of a firm plan for constituting an executive that seemed both safe and sufficiently energetic.[4]

Discussion and debate about the presidency took place in three phases: the first week in June, the middle of July, and the last part of August. Almost no progress was made; indeed, the discussions went in circles. Nobody had been able to devise a satisfactory mode of electing the president that would make him independent of Congress, and nobody was willing to vest real power in an office that was subordinate. It seemed safer simply to lodge executive authority directly in Congress, and, accordingly, the draft constitution as it stood in early September—a scant eight days before the final version was written—deposited most of the traditional domestic executive powers in Congress and lodged the federative powers in the Senate.[5]

Then, building upon a suggestion made by Pierce Butler of South Carolina, the convention worked out the electoral college system in a matter of three days. Suddenly the constitutional order clicked into place. All that remained was to transfer a few powers from the Senate to the executive, and the presidency had been born.

———— Edmund Randolph "opened the main business" of the convention on Tuesday, May 29. He analyzed at length the defects of the Articles of Confederation—he did not include the absence of an executive among them—and proposed fifteen resolutions as the outline of

4. Forrest McDonald, "*Ne Philosophos Audiamus:* The Middle Delegates in the Constitutional Convention," *Political Science Reviewer* 17 (1987):175–191; John P. Roche, "The Founding Fathers: A Reform Caucus in Action," *American Political Science Review* 55 (1961):799–816; William E. Nelson, "Reason and Compromise in the Establishment of the Federal Convention, 1787–1801," *William and Mary Quarterly* 44 (1987):458–484.

5. For a day-by-day record of the Convention I used *The Records of the Federal Convention of 1787,* ed. Max Farrand, 4 vols. (New Haven, CT, 1937); for a lively, readable account, see Jeffrey St. John, *Constitutional Journal: A Correspondent's Report from the Convention of 1787* (Ottawa, IL, 1987). See also Clinton Rossiter, *1787: The Grand Convention* (New York, 1966), and Catherine D. Bowen, *Miracle at Philadelphia: The Story of the Constitutional Convention* (Boston, 1966).

a national government. The seventh was "that a National Executive be instituted; to be chosen by the National Legislature for the term of ———— years, . . . and to be ineligible a second time; and that besides a general authority to execute the National laws, it ought to enjoy the Executive rights vested in Congress by the Confederation." The eighth resolution proposed "that the Executive and a convenient number of the National Judiciary" should compose a council of revision with a provisional veto of legislation.[6]

Discussion of the executive resolutions got off to a confused and tentative start on Friday, June 1. Wilson moved that the executive consist of a single person. A lengthy, embarrassed silence ensued. Benjamin Franklin (who favored a plural, preferably three-person, executive) at last broke it by urging the delegates to "deliver their sentiments" on this "point of great importance" before the question was put. Rutledge arose and announced his support for the motion so long as the executive was not given "the power of war and peace." Sherman then took a strange position. Declaring the executive to be merely an implement of the legislature, he said that the number should not be constitutionally fixed but that "the legislature should be at liberty to appoint one or more as experience might dictate." Randolph argued vehemently for a plural executive—a position that more than a quarter of the other delegates espoused. The motion was postponed; it was decided the following Monday, seven votes in favor of a single executive, three opposed.[7]

Meanwhile, Madison suggested that before determining whether the executive should be singular or plural, it would be best to decide what powers should be vested in the office or offices. He proposed

6. Farrand, ed., *Records*, 1:18–21.

7. Ibid., 1:102n., 65, 66, 97. Randolph said that a single executive was "the foetus of monarchy." For those in favor of a plural executive, see Forrest McDonald, *Novus Ordo Seclorum* (Lawrence, KS, 1985), 240 and n. 48. Much has been written about Franklin; see, for example, Esmond Wright, *Franklin of Philadelphia* (Cambridge, MA, 1986), Carl VanDoren, *Benjamin Franklin* (New York, 1938), Carl Becker, *Benjamin Franklin* (Ithaca, NY, 1946), Edward S. Corwin, "Franklin and the Constitution," *Proceedings of the American Philosophical Society* (Fall, 1956):283–288, Verner Crane, *Benjamin Franklin and a Rising People* (Boston, 1954), and William George Carr, *The Oldest Delegate: Franklin in the Constitutional Convention* (Newark, DE, 1990).

that the executive have power to carry the laws into effect, to appoint to offices "in cases not otherwise provided for," and to execute such functions as the legislature should assign him. The last was rejected, but the rest of the motion carried.[8]

By the time the decision for a single executive had been made, it had been agreed that the executive should be elected by the national legislature for a seven-year term, should be ineligible for reelection, and should be removable on impeachment and conviction of "malpractice or neglect of duty." (The convention rejected Dickinson's proposal that the executive be removable by the national legislature on application by a majority of the state legislatures, and it rejected Sherman's suggestion that the national legislature should be able to remove him at will.) It was also agreed that the executive should have a veto—the word "negative" was used—subject to being overridden by two-thirds majorities in both houses of the national legislature. The resolution calling for a council of revision was dropped as an improper mixing of executive and judicial powers.[9]

Deliberation on Randolph's resolutions was completed June 13, whereupon alternative plans were offered. The "small states plan," presented by William Paterson of New Jersey on June 15, proposed a unicameral congress and a plural executive elected by the congress. A plan presented by Hamilton on June 18 proposed a powerful unitary executive chosen for life by electors named by the people in election districts. Both plans were rejected, Paterson's after heated discussion by a vote of seven states to three and one divided, Hamilton's with neither discussion nor a vote.[10]

8. Farrand, ed., *Records,* 1:66–67.

9. Monday was June 4, Farrand, ed., *Records* 1:93–97, 98–104; the debates on Saturday, June 2, are 1:81, 85, 87, 88. For Dickinson's role during the convention see Forrest McDonald and Ellen Shapiro McDonald, "John Dickinson, Founding Father," in *Delaware History* 23 (1988):24–38; see also Milton E. Flower, *John Dickinson: Conservative Revolutionary* (Charlottesville, VA, 1983), M. E. Bradford, "A Better Guide than Reason: The Politics of John Dickinson," in *A Better Guide Than Reason: Studies in the American Revolution* (LaSalle, IL, 1979), and James H. Hutson, "John Dickinson at the Federal Constitutional Convention," *William and Mary Quarterly* 40 (1983):256–282.

10. Farrand, ed., *Records,* 1:242–280, 282–311, 313, 322. For Paterson, see John E. O'Connor, *William Paterson: Lawyer and Statesman, 1745–1806* (New Brunswick, NJ, 1979).

Otherwise the question of the executive branch was not discussed during the six weeks after June 5. The burning issue throughout that period was whether representation in the upper house would be equal by states or proportional to their population (proportionality in the lower house had long since been agreed upon). When equal representation finally received assent on July 17, the result was that the senate would be essentially a continuation of the old Congress except that each state would now have two votes instead of one. The implication, for executive purposes, was that this transformed Confederation Congress would continue to exercise the federative powers as representative of the still partly sovereign states. The executive, virtually an officer of the new congress, would have been scarcely more potent than the president of the old.[11]

———— Serious debate regarding the executive resumed on July 17. The first task, from the point of view of friends of executive power, was to pry the office loose from its dependence on the congress. Gouverneur Morris, who had been absent during the earlier round of discussions, took the lead. Declaring that election by the national legislature would "be the work of intrigue, of cabal, and of faction," he scored heavily by likening legislative election to the election of a pope or, in his second denunciation of the procedure, to the election of the Polish king by the Diet. He proposed instead that the executive be elected by the freeholders at large. Sherman objected that the voters would not be well enough informed to make an intelligent choice, that they would never give a majority to any man, and that they would generally vote for someone in their own state. Wilson countered by suggesting that if no one got a majority, the legislature could make the final decision; popular election would thus at least "restrain the choice to a good nomination." Charles Pinckney supported Sherman, saying that the people would be led "by a few active & designing men." Morris answered that designing men would find it

11. For a discussion of the "presidents" of the old Congress who "exercised the first glimmerings of executive power under the central government," see Richard B. Morris, "The Origins of the American Presidency," in *Essays in Honor of James Mac-Gregor Burns,* ed. Michael Beschloss and Thomas Cronin (Englewood Cliffs, NJ, 1989), 26–32.

much easier to manipulate the congress than a nationwide electorate and that if the executive were elected by the legislative, "he will not be independent on it; and if not independent, usurpation & tyranny on the part of the Legislature will be the consequence."[12]

But Sherman was right, or seemed to be. In 1787 Washington and a number of other men, heroes of the revolutionary struggle, were nationally known figures, but memories would fade, and it seemed probable that in normal times, given the primitiveness of communication and transportation and the size of the country, few Americans would even know the names of anybody outside their own states. Besides, many delegates believed that a congressionally elected executive would be independent so long as he was not eligible for reelection. Accordingly, Morris's motion was overwhelmingly rejected, only Pennsylvania voting for it.[13]

A confused debate followed. Luther Martin proposed and Jacob Broom seconded a motion that the executive be chosen by electors selected by the state legislatures; they were supported only by their own delegations, Maryland and Delaware. Then William Houstoun of Georgia proposed that the executive be made reeligible. Quite inconsistently, Morris spoke in favor of the motion, and somewhat surprisingly, it passed. Madison, appalled, said the vote would make the executive entirely dependent, and he cited Montesquieu's dictum

12. Farrand, ed., *Records,* 2:29–32. Everyone present remembered that foreign intrigue had led to the partition of Poland only fifteen years earlier, and it was commonly offered as "the horrible example." Wilson, interestingly, tried to blunt the force of Morris's argument by asserting that the cases were "totally dissimilar." For Charles Pinckney, see Frances Leigh Williams, *A Founding Family: The Pinckneys of South Carolina* (New York, 1978), and Mark D. Kaplanoff, "Charles Pinckney and the American Republican Tradition," in *Intellectual Life in Antebellum Charleston,* ed. Michael O'Brien and David Moltke-Hansen (Knoxville, TN, 1987), 85–122. In 1816 Rufus King, addressing the Senate, argued for election by freeholders in districts: "Nobody is so competent as the great body of freeman to make a proper selection." He also asserted that "a pure elective majority" had been "the object intended by the Constitution" (*The Life and Correspondence of Rufus King,* ed. Charles R. King, 6 vols. [New York, 1894–1900], 6:7).

13. Farrand, ed., *Records,* 2:32; for Morris's recollection and summary of the discussion, see *The Life of Gouverneur Morris, with Selections from His Correspondence and Miscellaneous Papers,* ed. Jared Sparks, 3 vols. (Boston, 1832), 3:174–176.

that unifying the legislative and executive would mean that "tyranni-cal laws may be made that they may be executed in a tyrannical manner." To dramatize their position, supporters of an independent executive moved that tenure be for life, and four of the ten delega-tions supported the motion. That vote had a sobering effect, and on the next day the delegates agreed unanimously to reconsider the whole subject.[14]

They did so on Thursday, July 19. After Morris gave a long speech about the principles that should guide the constituting of the execu-tive, a number of delegates spoke in favor of having electors make the choice. Ellsworth then renewed the motion, rejected two days ear-lier, that the executive be elected by electors picked by the state legislatures, adding a rider that the states be allotted one, two, or three electors according to the size of their populations. Massachu-setts was divided on the question, but the other states save Virginia and South Carolina voted aye. Thus for the first time the delegates agreed to having the executive elected by somebody other than the national legislature.[15]

After two days spent on making the executive impeachable, reject-ing again a proposed executive-judicial council of revision (a favorite scheme of Madison's), and denying the executive power to appoint judges (the choice was left to the senate), the convention recon-sidered the mode of election. During the discussions, another dimen-sion became evident. It was assumed that if some sort of electoral college were created, the electors would convene in the national

14. Farrand, ed., *Records,* 2:33–36, 40–41 (July 17 and July 18). Paul S. Clarkson and R. Samuel Jett have written a thorough study of Luther Martin (Baltimore, 1970). William W. Campbell published a thirty-seven-page "Life and Character of Jacob Broom," in the *Papers of the Delaware Historical Society* 51 (1909) and Broom is discussed in John A. Munroe, *Federalist Delaware* (New Brunswick, NJ, 1954). See also John A. Munroe, "Delaware and the Constitution: An Overview of Events Leading to Ratification," *Delaware History* 22 (1987):219–238. For William Hous-toun, see Edith Duncan Johnston, *The Houstouns of Georgia* (Athens, GA, 1950), 317–342.

15. Farrand, ed., *Records,* 2:52–59. William Garrott Brown, *The Life of Oliver Ells-worth* (New York, 1970), Purcell, *Connecticut in Transition,* and William C. Dennis, "A Federalist Persuasion: The American Ideal of the Connecticut Federalists," Ph.D. diss., Yale University, 1971.

capital, presumably Philadelphia or New York. Those cities were conveniently accessible from most states but remote from New Hampshire, Georgia, and the Carolinas. Houstoun of Georgia and Richard Dobbs Spaight of North Carolina, who reopened the question, declared that electors "from the more distant States" would be disinclined to make the long and difficult trip just to cast a single ballot and thus election by state-chosen electors would effectively disfranchise them. Delegates from the Carolinas and Georgia, who had opposed electors on the nineteenth, were joined by those from New Hampshire (who had just arrived), Massachusetts (which had been divided earlier), and New Jersey and Delaware (which, without saying why, reversed their earlier vote). The convention was back to congressional election, and there was little cheer in the room. Indeed, the rest of the day was spent in rancorous and confused debate over ways to make the executive independent.[16]

Rancor and confusion were present the next day as well. Ellsworth proposed a mixed scheme whereby the national legislature would make the choice for an executive's first term, but should he seek reelection, electors designated by the state legislatures would then vote. That plan whereby "a deserving Magistrate may be reelected without making him dependent on the Legislature" was rejected, seven states to four. Next Charles Pinckney offered a Harringtonian "rotation," by which the national legislature would elect the executive but no person should be eligible for the office "for more than 6 years in any twelve years." The motion was rejected, after long discussion, by a vote of six to five.[17]

Some potentially influential observations were made between the two votes, however. Madison offered one during the course of a long analysis in which he disapproved of all methods of election except by the people, through electors or directly. If the national legislative elected the executive, he declared, the "Ministers of foreign powers would have and make use of" opportunities "to mix their intrigues & influence with the Election," and he repeated Morris's

16. Farrand, ed., *Records*, 2:99–101 (July 24). Shlomo Slonim, "Designing the Electoral College," in *Inventing the American Presidency*, ed. Thomas E. Cronin (Lawrence, KS, 1989), 33–60.

17. Farrand, ed., *Records*, 2:108–109, 111–112, 115 (July 25).

admonition about Poland, where the election had "slid entirely into foreign hands." That caution nudged a number of delegates in the direction of favoring a decentralized election. The other observation was an offhand comment by Hugh Williamson that contained within it a positive step toward a solution. It had several times been repeated that electors, however chosen, would tend to vote for citizens of their own states, which would put the smaller states at a disadvantage. A few small-state delegates supported congressional election for that reason, and other delegates thought the tendency to vote for favorite sons would lead regularly to the election of mediocrities. To avoid the difficulty, Williamson suggested that electors vote for three candidates, in which case they would probably vote for one or two outstaters, who would quite likely be from small states. Morris immediately seized upon the idea and refined it: The electors should vote for two persons, "one of whom at least should not be of his own State." Madison, too, liked the notion but suggested a mandatory rotation of the executive from state to state. (Had that proposal been adopted, there would have been no Virginia dynasty and probably no presidency of James Madison.)[18]

At that point Elbridge Gerry threw in a comment that was not helpful. "The ignorance of the people," said this former champion of the people, "would put it in the power of some one set of men dispersed through the Union & acting in Concert to delude them into any appointment." The set of men he had in mind, he said, was the Society of the Cincinnati—the fraternal order of former officers of the continental line, which, when it had been organized in 1783, aroused hysterical fears of hereditary aristocracy in the hearts of republican ideologues. The prospect Gerry raised considerably dampened enthusiasm for a decentralized election.[19]

The next day, July 26, the executive was returned to where it had

18. Ibid., 2:109–114. There is no full biography of Hugh Williamson; in 1820 David Hosack wrote *A Biographical Memoir of Hugh Williamson* (New York).

19. Farrand, ed., *Records*, 2:114; for opposition to the Society of the Cincinnati, see *Letters of Members of the Continental Congress,* ed. Edmund C. Burnett, 8 vols. (Washington, DC, 1921–1936), 7:416, 434, 516, 522, 8:208, 211–212, 350; and John Bach McMaster, *The History of the People of the United States,* 8 vols. (New York, 1883–1913), 1:167–176.

started, elected by the newly constituted bicameral congress for a term of seven years and ineligible for a second term. On that same day the convention turned its resolutions over to the committee of detail—Rutledge, Wilson, Ellsworth, Randolph, and Gorham—which was to organize the resolutions into a draft of a constitution. The convention itself adjourned until August 6.

————— The personnel of the committee of detail reflected a curious mixture of attitudes. Rutledge and Ellsworth were ardent national-ists in the sense that they believed in a strengthened national author-ity, including a strong executive, but they were also federalists in the sense that they wanted the government to be as much as possible the agency of the state governments, and they wanted the federative powers to reside in the branch that directly represented the states, namely the senate. The other members were nationalists who wanted states to have a minimal voice in the national government, but Ran-dolph was also an agrarian republican who preferred a plural execu-tive, and Wilson was so opposed to congressional election of the executive that he was loath to vest the office with significant power. That left Gorham as an unqualified champion of executive authority, and thus it is scarcely surprising that the executive as described by the committee's draft had precious little power.[20]

Article 10 of the committee's report stipulated that "the Executive Power of the United States shall be vested in a single person" who would be styled the "President of the United States of America." Wilson had expressly rejected the traditional prerogative as a guide to what the executive power in a republic should be, and the distribu-tion of the prerogative powers in the committee's draft confirmed that rejection. The royal powers to coin money, regulate trade, natu-ralize citizens, establish courts, appoint a treasurer, subdue rebel-lions, make war, raise armies, build and equip fleets, and muster the militia were assigned to congress, not to the president. The powers to make treaties, appoint ambassadors, and appoint the judges of the supreme court were vested solely in the senate. The president was

20. Gorham was not only on the committee of detail, he was also chairman of the committee of the whole; he had prospered in trade and had a distinguished public career including brief service as president of the Continental Congress.

empowered to appoint executive officers except the treasurer, to receive ambassadors, and to grant pardons and reprieves except (in keeping with English constitutional tradition) in cases of impeachment. He was also made commander in chief and given a conditional veto.[21]

For the first week and a half after the convention reassembled the powers of the congress were under consideration, and the presidency was discussed only in connection with the veto power. Madison, like Wilson and Morris and other advocates of a strong executive, feared legislative tyranny as much as their opposites feared executive tyranny; he wanted to shore up defenses against legislative excess beyond a mere conditional veto. Accordingly, on August 15, Madison moved that both the president and the supreme court be given a veto; if either should object to a bill, a two-thirds vote in both houses of congress would be necessary to override, and if both should object, a three-fourths vote would be required. The motion was rejected, eight to three.[22]

Gouverneur Morris then offered a pair of novel suggestions for prohibiting hasty and ill-considered legislation. He proposed that a three-fourths majority be required to repeal legislation, if the president vetoed, the thought being that difficulty of repeal would make legislators cautious about enacting unwise laws. As the proposal received no support, Morris wondered aloud at the desirability of giving the president an absolute veto. That "might have its inconveniences," he admitted, but he emphasized "the danger on the other side. The most virtuous citizens will often as members of a legislative body concur in measures which afterward in their private capacity they will be ashamed of." The tendency of the "popular branch" toward absolutism was ever-present, he continued, pointing out that the "Ephori at Sparta became in the end absolute" and adding that if the popular branch overturned the executive, "as happened in Eng-

21. Farrand, ed., *Records,* 2:185, 181–182, 183 (Madison's notes, August 6). Again the word "veto" is not used; bills were to be presented to the president "for his revision." Regarding the exception of impeachments from the pardoning power, see David Gray Adler, "The President's Pardon Power," in Cronin, ed., *Inventing the American Presidency,* 213–214.

22. Farrand, ed., *Records,* 2:298.

land" in the 1640s, "the tyranny of one man will ensue." He moved that the question be postponed, "to consider of some more effectual check than requiring" a two-thirds majority to override a presidential veto. Wilson spoke in support of Morris, but Gorham, Rutledge, and Ellsworth grumbled at the endless delays and "the tediousness of the proceedings."[23]

Hugh Williamson proposed, as a step closer to an absolute veto, that the majority necessary to override be increased from two-thirds to three-fourths. That motion carried by a six-to-four vote, one state being divided. Madison noted that Congress could get around the veto power by calling its actions something other than bills. It was too late in the day to act on the matter, but on the next day the veto was extended to cover "every order resolution or vote, to which the concurrence of the Senate & House of Reps. may be necessary."[24]

Yet another day later, a change and an exchange took place on a matter of crucial importance. The committee of detail's draft had vested in Congress power "to make war." On August 17 Charles Pinckney suggested that the power should reside in the Senate, the whole Congress being too unwieldy. Pierce Butler said the Senate itself was too unwieldy and favored giving the power to the president, "who will have all the necessary qualities" for acting wisely and with dispatch and "will not make war but when the Nation will support it." At that point Madison and Gerry moved to substitute "declare" war for "make" war, "leaving to the Executive the power to repel sudden attacks." Sherman objected, wanting Congress to control the waging of war as well as the commencement of it. His colleague Ellsworth objected also, until King explained that "make" war "might be understood to 'conduct' it which was an Executive function." The change was approved, and in the finished Constitution the Congress was given the explicit and exclusive power to declare war. By implication the president was empowered to "make" or "conduct" war, but whether the power, as Madison put it, "to repel sudden attacks" extended to the repelling of threatened attacks

23. Ibid., 2:299–301 (August 15).
24. Ibid., 2:301, 304–305. Richard A. Watson, "Origins and Early Development of the Veto Power," *Presidential Studies Quarterly* 17 (1987):401–411.

or the defense of American interests abroad was left entirely unsettled. The question would remain a vexing one for more than 200 years.[25]

The next executive matter to come up concerned a council. The subject had been discussed in desultory fashion several times, and most delegates assumed that the creation of such a body was desirable, but it was first seriously considered on August 18. Ellsworth opined that there should be one to "advise but not conclude the President" and suggested that it should consist of the president of the Senate, the chief justice, and the heads of the departments of foreign and domestic affairs, war, finance, and marine. Pinckney objected and asked that the proposal be deferred until Morris arrived since Morris had given notice that he had a similar proposal. Gerry spoke against allowing heads of departments, and especially finance, to have any advisory capacity regarding legislation. Dickinson declared that department heads might be properly consulted by the president if they were appointed by the legislature, which he favored, but not if they were appointed by the president himself. On that note the subject was postponed until the following Monday, at which time Morris proposed an executive council much like the one Ellsworth had suggested, except that the president of the Senate was not included. The proposal was referred to a committee—which never reported on it.[26]

On August 24 the convention finally got to the article of the committee of detail's report that sketched out the presidency. It became evident during the course of a long day that there was dissatisfaction with every way of constituting the presidency that had been considered so far. Moreover, as Gorham had remarked a few days earlier, some delegates could not agree upon form until powers were defined, and others could not agree upon powers until form was decided. Amid objections from four of the smaller states, the convention voted to have the president elected by joint ballot of the two houses of Congress. It rejected by a six-to-five vote a motion that in such an election each state have one vote, rejected by the same mar-

---

25. Farrand, ed., *Records,* 2:318–319 (August 17). See also chapter 14 of this book.
26. Farrand, ed., *Records,* 2:328–329, 342–344.

gin a motion that the president be elected by popularly chosen electors, and rejected by a tie vote an abstract question that electors, however selected, should make the choice.[27]

A few odds and ends were considered late in August and early in September. On August 27 a question arose regarding succession in the event of the death, disability, or removal of the president. It had been agreed that the president of the Senate should succeed until a new president was elected; several objections were raised, but the problem was postponed. Two small but important points were settled. Luther Martin proposed that the pardoning power be limited to cases after conviction, but Wilson said that "pardon before conviction might be necessary in order to obtain the testimony of accomplices," and Martin withdrew his motion. Sherman, who like other old republicans had a fear of standing armies, succeeded in limiting the president's command of the state militias to occasions when they were called into the active service of the national government. On September 3 a somewhat random discussion of the dangers of plural officeholding—whether forbidding it would or would not strengthen the executive—took place. The result was a complex set of restrictions in the completed Constitution: the prohibition in Article 1, Section 6, of dual officeholding by congressmen and the ban against appointing members "to any civil Office under the Authority of the United States, which shall have been created, or the Emoluments whereof shall have been encreased during such time." That restriction limited the capacity of presidents and their "ministers" to manipulate votes in Congress by passing out lucrative or prestigious jobs.[28]

It will facilitate understanding of the decisions that followed if we pause to consider what the convention had wrought so far. There was to be a bicameral legislature, one house representing people, the other representing states. The Senate, whose members were to be elected by the state legislatures, would exercise most of the federative powers including the sending of ambassadors and the negotiation of

27. Ibid., 2:300, 401–404.
28. Ibid., 2:426–427, 489–492. Richard M. Nixon would later have good reason to be grateful for the position that Wilson and the convention took; Adler, "President's Pardon Power," in Cronin, ed., *Inventing the American Presidency,* 209–210, 212–218.

treaties. The other great federative power, the waging of war, was shared with the lower house of the legislature, as were most of the traditional executive powers. There was to be a Supreme Court, whose justices were to be appointed by the Senate, and inferior courts if Congress chose to establish them. And there was to be a president, elected by the Congress in joint session, serving a seven-year term unless removed on impeachment by the House and conviction by the Supreme Court. He was ineligible for reelection and had virtually no power of appointment and none of removal. He was commander in chief, had a conditional veto over legislation, and had power to grant pardons and reprieves. In sum, this was government by a reconstituted Congress, despite the objections that had been voiced against legislative supremacy.

———— But a grand breakthrough was in the offing. A few days earlier, on Friday, August 31, a catchall committee of one member from each state had been appointed to resolve matters that had been postponed and consider reports not yet acted upon. At some point in the deliberations Pierce Butler hatched a cumbersome scheme for electing the president that took care of the objections that had been raised against all other methods. The plan called for a president and a vice-president, which satisfied those delegates who had been concerned about succession in the event of the death, disability, or removal of the president. It provided that electors be chosen in each state by whatever method the state legislature determined. This overcame the objections of those who opposed popular elections, for it left the legislatures free to choose the electors themselves if they were so disposed. Each state was to have a number of electors equal to its combined number of senators and representatives, this being a compromise between equal and proportional allocation. The electors were to meet in their respective states, which solved the problem of distance of travel and minimized the danger of foreign intrigue, and were to vote for two candidates, at least one of whom must be a citizen of another state. Whoever received the most votes, if the vote was a majority of the electors, would become president; the one with the second most votes would become vice-president. In the expectation that a president elected in this manner would be sufficiently independent of Congress, the proposal also vested him with a share in the executive powers previously entrusted to the Senate. The president would appoint ambassadors, judges, and other officers (except the head of the Treasury Department, who would be chosen by joint ballot), and he would make treaties with the consent of two-thirds of the Senate. As part of the package, the power of trying impeachment cases was shifted from the Supreme Court to the Senate, except that in cases of impeachment of a president, the chief justice, not the vice-president, would preside, for obvious reasons.[29]

It was a strange proposal, though as Abraham Baldwin said, it was "not so objectionable when well considered, as at first view"; but there was more, a backup plan that many Framers did find objectionable. The scheme provided that if no one had a majority, the Senate should make the choice from the five leading vote-getters, and that if two persons tied, each having a majority, the Senate should choose between them. Most delegates thought that normally no candidate would get a majority and therefore that the Senate would usually elect the president from "nominees" proposed by the electors.[30]

Three days of heated discussions ensued. Gouverneur Morris, who generally favored the plan, insisted that one candidate would probably get a majority though he applied spurious arithmetic to arrive at that conclusion. Some delegates favored having both houses of Congress play the deciding role proposed for the Senate. Madison and Williamson moved to require that one-third of the electors constitute a choice rather than a majority. Quite a number of delegates expressed general uneasiness that the Senate was being given excessive

29. Farrand, ed., *Records*, 2:497–499 (September 4). For Butler's role, see McDonald, *Novus Ordo Seclorum*, 251 and n. 65, and Farrand, ed., *Records*, 3:302; Lewright B. Sikes, *The Public Life of Pierce Butler, South Carolina Statesman* (Washington, DC, 1979), Sidney Ulmer, "The Role of Pierce Butler in the Constitutional Convention," *Review of Politics* 22 (1960):361–374, Ernest M. Lander, Jr., "The South Carolinians at the Philadelphia Convention, 1787," *South Carolina Historical Magazine* 57 (1956):134–155, and Malcolm Bell, Jr., *Major Butler's Legacy: Five Generations of a Slaveholding Family* (Athens, GA, 1987), 19–97.

30. Farrand, ed., *Records*, 2:501, 499–502. Henry C. White, *Abraham Baldwin: One of the Founders of the Republic and Father of the University of Georgia* (Athens, GA, 1926), and E. Merton Coulter, *Abraham Baldwin: Patriot, Educator, and Founding Father* (Arlington, VA, 1987).

powers and a dangerous aristocracy was thus being created. Wilson in particular thought that given the executive powers lodged in the Senate and the expectation that it would function more or less as an executive council, to involve the upper house to such a degree in the election of the president would be especially dangerous.[31]

Despite grumbling and expressions of disapproval, every motion to abandon or fundamentally modify the proposed electoral college was rejected, and late in the day of September 6 Roger Sherman produced a change that made the system acceptable to all but a handful. He proposed that the House of Representatives make the choice in cases of ties or no majority, the members from each state having one vote for the purpose. With virtually no discussion, the motion was carried, ten states to one, only Delaware dissenting.[32]

Some minor tinkering and discussion followed the next day—Gerry, for instance, expressed concern that the role of the vice-president in presiding over the Senate might be improper because of the "close intimacy that must subsist between the President & vice-president," to which Morris responded that "the vice president then will be the first heir apparent that ever loved his father."[33]

By September 8 the work of the convention was substantially complete, and its resolutions were turned over to a committee of style, headed by Morris. The committee's draft of the Constitution was ready by September 12; only fine tuning remained. One point of consequence concerned the veto. Almost all the delegates agreed that the veto was necessary, mainly to enable the president to check legislative encroachment on the executive and to prohibit rash action by the Congress, but many now thought that a three-fourths majority to override was too high. A motion to pare it back to two-thirds carried by a close vote (the two future presidents in the convention, Washington and Madison, voted against the change). Another point, settled on September 14, had strong implications for the executive branch though it involved Article 1, Section 8, enumerating the powers of the legislative branch. The delegates voted to delete the power of

31. Farrand, ed., *Records*, 2:499–502, 511–515, 521–525.
32. Ibid., 2:527. In the only election in which there was a tie vote, that of 1800–1801, it was Delaware's representative James Bayard whose vote was pivotal.
33. Ibid., 2:536–537.

Congress to appoint a treasurer by joint ballot; rather, the head of the treasury would be an executive appointment as were the other department heads.[34]

———— Because of the way the presidency evolved in the convention, the Constitution did not adhere to the Montesquieuan doctrine of the separation of powers even though most delegates endorsed the doctrine as an abstract principle. Instead, they fashioned a government in which the various branches were separate and independent in terms of personnel but the powers were intermingled. Most of the traditional domestic prerogative powers and some of the federative were lodged in one or both houses of Congress. The executive branch shared in the lawmaking power by virtue of the veto, the authority to recommend legislation, and the vice-president's presiding over the Senate. The actual execution of the laws—despite a provision charging the president to "take Care that the Laws be faithfully executed"— would rest in the courts and their marshals and clerks. Congress shared in the judicial power through its power to impeach, its authorization to ordain and establish inferior courts, and its power to regulate jurisdictions. As Madison explained in *Federalist* 47–51, mixing powers had been necessary to ensure a system of checks and balances.[35]

34. Ibid., 2:554, 585–587, 614–615. The committee of style consisted of Morris, Madison, Hamilton, King, and William Samuel Johnson of Connecticut. On Johnson, see Elizabeth P. McCaughey, *From Loyalist to Founding Father: The Political Odyssey of William Samuel Johnson* (New York, 1980), and George C. Groce, Jr., *William Samuel Johnson: A Maker of the Constitution* (New York, 1937).

35. John Quincy Adams wrote of the question in "The Jubilee of the Constitution: A Discourse Delivered at the Request of the New York Historical Society," April 30, 1839, that "the legislative, judicial, and executive powers, like the prismatic colours of the rainbow, are entirely separate and distinct; but they melt so imperceptibly into each other that no human eye can discern the exact boundary line between them. The broad features of distinction between them are perceptible to all; but perhaps neither of them can be practically exercised without occasional encroachment upon the borders of its neighbour." This question whether the Constitution embodied a Montesquieuan separation of powers fueled many a debate during ratification; see *The Complete Anti-Federalist,* ed. Herbert J. Storing, 7 vols. (Chicago, 1981), 1:54–56, and chapter 8 of this book. Historians and political scientists still argue the matter forcefully; see Harvey Mansfield, *Taming the Prince* (New York, 1989), 260–264,

Powers were prospectively mixed in another curious and unintended way as well. When the appointment power was shifted from the Senate to the president with senatorial confirmation, the delegates were tired and irritable and anxious to go home. In these circumstances they neglected to provide a method for removing appointees except through the impeachment process. The delegates were not implying that administrative appointees should "hold their Offices during good Behaviour," as judges were to do, or that impeachment was the normal means of removal. But if the president required senatorial approval for appointing, it was reasonable to assume that, as Hamilton argued in *Federalist* 77, "the consent of that body would be necessary to displace as well as to appoint." That would mean that administrators would tend to remain in office at the pleasure of the Senate, Hamilton thought, even after the election of new presidents.

Whatever their views as to the role of the Senate in removing executive officers, most delegates apparently thought of the Senate somewhat on the lines of the old royal privy council, or more precisely, the colonial executive councils, which had doubled as upper legislative houses. Some delegates, George Mason for instance, strongly objected to the Constitution because it did not specifically provide for a small nonsenatorial executive council, but most apparently believed that the Senate would so serve, as is attested by the frequency of casual remarks that the Senate would sit almost continuously whereas there would scarcely be enough legislative business to justify an annual convening of the whole Congress.[36]

William Kristol, "The Problem of the Separation of Powers: *Federalist* 47–51," in *Saving the Revolution: The Federalist Papers and the American Founding*, ed. Charles R. Kesler (New York, 1987), 100–130, and Forrest McDonald and Ellen Shapiro McDonald, "The Constitution and the Separation of Powers," in *Requiem* (Lawrence, KS, 1988), 149–163. And yet more than 200 years of practice under the Constitution suggest that the inherent fluidity and the system of checks and balances render a strict separation impossible.

36. Farrand, ed., *Records*, 1:70–74, 97, 110, 2:198–199, 293, 328–329, 335–337, 342–344, 367, 533, 537, 539, 541–543. Many anti-Federalists objected to the Constitution on the ground that the Senate in its role as advisory council to the executive would constitute a "baneful aristocracy"; see, for example, Cincinnatus, "Essay 4," Nov. 22 1787, in Storing, ed., *Complete Anti-Federalist*, 6:18.

Irrespective of the part the Senate was to play in the exercise of executive power, two broad sets of presidential functions were itemized in the Constitution. One was administrative, as indicated in the "take care" clause, the authorization to appoint executive officers, the state of the union clause, and the authorization to grant reprieves and pardons. The other was the conduct of foreign relations: The president was to be commander in chief (but could not declare war, though he could negotiate a peace treaty), and he was to send and receive foreign ministers.[37]

Left unanswered was the delegates' understanding of what they meant by the words in Article 2, "The executive Power shall be vested in a President of the United States of America." That language differs sharply from that of Article 1: "All legislative Powers *herein granted* shall be vested in a Congress of the United States" (emphasis added). The more general vesting in Article 2, combined with the specification of certain presidential functions and duties, presupposes that "executive power" had an agreed-upon meaning. Given the delegates' knowledge of the subject from history, political philosophy, and experience, it seems evident that some of them, at least, thought of executive power as contingent and discretionary: the power to act unilaterally in circumstances in which the safety or the well being of the republic is imperiled; power corresponding to that of ancient Roman dictators, or to Bracton's *gubernaculum,* or to Fortescue's *dominium regale;* power, in sum, that extends beyond the ordinary rules prescribed by the Constitution and the laws.

37. For sources illuminating each clause of each article of the Constitution, see *The Founders' Constitution,* ed. Philip B. Kurland and Ralph Lerner, 5 vols. (Chicago, 1987).

CHAPTER

Ratification

In 1821 James Madison, who was widely rumored to have made and retained copious notes of the debates at the Constitutional Convention of 1787, confirmed that he had indeed "materials for a pretty ample view of what passed in that Assembly." He belittled the importance of his notes, however, as clues to the original understanding of the Constitution. "As a guide in expounding and applying the provisions of the Constitution," he wrote, "the debates and incidental decisions of the Convention can have no authoritative character. . . . The legitimate meaning of the Instrument must be derived from the text itself." Besides, he insisted, "if a key is to be sought elsewhere, it must be not in the opinions or intentions of the Body which planned & proposed the Constitution, but in the sense attached to it by the people in their respective State Conventions where it [received] all the authority which it possesses."[1]

Though Madison had in fact implicitly rejected that interpretation earlier—on at least two occasions he had argued constitutional posi-

1. James Madison to Thomas Ritchie, Sept. 25, 1821, in *The Records of the Federal Convention of 1787,* ed. Max Farrand, 4 vols. (New Haven, CT, 1937), 3:447–448. For an appraisal of the quality of the record, see James H. Hutson, "The Creation of the Constitution: The Integrity of the Documentary Record," *Texas Law Review,* 65 (1986):1–39.

tions in the House of Representatives by referring to the proceedings of the convention—the soundness of his doctrine, as a point of constitutional theory, is unquestionable. In the nature of things, the convention had been able to do no more than propose a constitution; only the people, in their capacity as people of the several states, severally, had the authority to make it into a living body of law.[2]

Moreover, the records of the contests over ratification of the Constitution are several times as abundant as those of its drafting. In addition to the celebrated *Federalist* essays, the equivalent of a dozen or more volumes of pamphlets and newspaper articles for and against the Constitution, expounding and defending or attacking its every clause, was widely disseminated; and the debates in the more important state ratifying conventions were recorded and published. Beyond that, a huge quantity of personal correspondence, commenting on the meaning of the Constitution and on the intentions of its Framers, has become readily available in recent years.[3]

In certain respects, to be sure, the documentary record of the ratification can be misleading, particularly in regard to the presidency. One reason is that the federal government contemplated by the original Constitution was minuscule in comparison with the behemoth that grew in the twentieth century; the trick is to discover

2. Regarding Madison's use of the proceedings, see *Abridgment of the Debates of Congress, from 1789 to 1856,* volume 1, ed. Thomas Hart Benton (New York, 1857), 274–278, 306–308 (Feb. 2, 8, 1791), and Farrand, ed., *Records,* 3:361 (April 22, 1790). By 1796, however, he was arguing to the contrary, in keeping with his 1821 position (Farrand, ed., *Records,* 3:372–375 [April 6, 1796]). For a lucid explanation of the principle underlying the proposition that the Constitution was an "act of the people . . . in their capacities as citizens of *the several members of our confederacy,*" see "A Freeman I" (Tench Coxe) in the Philadelphia *Pennsylvania Gazette,* Jan. 23, 1788, in *The Documentary History of Ratification,* ed. Merrill Jensen and John P. Kaminski et al., 8 vols. to date (Madison, WI, 1976–1988), 15:457.

3. The *Federalist* is available in a number of editions; I used that edited by George W. Carey and James McClellan (Dubuque, IA, 1990). *The Complete Anti-Federalist,* ed. Herbert J. Storing, 7 vols. (Chicago, 1981), is an almost complete collection of the published writings of opponents of ratification; Jensen and Kaminski, *Documentary History of Ratification,* will include—in some instances two or three times—virtually all the contemporary comment on the subject, pro or con, though that project is years from completion. I worked my way through the newspaper and pamphlet literature before it began to be conveniently collected.

whether twentieth-century practice and eighteenth-century principles are compatible. Another problem is that advocates and opponents were not always consistent in their arguments. Many anti-Federalists, for instance, contended that the presidency was the "foetus of monarchy," as Edmund Randolph had put it at the Constitutional Convention, but some argued persuasively that the presidency would be too weak to restrain the Senate or the Congress as a whole.[4]

Another somewhat misleading aspect of the verbiage employed in the contests derived from their partisan nature. Anti-Federalists, in their efforts to persuade voters that the Constitution posed grave threats to their liberties, interpreted its clauses in ways that justified their greatest fear, the maximization of the power of the central government and especially that of the president; the Federalists, many of whom actually desired such a maximization, found it expedient in their propaganda to belittle the amount of power that the Constitution would bestow on the central government. In other words, anti-Federalist spokesmen in 1787–1788 anticipated the "loose constructionist" interpretive line that Alexander Hamilton would espouse to justify the incorporation of the Bank of the United States in 1791, while some Federalists in 1787–1788 assumed a "strict constructionist" stance more like the position that Jefferson and Madison would take on the later occasion.[5]

Furthermore, in the heat of debate during the ratifying conventions speakers sometimes inadvertently said things that they clearly could not have meant. In the Virginia convention, for example, as seasoned and careful a debater as James Madison made one such gaffe. In a discussion of the pardoning power, which anti-Federalists

4. Farrand, ed., *Records,* 1:166 (Madison's notes, June 1); Jensen and Kaminski, ed., *Documentary History of Ratification,* 2:508–509, 511, 512. See also Paul A. Rahe, *Republics Ancient & Modern* (Chapel Hill, NC, 1992), 605–616.

5. The generalizations in this paragraph will be documented in the remainder of the chapter. For the classic formulations of loose and strict construction see "Opinion on the Constitutionality of an Act to Establish a Bank, "Feb. 23, 1791, in *The Papers of Alexander Hamilton,* ed. Harold C. Syrett et al., 26 vols. (New York, 1961–1979), 8:97–134, and *The Papers of Thomas Jefferson,* ed. Julian Boyd et al., 24 vols. to date (Princeton, NJ, 1950–1990), 19:275–280. I am indebted to M. E. Bradford for calling to my attention the point of this paragraph; see "The Authoritative Constitution: A Reading of the Ratification Debates," *Texas Tech Law Review* 21 (1990):2349–2374.

maintained should not be vested in the presidency since presidents were the most likely persons to be engaged in conspiracies to usurp absolute power, Madison referred to a security "to which gentlemen may not have adverted." If the president should "be connected, in any suspicious manner, with any person, and there be grounds to believe he will shelter him, the House of Representatives can impeach him; they can remove him if found guilty; *they can suspend him when suspected,* and the power will devolve on the Vice-President." The reason "gentlemen may not have adverted" to this point is that nothing about suspension is in the Constitution.[6]

Despite the pitfalls, it remains true that the ratification process gave the Constitution and the presidency their legitimacy. If the records of the process are studied with appropriate caution, they can reveal much about the validity of presidential claims to power as the office evolved over the years.

The crucial point to know is that the original understanding of the presidency confirms what is apparent from a reading of the text of Article 2, namely that the Constitution authorizes either an active or a passive presidency. If a presidential administration is appropriately motivated, politically skilled, and sufficiently popular, it can overcome the various constitutional checks and establish in effect a presidential government—without violating the primary design that government be limited in scope. Absent these qualities, the government of the United States can be (and often has been) congressional government or government by judiciary

——— A brief account of the ratification of the Constitution will place the attending debates, discussions, and explanations of the executive branch in perspective. The Philadelphia convention recommended that the procedures for amendments to the Articles of Confederation—which required approval by Congress and the legislatures of all thirteen states—be bypassed and that Congress instead send the Constitution to the several states, whose legislatures in turn were to call popularly elected special conventions to consider ratification. If and when nine state conventions ratified, the Constitution

6. Italics added. *The Debates in the Several State Conventions on the Adoption of the Federal Constitution,* ed. Jonathan Elliot, 2d ed., 5 vols. (Philadelphia, 1941), 3:498.

would become binding on those states. The others would remain at liberty to come under the Constitution or not.[7]

Some members of Congress, led by Richard Henry Lee of Virginia and Nathan Dane of Massachusetts, balked, protesting that the revised procedure was illegal, that the Constitution was defective in not being "bottomed" on a bill of rights, and that the executive branch would be dangerous without the restraint of "a Council of State or Privy Council." Lee proposed amendments to rectify these supposed defects, including provisions that a privy council "and not the Senate shall be joined with the President in the appointment of all Officers" and that the office of vice-president be abolished. Federalists, on the other hand, sought a positive congressional resolution recommending ratification. By way of compromise, on September 28—eleven days after the Constitution had been signed in Philadelphia—Congress agreed, unanimously, to follow the recommended ratification procedure but without commenting pro or con on the merits of the Constitution.[8]

The Federalists, as supporters of the Constitution designated themselves, got off to a fast start. By mid-December ten state legislatures had called for elections to ratifying conventions, and early in the new year two more followed. Three state conventions met and ratified the Constitution before the end of December; two more voted yes by January 9, 1788. Three of the early ratifiers—Delaware, New Jersey, and Georgia—approved the Constitution by unanimous convention votes, Connecticut approved by a more than three-to-one majority, and the Pennsylvania convention voted two-to-one in favor. Only in Pennsylvania, where Federalists triumphed through artful, devious, and high-handed tactics, was the opposition particularly serious.[9]

7. Article 13 of the Articles of Confederation and Resolutions of the Convention Recommending the Procedures for Ratification, in Jensen and Kaminski, ed., *Documentary History of Ratification,* 1:93, 317–318.

8. Proceedings of Congress on the Constitution, Sept. 20–28, ibid., 1:325–340, and Madison to Washington, Sept. 30, 1787, ibid., 1:343–345. Lee's amendments regarding the executive, which reflected the objections that his neighbor and political ally George Mason had made in Philadelphia, are at 338. Richard H. Lee, *Memoir of the Life of Richard Henry Lee, and His Correspondence,* 2 vols. (Philadelphia, 1825).

9. Volumes 2 and 3 of Jensen and Kaminski, ed., *Documentary History of Ratification,*

Indeed, Federalists acted for a time almost as if they thought the Constitution would ratify itself. Many newspapers praised the document in the abstract, repeatedly lauding the greatness of its Framers (especially Washington and Franklin). But, except for four essays written by Tench Coxe of Philadelphia and published under the pseudonym "An American Citizen," a speech delivered by James Wilson in Philadelphia and widely published elsewhere, and an essay signed "Curtius" by an anonymous New Yorker (also widely distributed), Federalists published no major analyses of the Constitution before Hamilton, Madison, and Jay began their essays signed Publius—the *Federalist*—on October 27. And, monumental as that commentary was, it failed utterly in its purpose of persuading New Yorkers to support ratification. When elections in that state were held in the spring, antiratification candidates received more than 14,000 votes as against 6,500 for Federalists; forty-six antis were elected delegates and only nineteen Federalists.[10]

---

cover ratification in these first five states. For the Carlisle, Pennsylvania, riots in response to ratification, see ibid., 2:642ff.; even in so "easy" a state as Delaware political disputation fostered mob violence; see ibid., 3:58–78. For the turbulence and civil disorder accompanying ratification in North Carolina, see *Ratifying the Constitution,* ed. Michael Allen Gillespie and Michael Lienesch (Lawrence, KS, 1989), 348–349. For a narrative account of the entire process, see Forrest McDonald, *E Pluribus Unum* (Indianapolis, IN, 1979), 333–371; for the personnel and politics, see Forrest McDonald, *We the People* (New Brunswick, NJ, 1992), 113–346; for a useful collection of essays, state by state, see Gillespie and Lienesch, ed., *Ratifying the Constitution.*

10. "An American Citizen: On the Federal Government," Sept. 26, 28, 29, Oct. 21, 1787, in Jensen and Kaminski, ed., *Documentary History of Ratification,* 13:247ff; James Wilson, "Speech in the State House Yard," Oct. 6, 1787, ibid., 2:167–172, 13:337–344; "Curtius," New York *Daily Advertiser,* Sept. 29, 1788, ibid., 13:268–272; editor's note, "Publius," *Federalist* 1, Oct. 27, 1787, ibid., 13:486–494. As for the New York elections, a summary of returns for five counties is in the *New York Journal* for June 5, 1788; for Orange County see the New York *Daily Advertiser,* June 14, 1788; for Queens County (improperly called Suffolk therein), New York *Daily Advertiser,* June 7, 1788; for Dutchess County the Poughkeepsie *Country Journal,* June 3, 1788; and for Westchester County the *Daily Advertiser,* June 3, 1788. For studies of John Jay, see Herbert Alan Johnson, *John Jay, 1745–1829* (Albany, NY, 1970), Frank Managhan, *John Jay: Defender of Liberty* (Indianapolis, IN, 1935), and Richard B. Morris, "John Jay and the Adoption of the Federal Constitution in New York: A New Reading of Persons and Events," *New York History* 63(1982):133–164.

These early victories obscured the extent of the anti-Federalists' propaganda initiative; their assault against the Constitution was massive. The material took a variety of forms. Erstwhile members of the Philadelphia convention who had either walked out on the proceedings or stayed until the end and refused to sign the document published their objections: John Lansing and Robert Yates of New York, Luther Martin of Maryland, Elbridge Gerry of Massachusetts, and George Mason and Edmund Randolph of Virginia. In addition several major series of essays began to appear almost immediately after the Constitution was published and continued until the spring of 1788; the most important of these were essays signed "Cato," "Brutus," "Centinel," and the "Federal Farmer." A pair of documents published by dissenters in Pennsylvania also appeared. Additionally, minor writers penned scores of small pieces attacking the Philadelphia convention as an aristocratic conspiracy, assailing particular features of the Constitution, claiming that Franklin had signed the instrument against his better judgment, and objecting in numerous petty ways.[11]

Moreover, anti-Federalists circulated their publications widely. The principal figures behind the organization of anti-Federalism nationwide were George Clinton, governor of New York, and his associates; the Clintonian responsible for directing the flow of propaganda was John Lamb, collector of the (state) customs in New York City, whose office served as a clearinghouse. From it, for example, thousands of copies of *The Letters from the Federal Farmer* were circulated in Connecticut and Massachusetts, as were the essays of "Centinel."[12]

11. The objections of the convention members are in Storing, ed., *Complete Anti-Federalist,* 2:3–98; the Cato, Brutus, Centinel, and Farmer essays are ibid., 2:101–452; the objections of the minority in Pennsylvania are in Jensen and Kaminski, ed., *Documentary History of Ratification,* 2:112–117, 617–640. For anti-Federalists in general, see Robert Allen Rutland, *The Ordeal of the Constitution: The Antifederalists and the Ratification Struggle of 1787–1788* (Norman, OK, 1966), and Stephen R. Boyd, *The Politics of Opposition: Antifederalists and the Acceptance of the Constitution* (Millwood, NY, 1979). For "Brutus," see Ann Diamond, "The Anti-Federalist 'Brutus,'" *Political Science Reviewer* 6 (1976):249–281.

12. Jensen and Kaminski, ed., *Documentary History of Ratification,* 14:17, 169–172; Isaac Q. Leake, *Memoir of the Life and Times of General John Lamb* (Albany, 1850), 305–316; Lamb Papers, New York Historical Society, passim; E. Wilder Spaulding, *His*

Belatedly, Federalists stepped up their efforts, but they had lost the momentum. When the Massachusetts convention gathered in Boston on January 9, a sizable majority of the delegates, not least among them the old republican heroes Sam Adams and John Hancock, were ill-disposed toward ratification. The Federalists had the weight of prestige and talent, however, and they shrewdly arranged to debate the Constitution clause by clause. That gave them time to work feverishly to cut backstage deals and, since the debates were recorded, incidentally left history with a thorough statement of their under-standing of the Constitution's provisions. At last, on February 6, after Federalists won John Hancock by promising him their support for the vice-presidency (or, if Virginia failed to ratify, the presidency itself), Massachusetts voted to ratify, 187 votes to 168.[13]

About a week later, the New Hampshire convention met and re-fused to ratify. A large majority of the delegates were opposed, but Federalist leaders persuaded them to make no definite decision and instead to adjourn until June. In the interim, two more states voted to ratify: Maryland in April by a comfortable 63-to-11 convention vote, South Carolina in May by a 149-to-73 vote. Yet also in the interim Rhode Island refused to call a convention, anti-Federalists won the elections for delegates in New York and in North Carolina, and the elections in Virginia seemed indecisive. Thus in June of 1788 eight states had ratified, but the necessary ninth appeared difficult to find.[14]

Excellency George Clinton (New York, 1938); Linda Grant De Pauw, *The Eleventh Pillar: New York State and the Federal Constitution* (Ithaca, NY, 1966); John P. Kaminski, "New York: The Reluctant Pillar," in *The Reluctant Pillar: New York and the Adoption of the Federal Constitution,* ed. Stephen L. Schechter (Troy, NY, 1985), 48–117.

13. Elliot, ed., *Debates,* vol. 2. See also Samuel B. Harding, *The Contest over the Ratification of the Federal Constitution in the State of Massachusetts* (New York, 1896); M. E. Bradford, "A Dike to Fence Out the Flood: The Ratification of the Constitution in Massachusetts," *Chronicles* 11 (1987); John C. Miller, *Sam Adams* (Boston, 1936); Herbert S. Allan, *John Hancock: Patriot in Purple* (New York, 1948); and McDonald, *E Pluribus Unum,* 341–345 and the sources cited therein.

14. Louise I. Trenholme, *The Ratification of the Federal Constitution in North Carolina* (New York, 1932), 107–132; William H. Masterson, *William Blount* (Baton Rouge, LA, 1954), 142–144; Archibald Maclaine to James Iredell, Jan. 15, 1788, in Griffith J.

The contest reached a climax in the summer. On June 21 New Hampshire became the ninth state when it approved by a ten-vote margin. Virginia, after a long and brilliant debate, followed suit four days later, likewise by a ten-vote majority. On July 26, after a longer round of debates, New York ratified with a margin of three votes. All three states proposed constitutional amendments as part of their decisions, as had Massachusetts, but they stopped short of making their ratifications conditional upon the adoption of the amendments. North Carolina's convention met in August and, after some debate, rejected the Constitution outright. (It did not ratify until November, 1789; Rhode Island finally approved in May, 1790.)¹⁵ The debates in Massachusetts, Virginia, New York, and North Carolina, together with the proposed amendments, round out the record of ratification.

———— Anti-Federalist writings about the presidency were a grab bag of interpretations, charges, fears, and analyses. Occasionally they engaged in ingenious, if nit-picking, constitutional exegesis. For example, at least three writers pointed out that though the Constitution specifies that presidents hold office "during the Term of four

---

McRee, *Life and Correspondence of James Iredell,* 2 vols. (New York, 1857–1858), 2:216; M. E. Bradford, "Preserving the Birthright: The Intention of South Carolina in Adopting the U.S. Constitution," *South Carolina Historical Magazine* 89 (1988):90–101; *New York Journal,* April 24, June 5, 1788; Papers Relating to the Adoption of the Federal Constitution, 17–36, in Rhode Island Archives; David Henley to Samuel Henley, April 18, 1788, in Personal Miscellaneous File, Library of Congress (containing a county-by-county breakdown of the returns in Virginia); George Nicholas to James Madison, April 5, 1788, in *The Writings of James Madison,* ed. Gaillard Hunt, 9 vols. (New York, 1900–1910), 5:114; Moncure Daniel Conway, *Omitted Chapters in History Disclosed in the Life and Papers of Edmund Randolph* (New York, 1888), 101; William Grayson to John Lamb, June 9, 1788, Lamb Papers; Jackson Turner Main, *The Anti-Federalists: Critics of the Constitution, 1781–1788* (Chapel Hill, NC, 1961), 187–248; Gregory A. Stiverson, "Maryland's Antifederalists and the Perfection of the U.S. Constitution," *Maryland Historical Magazine* 83 (1988):18–35.

15. These developments are narrated and documented in McDonald, *E Pluribus Unum,* 352–364, 369–370. For a good, concise account of the Virginia ratifying convention, see William Lee Miller, *The Business of May Next* (Charlottesville, VA, 1992), 194–216.

Years" it does not actually require that they be elected every four years—whereas, in the case of representatives and senators, it is specifically mandated that these legislators be elected every two and every six years. Congress is given power to determine when presidential electors are chosen and when they vote, and it is empowered to prescribe what officer shall act as president in the event that both the presidential and vice-presidential offices should become vacant. But suppose, as a Maine anti-Federalist did, that Congress "should think it for the publick good, after the first election, to appoint the first Tuesday of September, in the year *two thousand,* for the purpose of chusing the second President; and by law empower the Chief Justice of the Supreme Judicial Court to act as President until that time." Farfetched as this scenario might appear, there is no constitutional way to prevent such a usurpation; indeed in the fourth presidential election in 1800–1801, a similar scheme was contemplated and came close to being executed.[16]

Many anti-Federalists expressed objections to the method of electing the president, though their reasons varied considerably. A few critics thought the four-year term was too long. More thought, as several members of the Philadelphia convention had, that elections would usually fail to produce a majority for anyone and thus that the choice ultimately would be made in the House of Representatives— in which case corruption and foreign intrigue would be rife. The author of *Letters from the Federal Farmer,* probably the ablest and most influential of the anti-Federalist pamphleteers, opined that the electoral college system was an admirable invention, but he fiercely opposed the president's eligibility to succeed himself, a position shared by a goodly number. Surprisingly, a few opponents maintained that the executive would be unstable unless presidents were chosen to serve for life. None foresaw the development of parties as a means of narrowing the choice of presidents, none foresaw the development of the two-term tradition, and none imagined that the strains of the

16. The quotation is from "A Customer" in the Portland, Maine, *Cumberland Gazette,* March, 1788, in Storing, ed., *Complete Anti-Federalist,* 4:202–203. For a similar argument, see "Letters of Cato," and for another critique of the vagueness of the provisions, see "William Symmes," ibid., 2:113, 4:60–61. The election of 1800–1801 is discussed in chapter 10 of this book.

office would be so great as to minimize the temptation to hold it indefinitely.[17]

Several anti-Federalist writers objected to specific powers granted to the president. Some authors opposed the appointment power, one because he thought the power should be placed in a council of appointment like New York's, another on the arch-republican ground that it made the president the "fountain of honor" after the way of a monarch, others simply because they thought it generally dangerous. A number of antis opposed the veto, sometimes on general grounds but more commonly as an improper mixture of executive and legislative powers. Many opponents disapproved of the president's being commander in chief—a disapproval that was regularly accompanied by a tirade against the evil of standing armies. The tirade, in turn, was frequently linked with the observation that in Britain standing armies were better provided against because military appropriations there were made for one year, whereas the Constitution provided for two-year appropriations. Often, too, anti-Federalists reminded their readers that had George Washington "been possessed of the spirit of a Julius Cesar or a Cromwell, the liberties of this country, had in all probability, terminated with the war."[18]

Some powerful attacks upon the constitutional institution of the

17. Genuine Information (Luther Martin), Letters of Cato, Letters from the Federal Farmer, Old Whig, Cornelius, A Maryland Farmer, Samuel Chase in the Maryland Ratifying Convention, Cato (South Carolina), Tamony, Rawlins Lowndes in the South Carolina legislature, Rusticus, Denatus, the Albany Antifederal Committee, in Storing, ed., *Complete Anti-Federalist,* 2:66, 114, 309–310, 3:37, 4:145, 5:42, 44, 87, 139–141, 146–147, 153, 167–168, 266, 6:124; speeches of William Grayson and George Mason in the Virginia Ratifying Convention, in Elliot, ed., *Debates,* 3:490–493; James Haw, "Samuel Chase and Maryland Antifederalism: A Study in Disarray," *Maryland Historical Magazine* 83 (1988):36–49.

18. Regarding the appointment and veto powers, see Federal Farmer, Brutus, Old Whig, An Officer, Pennsylvania Minority, William Penn, Samuel Chase, Richard Henry Lee, An Impartial Examiner, and Albany Antifederal Committee, in Storing, ed., *Complete Anti-Federalist,* 2:304–306, 371, 3:37, 93, 158, 173–174, 5:87, 113, 194–196, 6:124. Regarding the commander in chief and standing armies, see Cato, Brutus, Old Whig, Philadelphiensis, Maryland Farmer, Georgian, South Carolina Cato, and Denatus, ibid., 2:114, 413–414, 3:37–38, 128–129, 5:25, 44, 133–134, 139–141, 266. The quotation is from Brutus, ibid., 2:413–414.

presidency were generalized. Anti-Federalist propagandists repeatedly charged that the presidency would be a kingship in everything but name. The presidency was compared with the British crown or another monarchy, parallels were drawn with Sweden and the Netherlands, and often the collapse of the Roman republic was recalled. Several writers warned that "the federal city," the District of Columbia, would, as Montesquieu had written of monarchical capitals, become as "the court of a president" the scene of *"ambition with idleness—baseness with pride—the thirst of riches without labour—aversion to truth—flattery—treason—perfidy—violation of engagements—contempt of civil duties—hope from the magistrate's weakness; but above all, the perpetual ridicule of virtue."* There are those who would argue that this doomsaying was prescient.[19]

The significance of the extravagant prophesies lies partly in the lingering fears of monarchies that such predictions both reflected and sought to exploit, but mainly it inheres in the understanding of the vesting clause ("the executive power shall be vested in a President") that it reveals. Clearly, anti-Federalists regarded the clause not as an abstract general statement, given substance only by the specifically enumerated powers that follow, but as a positive, comprehensive, unspecified, and ominous grant of authority.

———— Vociferous as some anti-Federalists were in their denunciation of the presidency and its powers, the creation of an executive branch was not the main source of opposition to the Constitution. By and large, opponents were more disturbed about the absence of a bill of rights, by what they saw as the tendency of the Constitution toward establishing a "consolidated national government" that would swallow up the states, by what they called the "unlimited" taxing powers of Congress, and by the "aristocratic" tone of the instrument.[20]

19. See the writers cited in the two preceding notes. The quotation is from "Letters of Cato," ibid., 2:114–115. See also index entries under "federal city," ibid., vol. 7, and Thomas Tredwell's remarks in the New York ratifying convention, in Elliot, ed., *Debates,* 2:402.

20. These comments are based upon the previously cited anti-Federalist sources, but see also Raymond B. Wrabley, Jr., "Anti-Federalism and the Presidency," *Presidential Studies Quarterly* 21 (1991):459–470.

One feature of the Constitution almost uniformly troubled the antis: the constitutional yoking of the president with the Senate in matters of appointments and the conduct of foreign relations. At first glance opposition to the admixture may seem surprising, for it was by no means an innovation. As we have seen, in most of the colonial governments and in several of the state constitutions the upper legislative chamber doubled as an executive council. In a number of places, however, notably Massachusetts, Virginia, and North Carolina, the experience with royal governors and their senates/councils had been bitter, especially on the eve of independence, and in those places opposition to the combination tended to be strongest.[21]

Objections were usually grounded on the abstract principle that the Senate's powers violated the doctrine of the separation of powers. Repeatedly, antis pointed out that the Senate was vested with legislative, executive, and (in being the court to try impeachments) judicial powers. Again and again, they quoted or paraphrased one sentence from Montesquieu: "When the legislative and executive powers are united in the same person, or in the same body of magistrates, there can be no liberty, because apprehensions may arise, lest the same monarch or *senate* should enact tyrannical laws, to execute them in a tyrannical manner."[22]

Antis did not entirely agree upon the practical implications of the mixing. Generally their belief seemed to be that senators would be mere minions of the president. Given the record of poor attendance that the old Congress had had, given the expectation that the Senate would be in almost continuous session, and given the smallness of the Senate—twenty-six members, of whom, anti-Federalists never tired of pointing out, fourteen constituted a quorum, of which eight was a majority—it was easy enough to think of the president and Senate as a prospective king and privy council. Moreover, this small group would exercise what antis described as two-thirds of the legislative power, all the executive power, and, by virtue of the appointment

21. See chapter 5 of this book and volumes 3 and 4 of Elliot, ed., *Debates*. For a defense of the mixture by a Federalist former governor of Massachusetts, see James Bowdoin's speeches in the Massachusetts Ratifying Convention, ibid., 2:127–128.

22. See, for example, the Pennsylvania Minority and Cincinnatus, in Storing, ed., *Complete Anti-Federalist*, 3:161 and 6:20–21.

power and the Senate's power to try impeachments, indirect control of the judicial branch as well.[23]

A few anti-Federalists took the opposite point of view, holding that the Senate would have all the power, dominating every branch. The Federal Farmer said that the Senate "will not, in practice, be found to be a body to advise, but to order and dictate in fact: and the president will be a mere *primus inter pares*." The remedy, he suggested, would be to strip the Senate of its executive powers and to provide the independent executive thus established with a responsible executive council—a proposal emphatically endorsed by George Mason in the statement he made justifying his refusal to sign the Constitution. A Massachusetts anti who signed his articles "John DeWitt" said that the president would be "infinitely less apt to disoblige [the senators], than they to refuse him. It is far easier for twenty to gain over one, than one twenty. . . . It is also highly improbable but some of the members, perhaps a major part, will hold their seats during their lives." The Pennsylvania minority address declared that the "president general is dangerously connected with the senate; his coincidence with the views of the ruling junto in that body, is made essential to his weight and importance in the government, which will destroy all independency and purity in the executive department."[24]

A writer styling himself "Cincinnatus" (probably Richard Henry Lee's brother Arthur Lee) insisted that the combination would be fatal whether the senators proved to be minions or masters. The "absurd division" of the executive power, he wrote, "must be productive of constant contentions for the lead, must clog the execution of government to a mischievous, and sometimes to a disgraceful de-

23. For examples of such thinking, see William Symmes, John Francis Mercer, Richard Henry Lee, and "Impartial Examiner," ibid., 4:60, 5:104, 113, 196–197, and the remarks of William Lenoir in the North Carolina ratifying convention, in Elliot, ed., *Debates*, 4:204–205.

24. One of the Pennsylvania anti-Federalists, William Findley, added his opinion that the Senate might fall victim to the intrigues of foreign powers in which case the people would be obliged "to seek their refuge in the arms of the *monarch*, or PRESIDENT GENERAL" (Storing, ed., *Complete Anti-Federalist*, 2:11–12, 304–307, 3:94, 162, 4:26–27). See also Gilbert Livingston's comments in the New York ratifying convention, in Elliot, ed., *Debates*, 2:287.

gree." On the other hand, if the president and Senate "should unhappily harmonize in the same objects of ambition, their number and their combined power, would preclude all fear of that responsibility, which is one of the great securities of good, and restraints on bad governments." Quoting De Lolme to the effect that dividing the executive produces continual contention and leads to "absolute power," he cited De Lolme's dictum that "for the tranquility of the state it is necessary that the executive power should be in one." Cincinnatus added that "this singlehood of the executive, is indispensably necessary to effective execution, as well as to the responsibility and rectitude of him to whom it is entrusted."[25]

The specific power of a split executive most dreaded by the antis was the making of treaties that become part of the supreme law of the land. The supreme law clause is worded interestingly. The Constitution and laws "made in pursuance thereof"—which is to say as an exercise of one or more of the powers delegated in Article 1, Section 8—are part of the supreme law, as are "treaties made, or which shall be made, under the authority of the United States." A narrow reading of the "treaties made" language—which anti-Federalists and ultimately the Supreme Court gave it—would indicate that so long as treaties are made by the president or his agents with the concurrence of "two-thirds of the senators present" (Article 2, Section 2), they are part of the supreme law, irrespective of whether they conflict with the rest of the Constitution. Treaties, in other words, do not have to be constitutional to be supreme law.[26]

Southerners were especially wary about the treaty-making power and for good reason. In one of the few instances of serious sectional

25. "Cincinnatus," in Storing, ed., *Complete Anti-Federalist,* 6:21–22. For Lee's probable authorship, see Jensen and Kaminski, ed., *Documentary History of Ratification,* 13:529–530. Writing in rebuttal, Alexander White cited the Roman commonwealth, Carthage, and Sparta as proofs that the connection of senate and president was not dangerous, ibid., 8:442.

26. See the objections of Elbridge Gerry, George Mason, "Cato," "Samuel," Mercer, Lee, Lowndes, "Reply to Cassius," and "Sentiments of Many," in Storing, ed., *Complete Anti-Federalist,* 2:6–7, 12, 115, 4:194, 5:104, 113, 158, 203, 276. The Supreme Court case upholding, solely on the strength of a treaty, a law that had previously been declared unconstitutional is *Missouri* v. *Holland,* 252 U.S. 416 (1920).

animosity that had surfaced in the new country, northerners had in 1786 been willing to bargain away American rights to navigation on the Mississippi River in exchange for commercial concessions from Spain. The issue arose in the ratifying conventions of Virginia and North Carolina, where anti-Federalists used it in their attack on the constitutional provisions concerning treaties. Patrick Henry, William Grayson, James Monroe, and John Dawson led the onslaught in Virginia. Grayson, who had been in Congress during the debates over the Mississippi, pointed out that seven states had supported the abandonment of navigation rights, and other antis observed that the senators from only five states—ten, being two-thirds of a bare quorum of fourteen   were sufficient to ratify a treaty. Henry played on the Mississippi question, but he also raised a grave issue that would haunt the conduct of American foreign relations repeatedly in the twentieth century. Treaties, Henry said, rested on "the laws and usages of nations," and to make them "municipal"—meaning internal law—was "a doctrine totally novel" and to make them superior to domestic law and the Constitution was a monstrous innovation. In North Carolina, anti-Federalists Samuel Spencer, Joseph M'Dowell, and William Porter evoked the same arguments as their Virginia counterparts.[27]

Two more features of the relationship between president and Senate drew anti-Federalist fire: the president's power to grant pardons and the Senate's power to try impeachments. Steeped as they were in knowledge of the conspiracies that had plagued the Roman republic and seventeenth-century England, anti-Federalists assumed that if a serious plot against American liberty were forthcoming, it would arise from collaboration between presidents and senators. This, anti-

27. Elliot, ed., *Debates*, 3:221, 500–503, 609–610, 4:115–119, 124–125. Regarding the 1786 Spanish-American negotiations, see Samuel F. Bemis, *Pinckney's Treaty* (Baltimore, 1926); *Journals of the Continental Congress,* ed. Worthington C. Ford et al., 34 vols. (Washington, DC, 1904–1937), 31:574–613 (Aug. 29–31, 1786); Edmund Cody Burnett, *The Continental Congress* (New York, 1941), 654–659. For Henry, see Robert Douthat Meade, *Patrick Henry: Patriot in the Making* (Philadelphia, 1957), Richard R. Beeman, *Patrick Henry: A Biography* (New York, 1974), and M. E. Bradford, "The Trumpet Voice of Freedom: Patrick Henry and the Southern Political Tradition," *Southern Partisan* 8 (1988):16–22.

Federalists insisted, made a mockery of both impeachments and pardons. To whom is the president responsible in case of misbehavior, James Monroe asked. "To the Senate, his own council. If he makes a treaty, bartering the interests of his country, by whom is he to be tried? By the very persons who advised him to perpetrate the act." As for the pardoning power, George Mason echoed the protest of the Pennsylvanians who had said that "having the power of pardoning without the concurrence of a council, he may skreen from punishment the most treasonable attempts that may be made on the liberties of the people, when instigated by his coadjutors in the senate."[28]

Thus the presidency as seen through the eyes of opponents of the Constitution.

——— Only a handful of Federalists attempted anything like a thorough analysis of the proposed executive authority. Their relative silence derived mainly from the character of the rhetorical warfare: Anti-Federalists, though advancing negative arguments, were on the attack; at least half the Federalists' writings were defenses against anti-Federalist charges. As a leading scholar of the antis has written, "It is hardly too much to say that among the 'front-line' debaters, the Anti-Federalists criticized the Constitution and the Federalists criticized the Anti-Federalists."[29]

The first lengthy set of essays defending the Constitution, however—Tench Coxe's series signed "An American Citizen"—was only indirectly responding to attacks. Throughout 1787 rumors had circulated that the convention was planning to erect a monarchy, and some people believed, along with an anonymous Marylander, that to estab-

28. Elliot, ed., *Debates,* 3:220–221, 485, 489, 491, 494, 497, 4:263. Centinel and Pennsylvania Minority in Storing, ed., *Complete Anti-Federalist,* 2:142, 3:162. An answer by "An Impartial Citizen" that "all civilized nations" have included the pardon power cited not merely legal commentators such as Blackstone but also Demosthenes, Seneca, Cicero, and Diodorus Siculus (Jensen and Kaminski, ed., *Documentary History of Ratification,* 8:428).

29. Herbert J. Storing, "The 'Other' Federalist Papers: A Preliminary Sketch," *Political Science Reviewer* 6 (1976):215. Storing was considering "one hundred or so essays and pamphlets."

lish "*a first Magistrate* possessed exclusively of the Executive power" would be "the same" as monarchy.[30]

Accordingly, Coxe launched a preemptive strike against the not-yet-leveled attack that the American presidency was patterned after and closely resembled the British crown. The crown, Coxe pointed out, was the head of an established church, but there was no danger of "ecclesiastical tyranny" in America because "all religious funds, honors and powers" were diffused among countless congregations. The British king was king for life, but (Coxe added, ingenuously or disingenuously) "our president will always be *one of the people* at the end of four years." The hereditary king "may be an idiot, a knave, or a tyrant by nature," and "*he can do no wrong.*" The president "cannot be an idiot, probably not a knave or a tyrant," for these qualities would have become manifest before he reached the constitutional age of thirty-five; and far from claiming that he can do no wrong, the Constitution "pre-supposed he may and will sometimes do wrong" by providing for impeachment and "*peaceable*" removal. The king had legislative power, the president only a qualified veto that amounted "to no more, than a serious duty imposed upon him to request both houses to reconsider any matter on which he entertains doubts or feels apprehensions." And the president could not make treaties without two-thirds of the Senate.[31]

Coxe then considered the protections against corrupt executive influence. The president could create no nobility or titles of honor, and he could make no major appointments without the approval of the Senate, "which will remove the idea of *patronage and influence.*" This curious conception of the president's political power as being limited, indeed almost nonexistent, was accented by Coxe's significant assertion that the president would not have the power to remove appointees: He cannot "take away offices during good behaviour." (In a subsequent essay, Coxe added that the Senate could not properly be likened to the House of Lords, not being hereditary and being

30. On the question of monarchy and rumors thereof, see Jensen and Kaminski, ed., *Documentary History of Ratification*, 13:89, 168–178. For Tench Coxe, see Jacob E. Cooke, *Tench Coxe and the Early Republic* (Chapel Hill, NC, 1978).

31. "An American Citizen," 1, Sept. 26, 1787, Jensen and Kaminski, ed., *Documentary History of Ratification*, 13:249–250.

subject to the "controul" of the president and "the mighty check" of the House of Representatives.)[32]

The next extended Federalist commentary on the executive was made by James Wilson during the Pennsylvania ratifying convention. Wilson, as the chief spokesman for the Constitution there, was in a peculiar situation. As indicated, the anti-Federalists in Pennsylvania took the position that the presidency was too weak, lacking independence and being subordinate to the Senate. Considerations of rhetorical strategy thus imposed upon Wilson the task of demonstrating that the presidency was sufficiently energetic and independent and yet at the same time—because Wilson's speeches were published and widely disseminated as Federalist propaganda—of reassuring voters in other states who distrusted executive power that there was no cause for alarm.[33]

He walked this forensic tightrope with considerable skill though scarcely with enough to justify the arrogance and contempt that he showed toward his opponents. The independence of the president from Congress, he said, was ensured through the mode of election by the electoral college, and he rehearsed the difficulties the Constitutional Convention had had in hitting upon that mode. Independence was further guaranteed by the provision that the president be paid a fixed stipend that could not be reduced during the term for which he was elected. The powers to veto legislation and to grant pardons were potent instruments granted to the president. The Senate's power to try impeachments would not make the president its "tool," for that power could be exercised only if the House brought impeachment charges. Most tellingly—though he soft-pedaled the proposition—Wilson declared that the executive powers given to the Senate were exceptions to the general grant contained in the vesting clause.[34]

32. "An American Citizen," 1 and 2, Sept. 26, 28, 1787, ibid., 13:250–251, 264–266.

33. For objections to the weakness of the executive among anti-Federalists at the Pennsylvania convention, see ibid., 2:465, 508–509, 512; regarding the publication of the debates, see the editor's notes, ibid., 2:39–42.

34. These points are recorded ibid., 2:451, 452–453, 480, 487–488, 566–568; regarding Wilson's contemptuous treatment of the antis, see the nasty exchange, ibid., 2:532, 551, concerning The . . . Universal History (London, 1761), Blackstone, and trial by jury in Sweden.

On the other side, Wilson advanced reasons for confidence that the presidency would not be dangerous. As for the treaty-making power, it was adequately checked. In a careful analysis, Wilson skirted the problem of whether treaties must conform to the Constitution and laws by saying that Parliament sometimes had to change the laws before a treaty could be promulgated; by implication, acts of Congress would sometimes be necessary to give life to treaties. On another subject, Wilson pointed out that the restrictions regarding plural officeholding would prevent British-style corruption. He scored significantly by emphasizing that treason in monarchies was defined by the king but that in America the president had no such power because treason is narrowly defined in the Constitution itself. Finally, Wilson came full circle to the method of election, which made the president "the MAN OF THE PEOPLE," the one governmental official who was elected to represent the entire country.[35]

Wilson's counterparts in the South were also on the defensive, but there they had to defend against the charge that the president, with or without senatorial collusion, would be excessively strong. James Iredell, the most articulate Federalist in the first North Carolina convention, addressed telling remarks to the criticism that the Constitution provided no executive council. The antis' reasoning on the subject, he declared, was based upon a misunderstanding of the British model. A council was necessary in Britain because the king was above the law, and Parliament could punish executive wrongdoing only by going after the ministers who were assumed to be responsible. To create a council for the president, who was not above the law, would be to reduce his responsibility for his actions by enabling him to use the councillors as a shield. Besides, Iredell foresaw the evolution of the department heads as an advisory cabinet, and—unlike such anti-Federalists as "Cato" and George Mason, who argued that a cabinet of department heads was "the most dangerous council in a free country," probably because it resembled the post-Walpolean ministry in England—he regarded a cabinet as a positive good. No one,

35. Jensen and Kaminski, ed., *Documentary History of Ratification*, 2:452–453, 498 (including references to Strabo and Necker), 515–516, 561–563; Elliot, ed., *Debates*, 2:472–473, 504–507, 510–513.

said Iredell, would be better informed about public affairs than the heads of the great departments, they would normally be in close proximity to the president, and the president's authority to require their opinions in writing would result in a record that would make it possible to discern who had advised what and create a public framework for responsible opinion.[36]

Iredell discussed several other aspects of the presidency. In general he seemed to endorse the vesting clause as a positive grant, mentioning such nonenumerated powers of the president as directing espionage against foreign enemies and granting blanket pardons that amounted to dispensings or suspensions of the law. (He did implicitly contradict himself slightly. He said that the pardoning power "is naturally vested in the President, because it is his duty to watch over the public safety"; but if it were naturally part of his duty, why did the Constitution enumerate it?) As for the impeachment process, Iredell found it appropriate that the representatives of the people, the House, bring and prosecute impeachments and that the representatives of the states, the Senate, try them as an expression of the states' residual sovereignty. The same residual sovereignty, he contended, justified the Senate's participation in the making of treaties: The senatorial share of the power would protect the individual states from being bargained away.[37]

Federalists in Virginia and Maryland discussed essentially the same subjects as Iredell, and only in two particulars did they add to his arguments. George Nicholas, one of the half-dozen leading Federalist spokesmen in the Virginia ratifying convention, rebutted anti-Federalist arguments about the treaty-making power by demonstrating that treaties would be in practice considerably more difficult to get through under the Constitution than under the existing Articles of Confederation, a point that had been made also by Nathaniel

---

36. Elliot, ed., *Debates*, 4:107–110. For the objections of "Cato" and Mason, see Jensen and Kaminski, ed., *Documentary History of Ratification*, 14:9, 150.

37. Elliot, ed., *Debates*, 4:110–114, 125–129. See also Iredell's remarkably erudite essays signed "Marcus," published in Norfolk in February and March 1788, in Jensen and Kaminski, ed., *Documentary History of Ratification*, 16:163–169, 242–248, 322–326, 379–386, 427–430. These were written in rebuttal of George Mason's published objections.

Gorham and Rufus King in the Massachusetts ratifying convention. Francis Corbin, another Virginia Federalist, offered a significant and somewhat surprising interpretation of the supreme law clause as it applied to treaties. The supreme law clause binds "the judges in every state"; it is silent as to judges in the federal district though all "judicial officers" are required to take an oath to "support" the Constitution. Corbin, addressing the anti-Federalist contention that treaties can be "paramount to the Constitution itself, and the laws of Congress," said, "It is as clear as that two and two make four, that the treaties made are to be binding on the states only." Experience had shown, he added, that treaties "would never be complied with, if their observance depended on the will of the states"—he might also have added, but did not need to, that Virginia had violated the peace treaty of 1783 in various ways—and that "the consequences would be constant war." In this interpretation Corbin was emphatically supported by James Madison.[38]

———— The most thorough and systematic Federalist analysis of the executive branch was that made by Alexander Hamilton in *Federalist* essays 67 through 77. The first three of these were essentially defensive. In 67 Hamilton ridiculed various anti-Federalist charges, singling out one in particular: "Cato" had written that the president's influence over the Senate would be enhanced by his authority to make temporary appointments to fill vacant seats that occurred in that body, whereas the Constitution (Article 1, Section 3) actually vests that power in the state governors. In 68 he defended the electoral college system and offered his opinion that there would be "a

38. Elliot, ed., *Debates*, vol. 3, generally; for the Corbin argument and Madison's endorsement, 3:510, 515. For Nicholas, 3:357, 499, 506–507; for Gorham and King, see Jensen and Kaminski, ed., *Documentary History of Ratification*, 13:553–554 (unpublished notes for a speech or speeches presumably given in the Massachusetts convention). One fairly important Maryland Federalist, Alexander Contee Hanson writing as "Aristides," described the presidency much as Iredell and the Virginia Federalists did (ibid., 15:517–551, and especially at 525, 528, 529–531). Only one southern Federalist who devoted much attention to the presidency treated the vesting clause as merely declaratory and explicitly regarded the office as one of purely enumerated powers: "Americanus," 1 and 2 (ibid., 8:203–204, 245–246).

constant probability of seeing the station [of the presidency] filled by characters preeminent for ability and virtue." In 69 he compared the presidency to the British crown and the governorship of New York, finding the presidency far less potent than the crown and, except for the "concurrent authority" with the Senate in making treaties, not appreciably more powerful than the governor.[39]

Then Hamilton raised the tone, penning a philosophical analysis of the nature of executive power, its role in a free government, and the constitutional arrangements that would make it both adequate and safe. The key was energy: "Energy in the executive," he wrote, "is a leading character in the definition of good government." This quality, which he also described as "decision, activity, secrecy, and dispatch" and as "vigor and expedition," was essential for national defense, a "steady administration of the laws," protection of property against unlawful combinations, and "security of liberty against the enterprises and assaults of ambition, of faction and of anarchy." He cited the repeated necessity of the Roman republic to resort to a dictator, "as well against the intrigues of ambitious individuals, who aspired to the tyranny, and the seditions of whole classes of the community, whose conduct threatened the existence of all government, as against the invasions of external enemies, who menaced the conquest and destruction of Rome."[40]

The ingredients that constituted energy in the executive, Hamilton continued, were unity, duration, adequate provision for support, and competent powers. In his discussion of unity, he rejected the idea of a plural executive on the ground that it led to dissensions, rivalries, and paralysis in times of emergency. He also rejected a council "whose concurrence is made constitutionally necessary to the operations of the ostensible executive," for cabals in the council would "enervate the whole system of administration." Even absent cabals the diversity of views would embue the executive with "habitual feebleness and dilatoriness." Either kind of plurality tended to "conceal faults, and destroy responsibility" by making it impossible to allocate blame in cases of executive wrongdoing. The responsibility and accountability

39. *Federalist* 67, 68, 69.
40. *Federalist* 70.

arising from the vesting of the office in a single person Hamilton considered as the greatest safeguard against executive abuse. (He did not anticipate the emergence of the enormously bloated staffs of the modern presidency, but his observations about plural executives and councils would have applied equally to those.)[41]

A presidential term of considerable duration, Hamilton believed, was necessary to give firmness to the executive magistrate. If the term were too short, the president would be unwilling to jeopardize the chance of reelection by taking stands that were unpopular but necessary for the public good. Whether four years was adequate, Hamilton would not say (though he had thought not in the Constitutional Convention), but he did opine that as time for reelection approached, a president's firmness would tend to decline and he would be apt to court popular favor even at the expense of sound policy. Another reason for making the term of office fairly long, Hamilton wrote, was to lend stability to administration. Every new president would be disposed to institute new men and measures, especially if he had unseated an incumbent, and such changes, Hamilton added with hyperbole, "could not fail to occasion a disgraceful and ruinous mutability in the administration of the government."[42]

The same line of thinking led Hamilton to reject suggestions that limitations be placed on the number of terms a president could serve— though he cast his argument, as did many friends of executive power, in Humean terms. "The desire of reward is one of the strongest incentives of human conduct," he wrote, and thus "the best security for the fidelity of mankind is to make their interest coincide with their duty. Even the love of fame," which Hamilton described as "the ruling passion of the noblest minds," would be minimal in its effects if a president "foresaw that he must quit the scene" before finishing what he had set out to do and must turn his projects, "together with his own reputation, to hands which might be unequal or unfriendly to the task."[43]

41. Ibid.

42. *Federalist* 71 and 72. In *Federalist* 77 Hamilton said that stability would be increased because the approval of the Senate would be necessary for removals as well as for appointments; that rather contradicts the dire prophecy put forth here.

43. *Federalist* 72.

The third requisite for energy in the executive, "adequate provision for its support," Hamilton could treat in a few words. His audience was familiar enough with colonial history to know that colonial governors had often been reduced to impotence when assemblies withheld appropriations. "There are men who could neither be distressed nor won into a sacrifice of their duty; but this stern virtue is the growth of few soils: And in the main it will be found, that a power over a man's support is a power over his will." Accordingly, the Constitution's provision that a president's compensation could not be increased or diminished during his term was a prudent one.[44]

Hamilton devoted the remainder of the executive essays to an analysis of the expressly granted powers of the president. Before doing so, however, he had already taken up, as an introduction to his discussion of stability, the powers that inhere in the office simply by virtue of their being "peculiarly within the province of the executive department." He recited them under the general rubric of administration, by which he meant approximately what Bracton had meant by *gubernaculum* five centuries earlier. These were "the actual conduct of foreign negotiations, the preparatory plans of finance" or budget-making power, "the application and disbursement of the public moneys, in conformity to the general appropriations of the legislature," and the war powers. None of these powers is expressly granted in Article 2; without saying so, Hamilton clearly inferred them from the vesting clause and from his understanding of the nature of executive power.[45]

Then Hamilton turned to the enumerated special powers, starting with the veto. He considered the veto necessary to enable the president to defend against attacks by Congress "upon the constitutional rights of the executive" and useful also as "an additional security against the enaction of improper laws." The propriety of making the president commander in chief Hamilton regarded as self-evident, and the provision for requiring the opinions, in writing, of the depart-

44. *Federalist* 73.

45. *Federalist* 72. See also Harvey Flaumenhaft, "Hamilton's Administrative Republic and the American Presidency," in *The Presidency in the Constitutional Order*, ed. Joseph M. Bessette and Jeffrey Tulis (Baton Rouge, LA, 1981), 65–112.

ment heads he considered a "redundancy," a power inherent in the office. The pardoning power he defended in the same manner that Wilson and Iredell had, and like them he considered the power as amounting to a dispensing or a suspending power. Hamilton found acceptable the Senate's "concurrent" role in the making of treaties, yet, as indicated, he insisted that the "actual conduct of foreign negotiations" belonged exclusively to the president—a point on which he and Madison would differ during Washington's second administration. He likewise defended the Senate's sharing in the appointment power though he commented that senatorial disapproval of presidential nominees would be rare. (He did not foresee, but would not have been surprised at, the practice of senatorial courtesy, whereby presidents cleared prospective nominees in a given state with the senior senator of the state.) In conclusion, Hamilton dismissed such minor powers as the State of the Union message, the receiving of ambassadors, and the like because no one had raised serious objection to them.[46]

Two more points about Hamilton's view of the presidency are in order. First, he had more in mind than he set down on paper in 1788: He hoped to be able to transform the executive into an office approximating the British system of government by cabinet ministers, and he would go a long way toward succeeding. Second, he viewed executive authority as being extensive. In earlier essays he had addressed in general terms "the principal purposes to be answered by the Union," most of which were partly or totally executive in nature. Granted, these purposes were limited: the common defense, "the preservation of the public peace as well against internal convulsions as external attacks," regulation of interstate and foreign commerce, and superintending foreign relations. The powers necessary to the implementation of these ends, however, "ought to exist without limitation: *Because it is impossible to foresee or define the extent and variety of national*

---

46. *Federalist* 73–77. Regarding Hamilton's later difference with Madison in the matter of foreign relations, see the discussion of his Pacificus letters in chapter 9 of this book. For a study of the more general attitude, see Ronald C. Moe, "The Founders and Their Experience with the Executive Veto," *Presidential Studies Quarterly* 17 (1987):413–432.

exigencies, or the correspondent extent and variety of the means which may be necessary to satisfy them."[47]

In other words, Hamilton believed that in the final analysis the federal government and particularly the executive branch must have whatever power was needed to protect the safety and well being of the republic.

47. *Federalist* 23; see also 24 and 35 and chapter 9 of this book.

CHAPTER 9

The Washington Administration

It was a foregone conclusion, from the moment the Constitution was published, that Washington would be the choice of the electoral college. Students who encounter contemporary documents for the first time are amazed at the adulation lavished upon the man. In Europe as well as in America he was heralded as the Greatest Character of the Age. His customary designation as the Father of His Country was an appellation far more exalted than the Father of His People that was applied to monarchs. It is no exaggeration to say that Americans were willing to venture the experiment with a single, national republican chief executive only because of their unreserved trust in George Washington.[1]

1. For a sampling of the adulation, see Patricia A. Anderson, *Promoted to Glory: The Apotheosis of George Washington* (Northampton, MA, 1980). The anti-Federalist historian Mercy Warren wrote, "Had any character of less popularity and celebrity been designated to this high trust [as president], it might at this period have endangered, if not proved fatal to the peace of the union. Though some thought the executive vested with too great powers to be entrusted to the hand of any individual, Washington was an individual in whom they had the utmost confidence" (Warren, *The History of the . . . American Revolution,* ed. Lester H. Cohen, 2 vols. [1805; repr., Indianapolis, IN, 1988], 2:662). Pierce Butler wrote that the president's "powers are full great, and greater than I was disposed to make them. Nor, Entre Nous, do I believe they would have been so great had not many of the members cast their eyes towards General

Less certain was whether he would answer the call. He had announced when he resigned as commander in chief that he would never again hold public office, and he regarded that pledge as a sacred promise. He sincerely questioned his ability to fill the presidential office effectively, for even though he had successfully commanded the army and administered his vast plantations with great system and skill, he had had virtually no experience in governing. Beyond these reservations, he positively dreaded the thought of leaving the serenity of his beloved Mount Vernon to take up the cares of renewed public service. Compounding the uncertainty was his reluctance to discuss the matter lest that "be construed into a vain-glorious desire of pushing myself into notice as a candidate."[2]

A number of friends and associates broached the subject in letters, but it was probably his former aide-de-camp Alexander Hamilton whose persuasion was decisive. Hamilton initiated an exchange of letters in which he argued that by signing and recommending ratification of the Constitution Washington had pledged himself to do everything he could to give it life. "It is to little purpose to have *introduced* a system," he wrote, "if the weightiest influence is not given to its firm *establishment,* in the outset." Then Hamilton rather presumptuously said, "It would be inglorious in such a situation not to hazard the glory however great," which Washington had "previously acquired." This appeal to a combination of duty and courage was irresistible.[3]

Washington as President; and shaped their Ideas of the Powers to be given to a President, by their opinions of his Virtue" (*The Records of the Federal Convention of 1787,* ed. Max Farrand, 4 vols. [New Haven, CT, 1937], 3:302).

2. See, for example, Washington to Hamilton, Aug. 28, Oct. 3, 1788 (source of the quotation), to Henry Lee, Sept. 22, to Benjamin Lincoln, Oct. 26, to Gouverneur Morris, Nov. 28, and to Jonathan Trumbull, Dec. 4, 1788, in *The Writings of George Washington,* ed. John C. Fitzpatrick, 39 vols. (Washington, DC, 1931–1944), 30:66–67, 109–112, 97–98, 117–121, 143, 149–150. Washington's attitudes are made quite clear in *David Humphreys' "Life of General Washington,"* ed. Rosemarie Zagarri (Athens, GA, 1991), 43, 45–51. See also Richard Norton Smith, *Patriarch: George Washington and the New American Nation* (New York, 1992).

3. Hamilton to Washington, Aug. 13, Sept., Nov. 18, 1788, Washington to Hamilton, Aug. 28, Oct. 3, Nov. 6, 1788, in *The Papers of Alexander Hamilton,* ed. Harold C. Syrett et al., 26 vols. (New York, 1961–1979), 5:201–202, 206–208, 220–222, 222–224, 233.

Hamilton foresaw another barrier to a suitable beginning for the Constitution. Federalists had generally agreed to support Washington for president and John Adams for vice-president, but since electors voted for two candidates, the tally could result in an awkward and embarrassing tie. The obvious solution was to induce some electors to waste their second ballots, but there was danger in that tactic. Anti-Federalists, according to rumors, intended to support George Clinton for vice-president; if they did and if Federalists threw away too many second ballots, the consequence would be the humiliation of having a foremost opponent of the Constitution in a position to succeed to the presidency. (The danger was dramatized when Washington almost died of anthrax during his first few weeks in office and again a month or two later when he nearly died of pneumonia.) Hamilton headed off the possibility by writing to Federalist leaders and orchestrating an appropriate distribution of the electoral votes.[4]

Washington, meanwhile, agreed to serve. But he expressed his misgivings poignantly in a letter to Edward Rutledge, written shortly after his inauguration. "I greatly apprehend that my Countrymen will expect too much from me. I fear, if the issue of public measures should not corrispond with their sanguine expectations, they will turn the extravagant (and I may say undue) praises which they are heaping upon me at this moment, into equally extravagant (though I will fondly hope unmerited) censures."[5]

It seemed, during the first term, that Washington's misgivings had been unjustified. The executive departments and the federal court system established, the president filled government offices with men of high quality, the public debts (which had been devastating) were ordered in a way that increased the nation's prosperity, and the divisions left by the ratification process had been bridged. In 1792,

4. Hamilton to Theodore Sedgwick, Oct. 9, Nov. 9, 1788, Jan. 29, 1789, Sedgwick to Hamilton, Oct. 16, Nov. 2, Hamilton to Madison, Nov. 23, 1788, Hamilton to James Wilson, Jan. 25, 1789, Jeremiah Wadsworth to Hamilton, Feb. 1789, ibid., 5:225, 226, 228, 230–231, 235–237, 247–249, 250–251, 252. The problems inherent in the original arrangements for electing the president and vice-president became acute in the election of 1800–1801 and necessitated the adoption of the Twelfth Amendment.

5. Washington to Edward Rutledge, May 5, 1789, in Fitzpatrick, ed., *Writings of Washington*, 30:309.

the uncertainty of affairs in Europe, combined with the fact that the presidential experience had not been especially unpleasant, made it possible for supporters to prevail upon Washington to serve a second term. His luster untarnished, he was elected again by the unanimous vote of the electoral college.[6]

The second term, however, proved to be a nightmare. As would happen in most two-term presidencies, the second term saw the country imperiled by foreign wars and rent by violent political confrontations at home. The Father of His Country was indeed beset by "unmerited censures" of the vilest kind, and the psychic cost of the second term was more than any person could reasonably be expected to bear. That would be true of most of his successors.[7]

But Washington had defined the presidency, grounded it on firm foundations, and made it central to the survival of the republic by the time he retired in 1797. Not all the precedents he established would last, not even until the end of the century. Yet he made the office viable, an institution of great flexibility and energy that could exert its will while remaining under the ultimate control of the law.

———— The new government started inauspiciously. Congress, scheduled by the Confederation Congress to convene in New York on March 4, 1789, did not obtain a quorum until April 6. Any man other than Washington might have been on the scene, ready to launch the ship of state, for he and everyone else knew that he had been elected president, but to avoid seeming eager he remained at home awaiting official notice. Congress accordingly counted the votes and dispatched a messenger to notify him; even then he made a leisurely trip northward, gratified but somewhat distressed by the overwhelming popular acclaim shown him along the way. He finally arrived—to be inaugurated on April 30.[8]

6. Regarding the first term in general, see James Hart, *The American Presidency in Action: 1789: A Study in Constitutional History* (New York, 1949), and Leonard D. White, *The Federalists: A Study in Administrative History* (New York, 1948).

7. This problem is developed at greater length in Forrest McDonald, "A Mirror for Presidents," *Commentary* (December 1976):34–41, and in Bill Moyers, *A World of Ideas* (New York, 1989), 111–118.

8. For a colorful contemporary description of Washington's trip to New York to be

During the week before he got to the city, and for two weeks afterward, the Senate was engaged in a debate over an appropriate form of address for the president. John Adams, having spent many years as American minister in the courts of Europe, had acquired a taste for royal pomp and had convinced himself that something approaching regal "dignity and splendor" would be necessary if people were to respect the new government. He insisted to the senators, to whom he regularly pontificated, that only an exalted system of titles would infuse the people with adequate awe and veneration to lend permanence and weight to the government. A goodly number of senators, thinking of their body as an American House of Lords, seemingly agreed. Richard Henry Lee, who had earlier been as ardent a radical republican as Adams had been, was among this group: At one point Lee rose and "read over a list of the Titles of all the Princes and Potentates of the Earth, marking where the Word Highness occurred." Oliver Ellsworth observed that the "appellation of President" was too common for the chief executive of a nation, inasmuch as there were presidents "of Fire Companies & of a Cricket Club." Various titles were proposed, including "his elective majesty" (the title of the king of Poland), until the Senate fixed upon "His Highness the President of the United States and Protector of the Rights of the Same." The House of Representatives balked, refusing to accept any title but the simple constitutional formulation, "President of the United States."[9]

President Washington was mightily embarrassed by this, not least because the debate and other indicators revealed the existence of a "court party" in the Senate that wanted to make the presidency quasi-monarchical; he himself was searching for rules of comport-

inaugurated, see David Ramsay, *The History of the American Revolution,* ed. Lester H. Cohen, 2 vols. (Indianapolis, IN, 1990), 2:656–660.

9. *The Diary of William Maclay and Other Notes on Senate Debates,* ed. Kenneth R. Bowling and Helen E. Veit, vol. 9, *Documentary History of the First Federal Congress of the United States of America* (Baltimore, 1988), quotations at 28, 29; see also 53. The proceedings of the Senate were closed to the public; Maclay's diary is the primary source for what occurred in the Senate during its first two years. Page Smith, *John Adams,* 2 vols. (Garden City, NY, 1962); Peter Shaw, *The Character of John Adams* (Chapel Hill, NC, 1976).

ment suitable to a republican executive. He had scarcely taken up residence in a large rented house when throngs of visitors began to call, most come to gape at the Great Man or to solicit jobs. All acted as if they had a constitutional right to be there. From breakfast to bedtime, Washington complained, it was impossible to be "relieved from the ceremony of one visit before I had to attend to another." Upon inquiring about the practice of the presidents of the Confederation Congress, he learned that they had been "considered in no better light than as a Maitre d'Hôtel . . . for the table was considered as a public one." After two days of harassment, Washington published a notice in the newspapers that he would thereafter receive "visits of compliment" between 2:00 and 3:00 P.M. on Tuesday and Friday and that he would "neither return visits nor accept any invitations."[10]

That elicited complaints in some quarters. Pennsylvania senator William Maclay grumbled that Washington proposed "to be seen only in public on Stated times like an Eastern Lama." Washington sought the advice of Madison, Jay, Adams, and Hamilton. He needed rules of behavior, he told them, that would strike a balance between "too free an intercourse and too much familiarity," which would reduce the dignity of the office, and "an ostentatious show" of monarchical aloofness, which would be improper in a republic. A "line of conduct" was worked out. Dinners were to be held every Thursday at 4:00 P.M. for government officials and their families on a regular system of rotation to avoid favoritism. Two occasions a week were established for greeting the general public, a levee for men on Tuesdays from 3:00 to 4:00 P.M. and tea parties for men and women on Friday evenings. Anyone respectably dressed could attend without invitation or prior notice.[11]

10. Washington to David Stuart, July 26, 1789, in Fitzpatrick, ed., *Writings of Washington,* 30:360–362; James Thomas Flexner, *George Washington and the New Nation (1783–1793)* (Boston, 1969), 192–209; Hart, *American Presidency,* 11–16. Attention to etiquette and ceremony was evidence of Washington's "deliberate intention to *lead* . . . in 'tone-setting,' moral ways" (Ralph Ketcham, *Presidents Above Party: The First American Presidency, 1789–1829* [Chapel Hill, NC, 1984], 91).

11. Bowling and Veit, ed., *Diary of Maclay,* 21; Queries on a Line of Conduct to be Pursued by the President, May 10, 1789, Washington to Madison, May 11, 1789, to David Stuart, July 26, 1789, in Fitzpatrick, ed., *Writings of Washington,* 30:319–322, 361–362.

Three other matters of protocol were given careful attention. One concerned the president's salary. Washington had refused to accept a salary during the Revolutionary War, and in his inaugural address he asked not to be compensated except by an expense account. Congress, however, took the position that the Constitution mandated a "fixed compensation" for the president and voted a salary of $25,000 per year. (For Washington's eight years of service that should have amounted to $200,000, but he drew $196,121, the difference being the salary for the fifty-six or fifty-seven days his first administration fell short of being four full years. Such scrupulousness was characteristic of the man.)[12]

A second concern was the inauguration ceremony. Washington took the oath of office in the Senate chamber, where both houses of Congress had gathered, and then he delivered his address. This procedure was consciously patterned after the arrangements in England, where the king, at the beginning of each session of Parliament, addressed both houses in the chamber of the Lords. Each house of Congress completed the ritual by calling on the president later with a formal answer, as the Lords and Commons customarily did. That pattern was repeated annually on the occasion of the State of the Union address. But Washington took some of the monarchical edge off the proceedings by wearing a suit of brown broadcloth made in Connecticut.[13]

A third matter had to do with the niceties of federal-state relations. After the first session of the First Congress adjourned in the fall of 1789, Washington made a good-will tour through New England, avoiding Rhode Island, which had not yet ratified the Constitution, and Vermont, which was governing itself as an independent republic. As he approached Cambridge, Massachusetts, he was invited to review the militia troops there; he declined, "otherwise than as a pri-

12. Inaugural Address, in Fitzpatrick, ed., *Writings of Washington*, 30:295–296 and n. 40.

13. A detailed description of the inauguration is in Flexner, *Washington and the New Nation*, 182–191. Washington also had it in mind to promote American manufactures; he praised Connecticut's "superfine broad" cloth and noted, "I use no Porter or Cheese in my family, but such as is made in America" (Zagarri, ed., *Humphreys' "Life of Washington,"* 79–80).

vate man," because they were under state jurisdiction. Having deferred to state sensibilities in that regard, he similarly refused John Hancock's invitation to stay in the governor's residence in Boston but agreed to have dinner together—on the assumption that Hancock would acknowledge the subordinate position of governors by first paying the president a courtesy call. Hancock instead sent a message that he was crippled with gout and could not leave home, whereupon Washington flatly refused to see him except in Washington's own lodgings. Next day the governor, heavily swathed in bandages, called upon the president.[14]

Such concerns can be regarded as trivial—some contemporaries thought them pretentious or comical—but Washington did not so view them, and he was right. He fully understood, if only intuitively, that the presidency, if properly established, would be dual in nature, chief executive officer but also ritualistic and ceremonial head of state, and that the latter function was quite as vital as the more prosaic administrative one. Moreover, it was his task to enable the American people to make the transition from monarchy to republicanism by serving as the symbol of nationhood and to institutionalize that symbol by investing it in the office, not in the man. To that end, he behaved as if his every move was being closely scrutinized, which to a considerable extent it was. He even opened a correspondence with a Virginia friend who could mingle with ordinary folks and inform him how people were responding to the president's doings. When the correspondent wrote that certain actions had led some people to endorse Patrick Henry's assertion that the presidency "squinted toward monarchy," Washington made appropriate adjustments in his behavior.[15]

14. Washington to Hancock, Oct. 22, 23, 26, 1789, in Fitzpatrick, ed., *Writings of Washington,* 30:450–453 and notes; Flexner, *Washington and the New Nation,* 230; Hart, *American Presidency,* 18–20.

15. Hart, *American Presidency,* 13–14; Washington to David Stuart, July 26, 1789, in Fitzpatrick, ed., *Writings of Washington,* 30:359–366. On May 5, 1789, Washington wrote to Madison, "As the first of every thing, *in our situation* will serve to establish a Precedent, it is devoutly wished on my part, that these precedents may be fixed on true principles" (*The Papers of James Madison,* volume 12, ed. Charles F. Hobson et al. [Charlottesville, VA, 1979], 132). Washington's role as chief of state may be viewed in

Washington was able to succeed, partly because of a natural gravity and dignity combined with simplicity of tastes and manners, but more importantly because he was a consummate actor who had self-consciously been role-playing throughout his adult life. Lest that observation be taken as pejorative, additional observations are in order, particularly in regard to the eighteenth-century concept of character. The word was rarely used to denote internal qualities. Its most common signification meant reputation: One had a character for honesty, fickleness, perspicacity. But it also meant, in polite society and in public life, a persona that one deliberately selected and always wore; it was conventional practice to pick a role, like a part in a play, and attempt to act it consistently, always to "be in character." If one chose a character that one could play comfortably and played it long enough and well enough, by degrees it became a "second nature" that superseded one's primary nature, which was generally thought to be base. One became, in other words, what one pretended to be. Washington differed from ordinary mortals by picking a progression of characters during his lifetime, each nobler and grander than the last, and by playing each so well that he ultimately transformed himself into a man of extrahuman virtue.[16]

---

light of Harold M. Barger's "The Prominence of the Chief of State Role in the American Presidency," *Presidential Studies Quarterly* 8 (1987):127–139; his symbolic role is developed in Forrest McDonald, *The Presidency of George Washington* (Lawrence, KS, 1974). Glenn A. Phelps, "George Washington: Precedent Setter," in *Inventing the American Presidency,* ed. Thomas E. Cronin (Lawrence, KS, 1989), 261, justly takes me to task for underrating Washington's tangible achievements; one hopes the present chapter rectifies that. See also Glenn A. Phelps, "George Washington and the Founding of the Presidency," *Presidential Studies Quarterly* 17 (1987):345–361.

16. See Forrest McDonald and Ellen Shapiro McDonald, *Requiem* (Lawrence, KS, 1988), 14–15; Forrest McDonald, *Novus Ordo Seclorum* (Lawrence, KS, 1985), 193–199. For the best contemporary description of the concept of character that I have found, see Fanny Burney's novel *Cecilia, Or, Memoirs of an Heiress,* 5 vols. (London, 1782). See also Paul K. Longmore, *The Invention of George Washington* (Berkeley, CA, 1988), 9–11, 14–16, 51–52, 179–183; Barry Schwartz, *George Washington: The Making of an American Symbol* (New York, 1987), 81–89, 125–126, 128–130, 147; Forrest McDonald, "Washington, Cato, and Honor: A Model for Revolutionary Leadership," in *American Models of Revolutionary Leadership: George Washington and Other Founders,* ed. Daniel J. Elazar and Ellis Katz (Lanham, MD, 1992), 43–58.

That concept and practice underwent substantial modification in the nineteenth century, but in a vulgarized form—politically creating and acting in accordance with a "public image"—it survives; the need for it inheres in the presidency and in the nature of popular politics. It may also be true that great leaders must be polished actors having a flair for the dramatic, lest they be leaders whom no one will follow.[17]

———— Preoccupation with ritual was appropriate during the first few months, for until Congress enacted the legislation, there were almost no laws to be executed, no executive departments to administer them, and no courts to adjudicate them. As the first session unfolded, the doings in the Congress amounted almost to a second constitutional convention, for they organically defined, shaped, and gave life to a government that the Constitution only authorized.

Washington had thought of actively directing the process, but then he decided it would be prudent to let others lead. He had written a sixty-two-page statement of maxims, principles, and proposals but scrapped it and instead presented a handful of legislative recommendations in his inaugural address. These concerned his duties in treaty-making or as commander in chief: a proposal for bringing the minuscule existing military establishment into conformity with the Constitution, one establishing a temporary commission to treat with southern Indians, and one authorizing the calling of the militia in the Ohio country if needed. All three were acted upon. Perhaps it was Congress' apparent willingness to grant him blanket authority in such matters, together with the demonstrated court-party inclinations of the Senate and the advice of the people he consulted most frequently (Madison, Hamilton, Jay), that induced him to play a passive role in the definition of the executive power in 1789. In any event, most people in government seemed anxious to clothe the pres-

17. See Longmore, *Invention of George Washington*, 11, 15, 32, 52, 80, 181–183; Erwin C. Hargrove, *Presidential Leadership: Personality and Style* (New York, 1966), esp. chap. 1, "Theodore Roosevelt: The Dramatizing Leader"; Thomas A. Bailey, *Presidential Greatness: The Image and the Man From George Washington to the Present* (New York, 1966), 129–130, 143–145, 157–161, 205–206. The subject of presidential images is developed in chapter 15 of this book.

ident with adequate powers, which spared him the unpleasant necessity of seeking the powers himself.[18]

The extent to which Congress expected the executive branch to exercise discretionary powers is revealed by the process of making appropriations. The appropriations act of 1789, consisting of 125 words, allotted a "sum not exceeding" $216,000 for salaries and operations of the government, a limit of $137,000 for the War Department, a maximum of $190,000 for redeeming warrants issued by the former treasury board, and up to $96,000 for pensions to war invalids. From the outset, however, it was understood that executive officers could divert funds from the objects for which they had been appropriated to meet special contingencies. For example, in 1793 Jefferson and Madison approved the advance of money to French refugees from Santo Domingo even though no funds had been appropriated for the purpose and though both men thought Congress had no constitutional authority to make such an appropriation. From time to time Congress attempted to bring spending more fully under its control, but it was simply unable to micromanage the budget.[19]

A significant decision regarding executive power arose in the House debates concerning the creation of the executive departments. William Loughton Smith of South Carolina, citing Hamilton's *Federalist* 77, contended that senatorial approval would be necessary for presidential removal of executive officeholders just as it was for appointment. Madison, who had rapidly emerged as the principal court-party spokesman in the First Congress, summarized the arguments. Four general positions had been advanced: that the matter was for Congress to decide; that "no removal can take place otherwise than by impeachment"; that the power was "incident to that of appointment, and therefore belongs to the President & Senate"; and that the power of removal was vested solely in the president. The last of these prevailed by a sizable majority.[20]

18. First Inaugural Address, and Proposed Address to Congress, in Fitzpatrick, ed., *Writings of Washington,* 30:291–308 and notes; Hart, *American Presidency,* 57–58, 141.

19. White, *Federalists,* 323–334; Lucius Wilmerding, Jr., *The Spending Power: A History of the Efforts of Congress to Control Expenditures* (New Haven, CT, 1943), 7 and passim.

20. Madison's speeches of May 19, June 16, 17, 18, 22, Madison to Edmund Randolph, June 17, to Samuel Johnston, June 21, to Jefferson, June 30, 1789, in Hobson,

That decision did not bind future congresses or presidents; the question would be raised again on several pivotal occasions in American history. But the constitutional reasoning underlying the decision became established doctrine. The Constitution, Madison declared, vested the executive power in the president, with the exception that the Senate shares the appointment and treaty-making powers. Congress is not authorized to add other exceptions. Madison then asked, "Is the power of displacing an executive power? I conceive that if any power whatsoever is in its nature executive it is the power of appointing, overseeing, and controlling those who execute the laws." If the Constitution had not required senatorial approval of appointments, the president "would have the right by virtue of his executive power to make such appointment." This was an endorsement of the view that the president has certain unspecified but real powers that he exercises by virtue of the vesting clause; the vesting clause was a positive grant, not an abstract generalization.[21]

Senator Maclay was unhappy with the House's decision, perceiving it as undercutting the Senate's special relationship with the executive. Indeed, he objected to the creation of departments by ordinary legislative process. The proper way, he contended, was for the president to communicate "to the Senate that he finds, such & such officers necessary in the Execution of the Government. and nominates the Men. if the Senate approve they will concur in the Measure. if not refuse their Consent." When the appointments are made, Maclay went on, the president should notify the House and request adequate salaries. The House could then "shew their concurrence or disapprobation by providing for the Officer or not."[22]

---

ed., *Papers of Madison,* 12:170–174, 225–230, 232–239, 244–245, 249–251, 254–256, 270–271. The debates are summarized at length in Hart, *American Presidency,* 155–184. George C. Rogers, *Evolution of a Federalist: William Loughton Smith of Charleston, 1758–1812* (Columbia, SC, 1962).

21. Speech of June 16, 17, 1789, in Hobson, ed., *Papers of Madison,* 12:225–229, 232–239; Louis Fisher, *Constitutional Conflicts between Congress and the President,* 3d ed., rev. (Lawrence, KS, 1991), 54–58. The removal power is treated in chapter 12 of this book.

22. Bowling and Veit, ed., *Diary of Maclay,* 110.

Maclay received little support on that proposal, but he was strongly backed on a related one. The House bill establishing the State Department provided for the appointment by the secretary of a chief clerk who was to become acting secretary if the president should remove *"the said principal Officer."* Maclay objected that the provision unconstitutionally bypassed the Senate. Half the senators agreed with him and voted to strike the offending provision; Adams broke the tie by supporting the House's bill.[23]

Signs of strain between president and Senate soon appeared. Congress had enacted the first revenue act, establishing duties on imported goods and providing for collectors, and early in August Washington sent to the Senate a list of nominees for collectorships. Among these was Benjamin Fishbourn, whom Washington had known as a good army officer during the war and who had been serving as the customs collector for Savannah under Georgia's import laws. The Senate approved the other nominees but without saying why rejected Fishbourn, whereupon Washington promptly submitted another nominee. But the Senate also adopted a resolution that senatorial "advice, and consent to the appointment of Officers should be given in the presence of the President." Then it appointed a three-man committee to confer with Washington "on the mode of communication proper to be pursued between him and the Senate, in the formation of Treaties, and making appointments to offices." Washington told the committee that oral communications seemed necessary with regard to treaties and possibly for foreign ministers though details of how to conduct such discussions would have to be worked out; communications respecting other appointments, however, should be written in order to avoid the awkwardness that personal confrontations might entail. The Fishbourn episode is sometimes cited as the first example of senatorial courtesy, but a more likely candidate came two weeks later, when Georgia's senators objected to the appointment of one of the commissioners to negotiate with Indians in Georgia, and the Senate voted to postpone confirmation.[24]

23. Ibid., 110–115, 117.

24. Hobson, ed., *Papers of Madison*, 12:328–329, n. 1; Fitzpatrick, ed., *Writings of Washington*, 30:370–371, 373–374; Fisher, *Constitutional Conflicts*, 33–35.

The course of those Indian negotiations strained relations between president and Senate further and established an important precedent. On Saturday, August 22, after several days of interchange about who would sit where when the president called on the Senate for consultation, Washington appeared with Henry Knox, the acting superintendent of war. Knox handed Washington a paper with seven points on which advice and consent was being sought; Washington handed it to Adams, who read it aloud, rapidly. Carriages outside made such a noise that no one understood "one Sentence of it." After the doorkeeper closed the windows, Adams read the first point, which contained several references to the whole paper. Robert Morris rose to say he had not been able to hear the paper and asked that it be read again. It was. Then Adams put the question on the first point, yes or no. An embarrassed silence followed. Maclay broke it by requesting that before an answer be given the treaties involved should be read, along with the instructions issued by the old Congress to the negotiators. The senators then raised a cacophony of voices, speaking of every manner of thing, at which Washington grew progressively angrier. Finally, he "started up in a Violent fret" and declared, *This defeats every purpose of my coming here.*" Tempers gradually cooled, but following another fruitless session on Monday Washington resolved never to enter the Senate for a consultation again.[25]

He kept that vow, and thus the idea that the Senate would serve as an executive council was stillborn. In future Washington consulted with senators occasionally in his own office, individually or in small groups, and he received committees of the Senate, but by and large he dealt formally with the whole Senate only in writing, and he sought its consent after he had initiated and concluded negotiations with foreign powers. (Most of his successors followed his example.)[26]

25. Bowling and Veit, ed., *Diary of Maclay,* 128–132. For a study of Henry Knox, see North Callahan, *Henry Knox: George Washington's General* (New York, 1958).

26. Louis W. Koenig, "The Modern Presidency and the Constitution: Foreign Policy," in *The Constitution and the American Presidency,* ed. Martin L. Fausold and Alan Shank (Albany, NY, 1991), 171–193; Gary J. Schmitt, "Executive Privilege: Presidential Power to Withhold Information from Congress," in *The Presidency in the Constitutional Order,* ed. Joseph M. Bessette and Jeffrey Tulis (Baton Rouge, LA, 1981), 154–194; Raoul Berger, *Executive Privilege: A Constitutional Myth* (New York,

Yet he continued to regard the Senate as constitutionally more important than the House because of its share of the executive authority, an attitude that led him to consider exercising the veto. Early in September he sent a letter asking Madison's advice on a variety of matters, including the query, "Being clearly of opinion that there ought to be a difference in the wages of the members of the two branches of the Legislature"—the appropriations bill had provided equal pay—"would it be politic or prudent in the President when the Bill comes to him to send it back with his reasons for non-concurring?" Apparently Madison advised against the veto, for it was not exercised. Thereafter Washington grew extremely reluctant to veto legislation and did not use the power until April of 1792, on a bill that was patently unconstitutional and only after Jefferson urged him to veto something lest the power fall into disuse, as it had in England. He vetoed but one more bill during his presidency, on the eve of his departure from office.[27]

The question of the president's status arose again during the first session of the Senate, albeit unofficially and indecisively; on July 14 Oliver Ellsworth referred to the president, saying, "It is Sacrilege to touch an Hair of his head." Next day, Charles Carroll made a number of references to the British king in regard to the presidency, saying, *"The king can do no wrong,* if anything improper is done, it should be the Ministers that should answer." Later, near the end of the session,

---

1975); Ralston Hayden, *The Senate and Treaties, 1789–1817* (New York, 1920), 104–105 and passim; Fisher, *Constitutional Conflicts,* 216–222.

27. Washington to Madison, ca. Sept. 8, 1789, in Hobson, ed., *Papers of Madison,* 12:390–391; Carlton Jackson, *Presidential Vetoes, 1792–1945* (Athens, GA, 1967), vii–ix, 1–4; Harry C. Thomson, "The First Presidential Vetoes," *Presidential Studies Quarterly* 8 (1978):27–32; White, *Federalists,* 65–66. Neither Adams nor Jefferson exercised the veto, Madison vetoed seven bills, Monroe one. Seven of the first fifteen presidents vetoed no bills. As to grounds for exercising the veto, Washington first used it (to veto "an act for an apportionment of Representatives") because the bill violated the Constitution; he used it a second time because a bill decommissioning five companies of light dragoons was poorly crafted, inconvenient and injurious to the public, and did not "comport with economy" (*Messages and Papers of the Presidents,* comp. James D. Richardson, 10 vols. [Washington, DC, 1889–1905], 1:124, 211–212).

Maclay recorded a discussion involving himself, Ellsworth, John Adams, Fisher Ames, and Philip Schuyler concerning whether federal court writs should run in the name of the president, as British writs ran in the name of the king. In that context Ames "said the President personally was not subject to any process whatever, could have no action Whatever brought against him, was above the power of all Judges Justices &ca." The others except Maclay agreed, Schuyler adding that he was no lawyer, "but I think the President a kind of Sacred Person."[28]

Nothing was settled by these discussions, of course; the decisive precedents came during Jefferson's presidency. But two points want notice. Federal court writs have always been issued in the name of the president, and at least until the Nixon administration the president has always in practice been beyond the reach of the courts except when the Senate sits as a court of impeachment.[29]

———— Congress created the executive departments before the end of summer, 1789: State Department, War Department, and Treasury Department. Congress also established two executive agencies that had less than departmental status. The Post Office was simply carried over from the Confederation, though Washington replaced the postmaster general. The Judiciary Act created the office of attorney general, consisting of a lawyer on retainer to advise the president in regard to constitutionality and law; he would prepare and argue cases before the Supreme Court and could continue a private practice. Federal district attorneys to enforce the laws (except revenue laws, which were entrusted to Treasury) were subordinate not to the attorney general but to the secretary of state. The actual execution of the laws was the function of federal marshals, who were officers of the federal district courts.

As a result of this legislation, Washington found himself with nearly a thousand offices to fill. He was besieged with applications, but he

28. Bowling and Veit, ed., *Diary of Maclay*, 112, 168. Winfred E. A. Bernhard, *Fisher Ames: Federalist and Statesman, 1758–1808* (Chapel Hill, NC, 1965).

29. Hart, *American Presidency*, 42–43; see also chapter 10 of this book. In *Youngstown Sheet and Tube Company* v. *Sawyer*, the action was brought against Secretary of Commerce Charles Sawyer, not against President Truman.

shunned the opportunity to develop a patronage system. His appointments were scrupulously nonpartisan except that he refused to appoint known enemies of the Constitution. No one was appointed unless Washington knew him personally or someone Washington trusted attested to his character. For the major appointments, the president consulted at length with several intimates, notably Madison. For secretary of state he preferred John Jay, but he bowed to Jay's wish to be chief justice and instead chose Thomas Jefferson, who was returning to Virginia on leave from his post as minister to France. Henry Knox continued in the War Department, Alexander Hamilton was appointed secretary of the treasury after Robert Morris turned it down, Edmund Randolph became attorney general, and Samuel Osgood of Massachusetts became postmaster general.[30]

The chain of responsibility was curiously mixed. The statutes establishing State and War used identical language to describe the secretaries' duties: "He shall perform and execute such duties as shall, from time to time, be enjoined on or entrusted to him by the president . . . agreeable to the constitution." The Post Office was different. Congress chose to exercise its constitutional authority to "establish Post Offices and post Roads" directly instead of delegating the function to the executive branch, and since Washington was not especially interested in the department, it operated without presidential direction. Timothy Pickering, who succeeded Osgood, went so far in the discretionary exercise of authority as to drop the customary practice of advertising for bids for mail contractors, until Congress made the practice mandatory in 1792.[31]

The Treasury Department was put on a special footing. Despite recognizing the need for discretionary authority in spending, most members of the House of Representatives were anxious to retain a general managerial control over the operations of the Treasury. Several of them feared that the treasury secretary might evolve into a British-style prime minister. For these reasons, the secretary was

30. Fitzpatrick, ed., *Writings of Washington,* vol. 30, passim; Hart, *American Presidency,* 111–133.

31. Hart, *American Presidency,* 220; White, *Federalists,* 176–183; Gerald H. Clarfield, *Timothy Pickering and the American Republic* (Pittsburgh, PA, 1980).

required by law to report directly to the House as well as to the president. The secretary was empowered to appoint his assistant, superintend the collection of the revenues, decide upon the forms for keeping accounts, and prepare and report budgetary estimates. He was also "to digest and prepare plans for the improvement and management of the revenue, and for the support of public credit." The secretary must make reports "and give information to either branch of the Legislature, in person or in writing (as he may be required) respecting all matters referred to him" or that pertained to the office. The aim of the statute was to keep the Treasury Department on a congressional leash; the effects were to endow it with authority to initiate legislation and to place the power of the purse partially in the executive branch.[32]

Washington oversaw the work of the department heads closely though he gave them free rein in dealing with their subordinates. The essence of his administrative method was not to direct but to channel executive affairs. He referred letters he received to the appropriate secretary, and they referred letters they received to him, along with drafts of proposed replies. Sometimes he suggested changes or called consultations. "By this means," Jefferson later recalled in a memorandum to his own department heads, Washington was "always in accurate possession of all facts and proceedings in every part of the Union, and to whatsoever department they related; he formed a central point for the different branches; preserved a unity of object and action among them"; and assumed responsibility for whatever was done. This system generated a huge amount of paperwork, but it kept Washington fully in charge.[33]

There were, however, variations in the routine that stemmed from differences in temperaments and talents. Washington was an expert in foreign affairs and war, and thus he tended to be his own foreign secretary and war secretary, Jefferson and Knox being reduced almost to clerical status. Jefferson, not fond of routine clerical work, tended

32. *The Laws of the United States of America* (Philadelphia, 1796), 1:36–40; *Abridgment of the Debates of Congress*, volume 1, ed. Thomas Hart Benson (New York, 1857), 92–94, 109, 111–112.

33. Jefferson to heads of departments, Nov. 6, 1801, quoted in McDonald, *Presidency of George Washington*, 40–41.

to be lackadaisical in carrying out his duties—at least until the international arena began to heat up. For example, in 1791 he wrote to the American chargé in Spain, William Carmichael, complaining mildly that Carmichael had sent no communication in two years; but Jefferson had written to him only once during that period. Knox adored his boss and happily did what he was told, but his competence was limited, and he devoted much of his energies to private land speculations. Hamilton, by contrast, was brilliant in the field of finance, which was beyond Washington's ken or interest. That, and his special relationship with the House, gave Hamilton a freer hand than the other secretaries had. Besides, Hamilton was extremely energetic and a compulsive meddler; when matters in the domain of War or State interested him, he often took the liberty of initiating policy by submitting unsolicited proposals to Washington. At one point, when Knox was away on private business for an extended period, Hamilton actually ran the War Department as well as Treasury.[34]

Perhaps because Washington sensed that his chief administrators were not especially compatible as a group, he did not consult them collectively during his first term. When his perceived need for an advisory body increased, upon the outbreak of the French revolutionary wars, he began to consult them, but he also turned to the Supreme Court. In the summer of 1793 he framed (actually Hamilton framed for him) a series of questions about international law and treaty obligations, and he forwarded these to the Court for an opinion. Chief Justice Jay had been a frequent presidential adviser, and he and the other justices would have been eager to become an ex officio advisory council—but for a flukish circumstance. Shortly before, Congress had assigned the Court the administrative duty of reviewing pension claims of war veterans. The justices, not wishing to take on the onerous and somewhat demeaning task, indignantly refused, saying that they were already overworked, that the function was not judicial, and that it violated the principle of the separation of powers. Now, asked to assume an executive role, the Court could not with good grace reverse its stand. It accordingly refused. Thereafter, Wash-

34. White, *Federalists,* 116–155; Forrest McDonald, *Alexander Hamilton* (New York, 1979), 133–140, 217–222.

ington regularly called the department heads together for meetings—and thus was born the presidential cabinet.[35]

——— In the Constitutional Convention Hamilton had declared his warm admiration for the British government. His proposal to establish one like it was supported by no one, and he had little influence in shaping the finished Constitution. But he perceived that the Constitution did not preclude a functioning system of government closely patterned after the British model. Congress, in organizing the Treasury Department and specifying the duties of the secretary, facilitated the fashioning of such a system by making Hamilton virtually a nonvoting member of the House. His position was almost analogous to that of the chancellor of the exchequer; he saw himself, mutatis mutandis, as Sir Robert Walpole to Washington's George II. Or as Madison put it many years later, Hamilton sought "to administer the Government . . . into what he thought it ought to be."[36]

To pull it off, Hamilton would have to devise and then persuade Congress to enact a system of public finance that would make the operations of the Treasury Department permanently indispensable, not only to the functioning of the federal government but also to the ordinary conduct of private business. The initial step was Hamilton's First Report on the Public Credit, presented to Congress on January 9, 1790. The public debts were of three descriptions: a foreign debt of about $11 million, a domestic debt of about $40 million accumulated to finance the war, and state war debts of about $25 million. Hamilton proposed to refinance the foreign debt at lower interest with Dutch bankers, which was easy enough now that the government had a taxing power. He proposed that the federal government assume the state debts and "fund" them as well as the domestic debt at par but at a reduced interest rate—that is, he asked Congress to pledge as a first priority against all revenues sufficient funds to provide interest payments at an average of just over 4 percent (instead of the 6 percent at which the money had been borrowed). Various compensatory op-

35. Draft of Questions to be Submitted to Justices of the Supreme Court, July 18, 1793, in Syrett, ed., *Hamilton Papers*, 15:110–116 and notes.
36. Hamilton's speech of June 16, 1787, and Nicholas P. Trist memorandum, Sept. 27, 1834, in Farrand, ed., *Records*, 1:288, 3:534.

tions, such as a tontine and public lands, were to be offered to induce creditors to accept the cut. Except for a modest "sinking fund," which was to make open market purchases of government securities with the profits earned by the Post Office, no provision was to be made for retiring the principal of the debts.[37]

Congress enacted the proposals into law with minor changes, though not without a bit of management by Hamilton. In the House, Madison proposed to discriminate between original holders of government paper and present holders, but as Hamilton explained, that would be to announce to future creditors that government paper was not freely negotiable—and thus could not be used as a stable basis for currency, as Hamilton intended it should. Madison's idea was defeated by a large margin. Somewhat stickier was the plan for assuming the state debts, which was defeated on the first vote, mainly by representatives from the southern states that had largely repudiated their debts. Then occurred a famous dinner at Jefferson's, whereat Madison and Jefferson promised Hamilton enough southern support for assumption if he would deliver northern votes to locate the permanent capital on the Potomac. The deal was consummated, and the bill was passed.[38]

The task that followed called not for financial or political skill but for administrative genius. The complexity of servicing the public debt can be seen by observing just one part of it, that of making quarterly interest payments. Regular transactions with about twenty-five thousand individuals were involved. Payments were fixed on the first days of January, April, July, and October at the Treasury and at thirteen state loan offices, distributed over a thousand-mile area and as much as two weeks' travel time from the Treasury. There were only six banks in the country. The main source of revenue was sixty-seven customs offices, which collected unpredictable, widely varying, and seasonally fluctuating amounts. On the days that interest payments fell due, Hamilton needed to know how much money was available in what forms and where, and he needed to be able to move

---

37. McDonald, *Hamilton,* 143–188.

38. Ibid., 158, 177–178, 181–187; First Report on the Public Credit, Jan. 9, 1790, in Syrett, ed., *Hamilton Papers,* 6:73–78.

it appropriately. Considering the slowness of transportation and communication, smooth operation would appear impossible, but during Hamilton's five-and-a-half years in office there was never a complaint of delay or error in the disbursement of interest.[39]

Hamilton was able to consolidate his position as "prime minister" in part because on a workaday basis he and his department, with more than five hundred employees as compared to a total of twenty-two in the other departments, were the government during Washington's first term. Congress and the courts were normally in session three or four months of the year; the monumental outpouring of congressional legislation in 1789 ran to seventy-six printed pages. The president and the other secretaries were in the capital much of the year, but they had little to do. Treasury alone worked full time the year around.[40]

Hamilton cemented his position further by keeping the Treasury above reproach and by being careful to avoid offending a citizenry accustomed to regarding tax collectors as the embodiment of tyranny. For example, he instructed the captains of cutters in the newly founded Coast Guard (established by Congress to prevent violations of the revenue laws) that they must "always keep in mind that their Countrymen are Freemen. . . . They will therefore refrain with the most guarded circumspection from whatever has the semblance of haughtiness, rudeness or insult."[41]

The next step in Hamilton's program elicited a storm of opposition, though not entirely on its merits. When Congress adjourned after its second session ended in August, 1790, it instructed Hamilton to draw up further provisions for the public credit, which was generally understood to comprehend supplementary taxes and a na-

39. Nathaniel Appleton to Hamilton, March 16, 1791 (two letters), Appleton to Hamilton, May 15, 1791, Treasury Department Circular Letter to the Collectors of the Customs, June 1, 1791, in Syrett, ed., *Hamilton Papers,* 8:191–193, 341–342, 409; Bray Hammond, *Banks and Politics in America from the Revolution to the Civil War* (Princeton, NJ, 1957), 125; White, *Federalists,* 119–127, 349–352.

40. White, *Federalists,* 42–43, 122–123, 135–136, 146–147; Hart, *American Presidency,* 70.

41. Treasury Department Circular to the Captains of the Revenue Cutters, June 4, 1791, in Syrett, ed., *Hamilton Papers,* 8:426–433; the quote is on 432.

tional bank. Hamilton submitted his report on a bank when Congress reconvened in December. The essential features were that the bank was to be incorporated by Congress as a private institution, that the federal government would subscribe to one-fifth of the stock and have inspection rights, and that three-quarters of the subscription price of the stock held by private investors could be paid in the highest grade government securities. In effect, government debt—the certificates of which had reached par on the open market and were therefore "as good as gold"—was to be used as the basis for money, as it would be through most of the nation's history. It was a sound scheme, destined to provide the country with a convenient, necessary, stable, and elastic currency, though it struck some people as resembling sleight of hand or mirror tricks. Indeed, Hamilton himself said that "opinion" was the "soul of credit," and that it was "affected by appearances, as well as realities."42

Some members of Congress, steeped in the suspicions and hostility toward paper transactions of the English country-party ideology, reacted instantly and strongly against the bank proposal. The more serious threat came from two sources that were related to one another but only tangentially to the bank. Both concerned the location of the capital. The act providing for the Potomac as the permanent site also provided that Philadelphia should be the capital until the federal city was constructed. When Jefferson and Madison arrived in Philadelphia for the December, 1790, session of Congress, they were shocked to learn that the Pennsylvania delegates were openly declaring "that they never intended to aid in a removal" of the capital; indeed, the Pennsylvania legislature had appropriated money to build permanent federal buildings in Philadelphia. Virginians and Marylanders feared that if the bank were established in Philadelphia, it would be impossible to move the capital. Accordingly, Madison worked feverishly to limit the duration of the bank's charter to ten years so that it would expire when the capital was scheduled to be moved. When the effort failed Madison adopted the stance that Congress had no constitutional authority to incorporate a bank, but

42. McDonald, *Hamilton,* 192–195; Report on a National Bank, Dec. 13, 1790, in Syrett, ed., *Hamilton Papers,* 7:305–342; the quoted passages are at 6:97.

the House rejected his argument by an almost two-to-one margin. Nearly two-thirds of those who sided with Madison were from Virginia and Maryland.[43]

President Washington was seriously upset by the raising of the constitutional issue, partly because he trusted Madison's judgment in such matters but also because of another concern. The law had required the president to appoint a commission to choose among various sites for the capital on the Potomac between two designated points. Instead Washington picked the area himself, three miles further downstream from the southeasternmost designated spot. The choice was nearer to Mount Vernon and increased the value of his holdings, as he admitted. It was generally assumed that whenever a president found it expedient to act contrary to law, he should at the first opportunity ask Congress for indemnification, which Washington proceeded to do. The House promptly passed the measure, but champions of the bank in the Senate held back, using indemnification as insurance against a veto of the bank bill. Thus while Randolph, Jefferson, and Hamilton were giving their solicited opinions on the constitutionality of the bank—the celebrated "strict constructionist" arguments of the first two and the "loose constructionist" argument of the third—the question whether Washington would sign the bank bill hinged on an entirely different pivot. On the tenth day after the bill passed Congress (the constitutionally mandated last day for signing), Washington signed. Immediately the Senate approved the indemnification bill.[44]

43. Theodore Sedgwick to Mrs. Sedgwick, Dec. 26, 1790, Joseph Jones to James Monroe, Jan. 27, 1791, and William L. Smith's *Politics of a Certain Party*, all as quoted in Kenneth R. Bowling, "Politics in the First Congress, 1789–1791," Ph.D. diss., University of Wisconsin, 1968, 233–235; editorial note on locating the federal district, in *The Papers of Thomas Jefferson*, ed. Julian Boyd et al., 24 vols. to date (Princeton, NJ, 1950–1990), 19:3–58; Fisher Ames to Thomas Dwight, Feb. 7, 1791, and to George Richards Minot, Feb. 17, 1791, in *The Works of Fisher Ames*, ed. William B. Allen, 2 vols. (Indianapolis, IN, 1983), 2:862–865; Benton, ed., *Abridgment of Debates in Congress*, 1:274–278, 306–308 (Feb. 2, 8, 1791).

44. These matters are analyzed and documented at length in McDonald, *Hamilton*, 202–210. See also Benjamin B. Klubes, "The First Federal Congress and the First National Bank: A Case Study in Constitutional Interpretation," *Journal of the Early Republic* 10 (1990):21–41; Kenneth R. Bowling, "The Bank Bill, the Capital City, and President Washington," *Capitol Studies* 1 (1972):59–71.

———— One byproduct of the clash over the bank was a development that the Framers of the Constitution had totally failed to anticipate: the emergence of political parties. Parties were not unprecedented in America, to be sure. Several colonies had had rudimentary
court parties and country parties, Pennsylvania had a well-developed
two-party system, and a powerful faction had gathered around
George Clinton in New York; but these were local or transient affairs.
It was almost universally believed that parties—or factions, as they
were commonly called—posed a mortal threat to republics because
they were by definition (as Madison put it) "a number of citizens,
whether amounting to a majority or minority of the whole, who are
united and actuated by some common impulse . . . adverse to the
rights of other citizens, or to the permanent and aggregate interests
of the community." Madison argued persuasively in *Federalist* 10 that
the structure of the government under the Constitution, together
with the extent and the diversity of the country, would prevent any
faction from obtaining and holding a majority for a dangerous length
of time.[45]

He changed his mind in the spring of 1791 after Jefferson became
convinced and then convinced him that Hamilton had organized a
"money phalanx" through which he dominated Congress and by
which he intended to implement his sinister ends. The occasion for
Jefferson's conversion to all-out opposition was a dinner party held
about two months after Washington approved the bank bill. Jefferson was engaging in conversation with Hamilton and John Adams
when Adams said that if the British government were purged of its
corruption and if representation in the Commons were made more
democratic, "it would be the most perfect constitution ever devised
by the wit of man." Hamilton, echoing an observation made by
David Hume, replied that if the English government were purged of
corruption and representation were equalized, "it would become an
impracticable government: as it stands at present, with all its sup-

45. On the matter of parties generally, see Ketcham, *Presidents Above Party*. In
Federalist 10 Madison also developed the idea of filtering popular views through "a
chosen body of citizens, whose wisdom may best discern the true interest of their
country, and whose patriotism and love of justice will be least likely to sacrifice it to
temporary or partial considerations."

posed defects, it is the most perfect government which ever existed." Upon hearing these words, Jefferson concluded that the whole tenor of Hamilton's system—which he had previously thought of simply as a series of measures to establish public credit—revealed a design to corrupt America and reduce it under a monarchy.[46]

Consciously or unconsciously, Jefferson set out to thwart Hamilton in ways that Bolingbroke had prescribed to check Walpole more than half a century earlier. Bolingbroke had suggested an appeal to a Patriot King; Jefferson appealed to Washington, but Washington, remembering his years as head of an ill-supplied and ill-paid army, regarded Hamilton's establishment of public credit as virtually miraculous and could not be persuaded that Hamilton was the principal behind a nefarious plot. Bolingbroke, it will be recalled, had also suggested the organization of a party—not a narrow and self-interested one of the sort Madison had described but a country party of the whole people. Such a party would exist until it could gain control of government and undo the evil work; then, the Constitution restored to its original purity, the party would wither away.[47]

Jefferson and Madison began to organize their "republican" party forthwith, presumably with a view toward gaining control of Congress in the 1792 elections and, if Washington should retire as expected, of the presidency itself. They established contact with anti-Hamilton political leaders in New York (Clinton, Robert R. Livingston, Aaron

---

46. *The Anas of Thomas Jefferson,* ed. Franklin B. Sawvel (New York, 1970), 36–37. Hamilton had expressed the same sentiment in the Constitutional Convention; speech of June 22, 1787, in Syrett, ed., *Hamilton Papers,* 4:216–217 (Yates's minutes). For David Hume's original formulation, see *Essays Moral, Political, and Literary,* ed. Thomas Hill Green and Thomas Hodge Grose, 2 vols. (1964; repr. of London, 1882 ed.), 3:120–121.

47. *The Literary Bible of Thomas Jefferson: His Commonplace Book of Philosophers and Poets,* ed. Gilbert Chinard (Baltimore, 1928), 20, 34, says that Bolingbroke was possibly the strongest single influence on Jefferson's thinking. See, for example, Jefferson to Washington, May 23, and to Lafayette, June 16, 1792, in *Thomas Jefferson: Writings,* ed. Merrill D. Peterson (New York, 1984), 985–991. See also Lance Banning, *The Jefferson Persuasion: Evolution of a Party Ideology* (Ithaca, NY, 1978). For Bolingbroke on the Patriot King and parties, see chapter 3 of this book. For Jefferson's account of Washington's reaction, see his *Anas,* Oct. 1, 1792, in Peterson, ed., *Jefferson: Writings,* 681–682.

Burr). They set up an opposition newspaper and managed to subsidize it at government expense: Jefferson took on its editor, Philip Freneau, as a superfluous translator in the State Department; Madison pushed through Congress a cheap postal rate for newspapers. And they coordinated a series of attacks against Hamilton to commence when Congress reconvened in November of 1791. The offensive continued throughout 1792, both in newspapers and by Madison and his supporters in Congress. Washington was spared personal assault until his second term, but he took criticism of his administration as criticism of himself.[48]

Hamilton and Washington were confused and angered by it all. They were conscious of their rectitude and of the value of their services to the country; they could not imagine that anything other than the basest motives were behind the attacks. Furthermore, in the absence of a concept of a loyal opposition—which began to evolve in England in the 1820s but not in America until later—they tended to regard attacks upon governmental policy as attacks upon government, as sedition. Recollection of recent American history, of armed resistance to the federal tax on whiskey in the back country of North Carolina and Pennsylvania and of the open use of seditious language by some of the administration's critics, exacerbated their defensiveness.

All this boded ill for the tranquillity of the republic.

48. The standard work on the subject is Noble E. Cunningham, Jr., *The Jeffersonian Republicans: The Formation of Party Organization, 1789–1801* (Chapel Hill, NC, 1957). See also Lewis Leary, *That Rascal Freneau* (New Brunswick, NJ, 1941); Harry M. Tinkom, *The Republicans and Federalists in Pennsylvania, 1790–1801* (Harrisburg, PA, 1950); Carl E. Prince, *New Jersey's Jeffersonian Republicans: The Genesis of an Early Party Machine, 1789–1817* (Chapel Hill, NC, 1967); Alfred F. Young, *The Democratic Republicans of New York: The Origins, 1763–1797* (Chapel Hill, NC, 1967); Morton Borden, *Parties and Politics in the Early Republic, 1789–1815* (New York, 1967); William N. Chambers, *Political Parties in a New Nation: The American Experience, 1776–1809* (New York, 1963); Adrienne Koch, *Jefferson and Madison: The Great Collaboration* (New York, 1950); George Dangerfield, *Chancellor Robert R. Livingston* (New York, 1960); Herbert S. Parmet and Marie B. Hecht, *Aaron Burr: Portrait of an Ambitious Man* (New York, 1967); Samuel H. Wandell and Meade Minnigerode, *Aaron Burr,* 2 vols. (New York, 1925). Much of the literature on the subject exhibits an anti-Hamilton bias.

———— The timing of the formation of an opposition party was unfortunate, for it coincided with revolutionary France's intrusion into American affairs. The United States was tied to France by gratitude for its help in winning independence and by the "perpetual" treaty of alliance of 1778. Most Americans cheered when the French Revolution began in 1789, perceiving it as a reform movement approved by Louis XVI, whom they regarded as a great champion of liberty; most, except the more ardent republican ideologues, had stopped cheering by the time they learned of the king's execution in 1793. Meanwhile, France declared war against Prussia and Austria, and shortly afterward it dispatched Citizen Edmond Genet as a special minister to enlist the United States in the cause of liberating the world. The Americans were not expected to join France as a belligerent—the alliance extended only to defensive wars—but to work in concert to extend the "empire of liberty" and to punish colonial powers by cutting off trade with them. Genet was assigned three specific duties: obtain American foodstuffs for France, use American ports as bases for privateering, and enlist American citizens in private expeditions to reconquer Canada, Florida, and Louisiana. Genet arrived in Charleston in April, 1793, and began a tour northward toward Philadelphia, handing out privateering commissions along the way.[49]

Washington, understanding that to incur the hostility of Great Britain could be catastrophic, asked his cabinet for ideas about how to preserve neutrality. Jefferson, who usually took the position that the management of foreign affairs was exclusively an executive function, now let francophilia sway his judgment, arguing that since only Congress could declare war, it alone could declare neutrality; a presi-

49. Harry Ammon, *The Genet Mission* (New York, 1973), 25–53; Alexander De-Conde, *Entangling Alliance: Politics & Diplomacy under George Washington* (Durham, NC, 1958), 197–203. See also editor's note to cabinet meeting of April 19, 1793, in Syrett, ed., *Hamilton Papers*, 14:329. Regarding Washington's early thinking about the Revolution, see Jefferson's account of a conversation of December 27, 1792, in Sawvel, ed., *Anas of Jefferson*, 100–102; his changed attitude is implicit in his letter to Jefferson and Hamilton, April 12, 1793, in Fitzpatrick, ed., *Writings of Washington*, 32:415–416; his conviction that internal instability would doom revolutionary France is expressed in a letter to Henry Lee, May 6, 1793 (32:450).

dential proclamation of neutrality would be unconstitutional. Hamilton and Knox urged that such a proclamation could and should be issued. (Hamilton even induced Jay to draft one. So much for protestations about the separation of powers.) Washington agreed with them, and on April 22 he issued the proclamation.[50]

There followed a war of words between Hamilton and Madison, conducted under pseudonyms in the newspapers, over the nature and extent of presidential authority. Hamilton, in articles signed Pacificus, maintained that the executive was constitutionally "the *organ* of intercourse between the Nation and foreign Nations," that the president's power to receive ambassadors and other foreign ministers carried with it power to recognize or deny recognition to a regime, that the Senate's authority to ratify treaties and confirm diplomatic appointments were minor exceptions to the general grant of presidential power conveyed by the vesting clause, and that those exceptions "ought to be extended no further than is essential to their execution." He did not contend that the president could by proclamation make new law, but he held that the neutrality proclamation merely "proclaims a *fact* with regard to the *existing state* of the Nation." Hamilton based his argument on the "broad and comprehensive ground" that the federative powers inhere in the executive; he said he could also have justified the proclamation solely on the constitutional clause charging the president to "take care that the laws be faithfully executed," for "our Treaties and the laws of Nations form a part of the law of the land." To the end of executing the laws, the proclamation informed citizens what the laws were and warned "that these laws will be put in execution against the Infractors."

50. Washington to Gouverneur Morris, March 25, to David Stuart, April 9, to Jefferson, April 12, to Hamilton, April 12, to Knox, April 12, Proclamation of Neutrality, April 22, 1793, in Fitzpatrick, ed., *Writings of Washington*, 32:402–403, 414, 415–417, 430–431; "For the Gazette of the United States," March-April 1793, Hamilton to Jay, April 9, 1793 (two letters), Jay to Hamilton, April 11, 1793, Washington to cabinet members, April 18, 1793, cabinet meeting, April 19, 1793, Carrington to Hamilton, April 26, 1793, Hamilton and Knox to Washington, May 2, 1793, in Syrett, ed., *Hamilton Papers*, 14:267–269, 297–298, 299–300, 307–308, 326–329, 346–352, 367–396; entries of April 18, May 7, 1793, in Sawvel, ed., *Anas of Jefferson*, 118–121.

Clearly, Washington shared Hamilton's interpretation; he issued proclamations with some frequency through the remainder of his term.[51]

Madison, writing under the pseudonym Helvedius, took a stance at variance with the position he and Jefferson would hold as presidents. Defying history and logic he insisted that neither the power to declare war nor the power to make treaties was properly executive in nature. "The natural province of the executive magistrate is to execute laws, as that of the legislature is to make laws." The president could serve as "a convenient organ" of communication in dealing with foreign governments, which might influence Congress' decisions, but he could have no part in the decisions themselves. The war and treaty powers were more nearly legislative than executive, Madison maintained, as was the power to recognize the legitimacy of a regime. As for the fact that the Constitution gave the treaty-making power to the president and two-thirds of the Senate as opposed to the simple majority required "in all other cases," Madison saw that as a "substitute or compensation" for participation by the House as in other legislation. The statement, in addition to being wrong about "all other cases," was scarcely the most persuasive argument Madison ever made.[52]

51. "Pacificus 1," in Syrett, ed., *Hamilton Papers,* 15:33–43. Hamilton does not use the term federative power, but as Robert Scigliano points out in "The War Powers Resolution and the War Powers," in Bessette and Tulis, ed., *Presidency in the Constitutional Order,* 151 n. 37, Hamilton's description of the executive power in *Federalist* 78 is almost identical to Locke's in *Two Treatises,* second treatise, chap. 1, para. 3. For examples of other presidential proclamations, see, for instance, Fitzpatrick, ed., *Writings of Washington,* 33:304, 305, 457–461, 507–509, concerning disturbances in the west and resistance to the federal excise. The arguments of both Hamilton and Madison are succinctly summarized in the introduction by Richard Loss to *The Letters of Pacificus and Helvidius with the Letters of Americus* (Delmar, NY, 1976), v-xiii.

52. "Helvidius," 1 and 3, in *The Papers of James Madison,* volume 15, ed. Thomas A. Mason et al. (Charlottesville, VA, 1985), 15:69–73, 97–98. In other numbers Madison scored against Hamilton by quoting his narrower descriptions of executive power in the *Federalist.* The pseudonym Helvidius was adopted from Helvidius Priscus, a first-century A.D. Roman who defended the privileges of the Senate against encroachments by the emperors.

To proclaim neutrality was one thing, to enforce it quite another. French agents boldly used American ports to equip privateers, and French consuls, on Genet's instructions, acted as prize courts. The obvious agents for policing such activity were the customs collectors, but when Hamilton proposed employing them Jefferson protested vehemently, saying that to do so would make them "an established corps of spies or informers against their fellow citizens." Instead, Jefferson proposed using grand juries, an ineffectual method. Randolph did bring proceedings against two Americans who were serving on board a French privateer, but absent a federal law against recruiting and given his uncertain grasp of the law of nations Randolph based the prosecution on the common law offense of disturbing the peace. Both Americans were acquitted. Washington thought it best to employ the state governors to enforce the neutrality proclamation. The governors were inadequate to the task, and in August Washington adopted Hamilton's original suggestion.[53]

Genet's activities were tangentially connected with another law enforcement problem. He had promoted the organization of about three dozen "democratic-republican societies," political action clubs that formed the extreme left wing of the republican party. The most radical societies were in western Pennsylvania, a hotbed of resistance to the collection of the federal excise on whiskey. In the summer of 1794 the members and assorted hooligans engaged in a good deal of violence, launching an armed attack against and burning the house of the excise inspector, robbing the mails, tarring and feathering collectors, defying court orders, and organizing a march on Pittsburgh by a mob of five or six thousand armed men. County and state officials, when they did anything, supported the insurgents.[54]

53. John J. Reardon, *Edmund Randolph* (New York, 1975), 231–232; Hamilton to Washington, May 15, and editor's note thereto, Treasury Circular to Customs Collectors, May 30, Jefferson to Hamilton, June 1, Hamilton to Rufus King, June 15, 1793, in Syrett, ed., *Hamilton Papers*, 14:451–460, 499, 508–510, 547–549; entry of May 20, 1793, in Sawvel, ed., *Anas of Jefferson*, 122–123; White, *Federalists*, 215–217; Charles Warren, *The Supreme Court in United States History*, 2 vols. (Boston, 1922, 1926), 1:105–117. The Supreme Court declared the prize courts illegal in 1794.

54. Eugene Perry Link, *Democratic-Republican Societies, 1790–1800* (New York, 1942), 145–148 and passim; Leland D. Baldwin, *Whiskey Rebels: The Story of a Frontier*

Orders to desist being ignored, Washington determined to suppress the rebellion by force. Under the Militia Act of 1792, the president was authorized to call out the militia if a federal judge certified that the laws of the United States were being opposed "by combinations too powerful to be suppressed by the ordinary course of judicial proceedings." Justice James Wilson so certified in August, and Knox, on the president's instructions, wrote to the governors of New Jersey, Pennsylvania, Maryland, and Virginia to mobilize a total of 12,950 men. In September the forces were assembled and began marching westward with Washington himself in command. He stayed with the troops for three weeks, then turned them over to Gov. Henry "Light-Horse Harry" Lee. Resistance disappeared; several thousand men fled down the Ohio to Kentucky, a few score people were arrested, twenty were taken to Philadelphia and tried for treason, and two were convicted. Washington pardoned them.[55]

Though Jefferson, who had long since left the government, scoffed that "an insurrection was announced and proclaimed and armed against, but could never be found," Washington's handling of the episode was skillful. The guiding principle was, as Hamilton put it in another context, "Whenever the Government appears in arms it ought to appear like a *Hercules*," for the respect it thus inspires is likely to prevent the necessity for bloodshed. Presidents who followed that maxim in suppressing rebelliousness generally succeeded. Washington also set a key precedent in the aftermath of the Whiskey Rebellion. Through General Lee, he granted a blanket amnesty to the insurgents—thereby simultaneously indicating that the president's pardoning power extends to a general dispensing of the laws and

Uprising (Pittsburgh, PA, 1939), 10, 25–28, 73, 92–98, 108–109, 113–155; Thomas P. Slaughter, *The Whiskey Rebellion: Frontier Epilogue to the American Revolution* (New York, 1986); deposition of Francis Mentges, Aug. 1, Hamilton to Washington, Aug. 5, 1794, in Syrett, ed., *Hamilton Papers,* 17:2–6, 49–58, and notes thereto; Jacob E. Cooke, "The Whiskey Insurrection: A Re-evaluation," *Pennsylvania History* 30 (1963): 316–346.

55. Cooke, "Whiskey Insurrection"; McDonald, *Hamilton,* 299–302; M. E. Bradford, " 'Light Horse Harry' Lee, A Forgotten Forefather," in *Against the Barbarians and Other Reflections on Familiar Themes* (Columbia, MO, 1992), 114–127.

showing a magnanimity that strengthened his administration in the eyes of the public.[56]

Other major issues regarding the executive arose from a diplomatic mission that was under way even as the Whiskey Rebellion was being suppressed. During the previous winter, Britain had evoked a questionable doctrine in international law to seize about 300 American ships in the West Indies. Federalists as well as Republicans clamored for war. Washington, heeding the advice of Hamilton and a handful of senators, followed a policy of preparing for war but negotiating for a peaceful settlement of differences. He sent Chief Justice Jay to London as a minister plenipotentiary. The resulting treaty was not unflawed from an American point of view, but it preserved the peace, secured some commercial concessions, and pioneered the settlement of international disputes by arbitration commissions. Republicans organized protest rallies and petition drives against ratification. They had not actually seen the treaty, for its terms were kept secret until it was considered by the Senate; but they opposed any amicable agreement with Britain and sensed that the treaty could be turned into an advantageous political issue. Despite their efforts, the Senate ratified during the summer of 1795 by the narrowest constitutional margin, twenty to ten. The extent of the opposition, however, caused Washington to hesitate, and Randolph (who had succeeded Jefferson at State) urged him not to sign it. Then documents were intercepted, seemingly showing that Randolph had sought French bribes to influence American policy. In a fit of rage, Washington reacted by signing the treaty.[57]

56. John Alexander Carroll and Mary Wells Ashworth, *George Washington: First in Peace* (New York, 1957), 217, n. 23; Hamilton to James McHenry, March 18, 1799, in Syrett, ed., *Hamilton Papers,* 22:552–553. Equally skillful was Washington's handling of the rebellion in North Carolina. Inaccessibility made a massive military incursion impossible, and so he did not venture one. Instead he used the proclamation power and then ignored noncompliance; Jeffrey J. Crow, "The Whiskey Rebellion in North Carolina," *North Carolina Historical Review* 66 (1989):1–28, interprets the episode differently.

57. The standard work on the subject is Samuel Flagg Bemis, *Jay's Treaty* (New York, 1923); see also Jerald A. Combs, *The Jay Treaty: Political Battleground of the Founding Fathers* (Berkeley, CA, 1970). My own analyses are in McDonald, *Hamilton,* 290–294, 315–319, and *Presidency of Washington,* 134–136, 141–144, 149–156, 160–165.

The matter did not end there. In March of 1796 Congressman Edward Livingston of New York introduced a resolution requesting the president to provide the House with copies of the papers relevant to the negotiation of Jay's Treaty. The partisan expectation was that the papers would reveal politically juicy information for use in the upcoming elections. The constitutional question, whether the House had a right to see the papers, turned on the point that arbitration commissions provided by the treaty would require appropriations—which could be initiated only in the House. The deeper issue, one that has never been and perhaps cannot be answered satisfactorily, centered on how much information the executive could properly withhold from Congress or the public in the interest of national security. The House debated the resolution for three weeks, passing it on March 24 with the significant qualification, "excepting such of the said papers as any existing negotiation may render improper to be disclosed."[58]

Washington responded with a thundering refusal. Placing his damaged but still great prestige on the line, he said that the papers were not "relative to any purpose under the cognizance of the House of Representatives, except that of an impeachment, which the resolution has not expressed." He went on to lecture Congress: Secrecy in the conduct of foreign relations was occasionally necessary, he said, and though that could be dangerous, the Constitution reduced the danger by making the Senate, but not the House, privy to these matters. The purpose of employing the Senate in that way was to protect the states; senators represented states as states, and accord-

---

Jay's mission was, of course, another example of mixing judicial and executive powers. Mercy Warren, in her *History of the Revolution,* 2:667, says that "sensible protests were entered in the senate, against the blending of office." On the "affair Randolph," see Irving Brant, "Edmund Randolph, Not Guilty!" *William and Mary Quarterly* 7 (1950):180–198; Mary K. Bonsteel Tachau, "George Washington and the Reputation of Edmund Randolph," *Journal of American History* 73 (1986):15–34.

58. White, *Federalists,* 63–64; James Thomas Flexner, *George Washington: Anguish and Farewell (1793–1799)* (Boston, 1972), 265–276; Hamilton to William L. Smith, March 20, and to King, April 15, 1796, in Syrett, ed., *Hamilton Papers,* 20:72–74, 114–115; William B. Hatcher, *Edward Livingston: Jeffersonian Republican and Jacksonian Democrat* (Baton Rouge, LA, 1940).

ingly the Senate was vested with certain powers not shared with the House. Washington concluded by observing that the House had been implementing treaties for seven years without ever asserting a right to do otherwise and that the Constitutional Convention had explicitly rejected a motion that treaties not be binding until they were ratified by a law. After a month of sometimes angry debate, the House voted by a narrow margin to appropriate the funds without seeing the requested papers.[59]

————— Washington's decision to retire at the end of his second term had both positive and negative sources. On the one hand, he could take satisfaction in knowing that the government and the presidency had been firmly established as viable and stable institutions. On the other, the level of political discourse had degenerated so abysmally as to make continued service unacceptable to him. For more than three years he had been forced to endure calumnies that mounted steadily in shrillness and intensity. He was charged with being "infamously niggardly" in private dealings; it was said that "gambling, reveling, horseracing and horse whipping" had been the essentials of his education, that he was "a most horrid swearer and blasphemer," even that he had taken British bribes when he commanded American troops. His subordinates fared no better, being denounced variously as rascals, liars, jackals, drunks, demagogues, atheists, and fops. In public, Washington retained his poise, but in private, as Jefferson later recalled, he suffered "more than any person I ever yet met with," and many a time he interrupted cabinet meetings to indulge in tirades against the opposition press or in fits of self-pity.[60]

Nor did matters improve under his successor. John Adams was

59. Washington's message, March 30, 1796, is in Fitzpatrick, ed., *Writings of Washington,* 35:2–5. Pres. Richard Nixon cited the precedent, but the circumstances were different: In Nixon's case the House actually was considering impeachment. The question of secrecy in the conduct of foreign relations in modern times is treated in chapter 14 of this book.

60. McDonald, *Presidency of Washington,* 184; *New-York Journal,* Dec. 7, 1793; *National Gazette,* March 2, 1793; Jefferson to Madison, June 9, 1793, in Peterson, ed., *Jefferson: Writings,* 1011. For a new approach to the second term, see North Callahan, *Thanks, Mr. President: The Trail-Blazing Second Term of George Washington* (New York, 1992).

elected president in 1796 by a three-vote margin over Jefferson, with the result that the country had a president and a vice-president from opposing political parties. Adams, uncertain as to appropriate procedures, retained Washington's cabinet until 1800, when he suddenly became convinced that they were Hamilton's lackeys and summarily fired the lot of them. Meanwhile, he had blundered the nation into an undeclared (but congressionally sanctioned) naval war with France, then wrecked his party by initiating a peace move that resulted in an abrogation of the 1778 treaties. While the quasi-war was being fought, Virginia threatened to take up arms against the United States and a band of rebels in Pennsylvania actually did so.[61]

Thus it was that the need for presidential leadership was as great in 1800 as it had been in 1789.

61. For the Adams presidency, see Ralph A. Brown, *The Presidency of John Adams* (Lawrence, KS, 1975); Stephen G. Kurtz, *The Presidency of John Adams: The Collapse of Federalism, 1795–1800* (Philadelphia, 1957); and Manning Julian Dauer, *The Adams Federalists* (Baltimore, 1968).

CHAPTER **10**

The Jeffersonians

Thomas Jefferson came almost as close to being indispensable during the transitional period 1800–1801 as Washington had been during the transition of 1787–1789. The nation was blessed with freedom, prosperity, and peace, and yet for five years its public councils had been plagued by rancor, divisiveness, and mistrust so extreme as to border on paranoia. Federalists referred to Republicans as "the sect," "the faction," or "the democrats," using each term pejoratively, and were perfectly convinced that if the Republicans came to power the result would be Jacobinism and the guillotine. (At stake, Hamilton said, was "true liberty, property, order, religion and of course *heads*.") The Republicans referred to Federalists as "the sect," "the faction," or "the monocrats," again pejoratively, and were entirely certain that if they remained in power the result would be monarchy and hereditary aristocracy. In these circumstances, for a variety of reasons, Jefferson and possibly Jefferson alone could restore tranquillity and sanity to the body politic and ensure that the transfer of power be constitutional, orderly, and safe.[1]

1. The Hamilton quotation is from Hamilton to Robert Troup, April 13, 1795, in *The Papers of Alexander Hamilton,* ed. Harold C. Syrett et al., 26 vols. (New York, 1961–1979), 18:329. For a similarly unrestrained view from the other side, see Jefferson to Stephens Thomson Mason, Oct. 11, 1798, in *The Writings of Thomas Jefferson,*

Not least among the reasons was a negative: When Jefferson and his Republican minions won control of government, they would not be cursed with having Jefferson and his Republican minions in opposition. Some Federalist newspapers attacked Jefferson viciously, but most Federalists found distasteful the rough and tumble of popular politics at which Republicans excelled; and the Federalist party, which had never been particularly well organized, rapidly began to fade. When Jefferson proved to be a champion of a strong executive branch— as Hamilton had predicted, over the skepticism of other Federalists— it became easier and easier to accept his regime. Ultras remained in opposition, but so thoroughly did the Republicans dominate politics that by 1804 internal schisms posed a greater threat to the administration than Federalists did. By 1807 even John Quincy Adams, the son of the Federalist former president, was calling himself a Republican.[2]

On the positive side Jefferson could pose and be depicted by his partisan press as a man of the people, which neither of his predecessors had been able (or willing) to do, and that endeared him to the multitudes. He was in fact a member of what he called the "natural aristocracy," one of the common herd whom the common herd recognizes as being of them but better. Beyond that, Jefferson was widely known as the author of the Declaration of Independence; he could be and was described as the Father of American Liberty, even as Washington was understood to be the Father of His Country.[3]

The elements that made Jefferson the man for the occasion in 1800–1801 were idiosyncratic. In keeping with the best traditions of the Virginia gentry, he felt obliged to devote his life to public service,

---

ed. Andrew A. Lipscomb and Albert Ellery Bergh, 20 vols. (Washington, DC, 1903–1904), 10:61–62. The partisan newspapers of the period teem with near-paranoia.

2. Regarding the inept efforts of Federalists to adapt to popular politics, see David Hackett Fischer, *The Revolution in American Federalism: The Federalist Party in the Era of Jeffersonian Democracy* (New York, 1965). See also William N. Chambers, *Political Parties in a New Nation, 1776–1809* (New York, 1963), and Linda K. Kerber, *Federalists in Dissent: Imagery and Ideology in Jeffersonian America* (Ithaca, NY, 1970).

3. For an excellent study of the subject of which this paragraph is a small part, see Merrill Peterson, *The Jeffersonian Image in the American Mind* (New York, 1960). Regarding the natural aristocracy, see Jefferson to John Adams, Oct. 28, 1813, in Lipscomb and Bergh, ed., *Writings of Jefferson*, 13:394–403.

and he spent thirty-five years in various offices; but he rarely found it pleasurable. He was an intensely private man, never comfortable in large groups. He had a passionate aversion to (one might say almost a fear of) confrontation, argument, and disharmony. He was therefore polite, deferential, and conciliatory even in dealing with people he despised. His enemies regarded him as timid, irresolute, and spineless, and when he acted differently behind their backs from the way he did in their presence, devious, slippery, and hypocritical. However accurate their assessment, one does not have to be an utter cynic to recognize that deviousness, slipperiness, and hypocrisy—if combined, as they were in Jefferson, with persuasiveness, charm, and a firm sense of purpose—are priceless political assets.[4]

The implication of these personality traits for the presidency is that they led Jefferson to wield power, not by direct exercise of his constitutional authority, but by bargaining, persuasion, and the careful husbanding or expenditure of his counters in the political game. He endeavored, successfully, to create the impression that Congress, representing the people, was the branch of government that properly expressed the popular will and that the president's function was simply to carry that will into execution. Yet he and his subordinates drafted and steered through Congress more legislation than the Washington and Adams administrations combined, and his requests for legislation were rarely rejected. In sum, he ran the government masterfully and more thoroughly than his predecessors and all but a handful of his successors, and he took bold foreign policy initiatives into the bargain.[5]

4. This sketch of Jefferson is drawn from a study of his writings, the observations made by such enemies as Hamilton and such converts to admiration as Federalist Sen. William Plumer of New Hampshire (in *William Plumer's Memorandum of Proceedings in the United States Senate, 1803–1807,* ed. Everett Somerville Brown [New York, 1923]), and the various major biographies of Jefferson. Especially interesting in regard to the interplay between his personal makeup and his style of leadership is Robert M. Johnstone, Jr., *Jefferson and the Presidency: Leadership in the Young Republic* (Ithaca, NY, 1978), 32ff. and passim. Johnstone argues convincingly that Jefferson's presidency is a good case study of leadership in accordance with the principles analyzed in Richard Neustadt's influential book, *Presidential Power* (New York, 1964).

5. Johnstone, *Jefferson and the Presidency;* Noble E. Cunningham, Jr., *The Jeffersonian Republicans in Power: Party Operations, 1801–1809* (Chapel Hill, NC, 1963), passim; Gary J. Schmitt, "Jefferson and Executive Power: Revisionism and the 'Rev-

But there was a flaw in his scheme of things. His methods could be effective only with a man of Jefferson's gifts at the helm. The other "Jeffersonian" presidents—Madison, Monroe, and John Quincy Adams—more or less failed because the machinery that Jefferson had employed to exert his will could be and was used to frustrate the will of his successors.

——— Jefferson's presidency saved the office and possibly the Union, but the process by which he became president imperiled both. Indeed it triggered a nearly fatal constitutional crisis, for the outcome of the presidential election of 1800, far from being a triumph of the people over special interests, as Jeffersonian mythmakers had it, resulted from the machinations of wily backstage political operators. Almost two-thirds of the 138 electors were chosen by state legislatures, not the voters. President Adams actually gained electoral votes over the number he had received in 1796—except in New York. Aaron Burr, by consummate manipulation, enabled the Republicans to take control of that state's legislature, and hence its twelve electoral votes, in the April state elections. Hamilton proposed to Gov. John Jay to call the outgoing legislature, which was Federalist-dominated and would not expire until fall, into a special session and urge it to change the election laws in the direction of democracy. Specifically, he wanted New Yorkers to vote directly by districts for presidential electors. That would have ensured the defeat of the Jefferson-Burr ticket though not necessarily the election of Adams, for Hamilton planned that some Federalist electors should vote for Adams's "running mate," Charles Cotesworth Pinckney, but not for Adams—thus making Pinckney president. Jay, however, declined to interfere, and the two Republicans carried New York and received a total of seventy-three electoral votes apiece, a majority and a tie.[6]

---

olution of 1800,'" in *American Models of Revolutionary Leadership,* ed. Daniel J. Elazar and Ellis Katz (Lanham, MD, 1992), 149–171.

6. Bureau of the Census, *Historical Statistics of the United States: Colonial Times to the Present* (Washington, DC, 1961), 681; introductory note for Hamilton to Theodore Sedgwick, May 4, Hamilton to Jay, May 7, Hamilton to Sedgwick, May 8, 10, introduc-

The tie dramatized the need for a constitutional amendment, and the events that followed made it all the more pressing. The Constitution provided that in such circumstances the election should be decided in the House of Representatives, in which, for the occasion, each state's delegation would have one vote. As it happened, the Federalists had a majority in the outgoing House, but they controlled only six delegations. Eight were dominated by Republicans, and two were evenly divided, meaning that without Federalist votes Jefferson could not be elected. When the balloting began on February 11, 1801, Federalists lined up solidly for Burr, even though the Republican electors had clearly intended that Jefferson be president.[7]

The deadlock continued, day after day, and time became a factor. The Sixth Congress would expire on March 4; the newly elected Seventh Congress was not scheduled to convene until late in the year. It began to appear that if the Federalists continued to hold out, one of two possibilities might result. Perhaps Burr could persuade a few Republicans to switch and vote for him; a handful of venal representatives were available for the purpose. The other prospect was as ominous. The Constitution (Article 2, Section 1, paragraph 6) empowers Congress to designate by law the officer who succeeds to the presidency in case both the presidency and the vice-presidency become vacant—as would have happened if the House reached no decision by March 4—and Federalists began to talk of passing a presidential succession act, whereby the president pro tem of the Senate would become president and serve until the next election, in 1804. It

---

tory note for Hamilton to Benjamin Stoddert, June 6, Letter . . . Concerning the Public Conduct and Character of John Adams, Oct. 24, 1800, in Syrett, ed., *Hamilton Papers*, 24:443–453, 464–467, 470, 474–475, 574–585, 25:169–234; Noble E. Cunningham, Jr., *The Jeffersonian Republicans, 1789–1801* (Chapel Hill, NC, 1957), 176–185; Morton Borden, "The Election of 1800: Charge and Countercharge," *Delaware History* 5 (1952):42–62; Beatrice G. Reubens, "Burr, Hamilton, and the Manhattan Company," *Political Science Quarterly* 72 (1957):578–607 and 73 (1958):100–125. For Burr, see *Political Correspondence and Public Papers of Aaron Burr*, ed. Mary-Jo Kline, 2 vols. (Princeton, NJ, 1983), and Milton Lomask, *Aaron Burr: The Years from Princeton to Vice President, 1756–1805* (New York, 1979).

7. Cunningham, *Jeffersonian Republicans, 1789–1801*, 239–244; Jefferson to Tench Coxe, Feb. 11, 1801, in Lipscomb and Bergh, ed., *Writings of Jefferson*, 10:198.

was widely reported that John Marshall, recently appointed as chief justice, had given a legal opinion that Congress under those conditions could appoint a president, and it was rumored that Marshall himself was being contemplated for the office.[8]

To have the election stolen, even if constitutionally done, would have been intolerable to Republicans. As Jefferson wrote, they declared "openly and firmly, one and all, that the day such an act passed, the Middle States [including Virginia] would arm, and that no such usurpation, even for a single day, should be submitted to." Furthermore, the Republicans would call "a convention to reorganize the government, and to amend it. The very word convention," Jefferson added, infused Federalists with "the horrors," given "the present democratical spirit of America." Faced with those prospects, the Federalists attempted to negotiate terms. Whether they obtained them was and is disputed, but in any event enough representatives changed their votes on February 17 to elect Jefferson president.[9]

The crisis passed, and the transition was completed without further incident. But the electoral college system was clearly not working the way it was designed to work, and another tie at another time might not be peacefully resolved. Accordingly, before the next election Congress passed and the requisite number of states ratified the Twelfth Amendment, requiring electors to vote separately for president and vice-president.

——— To Jefferson's way of thinking, the roles of chief of state and harmonizer were of one piece. Despising and fearing the tendencies

8. Jefferson to Monroe, Feb. 15, to Madison, Feb. 18, 1801, in Lipscomb and Bergh, ed., *Writings of Jefferson,* 10:201–204; Charles Warren, *The Supreme Court in United States History,* 2 vols. (Boston, 1922, 1926), 1:182–183. The literature about John Marshall is large; see, for example, Albert J. Beveridge, *The Life of John Marshall* (Boston, 1944), Robert Kenneth Faulkner, *The Jurisprudence of John Marshall* (Princeton, NJ, 1968), William Melville Jones, *Chief Justice John Marshall: A Reappraisal* (Ithaca, NY, 1956), and R. Kent Newmyer, *The Supreme Court under Marshall and Taney* (New York, 1968).

9. Jefferson to Monroe, Feb. 15, 1801, in Lipscomb and Bergh, ed., *Writings of Jefferson,* 10:201–202; Merrill D. Peterson, *Thomas Jefferson and the New Nation: A Biography* (New York, 1970), 643–651; Dumas Malone, *Jefferson the President: First Term, 1801–1805* (Boston, 1970), 11–14, 487–493.

he perceived as monarchical in the Washington and Adams administrations and attributing the bitter discord to them, he set out to republicanize the presidency in a manner he believed accorded with the desires of all but a handful of extremists. His fusion of the roles was evident at his inaugural, where he appeared the epitome of simplicity and moderation. Shortly before noon on March 4 he left the boarding house where he shared common table with more than thirty others, walked to the Capitol, took the oath of office, and delivered an inaugural address on which he had labored long and hard.[10]

"The genius of the address," as Merrill Peterson has written, "lay in its seemingly artless elevation of the Republican creed to a creed of Americanism." Listing "the essential principles of our Government," Jefferson included "equal and exact justice to all men, of whatever state or persuasion, religious or political; peace, commerce, and honest friendship with all nations, entangling alliances with none"; preservation of the rights of states in domestic affairs and of the general government "in its whole constitutional vigor" in relation to other nations; majority rule, tempered by reason and protection of the rights of the minority; "economy in the public expense"; "the honest payment of our debts and sacred preservation of the public faith" (Federalists had feared that Jefferson would repudiate the public debt); reliance on the militias "in peace and for the first moments of war, till regulars may relieve them"; "encouragement of agriculture, and of commerce as its handmaid"; and "freedom of religion; freedom of the press, and freedom of person." He believed that Americans, except for a few diehard monarchists, supported these principles, and indeed most Federalists approved them; Hamilton regarded the address as "virtually a candid retraction" of the positions Jefferson had held when in opposition.[11]

Jefferson urged Americans to "unite with one heart and one mind" to avoid recapitulating the violence and fanaticism of the Old World.

10. The inauguration is described in the Washington *National Intelligencer,* March 6, 1801; see also Malone, *Jefferson: First Term,* 1–2.

11. Peterson, *Jefferson,* 655; James D. Richardson, comp., *Messages and Papers of the Presidents,* 10 vols. (Washington, DC, 1889–1905), 1:321–324; "An Address to the Electors of the State of New-York," March 21, 1801, in Syrett, ed., *Hamilton Papers,* 25:365.

Americans differed on political matters, "but every difference of opinion is not a difference of principle. We have called by different names brethren of the same principle. We are all republicans, we are all federalists." Some "honest men," he continued, "fear that a republican government can not be strong," but he believed the American government, "the world's best hope," to be "the strongest Government on earth," for it was "the only one where every man, at the call of the law, would . . . meet invasions of the public order as his own personal concern." Recent American history belied much of this, as Jefferson knew full well, but he understood that a president must speak to the higher aspirations of the people, that they strive together to be better than they are.[12]

As for the ceremonial, ritualistic, and symbolic functions of the presidency, Jefferson seemed to reject them entirely. In actuality he adapted them to republicanism. He ostentatiously disdained ostentation. He shunned display, protocol, and pomp; he gave no public balls, held no levees, had no public celebrations of his birthday. He abandoned the monarchical ritual of appearing in person before the legislative branches and afterward exchanging formal messages. When Jefferson had anything to say to Congress, he sent his secretary with a written note. He refused to follow Washington's precedent of making a grand tour of the country, being "not reconciled to the idea of a chief magistrate parading himself through the several states as an object of public gaze." He staged no entertainments for the public, but he kept his doors open to every citizen. He never held court for government officials or, though he understood the ritualized niceties of European diplomacy, for foreign ministers. Instead, he held an endless succession of small dinner parties, invitations to which were handwritten and signed not "The President of the United States," as Washington and Adams had signed, but simply "Th: Jefferson." There were rarely more than twelve guests at a time, and the seating was pell-mell. The wines and food were superb (his entertainment costs ate up much of his salary), but the atmosphere was one of studied

---

12. Richardson, comp., *Messages and Papers of the Presidents*, 1:322. Richardson capitalizes "Republicans" and "Federalists," but see Peterson, *Jefferson*, 656, which makes it clear that Jefferson used lowercase letters.

casualness, of the country squire at home to friends. Unwigged, casually dressed, Jefferson charmed his guests with easy conversation that ranged from art and architecture through mathematics and music to zoology. By stripping from everyone pretense and the trappings of status, he established a milieu in which he was quite without a peer. In the intimate surroundings in which he was host and master of the house, he was clearly the first among equals.[13]

By his manner and with the help of a partisan press that praised him endlessly, Jefferson won a popularity that matched that of Washington. There was, however, a fundamental difference between Jefferson's popularity and Washington's. Washington had been revered as a demigod and as the symbol of the nation. Jefferson, by completing the transition from monarchy to republicanism, humanized the presidency and served as a symbol not of the nation but of the people. That gave the presidential office a prestige and an informal set of powers that transcended by far the formal authority granted by the Constitution—powers that would be operative even during the numerous administrations when the White House was occupied by mediocrities or worse.[14]

——— Though the Republicans initiated the party system and used the party as a means of gaining and exercising power, there were Bolingbrokean limits beyond which they would not go. Neither Jefferson nor his Republican successors, for example, deigned to campaign actively or to solicit votes directly. Nor did they use federal patronage to win votes. That would have smacked too much of Walpole or, as Republicans believed, of Hamilton.[15]

13. Brown, ed., *Plumer's Memorandum*, 211–213, 543–547; Jefferson to Nathaniel Macon, May 14, 1801, in Lipscomb and Bergh, ed., *Writings of Jefferson*, 10:260–262; Jefferson to James Sullivan, June 19, 1807, as quoted in Johnstone, *Jefferson and the Presidency*, 235; Malone, *Jefferson: First Term*, 92–95, 370–376; Robert R. Davis, Jr., "Pell-Mell: Jeffersonian Etiquette and Protocol," *Historian* 43 (1981): 509–529.

14. Johnstone, *Jefferson and the Presidency*, 36–41 and passim; Peterson, *Jeffersonian Image*, 3–14 and passim.

15. See Ralph Ketcham's persuasive study, *Presidents Above Party* (Chapel Hill, NC, 1984). See also Sidney H. Aronson, *Status and Kinship in the Higher Civil Service: Standards of Selection in the Administrations of John Adams, Thomas Jefferson, and Andrew Jackson* (Cambridge, MA, 1964).

Indeed, Jefferson at first intended to make minimal changes in personnel. He considered Adams's "midnight appointments"—those made between December of 1800, when the results of the voting in the electoral college were known, and March 3, 1801, when Adams was still signing commissions—to be null and void. Judicial appointees who had been delivered their commissions were beyond his reach, but for the others Jefferson summarily refused to recognize the validity of their appointments. A dozen or two officeholders he removed on grounds of misconduct. He intended to dismiss none for differences of political opinion except those who proved to be irreconcilably and overtly monarchists. The federal marshals and district attorneys, he believed, needed to be replaced, partly because many of them packed juries and because Federalists did monopolize the federal bench. Otherwise, except at the cabinet level, he planned to appoint Republicans to fill vacancies as they occurred, without resorting to his removal power.[16]

Pressure from supporters hungry for federal jobs, however, especially in New York and New England, impelled him to modify that approach. In July of 1801 he published a reply to a remonstrance from a committee of merchants in New Haven, therein announcing a revised policy. Certain remarks in his inaugural address, he wrote—declarations "in favor of *political tolerance,* exhortations to *harmony* and affection . . . and to respect for the *equal rights* of the minority"—had been "misconstrued into assurances that the tenure of offices was to be undisturbed." The "will of the nation," he continued, "calls for an administration of government according with the opinions of those elected." The number of vacancies occurring through death were few and by resignation none, and thus some officers must be removed. (Elsewhere he suggested that Republicans should have at least half the important offices, whereas a survey indicated that as of September 198 of these were held by Federalists and only 30 by Republicans.) The chore was painful, Jefferson declared, but it was his duty and he would meet it, proceeding cautiously so that it might

16. Jefferson to William B. Giles, March 23, to Henry Knox, March 27, to Elbridge Gerry, March 29, 1801, in Lipscomb and Bergh, ed., *Writings of Jefferson,* 10:238–243, 246–247, 251–255.

"injure the best men least, and effect the purposes of justice and public utility with the least private distress; that it may be thrown, as much as possible, on delinquency, on oppression, on intolerance, on ante-revolutionary adherence to our enemies."[17]

There was a turnover, but nothing like wholesale change. Two years after the reply to the New Haven merchants, it was estimated that of the revenue officers, marshals, and district attorneys, 151 were Republicans, 15 neutrals, and 122 Federalists. How many Federalists were removed solely for political reasons cannot be determined. In the summer of 1802 Jefferson drew up a list of twenty-four such, but a year later he reclassified the causes of removals—he had by then removed about a third of the officers subject to his direct removal—and assigned different reasons, so that none was classified as purely political.[18]

Jefferson's Republican successors were more sparing in their use of the removal power. Madison removed twenty-seven during his eight years in the White House. (William H. Crawford once observed that Madison could not bring himself to fire people for "simple incapacity.") Monroe removed the same number during his eight years, and John Quincy Adams removed twelve during his four years, even though the number of officers had increased a great deal since 1816.[19]

Before the Jeffersonian era came to a close, however, the seeds of a radical change had been sown and would bear bitter fruits under the Jacksonian presidents and long afterward. Though it had generally been conceded that the removal power belonged exclusively to the president, in 1820 Congress altered the rules by passing a Tenure of Office Act, providing that district attorneys and the principal officers who had anything to do with the collection and disbursement of

17. Jefferson to Elias Shipman and others, July 12, 1801, ibid., 10:268–273; Cunningham, *Jeffersonian Republicans in Power*, 18–29.

18. Cunningham, *Jeffersonian Republicans in Power*, 60–63.

19. Leonard D. White, *The Jeffersonians: A Study in Administrative History, 1801–1829* (New York, 1951), 379–380; Mary W. M. Hargreaves, *The Presidency of John Quincy Adams* (Lawrence, KS, 1985); J. E. D. Shipp, *Giant Days or the Life and Times of William H. Crawford* (Americus, GA, 1909); Harry Ammon, *James Monroe: The Quest for National Identity* (New York, 1971); George Dangerfield, *The Era of Good Feelings* (New York, 1952).

money should thenceforth be appointed to serve fixed terms of four years. Present incumbents would be phased out at stated intervals, the last of them leaving office on September 30, 1821. Jefferson and Madison both thought the act unconstitutional and a dangerous reduction of necessary presidential responsibility. So did Monroe, who had signed it into law before someone called the issue to his attention and caused him to revise his opinion. The way for the introduction of the spoils system opened by the act was broad and inviting.[20]

———— In matters of administration, Jefferson's primary goal was to undo the Hamiltonian fiscal system, and in that effort he had mixed results. He was unable to abolish the budgeting and spending practices that he had railed against when he was in the opposition. As early as 1802 he was writing, "When this government was first established, it was possible to have kept it going on true principles, but the contracted, English, half-lettered ideas of Hamilton, destroyed that hope in the bud. We can pay off his debt in 15. years: but we can never get rid of his financial system." Jefferson's secretary of the treasury, Albert Gallatin, sought diligently for a time to get Congress to make itemized appropriations, but he finally gave it up as impractical. Indeed, the Jeffersonians resumed the Hamiltonian practice of taking money that had been appropriated for one purpose and using it for another—and went even further. In 1803, for example, Jefferson bound the government to spend $15 million for the purchase of Louisiana (only $2 million had been appropriated, and that secretly). In 1807, in the wake of the British firing on USS *Chesapeake,* Jefferson ordered the spending of considerable sums for naval armament without waiting for Congress to reconvene and appropriate the money; he was by law authorized to make emergency expenditures, and Congress subsequently formally approved his action.[21]

20. White, *Jeffersonians,* 387–388.

21. Jefferson to Dupont de Nemours, Jan. 18, 1802, as quoted ibid., 146–147; ibid., 112–115; Louis Fisher, *Constitutional Conflicts between Congress and the President,* 3d ed., rev. (Lawrence, KS, 1991), 248. Lucius Wilmerding, Jr., *The Spending Power* (New Haven, CT, 1943), 4, 6–7, 9–12, 13, 55, 63–64 and n. 25, 75–76, 194; Alexander Balinky, *Albert Gallatin: Fiscal Theories and Policies* (New Brunswick, NJ, 1958).

In one minor instance Jefferson temporarily declined to spend money that had been appropriated. Early in 1803 Congress had voted $50,000 for fifteen gunboats to patrol the Mississippi River. When the Louisiana Purchase was consummated, the patrol no longer seemed necessary, and for about a year Jefferson "impounded" the funds. That raised but did not settle a constitutional question: whether appropriations are mandatory or permissive. The clause requiring the president to "take Care that the Laws be faithfully executed" (Article 2, Section 4) would seem to indicate that they are mandatory, but the negative wording of the appropriations clause (Article 1, Section 9) would suggest the opposite: "No Money shall be drawn from the Treasury, but in Consequence of Appropriations made by Law." As will be seen, a number of presidents impounded funds occasionally during the nineteenth century, and it became a common practice during the twentieth.[22]

In two respects the Jeffersonians did undo Hamilton's system. The first was temporary. In 1811 the charter of the Bank of the United States expired, and though both Madison (by then president) and Gallatin (still secretary of the treasury) had come to regard it as necessary under the meaning of the "necessary and proper" clause of the Constitution and urged its recharter, Congress rejected it. The Bank went out of business just in time for the War of 1812, with the result that the capacity of the government to raise funds was totally deranged. Too late, a chastened Congress chartered the second Bank in 1816.[23]

The other achievement had to do with reduction of the public debts. By instituting stringent (and, insofar as they concerned military preparedness, short-sighted) economies, Gallatin cut the debt from $83 million to $45 million by the beginning of the war, despite the Louisiana Purchase. The debt soared during the war, reaching $127 million in 1816. Under Monroe and John Quincy Adams it was

22. See chapter 11 of this book. Arthur M. Schlesinger, Jr., *The Imperial Presidency* (Boston, 1973), 235, belittles the Jefferson precedent for impoundment; it was indeed minor, but it was a precedent. See also Fisher, *Constitutional Conflicts*, 128–129.

23. Bray Hammond, *Banks and Politics in America from the Revolution to the Civil War* (Princeton, NJ, 1957), 209–226, 230–243.

reduced by more than half, and in Jackson's last year it was fully retired.[24]

One more point about administration under the Jeffersonians is noteworthy. Jefferson's cabinet meetings, which were frequent, were invariably harmonious; the members were able men who respected and liked one another and saw eye to eye on matters of consequence, and, as Jefferson put it, "the power of decision in the President left no object for internal dissension." Under his successors there was considerable disharmony. Madison saw fit to ask for the resignation of his war and navy secretaries because of policy disagreements, and Monroe insisted on imposing conditions before he agreed to serve as Madison's secretary of state. Monroe assembled a stellar cabinet when he became president, but its meetings were frequently attended with rancor as department heads jockeyed to succeed him. The climax came when he and Secretary of the Treasury Crawford got into a heated argument about appointments. As John Quincy Adams described the scene, Crawford made a petulant remark, whereupon "Mr. Monroe replied with great warmth, saying that he considered Crawford's language as extremely improper and unsuitable to the relations between them." Crawford turned to him, "raised his cane, as in the attitude to strike, and said, 'You damned infernal old scoundrel!' Mr. Monroe seized the tongs at the fireplace for self-defence" and said he would ring for servants to "turn him out of the house." Crawford calmed down, said he had intended no insult, and left. "They never met afterwards."[25]

———— In dealing with Congress, Jefferson framed a conception of the role of the executive that made a lasting contribution to the presidency. His predecessors had been essentially passive in their relations with Congress. That is to say, they supplied Congress with facts, called problems to its attention, and sometimes suggested that

24. Bureau of the Census, *Historical Statistics of the United States* (Washington, DC, 1961), 721.

25. White, *Jeffersonians*, 60–67; Jefferson to Desutt de Tracy, Jan. 11, 1811, as quoted in Johnstone, *Jefferson and the Presidency*, 86; *The Diary of John Quincy Adams, 1794–1845*, ed. Allan Nevins (New York, 1969), 353–354, Dec. 14, 1825; Ketcham, *Presidents Above Party*, 124–130.

Congress might want to consider legislation on a particular subject, but they did not think it proper to propose specific laws, let alone draft legislation to submit to Congress. Jefferson perceived that to rely upon Congress to generate its own leadership was to invite drift, lack of system, or—what was worse—sporadic stampedes that produced such legislation as the Alien and Sedition Acts. The president and his cabinet were in a better position to be well informed than congressmen were; the president alone, as Jefferson put it, could "command a view of the whole ground" as representative of the nation and not merely of a state or a congressional district; the concentration of authority in one disinterested servant of the whole gave him a decisiveness as well as a vision that the other branches lacked. In his inaugural address Jefferson asked Congress to "guide and support" his efforts to "steer . . . the vessel," but it was he who would do the steering.[26]

Yet he was extremely careful not to offend the amour propre (what Americans at the time called self-love) of the congressmen, collectively or individually. He was always deferential to them, referring to them as the "grand council" to whom was entrusted "the sovereign functions of legislation." He made sure that they had repeated opportunities to share his table, taking care that his invitees formed compatible company. He rarely drafted proposed legislation, and when he did he avoided the appearance of violating the principle of the separation of powers by having a trusted intimate in Congress introduce the measure as the congressman's own. Gallatin drew up a great deal of proposed legislation and worked closely with the House in seeing it enacted—a practice Republicans had protested fiercely when Hamilton had done it—but that, too, was acceptable to Congress because Gallatin had been the Republicans' financial brain during his six years in the House; his activity as secretary was simply a continuation of the role the members were accustomed to. Those exceptions aside, Jefferson had merely to hint at what he wanted, and Congress gave it to him. For example, in his first annual message, he wrote, "The judiciary system of the United States, and especially that por-

26. Richardson, comp., *Messages and Papers of the Presidents*, 1:324; Johnstone, *Jefferson and the Presidency*, 114–161; White, *Jeffersonians*, 45–59.

tion of it recently erected, will of course present itself to the contemplation of Congress"; no one could fail to understand that he was calling for the repeal of the Judiciary Act of 1801. Repeal came soon.[27]

Not least among the reasons for Jefferson's success as legislator-in-chief was the support of his party, which had been organized and at least at first held together to implement a limited set of policy objectives. To ensure that this ready-made backing stayed in line, Jefferson used two institutional mechanisms that had been developed by congressional Republicans. The first was the caucus: informal meetings of party members designed at the beginning for nominating candidates but rapidly transformed into sessions devoted to working out legislative positions and strategy. The other was the floor leader. When Jefferson took over, congressmen such as John Randolph of Roanoke, William Branch Giles, Joseph H. Nicholson, and Nathaniel Macon had already won positions of leadership among Republicans, and Jefferson worked through them. As time went on, he and his successors tended to designate floor leaders (often more than one at a time) who obtained their support not from their own prior achievements but from having the ear and the blessings of the president.[28]

The close harmony between president and Congress was marred by a few sour notes during Jefferson's second term. Part of the discord came from John Randolph of Roanoke, who broke with Jefferson over various policy decisions, but Randolph and his "Tertium Quid" were never able to mount much opposition. Other dissonance re-

27. White, *Jeffersonians*, 50–53; Johnstone, *Jefferson and the Presidency*, 171–176; Richardson, comp., *Messages and Papers of the Presidents*, 1:331. A revealing letter concerning Jefferson's ways with Congress is Jefferson to Barnabas Bidwell, July 5, 1806, in Lipscomb and Bergh, ed., *Writings of Jefferson*, 11:114–118.

28. Johnstone, *Jefferson and the Presidency*, 130–139; Cunningham, *Jeffersonian Republicans in Power*, 71–100, and Noble E. Cunningham, Jr., *The Process of Government under Jefferson* (Princeton, NJ, 1978). William C. Bruce, *John Randolph of Roanoke, 1773–1833*, 2 vols. (New York, 1922); Russell Kirk, *John Randolph of Roanoke* (Chicago, 1964); Dice R. Anderson, *William Branch Giles* (Menasha, WI, 1914); William E. Dodd, *The Life of Nathaniel Macon* (Raleigh, NC, 1903); Noble E. Cunningham, Jr., "John Beckley: An Early American Party Manager," *William and Mary Quarterly* 13 (1956): 40–52; "William Plumer's Biographical Sketches of James A. Bayard, Caesar A. Rodney, and Samuel White," ed. John A. Munroe, *Delaware History* 4 (1950/1951): 354–377.

sulted from a mistake that Jefferson made early in the second term when he announced that he would follow Washington's precedent and retire after having served eight years. As Sen. William Plumer recorded in his diary, *"Most men shun* [a setting] *but all seek the rising sun. . . .* as soon as its known that the incumbant at the end of the term is to return to private life—a vast multitude that would be his advocates— trumpeters of his fame—turn their attention to his successor—& make a merit of blaming—censuring—& perhaps, defaming the incumbent." Plumer's prediction came to pass and caused Jefferson great pain, but it only slightly impaired his legislative effectiveness.[29]

Two aspects of Jefferson's relations with Congress were of ongoing importance. An ancient maxim, cited by Taube among others, was that *delegata potestas non potest delegari*—"delegated power cannot be delegated"—but practice showed it was sometimes necessary to delegate legislative powers. The precedent was not original with Jefferson's Congress—the act authorizing Washington to pick a site for the District of Columbia was regarded by some people as an unconstitutional delegation—but it became a norm under Jefferson. The discretionary power to reassign appropriations from one object to another confirmed a pattern that was repeatedly followed under his successors. The Non-Intercourse Act of 1809, for instance, closed American trade with Britain and France but authorized President Madison to reopen trade with either if in his opinion certain conditions were met. On the basis of misinformation he opened trade with Britain; when he learned of his mistake he closed it again by presidential proclamation having the force of law.[30]

Another concern was secrecy in government. Common sense supported the view shared by Washington and Hamilton that "confiden-

29. Cunningham, *Jeffersonian Republicans in Power*, 71–100; Brown, ed., *Plumer's Memorandum*, 453; Lynn W. Turner, *William Plumer* (Chapel Hill, NC, 1962). Though Jefferson's intention to retire after the second term was not public knowledge until late winter of 1806, he had informed friends of his plans more than a year earlier; Jefferson to John Taylor, Jan. 6, 1805, in Lipscomb and Bergh, ed., *Writings of Jefferson*, 11:56–58. He said also that he would have preferred it if the president had been chosen for a single seven-year term and been ineligible for reelection.

30. The question of delegation of legislative power to the executive is discussed in Fisher, *Constitutional Conflicts*, 85–88.

tiality" was sometimes necessary in the executive, especially in the conduct of foreign relations, but the Republicans in opposition had denounced executive secrecy as impermissibly dangerous in a republic. Once in power, they practiced secrecy and outright deception in dealing with Congress and the public. For instance, in his annual message to Congress in December of 1802, Jefferson made only passing reference to the Spanish retrocession of Louisiana to France, though the administration was so concerned that Jefferson was considering negotiating an alliance with the despised British. Two days later, in an action that was made to appear spontaneously hostile to the president but was in fact carefully orchestrated, the House adopted a resolution demanding to see the executive papers relating to the recent closing of New Orleans to American trade. That stratagem was designed to and did accomplish a dual purpose. It convinced the French minister to the United States that Jefferson would be forced by his own partisans to adopt an aggressive policy toward Louisiana, perhaps involving seizure of New Orleans. And it disarmed Federalists who desired an aggressive policy. Shortly thereafter, upon hearing that Napoleon might be disposed to sell New Orleans, Jefferson asked for and got a secret appropriation of $2 million for the purpose.[31]

Perhaps the most striking instance of secrecy and deception occurred in 1805. Through much of that year Jefferson took a well-publicized bellicose stance against Spain, preparing the public for a contemplated seizure of Florida. In November, however, he changed his mind and decided he could persuade Napoleon to exert pressure on Spain to sell Florida. It would be difficult to reverse positions publicly, given the hostility that he had aroused toward France and Spain. To get around the problem, he opted to be candid with Congress but quite otherwise with the public. Accordingly, he prepared two messages for the upcoming congressional session—one official and public, the other to be read behind closed doors. The public

31. Richardson, comp., *Messages and Papers of the Presidents,* 1:343; Henry Adams, *History of the United States during the Presidencies of Thomas Jefferson and James Madison,* 9 vols. (New York, 1889–1891), 1:427–433; Robert W. Tucker and David C. Hendrickson, *Empire of Liberty: The Statecraft of Thomas Jefferson* (New York, 1990), 108–110, 114.

version, delivered in the formal message presented on December 3, was hostile toward Spain and suggested the need to prepare for war. The private version informed Congress of the new turn in policy and asked for a secret appropriation of $2 million to supplement the secret appropriation of 1802, which had not been spent and remained essentially impounded.[32]

Obviously the Senate allowed Jefferson a free hand in the conduct of foreign relations, and the latitude became institutionalized and was passed to his successors. The extent to which the Senate abdicated its claims was dramatically encapsulated in a resolution of the Senate Committee on Foreign Relations, adopted on February 15, 1816, "The President," the committee opined, "is the constitutional representative of the United States with regard to foreign nations." He manages such matters "and must necessarily be most competent to determine when, how, and upon what subjects negotiation may be urged with the greatest prospect of success." He is responsible not to the Senate but "to the Constitution. The committee consider this responsibility the surest pledge for the faithful discharge of his duty. They think the interference of the Senate in the direction of foreign negotiations calculated to diminish that responsibility and thereby to impair the best security for the national safety." Dealing with foreign nations, the committee concluded, "requires caution and unity of design" and "frequently depends on secrecy and dispatch."[33] Hamilton himself could scarcely have expressed this Jeffersonian committee's views more clearly.

————— Jefferson also had occasion to exercise the executive's so-called war powers—powers as commander in chief—even though the country was not officially at war during his tenure, and he established a tentative beginning of a long series of precedents. Shortly after he took office a petty tyrant of a paltry satrapy, the pasha of Tripoli, declared war on the United States. For several years the United States,

32. Adams, *History of the United States,* 3:91, 99–102, 106–108, 111–139; Tucker and Hendrickson, *Empire of Liberty,* 180–187.

33. Senate Committee on Foreign Relations, resolution of Feb. 15, 1816, in *The Founders' Constitution,* ed. Philip B. Kurland and Ralph Lerner, 5 vols. (Chicago, 1987), 4:88–89.

like most other commercial nations having weak navies, had paid annual bribes called tribute to the assorted Barbary Coast princes in exchange for which the pashas and deys and beys abstained from plundering the private shipping of the paying nations. The pasha of Tripoli, having recently murdered his brother and usurped the throne, learned that Tripoli was receiving smaller payments than Algiers and Morocco were. Piqued by jealousy (and short on cash) he cut down the American flag, the traditional local way of announcing the opening of hostilities.[34]

In response, and in the absence of authorization by Congress, which would not be in session for months, Jefferson dispatched a four-ship squadron to protect American shipping in the region. The American warship *Enterprise* chanced upon, attacked, and almost destroyed a fourteen-gun Tripolitan vessel but permitted it to limp back to port without its guns and virtually without sails. Commodore Richard Dale, in command of the squadron, had been given blanket authority to seek out and destroy any Tripolitan craft he could find; he did not destroy this enemy vessel because he was under orders to proceed first to Malta for supplies. Later the squadron returned to chase and sink Tripolitans.[35]

That was not the way Jefferson chose to describe the episode to Congress in his first annual message on December 8, 1801. Instead, he painted an exaggerated picture of dangers to American shipping, described *Enterprise*'s encounter in heroic terms, and told Congress that the Tripolitan vessel had been released because he lacked constitutional authorization "without the sanction of Congress, to go beyond the line of defense." He asked Congress to authorize "measures

34. A. B. C. Whipple, *To the Shores of Tripoli: The Birth of the U.S. Navy and Marines* (New York, 1991); Louis B. Wright and Julia H. Macleod, *The First Americans in North Africa: William Eaton's Struggle for a Vigorous Policy against the Barbary Pirates, 1799–1805* (Princeton, NJ, 1945); Gardner W. Allen, *Our Navy and the Barbary Corsairs* (Boston, 1905); David A. Carson, "Jefferson, Congress, and the Question of Leadership in the Tripolitan War," *Virginia Magazine of History and Biography* 94 (1986):409–424.

35. Gary J. Schmitt, "Thomas Jefferson and the Presidency," in *Inventing the American Presidency,* ed. Thomas E. Cronin (Lawrence, KS, 1989), 337; Francis D. Wormuth and Edwin B. Firmage, *To Chain the Dog of War: The War Power of Congress in History and Law* (Urbana, IL, 1989), 23–25, 63.

of offense also." Accordingly, on February 6, 1802, Congress passed an act empowering the president to "employ such of the armed vessels of the United States" as he saw fit to protect American shipping against the Tripolitans and to "subdue, seize, and make prize of all vessels, goods and effects, belonging to the Bey of Tripoli, or to his subjects," and to order "all such other acts of precaution or hostility as the state of war will justify, and may, in his opinion, require."[36]

Under that act Jefferson sent a larger squadron in 1803 to blockade not just Tripoli but Algiers and Morocco as well. The war continued two more years, and the United States lost a superb vessel, the thirty-eight-gun frigate *Philadelphia,* but the blockade was immensely effective. For the first time in living memory, piracy vanished from the Mediterranean; no pirate at sea could get home, and none in port could go to sea.[37]

Madison had occasion to follow Jefferson's example. During the War of 1812 Algerian pirates resumed their plundering, and immediately after the war Madison sent a ten-vessel fleet to scour the seas of the brigands. Under Stephen Decatur the fleet did so, exacting tribute from the rulers of Tunis and Tripoli in the bargain. To make sure the pirates never rose again, Madison negotiated a deal with Spain whereby the navy established a permanent base at Port Mahon, on the island of Majorca, and cruised the Mediterranean on "friendly" visits for many years afterward. No longer did American merchantmen fear attack by the North Africans.[38]

36. Richardson, comp., *Messages and Papers of the Presidents,* 1:326–327; terms of the act as quoted by David Gray Adler, "The President's War-Making Power," in Cronin, ed., *Inventing the American Presidency,* 134–135. Adler fails to observe that Commodore Dale was under orders to go directly to Malta.

37. See the works cited in note 34 of this chapter and Christopher McKee, *Edward Preble: A Naval Biography, 1761–1807* (Annapolis, MD, 1972). Regarding *Philadelphia,* Tripolitans captured it when it ran aground in treacherous shallows, and the Americans destroyed it to keep them from using it. In considering Jefferson's handling of the matter, readers who are reminded of the Gulf of Tonkin Resolution and its aftermath (except for the dissimilarity of outcomes) are not indulging overactive imaginations.

38. Forrest McDonald, *The Boys Were Men: The American Navy in the Age of Fighting Sail* (New York, 1971), 144–145. Madison asked Congress for a declaration of war against Algiers; instead it only authorized the use of force against the dey of Algiers.

Madison also engaged in a form of warfare that Jefferson had contemplated, namely filibustering operations. Though these had been forbidden by an act of Congress, American civilians, with covert presidential approval and/or connivance, repeatedly moved as "settlers" into thinly inhabited territory possessed by Spain or (later) by Mexico, declared independence, won it after minor fighting, and asked to be annexed to the United States. (There is evidence, though it is not conclusive, that Aaron Burr's ill-fated expedition down the Mississippi was intended with Jefferson's approval as a filibustering venture.) In 1809 Madison covertly approved the movement of settlers into the area around Baton Rouge, on the Spanish side of the Mississippi. By the next spring the Americans had grown numerous enough (and Spain weak enough) that an attack on the Spanish became feasible. The Americans attacked in July, triumphed, declared themselves the independent Republic of West Florida, and invited the United States to annex them. On October 27, 1810, Madison issued a proclamation declaring that the area was a part of the Territory of Orleans.[39]

The following January Madison, taking the position (as Jefferson had) that the Louisiana Purchase had included Florida, obtained the secret approval of Congress to send former governor George Mathews of Georgia to "liberate" the Gulf Coast portion of Spanish Florida. Mathews was expressly ordered to take the place only if the inhabitants approved, but in light of what had happened at Baton Rouge he apparently assumed that stipulation to be merely a diplomatic nicety, designed to give the president a shield that would later become known

---

The action against Tunis and Tripoli was an executive extension, even as Jefferson's had been. Richardson, comp., *Messages and Papers of the Presidents*, 1:554, 562–563; Adams, *History of the United States*, 9:87, 105; Wormuth and Firmage, *To Chain the Dog of War*, 63–64. The latter work refers to the authorizations as "declarations of war," which strains the definition.

39. Johnstone, *Jefferson and the Presidency*, 195; Richardson, comp., *Messages and Papers of the Presidents*, 1:480–481, 484; Rembert W. Patrick, *Florida Fiasco: Rampant Rebels on the Georgia-Florida Border, 1810–1815* (Athens, GA, 1954), 8–11; Isaac J. Cox, *The West Florida Controversy, 1798–1813* (Baltimore, 1918). Regarding the possible complicity of Jefferson in Burr's western adventures, see my analysis in *The Presidency of Thomas Jefferson* (Lawrence, KS, 1976), 110–114, 120–128, 133–134.

as "deniability" in the event that something went wrong. In any case, in the fall Mathews marched with a force of 200 volunteers, but complications set in and Madison withdrew the navy, frustrating Mathews's plan to attack Saint Augustine. The forays into Florida established important precedents, however, for the way by which Jefferson's American Empire of Liberty would expand across the continent during the nineteenth century.⁴⁰

———— In dealing with the federal judiciary, Jefferson scored some points but was ultimately frustrated. His actions and policies concerning the courts derived partly from political and personal considerations, but they were grounded firmly in an interpretation of the Constitution that he and his adherents believed proper. Most Federalists believed that the final arbiter of constitutional questions was the Supreme Court. After 1800 it was in their political interest to take that position, since Republicans controlled the elective branches of government and Federalists totally dominated the judiciary—but the belief was nonetheless sincere. Jefferson believed, on the contrary, that the Constitution gave each branch the equal and coordinate power and duty to pass on constitutionality regarding matters entrusted to it; the states had such power and duty as well, in their respective spheres. The opinion, Jefferson insisted, that gave federal judges "the right to decide what laws are constitutional, and what not, not only for themselves in their own sphere of action, but for the legislature and executive also, in their spheres, would make the Judiciary a despotic branch."⁴¹

40. Patrick, *Florida Fiasco*, 14–15, 72–73, passim; Cox, *West Florida Controversy*, 328–332, 437–486; G. Melvin Herndon, "George Mathews, Frontier Patriot," *Virginia Magazine of History and Biography* 77 (1969):307–328; Paul Kruse, "A Secret Agent in East Florida: General George Mathews and the Patriot War, 1811–1812," *Journal of Southern History* 18 (1952):193–217. For Jefferson's concept of an "empire of liberty," see Drew R. McCoy, *The Elusive Republic: Political Economy in Jeffersonian America* (Chapel Hill, NC, 1980), 203–204; Wormuth and Firmage, *To Chain the Dog of War,* 66, 130.

41. Jefferson to Abigail Adams, Sept. 11, 1804, in Lipscomb and Bergh, ed., *Writings of Jefferson,* 11:51. Jefferson proposed to put his constitutional theory in the first annual message to Congress, but Madison and Gallatin persuaded him to delete the statement so as not to arouse unnecessary Federalist opposition; Johnstone, *Jefferson*

Jefferson's first significant use of his constitutional authority reflected that attitude. Republicans had fiercely objected to the Sedition Act of 1798, under which twenty-five Republican editors and printers had been prosecuted for seditious libel and ten were convicted and jailed or fined or both. The act had expired the day before Jefferson took office, but, wanting to underscore his position, he pardoned those who had already been convicted and stopped the prosecution of a case that was pending. At his request Congress voted to restore the fines with interest. The president explained his action: "The judges, believing the law constitutional, had a right to pass a sentence of fine and imprisonment; because the power was placed in their hands by the Constitution. But the executive, believing the law to be unconstitutional, were bound to remit the execution of it; because that power has been confided to them by the Constitution." He believed the law to be unconstitutional because the power to legislate on the subject of the press was not given to Congress at all. Yet, "while we deny that Congress have a right to control the freedom of the press, we have ever asserted the right of the States, and their exclusive right, to do so."[42]

The pardons might have been interpreted by the Federalists as throwing down a gauntlet except that they had beaten Jefferson to it. The Judiciary Act of 1801, enacted four days before Jefferson was inaugurated, embodied needed reforms, including that of relieving Supreme Court justices of the onerous burden of riding circuit, imposed by the organic Judiciary Act of 1789; but it also contained highly partisan trickery. It created sixteen new circuit judgeships,

---

and the Presidency, 167–168 and n. 13. As for the states, he wrote in the Kentucky Resolutions of 1798 that each had "an equal right to judge for itself" whether an act of Congress was constitutional (*Thomas Jefferson: Writings,* ed. Merrill D. Peterson [New York, 1984], 449). Charles Warren, in *Supreme Court,* 1:219–220, points out that among Jefferson's followers in Virginia and Kentucky, control of the federal judiciary was less a matter of constitutional principle than of concern about land titles—an observation that is reinforced by Kathryn Turner in "Federalist Policy and the Judiciary Act of 1801," *William and Mary Quarterly* 22 (1965):3–32.

42. Jefferson to Abigail Adams, Sept. 11, 1804, in Lipscomb and Bergh, ed., *Writings of Jefferson,* 11:50–51; James Morton Smith, *Freedom's Fetters: The Alien and Sedition Laws and American Civil Liberties* (Ithaca, NY, 1956).

which Adams promptly filled, and it took a slap at Jefferson by providing that when the next vacancy on the Supreme Court occurred, the number of justices would be reduced from six to five so that Jefferson could not make an appointment. As indicated, Congress repealed the 1801 act early in 1802, but Federalists protested that the repeal was unconstitutional because it removed the new circuit judges from their positions, which they constitutionally held "during good Behavior." To forestall a Supreme Court ruling on the matter, the time for the Court's sitting was changed so that it would not convene until 1803.[43]

This conflict set up the first of several confrontations that permanently affected the relations between the executive and judicial branches—the case of *Marbury* v. *Madison*. William Marbury had been one of Adam's midnight appointees (to a justiceship of the peace in the District of Columbia), but his commission, though signed, had not been delivered when Adams left the presidency. Marbury and three others sued Secretary of State Madison, who, though the law required him to deliver the commissions, was under direct orders from the president to withhold them. The Supreme Court declared that the commissions were due and that the proper remedy was a writ of mandamus against Madison. Having said that, the Court ruled that it did not have jurisdiction in the case because of a constitutional flaw in the Judiciary Act of 1789.[44]

Jefferson and his adherents struck back angrily, not at the Court's declaring part of an act of Congress unconstitutional—that was within what Jefferson called its proper "sphere"—but at Chief Justice John Marshall's asserting that the executive had violated the law and his implying that the executive branch was subject to orders from the Court. At Jefferson's gentle urging, Republicans in Congress set out to purge the bench through the impeachment process. As a test run, in 1803 the House impeached and in 1804 the Senate convicted and removed a federal district judge. Shortly afterward they trained their

43. Turner, "Federalist Policy and the Judiciary Act of 1801"; Warren, *Supreme Court*, 1:185–189, 204–222.

44. *Marbury* v. *Madison*, 1 Cranch 137; for an extended discussion, see Warren, *Supreme Court*, 1:231–268. See also Robert Lowry Clinton, *Marbury v. Madison and Judicial Review* (Lawrence, KS, 1989).

guns on the most vulnerable of the Supreme Court justices, Samuel Chase. Chase was not accused of "Treason, Bribery, or other high Crimes and Misdemeanors," the constitutionally specified grounds for impeachment, but of such indiscretions as browbeating young Republican attorneys and haranguing grand juries about the evils of democracy. Whether he would be convicted and removed would hinge upon whether the trial in the Senate was conducted on a political or a judicial basis, which in turn would depend largely on the outgoing vice-president, Aaron Burr, who would preside over the lame-duck session of the Senate early in 1805. Possibly to influence the outcome, Jefferson appointed Burr's relatives and friends to important positions in the Louisiana Territory, but Burr presided over the trial with rigorous impartiality, and Chase was acquitted. Plans for impeaching other justices were scrapped.[45]

The independence of the judiciary was thus ensured, but another round in the fight between Jefferson and Marshall was yet to come. In 1807 Marshall presided over the circuit court trial of Burr for treason, and during the proceedings Marshall issued a subpoena *duces tecum* to Jefferson, ordering the president to appear in the court and to bring certain documents with him. Jefferson refused to comply beyond submitting some, not all, of the subpoenaed documents to the district attorney, not to the court, with instructions that the attorney withhold such parts of the documents as he considered not "directly material for the purposes of justice." There was nothing that Marshall could do, and that was that.[46]

The results of the conflicts were mixed. On the one hand, the

45. Warren, *Supreme Court,* 1:269–297; Johnstone, *Jefferson and the Presidency,* 180–187; Adams, *History of the United States,* 2:143–159, 218–244; William H. Rehnquist, *Grand Inquests: The Historic Impeachments of Justice Samuel Chase and President Andrew Johnson* (New York, 1992), 11–132; James Haw et al., *Stormy Patriot: The Life of Samuel Chase* (Baltimore, 1980); John S. Elsmere, *Justice Samuel Chase* (Muncie, IN, 1980); *Report of the Trial of the Hon. Samuel Chase . . . Taken Shorthand by Charles Evans* (Baltimore, 1805); Richard B. Lillich, "The Chase Impeachment," *American Journal of Legal History* 4 (1960):49–72.

46. Dumas Malone, *Jefferson the President: Second Term, 1805–1809* (Boston, 1974), 314–325; *Reports of the Trials of Aaron Burr . . . Taken in Short Hand by David Robertson,* 2 vols. (Philadelphia, 1808), 1:114–172, 209–210; Johnstone, *Jefferson and the Presidency,* 202–207.

president was seemingly beyond the reach of the Court. On the other, the Court survived relatively unscathed and seemingly safe from political attack. But the balance was such that the Court did not declare another act of Congress unconstitutional for more than half a century.[47]

———— The one unmitigated failure of Jefferson's tenure in office, the embargo policy, demonstrated among other things that a president can maintain a firm grip on the reins of power and yet lose control of the course of events. The embargo, enacted in December, 1807, as a belated response to the British attack on USS *Chesapeake,* prohibited American vessels from obtaining clearances for foreign parts; it was variously considered as a step preparatory to war or as a means of avoiding war by reducing the likelihood of confrontations on the high seas. It swiftly evolved, however, through new enactments and executive policy, into an effort to prohibit trade with the outside world, by which means Jefferson fancied the United States could starve the European powers into ending their insane wars and their oppressive commercial restrictions. The experiment—a pioneering attempt to employ economic sanctions to end a war—may have been high-minded, but it was also simpleminded. It was as if a flea had tried to stop a dogfight by threatening suicide. Nonetheless, Jefferson employed ever more draconian means to enforce the policy, almost to the very end of his term.[48]

Jefferson grossly underrated the resistance the embargo policy would elicit in America. Opposition was minimal for a bit over two months, while the northern ports were still frozen; as soon as the

47. In 1838 the Supreme Court did rule that the circuit court for the District of Columbia could issue writs of mandamus to members of the executive branch in respect to the performance of "purely ministerial" (as opposed to "executive") duties. *Kendall v. U.S.,* 12 Peters 524; Warren, *Supreme Court,* 2:43–49. See also chapter 11 of this book.

48. For Jefferson's original understanding of the limited purposes of the embargo, see Jefferson to John Taylor, Jan. 6, 1808, in Lipscomb and Bergh, ed., *Writings of Jefferson,* 11:414; for the evolution toward use of it for economic sanctions, see McDonald, *Presidency of Jefferson,* 144–147; for a fuller account, see Adams, *History of the United States,* 4:152–177, and Tucker and Hendrickson, *Empire of Liberty,* 204–213, 222–228.

thaw began, ships cleared port in defiance of the law. Jefferson responded by asking for and obtaining from Congress legislation empowering collectors of the revenues to seize ships and cargoes, without warrants or the prospect of trial, upon the mere formation of a suspicion that a shipper or a merchant contemplated violating the embargo. He also obtained congressional authorization to use the army and navy to enforce the law. He declared, by proclamation, that the region around Lake Champlain—where some entrepreneurs from Vermont and upstate New York were transporting goods to Canada on rafts—was in a state of insurrection. He ordered state and federal officials, "and all other persons, civil and military, who shall be found within the vicinage," to suppress the supposed rebellion "by all means in their power, by force of arms or otherwise."[49]

Toward the end of May the enforcement policy received a setback in the courts, but not for long. The collector at Charleston had refused clearance for a ship with a cargo of cotton and rice consigned to Baltimore, not because he suspected any intention to violate the embargo but because he was bound by executive order. To Jefferson's chagrin, his own Supreme Court appointee, Justice William Johnson, issued a writ of mandamus ordering the clearance on the ground that the law empowered collectors (not the president) to detain on suspicion; the president had thus exceeded his legal authority in ordering a blanket policy. Jefferson's attorney general, Caesar Rodney, promptly issued a contrary opinion, which the administration followed thereafter—disregarding Johnson's decision. Rodney's opinion also rebuked Johnson harshly for interfering with the executive, and Congress subsequently overturned the ruling, in effect, by giving the president the general authority omitted in the earlier act.[50]

49. Adams, *History of the United States,* 4:249–289; Richardson, comp., *Messages and Papers of the Presidents,* 1:450–451; Leonard W. Levy, *Jefferson and Civil Liberties: The Darker Side* (New York, 1973), 107, 130–131, and passim; Walter W. Jennings, *The American Embargo, 1807–1809* (Iowa City, IA, 1921); Louis M. Sears, *Jefferson and the Embargo* (Durham, NC, 1927); Irving Brant, *James Madison: Secretary of State, 1800–1809* (Indianapolis, IN, 1953), 402–403.

50. Malone, *Jefferson the President: Second Term,* 592–594 and n. 28; Warren, *Supreme Court,* 1:324–338; Donald G. Morgan, *Justice William Johnson: The First Dissenter* (Columbia, SC, 1954), 55–74.

As the crisis wore on, as popular determination to resist and the administration's determination to suppress mounted, and as the Bill of Rights was repeatedly trampled, a significant feature of the constitutional order—one that would appear repeatedly in future—became manifest. In times of perceived national emergency the judiciary and the Congress usually offer no barriers to, and often abet, the exercise of power by the president. As Jefferson put it in 1808, in times of emergency "the universal resource is a dictator."[51]

Another feature evident from study of the crisis is that, though Jefferson was right when he said that the president is the only person in government who can "command a view of the whole ground," there are circumstances under which he can develop myopia. Specifically, the calamitous experience of the embargo showed that when the president has become accustomed to having his own way in running government he is apt to forget that there are limits to what government can do, no matter how skillfully it is managed. (Gallatin, who disapproved of the embargo from the outset, had some wise advice—paraphrased from Adam Smith—that the president unfortunately did not heed. "Governmental prohibitions," said Gallatin, "do always more mischief than had been calculated; and it is not without much hesitation that a statesman should hazard to regulate the concerns of individuals as if he could do it better than themselves.")[52]

———— Despite the continued success of his political party, Jefferson himself did not prove to be immune to the high cost in personal suffering that had afflicted Washington late in his second term and would beset other two-term presidents as well. During the winter of 1807–1808 Jefferson was rendered virtually helpless by migraine headaches, and they plagued him periodically for the remainder of his term. During his last four months in office he all but abdicated (except in regard to enforcing the embargo), saying that he preferred being "but a spectator" and pleading that he did not want to institute "measures which those who are to execute them"—the Madison ad-

51. Quotation from Jefferson to James Brown, Oct. 27, 1808, in Lipscomb and Bergh, ed., *Writings of Jefferson*, 12:183.

52. Quotation from Gallatin to Jefferson, Dec. 18, 1807, in *The Writings of Albert Gallatin*, ed. Henry Adams, 3 vols. (Philadelphia, 1879), 1:368.

ministration—"would disapprove." And to a friend, just before the end, he wrote, "Never did a prisoner, released from his chains, feel such relief as I shall on shaking off the shackles of power."[53]

In long-range terms Jefferson had established precedents and demonstrated techniques that vigorous presidents could employ to their advantage, but in the short run he spoiled things for those who immediately followed him. He bequeathed a foreign policy mess that the inept Madison could only worsen.[54] He left people in general and members of Congress in particular fed up with executive authority. The institutions he had employed effectively to manage Congress—a powerful Speaker of the House, floor managers, party caucuses—were used by congressional leaders to frustrate future presidents. Finally, Jefferson and his immediate successors displayed what became a pattern: With few exceptions, vigorously active presidents are likely to be followed by at least one or two chief executives who are considerably less so.

53. Jefferson to Levi Lincoln, Nov. 13, 1808, as quoted in Johnstone, *Jefferson and the Presidency*, 286; Jefferson to Dupont de Nemours, March 2, 1809, in Lipscomb and Bergh, ed., *Writings of Jefferson*, 12:259–260.

54. For a different, but persuasive, appraisal of the two presidents in terms of foreign affairs, see Robert Allen Rutland, *The Presidency of James Madison* (Lawrence, KS, 1990), 210–211.

Three

Evolution

It is a commonplace among students of the presidency that the two-plus centuries of American experience under the Constitution have been characterized by a general if irregular drift of authority and responsibility toward the executive branch. In truth, the preponderance of power has flowed in long-term trends from one branch to another, and now and again a balance has been reached. During the better part of the nineteenth century Congress predominated, as most though not all the Founders intended that it should. Legislative supremacy reached its peak upon the triumph of the Radical Republicans in Congress after the Civil War, at which time both the president and the Supreme Court were reduced to veritable ciphers. Soon thereafter corruption and incompetence ended the dominance of Congress; in the absence of vigorous executives and the lack of a tradition of a strong presidency, the Supreme Court was the most potent and effective instrument of government for roughly the last three decades of the century.

Then came a new equilibrium. By the end of the 1890s Congress had restored itself to respectability and infused its membership with discipline. The presidency was also energized. The presidents from McKinley through Hoover were much more active than any of their nineteenth-century predecessors save Jefferson and Lincoln. Consequently, for perhaps the only time in American history the three branches reached an approximate balance of power without impairing the effectiveness of the federal government.

The balance ended during Franklin Roosevelt's New Deal, and for almost forty years after Roosevelt's inauguration presidential power grew at a dazzling pace. Then, in reaction to the presidencies of Lyndon Johnson and Richard Nixon, Congress reasserted itself, passing a large number of enactments aimed at making the executive responsible to the legislative.

In one crucial respect, however, inflation of the presidency has been virtually uninterrupted, and that is in the area of what the people expect of their presidents. Because, as John Locke taught, the executive (unlike the other branches) is on continuous duty and must sometimes "act according to discretion, for the publick good, without the prescription of the Law, and sometimes even against it"; because, as Alexander Hamilton declared, "Energy in the Executive is a lead-

278 PART THREE: EVOLUTION

ing character in the definition of good government"; because, as Gouverneur Morris said, the office of the president was "so constituted as to be the great protector of the Mass of the people"; because, as Jefferson maintained, circumstances "sometimes occur" when the president must "assume authorities beyond the law" in keeping with the "*salus populi* . . . , the laws of necessity, of self-preservation, of saving our country when in danger"; for all these reasons, the president was and is the most visible representative and symbol of the nation. Accordingly, what the nation expects of itself it expects in turn of the president, and as the one increases, so does the other.

The level of expectation has been accelerated over the years by developments in the technology of communications—mass printing, then radio, then television—and by the companion development of a special relationship between journalists and presidents. Ever since the emergence of partisan politics in America, presidents and their parties have manipulated the images of incumbents and candidates. Ever since the coming of mass media, White House correspondents have earned their keep by feeding the appetites of the people for news of their presidents. Both sets of activities stimulate a popular craving for the president to do something—or to appear to be doing something.

As was indicated at the outset, I take no position on the question whether these changing perceptions of the presidency are good or bad, wholesome or unwholesome; my concern is with describing how they came to pass. But it must be said that there are perils inherent in the ways the presidency and expectations of it have evolved. Many people believed, for example, that Franklin Roosevelt, Lyndon Johnson, and Richard Nixon extended the powers of the office so far as to undermine the constitutional order. Yet when Congress attempted to wrest back powers that the original Constitution had vested in it, particularly in the area of foreign relations, it incited subsequent presidents and their subordinates to operate outside the law in a sense that is qualitatively different from Locke's federative power or Jefferson's *salus populi*. Moreover, to the extent that efforts to curb the president have proven effective, they have prevented him from living up to popular expectations and thus have contributed to widespread popular frustration and disillusionment. As for the relationship between the media and the presidency, it can be symbiotic, but it can also be adversarial. If for any reason the press perceives a president as ineffectual, its perception becomes a self-fulfilling prophecy, for the press can undermine the credibility the president needs to succeed.

Part Three describes these and related developments from several perspectives, starting with the presidency of Andrew Jackson and ending with that of George Bush. Chapter 11 considers law enforcement; 12, administration; 13, legislation; 14, foreign relations; 15, imagery and symbolism; and 16, the present condition of the office. Along the way, it has been necessary to make judgments about how well or poorly individual presidents have performed their various functions. I have tried to maintain a balance in my sources, drawing on Democrats and Republicans, liberals and conservatives, statists and libertarians; but the judgments are my own, and I know I cannot please everyone.

II

The President and the Law

The president's responsibility to "take care that the Laws be faithfully executed"—if the duty is construed to mean causing his subordinates to institute and prosecute civil or criminal proceedings in federal courts for violations of congressional enactments—has turned out to be among the least important of his functions. For the better part of a century the volume of laws to be enforced was relatively minuscule: The vast majority of Americans rarely came in contact with the federal government except for receiving occasional letters in the mails or serving in some capacity in times of war. The scope of executive authority is suggested by the size of the White House staff. Until 1857 Congress did not appropriate funds for a presidential clerk. By the time of Grant's presidency the staff had swollen to six, and by McKinley's it had more than quadrupled to twenty-seven. Afterward, and throughout the twentieth century, as government expanded, enforcement of its multitudinous laws and regulations was largely entrusted to regulatory bodies that were indirectly responsible to the president, if at all.[1]

1. Edward S. Corwin, *The President: Office and Powers, 1789–1957* (New York, 1957), 300–301; Joseph E. Kallenbach, *The American Chief Executive: The Presidency and the Governorship* (New York, 1966), 440–441. Homer Cummings and Carl McFarland, *Federal Justice: Chapters in the History of Justice and the Federal Executive* (New

At the beginning and through much of the nineteenth century, Congress chose to rely upon state and local sheriffs and police to enforce its legislation rather than create a federal enforcement apparatus. That system was sometimes effective, sometimes not, depending upon whether the states agreed that the congressional act was desirable. A case in point is the Fugitive Slave Act of 1793, under which runaway slaves were to be arrested by state officials and returned at their owners' expense. State officials enforced the law until a number of northern legislatures, beginning with Indiana's in 1824, passed "personal liberty" laws. In the early 1840s Vermont, and subsequently other states, made it a crime for any citizen to aid in the capture of a runaway slave. In 1842, in *Prigg* v. *Pennsylvania*, the Supreme Court held that state officials could not be compelled to enforce federal laws if state law prohibited them from doing so. As part of the Compromise of 1850, a new enforcement mechanism was established: Special commissions, appointed by the federal courts, would order the return of runaways brought in by marshals, who had long since been vested with the powers of local sheriffs. This machinery, however, proved generally unworkable, largely because of popular opposition.[2]

York, 1937), 466ff., list the federal crimes as codified in acts of 1790 and 1825 that were on the books most of the nineteenth century: treason, sedition, theft of federal property, counterfeiting, forgery of government documents, perjury, and attempts to subject ambassadors to the execution of the laws. For the size of the White House staff, see John Hart, *The Presidential Branch* (Elmsford, NY, 1987), 18–21, 97–109. The mushrooming of the White House staff is a recent phenomenon; as late as 1952 the whole of the president's personal staff consisted of twenty-two full-time and three part-time civilian officials and three military aides (*The Truman White House: The Administration of the Presidency 1945–1953*, ed. Francis H. Heller [Lawrence, KS, 1980], 93).

2. Cummings and McFarland, *Federal Justice*, 174–182, 367; Leonard D. White, *The Federalists* (New York, 1948), 402–404; idem, *The Jeffersonians* (New York, 1951), 539–545; idem, *The Jacksonians: A Study in Administrative History, 1829–1861* (New York, 1954), 522–529; Alfred H. Kelly and Winfred A. Harbison, *The American Constitution: Its Origin and Development*, 4th ed. (New York, 1970), 359–362, 378–380; Paul Finkleman, *An Imperfect Union: Slavery, Federalism, and Comity* (Chapel Hill, NC, 1981), 92–96, 131, 132–136; Louis Fisher, *American Constitutional Law* (New York, 1990), 947; Paul Finkleman, "Prigg v. Pennyslvania and the Northern State Courts: Anti-Slavery Uses of a Pro-Slavery Decision," *Civil War History* 25 (1979):5–35; *Prigg* v. *Pennsylvania*, 16 Peters 539.

The executive departments that did the greatest volume of business with the public and, until relatively recent times, were therefore most involved in law enforcement were Treasury and the Post Office. The Treasury Department, through its port collectors, secret service, and Coast Guard, was charged with preventing counterfeiting, smuggling, piracy, and the slave trade. Through the 1820s suits for debts owed the United States were prosecuted by federal district attorneys under instructions of an auditor in Treasury, not the attorney general's office. A similar arrangement prevailed in the Post Office. In 1830 a new office, Solicitor of the Treasury, was created, and for the next three decades the solicitor directed the district attorneys in all federal civil litigation except that of the Post Office. Only in appeals of suits to the Supreme Court did the attorney general participate.[3]

The attorney general's office evolved slowly. William Wirt, one of the more distinguished early incumbents (1817–1829), bespoke the original conception of the position when he said that "I do not consider myself as the advocate of the government, but as a judge, called to decide a question of law with the impartiality and integrity which characterizes the judician." He was, in sum, a part-time legal adviser to the president and to the department heads when ordered by the president or required by law, and he was allowed to continue a private practice. Wirt did represent the United States in trial courts more than any other attorney general, but he did so as private counsel and received sizable fees for his services—$1,500 for prosecuting pirates in Baltimore, for example, and $1,000 for prosecuting mail robbers. As for the opinions of the attorney general, Wirt could find no record of the activities of his predecessors. The opinions were gathered and published for the first time in 1840 and were published from time to time thereafter.[4]

3. White, *Jacksonians*, 165–174; Cummings and McFarland, *Federal Justice*, 100, 146–147, 164.

4. Cummings and McFarland, *Federal Justice*, 90–91; Luther A. Huston, *The Department of Justice* (New York, 1967), 19–21; John P. Kennedy, *Memoirs of the Life of William Wirt, Attorney-General of the United States*, vol. 2 (Philadelphia, 1851), 52–61, 70; Nancy V. Baker, *Conflicting Loyalties: Law and Politics in the Attorney General's Office, 1789–1990* (Lawrence, KS, 1992), 15–16, 126–130; Susan Low Bloch, "The

Meanwhile, the office became highly political and began to be saddled with administrative duties but lacked adequate clerical assistance. Politicization was most blatant under Andrew Jackson, when Roger Brooke Taney, one of Jackson's three attorneys general, advised Jackson (in reference to his war on the Bank of the United States and the Supreme Court's earlier ruling in *M'Culloch* v. *Maryland* that the Bank was constitutional) that the president was not bound by Supreme Court decisions. New duties were added in the 1840s and 1850s, including the administration of applications for pardons; the attorney general had one clerk and one messenger until a second clerk was provided in 1850. President Polk recommended the creation of a justice department, in which the various solicitors would be placed under the attorney general, but Congress declined to act. A few years later, the secretary of the newly established Interior Department suggested the creation of a justice department, but nothing came of the suggestion, though in 1855 the attorney generalship was made a full-time job, the salary being increased and the maintenance of a private practice being forbidden. Despite that change, the federal district attorneys "remained all but completely independent" until August of 1861, when Congress, in an act necessitated by the enormously complex legal issues arising from the Civil War, placed them under the direction of the attorney general.[5]

The revised system broke down under the huge increase in litigation engendered by the war, even though the executive departments and the recently established court of claims handled much of the business with their own solicitors. Congress, occupied with Reconstruction of the South and also seeking to reduce the war-bloated federal establishment, balked at reform for a time, but in 1870 it

---

Early Role of the Attorney General in Our Constitutional Scheme: In the Beginning There Was Pragmatism," *Duke Law Journal* 1 (1989): 561–653.

5. Robert V. Remini, *Andrew Jackson and the Course of American Democracy, 1833–1845* (New York, 1984), 95–97, 105–107, 122; idem, *Andrew Jackson and the Bank War: A Study in the Growth of Presidential Power* (New York, 1967), 63, 72, 82, 118–119; Bray Hammond, *Banks and Politics in America from the Revolution to the Civil War* (Princeton, NJ, 1957), 423–429, 417–421; Huston, *Department of Justice*, 22; Cummings and McFarland, *Federal Justice*, 100–110, 148, 153–156, 170; Baker, *Conflicting Loyalties*, 61, 68–71.

passed an act consolidating "all the law officers of the Government" under a Department of Justice, headed by the attorney general. The office of solicitor general and several new assistants to the attorney general were created to handle the actual litigation of cases, and the practice of hiring outside counsel to try government cases was stopped.[6]

Two additional developments were necessary before the consolidated and expanded Justice Department could become an effective law enforcement agency. One was the establishment of federal prisons. For the first hundred years of the federal government, it contracted with state governments for the incarceration of convicts (originally paying the states fifty cents a month for the service). Scandals involving the states' leasing of prisoners as slave labor, together with various reform impulses, led in the 1880s to a movement for the building of federal prisons, and in the 1890s the first two, at Atlanta and Leavenworth, were established. For some time it was an informal practice to reduce sentences for good behavior, and in 1910 the parole system was initiated.[7]

The other development concerned investigative activity. Though most departments contained investigative arms, the Justice Department did not obtain a regular one until the twentieth century; commonly, when it wanted to conduct an investigation, it relied on the ancient inquisitorial institution of the grand jury or borrowed detectives from other agencies. When Charles J. Bonaparte became attorney general in 1906 he complained to Congress that a "Department of Justice with no force of permanent police in any form under its control is assuredly not fully equipped for its work." Such was the general aversion to and fear of "secret police," however, that Con-

6. Louis Fisher, *Constitutional Dialogues: Interpretation as Political Process* (Princeton, NJ, 1988), 24–25; Daniel J. Meador, *The President, the Attorney-General, and the Department of Justice* (Charlottesville, VA, 1980), 7–10; Baker, *Conflicting Loyalties,* 62–63; Cummings and McFarland, *Federal Justice,* 218–229; Charles Fried, *Order and Law: Arguing the Reagan Revolution—A Firsthand Account* (New York, 1991), 14.

7. Cummings and McFarland, *Federal Justice,* 352–360; Paul W. Keve, *Prisons and the American Conscience: A History of U.S. Federal Correction* (Carbondale, IL, 1991), 11–17, 29–35, 36–50. Actually the first federal penitentiary was opened in 1831 beside the Anacostia River; it was under the Department of the Interior and was to serve the District of Columbia by providing cells for 150 men and 64 women. It closed in 1862.

gress responded by prohibiting Justice from borrowing secret service operatives from Treasury. After a good deal of friction between Theodore Roosevelt and Congress over the matter, Congress resumed its practice of voting funds to Justice for investigations by personnel from other departments, and in 1909 Taft's attorney general, George W. Wickersham, formally created a "Bureau of Investigation" inside the department. In 1924 this bureau came under the direction of J. Edgar Hoover, who headed it until his death in 1972.[8]

———— The efforts of presidents and their attorneys general to enforce federal law have met with varying success, but for a variety of reasons the overall trend throughout the twentieth century has been toward a breakdown of the capacity for enforcement. A major reason is the penchant of Congress to enact bad legislation—bad in the sense of being poorly crafted, or extending into areas that are best left to state and local authorities, or simply being unenforceable at any level of government. In 1910, for example, Congress passed the Mann Act, also known as the White Slave Act, which made it illegal to transport a female across state lines for "immoral purposes." Soon thereafter came the Eighteenth Amendment and the 1919 Volstead Act, prohibiting the manufacturing, transportation, or sale of alcoholic beverages. Failing to learn from those experiences that attempts to legislate morality are apt to breed worse evils than the ones they seek to eradicate, Congress began in the 1950s to outlaw a host of "controlled substances"; but despite ever more draconian methods of enforcement, the use of drugs grew apace. In 1968 came the Omnibus Crime Control and Safe Streets Act, since the enactment of which the streets have grown progressively less safe. Examples of "bad" legislation abound.[9]

8. Lewis L. Gould, *The Presidency of Theodore Roosevelt* (Lawrence, KS, 1991), 291–293; Cummings and McFarland, *Federal Justice*, 366–383; Max Lowenthal, *The Federal Bureau of Investigation* (New York, 1950), 83–92. The number of Secret Service agents had increased from 167 at the end of McKinley's administration to 3,000 at the end of Theodore Roosevelt's (*New York Times,* Feb. 12, 1909, 4:4).

9. Cummings and McFarland, *Federal Justice,* 475–476, 480; Omnibus Crime Control and Safe Streets Act of 1968, 18 U.S. Code 2510–2520; Lawrence M. Friedman, *American Law: An Introduction* (New York, 1984), 137, 160–162; Thomas Cronin,

Another reason for the decline in law-enforcement capability is that presidents or their attorneys general, since Theodore Roosevelt pioneered the technique, have found almost irresistible the temptation to transform enforcement into theater for short-range political advantage. Roosevelt gained a reputation as a trustbuster without

Tania Z. Cronin, and Michael E. Milakovich, *U.S. v Crime in the Streets* (Bloomington, IN, 1981), passim; Allen J. Owens, "The Opiate of the Politicians," *Humanist* (Sept./Oct. 1990): 5–6. In the matter of crime, it is worth noting that in 1932, when Joseph Zangara killed Mayor Anton Cermack of Chicago in an attempt to assassinate President-elect Roosevelt, Zangara was tried, convicted, and executed in less than six weeks. Today convicted murderers commonly are jailed for ten years and more before being executed. See William Tucker, "Toward an Ecology of Crime," in *Public Interest Law Review: 1992,* ed. Terry Eastland (Durham, NC, 1992).

For the playing out of "bad" legislation, how it is implemented and enforced, see specific studies. For example, Robert L. Sansom, *The New American Dream Machine: Toward a Simpler Lifestyle in an Environmental Age* (Garden City, NY, 1976), 35, says of EPA that "the ultimate difficulty lay in the law. EPA was forced by legislative deadlines, often imposed on the administrator by court decisions in response to citizen suits, to act on the basis of weak technical knowledge." Charles Noble, *Liberalism at Work: The Rise and Fall of OSHA* (Philadelphia, 1986), accounts for "why OSHA has been unable to provide workers with the kind of protection that Congress intended" from a Marxist perspective, but he does not question the flawed nature of the act that made it unenforceable and guaranteed its politicization: "At bottom reformers created a paper state—long on statutes and regulations, but short on effective social power" (240). Gary C. Bryner, *Bureaucratic Discretion: Law and Policy in Federal Regulatory Agencies* (New York, 1987), criticizes "broad statutory statements of general purpose" that offer little specific guidance for meeting goals, statutes that "promise dramatic improvement and even absolute achievement" without "discussion of how the costs are to be distributed and how competing policy goals are to be achieved" and without "providing adequate resources for implementation" (1–6 and passim). His discussion of EPA, 92–118, is instructive. See also Terry M. Moe, "The Politics of Bureaucratic Structure," in *Can the Government Govern?* ed. John E. Chubb and Paul E. Peterson (Washington, DC, 1989), 267–329. On congressional deferment of policymaking authority to agencies, see Martin M. Shapiro, "Prudence and Rationality under the Constitution," in *The Constitution and the Regulation of Society,* ed. Gary C. Bryner and Dennis L. Thompson (Provo, UT, 1988), 219–235; for a quick summary of the legislative/regulatory "Binge, 1969–1979," see Theodore J. Lowi, "Liberal and Conservative Theories of Regulation," ibid., 11–14. For a classic example of Congress' leaving it to the courts to give "meaning" to legislation, see the Americans with Disabilities Act, 1992. See also Gary L. McDowell and Eugene W. Hickok, *Justice vs. Law: Courts and Politics in American Society* (New York, 1993).

actually harming any trusts and by such means was able to become the first vice-president who, having succeeded to the presidency upon the death of an incumbent, managed to be elected to the office. In 1919 Attorney General A. Mitchell Palmer, looking toward capturing the Democratic nomination for president the next year, launched a series of raids in which thousands of radicals or suspected radicals were jailed without trial or formal arrest, then released; he formally arrested more than 5,000, turned about one-third over to state authorities for prosecution, and deported more than 500. In 1934 and 1935 Franklin Roosevelt, looking toward reelection in 1936, declared war on "racketeers" and "gangsters" and ordered federal agents to "shoot on sight" the likes of bank robber John Dillinger, which they did. In 1962 and 1963 Attorney General Robert Kennedy, looking toward his brother's reelection, got together with segregationist governors Ross Barnett of Mississippi and George C. Wallace of Alabama to stage elaborate "confrontations" between federal marshals and state officials over the integration of universities. Tops in the law-enforcement-as-theater department was George Bush's deployment of armed forces in December of 1989 to invade Panama, oust Pres. Manuel Noriega, and transport him to Florida, where he had been indicted in two federal courts on drug trafficking charges. In April of 1992, he was convicted on eight drug and racketeering counts, largely on testimony of drug kingpins who won immunity from prosecution in exchange for their services. Triumphantly, President Bush heralded the conviction as a powerful message to drug kingpins.[10]

10. For Theodore Roosevelt's trustbusting, see n. 12 of this chapter; for Palmer, see Stanley Cobin, *A. Mitchell Palmer: Politician* (New York, 1963), 217–245; Robert K. Murray, *Red Scare: A Study in National Hysteria* (New York, 1964), and Baker, *Conflicting Loyalties,* 108–115; for FDR, see Richard Ged Powers, *G-Men: Hoover's FBI in American Popular Culture* (Carbondale, IL, 1983), 33–50, 112–138; in 1934 the Justice Department published a list of 6,000 gangsters it would pursue, and Roosevelt signed six bills designed to wipe out gangsters (*New York Times,* July 27, 1:2 and May 19, 1:2); for Kennedy and Barnett, see *American Journey: The Times of Robert Kennedy,* interviews by Jean Stein, ed. George Plimpton (New York, 1970), 104–105, and *The Growth of Presidential Power: A Documented History,* ed. William M. Goldsmith, 3 vols. (New York, 1974), 3:1658–1665, 1675–1678; for Wallace, see "Former Top Aid Rips Wallace," *Tuscaloosa News,* April 10, 1992; for Bush, see any newspaper, Dec. 1989, *New York Times,* Jan. 4, 1990, A, 1:6, 12:1, Jan. 5, 1990, A, 1:6, and any newspaper for April 10, 1992.

The effects of bad legislation and presidential theater in enforcement are well illustrated by the history of efforts to enforce the
Sherman Antitrust Act. The act, as first passed in 1890, was a classic
case of bad law: It declared illegal "every contract, combination . . .
or conspiracy" to restrain or monopolize "any part of the trade or
commerce among the several states, or with foreign nations." As
Attorney General Richard Olney said, "As all ownership of property
is of itself a monopoly, and as every business contract or transaction
may be viewed as a combination which more or less restrains some
part or kind of trade or commerce, any literal application of the
provisions of the statute is out of the question." The first effective
employment of the act, moreover, was not against a business combination but against a labor union.[11]

Then six months after Theodore Roosevelt took office, he ordered
Attorney General Philander Knox to institute an antitrust suit against
the Northern Securities Company. That was a bold and shrewd move,
carefully calculated to bring favorable publicity to the young president. The choice of target was equally bold and clever. The company
was well known; it had been recently formed as a holding company
after a highly publicized battle for control of the railroads in the
Northwest and was widely portrayed as an evil monopoly. Most
people believed, mistakenly, that it was a favorite creation of the
powerful investment banker J. P. Morgan and that it encompassed an
enormous railroad system. It could actually be dissolved with minimal disruption in the financial community, and the government's
case was so framed that the principals could make money out of
losing the case. Indeed, all the involved parties contributed heavily
to Roosevelt's reelection campaign even though he was indelibly
stamped as a champion of the "little fellow" against "big business."
Of the forty-three other antitrust suits the Roosevelt administration

11. The Sherman Act can be seen in any good documents collection, for instance
Documents of American History, ed. Henry Steele Commager, 7th ed. (New York,
1963), 586–587; 26 U.S. Statutes at Large, 209; Olney as quoted in Cummings and
McFarland, *Federal Justice,* 322; *In re Debs,* 158 U.S. 564 (1895); William Letwin, *Law
and Economic Policy in America: The Evolution of the Sherman Antitrust Act* (New York,
1965), 117–121, 123–128; Robert H. Bork, *The Antitrust Paradox: A Policy at War with
Itself* (New York, 1978), 19–20.

instituted, only one—that against the so-called beef trust—resulted in a victory of any consequence by the government.[12]

After an interim term, the presidency of William Howard Taft, during which the Sherman Act was rigorously enforced and a considerable number of large firms were broken up, Woodrow Wilson brought a new approach to the subject. In 1914, at Wilson's behest, Congress passed the Clayton Antitrust Act and the Federal Trade Commission Act, aimed not at breaking up industrial giants or even at punishing wrongdoers but at preventing wrongdoing. Various "unfair" business practices, such as price discrimination, were defined, and the Federal Trade Commission (FTC) was authorized to investigate businesses, require annual financial reports from them, and publicize its findings. These changes reflected Wilson's belief in publicity—doing nothing behind closed doors that would not bear public scrutiny—and in voluntarism, the belief that most businessmen would do the right thing without being coerced by government if they were taught to and allowed to and were policed by an informed public opinion. In keeping with those views, businesses were invited to send their lawyers to Washington for free advice from Justice Department lawyers and FTC staff members. Among others, Ford Motor Company and American Telephone and Telegraph availed themselves of this free antitrust insurance; over the next two decades a great new wave of corporate consolidation took place, and though the Sherman Act was still on the books, antitrust suits for practical purposes ceased to be brought.[13]

Franklin Roosevelt steered an erratically vacillating course. For a time he moved in the direction of encouraging monopoly on a grand scale. At his direction the National Recovery Administration (NRA)

12. Gould, *Theodore Roosevelt*, 49–53, 106, 212, 213–214, 218, 246–247, 279–280; Robert H. Wiebe, "The House of Morgan and the Executive, 1905–1913," *American Historical Review* 65 (1959):49–60; Letwin, *Law and Economic Policy*, 184–207, 245–246; Forrest McDonald, *The Phaeton Ride: The Crisis of American Success* (Garden City, NY, 1974), 70–71.

13. Paolo E. Coletta, *The Presidency of William Howard Taft* (Lawrence, KS, 1973), 153–163; Letwin, *Law and Economic Policy*, 273–278; Benjamin J. Klebaner, "Potential Competition and the American Antitrust Legislation of 1914," *Business History Review* 38 (1964):175, 179–180; Goldsmith, ed., *Growth of Presidential Power*, 3:1373–1378, 1381, 1383.

requested every industry to draw up "codes of fair practice" that would fix uniform prices, wages, and working conditions and integrate each industry, through its trade associations, into what was in effect a single whole. The codes were hastily and carelessly drawn, and they violated the first principle of the rule of law, namely that law be knowable. In the "Hot Oil" cases, argued before the Supreme Court in 1934, counsel against the government declared that his client "was arrested, indicted and held in jail for several days and then had to put up bond for violating a law that did not exist, but nobody knew it." Counsel for the government conceded that there were hundreds of codes that "would be rather difficult to find," for there was no official or general publication of them.[14]

After the NRA was declared unconstitutional in 1935, Roosevelt discovered that "big businessmen hate me," announced that "I welcome their hatred," and promptly began to show it. One way of doing so was contained in the Robinson-Patman Act, passed at his urging in 1936, which made it a crime, among other things, to sell goods at "unreasonably low prices for the purpose of destroying competition or eliminating a competitor." That worked at cross-purposes with antitrust: The original intention had been to preserve competition as a means of benefiting consumers; now the intent was to protect small businesses as such at the expense of the consumer. Under this law, furthermore, the FTC proved to be "notoriously hostile to efficiency."[15]

The companion piece to favoring small business was an all-out attack on big business by Thurmon Arnold, who in 1938 was brought in by Roosevelt as a special agent of the Antitrust Division of the

14. Corwin, *President*, 394–395, quoting the *Washington Post*, Dec. 11, 1934; Ellis W. Hawley, *The New Deal and the Problem of Monopoly: A Study in Economic Ambivalence* (Princeton, NJ, 1966). The *Federal Register* now publishes all presidential proclamations and orders; it began doing so on March 14, 1936. On the NRA in general by the man who directed it, see Hugh Johnson, *The Blue Eagle from Egg to Earth* (Garden City, NY, 1935).

15. Bork, *Antitrust Paradox*, 77, 252, 383–386; Frederick M. Rowe, *Price Discrimination Under the Robinson-Patman Act* (Boston, 1962), 551–555 and passim; Milton Handler, *Twenty-Five Years of Antitrust*, vol. 2 (New York, 1973), 901–902; *The Federal Trade Commission since 1970: Economic Regulation and Bureaucratic Behavior*, ed. Kenneth W. Clarkson and Timothy J. Muris (New York, 1981), 95.

Justice Department. Arnold pledged to pursue a "vigorous" policy; he instituted 215 investigations and directed the prosecution of suits against corporate giants like General Electric and DuPont. None of the major suits, however, was settled when the United States entered World War II. Roosevelt recognized that these corporations were indispensable to wartime production and suspended the suits until the end of the war. Truman resumed the suits, with peculiar results: A number of enormous fortunes were made from the breakup of established businesses, as happened in the aluminum industry; and elements of irrationality were mandated, such as prohibitions on the exchange of defense technology.[16]

During the Eisenhower years antitrust activity tapered off, and the targets were mostly small potatoes. But then came the never-never land of the sixties and seventies. At a time marked by race riots, student demonstrations, a rising drug culture, assassinations, and a general breakdown of law and order, the nation was swept by a wave of anticorporate hysteria.[17]

16. Corwin D. Edwards, "Thurman Arnold and the Antitrust Laws," *Political Science Quarterly* 58 (1943):338–355; Edwards says that in five years Arnold instituted 44 percent of all proceedings under antitrust during the fifty-three years of the Sherman Act (339). Wilson D. Miscamble, "Thurman Arnold Goes to Washington: A Look at Antitrust Policy in the Later New Deal," *Business History Review* 56 (1982):1–15. Thurman Arnold, *Fair Fights and Foul: A Dissenting Lawyer's Life* (New York, 1951), 113–115; on 144 Arnold contests Rexford Tugwell's statement that "trust busting was quietly put away for the duration" of the war; he attempts to maintain that "the Antitrust Division was just as important during the war as it was prior to the war." Edwards, 351–352, notes wartime postponements in the cases of DuPont, General Electric, Bendix, and others; in March 1942 the Department of Justice agreed to suspend proceedings "when in the opinion of the War or Navy Department immediate prosecution would interfere with war production." See also Gene M. Gressley, "Thurman Arnold, Antitrust, and the New Deal," *Business History Review* 38 (1964):214–231. For Truman's antitrust policy see Robert Griffith, "Forging America's postwar order: domestic politics and political economy in the age of Truman," in *The Truman Presidency,* ed. Michael J. Lacey (Cambridge, Eng., 1989), 75–79, 111–113, 124–125; Donald R. McCoy, *The Presidency of Harry S. Truman* (Lawrence, KS, 1984), 181–182.

17. Richard A. Posner, "A Statistical Study of Antitrust Enforcement," *Journal of Law and Economics* 13 (1970):366, 371–372, 411–413, offers data showing that the number of antitrust suits instigated by the Department of Justice did not increase

The most notorious of the antitrust actions were instituted in 1968 and 1969 against American Telephone and Telegraph, IBM, Exxon, the Kellogg Food Company, and others. Each of these cases dragged along for years without anyone's ever knowing quite what violations of the law were being alleged. The Exxon proceedings, for example, "employed the energies of more than 200 FTC staff attorneys during a ten-year period, ending up with not much more than thousands of pages of microfilmed company documents and reams of internal memoranda," and the proceedings against Kellogg followed a similar course. The IBM case has been described as "the all-time champion lawsuit in size. The documents could fill a dozen warehouses. Costs on both sides were staggering." It appeared that the case "would literally go on forever." Finally on January 8, 1982, "the Reagan administration threw in the towel and the mighty lawsuit fizzled out, after millions of dollars, millions of documents, and millions of hours." At the same time AT&T capitulated and "agreed to divest itself of all its regional Bell operating companies." Most of the other pending cases were abandoned, with no tangible results, and "no monopolization cases have been filed since that day."[18]

---

substantially: 1953–1961, 277 suits; 1961–1969, 330. But the number of private antitrust suits preceded by Department of Justice judgments increased dramatically: 1951–1960, 477; 1961–1963, 880. See also Joseph C. Gallo, Joseph L. Craycraft, and Steven C. Bush, "Guess Who Came to Dinner: An Empirical Study of Federal Antitrust Enforcement for the Period 1963–1984," *Review of Industrial Organization* 2 (1985–1986):106–127; McDonald, *Phaeton Ride,* 116, 140–143; Terry Eastland, in "Reagan Justice: Combating Excess, Strengthening the Rule of Law," *Policy Review* (Fall 1988):16–17, notes a drastic change in enforcement policy: "Bigness was equated with badness and constituted a sufficient reason for government intervention." Indeed, "exotic" enforcement theories in the 1970s included the FTC's Michael Pertschuk's view that antitrust "must address 'the social and environmental harms produced as unwelcome byproducts of the marketplace.'" The Reagan administration returned antitrust law to a concern with economic efficiency and consumer welfare. In 1982 its "Merger Guidelines" reintroduced a measure of sanity to the proceedings.

18. William F. Shughart II, "Antitrust Policy in the Reagan Administration: Pyrrhic Victories?" in *Regulation and the Reagan Era: Politics, Bureaucracy and the Public Interest,* ed. Roger E. Meiners and Bruce Yandle (New York and London, 1989), 94; Friedman, *American Law,* 285. James G. Stewart, "The World of Business: Whales

Such disparate enforcement policies, coupled with the Watergate and Iran-Contra scandals, repeated revelations of law violations by presidents, bureaucrats, and executive-branch staffers, together with exposés of the many ways in which congressmen set themselves above the law, resulted by the early 1990s in widespread skepticism about the law, lawmakers, and law enforcers.[19] And without that trust, as Locke taught long ago and the Framers understood well, there can be no government of laws.

———— While presidential enforcement of acts of Congress was following its erratic course, the presidency was simultaneously expanding into a wide range of activities, including the making of law and the coercion of individuals and groups, not in accordance with law but consonant with its conception of the public good.

Much of the expansion resulted from delegation of powers by Congress, which started harmlessly enough in the nineteenth century but evolved monstrously during the twentieth. A tariff act of 1890 empowered the president to suspend some of its provisions if spe-

---

and Sharks," *New Yorker,* Feb. 15, 1993, 38; Stewart makes an intriguing and convincing argument that the collapse of "Big Blue" in 1992–1993 was directly related to the dropping of the suit whereas the vitality of AT&T arose from its dismemberment (37–43).

19. F. Christopher Arterton, "Watergate and Children's Attitudes toward Political Authority Revisited," *Political Science Quarterly* 90 (1975–1976):477–495; Chester A. Newland, "Faithful Execution of the Law and Empowering Public Confidence," *Presidential Studies Quarterly* 21 (1991):673–686; *Roosevelt to Reagan: The Development of the Modern Presidency,* ed. Malcolm Shaw (London, 1987), 297–298, 304–306, 309; Arthur M. Schlesinger, Jr., *The Imperial Presidency* (Boston, 1973), 410–411. The scandals and revelations can be followed dispassionately in the *Congressional Quarterly Almanac;* see, for example, 1989:639–653 for the HUD scandals involving eighteen hearings and three different committees. See also 1989:653, which reports that since the enactment of the independent-counsel law in 1978 there have been eleven special prosecutors. *Gallup Poll Monthly,* Oct. 1991, 36, reported confidence in major institutions at an all-time low: "At the bottom is Congress," with an 18 percent confidence rating; the Supreme Court at 39 percent "received its lowest rating ever"; the presidency had "the highest public confidence of the three main branches," at 50 percent. A *New York Times* editorial, Feb. 10, 1993, A, 14:1, begins, "It's no secret that the U.S. Congress is inefficient. The real mystery is how it gets anything done at all."

cified conditions prevailed. By 1922 Congress was authorizing the president to determine costs of production worldwide and to adjust tariff rates accordingly; by 1932 it was authorizing him to raise or lower up to 50 percent the rates set by statute. By 1970 the habit of delegating had become so entrenched that Congress granted President Nixon authority "to issue such orders and regulations as he may deem appropriate to stabilize prices, wages, and salaries," and three months later fifty-eight House Democrats sent the president a letter urging him to impose controls. In 1975 President Ford retaliated against the Organization of Petroleum Exporting Countries (OPEC) oil embargo by imposing a "fee" of three dollars a barrel on imported oil; the Supreme Court upheld this president-mandated tax as it had most delegations of power even though it continued to pay lip service to the doctrine of *delegata potestas non potest delegari*.[20]

Equally instrumental in drawing powers to the presidency has been the "stewardship theory" first enunciated by Theodore Roosevelt, followed by most presidents since, and mirrored in most Americans' increased expectations of the office. Roosevelt insisted, he wrote in his autobiography, "that the executive power was limited only by specific restrictions and prohibitions appearing in the Constitution or imposed by the Congress under its Constitutional powers. . . . I declined to adopt the view that what was imperatively necessary for the Nation could not be done by the President unless he could find some specific authorization to do it. . . . I acted for the public welfare, I acted for the common well-being of all our people, whenever and in whatever manner was necessary, unless prevented by direct constitutional or legislative prohibition."[21]

In part, Roosevelt-style activism—which actually began before

---

20. John Day Larkin, *The President's Control of the Tariff* (Cambridge, MA, 1936), 43–47, 49–53, 55–57, 104–108, 143–150; Corwin, *President*, 124; Louis Fisher, *Constitutional Conflicts between Congress and the President*, 3d ed., rev. (Lawrence, KS, 1991), 96–98; F. W. Taussig, *The Tariff History of the United States*, 8th ed. (New York, 1967), 279, 478–480; *New York Times*, Aug. 18, Nov. 24, Nov. 26, 1970, 20:1, 63:3, 71:4. In the mid-1930s the Supreme Court declared unconstitutional the NRA and other delegations of power; *Schechter Poultry Corp.* v. *U.S.*, 295 U.S. 495 (1935); *Carter* v. *Carter Coal Co.*, 298 U.S. 238 (1936). It has rarely if ever done so since.

21. Quoted in Corwin, *President*, 153, and Gould, *Theodore Roosevelt*, 197.

Roosevelt—was in the nature of president as conservator of the peace, as if he were a medieval king. The exercise of that function is epitomized by presidential interventions in labor disputes. In 1877 the area from Baltimore to Chicago and beyond was hit by a violent strike of railway workers. The Constitution provides that the United States shall protect the states from domestic violence, but only "on Application of the Legislature, or of the Executive (when the Legislature cannot be convened)." President Hayes, however, on the informal request of a few governors and without notification as to whether the legislatures could be convened, dispatched army troops and sent arms to state militias to suppress the strike. Seventeen years later President Cleveland sent troops to Chicago, over the vehement opposition of Gov. John Peter Altgeld, ostensibly to protect federal property and to "remove obstructions to the United States mails" but in fact to crush the Pullman strike. In 1902 Theodore Roosevelt negotiated a settlement to a crippling anthracite coal strike, but he wrote in his autobiography that had the negotiations failed he would have arranged for the governor to request help, put the army under a "first-rate" general, and ordered him to "dispossess the operators and run the mines as a receiver." During the next half century, as E. S. Corwin wrote in his classic study of the presidency, presidents intervened in twenty-five major industrial disputes "without specific legal authorization, or even to the derogation of the law in some instances."[22]

The new activism also involved the issuing of decrees that had the force of law. The oldest form of decree was the proclamation: Some proclamations were commemorative such as designating Thanksgiving Day or National Secretaries Month; others were substantive. Court decisions on the subject have been inconsistent. As was indi-

22. Constitution of the United States, Article 4, Section 4; Corwin, *President*, 134, 153–155. Bennett Milton Rich, *The Presidents and Civil Disorder* (Washington, DC, 1941), 72–107; Ari Hoogenboom, *The Presidency of Rutherford B. Hayes* (Lawrence, KS, 1988), 79–92; Richard E. Welch, Jr., *The Presidency of Grover Cleveland* (Lawrence, KS, 1988), 141–157; McCoy, *Harry Truman*, 59–60, 290–293; Goldsmith, ed., *Growth of Presidential Power*, 2:1135–1158, 1168–1176. The idea that there is a national peace to be preserved was first advanced by the Court in the case *In re Neagle*, 135 U.S. 1–2 (1890); Goldsmith, ed., *Growth of Presidential Power*, 1143–1147.

cated earlier, in English law after the Glorious Revolution and in American law at first, substantive proclamations could not create new law but could only be declarative of what the existing law was or proclaim that conditions made certain laws operative. In many instances that doctrine still holds true: When a president declares a drought-stricken location a "disaster area," for example, he has thereby indicated that affected farmers are eligible for relief as provided by act of Congress. But modern presidents have gone far beyond the rule, as President Nixon did in 1971 for instance when he imposed a 10 percent surcharge on dutiable imports. A court upheld that action, which would be explicable given the presidential latitude in setting tariff rates that Congress had established—except that the court relied on the 1917 Trading with the Enemy Act and vague references to the president's power to conduct foreign affairs. In 1980, by contrast, a federal judge struck down President Carter's imposition of a fee on imported oil as not falling "within the inherent powers of the President."[23]

A more common form of presidential legislation, especially since Franklin Roosevelt, has been executive orders. The courts hold that these have the force of law only when they are justified by the Constitution or when the power has been delegated by Congress, but in practice most executive orders are either upheld or unchallenged. Between 1941 and 1951, for example, no such order was declared invalid by the Supreme Court though during that period Roosevelt seized aviation plants, shipbuilding companies, a shell plant, and nearly 4,000 coal companies in palpable violation of the Fifth Amendment's "taking" clause. Harry Truman employed equally far-reaching measures. Every president from Roosevelt through Nixon issued executive orders prohibiting racial discrimination by companies supplying the government or receiving federal assistance on private projects, though the policy was not yet authorized by statute and may have violated statutory law. President Kennedy established the Peace Corps temporarily by executive order in 1961, and until Congress got

23. Glendon A. Schubert, Jr., *The Presidency in the Courts* (Minneapolis, MN, 1957), 302ff. and 308–311; Fisher, *Constitutional Conflicts*, 104–105, and *U.S. v. Yoshida Int'l, Inc.*, cited ibid., 105n; *Alcan Aluminum Corp. v. U.S.*, 429 U.S. 986 (1976); *New York Times*, Aug. 17, 1971, 17:5, May 13, 1980, D, 18:4 and May 14, 1980, 1:5.

around to funding it, he financed it by transferring funds appropriated for another purpose. Just how many executive orders have been issued is unknown. They have been numbered consecutively since 1907, and late in 1990 Executive Order 12,735 was issued; but there are also fractions, so the total might be as many as 50,000. In addition, there are secret orders called National Security Decision Directives, about three quarters of which are not made public and are not therefore subject to review by the press, Congress, the courts, or the public.[24]

The two main aspects of the stewardship presidency, direct action and lawmaking, have been most effective at aggrandizing the powers of the office, when the nation has been deemed to be in a state of emergency. Between the Civil War and the Korean conflict, Congress and the courts proved willing during wartime to cede—and presidents proved eager to accept—powers virtually amounting to a suspension of the Constitution. Many nonwar emergencies have also been declared, and presidents sometimes have neglected to declare them ended. Franklin Roosevelt declared thirty-nine emergencies during his first six years in office, and in 1971 Congress was surprised to learn that the national emergency proclaimed during the banking crisis of March, 1933, was still nominally in effect. So too were emergencies declared by Truman in 1950 and by Nixon in 1970 and 1971. The Senate set up a special committee to study the matter. The committee's 1973 report indicated that the four proclamations combined activated 470 provisions of federal law which empowered the president, among other things, to "seize property, organize and control the means of production, institute martial law, control all transportation and communication, and restrict travel." Legislation passed in 1976 and revised in 1985 provided that Congress could terminate a

24. McCoy, *Harry Truman*, 108–109, 170, 254–256; Fisher, *Constitutional Conflicts*, 106–110; *New York Times*, March 2, 1961, 1:8 and 12:1, 2. Schubert, *Presidency in the Courts*, 309–311, 361–365. The second group of pages is Appendix A, a table of cases holding presidential actions unconstitutional. In it, three cases are listed between 1936 and 1952, only one of them being by the Supreme Court, and that concerned regulations promulgated by the navy. For more modern experience with executive orders, see Robert A. Shanley, "Presidential Executive Orders and Environmental Policy," *Presidential Studies Quarterly* 13 (1983):405–416.

presidentially declared state of emergency by joint resolution, but as of 1992 it had not yet seen fit to exercise the power.[25]

———— In modern times it has come to be expected that presidential excesses will be restrained by the Supreme Court, but Court orders to the president are recent and possibly transient phenomena that run counter to the history of the relationship between the two branches. Apart from the defiance of John Marshall by Jefferson and Jackson, there were no major clashes between the Court and the presidency until the Civil War, and when those clashes came it was evident that the judiciary was, as Hamilton had described it, "the least dangerous" branch of the federal authority. The first serious collision occurred in 1861, when Lincoln suspended the writ of habeas corpus in border areas and ordered military commanders to arrest and imprison suspected rebel sympathizers without evidence, charges, or trial. Under those orders an army officer arrested John Merryman, a Baltimore secessionist, and imprisoned him without formal charges. Merryman petitioned Chief Justice Roger Brooke Taney, sitting as a circuit judge, for a writ of habeas corpus, and Taney issued the writ. When the officer refused to release the prisoner, Taney cited him for contempt and declared that power to suspend the writ was vested in Congress, not in the president. Lincoln ignored the decision and continued to order military commanders to suspend habeas corpus as they saw fit. The courts could do nothing about it.[26]

25. Fisher, *Constitutional Conflicts,* 258–260; Thomas Cronin, "A Resurgent Congress and the Imperial Presidency," *Political Science Quarterly* 95 (1980):213; Schubert, *Presidency in the Courts,* 241ff., 296; Schlesinger, *Imperial Presidency,* 320–321, 323–324; Richard M. Pious, *The American Presidency* (New York, 1979), 44–45, 55–60; *New York Times,* Sept. 15, 1976, 24:1; Daniel P. Franklin, *Extraordinary Measures: The Exercise of Prerogative Powers in the United States* (Pittsburgh, PA, 1991).

26. *Ex parte Merryman,* 17 Fed. cases No. 9487 (1861). Kelly and Harbison, *American Constitution,* 439–441. In 1866, after the fighting had ended, the Court more or less apologized for its wartime conduct. *Ex parte Milligan,* 4 Wallace 2 (1866). Mark E. Neely, Jr., *The Fate of Liberty: Abraham Lincoln and Civil Liberties* (New York, 1991), contends that though the suspension of civil liberties during the Civil War was fairly hair-raising, Lincoln personally had little to do with it and was probably unaware of most of the trials by military commissions.

Even more definitive of the Court's limitations was a case that arose in 1867. The constitutionality of the two reconstruction acts of March 1867 was challenged by attorneys for the state of Mississippi, who requested of the Supreme Court permission to seek an injunction against Andrew Johnson and the district military commander restraining them from executing and enforcing the acts. Chief Justice Salmon P. Chase, speaking for the Court, dismissed the suit as "absurd and excessive" and in a series of hypothetical questions described what would happen if the Court granted Mississippi's request. If it served an injunction on the president, he would either refuse to heed it, in which case the Court would have no way of enforcing its order, or he would obey it, in which case he would be making himself liable to impeachment for failing to execute an act of Congress. If he were impeached for obeying a Court order, the Court could not protect him by issuing an injunction preventing the Senate from carrying out its constitutional function of trying impeachment cases. "These questions," as Chase put it, "answer themselves."[27]

The commonsense passivity or restraint displayed by the judges in these two cases was in accordance with the doctrine of the "political question," more or less a subdivision of the doctrine of the separation of powers. Theoretically, each of the branches has its proper spheres of action; certain activities are the function of the political branches—those that are elected, namely the legislative and the executive—whereas the adjudication of "cases and controversies" between individuals or groups who have "standing" is a function of the judiciary. In practice the doctrine is simply a recognition by the judges that in the ordinary course of events they have no means of coercing a legislature or an executive.[28]

Superficially, it would seem that the Court departed from traditional doctrine in 1952 when it ruled that Harry Truman's seizure of the steel industry to stop a strike was illegal. The ruling was a departure from precedent, given the frequency with which the Court had upheld seizures in industrial disputes before, but it was not a depar-

27. *Mississippi* v. *Johnson,* 4 Wallace 475 (1867).

28. The leading case pronouncing the political-questions doctrine was *Luther* v. *Borden,* 7 Howard 1 (1849). It was adhered to until the 1960s; see text at n. 32 of this chapter. See also Franklin, *Extraordinary Measures,* 136.

ture from the proposition that the president is immune to court orders. The order was given to Secretary of Commerce Charles Sawyer, not the president, and most of the justices were careful to confirm that the president has emergency powers in "catastrophic situations." The problem was that in this instance Truman was obliged by the Taft-Hartley Act to follow different procedures in dealing with the strike. The decision, however, was muddled; it was a six-to-three vote, and each of the six in the majority wrote a separate opinion, contradicting the others on various points. Although Truman "grumbled" about the decision, he did not contest or defy it: "The government immediately relinquished control of the steel mills."[29]

Indeed, during the early 1950s the Court was still in a period of passivity and permissiveness toward actions by the political branches that had begun in 1937. This was the era of "McCarthyism," and the Court was in no mood to incur the wrath of witch-hunters. On the contrary, it ruled in their favor in a number of key cases; it did not begin to rediscover the Bill of Rights until the frenzy had died and McCarthy had been repudiated. Perhaps the nadir was hit at the very beginning of the decade, in cases involving persons accused of disloyalty. In oral argument in one such case, counsel for the Justice Department refused to give the grounds for ordering an alien to be excluded as a security risk; asked if he knew the grounds, he answered that he did but would not tell the Court. On the basis of this "secret evidence," the Court upheld the government.[30]

The Court, however, was on the verge of a resurgence of power. It amassed an enormous amount of moral capital by its desegregation decisions, beginning with *Brown* v. *Board of Education* in 1954; the respect it won was augmented by the lack of cooperation and sometimes deliberate obstruction by the political branches. As its prestige

29. *Youngstown Sheet and Tube Company* v. *Sawyer,* 343 U.S. 579 (1952); Maeva Marcus, *Truman and the Steel Seizure Case: The Limits of Presidential Power* (New York, 1977), 209, 215–227, 228–229; McCoy, *Harry Truman,* 291–293; Corwin, *President,* 156–157; Kallenbach, *American Chief Executive,* 558–559; Schubert, *Presidency in the Courts,* 284–285; Fisher, *Constitutional Conflicts,* 250–251; Franklin, *Extraordinary Measures,* 135.

30. *U.S. ex rel Knauff* v. *Shaughnessy,* 338 U.S. 537 (1950); Schubert, *Presidency in the Courts,* 22–24, 127–130, 345.

soared, its boldness increased, and it set out actively to reshape society irrespective of constitutional niceties and precedents. Some of its decisions, such as the outlawing of prayer in public schools, elicited howls of protest in some quarters, but most of its rulings to protect First Amendment rights and the rights of accused felons added to its growing reputation as the defender of the weak against what was coming to be called "the Establishment."[31]

The Court's most daring and potentially explosive decisions were those reached between 1960 and 1964 mandating the reapportionment of representation in state legislatures to make them conform to a newly discovered constitutional principle, that of "one person, one vote." These decisions radically reversed the political-questions doctrine and were, as the Court had held as recently as 1946, beyond the range of what courts could enforce—if the legislatures resisted. But the time was not one for resistance. The nation had been urbanizing at an ever-accelerating pace, and in most state constitutions representation was apportioned to reflect the bygone rural past; the result was gross imbalance and disproportionate legislative influences for rural and small-town districts that almost amounted to rotten boroughs. Furthermore, the direct targets of the decisions were southern states, which, having recently become discredited by their resistance

31. *Brown* v. *Board of Education,* 347 U.S. 483 (1954); the school prayer case was *Engel* v. *Vitale,* 370 U.S. 421 (1962); important criminal rights cases were *Escobedo* v. *Illinois,* 378 U.S. 478 (1964), and *Miranda* v. *Arizona,* 384 U.S. 436 (1966); for the First Amendment cases, see Fisher, *American Constitutional Law,* chaps. 10, 11, 12. For an open espousal of an activist noninterpretivist judicial position, see William J. Brennan, Jr., "The Georgetown Speech, October 12, 1985," in *Major Problems in American Constitutional History: Volume II,* ed. Kermit L. Hall (Lexington, MA, 1992), 557–566, in which Brennan says that "the Constitution embodies the aspiration to social justice, brotherhood, and human dignity. . . . [It] is the lodestar for our aspirations"; see also Michael Perry, *The Constitution, the Courts, and Human Rights: An Inquiry into the Legitimacy of Constitutional Policymaking by the Judiciary* (New Haven, CT, 1982), esp. 126–138; Richard B. Saphire, "Making Noninterpretivism Respectable: Michael Perry's Contributions to Constitutional Theory," *Michigan Law Review* 81 (1983):801ff.; Bruce Ackerman, *Reconstructing American Law* (Cambridge, MA, 1984), 72–104. For two interpretivist views, see Henry P. Monaghan, "Our Perfect Constitution," *New York University Law Review* 56 (1981):353–396, and J. Clifford Wallace, "A Two Hundred Year Old Constitution in Modern Society," *Texas Law Review* 61 (1982/83):1575–1586.

to racial integration, could scarcely stand up now for principles of federalism and local self-government. Accordingly, no effective opposition was forthcoming.[32]

Interference in political questions, however, did not yet extend to the presidency, for presidential power was just then approaching the zenith of an ascent that had continued, with few interruptions, for nearly seven decades. Lyndon Johnson dominated the federal government more thoroughly than had any predecessor save possibly Jefferson, and he doubtless would have continued to prevail had not popular and media protests against his Vietnamese policy persuaded him not to seek reelection in 1968. Richard Nixon, a master in matters of foreign relations, was no equal to Johnson in managing the unwieldy machinery of domestic government; yet so accustomed had the nation become to presidential rule that he and his staff could proclaim broad domestic policies and encounter virtually no resistance.[33]

Then came the Watergate scandal, and president and Court were soon involved in a direct confrontation. During the election of 1972 a group from the Republican Committee to Reelect the President

32. *Gomillion* v. *Lightfoot,* 364 U.S. 339 (1960); *Baker* v. *Carr,* 369 U.S. 186 (1962); *Reynolds* v. *Sims,* 377 U.S. 533 (1964).

33. The bibliography on both presidencies is immense. For Johnson's, good places to begin are Vaughn Davis Bornet, *The Presidency of Lyndon B. Johnson* (Lawrence, KS, 1983); Rowland Evans and Robert Novak, *Lyndon B. Johnson: The Exercise of Power* (New York, 1966); and Doris Kearns, *Lyndon Johnson and the American Dream* (New York, 1976). For Nixon, the most balanced account is Stephen E. Ambrose, *Nixon,* 3 vols. (New York, 1987–1991). See also William Safire, *Before the Fall: An Inside View of the Pre-Watergate White House* (Garden City, NY, 1975), and Rowland Evans, Jr., and Robert D. Novak, *Nixon in the White House: The Frustration of Power* (New York, 1971). For an interesting example of Nixon's use of executive power, see J. Larry Hood, "The Nixon Administration and The Revised Philadelphia Plan for Affirmative Action: A Study in Expanding Presidential Power and Divided Government," *Presidential Studies Quarterly* 23 (1993):145–167; for a short summary of Nixon's executive/legislative style, see Bert A. Rockman, "Tightening the Reins: The Federal Executive and the Management Philosophy of the Reagan Presidency," *Presidential Studies Quarterly* 23 (1993):104–105. For examples of Nixon's economic proclamations, see Ambrose, *Nixon,* 2:458–459; these included a freeze on prices and wages, repeal of an excise tax on automobiles, a job-development credit, a cut in federal spending, a surtax on imports, and suspension of the convertibility of the dollar into gold.

burglarized the Democratic party premises in the Watergate complex in Washington, and during the next year a Senate committee conducted an investigation of the break-in and the subsequent White House "cover-up" of the episode. During this investigation it came to light that White House conversations had routinely been recorded on tape. A flurry of court actions aimed at securing the tapes ensued, culminating in a Supreme Court order directing the president to deliver them. That was on July 24, 1974.[34]

Had circumstances been different, Nixon would no doubt have defied the order, though if circumstances had been different the Court probably would not have issued it. But six days after the Court handed down the order, the House Judiciary Committee referred three articles of impeachment to the full membership. In another six days Nixon bowed to the order and surrendered the tapes, and on the evening of August 8 he announced his resignation in a nationally televised speech. Clearly, it was the threat of action by the other political branch that led the president to bow to the judiciary.[35]

Even so, during the remainder of the decade, as the political branches were deadlocked and ineffectual, the "least dangerous" branch surged ahead as the most powerful. Presidents and Congress alike avoided making controversial decisions, deferring instead to the judiciary, and apologists for the Supreme Court declared that the Court could redefine the Constitution in the interest of "social justice." The Court, in turn, became as disdainful of the letter and spirit of the Constitution as any recent president had been.[36]

34. *U.S. v. Nixon*, 418 U.S. 683 (1974); Schlesinger, *Imperial Presidency*, 269–272; Michael A. Genovese, *The Nixon Presidency: Power and Politics in Turbulent Times* (Westport, CT, 1990); and Bob Woodward and Carl Bernstein, *The Final Days* (London, 1976).

35. *New York Times*, July 30–Aug. 10, 1974, especially Aug. 9, 1:7, 2:1. For the articles of impeachment, see Goldsmith, ed., *Growth of Presidential Power*, 3:2212–2216. The impact of the threat of impeachment was verified to me during a conversation with Richard Nixon, Oct. 30, 1992.

36. For an excellent summary of these developments, see Lino A. Graglia, "How the Constitution Disappeared," in *Still the Law of the Land? Essays on Changing Interpretations of the Constitution* (Hillsdale, MI, 1987), 37–61; see also Robert H. Bork, *The Tempting of America: The Political Seduction of the Law* (New York, 1990), and James McClellan, "The Judicialization of the American Republic," in *Judges War:*

When Ronald Reagan assumed the presidency in 1981, checking the tendencies of the Court was high on his agenda. He sought to rein in the Court less as a matter of freeing the president's hands—though that must have entered his calculations—than as a means of coping with social issues that concerned a large portion of his supporters. He believed that the way to check the Court was through the president's power to appoint federal judges. For the most part, his predecessors had appointed justices and judges as political prizes or for political ends, paying little attention to the quality or the ideas of the appointees. Harry Truman appointed cronies or friends of cronies; Jimmy Carter filled the district and circuit benches with as many "minorities" as he could. When presidents had appointed with a view toward ensuring desired rulings, the appointments often backfired. For example, Lincoln appointed Chase as chief justice thinking that he would uphold the paper money Chase had instituted as secretary of the treasury (he did not), and Wilson appointed Brandeis at least partly because of his ideas on antitrust policy (Brandeis wrote only one decision on the subject).37

President Reagan, on the other hand, scrupulously screened prospective nominees for ability and integrity, but more importantly for judicial philosophy, the idea being to appoint people who believed in

---

The Senate, Legal Culture, Political Ideology and Judicial Confirmation, ed. Patrick B. McGuigan and Jeffrey P. O'Connell (Washington, DC, 1987), 61–100; Edwin Meese III, *With Reagan: The Inside Story* (Washington, DC, 1992), 315–316. A midway position is taken by Fried, *Order and Law,* 56–70. For defenses of the Court's activism, see William J. Brennan, Georgetown University speech of Oct. 12, 1985, in *New York Times,* Oct. 13, 1985, A, 1:2 and A, 36:3; John Paul Stevens's remarks, *New York Times,* Oct. 26, A, 1:1 and 11:4; John Hart Ely, *Democracy and Distrust* (Cambridge, MA, 1980).

37. Evan A. Evans, "Political Influences in the Selection of Federal Judges," *Wisconsin Law Review* (May 1948):330–351; Griffin B. Bell, "Federal Judicial Selection: The Carter Years," in *Judicial Selection: Merit, Ideology, and Politics* (Washington, DC, 1990), 25–32; David F. Pike, "The Court-Packing Plans," in Fisher, *American Constitutional Law,* 168–169; George C. Smith, "Judicial Qualifications and Confirmation: The Carter Years," in McGuigan and O'Connell, ed., *Judges War,* 135–154; David M. O'Brien, *Judicial Roulette* (New York, 1988), 40–44, 58–64; Forrest McDonald, "Supreme Court Nominees: A Look at the Precedents," *Wall Street Journal,* Sept. 16, 1987.

judicial restraint and the doctrine of "original intent." This selection process was designed to take judges "out of politics in two senses— first by minimizing if not eliminating entirely the problem of crony- ism, and second by ensuring that the nominees were selected, not for their views on particular issues, but for their understanding of the judicial role and their fidelity to the Constitution." It reflected an effort to restore a separation of powers and to effect a balance be- tween executive and judicial. Of the 761 district and appellate judge- ships in the federal judiciary, Reagan appointed 371.[38]

The effectiveness of Reagan's approach, however, is questionable. For one thing, conservative appointees to the Supreme Court proved to be as unpredictable as Chase, Brandeis, and many others had been. For another, George Bush did not continue Reagan's policy, and he was dilatory in making judicial appointments. During his last year in office the Senate Judiciary Committee held up a number of nomina- tions, with the result that President Clinton had more than a hun- dred district and circuit judgeships to fill and faced the possibility of appointing several Supreme Court justices as well.

———— There remain to be considered the presidential powers that are or seem to be contradictory to the "take care" clause. The most striking of these would appear to be the president's enumerated au- thority to grant reprieves and pardons, though as we have seen its design was at least in part to facilitate the execution of the laws. It

38. Meese, *With Reagan,* 316–320, quote at 320. Stephen J. Markman, "Judicial Selection: The Reagan Years," in *Judicial Selection,* 33–47; Bruce E. Fein, "Politics: The Art of Public Education," in *Steering the Elephant: How Washington Works,* ed. Robert Rector and Michael Sanera (New York, 1987), 20; Tinsley E. Yarbrough, "Reagan and the Courts," in *The Reagan Presidency: An Incomplete Revolution?* ed. Dilys M. Hill, Raymond A. Moore, and Phil Williams (Southampton, Eng., 1990), 68–93; and especially William French Smith, *Law and Justice in the Reagan Adminis- tration* (Stanford, CA, 1992). The politicization of the judicial appointment process by the liberal Democrats on the Senate Judiciary Committee emerged clearly during the bitter hearings concerning the nominations of Robert H. Bork in 1987 and Clarence Thomas in 1991. Bork was rejected; Thomas was confirmed; the flaws in the system were clear to partisans of both sides. From 1795 to 1992, eighteen Supreme Court nominations were either rejected or withdrawn because of the Senate's opposi- tion (O'Brien, *Judicial Roulette,* 67).

was thought that, in dealing with conspiracies in particular, plotters could be induced to betray their confederates by the prospect of a pardon for themselves. To some extent that has worked in practice. In recent years, for example, various leaders of organized crime syndicates have been imprisoned after underlings testified against them in exchange for immunity from prosecution for their own crimes; such bargains, however, are commonly struck under the executive prerogative not to prosecute (nolle prosequi) rather than under the authority to pardon.[39]

By far the most common use of the pardoning power has not been individual but wholesale, amnesty proclamations designed to restore order by showing mercy after periods of widespread resistance to the laws or the government. Washington's handling of the Whiskey Rebellion established the pattern; John Adams followed much the same course in dealing with the Fries Rebellion of 1799. Other presidents have granted general amnesties ever since. Madison granted amnesty in 1815 to a group of pirates. In 1863 Lincoln proclaimed amnesty for rebels who met certain conditions, as his successor Andrew Johnson did in 1865, 1867, and 1868. Theodore Roosevelt granted amnesty to the Filipino rebel Emilio Aguinaldo and his followers in 1902, and Wilson, Coolidge, and Franklin Roosevelt did to other classes of lawbreakers in 1917, 1924, and 1933. In 1952 Harry Truman pardoned 9,000 people who had deserted the armed forces (in peacetime). More recently, Jimmy Carter announced a general amnesty for Vietnam-era draft evaders in 1977, completing a process begun selectively by Gerald Ford.[40]

39. On pardoning in general, the standard authority is W. H. Humbert, *The Pardoning Power of the President* (Washington, DC, 1941); see also David Gray Adler, "The President's Pardon Power," in *Inventing the American Presidency,* ed. Thomas E. Cronin (Lawrence, KS, 1989), 209–235, and William Duker, "The President's Power to Pardon: A Constitutional History," *William and Mary Law Review* 18 (1977):475, 525, 535.

40. Humbert, *Pardoning Power,* 40, 42; Corwin, *President,* 159–160; Ralph A. Brown, *The Presidency of John Adams* (Lawrence, KS, 1975), 127–129; *Messages and Papers of the Presidents,* comp., James D. Richardson, 10 vols. (Washington, DC, 1889–1905), 1:181, 303, 6:213, 310, 547, 655, 708; *Public Papers of the Presidents of the United States, Harry S. Truman,* volume 1952–1953 (Washington, DC, 1966), 1233; Adler, "President's Pardon Power," in Cronin, ed., *Inventing the American Presidency,* 218–219;

The president's power to grant amnesties has never been seriously challenged. In 1869 the Senate Judiciary Committee did adopt a report denying the power, but the full Senate refused to approve the report, and significantly, the House had not included Johnson's grants of amnesty among the charges in the bill of impeachment against him the year before. The most fully reasoned statement regarding amnesties was formulated by William Howard Taft in 1891 when he was serving as solicitor general under Benjamin Harrison. If the president could pardon separately 10,000 individuals, Taft argued—and no one doubted that he could—it followed logically that he could issue one pardon for the same offenders as a group.[41]

In contrast to the implied power to proclaim amnesties, the nature and extent of the enumerated power to grant individual pardons have been tested in courts on a number of occasions. The first leading case involved a man named Wilson who had been indicted for crimes related to mail robbery, one of which carried the death penalty. Andrew Jackson pardoned him for the capital crime but not for the others. Wilson refused to accept the pardon as offered, and the federal district court was divided as to whether the pardon was effective anyway. When the case reached the Supreme Court, Chief Justice Marshall pronounced two doctrines about the nature of pardons. Like the English kings' pardon (to which Marshall expressly linked it), presidential pardon was a private, personal act of grace. And, "a pardon is a deed to the validity of which delivery is essential; and delivery is not complete without acceptance; it may then be rejected by the person to whom it is tendered; and if it be rejected, we have discovered no power in a court to force it to him."[42]

That decision has not entirely stood the test of time. The "act of

---

Jonathan T. Dorris, *Pardon and Amnesty under Lincoln and Johnson* (Chapel Hill, NC, 1953); Morris Sherman, *Amnesty in America* (Passaic, NJ, 1974).

41. Humbert, *Pardoning Power*, 37. It is now generally agreed that amnesties are distinguished from dispensings in only one vital particular: Though they (like individual pardons) can be granted prior to convictions for violating the law, they cannot be granted prior to the commissions of crimes.

42. Humbert, *Pardoning Power*, 64–65; Corwin, *President*, 159; *U.S.* v. *Wilson*, 32 U.S. 150 (1833); Peter M. Shane and Harold H. Bruff, *The Law of Presidential Power: Cases and Materials* (Durham, NC, 1988), 440.

grace" interpretation slipped into disuse, and the pardon became instead, as Justice Holmes opined in 1927, "a part of the Constitutional scheme. When granted it is the determination of the ultimate authority that the public welfare will be better served by inflicting less than what the judgment fixed." The ruling that no one is obliged to accept a pardon and that it is invalid if rejected has had a mixed history. In 1915 the Court had upheld the doctrine, but in the 1927 case just mentioned it ruled that the president could "commute" a death sentence to life imprisonment—deemed a less than "full" pardon—without the acceptance of the guilty party. Whether consent to a full pardon would still be required has not been recently adjudicated.[43]

The leading case defining the range and effect of a pardon arose during Reconstruction. In 1865 Congress passed an act prescribing an oath of office, requiring attorneys practicing before the federal bar to swear that they had never borne arms against the United States or given aid and comfort to its enemies. Andrew Johnson, in addition to the general amnesties he granted, individually pardoned another 13,500 former Confederates, including Augustus H. Garland, who had in 1860 been admitted to the federal bar. He sued to be allowed to practice and won a favorable decision by a five-to-four vote. The majority held that in Garland's case the oath act was both a bill of attainder and an ex post facto law and thus unconstitutional on those counts. It also ruled that the act could not nullify the force of the president's pardon. The pardoning power, the Court held, was "unlimited except in cases of impeachment." "It extends to every offense known to the law," which is to say federal law, "and may be exercised at any time" after the commission of the offense, whether before, during, or after trial. "Congress can neither limit the effect" of the president's pardon, "nor exclude from its exercise any class of offenders." A pardon, the Court went on, when it is full, "releases the punishment and blots out of existence the guilt, so that in the eye of the law the offender is as innocent as if he had never committed the

---

43. Humbert, *Pardoning Power*, 66–71; *Biddle* v. *Perovich*, 274 U.S. 480, 486 (1927); *Burdick* v. *U.S.*, 236 U.S. 79 (1915); Corwin, *President*, 158–162. Corwin asserted that the acceptance doctrine is dead; Humbert (73) deems Corwin's claim an overstatement.

offence. . . . it makes him, as it were, a new man." The Court during the twentieth century has made only minor exceptions to the "new man" interpretation.[44]

Another leading case, decided in 1925, established the principle that the pardoning power extends to criminal contempt of court rulings, though not to civil contempt. Philip Grossman, owner of a Chicago restaurant, was found to be selling alcohol illegally on his premises, and the federal district court issued an injunction to stop him. He continued to sell liquor despite the injunction, whereupon the court found him guilty of contempt and sentenced him to a year's imprisonment and a $1,000 fine. President Coolidge commuted the sentence to paying the fine. District Judge James Wilkinson ordered Grossman jailed anyway on the ground that if the pardon power extended to contempt, the president would become "the ultimate source of judicial authority" and the "very existence" of an independent judiciary would be undermined. The Supreme Court ruled otherwise and cited twenty-seven instances during the preceding eighty-five years in which contempt rulings had been overturned by pardons.[45]

The pardoning power is potentially awesome and dangerous, but despite occasional suspicions and charges, it has not been proved that the pardon has been used corruptly. Andrew Johnson was alleged to have taken bribes for granting pardons, and Congress examined his bank records in search of unusual deposits; the investigators found nothing incriminating. Richard Nixon was rumored to have pardoned Jimmy Hoffa in exchange for the political support of the Teamsters' Union, and Gerald Ford was suspected of having agreed to pardon Nixon in exchange for Nixon's stepping down to let Ford

44. *Ex parte Garland,* 71 U.S. 333, 334, 380–381 (1867); Lately Thomas, *The First President Johnson* (New York, 1968), 394–400; Adler, "President's Pardon Power," in Cronin, ed., *Inventing the American Presidency,* 218. Adler (231, n. 6) points out that the "new man" theory derives from Bracton, as does Duker, "The President's Power to Pardon," *William and Mary Law Review,* 534. Shane and Bruff, *Law of Presidential Power,* 440–442.

45. *Ex parte Grossman,* 267 U.S. 87, 118 (1925); Corwin, *President,* 162–164; Humbert, *Pardoning Power,* 57–58; *Cases and Other Authorities Selected from Decisions of State and Federal Courts,* ed. Walter F. Dodd (St. Paul, MN, 1932), 258–264; *New York Times,* Dec. 2, 1924, 6:4 and March 3, 1925, 25:1.

become president; the principals denied both allegations, and no evidence was found to substantiate the charges. H. R. Haldeman, Nixon's chief of staff during the Watergate scandal, proposed a corrupt use of the pardon—a blanket pardon for all persons connected with the episode—but Nixon rejected the advice.[46]

As a normal matter, of course, the use of the pardon has not been dramatic or controversial. Since 1891 the Office of the Pardon Attorney in the Justice Department has investigated routine applications for pardons and made recommendations to the attorney general, who in turn makes a recommendation to the president, who decides the matter. Between 1902 and 1936, the percentage of federal prisoners receiving some sort of executive clemency—that is, pardon to a lesser or greater degree—ranged from 1.8 to 13.5 annually, the average number of acts of clemency being around 300 a year. More recently, the numbers have declined, despite a much larger base of prisoners. Between 1953 and 1984, not counting the Vietnam-conflict amnesties, about 4,600 pardons and 500 commutations were granted, an average of about 170 a year. Ronald Reagan, during his eight years in office, issued about 380 pardons, fewer than 50 a year.[47]

————— Impoundment—a selective refusal to spend money that Congress has appropriated—is a device by which presidents from Jefferson onward have declined to enforce the law for a variety of reasons. In 1857 James Buchanan got into a spat with some congressmen from Illinois and to chastise them withheld funds that had been appropriated to construct various buildings in their districts. In 1876 President Grant approved a rivers and harbors bill but announced that he objected to some of the appropriations as being "of purely private or local interest" and that he would refuse to spend the funds. Every president from Franklin Roosevelt to Ronald Reagan impounded

46. Adler, "President's Pardon Power," in Cronin, ed., *Inventing the American Presidency,* 220–224, 228. I heard the rumor concerning Hoffa from an attorney for the Teamsters' Union; John M. Orman, "Exercise of the President's Discretionary Power in Criminal Justice Policy," *Presidential Studies Quarterly* 9 (1979):421, asserts it but without documentation.

47. Humber, *Pardoning Power,* 111–112; Adler, "President's Pardon Power," in Cronin, ed., *Inventing the American Presidency,* 212–219.

appropriations, sometimes on a small scale and for good reasons, at other times on a grand scale and for questionable reasons.[48]

Claims of presidential authority to impound funds have been grounded on four general bases: efficiency in management, statutory authorization, constitutional interpretation, and the doctrine of inherent power. The first was purely commonsensical. As Attorney General Judson Harmon declared in an 1896 opinion, appropriations are not mandatory "to the extent that you are bound to expend the full amount if the work can be done for less." Warren G. Harding's budget director, Charles G. Dawes, made the same point in the early 1920s. The House Appropriations Committee reported in 1950 that an appropriation of a set amount for a particular purpose was "only a ceiling upon the amount which should be expended for that activity" and that the administrative officials responsible for carrying it out should do so "with the smallest amount possible within the ceiling fixture fixed by the Congress."[49]

Statutory authorizations or mandates for the president to impound funds have been legislated many times. In 1933 Franklin Roosevelt was ordered to reduce spending as much as possible. In the Omnibus Appropriations Act of 1950 Harry Truman was directed to cut the budget by $550 million; the pruning itself was left to his discretion except that he was not to impair the national defense. On several occasions during the 1960s Congress directed spending cuts or enacted general budget ceilings, which implicitly granted impoundment powers, as did legal limits on the size of the public debt. Occasionally during that decade, specific, limited impoundments were also authorized—as, for example, in the Civil Rights Act of 1964, which empowers the president to withhold federal funds from programs in which there is racial discrimination.[50]

Constitutional authorization for impoundments has been claimed mainly in relation to the president's office as commander in chief. A case in point arose in 1948 when Congress voted funds for seventy air

48. Fisher, *Constitutional Conflicts,* 128–130; Richardson, comp., *Messages and Papers of the Presidents,* 9:4331; Louis Fisher, *Presidential Spending Power* (Princeton, NJ, 1975), 147–174; Pious, *American Presidency,* 278–288.

49. Fisher, *Presidential Spending Power,* 37–39, 148, 149.

50. Ibid., 40–41; Schlesinger, *Imperial Presidency,* 236–237.

groups even though Truman had requested fifty-five. He signed the bill, but declaring that a balance must be struck between considerations of national security and a healthy economy, he announced that he would place the extra $822 million in reserve. No one challenged his authority. Again, from 1961 to 1963 the Kennedy administration was at odds with Congress over the funding of the B-70 bomber; Congress voted far more money for the purpose than Kennedy thought proper, and though considerable maneuvering occurred to avoid the appearance of a confrontation, the money went unspent.[51]

The boldest claims to the impoundment power, those made by the Nixon administration, were sometimes justified on statutory or constitutional grounds, but it seems clear that President Nixon and his subordinates assumed that the power inhered in the presidential office and was virtually limitless. In December of 1972 and January of 1973—in the wake of his reelection by the largest margin in modern history—Nixon began a campaign of impoundments designed to end congressional programs in their entirety. The main targets were various subsidies for public housing, to farmers, and to local governments for developing water and sewer facilities, but it appeared that the net would be cast wider—until, some people feared, the whole domain of public spending would be ruled by presidential prerogative.[52]

In response, after a number of lawsuits successfully challenged certain of the impoundments and after the two houses failed to agree on legislation in 1973, Congress enacted the Congressional Budget and Impoundment Control Act of 1974. Impoundments were classified as being of two kinds, recissions and deferrals, the one being the outright cancellation of a budget authority, the other being a delay

51. *Truman in the White House: The Diary of Eben A. Ayers,* ed. Robert H. Ferrell (Columbia, MO, 1991), entry of April 21, 1948; *The Harry S. Truman Encyclopedia,* ed. Richard S. Kirkendall (Boston, 1989), 5–6. Fisher, *Presidential Spending Power,* 162–165, places the incident in 1949 and says that Congress voted for fifty-eight air groups; McCoy, *Harry Truman,* properly places the incident in 1948 but sets the final congressional allocation at sixty-six bomber groups. The *New York Times* in April and May, 1948, records the episode and sets the congressional allocation at seventy groups.

52. Richard Hodder, "The President and the Constitution," and David Mervin, "The President and Congress," in Shaw, ed., *Roosevelt to Reagan,* 40–41, 103–104; Fisher, *Presidential Spending Power,* 175–186; Schlesinger, *Imperial Presidency,* 237–244.

or a stretching out of a program. In taking either kind of action, the president was required to notify Congress. For a recission to take effect, both houses were required to ratify the impoundment within forty-five days. A deferral automatically became effective and remained in effect unless either house voted to veto it.[53]

The act might have been challenged on constitutional grounds. The White House had for decades maintained that appropriations were permissive, not mandatory, but Gerald Ford (when he succeeded to the presidency) chose to regard it as a new source of authority for impounding funds. That could be done because the legislation had been poorly and ambiguously drawn, and Ford used it to make more than a hundred policy impoundments a year, whereas Nixon had never exceeded a few dozen in a year. Congress reacted by making expenditures mandatory and by making appropriations ever more rigid.[54]

The impasse was broken in 1983 when the Supreme Court, in a case unrelated to the budget, declared that a one-house legislative veto was unconstitutional. Assuming that the ruling would be applied to the Impoundment Act if adjudicated, President Reagan and Congress agreed to restrict the use of deferrals. But then in 1985 Congress passed the Gramm-Rudman-Hollings Act, mandating budgetary restraints, and Reagan began to depend heavily on deferrals. In 1987, however, the Supreme Court ruled that the deferral authority was contingent on the one-house veto, and since the veto was unconstitutional the deferral authority could no longer be exercised. After that time the budget began once again to spin out of control.[55]

————— That turn of events, and the larger deadlock between legislative and executive of which it formed a part, was widely perceived

53. Fisher, *Presidential Spending Power,* 189–192, 198–199; Cronin, "Resurgent Congress," *Political Science Quarterly,* 215–216, 221–222; Fisher, *Constitutional Conflicts,* 129–197; Louis Fisher, *Court Cases on Impoundment of Funds* (Library of Congress: Congressional Research Service, Aug. 22, 1973); James MacGregor Burns, *The Power to Lead: The Crisis of the American Presidency* (New York, 1984), 174.

54. Fisher, *Presidential Spending Power,* 200–201.

55. Fisher, *Constitutional Conflicts,* 129–130; *Immigration and Naturalization Service v. Chada,* 462 U.S. 919 (1983); Fried, *Order and Law,* 148–151, 168.

as a crisis in government. The original constitutional understanding, that in domestic affairs Congress would make the law and presidents would see to its enforcement, had never worked in practice, and by the early 1990s it had largely been abandoned. No viable new arrangement had yet been devised in its place.[56]

---

56. See chapter 14 of this book. See also James J. Kilpatrick, "The Getting Is Still Good," *Tuscaloosa News,* May 13, 1992, 10A: "Last month President Bush attempted to slice some pork out of the federal budget. Last week the Senate made hash of his effort. The president had proposed to rescind 130 items. The Senate Appropriations Committee rejected 97."

CHAPTER 12

President and Administration

"The government does not govern," the historian Henry Adams, grandson of John Quincy Adams, wrote in 1870. "Congress is inefficient, and shows itself more and more incompetent." Meanwhile, "the Executive, in its full enjoyment of theoretical independence, is practically deprived of its necessary strength by the jealousy of the Legislature. Without responsibility, direct, incessant, and continuous, no government is practicable over forty millions of people and an entire continent, and no responsibility exists at Washington."[1]

The paralysis had come on slowly, and Adams perceived it as being constitutional in origin. The Constitution had been designed to restrain the federal government by pitting the presidency and the two houses of Congress as rivals as well as cooperators. But the scheme contemplated a small body of civil servants, no more than a few hundred, to administer government. By 1870 the number of government functionaries had grown to more than 50,000, and contention between Congress and presidency for the wealth and power that accompanied hiring and firing had brought about a deadlock.

1. Henry Brooks Adams, "The Session," in *North American Review* 111 (1870):60; also quoted in Leonard D. White, *The Republican Era: A Study in Administrative History, 1869–1901* (New York, 1958), 52.

When Adams wrote, control of the administrative machinery, after a series of struggles, had come temporarily to reside in Congress and particularly in the Senate. Yet movements were already afoot to remove administration from politics and to vest it instead in a career civil service of experts. Professionalization would become the rage for a half century, and the quality of government would improve considerably. Somewhere along the line, however, the bureaucracy became a fourth branch of government, over which the others continuously vied for dominance but none could control.

So far had the process gone by the 1990s that, despite endless efforts at reorganizing the machinery of administration, Congress was again widely regarded as "incompetent," the presidency was regarded as lacking "its necessary strength," and the impression was general that "no responsibility exists at Washington."

——— The introduction of the spoils system, as the political distribution of federal patronage was called, is generally (though not entirely accurately) associated with President Andrew Jackson, but Jackson thought of it as an instrument of reform, not of corruption. Before Jackson's accession to the presidency, federal officeholding, particularly at the higher levels, had tended to devolve almost exclusively upon well-educated, upper-class families. These people, Jackson declared, considered office "as a species of property" and saw "government rather as a means of promoting individual interests than as an instrument created solely for the service of the people." There was no need to confine offices to the highly educated few, for the "duties of all public officers are, or at least admit of being made, so plain and simple that men of intelligence may readily qualify themselves for their performance." Jackson further expressed a sentiment that had been recorded by De Lolme in the eighteenth century and would be echoed by advocates of term limits for legislators in the late twentieth: "I can not but believe that more is lost by the long continuance of men in office than is generally to be gained by their experience." Jackson asked Congress to enact a "general extension"—presumably to all federal employees—of the 1820 statute that limited certain officeholders to four-year terms. Such "rotation," as he called it, was "a leading principle in the republican creed." In practical terms, Jackson was proposing that political enemies be removed and replaced by partisan supporters or, as the Jacksonian senator William L. Marcy bluntly phrased it, that "to the victor belong the spoils."[2]

Jackson's position regarding appointments and removals engendered a great deal of opposition, but he turned over the personnel of the civil service less than was supposed at the time—though more than his predecessors had done—and his distribution of the spoils could scarcely be called a "system." Hordes "of all sorts of people, from the highest and most polished down to the most vulgar and gross in the nation" crowded the capital for Jackson's inauguration, most of them to seek appointments as well as to freeload on the refreshments furnished at the White House; Justice Joseph Story wrote that the "reign of King Mob" had begun.[3]

As for the volume of turnover, an administration newspaper reported after about eighteen months that 919 employees had been removed—of a total of 10,093—or a bit more than 9 percent. During the rest of Jackson's presidency somewhere between 10 and 20 percent more were replaced. In addition, however, the total number of federal employees nearly doubled. Though these numbers were minuscule by later standards, they were enough that, together with certain of Jackson's idiosyncrasies and the rejection of many of his nominees by the Senate, they required the president to spend an inordinate amount of time considering applicants and ensured that no uniform standards would be applied. Fitness for office was rarely considered.[4]

2. Leonard D. White, *The Jacksonians* (New York, 1954), 318; James D. Richardson, comp., *Messages and Papers of the Presidents,* 10 vols. (Washington, DC, 1889–1905), 2:448–449 (Dec. 8, 1829); Jean-Louis De Lolme, *The Constitution of England,* ed. John Macgregor (London, 1853), 167–168; *Register of Debates,* 22d Cong., 1st sess., p. 1325 (Jan. 24, 1832); Sidney H. Aronson, *Status and Kinship in the Higher Civil Service* (Cambridge, MA, 1964).

3. Carl Russell Fish, *The Civil Service and the Patronage* (1904; repr., New York, 1963).

4. Ibid., chap. 5, passim; White, *Jacksonians,* 308; Bureau of the Census, *Historical Statistics of the United States* (Washington, DC, 1961), 710; Erik McKinley Eriksson, "The Federal Civil Service under President Jackson," *Mississippi Valley Historical Review* 13 (1926/1927):527–528. It should be observed that figures on the number of government employees are of questionable reliability except in a general way; see Paul P. Van Riper, *History of the United States Civil Service* (Evanston, IL, 1958), 56–59. See a table in Robert Williams, "The President and the Executive Branch," in

Senatorial opposition to Jackson was based partly on self-interest—the Senate wanted a share of the patronage, or all of it—but it also derived from the conviction that Jackson and his policies were dangerous for the country, threatening economic ruin and virtual dictatorship. The opponents, led by Daniel Webster, Henry Clay, and (after 1832, when he resigned the vice-presidency and was elected to the Senate) John C. Calhoun, at first called themselves the National Republican party but later took the name Whigs, to dramatize themselves as opponents to "King Andrew the First."[5]

The climax of their opposition came in response to Jackson's war against the Bank of the United States. Jackson, sincerely albeit foolishly convinced that the Bank made "the rich richer and the potent more powerful" and would "destroy the liberties of our country," set out to kill it. To that end he ordered the secretary of the treasury, Louis McLane, to remove the government's deposits from the Bank. But McLane was required by law to remove the deposits only if he judged them to be unsafe; not so judging, he refused. Jackson replaced him with William Duane, who likewise refused to obey the president's order; Jackson summarily fired him and replaced him with Attorney General Taney, who withdrew the deposits. The Senate promptly adopted resolutions censuring Jackson, but the Whigs failed in their attempt to reverse the decision made in 1789 by requiring senatorial approval for removal as well as for appointment.[6]

––––––––

Roosevelt to Reagan, ed. Malcolm Shaw (London, 1987), 120, which shows the increase in the number of civil servants from 3,000 in 1800 to 50,000 in 1849, to 600,000 in 1932, and 3,000,000 in 1980—growth paralleling the creation of departments and agencies.

5. Thomas Payne Govan, *Nicholas Biddle: Nationalist and Public Banker, 1786–1844* (Chicago, 1959), 112–274; Robert V. Remini, *Henry Clay: Statesman for the Union* (New York, 1991); Merrill D. Peterson, *The Great Triumvirate: Webster, Clay, and Calhoun* (New York, 1987); and Gerald W. Johnson, *America's Silver Age: The Statecraft of Clay—Webster—Calhoun* (New York, 1939).

6. Richardson, comp., *Messages and Papers of the Presidents,* 2:576–591 (July 10, 1832); Govan, *Biddle,* 201–202; Bray Hammond, *Banks and Politics in America from the Revolution to the Civil War* (Princeton, NJ, 1957); White, *Jacksonians,* 40–42; Fish, *Civil Service,* 140–142; James Roger Sharp, "Andrew Jackson and the Limits of Presidential Power," *Congressional Studies* 7 (1980):63–80.

Interestingly, it was the Whigs who turned the spoils system into a semipermanent feature of federal politics, after some flukish turns of events. The Whigs captured the presidency in 1840 with the "Log Cabin and Hard Cider" campaign of William Henry Harrison and John Tyler and gained control of both houses of Congress. Harrison, an irresolute man with a somewhat bogus reputation as a military hero, capitulated entirely to Whig congressional leaders and their opposition to an energetic presidency. In his inaugural address, written largely by the secretary of state, Daniel Webster, he virtually repudiated the idea of presidential power, and apparently he agreed that executive decisions would be made by majority vote in the cabinet. As for patronage, his Whig masters rejected the spoils system in theory, but when a mob of 30,000 to 40,000 office-seekers showed up for the inauguration, the Whigs decided that it was prudent to throw the Jacksonian rascals out and replace them with their own. Before they could begin seriously implementing that policy, however, Harrison died—one month after taking the oath of office.[7]

Tyler, thus becoming the first vice-president to accede to the presidency upon the death of an incumbent president, was in an awkward position. In part his discomfort arose because members of both parties thought of him as an "acting" president, not a real one, and referred to him as "His Accidency." More importantly, Tyler was a Virginia republican of the old school who had been nominated by the Whigs solely to balance their ticket, and by the end of his first year he and the Whigs had broken with one another. Vainly hoping to build a power base for election in 1844, he removed many officials and named personal and political friends as replacements. The task became almost a full-time job, for the majority of his nominees were rejected by the Senate. Even so, it became generally accepted that appointments to public office were purely partisan and purely political.[8]

7. Richardson, comp., *Messages and Papers of the Presidents*, 4:5–21 (March 4, 1851); Leonard D. White, *The Jeffersonians* (New York, 1951), 46–47, 303–304; Fish, *Civil Service*, 143–144; Norma Lois Peterson, *The Presidencies of William Henry Harrison and John Tyler* (Lawrence, KS, 1989), 35–39.

8. Fish, *Civil Service*, 147–157; Peterson, *Harrison and Tyler*, 45–51, 71, 168–169, 197–198, 224–225, 236–241. Conflicts between the Senate and the president in later years did not produce a high level of rejection by the Senate of presidential nominees;

Except for Lincoln, who demonstrated during the emergency of the Civil War the great potential the presidency contained, the nineteenth-century presidents continued to be little more than chief clerks of personnel. Because control of the presidency changed parties in every election but one from 1840 through 1860, an enormous turnover in personnel occurred every four years. Zachary Taylor, for instance, removed nearly two-thirds of the presidential appointees during his first year, and more than one-third of all government employees resigned or were removed; when he died after two years the continuing turnover required that his successor, Millard Fillmore, spend almost half of every working day processing applications for office. James K. Polk differed from the others in using the patronage to effect policy, but he confined appointments to his own party. James Buchanan rounded out the spoils system: Though a Democrat, when he became president in 1857 he purged the civil service of the appointees of his Democratic predecessor, Franklin Pierce. Lincoln effected the most thorough change of all: 1,457 removals from the 1,639 "places within his gift." (According to Carl Russell Fish, the pioneer student of the subject, the first president to break the pattern of rotation was Theodore Roosevelt.)[9]

President Lincoln, though a man of iron will, was not immune to the difficulties arising from bickering about patronage. He avoided some friction by leaving the chore of dealing with Congress, which he found personally as well as philosophically unpalatable, largely to the cabinet officers, especially Secretary of War Edwin Stanton and

---

between 1961 and 1977 only four major nominations were rejected by a floor vote, nine by a committee vote, and twenty-seven were forced to withdraw (G. Calvin Mackenzie, *The Politics of Presidential Appointments* [New York, 1981], 177).

9. Fish, *Civil Service*, 159–160, 163, 166–170; Elbert B. Smith, *The Presidencies of Zachary Taylor and Millard Fillmore* (Lawrence, KS, 1988), 57–65, 159–163; Elbert B. Smith, *The Presidency of James Buchanan* (Lawrence, KS, 1975), 20–22, 67, 68, 84–85, 102–103. Polk wrote in his diary, "Will the pressure for office never cease! It is one year to-day since I entered on the duties of my office, and still the pressure for office has not abated. I most sincerely wish that I had no offices to bestow" (March 4, 1846, *The Diary of James K. Polk During His Presidency, 1845 to 1849*, vol. 1, ed. Milo Milton Quaife [Chicago, 1910], 261). For the pressures on Pierce, see Larry Gara, *The Presidency of Franklin Pierce* (Lawrence, KS, 1991), 49–51.

Secretary of the Treasury Salmon P. Chase; but they and Secretary of State William Seward were continually conspiring against each other and against the president himself. Moreover, Lincoln was squeezed between Chase, who demanded the right to approve Treasury employees, and Seward and New York Republican boss Thurlow Weed, who insisted that they (in consultation with the Senate) should manage all federal appointments in New York State. Chase ultimately resigned in response to the issue, and by the time of his reelection, Lincoln controlled neither the cabinet nor the Congress, in which Radical Republicans were on a collision course with the president.[10]

The collision came, but the assassination of Lincoln meant that it would be between Congress and Andrew Johnson, which made it more violent. For one thing, Johnson was neither patient nor skillful; his attitude toward Congress was truculent and stubborn. For another, Congress was overwhelmingly Republican; Johnson was a Democrat (for the third time, the nation had had a president and a vice-president from different parties). Moreover, Johnson was determined to return the seceded states to the Union quickly and with a minimum of conditions, and the Radicals in Congress, while not of one mind as to details, were determined to impose harsh conditions and inflict serious punishments.[11]

Disagreements over control of the patronage precipitated the clash. Johnson had intended to retain the civil service establishment appointed under Lincoln, but when the depths of his policy differences with Congress became evident—he vetoed twenty-one bills; fifteen vetoes were overridden—Johnson set out to solidify his power by appointing his supporters. Lashing back, in March of 1867 Congress

---

10. Edward S. Corwin, *The President, 1789–1957* (New York, 1957), 24, 324; Fish, *Civil Service*, 177; Harry J. Carman and Reinhard H. Luthin, *Lincoln and the Patronage* (New York, 1943).

11. The bibliography on Johnson and Reconstruction is huge and varies ideologically. See Martin E. Mantell, *Johnson, Grant, and the Politics of Reconstruction* (New York, 1973); James E. Sefton, *Andrew Johnson and the Uses of Constitutional Power* (Boston, 1980), 123, 137, 157–158; Kenneth M. Stampp, *The Era of Reconstruction, 1865–1877* (New York, 1965); Howard K. Beale, *The Critical Year: A Study of Andrew Johnson and Reconstruction* (New York, 1930); Eric L. McKitrick, *Andrew Johnson and Reconstruction* (Chicago, 1960); Eric Foner, *Reconstruction: America's Unfinished Revolution, 1863–1877* (New York, 1988).

passed (over the president's veto) the Tenure of Office Act, requiring senatorial approval of presidential removals. Cabinet officers were covered in a special clause: The act provided that they should hold office for the term of the president by whom they had been appointed, subject to removal by and with the advice and consent of the Senate. After some skirmishing, Johnson challenged the act in 1868 by removing Secretary of War Stanton.[12]

Apparently Johnson was hoping to set up a court case to test the constitutionality of the Tenure of Office Act, but instead the House voted to impeach him. Two of the articles of impeachment were trivial; the other nine were variations on the removal of Stanton. Attorneys for the president argued that the act was unconstitutional, citing Madison, the decision of 1789, and the precedents of seventy-nine years. Though the entire proceeding was a political vendetta, enough members of the Senate were sufficiently persuaded by constitutional scruples to oppose conviction—the impeachment falling short of the constitutionally required two-thirds majority by one vote.[13]

The Tenure of Office Act remained on the books for almost a generation, however, during which Congress for practical purposes controlled the patronage, despite efforts of some presidents to assert themselves.[14] It is small wonder that during that era the federal government virtually lost contact with the tide of events.

———— Calls for reform of the system, emanating from a variety of sources, were being heard throughout the period. Partly the calls were rooted in sheer disgust at the incompetence of government, as Henry Adams's had been, but there was in some quarters also a sense of moral outrage at the decadence of public life. It was not that

12. Fish, *Civil Service,* 188–197; William H. Rehnquist, *Grand Inquests* (New York, 1992), 184–202; Robert J. Spitzer, *The Presidential Veto: Touchstone of the American Presidency* (Albany, NY, 1988), 58. Johnson actually vetoed twenty-nine measures, a record to that time, but eight were pocket vetoes, not subject to override.

13. Rehnquist, *Grand Inquests,* 199–221; Michael Les Benedict, *The Impeachment and Trial of Andrew Johnson* (New York, 1973); David Miller Dewitt, *The Impeachment and Trial of Andrew Johnson* (New York, 1903).

14. Repeal came in 1886 (Fish, *Civil Service,* 206–208). Repeal was the work of Democrats, who regained control of the White House and Congress in the 1884 elections.

venality was especially more widespread than it had been; after all, in 1838 the collector of the port of New York, Samuel Swartwout, had absconded with $1,225,705.69—a sum that, as a percentage of the federal budget, would have been equivalent to about $160 billion in 1992. Nor was it the practice of levying "assessments" (a percentage of the salary of government employees collected to pay party expenses and fatten the purses of party leaders), though that was more blatant than it had been earlier.[15]

Rather, the moral stimuli for reform arose from at least three separate sources. Among better-educated Americans, who formed a disproportionately large number of the reformers, there was a painful sense of decline from the standards of public conduct that had graced the national councils during most of the time from Washington's presidency to that of John Quincy Adams. (The opposite side of the same phenomenon was encapsulated in H. L. Mencken's remark that Theodore Roosevelt became a reformer because he was "scandalized by the discovery that his town was run by men with such names as Michael O'Shaunnessy and Terence Googan.") A second stimulus was the spillover of the moral fervor that had accompanied the abolitionist movement, the Civil War, and Reconstruction; the flow of self-righteousness, once started, is difficult to stem. A third was the frequency of scandals during Grant's presidency, which arose less from an increase in corruption than from the shortsightedness of politicians in breaking one of their cardinal rules, namely that they respect each other's right to earn a living, however dishonestly. The major scandals of the Grant administration surfaced when professional politicians blew the whistle on other professionals.[16]

15. House Doc. 13, 25th Cong., 3d sess., Dec. 10, 1838, p. 29; White, *Jacksonians*, 424–428; Fish, *Civil Service*, 137–140; William E. Nelson, *The Roots of American Bureaucracy, 1830–1900* (Cambridge, MA, 1982), 120.

16. Nelson, *Roots of American Bureaucracy*, stresses the moral roots of the reform movement. Ari Hoogenboom, in *Outlawing the Spoils: A History of the Civil Service Reform Movement, 1865–1883* (Urbana, IL, 1961), is skeptical of the moral roots and emphasizes the self-interestedness of the reformers. The Mencken quotation is from *A Mencken Chrestomathy* (New York, 1962), 236. The classic work on the scandals of the Grant administration is Allan Nevins, *Hamilton Fish: The Inner History of the Grant Administration* (New York, 1936).

The civil service reformers gained ever-widening popular support as the nineteenth century wore on, for the disruptions attending the technological and industrial revolutions, together with massive urbanization and immigration, left millions of Americans feeling that they lived in a strange new world in which they had lost control over their lives. On the positive side, the new technology included such devices as the typewriter and adding machine, which appeared to bring "scientific" administration within reach, and the emergence of gigantic corporations seemed to provide models of scientific management as well as to necessitate scientific federal regulation.[17]

Similar forces were at work throughout the industrializing world, and American reformers were in communication with like-minded people in England, France, Germany, and New Zealand. Congressman Thomas Allen Jenckes of Rhode Island, Sen. Charles Sumner of Massachusetts, editor E. L. Godkin of the *Nation,* political editor George W. Curtis of *Harper's Weekly,* and a host of social scientists emerging from the newly instituted graduate schools formed part of an international network of champions of change. Their prescriptions varied in detail, but in essence what they sought was to remove power from professional politicians and legislative bodies, concentrate it in the executive branch, and place it in the hands of experts.[18]

The agenda was profoundly antidemocratic, but the reformers found ways to work around American "prejudices" in favor of popular government. One of the more interesting arguments was that offered by the young political scientist Woodrow Wilson. England and America were far behind Prussia and France in administrative efficiency, Wilson wrote in 1887, because the "English race . . . has

17. Paul P. Van Riper, "The American Administrative State: Wilson and the Founders," in *A Centennial History of the American Administrative State,* ed. Ralph Clark Chandler (New York, 1987), 22–24; Alfred D. Chandler, Jr., *The Visible Hand: The Managerial Revolution in American Business* (Cambridge, MA, 1978); Robert H. Wiebe, *The Search for Order, 1877–1920* (New York, 1967).

18. White, *Republican Era,* 297–302; Nelson, *Roots of American Bureaucracy,* 82–112; Fish, *Civil Service,* 209–213; Frederick C. Mosher, ed., *Basic Literature of American Public Administration, 1787–1950* (New York, 1981), 49–107; Hoogenboom, *Outlawing the Spoils,* 13–49; Peter J. Coleman, *Progressivism and the World of Reform: New Zealand and the Origins of the American Welfare State* (Lawrence, KS, 1987).

been more concerned to render government just and moderate than to make it facile, well-ordered, and effective." But the struggle for constitutional government having long since been won, it was now "imperatively necessary" to develop efficient administration. "We should not like to have had Prussia's history for the sake of having Prussia's administrative skill," Wilson admitted, "and Prussia's particular system of administration would quite suffocate us. It is better to be untrained and free than to be servile and systematic. Still there is no denying that it would be better yet to be both free in spirit and proficient in practice." The means to that end, he was confident, lay in the distinction between policy-making or politics on the one hand and ministering, administering, or executing on the other. The one was the exclusive domain of public opinion and the electoral process; the other should be the exclusive domain of experts trained in the science of administration.[19]

The first major fruit of the reformers' labors, except for an impotent civil service commission that had been set up in 1871 and allowed to die four years later, was the passage in 1883 of the Pendleton Act. Passage is generally attributed to reaction against the assassination of James A. Garfield by a disappointed office-seeker; the bill was signed into law by Chester A. Arthur, who had once been removed as collector for the port of New York for political reasons. The act created the Civil Service Commission and required open competitive examinations for certain classes of federal employment. This merit system governing appointments did not impair the president's power of removal, but it made possible contemplation of careers in federal service by deterring removals for purely partisan reasons. The act also empowered the president to extend the "classified service" by executive order. Every succeeding president for some time, except McKinley, did extend coverage, from about one-seventh of the total in 1883 to about half in 1901. Theodore Roosevelt and William Howard Taft extended the merit system rapidly, as did the Republicans in

19. Wilson, "The Study of Administration," in Mosher, ed., *Basic Literature of American Public Administration*, 66–81. The word "prejudice" is Wilson's (72). For a discussion of the policy/administration dichotomy, see Paul H. Appleby, ibid., 303–310. Wilson's article originally appeared in *Political Science Quarterly* 2 (1887):197–222.

the 1920s. By 1928 about 80 percent of the positions below policy-making level were covered.[20]

———— Accompanying the expansion of the meritocracy was an expansion of the regulatory functions assumed by the federal government. Functional expansion took place in two distinct ways which would engender complications as the administrative system matured. One way was to set up independent agencies, regulatory bodies unattached to any department. The first such agency, the Interstate Commerce Commission (ICC), was established by law in 1887 to regulate interstate railroads. Contrary to a widely held misconception, regulation of economic activity, including the rates charged by public utilities, had been the norm in America almost from the outset, as it had been under the common law in England, but such regulation was at the level of state and local governments. State efforts to regulate railroads, however, had often been marked by corruption, a punitive spirit, and ineffectiveness. Then in 1886, in the *Wabash* case, the Supreme Court ruled that state regulation of interstate railways was unconstitutional on the ground that the power of Congress to regulate commerce "among the several States" was exclusive. The passage of the Interstate Commerce Act, though the subject of political agitation for some time, came largely in response to the *Wabash* decision. And, contrary to another widely held perception, the act was ardently sought by most interstate railroad operators as a means of escaping the clutches of ignorant and avaricious state legislators.[21]

20. Hoogenboom, *Outlawing the Spoils,* 200–202, 217–219, 258; Fish, *Civil Service,* 217–221, 224–229; Nelson, *Roots of American Bureaucracy,* 119–125; Van Riper, *United States Civil Service,* 96–112, 120, 122, 126–127, 149–150, 172–174, 195–196, 201–203, 214–215, 308–309, 320; Justus D. Doenecke, *The Presidencies of James A. Garfield and Chester A. Arthur* (Lawrence, KS, 1981), 96–103; White, *Republican Era,* 297–302, 310, 317; Williams, "The President and the Executive Branch," in Shaw, ed., *Roosevelt to Reagan,* 123–125; Hugh Heclo, "The In-and-Outer System: A Critical Assessment," *Political Science Quarterly* 103 (1988):37–56. For William Howard Taft's views on civil service, see *Our Chief Magistrate and His Powers* (New York, 1916), chapter three.

21. Albro Martin, *Railroads Triumphant: The Growth, Rejection, and Rebirth of a Vital American Force* (New York, 1992), 329–330; *Wabash, St. Louis and Pacific Railway Company* v. *Illinois,* 118 U.S. 557 (1886); Gabriel Kolko, *Railroads and Regulation, 1877–1916* (Princeton, NJ, 1965); Lee Benson, *Merchants, Farmers, and Railroads: Railroad Regula-*

It took a full generation for the Interstate Commerce Commission to evolve into an effective regulatory body. The impetus for its development came partly from the Supreme Court, which held that regulated rates must be "reasonable," meaning they must permit a fair rate of return on capital investment, a fair rate being one sufficient to attract investors given prevailing interest rates. And change came partly from congressional amendments of the original act, especially the Hepburn Act of 1906, the Mann-Elkins Act of 1910, and the Physical Valuations Act of 1913.[22]

The creation of additional independent commissions, though supported by many members of Congress, by big business, and by progressives in general, proceeded slowly because each new agency was a groundbreaking operation. The next institution to be established was the Federal Trade Commission (1914), followed by the United States Shipping Board (1916, subsumed by the Commerce Department in 1933). The Federal Power Commission, established in 1920, was unique in that it was headed by the secretaries of war, interior, and agriculture, an arrangement that was scrapped in 1930 for a more conventional commission. The Federal Radio Commission (1927) was replaced in 1934 by the Federal Communications Commission. The Securities and Exchange Commission, the National Labor Relations Board, the Bituminous Coal Commission, and the United States Maritime Commission were established between 1934 and 1936. A number of temporary agencies were established during World War II, and a handful of permanent ones were added in the late forties and early fifties. A surge of activity came in the sixties and seventies, and by 1990 there were thirty-two "major" and twenty-three "minor" independent agencies.[23]

---

tion and New York Politics, 1850–1887 (Cambridge, MA, 1955). Regarding the regulatory tradition, see Forrest McDonald, Novus Ordo Seclorum (Lawrence, KS, 1985), 10–24, and for England, Sir William Blackstone, Commentaries (London, 1791), book 2.

22. Smyth v. Ames, 169 U.S. 466 (1898); Hepburn Act, Statutes at Large, 59th Cong., 34 (1906):584; Mann-Elkins Act, Statutes at Large, 61st Cong., 36 (1910):539; Physical Valuation Act, Statutes at Large, 62d Cong., 37 (1913):701. Smyth v. Ames involved state regulation of an intrastate railroad, but its principles were applicable to the ICC as well.

23. The President's Committee on Administrative Management (Brownlow Com-

The more common kind of the expansion of regulatory activities occurred haphazardly inside the framework of executive departments. When the Department of the Interior was created in 1849, for example, it was given functions previously lodged elsewhere: Control of public lands was transferred from the care of the Treasury Department; management of the patent office was removed from the State Department; overseeing pensions and Indian affairs was shifted from the War Department. By 1869 Interior had been assigned a variety of additional miscellaneous duties. By 1900 it contained more than twenty substantive agencies administering mostly unrelated activities, ranging from educational and eleemosynary functions to operating national parks. Moreover, it had no central accommodations, the component bureaus being scattered around Washington. The lack of physical or functional unity made supervision extremely difficult, and the various components operated almost independently. (Interior became the focus of a series of special interest groups targeting the separate bureaus.)[24]

The growth of agencies within the executive departments was rapid. And though many were created to respond to a perceived problem, they were rarely abolished even if the problem proved transitory or insoluble. President Reagan's director of the office of personnel management, the political scientist Donald Devine, tabulated the new and discarded federal units of government—agencies, bureaus, and so on—over time. As of 1923, there were 175 such units. Between 1924 and 1973, some 246 new units were established and 27 were eliminated, bringing the total to 394. Between 1974 and 1992, approx-

---

mittee), *Report of the Committee with Studies of Administrative Management in the Federal Government* (Washington, DC, 1937), 209–214; *Congressional Directory, 1989–1990; The 1990 Information Please Almanac* (Boston, 1990), 650–652; Nolan E. Clark, "The Headless Fourth Branch," in *The Imperial Congress: Crisis in the Separation of Powers,* ed. Gordon S. Jones and John A. Marini (New York, 1988), 268–292.

24. White, *Republican Era,* 175–195. Carl Schurz, head of the department, wrote to president-elect Garfield early in 1881, "The Interior Department is the most dangerous branch of the public service. It is more exposed to corrupt influences and more subject to untoward accidents than any other." The secretary faces "a ceaseless struggle with perplexing questions and situations" (ibid., 180).

imately 385 additional units were established and only 12 dropped, making a total of an estimated 767.[25]

———— From the point of view of administration, the history of the presidency in the twentieth century has been the history of presidents' attempts to gain control of the sprawling federal bureaucracy. As the century began, direct supervision of administration remained where it had been for a long time, in the hands of department and bureau chiefs and the related congressional committees. The president's influence lay almost solely in his powers of appointment and removal. The appointment power, though shrinking through the workings of the merit system, remained formidable. The removal power was a mixed affair. In 1926 the Supreme Court finally rendered a full-scale decision on the subject. In *Myers* v. *United States,* speaking for the majority in a divided court, Chief Justice Taft delivered a sweeping opinion holding that the president's power to remove his appointees was virtually absolute and that Congress in establishing executive offices may not constitutionally require senatorial consent for removals. "The power to remove inferior executive officers, like that to remove superior executive officers, is an incident of the power to appoint them, and is in its nature an executive power." Nine years later, however, the Court restricted the president's removal power somewhat by holding that the Federal Trade Commission, one of the independent agencies, was "neither political nor executive, but predominantly quasi-judicial and quasi-legislative," and thus, though its commissioners were presidential appointees (with senatorial approval), they could not be removed by the president except for "inefficiency, neglect of duty, or malfeasance in office" as specified by the organic act.[26]

25. Donald Devine, "When Government Becomes Too Complex, It Begins to Collapse," in *Human Events,* March 28, 1992, 14.

26. *Myers* v. *United States,* 272 U.S. 52 (1926); *Humphrey's Executor* v. *United States* (also styled *Rathbun, Executor* v. *United States*), 295 U.S. 602 (1935). John A. Rohr, *The President and the Public Administration* (Washington, DC, 1989), 15–29; see Fisher, *Constitutional Conflicts,* 61–64, for a summary of related later cases. Taft's decision was entirely in keeping with the view he expressed in *Our Chief Magistrate,* 76. Edward S. Corwin, *President,* 85–95, lambasts Taft for the ruling, as he does at greater length in

The battle for control of administration had long since been joined more directly. In 1903 Theodore Roosevelt had appointed a commission of policy-level career administrators to study the scientific work being done by agencies of the federal government and to recommend means of coordinating that work. The commission studied the matter for four months, found a great deal of overlap and duplication in the thirty scientific agencies, and suggested the consolidation of their activities into a single agency for the sake of efficiency and coordination. Roosevelt passed the proposal along to Congress, but Congress declined to act.[27]

Undaunted, Roosevelt was so pleased by the prospects for administrative reform that he appointed another commission—named for Assistant Secretary of the Treasury Charles H. Keep, who served as its chairman—to study a wider range of administrative affairs. The Keep Commission attracted considerable publicity by exposing some corruption. It found duplication, overlap, and a total lack of system in the acquisition of supplies. It learned that sizable numbers of civil servants were underemployed, many having almost nothing to do. It encountered powerful resistance to change of any sort; for example, office workers were loath to learn to use typewriters (the average government employee used twenty-three pencils a month), and bookkeepers were disdainful of adding machines, insisting that they were inaccurate. When it completed its investigation, the Keep Commission made eleven formal proposals, none of which Congress acted upon. Indeed, many congressmen were incensed by its very existence, for it represented a serious effort by the executive branch to assert its authority over the administration, "an authority previously the ex-

---

The President's Removal Power under the Constitution (New York, 1927), written in immediate response to the decision. A related recent case, *Morrison v. Olson*, 108 S.Ct. 2597 (1988), upheld the 1978 Ethics in Government Act establishing the office of independent counsel, who can be removed (apart from impeachment and conviction) only "by the personal action of the Attorney General and only for good cause."

27. Oscar Kraines, "The President Versus Congress: The Keep Commission; The First Comprehensive Presidential Inquiry into Administration," in *The First Branch of American Government: The United States Congress and Its Relations to the Executive and Judiciary, 1789–1989*, ed. Joel H. Silbey, 4 vols. (Brooklyn, NY, 1991), 1:201–250. The article first appeared in *Western Political Quarterly* 23 (March 1970):5–54.

clusive and unchallenged domain of Congress." In an amendment to an appropriation bill, Congress expressly prohibited the use of government funds for such commissions in future.[28]

William Howard Taft, however, was given an opportunity for seeking administrative control. Congress was in a stew about the recent frequency of deficits (eleven deficits in seventeen years), and it authorized Taft to study the bureaucracy thoroughly to find ways of reducing expenditures. As Taft told Congress, the real problem was that "the United States is the only great Nation whose Government is operated without a budget." The various departments had traditionally drawn up estimates of their required expenditures and submitted them directly to the appropriate congressional committees. Taft proposed to use his authorization as a means of bringing the budgetary system under the direct supervision of the president—which would place the entirety of the administration under presidential management. Congress refused to go along with the plan.[29]

President Wilson did not choose to follow Taft's agenda, despite his commitment to administrative centralization, for he had more pressing concerns. Nonetheless he greatly strengthened the presidency. As a political scientist he had been critical of the doctrine of the separation of powers and had warmly praised the British ministerial system. As president he became in effect his own prime minister, and the legislative reforms he steered through Congress during his first term reflected that activism. Moreover, during World War I Congress heaped emergency powers on him, and though ultimately Congress would turn against him, as was the norm with strong presidents, he laid the foundations for a managerial presidency of the kind Taft's commission had contemplated.[30]

28. Ibid. See also Peri E. Arnold, *Making the Managerial Presidency: Comprehensive Reorganization Planning, 1905–1980* (Princeton, NJ, 1986), 23–26, for a brief summary. Congress refused even to appropriate funds for the publication of the commission's report.

29. Arnold, *Making the Managerial Presidency*, 26–51, quote at 44. Taft's proposal bore fruit in the passage of the Budget and Accounting Act of 1921; see chapter 13 of this book.

30. An almost definitive account of Wilson's presidency is Arthur S. Link, *Wilson*, 5

The postwar years, a time when a rage for consolidation and reorganization in the interest of efficiency was sweeping America, saw the acceptance of the idea that the president should manage the bureaucracy. The decade of the twenties started out otherwise, with the formation of a joint congressional committee to reorganize administration. President Harding requested authority to appoint a member from the executive branch; the committee, surprisingly, agreed and made the president's man, Walter F. Brown, chairman. The chairmanship soon evolved into a commission that made its own study and recommendations to the joint committee, which reported them to Congress. Little change was enacted, but Congress did agree in principle that reorganization was a presidential function. That recognition was reinforced in 1932, when Congress, hoping to balance the federal budget, acceded to President Hoover's request for unilateral reorganization authority, subject to veto by either house. In December Hoover sent to Congress orders for changes in fifty-eight governmental activities. The House rejected them, but in the Economy Act of 1933 Congress granted the reorganization authority to Franklin Roosevelt, with a proviso that to stop an executive reorganization order, a vote by both houses, signed by the president, would be necessary.[31]

Roosevelt made little of the authority granted him, for he and Congress were so busy creating agencies to cope with the depression there was no time for reorganization, but immediately after Roosevelt's triumphant reelection in 1936 he set in motion a plan to concentrate executive power in his hands. Following what had become a tradition, he appointed a committee on administrative management, chaired by Louis Brownlow. Roosevelt wanted the committee to function as a quasi constitutional convention, and it complied by

vols. (Princeton, NJ, 1947–1965) (subtitles vary). See also Woodrow Wilson, *Congressional Government: A Study in American Politics* (1885; repr., Boston, 1913).

31. Arnold, *Making the Managerial Presidency,* 52–82. Regarding the consolidation and reorganization of business during the twenties, see, for example, Forrest McDonald, *Insull* (Chicago, 1962), 188–273; Forrest McDonald, *The Phaeton Ride* (Garden City, NY, 1974), 82–101; and Alfred P. Sloan, *My Years with General Motors* (Garden City, NY, 1964). Brown was an attorney from Toledo and a major figure in the Ohio Republican party.

drawing a blueprint for reorganization that would place all federal agencies (including the independent commissions, which it attacked as a "headless 'fourth branch' of the Government") under the direct and exclusive command of the president. In keeping with Wilson's 1887 formulation, it distinguished between policy and administration, policy being the function of president and Congress working together, administration being purely a presidential function. The Brownlow Committee's report met a storm of criticism in Congress, which was just then fighting over Roosevelt's court-packing scheme, and cries of "dictator!" were heard—but eventually most of the committee's proposals were enacted.[32]

Those enactments, together with Roosevelt's reelection for third and fourth terms, the great concentration of power in Washington during World War II, and the commencement soon afterward of the cold war, brought into existence what political scientists call the institutional presidency. A perceptive student of the subject, John A. Rohr, has observed that "the Brownlow Committee prepared Americans to accept President Truman's description of his office, that 'the buck stops here.'" Any earlier generation of Americans would have been puzzled by an assertion that the buck stopped anywhere, for they would have assumed "that it floated freely among such competing institutions as the Senate, the House, the courts, the presidency,

32. Brownlow Committee, *Report*, passim (quote at 32); Rohr, *President and Public Administration*; Arnold, *Making the Managerial Presidency*, 88–117; Rowland Egger, "The Period of Crisis: 1933 to 1945," in *American Public Administration: Past, Present, Future*, ed. Frederick C. Mosher (Tuscaloosa, AL, 1975), 49–96; Barry D. Karl, *Executive Reorganization and Reform in the New Deal: The Genesis of Administrative Management, 1900–1939* (Chicago, 1964); Louis Brownlow, *A Passion for Anonymity: The Autobiography of Louis Brownlow* (Chicago, 1958); *The Public Administration Dictionary*, ed. Ralph C. Chandler and Jack C. Plano, 2d ed. (Santa Barbara, CA, 1988), 166–168. The famous cry in the Brownlow Report (5) that "the President needs help" gave rise to the executive office of the president—a "presidential" branch within the executive branch (John Hart, "The President and His Staff," in Shaw, ed., *Roosevelt to Reagan*, 159–205); see also John Hart, *The Presidential Branch* (Elmsford, NY, 1987). Among the more sweeping grants of administrative power to Roosevelt was the 1941 first War Powers Act, which authorized him "to make such redistribution of functions among executive agencies as he may deem necessary"—a blank check (Peter Woll, *American Bureaucracy*, 2d ed. [New York, 1977], 212).

the bureaucracy, the states, foreign allies and enemies, and a host of private organizations."[33]

In reality, the buck continued to float and still does. What changed was an inflation in the perception of presidential responsibility by almost all Americans, including some who held the office. In due course, that inflated perception would make the office virtually impossible to manage, and the White House itself would turn into a bureaucracy.

——— During World War II, centralization of power had both positive and negative effects. On the plus side, mobilization occurred far more smoothly than it had during World War I and on twice the scale. And instead of the production bottlenecks and duplications that had accompanied the voluntarism of the first, the command economy during the second resulted in the greatest production for war that the world had ever seen. The minuses, however, were serious. Roosevelt could be petty and spiteful as well as grand, and sometimes his idiosyncracies cost lives as well as a great deal of money. Some people in the administration did foolish things: Vice-pres. Henry Wallace, for example, as head of the Bureau of Economic Welfare, instituted a program to stimulate production of wild rubber in the Amazon region, the result being that he got rubber for an average of $546 per pound, about 1,760 times as high as the average wartime procurement price of 31 cents a pound. Some defense contractors managed through political favoritism to grow extremely wealthy by producing inferior or unnecessary materiel. The federal government expanded its sphere of operation; it ventured into activities—the manufacture of false teeth, rum, eyeglasses, and ice cream, for instance—in which it had little or no competence, not to mention constitutional mandate. The momentum of expansion continued for several years after the war.[34]

33. Rohr, *President and Public Administration,* 41–42.

34. Interview with Samuel Insull, Jr., 1960; McDonald, *Phaeton Ride,* 138–144; John Willson, "World War II: The Great Liberal War," *Imprimis,* May 1992; Jesse Jones, *Fifty Billion Dollars: My Thirteen Years with the RFC, 1932–1945* (New York, 1951). The magnitude of the federal government's involvement in business activities in competition with private enterprise was revealed in hearings before the Senate

In reaction to the negatives, partisan cries to "clean up the mess in Washington" resulted (almost by accident) in reforms that genuinely if only temporarily improved the quality of government. Republicans won control of Congress in 1946 and looked forward confidently to capturing the presidency in 1948. As soon as Congress convened in January, 1947, it passed an act establishing a Commission on Organization of the Executive Branch of the Government, consisting of twelve members, four apiece to be chosen by the president, the Senate's president pro tem, and the Speaker of the House. The intention was to undo the economic and social programs that had been introduced by Roosevelt's New Deal and Truman's nascent Fair Deal.[35]

Two unforeseen developments upset the Republicans' plans. Truman was reelected along with a Democratic Congress, meaning that repeal of the targeted programs would be difficult if not impossible. And Herbert Hoover, whom the Republicans brought out of retirement to head the commission, acted as an engineer/manager rather than as an arch-conservative, insisting that reorganization for the sake of effective management should take precedence over questions of policy. The reports of the Hoover Commission, released to Congress during the first few months of 1949, made 277 specific proposals for shifting agencies and consolidating them to create "a clear line of command from the top to the bottom, and a return line of responsibility and accountability from the bottom to the top." More than half the proposals, among them the most important ones, were enacted into law or effected by executive orders.[36]

Select Committee on Small Business between 1953 and 1957; see, for example, hearings of April 16 and May 22, 1957 (Washington, DC, 1957).

35. Chandler and Plano, eds., *Public Administration Dictionary*, 193–194; David Burner, *Herbert Hoover: A Public Life* (New York, 1979), 336–337; Arnold, *Making the Managerial Presidency*, 120–126.

36. Arnold, *Making the Managerial Presidency*, 126–154, quote at 148. J. D. Williams, *Public Administration: The People's Business* (Boston, 1980), 193–194, says that of 273 recommendations, 72 percent were adopted, 111 by administration action, 85 by legislative action. See also Peri E. Arnold, "The First Hoover Commission and the Managerial Presidency," *Journal of Politics* 38 (1976):46–70, and William E. Pemberton, *Bureaucratic Politics: Executive Reorganization during the Truman Administration* (Columbia, MO, 1979).

For the next dozen years, and especially during the presidency of Dwight Eisenhower, the managerial presidency seemed at last to succeed. At the time, political observers tended to be deceived by Eisenhower's less-than-dynamic public speaking into thinking him a well-meaning but rather bumbling and ineffectual president. Critics seemed to believe that he fulfilled Harry Truman's prediction: "He'll sit right here and he'll say 'Do this, do that!!' And nothing will happen. Poor Ike—it won't be a bit like the Army. He'll find it very frustrating." But Truman and the pundits should have remembered that Eisenhower's successes as Supreme Allied Commander during World War II were not the product of military prowess but of administrative and political gifts, and he brought those to the presidency. That he appeared to be politically inept, historians now generally agree, was a carefully selected pose. As Fred Greenstein wrote of Eisenhower's "hidden hand" presidency, "On the assumption that a president who is predominantly viewed in terms of his political prowess will lose public support by not appearing to be a proper chief of state, Eisenhower went to great lengths to conceal the political side of his leadership."[37]

————— Then, after the ill-starred Kennedy dream of Camelot, came two presidents whose designs for the presidency knew no limits, and between them they reduced the prestige and power of the institution to a nadir it had not known since the days of Ulysses Grant. Lyndon Baines Johnson was masterful at having his way with Congress, but he seemed to believe that no problem was beyond the remedy of passing a law. The policies he pushed through, moreover, were rarely

37. Fred I. Greenstein, *The Hidden-Hand Presidency: Eisenhower as Leader* (New York, 1982), passim, quote at 5; Chester J. Pach and Elmo Richardson, *The Presidency of Dwight D. Eisenhower* (Lawrence, KS, 1991); Stephen Ambrose, *The Supreme Commander: The War Years of General Dwight D. Eisenhower* (Garden City, NY, 1970); Stephen Ambrose, *Eisenhower: The President,* vol. 2 (New York, 1984); Murray Kempton, "The Underestimation of Dwight D. Eisenhower," *Esquire,* Sept. 1967, 108ff.; John W. Sloan, "The Management and Decision-Making Style of President Eisenhower," *Presidential Studies Quarterly* 20 (1990):295–313; John W. Sloan, *Eisenhower and the Management of Prosperity* (Lawrence, KS, 1991); Walter Williams, *Mismanaging America: The Rise of the Anti-Analytic Presidency* (Lawrence, KS, 1990), 20–21, 109–110; Margaret Truman, *Harry S. Truman* (New York, 1973), 551–552.

thought out. To him an "idea" was "a suggestion produced on the spot," and as the columnist James Reston wrote, his administration was "poorly organized to administer the domestic programs he has introduced," producing "something almost unheard of here," namely criticism for "confusion and waste . . . from leading officials of the Johnson Administration itself." White House aide Joseph Califano said afterward that "often we didn't know where to put a program . . . and we didn't particularly care where it went; we just wanted to make sure it got enacted. That's one reason," he added in an understatement, "why the government is disorganized now."[38]

Most disruptively, Johnson pushed through a host of initiatives to shift administration away from the federal government to so called indirect or "third-party government." Responsibility for attaining congressionally mandated goals was increasingly delegated to government-sponsored enterprises, endowments, contractors, nonprofit corporations, state and local governments, and private businesses. Grants to such entities were funneled through a large number of federal agencies; the budgets of the largest departments came to support four indirect workers for every one on the federal payroll. In 1965 Democratic Sen. Abraham Ribicoff of Connecticut counted 150 federal agencies and more than 400 regional and area field offices servicing outside agencies through 456 different "program channels."[39]

38. Doris Kearns, *Lyndon Johnson and the American Dream* (New York, 1976), 218, said that Johnson's strategy was "pass the bill now, worry about its effects and implementation later." Tip O'Neill said of the Economic Opportunity Act, Johnson's "greatest accomplishment," that it "was put together a little too quickly. . . . Technically, the bill was a mishmash," in *Man of the House: The Life and Political Memoirs of Speaker Tip O'Neill,* with William Novak (New York, 1987), 185. Arnold, *Making the Managerial Presidency,* 232–236; *New York Times,* Nov. 23, 1966, 38:3; Eric Goldman, *The Tragedy of Lyndon Johnson* (New York, 1969); Harold Seidman and Robert Gilmour, *Politics, Position, and Power: From the Positive to the Regulatory State,* 4th ed. (New York, 1986), 117; Emmette S. Redford and Marlan Blissett, *Organizing the Executive Branch: The Johnson Presidency* (Chicago, 1981), 220–229; Williams, *Mismanaging America,* 116; Alonzo L. Hamby, *Liberalism and Its Challengers: From F. D. R. to Bush,* 2d ed. (New York, 1992), 256–265.

39. Seidman and Gilmour, *Politics, Position, and Power,* 119–125; Frederick C. Mosher, "The Changing Responsibilities and Tactics of the Federal Government," *Public*

When Richard Nixon became president he seemed almost oblivious of these developments. In his campaign he spoke repeatedly of the need "to get rid of the costly failures of the Great Society," and shortly after he took office he appointed an Advisory Council on Government Organization (chaired by Roy Ash), but he was really not interested in administration. He told a reporter, "All you need is a competent Cabinet to run the country at home. You need a President for foreign policy; no Secretary of State is really important; the President makes foreign policy." He also intended to have no chief of staff and to coordinate domestic policy through regular cabinet meetings. In less than a year, however, he abandoned both intentions. Cabinet meetings proved to be boring, tedious, and unproductive; department heads, briefed by the career bureaucrats under them, developed outlooks different from those of the president and found themselves with mixed loyalties. Nixon then decided to have as little to do with them as possible and concluded that the bureaucracy was his veriest enemy. As for the department heads, presidential aide John Ehrlichman said of them later, "We only see them at the annual White House Christmas party; they go off and marry the natives."[40]

Nixon's next approach was to set up a "counter-bureaucracy" inside the White House. He enlarged the executive office staff, doubling it to more than 4,000, renamed the Bureau of the Budget the Office of Management and Budget and moved it out of the White House to new quarters across Pennsylvania Avenue, and set up a Domestic Council under Ehrlichman. Ehrlichman and the council

Administration Review 40 (1980):541–548; Lester M. Salamon, "Rethinking Public Management: Third Party Government and the Changing Forms of Government Action," *Public Policy* 29 (1981):255–273; Arnold, *Making the Managerial Presidency,* 232.

40. Richard M. Nixon, *The Memoirs of Richard Nixon* (New York, 1978), 424; Seidman and Gilmour, *Politics, Position, and Power,* 101; Rowland Evans, Jr., and Robert D. Novak, *Nixon in the White House* (New York, 1971), 11; Richard P. Nathan, *The Administrative Presidency* (New York, 1983), 28–30; Arnold, *Making the Managerial Presidency,* 272ff.; Bradley H. Patterson, Jr., *The Ring of Power: The White House Staff and its Expanding Role in Government* (New York, 1988), 33, 44–45, 131; Hart, *Presidential Branch,* 121–122, 124, 190–191; James P. Pfiffner, "The President's Chief of Staff: Lessons Learned," *Presidential Studies Quarterly* 23 (1993):77, 82–85.

would meet for five or six hours a day for perhaps ten weeks with representatives of the various departments that had jurisdiction over a particular area and thrash out policy positions to present to the president. Increasingly, the staff of the Domestic Council took on the role of overseer, trying to micromanage administration and bypass department heads. In his bitter opposition to bureaucracy, noted *U.S. News & World Report,* Nixon "built his own bureaucracy."[41]

By 1971 or 1972, however, it became evident that the system was failing because it overloaded people at the top with operational trivia and left people at the bureau level in charge of actual policy—making substantive decisions, awarding grants, and promulgating rules. The administration thus came to realize that the policy/administration dichotomy was false; in the real world of domestic affairs, *"operations is policy."*[42]

President Nixon therefore reversed himself again, and on January 5, 1973, he announced that he was forming a sort of super cabinet. Thenceforth, direct access to the president would be limited to Haldeman and four other aides who would act as presidential assistants (and surrogates, having the authority to issue orders in the president's name) in designated areas: Ehrlichman in domestic affairs, Henry Kissinger in foreign affairs, Roy Ash in executive-management affairs, and George Shultz in economic affairs. Access to these presidential assistants was limited, with certain exceptions, to three counselors (the secretaries of agriculture, housing and urban development, and health, education, and welfare).[43]

41. Nathan, *Administrative Presidency,* 34–38; "Nixon's Top Command: Expanding in Size, Power," *U.S. News & World Report,* April 24, 1972, 74; Hart, *Presidential Branch,* 57, 122–123; "A Mini-Symposium: President Nixon's Proposals for Executive Branch Reorganization," ed. Douglas M. Fox, *Public Administration Review* 34 (1974):487–495.

42. Nathan, *Administrative Presidency,* 41, 45–46; Robert Wood, "When Government Works," *Public Interest* (1970):39–51.

43. *New York Times,* Jan. 6, 1973, 1:7; Seidman and Gilmour, *Politics, Position, and Power,* 75–76, 108–109; Nathan, *Administrative Presidency,* 51–52; Hart, *Presidential Branch,* 123–124; Richard P. Nathan, *The Plot That Failed: Nixon and the Administrative Presidency* (New York, 1975); Ron Seyb, "Nixon's Administrative Presidency Revisited: Aberration or Watershed?" *Journal of Policy History* 4 (1992):249–271. The three counselors were Caspar Weinberger, James T. Lynn, and Earl Butz (*New York Times,* May 11, 1973, 21:1).

These changes came to nothing because of Watergate: in April Ehrlichman resigned and in May Nixon quietly announced the abandonment of the "experiment" with counselors and the resumption of "a direct line of communication with the Cabinet." A panel of the National Academy of Public Administration later told the Senate that but for Watergate, the federal government might have been transformed into a Germanic "ideal type of monocracy, ruled from the top through a strictly disciplined hierarchical system" in which impeachment would be the only way to hold a president accountable. Ironically, Nixon's substantive domestic-policy legacy was an enormous increase in transfer payments—payments in cash or in-kind benefits such as food stamps, aid to mothers with dependent children, and medical care.[44]

As a result of the activities of the Johnson and Nixon administrations and of the efforts by Congress to regain powers lost over four decades, by 1974 the federal government was no longer the large and unwieldy but still manageable organism that John F. Kennedy had inherited from Dwight Eisenhower. It appeared rather to be a huge, amorphous blob, like a creature out of science fiction.[45]

44. *New York Times,* May 1, 1973, 1:7 and May 11, 1973, 1:8, 21:1; Seidman and Gilmour, *Politics, Position, and Power,* 108, 110; Hart, *Presidential Branch,* 124; Nathan, *Administrative Presidency,* 22–25 (transfer payments increased from $55.3 billion in 1969 to $150.4 billion in 1975 [ibid., 25]). See also Carl Lieberman, "Legislative Success and Failure: The Social Welfare Policies of the Nixon Administration," in *Richard M. Nixon: Politician, President, Administrator,* ed. Leon Friedman and William F. Levantrosser (New York, 1991), 107–131.

45. James L. Sundquist, "The Crisis of Competence in Our National Government," *Political Science Quarterly* 95 (1980/1981):183–208; George Reedy, *The Twilight of the Presidency* (New York, 1970); Peter F. Drucker, "The Sickness of Government," *Public Interest* (1969):3–23; John Adams Wettergreen, "Bureaucratizing the American Government," in Jones and Marini, eds., *Imperial Congress,* 68–99. Linda L. M. Bennett and Stephen Earl Bennett, *Living with Leviathan: Americans Coming to Terms with Big Government* (Lawrence, KS, 1990), conclude that "although big government may make all Americans queasy some of the time, it now makes only a tiny fragment nervous all of the time." For a dismal picture of morale among civil servants and public distrust of the federal bureaucracy as of 1989, together with some inane proposals for improving matters, see the National Commission on the Public Service (the Volcker Commission), *Leadership for America: Rebuilding the Public Service* (Washington, DC, 1989).

———— During the remainder of the 1970s it seemed as if the presidency might never recover. Gerald Ford, despite a long background in the House of Representatives, fought stubbornly to prevent what, from his new-found perspective as president, he saw as congressional encroachments on the executive, but his efforts were fruitless. Not least among his handicaps was that he was even more an "accidental" president than John Tyler, having been appointed (according to the Twenty-fifth Amendment) to the vice-presidency when Spiro Agnew resigned in disgrace and having succeeded to the presidency when Richard Nixon resigned in disgrace.[46]

Jimmy Carter entered the White House vowing to reorganize the "horrible bureaucratic mess" from the bottom up, only to find the undertaking quite beyond his abilities. He was a speed reader who could master the particulars of an operation quickly, but he bogged himself down in a morass of details and never grasped the larger significance of what needed to be done. Consequently, in the words of a specialist in the Congressional Research Service, his efforts "resulted in more, not fewer departments and agencies and in more agencies and programs being considered outside of direct accountability to the president." The "net effect . . . has been to further undermine the president's managerial authority."[47]

46. Thomas E. Cronin, *The State of the Presidency,* 2d ed. (Boston, 1980), 5, 46, 77, 210–213, 219; Thomas E. Cronin, "An Imperiled Presidency?" in *The Post-Imperial Presidency,* ed. Vincent Davis (New Brunswick, NJ, 1980), 137–151; Williams, "The President and the Executive Branch," in Shaw, ed., *Roosevelt to Reagan,* 143–144; Gerald R. Ford, *A Time to Heal: The Autobiography of Gerald R. Ford* (New York, 1979). Interestingly, the transition from Nixon to Ford was carefully and skillfully done; see Philip W. Buchen, "The Making of an Unscheduled Presidential Transition," in *The Presidency in Transition,* ed. James P. Pfiffner and R. Gordon Hoxie (Washington, DC, 1989), 69–73, and Kathy B. Smith, "The Transition from President Nixon to President Ford," ibid., 74–88. For a careful analysis of the press coverage of the transition, see Mark J. Rozell, *The Press and the Ford Presidency* (Ann Arbor, MI, 1992), 31–52; Rozell attributes the abrupt end of the honeymoon to Ford's pardon of Nixon.

47. Williams, *Mismanaging America,* 53–60; Arnold, *Making the Managerial Presidency,* 303–337; Joseph A. Califano, Jr., *Governing America: An Insider's Report from the White House and the Cabinet* (New York, 1981); Pfiffner, "President's Chief of Staff," *Presidential Studies Quarterly* 23:78, 98; Seidman and Gilmour, *Politics, Posi-*

Then came the Reagan revolution. Ronald Reagan, like Jefferson, brought to the presidency a fully conceived set of goals, and in domestic affairs his goals were, mutatis mutandis, much the same as Jefferson's had been. His aim regarding the administrative machinery of the federal government was not to manage it efficiently and economically but to minimize its functions and return as many of them as possible to the states or to private enterprise. He screened his appointees at the cabinet and subcabinet levels to make sure that they shared his views, and he took steps to ensure that they did not "go off and marry the natives." They were not briefed about their departments and agencies by veteran career civil servants, for example, but by conservative think tanks. They were regularly reminded of their mission, in the first term through meetings of "cabinet councils," in the second through an Economic Policy Council and a Domestic Policy Council. As presidential counsel Edwin Meese explained, Reagan used these "so that cabinet members feel closer to him than they do to their departments—and he gives them a lot of opportunity to remember that."[48]

---

tion, and Power, 112–118 (the quotation is from Ronald Moe's study, cited ibid., 118). In his own apologia for his presidency, Carter devoted fewer than three pages to his efforts to reorganize the bureaucracy (Jimmy Carter, Keeping Faith: Memoirs of a President [New York, 1982], 69–71). See also Bert A. Rockman, "Tightening the Reins," Presidential Studies Quarterly 23 (1993):105–106; Patterson, Ring of Power, 131–137, provides a revealing account of how the Carter government functioned in regard to one particular policy, concerning cities. In 1978 Carter did push through Congress a civil service reform package, billed as making it easier to fire incompetents (Volcker Commission, Leadership for America, 104–106).

48. It can be argued that Wilson and FDR also brought clear agendas to the presidency. Roland Evans and Robert Novak, The Reagan Revolution (New York, 1981) say that Reagan "was the first president since Roosevelt acting on a clear agenda" (20). Seidman and Gilmour, Politics, Position, and Power, 125–128; Rockman, "Tightening the Reins," Presidential Studies Quarterly, 23:106–111; Patterson, Ring of Power, 32–59, 63, 241–245, 252; Edwin Meese III, With Reagan (Washington, DC, 1992), 63, 76–78; Hart, Presidential Branch, 8, 61–62, 112, 123; Nathan, Administrative Presidency, 57–81; Pfiffner, "President's Chief of Staff," Presidential Studies Quarterly, 23:85–90; Donald J. Devine, "Political Administration: The Right Way," and Becky Norton Dunlop, "The Role of the White House Office of Presidential Personnel," in Steering the Elephant: How Washington Works, ed. Robert Rector and Michael

In addition to halting the increase in the activities of the federal government and trying to roll back the more useless or harmful of them, President Reagan sought to police closely the regulations promulgated by federal agencies. To this end, in 1981 and 1985 he issued Executive Orders 12291 and 12498 to "increase the accountability of agency heads for the regulatory actions of their agencies" and to "provide for presidential oversight of the regulatory process." These measures, though implemented as vigorously as possible, did not significantly untangle the regulatory snarl, but they did reduce the rate at which new regulations were being multiplied.[49]

The real Reagan revolution was a change in the way ordinary Americans thought about themselves, their government, and the presidency. Throughout the 1970s their feelings regarding all three had been overwhelmingly negative. "The one thing we know about Reagan," wrote *Washington Post* columnist Lou Cannon—scarcely Reagan's greatest fan—"is that he did revive confidence in the presidency." For a time, Reagan restored Americans to their accustomed self-confidence, optimism, and—a concept that had become unfashionable—patriotism. The *Newsweek* team that covered the 1984 election wrote that "Reagan had tapped into something old and deep in the national spirit, a dammed-up current of pride in the past and

---

Sanera (New York, 1987), 125–135, 145–155; Lawrence E. Lynn, Jr., "The Reagan Administration and the Renitent Bureaucracy," in *The Reagan Presidency and the Governing of America,* ed. Lester M. Salamon and Michael S. Lund (Washington, DC, 1984), 339–340, 368–370; Wallace Earl Walker, "Presidential Transitions and the Entrepreneurial Presidency: Of Lions, Foxes, and Puppy Dogs," *Presidential Studies Quarterly* 23 (1993):64–65. President Carter had also been consistent in his appointments—giving as many to minorities as possible (Califano, *Governing America,* 229–231).

49. Seidman and Gilmour, *Politics, Position, and Power,* 131; Nathan, *Administrative Presidency,* 77. The authors of these two books had strong reservations about the desirability of some of Reagan's policies but were warm in their admiration of his methods of implementing them. Negative evaluations of Reagan's effectiveness include Williams, *Mismanaging America,* and Richard W. Waterman, *Presidential Influence and the Administrative State* (Knoxville, TN, 1989), 106–108. See also Shirley Anne Warshaw, "Cabinet Government in the Modern Presidency," in Pfiffner and Hoxie, ed., *Presidency in Transition,* 129–146.

optimism about the future," and the voters reelected him in a landslide. He also modified the terms of political discourse, at least for a time. In the presidential election of 1988, George Bush was able to inflict heavy damage on the Democratic candidate Michael Dukakis by branding him as a "liberal," a label Democratic candidates formerly wore proudly.[50]

The momentum for Reagan-style conservatism, however, proved to be nonexistent; the impetus that Reagan had set in motion stopped the day he left the White House. His successor seemed to have no interest in or understanding of domestic affairs. The meetings in which agency and department heads had been regularly reminded of their mission immediately ceased, and the proliferation of regulations began again. It is true that when signs of weakness in the economy became obvious in 1991, President Bush, looking toward reelection, named an ad hoc committee headed by Vice-pres. Dan Quayle to investigate and terminate regulations that harmed business without appreciably improving the environment, working conditions, or other socially desirable goals. But by that time a significant portion of the American work force consisted of people whose sole activity was filling out required government forms, and the Code of Federal Regulations, "the official compendium of all formally promulgated

50. Lou Cannon, "A New Confidence in the Presidency," *Newsweek,* Jan. 9, 1989, 21; Peter Goldman, Tony Fuller, *Newsweek* election coverage team, *The Quest for the Presidency, 1984* (New York, 1985), 18; Michael Ruby, "The lessons of the Reagan era," *U.S. News & World Report,* Jan. 9, 1989, 19–26; Dilys Hill and Phil Williams regarded "The restoration of American pride and the regeneration of American power [as the] major achievements of the Reagan administration," in *The Reagan Presidency,* ed. Dilys M. Hill, Raymond A. Moore, and Phil Williams (Southampton, Eng., 1990), 6, 7, 235; see also Elizabeth Drew, "A Political Journal," *New Yorker,* Dec. 3, 1984, 100, 107. Tip O'Neill said that Reagan "quickly became as beloved a leader as this nation has ever seen." He "enjoyed a truly remarkable rookie year," but his "success didn't happen by accident"; among other things he had "enormous personal appeal" and "quickly became a folk hero" (*Man of the House,* 330, 341–344). O'Neill, though he thought it "sinful" that Reagan ever became president, also thought "he would have made a hell of a king" (ibid., 360). On the controversy over the "L" word, see for example, *New York Times,* Oct. 28, 1988, A, 35:2, and Elizabeth Drew, *Election Journal: Political Events of 1987–1988* (New York, 1989), 239, 264, 312, 335.

regulations," was approaching 200 volumes and totaling more than 100,000 pages.[51]

The government, to return to the words of Henry Adams, did not govern, and as in Adams's day the problem was institutional. Experience had demonstrated that Congress must have a powerful voice in policy-making and in overseeing administration lest the presidency or the bureaucracy become irresponsible. But Congress could perform its constitutionally mandated duties only if its members and their staffs were competent and dedicated to serving the public good and only if reasonable harmony existed between Capitol Hill and the White House. When Bill Clinton took the oath of office in 1993, these conditions had not been present for a quarter-century and more

51. Interview with Daniel Oliver, former chairman of the Federal Trade Commission, whose term overlapped the two presidencies, April 1992; Sigfredo A. Cabrera, "Overregulation Is Strangling U.S. Economy," in *Human Events,* April 4, 1992, 17; Brink Lindsey, "System Overload," *Policy Review* (Winter 1991):55. Environmentalist and consumerist groups were highly critical of deregulation. See also "Bush Extends Rules Freeze," in *USA Today,* April 30, 1992, 4A. The number of new federal regulations implemented annually declined from 7,745 in 1980 to 4,413 in 1991 though the number of regulation writers increased from 121,706 to 125,501. Quayle's Council on Competitiveness was abolished by President Clinton on January 22, 1993.

CHAPTER 13

President and Congress:

Legislation

In his First Annual Message, delivered on December 3, 1861, Abraham Lincoln complained about the quality and quantity of legislation that Congress had enacted during its seventy-two years under the Constitution. There had been passed, he said, "some 5,000 acts and joint resolutions, which fill more than 6,000 closely printed pages and are scattered through many volumes." A great number of provisions were obscure or conflicting, he added, making it "very difficult for even the best-informed persons to ascertain precisely what the statute law really is." He urged Congress to revise and rewrite the statutes, saying that he had been reliably informed that all the statutes "in force and of a permanent and general nature" could be "embraced in one volume (or at most two volumes) of ordinary and convenient size."[1]

Lincoln's figures suggest that, even allowing for statutes that had expired or been repealed, Congress had passed considerably fewer

1. *Messages and Papers of the Presidents,* comp. James D. Richardson, 10 vols. (Washington, DC, 1889–1905), 6:50.

than a hundred bills and resolutions a year and that the average enactment was less than one page long.[2] A century and a quarter later, in 1986, Congress passed a tax-code simplification act that ran 925 pages, and that was but one of 424 bills it enacted during the year. As many as 10,000 bills were being introduced in a session. In such circumstances, it was obviously impossible for members of Congress even to read, let alone seriously consider, more than a small fraction of the proposals on which they voted. Their ever-growing staffs—from about 4,300 in the 1950s to 11,500 in 1973 and to 32,000 in 1990—assumed responsibility for briefing them, staking out positions, writing their speeches, and advising them how to vote. Moreover, much of the drafting of legislation was being farmed out to private-sector lawyers and lobbyists. Having thus all but abdicated their duties as legislators, most congressmen devoted their attention to "constituent services," to exerting influence in the bureaucracy on behalf of voters and campaign contributors.[3]

Into the legislative vacuum, as it developed over time, drifted the president and the executive departments. During the nineteenth century presidents had used their veto power and the charge to "recommend to their Consideration such Measures as he shall judge necessary and expedient"—the president's constitutional share in the legislative power—sparingly and cautiously and often scarcely at all. In a series of steps beginning with Theodore Roosevelt, presidents assumed ever-greater roles as legislative leaders. By the 1950s executive

2. My tabulations of public bills and joint resolutions as indicated by Congresses in Bureau of the Census, *Historical Statistics of the United States* (Washington, DC, 1961), 690, show that during the first thirty-six Congresses, 1789–1861, a total of 4,294 public bills and 462 public joint resolutions were enacted—an average of just under 60 bills and 6.4 resolutions a year.

3. *Congressional Quarterly Almanac,* 1953:333, 1986:10, 523, 1987:10; Brink Lindsey, "System Overload," *Policy Review* (Winter 1991):55. Between 1945 and 1960 the number of bills per year ranged from about 5,000 to about 9,000, in the 1960s from around 9,000 to 12,000 (*Statistical Abstract of the United States,* 1962:370, 1972:368). In a 1991 poll of House administrative assistants (representatives' chiefs of staff), 56 percent attributed their bosses' success to "constituent services" and only 11 percent thought legislative activity most important (Lindsey, "System Overload," 56). The number of bills introduced annually in recent years has fallen off slightly due to the practice of lumping many subjects into one bill.

sponsorship of legislation had become so common that the chairman of a congressional committee could say to an inexperienced administration witness, "Don't expect us to start from scratch on what you people want. That's not the way we do things here—*you* draft the bills and *we* work them over."4

The chief executive had evolved into the legislator-in-chief. To perform the function required consummate skill and a great deal of luck, even when the president and Congress were nominally of the same party. When they were of different parties, as they were twenty of the twenty-four years before the election of 1992, the task was well-nigh impossible.

——— The first of the president's formal powers regarding legislation, the veto, seemed relatively straightforward when it was adopted, but it turned out to involve complications. For openers, there are two kinds of vetoes, regular and "pocket." The Constitution provides that every bill passed by both houses of Congress be submitted to the president, who has ten days (Sundays excepted) either to sign it, in which case it becomes law, or to return it with his objections. If two-thirds majorities in both houses vote to pass it despite his objections it becomes law, and if not, not. If he neither signs it nor returns it within the ten-day period, it becomes law without his signature. This feature prevents the president from holding a bill indefinitely, thereby turning his qualified veto into an absolute one. But the provision created a problem. If Congress should pass bills and adjourn, it could circumvent the veto power by making impossible the return of the bills with the president's objections. To obviate that contingency, the Framers added a qualification: In ten days a bill becomes law without the president's signature, "unless the Congress by their Ad-

4. Richardson, comp., *Messages and Papers of the Presidents,* vols. 4–9, passim; U.S. Constitution, Article 2, Section 3; quotation from Louis Fisher, *The Politics of Shared Power: Congress and the Executive* (Washington, DC, 1981), 23, citing Richard E. Neustadt, "Presidency and Legislation: Planning the President's Program," *American Political Science Review* 49 (1955):980, 1015. For one example of the literature on the subject, see J. Gregory Sidak, "The Recommendation Clause," *Georgetown Law Journal* 77 (1989):2079–2135. For a discussion of four presidential-legislative styles, see Patricia Lee Sykes, "The President as Legislator: A 'Superepresenator,'" *Presidential Studies Quarterly* 19 (1989):301–315.

journment prevent its Return, in which case it shall not be a Law." Bills killed by holding them at the end of a session came to be called pocket vetoes.[5]

Pocket vetoes have some quirky characteristics. They are absolute, not subject to override, and because of a tendency of Congress to complete much of its work at the end of sessions, the instrument became a potent one: 1,040 of the 2,453 bills killed by the presidents from George Washington through Ronald Reagan were pocket vetoes. On the other hand, the session-end rush made it difficult for presidents to read and sign bills they did not wish to pocket. To avoid this possibility, for the first 150 years presidents habitually went to the Capitol on the last day of a session in order to sign bills they supported before the adjournment; it was generally assumed that they could not sign a bill into law after the adjournment took place.[6]

Twentieth-century Supreme Court decisions modified and clarified the rules governing the exercise of the pocket veto. In 1929 the *Pocket Veto Case* addressed the question whether that means of killing bills applied only at the end of a Congress or also at the end of a session of Congress. The decision was in favor of the latter. That ruling was reversed by a court of appeals panel in 1985, but the Supreme Court refused to sustain the reversal. In the meantime, the Court had held that a brief recess was not an adjournment for veto purposes, and it had overturned the earlier understanding that the president could not sign a bill into law after Congress had adjourned.[7]

The regular veto procedure also turned out to contain complex-

5. U.S. Constitution, Article 1, Section 7. William Howard Taft, *Our Chief Magistrate and His Powers* (New York, 1916), 23–24.

6. Robert J. Spitzer, *The Presidential Veto* (Albany, NY, 1988), 72, 109. Spitzer's work is interpretively far richer than the earlier study, Carlton Jackson, *Presidential Vetoes, 1792–1945* (Athens, GA, 1967), which is merely a running account of vetoes; Jackson's work is a mine of information, however.

7. The *Pocket Veto Case*, 279 U.S. 644 (1929); *Wright* v. *U.S.*, 302 U.S. 583 (1938); *Edwards* v. *U.S.*, 286 U.S. 482 (1932); *Kennedy* v. *Sampson*, 511 F. 2d 430 (D.C. Cir. 1974); *Barnes* v. *Kline*, 759 F. 2d 21 (D.C. Cir. 1985); *Burke* v. *Barnes*, 479 U.S. 361 (1987); Spitzer, *Presidential Veto*, 114–155; Christopher H. Pyle and Richard M. Pious, *The President, Congress, and the Constitution: Power and Legitimacy in American Politics* (New York, 1984), 222; Louis Fisher, *Constitutional Conflicts between Congress and the President*, 3d ed., rev. (Lawrence, KS, 1991), 124–128.

ities, particularly in regard to pork-barrel legislation. At first, neither Federalists nor Jeffersonian Republicans believed that Congress had the power to authorize and pay for "internal improvements," meaning mainly the construction of inland transportation facilities. By the end of the War of 1812, however, it had become evident that improvements were necessary and that Congress had sufficient revenues and political incentives to authorize them. Presidents Madison and Monroe vetoed some such legislation on constitutional grounds, but it remained for Andrew Jackson to demonstrate the political possibilities. Jackson quietly signed into law appropriations for internal improvements amounting to perhaps twice as much as his predecessors combined, but in 1830, with great ostentation, he vetoed the Maysville Road bill. He declared that he was acting on grounds of constitutionality as well as policy since the road was entirely in Kentucky and thus the expenditure was not for the "general welfare" as the Constitution required. His real reason was less principled, namely to take a shot at his despised political enemy, Sen. Henry Clay of Kentucky.[8]

The political implication of this veto was not lost on members of Congress. When coupled with Jackson's subsequent claim that he had a right as the sole representative of all the people to be consulted prior to the enactment of legislation, the veto struck congressmen as a usurpation and a power play—a power play because the president could use the threat to veto internal-improvement projects in particular congressional districts to coerce individual legislators.[9]

8. Jackson, *Presidential Vetoes,* 15–27, gives a good account of the Maysville Road veto; Richardson, comp., *Messages and Papers of the Presidents,* 2:483ff. (May 27, 1830), contains the veto message; Jack N. Rakove, *James Madison and the Creation of the American Republic* (Glenview, IL, 1990), 171–172; Robert V. Remini, *Andrew Jackson and the Course of American Freedom, 1822–1832* (New York, 1981), 251–256; Claude G. Bowers, *The Party Battles of the Jackson Period* (Boston, 1922), 171, 175–176; Edward Campbell Mason, *The Veto Power: Its Origin, Development and Function in the Government of the United States* (Boston, 1890).

9. Jackson, *Presidential Vetoes,* 35, 40–41; Spitzer, *Presidential Veto,* 34–36; Leonard D. White, *The Jacksonians* (New York, 1954), 23, 25–27, 30; Remini, *Jackson and American Freedom,* 256, 266–267, 302–303, 323, 329; the right to prior consultation is in the Bank veto, in Richardson, comp., *Messages and Papers of the Presidents,* 2:576ff. (July 10, 1832). Edward S. Corwin, *The President, 1789–1957* (New York, 1957), 23,

To frustrate presidential meddling in what Congress considered its own preserve, congressmen during the course of the next generation developed the practice of adding riders to legislation. The Framers had been familiar with the practice (known in eighteenth-century England as "tacking") of heading off a veto by adding unrelated substantive features to appropriations bills or appropriations to unrelated substantive measures. The practice was so generally rejected in principle that the Framers thought it unnecessary to prohibit it in the Constitution. Bills were restricted to one subject, and that was that. From the middle third of the nineteenth century, however, the insertion of riders became the norm in America although the House of Representatives for a long time had a rule preventing it.[10]

After the Civil War, a new dimension, again concerning appropriations and the veto power, entered the relationship between president and Congress. Historically in England and America it was a cardinal principle that government could not take money from one taxpayer and give it to another except in payment for supplies or services, but from the Grant administration onward Congress began to violate the principle. One form of violation, the appropriation of funds for disaster relief, elicited little controversy and few vetoes. William McKinley requested such a measure for flood victims on the Mississippi River in 1897 and pointed to precedents in 1874 and 1882, "besides large sums in other years." Another form was extremely controversial: private bills granting pensions to Civil War veterans who claimed service related disabilities but whose claims had been rejected by the Pension Bureau. President Grant, believing many of these claims to

---

concluded that Jackson's "legislative role . . . was essentially negative, being confined for the most part to a vigorous use of the veto power," but in a note (322) he quotes a claim by a twentieth-century congressman that Richard Fletcher had asserted in an 1837 speech that "during Jackson's term of office, the principal function of the House Ways and Means Committee, of which Fletcher had been a member, was going through the form of approving laws which Jackson prepared and handed down to them for acceptance."

10. Spitzer, *Presidential Veto*, 7, 55–56, 123–124; Thomas Pitt Taswell-Langmead, *English Constitutional History from the Teutonic Conquest to the Present Time* (Boston, 1946), 613–614; Judith A. Best, "The Item Veto: Would the Founders Approve?" *Presidential Studies Quarterly* 14 (1984):183–188; Taft, *Our Chief Magistrate*, 25–27.

be fraudulent, vetoed forty private bills, and Grover Cleveland vetoed 482; this was more than twice as many vetoes as his twenty-one predecessors had exercised. Indeed, almost two-thirds of the bills vetoed during the Constitution's first two centuries were private bills, not public.[11]

Over the course of time, executive vigilance against congressional raids on the treasury greatly strengthened the prestige of the presidency, but the passage of legislation loaded with riders repeatedly frustrated the president's endeavors. To strengthen his hand, it has frequently been suggested, beginning with Grant, that he should be given an item veto by constitutional amendment; it has also been argued that the president actually has an item veto if he will but exercise it. It was rumored on several occasions that President Bush was determined to test the item veto in the courts, but he did not do it. The notion had a certain appeal in an age of runaway deficit financing, but it involved some impracticalities and one insuperable objection: At a time when the primary function of congressmen had become arranging favors and money for their constituents, the item veto could be used to reduce Congress to the status of a puppet show.[12]

11. Jackson, *Presidential Vetoes,* chap. 11; Spitzer, *Presidential Veto,* 72, 74, 81; Richardson, comp., quote from *Messages and Papers of the Presidents,* 10:21–22; *New York Times,* April 8, 1897, 3:5; Grant's and Cleveland's vetoes, Richardson, comp., *Messages and Papers of the Presidents,* vols. 7–9; William H. Glasson, *Federal Military Pensions in the United States* (New York, 1918), 277–279. In 1887 Cleveland did veto a bill to distribute seeds to farmers in drought-stricken areas of Texas (Richardson, comp., *Messages and Papers of the Presidents,* 8:557–558). According to the *U.S. Code,* private bills are "all bills for the relief of private parties, bills granting pensions, bills removing political disabilities, and bills for the survey of rivers and harbors" (Spitzer, *Presidential Veto,* 81). See also Richard E. Welch, Jr., *The Presidency of Grover Cleveland* (Lawrence, KS, 1988), 6, 10, 11, 14, 56, 62, 63, 73, 80, 89, 125, 217.

12. Louis Fisher, "The Constitution and Presidential Budget Powers: The Modern Era," in *The Constitution and the American Presidency,* ed. Martin Fausold and Alan Shank (Albany, NY, 1991), 163–168; Spitzer, *Presidential Veto,* 121–142; Best, "Item Veto," *Presidential Studies Quarterly* 14:183–188; Margaret N. Davis, "The Congressional Budget Mess," in *The Imperial Congress,* ed. Gordon S. Jones and John A. Marini (New York, 1988), 174–175; J. Gregory Sidak, "The President's Power of the Purse," *Duke Law Journal* (1989):1162–1253; J. Gregory Sidak and Thomas A. Smith, "Four Faces of the Item Veto: A Reply to Tribe and Kurland," *Northwestern University*

Other uses of the veto have varied with time and circumstances. After Cleveland's veritable orgy of vetoes, exercise of the power returned to a lower level until the presidency of Franklin Roosevelt. McKinley employed two regular vetoes of public bills, Theodore Roosevelt fifteen, though between them they pocket-vetoed more than sixty private bills. William Howard Taft and Woodrow Wilson, both stubborn men with strong constitutional convictions, faced hostile congresses for part of their terms. Each vetoed more than twenty public bills; six of Wilson's were overturned. Some important vetoes, presaging things to come, were of special-interest legislation. Both presidents vetoed immigration-restriction bills advocated by organized labor, for instance, and Wilson vetoed bills promising special benefits for farmers and veterans. The three Republicans who followed (Harding, Coolidge, and Hoover) had solid Republican congresses until 1931 and thus had fewer occasions for differences. Even so, they repeatedly felt obliged to veto veterans' bonus bills and bills to subsidize the marketing of farm products. Though most of their vetoes were sustained, Coolidge had the singular lot to witness four vetoes being overridden on one day. All told, of the 157 regular vetoes, public and private, employed by the presidents from McKinley through Hoover, 15 were overridden.[13]

Franklin Roosevelt's use of the veto was not entirely congruent with his public image. Though he is generally regarded as the first of the big-time spenders, he exercised the vast majority of his vetoes to

Law Review 84 (1990):437–479; Diane-Michele Krasnow, "The Imbalance of Power and the Presidential Veto: A Case for the Item Veto," Harvard Journal of Law and Public Policy 14 (1991):583–613; Stephen Glazier, "The Line-Item Veto: Provided in the Constitution and Traditionally Applied," in Pork Barrels and Principles: The Politics of the Presidential Veto (Washington, DC, 1988), 9–17, and Louis Fisher, "The Presidential Veto: Constitutional Development," ibid., 27–28; Terry Eastland, "George Bush into the Breach," National Review, Nov. 4, 1991, 42.

13. Statistics tallied from tables in Spitzer, Presidential Veto, 72 and 74. For a table of vetoes, 1789–1963, see also Joseph E. Kallenbach, The American Chief Executive (New York, 1966), 355; Taft, Our Chief Magistrate, 17; on the relationship between the number of vetoes and partisans in Congress, see Samuel B. Hoff, "Saying No, Presidential Support and Veto Use, 1889–1989," American Politics Quarterly 19 (1991): 310–323.

prevent public expenditures in ways that he thought were wasteful, unfair, or otherwise undesirable—veterans' bonus bills, for example, and a bill to restore a 15-percent cut that had been made in the salaries of government employees. Throughout his presidency he had huge Democratic majorities in Congress, and they usually gave him what he wanted; but surprisingly, he exercised the veto more often than Cleveland had, though to be sure he served twelve years to Cleveland's eight. Roosevelt used the veto as a method of cracking the whip, to keep Congress subordinate if not subservient. He also exercised the power in ways calculated to win favorable publicity. In 1935, for instance, he delivered a veto message in person to a joint session of Congress and simultaneously to the country through nationwide radio.[14]

The postwar presidents used the veto with varying effectiveness. Truman, who faced a hostile Republican Congress from 1947 to 1949, was highly combative and in addition to 70 pocket vetoes disapproved 137 private bills and 43 public bills—the best known being the Taft-Hartley Act, which was passed over his veto. He paid careful attention to his veto messages as a means of calling public notice to his policies. These messages and his peppery attacks on what he styled "the do-nothing Eightieth Congress" helped him win reelection in 1948. The other three Democrats (Kennedy, Johnson, and Carter), having strong majorities in Congress, vetoed public bills sparingly, just twenty-one times among them. Carter was overriden two times, the others none. Eisenhower and Reagan were essentially nonconfrontational. Both faced Democratic congressional majorities most of the time, and in the interest of keeping the doors open to successful negotiations they tried to avoid using the veto. Nixon and Ford, by contrast, wielded the veto as a weapon, but they met with little success against a Congress that was, by 1973, openly hostile. Of their seventy-one regular vetoes of public bills, more than a quarter

14. Jackson, *Presidential Vetoes*, 205–224, offers a good summary of Roosevelt's vetoes. Jackson places the total at 631, but Spitzer, *Presidential Veto*, 72, says that it was 635. It has hardly seemed worthwhile to make a tally to determine which (if either) is the accurate figure. See also James MacGregor Burns, *Roosevelt: The Lion and the Fox* (New York, 1956), 186–187, 190, 234; Arthur M. Schlesinger, Jr., *The Age of Roosevelt*, 3 vols. (Boston, 1956–1960), 2:554–557.

were overridden—the worst records except for the hapless Andrew Johnson and Franklin Pierce (who was overridden in five of his nine vetoes). George Bush exercised the veto freely, but his party had enough votes in the Senate to prevent overrides of his first thirty-five vetoes; on October 5, 1992, the 102d Congress overrode his thirty-sixth veto, of a bill regulating cable TV rates and standards.[15]

———— The other constitutional authority of the president regarding legislation, that of giving Congress, "from time to time," information on the "State of the Union" and recommending measures deemed "necessary and expedient," was exercised positively at first but soon lapsed into little more than a ritual. The early presidents and their cabinet officers had drafted bills and helped steer them through Congress. After the War of 1812 the decline of the first party system, combined with the emergence of congressional leaders whose personalities and wills were stronger than the president's, shifted the legislative initiative to Congress. Andrew Jackson tried to exert his powerful personality and will to reclaim a legislative role, but his attempt led to a backlash that reduced the presidency almost to impotence.

From Jackson's time until the end of the century the State of the Union messages, delivered annually in December, were formulaic rituals. Characteristically, the message reviewed relations between the United States and foreign nations as well as with Indian tribes;

15. Tallied from the table in Spitzer, *Presidential Veto,* 74; Donald R. McCoy, *The Presidency of Harry S. Truman* (Lawrence, KS, 1984), 98–99, 180–181, 258. The *New York Times* reported Ford's vetoes as if they were scores in an athletic contest: Ford overridden on 3 of 13 vetoes in 3¼ months in office, Nov. 22, 1974, 21:3; override of Ford veto third time in three weeks, Dec. 4, 1974, 1:6; override 4 Ford vetoes of 15 in 4 months, worst average since Pierce in the 1850s, Dec. 5, 1974, 34:5; see also April 11, 1976, D, 2:5, Sept. 4, 1976, 10:4, and Sept. 30, 1976, 32:1. The press "acknowledged the unquestionable success of Ford's veto strategy . . . [but] did not characterize that approach . . . as true 'leadership'" (Mark J. Rozell, *The Press and the Ford Presidency* [Ann Arbor, MI, 1992], 12). See also David McKay, "Presidential Strategy and the Veto Power: A Reappraisal," *Political Science Quarterly* 104 (1989):447–461. The override of Bush's thirty-sixth veto was reported on NPR's "Morning Edition," Oct. 6, 1992, as was Bush's comment that the override resulted from TV networks' intensive lobbying on Capitol Hill.

this survey normally took two-thirds or more of the message. Another sizable portion introduced the reports and legislative recommendations of the secretaries of departments and heads of administrative agencies. What little legislation the president himself recommended was almost invariably cast in terms of general policy such as approving or disapproving hard money, internal improvements, protective tariffs, or disposition of the public domain. Occasionally presidents proposed constitutional amendments; Jackson, for example, suggested that there should be two Supreme Courts, one for each side of the Appalachians, that the electoral college be abolished, and that the president be limited to a single term of four or six years.[16]

Lincoln was an exception to the pattern. After the firing on Fort Sumter in April of 1861 he declared an insurrection, called for a volunteer force of 75,000 men, ordered a blockade, and took various other steps, without legal or constitutional authorization; when Congress met in special session in July, he asked for and got retroactive legislation approving his actions. In his Second Annual Message he urged, largely as a war measure, the creation of a national banking system and a currency based upon government debt; Congress responded three months later by passing the National Banking Act. Also in that message he submitted a draft of a constitutional amendment providing for the gradual abolition of slavery (by 1900), for compensation to slaveholders, and for colonization of the freedmen somewhere outside the United States. Uninfluenced by Lincoln's relative activism, however, and warned by the fate of Andrew Johnson, subsequent presidents resumed the ways of Lincoln's predecessors.[17]

The style of the presidency in regard to legislation, though not yet

16. Jackson's proposals in Richardson, comp., *Messages and Papers of the Presidents*, 2:447–448, 461, 518–519, 557, 3:34; for samples of others, see 3:373ff. (Van Buren); 4:74–89 (Tyler); 4:385–416 (Polk); 5:9–24 (Taylor); 5:77–94 (Fillmore); 7:27–42 (Grant); 8:324–365 (Cleveland first term); 9:180–211 (Harrison); 10:26–50 (McKinley). For a careful analysis of modern State of the Union addresses, see Barbara Hinckley, *The Symbolic Presidency: How Presidents Portray Themselves* (New York, 1990).

17. Richardson, comp., *Messages and Papers of the Presidents*, Proclamations of April 15, April 19, April 27, 1861, Special Session Message, July 4, 1861, Second Annual Message, Dec. 1, 1862, 6:13–15, 20–31, 129–130, 136–142.

the substance, changed dramatically upon the accession of Theodore Roosevelt. The nation had undergone revolutionary changes during the three preceding decades, but one would think from the messages of the presidents that nothing unusual had taken place. Roosevelt, in his State of the Union messages, directed attention to the new conditions and called for an active federal response. He insisted that there must be "progressive regulation" of "our gigantic industrial development," and toward that end proposed a strengthening of the Interstate Commerce Commission, tougher antitrust laws, banking and currency reform, immigration restriction, conservation of natural resources, the establishment of a cabinet-level Department of Commerce and Industries, and similar measures.[18]

Though he vigorously advocated reform, Roosevelt was careful not to challenge the established order in Congress. He was almost obsequious in dealing with the old guard in the Senate, headed by Marcus Hanna of Ohio, Nelson Aldrich of Rhode Island, Orville Platt of Connecticut, William Allison of Iowa, and John C. Spooner of Wisconsin. He was at pains to curry favor with Speaker Joseph Cannon, who ran the House of Representatives like a house of correction. Courting Cannon, who was an uncouth, foul-mouthed, tobacco-chewing bumpkin, must have galled Roosevelt, who was upper-upper class, but Cannon and the senatorial old guard had restored discipline, and with it respectability and power, to a Congress that had forfeited those attributes in the 1870s. Cultivating these people was essential if Roosevelt were to exert influence.[19]

18. Ibid., 10:421–436, 452–453, 511–518.

19. L. White Busbey, *Uncle Joe Cannon: The Story of a Pioneer American* (New York, 1927), 219, quotes Cannon as saying, "I think Mr. Roosevelt talked over with me virtually every serious recommendation to Congress before he made it"; William Rea Gwinn, *Uncle Joe Cannon, Archfoe of Insurgency: A History of the Rise and Fall of Cannonism* (n.p., 1957); Blair Bolles, *Tyrant from Illinois: Uncle Joe Cannon's Experiment with Personal Power* (New York, 1951), 88–225; David Graham Phillips, *The Treason of the Senate*, ed. George E. Mowry and Judson A. Grenier (Chicago, 1964); Charles S. Dana, "Theodore Roosevelt and Tiberius Gracchus," *North American Review* 180 (1905):334; Lewis L. Gould, *The Presidency of Theodore Roosevelt* (Lawrence, KS, 1991), 53, 110; William H. Harbaugh, *Power and Responsibility: The Life and Times of Theodore Roosevelt* (New York, 1961), 152–156, 235–240, 242–243; John Morton Blum, *The Republican Roosevelt* (Cambridge, MA, 1954), 73–105; Nathaniel Wright

Roosevelt had some success, but what was more important was a tactic he employed, one that grew naturally from his exuberant soul and his sanguine spirit but that would become a standard device of presidents. He urged reform, but if it was not forthcoming, he picked out legislation that might loosely be described as reform and went on the hustings to claim responsibility for it. Sometimes the legislation was no reform at all; for example, the Elkins Act of 1903, prohibiting railroads from granting rebates to big shippers, was billed as a measure bringing railroads to brook but was actually designed for their protection. Sometimes the legislation was a supposed reform that others sponsored and Roosevelt took credit for; the Pure Food and Drug Act of 1906 was a response to years of self-interested lobbying by the chief chemist for the Department of Agriculture, Harvey W. Wiley. Roosevelt's showmanship in pretending to be the fountain of reform legislation transformed the expectations Americans had for their presidents and thus opened the door for the emergence of the legislative presidency.[20]

———— Congress remained cool toward presidential interference in the legislative process but the man who went through the door that

————
Stephenson, *Nelson W. Aldrich: A Leader in American Politics* (New York, 1930); Leland L. Sage, *William Boyd Allison: A Study in Practical Politics* (Iowa City, IA, 1956); Herbert David Croly, *Marcus Alonzo Hanna: His Life and Work* (New York, 1912), 371–376; Thomas Beer, *Hanna* (New York, 1929), 167–297; Dorothy Ganfield Fowler, *John Coit Spooner: Defender of Presidents* (New York, 1961), 193–370.

20. Harbaugh, *Power and Responsibility,* 236–252; Gabriel Kolko, *Railroads and Regulation,* 1877–1916 (Princeton, NJ, 1965), 95, 100n, 107–116; Ray Ginger, *Age of Excess: The United States from 1877 to 1914,* 2d. ed. (New York, 1975), 268–269; Stephen E. Ponder, "Executive Publicity and Congressional Resistance, 1905–1913: Congress and the Roosevelt Administration's PR Men," *Congress and the Presidency* 13 (1986):177–186; Blum, *Republican Roosevelt,* 55–72, 107–108; James E. Pollard, *The Presidents and the Press* (New York, 1947), 569–598; Gould, *Theodore Roosevelt,* 20–21, 105, 106, 153–154, 161–162, 163–164, 165–169; James Harvey Young, *Pure Food: Securing the Federal Food and Drugs Act of 1906* (Princeton, NJ, 1989), passim; Oscar E. Anderson, Jr., *The Health of a Nation: Harvey W. Wiley and the Fight for Pure Food* (Chicago, 1958), 172–196; Jack High and Clayton A. Coppin, "Wiley and the Whiskey Industry; Strategic Behavior in the Passage of the Pure Food Act," *Business History Review* 62 (1988):286–309.

Roosevelt had opened, Woodrow Wilson, was able to do so because of an interplay between a peculiar set of circumstances and a peculiar presidential psyche. Circumstances first. Wilson was the consummate outsider, an obscure state governor and erstwhile academician who was elected with 41.8 percent of the popular vote in a race against President Taft and former President Roosevelt. The Democrats gained control of the Senate for the first time in a generation and the second since the Civil War, and the five old guard Republican senators had either died or retired. The House had come under the Democrats' control in the 1910 elections, but before they took over, insurgent Republicans had risen against Speaker Cannon and stripped the speakership of many powers. The impact of the resulting decentralization was accentuated by the presence of 114 freshmen Democratic members in the House. In sum, the Democrats were ripe for leadership.[21]

Wilson's attitude toward the presidency fitted him for the role. The president, he wrote just before taking office, "must be the prime minister, as much concerned with the guidance of legislation as with the just and orderly execution of law, and he is the spokesman of the Nation in everything." Congress, "the law making part of the government," should "be very hospitable to the suggestions of the planning and acting part of it," the presidency. To stress the point, he abandoned precedent by appearing in person to address Congress.[22]

Radical as Wilson's conception of the presidency was, it was moderate compared to his conception of himself, which was little short of messianic. Indeed, the day after his election, the Democratic national chairman called on him to confer about appointments, only to be rebuffed by Wilson's statement, "Before we proceed, I wish it clearly

21. Arthur S. Link, *Woodrow Wilson: The New Freedom* (Princeton, NJ, 1956), 148; *Historical Statistics of the United States,* 682; *New York Times,* Dec. 29, 1912, 13:1. The new Democratic members were nearly two-fifths of the 290 Democrats in the House. See also *New York Times,* Nov. 7, 1912, 5:3, Nov. 10, 1912, 14:3; Henry F. Pringle, *Theodore Roosevelt: A Biography* (New York, 1931), 372–373.

22. Link, *Wilson: New Freedom,* 147; Stephen H. Balch, "Do Strong Presidents Really Want Strong Legislative Parties? The Case of Woodrow Wilson and the House Democrats," *Presidential Studies Quarterly* 7 (1977):233; Woodrow Wilson, *Congressional Government* (1885; repr., Boston, 1913), 68–82; Sidak, "Recommendation Clause," *Georgetown Law Journal* 77:2096–2098; Kallenbach, *American Chief Executive,* 336–340.

understood that I owe you nothing. Remember that God *ordained that I should be the next President of the United States.*" He was a master of oratory who described every issue, no matter how trivial, in terms of a great moral crusade, always with himself as the nation's (and later the world's) moral leader—and he believed what he was saying. Given that attitude, it followed that people who opposed him were un-enlightened or evil; it was therefore impossible to meet them halfway. Once, when the press reported that he was looking for a compromise on a particular piece of legislation, he assembled reporters and said to them, "When you get a chance, just say that I am not the kind that considers compromises when I once take my position. Just note that down so that there will be nothing more of that sort transmitted to the press." That kind of righteousness might have been self-defeating in a Congress whose members were entrenched and self-confident, but such was not the membership in 1913.[23]

Two more circumstances worked in Wilson's favor: a strong popular clamor for certain reforms and enthusiasm for an active presidency, awakened by Roosevelt and undimmed by the shortcomings of the unfortunate Taft. In particular, there was widespread popular support for reform of the banking and currency system, stimulated by the Panic of 1907 and the ensuing recession and by the revelations from a House committee of the existence of a "money trust"; for lowering the tariff, which remained extremely high despite reductions in 1909; and for revising the antitrust laws. Wilson was determined to drive and lead the Congress to enact appropriate legislation in these areas.[24]

23. Link, *Wilson: New Freedom,* 5, 149–154, 185; As Herbert Croly wrote, "Mr. Wilson seems to be one of those people who shuffles off their mortal coil as soon as they take pen in hand. They become tremendously noble. . . . They write only upon brass, and for nothing shorter than a millennium. They utter nothing which might sound trivial at the Last Judgment. . . . Moral enthusiasm is what he gives us, re-deemed only by the most abstract reference to living," in "The Other-Worldliness of Wilson," *New Republic,* March 27, 1915, 194; on 195, he warns that "being too noble is dangerous business."

24. On the background of the movement for reform of banking and currency, see Louis D. Brandeis, *Other People's Money and How the Bankers Use It* (New York, 1914), which popularized the "money trust" findings of the Pujo Committee, and H. Parker Willis, *The Federal Reserve System: Legislation, Organization and Operation* (New York,

The first to be considered, in a special session that Wilson called to meet in April, 1913, was tariff reduction, and in steering it through Congress Wilson employed tactics that could serve as textbook examples for would-be presidents. He began by casting the issue in moral terms. It is not easy to consider tariff revision as a burning moral crusade, but the Wilsonian Democrats managed it. To collect import duties for any other purpose than to raise necessary revenues, they declared, was "to tax one man for the benefit of another," and that was profoundly wrong. Secondly, Wilson applied a skillful combination of cooperation and coercion in drafting the bill. Before Congress met in the special session, he worked closely with the House Ways and Means Committee and especially its chairman, House Majority Leader Oscar W. Underwood of Alabama—ostentatiously bypassing the Speaker, which pleased many observers. The committee had a package ready by April 1. Then Wilson summoned Underwood to the White House and told him that the reductions were acceptable but that food, sugar, leather, and wool must be made duty free or he would veto the bill and there would be no tariff revision. Underwood complied. When the special session convened, it was greeted by Wilson's electrifying personal appearance and powerful speech in support of Underwood's revised bill. After two weeks of debate, the House passed the bill by a wide margin.[25]

1923). For the Payne-Aldrich Tariff of 1909 and the discontents arising from it that led to agitation for revision, see F. W. Taussig, *The Tariff History of the United States,* 8th ed. (New York, 1967), 361–408; George M. Fisk, "The Payne-Aldrich Tariff," *Political Science Quarterly* 25 (1910):35–68; Paolo E. Coletta, *The Presidency of William Howard Taft* (Lawrence, KS, 1973), 153–163. Regarding antitrust, see chap. 11 of this book; Benjamin J. Klebaner, "Potential Competition and the American Antitrust Legislation of 1914," *Business History Review* 38 (1964); William Letwin, *Law and Economic Policy in America* (New York, 1965).

25. Link, *Wilson: New Freedom,* 177–182; Taussig, *Tariff History,* 409–446; George Harvey, "The House Has Done Its Part," *Harper's Weekly,* May 17, 1913, 4; George Rothwell Brown, *The Leadership of Congress* (Indianapolis, IN, 1922), 176–177; Martin Torodosh, "Underwood and the Tariff," *Alabama Review* 20 (1967):115–130; Oscar W. Underwood, *Drifting Sands of Party Politics* (New York, 1928), 71, 124, 188–189, 198, 199, 213–214; John M. Blum, *Woodrow Wilson and the Politics of Morality* (Boston, 1956), 54.

The bill next went to the Senate, for years the graveyard of tariff-reduction legislation. The situation was analogous to that faced by people in the 1980s and 1990s who wanted to cut federal spending: Nearly everybody was in favor of cuts but not in regard to programs that benefited one's self or one's constituents. During the tariff battle in 1913, senators from Louisiana favored cutting everything but the protective tariff on sugar, those from Montana wanted to except wool from the general reduction, those from the Carolinas were willing to slash duties but not on textiles, and so on. As the debate in the Senate began, representatives of special interests started seeking exceptions.[26]

To head off the threat, Wilson conferred endlessly with particular senators. He talked with them in small groups, not individually, on the theory that the shame factor would be more effective that way. He made no promises, made no threats, twisted no arms. Instead, he simply appealed to senators to do what they knew was right for the country. Whenever a senator agreed to do so, Wilson followed up tellingly, as he did in a letter to Congressman Nathan P. Bryan of Florida, who agreed to waive protection for citrus fruits: "I congratulate the party and the country," he wrote, "upon having a man to serve them who sees so clearly and does his duty so fearlessly."[27]

Lobbyists had invaded Washington in droves, browbeating, threatening, cajoling, and making lavish promises to the beleaguered senators. Outraged, Wilson denounced the lobbyists in an appeal to the people to combat this "insidious" activity against the public interest, charging that the lobbyists were spending "money without limit" in order "to create an appearance of a pressure of public opinion antagonistic to some of the chief items of the tariff bill." He concluded by suggesting that Congress shared his indignation: "I know that in this I am speaking for the members of the two houses,

26. Taussig, *Tariff History,* 413–414, 417, 425, 426, 428; Link, *Wilson: New Freedom,* 183–184; *New York Times,* April 7, 1913, 1:8, and April 8, 1913, 1:8, also April 15, 1913, 2:2, April 17, 1913, 1:6, May 2, 1913, 2:6, and especially May 16, 1913, 2:2.

27. Link, *Wilson: New Freedom,* 184–186; *New York Times,* April 10, 1913, 1:3, and April 30, 1913, 2:4; "The Tariff in the Senate," *Nation,* May 22, 1913, 514. For Nathan P. Bryan, see *New York Times,* April 28, 1913, 2:3.

who would rejoice as much as I would, to be released from this unbearable situation."[28]

Then came a complicating twist. Democrats, bewildered by the unprecedented attack by the president on a perfectly legitimate activity, said lamely "that they knew of no lobbyists." Republicans, seeking to capitalize on the furor, demanded that a select Senate committee investigate the situation. When the Democratic senators learned that the president welcomed an investigation and wanted to make it as broad as possible, they seized the occasion to turn the inquest into a confessional by the senators themselves. The senators were examined in alphabetical order, and thus in the words of Wilson's biographer Arthur Link, "the country was treated to the spectacle of each senator coming dutifully before the committee and telling how many shares of cotton mill stock or how many acres of grazing or sugar land he owned and how many lobbyists he had talked with or heard from." In addition to embarrassing a goodly number of senators, the committee uncovered proof that the sugar lobby had spent enormous sums to fight for its protection. The Progressive Senator Robert La Follette of Wisconsin chortled that Wilson had thrown a "short-fuse missile. . . . Congress sneered. The interests cried demagogue. The public believed. The case is proved." Debate on the Underwood Tariff dragged on, but it was anticlimactical; early in September the bill passed.[29]

Wilson worked the Federal Reserve Act, the Clayton Antitrust Act, the Federal Trade Commission Act, and lesser legislation through Congress by means similar to those he employed with the Underwood Tariff, but his legislative influence began to wane after 1915. He was reelected in 1916 by a narrow margin in the electoral college and

28. Link, *Wilson: New Freedom,* 186–187; *New York Times,* May 27, 1913, 1:1; Karl Schriftgiesser, *The Lobbyists: The Art and Business of Influencing Lawmakers* (Boston, 1951), 38–44; James Deakin, *The Lobbyists* (Washington, DC, 1966), 74–75; "President's War on Tariff Lobby," *Literary Digest,* June 7, 1913, 1257–1258, and "Hunting the Insidious Lobbyist," ibid., July 5, 1913, 3–5.

29. Link, *Wilson: New Freedom,* 188–194; Taussig, *Tariff History; La Follette's Weekly Magazine,* July 12, 1913, 1; see also, for example, *New York Times,* May 28, 1913, 1:1, May 29, 1913, 1:3, June 6, 1913, 2:1, June 12, 1913, 1:4, June 15, 1913, B, 11:3, June 18, 1913, 1:6.

again by a minority of the popular vote. By then, having become frustrated domestically, he had directed his attention to saving the world "for democracy." In 1918 Republicans regained control of Congress, and they made life hell for Wilson. Nonetheless, he had indelibly impressed on the constitutional order the president's role as legislative leader.[30]

———— The Republican presidents of the 1920s continued the practice of drafting legislation and following its progress through Congress. They also produced—though they did not fully exploit—an instrumentality, created by the Budget and Accounting Act of 1921, that would prove effective in supervising legislation. No longer would federal agencies submit separate estimates of funds needed for the coming fiscal year; now the president, with the aid of the Bureau of the Budget, would decide and request. Within a few months the bureau issued a circular ordering every agency having proposals for legislation or having opinions on pending legislation to submit them, if they in any way involved spending money (which practically all legislation does), to the Bureau of the Budget for clearance. Rigorous enforcement of the procedure began in 1924.[31]

President Hoover was legislatively more active than Harding and Coolidge, especially in proposing measures to combat the steadily worsening depression that had begun shortly after he took office. In December, 1931, he proposed sixteen major bills; of the four that

30. Balch, "Do Strong Presidents Really Want Strong Legislative Parties?" *Presidential Studies Quarterly* 7:234–237; Alex M. Arnett, *Claud Kitchin and the Wilson War Policies* (Boston, 1937), 249–270; Link, *Wilson: New Freedom,* 200–471, and Arthur S. Link, *Woodrow Wilson: Confusion and Crises, 1915–1916* (Princeton, NJ, 1964) and *Woodrow Wilson: Campaigns for Progressivism and Peace, 1916–1917* (Princeton, NJ, 1965).

31. Richard E. Neustadt, "Presidency and Legislation: The Growth of Central Clearance," *American Political Science Review* 48 (1954):641–647. Coolidge and Hoover used the new budget policy primarily as a device to keep government spending to a minimum, not as a way of coordinating substantive policy although that had been anticipated in the 1921 act. See also John Hart, *The Presidential Branch* (Elmsford, NY, 1987), 30–32; *New York Times,* June 11, 1921, 8:1, and June 30, 1921, 1:3, 9:1, 16:1; J. P. Chamberlain, "American Budgetary Reform," *Nation,* June 21, 1919, 976–978.

were enacted (Democrats had gained control of the House in the 1930 elections), the Glass-Steagall Act was by far the most important. Designed to counteract the devastating contraction of currency and credit, it broadened the kinds of commercial paper that were acceptable for rediscount (and thus usable as the basis for the issuance of money) in the Federal Reserve System, and it also made government debt acceptable for the purpose. Politicians took awhile to perceive the implication for fiscal policy: The more the federal government borrowed, the greater was the potential money supply. That innovation, coupled with the income tax on personal and corporate incomes authorized by the Sixteenth Amendment, made the growth of the Leviathan state and the imperial presidency fiscally possible.[32]

In contrast to Hoover, Franklin Roosevelt succeeded with Congress, and during the hundred days of an emergency session in 1933 he pushed through major legislation on a scale that would stand as the exemplar of the legislative presidency. Congress was positively eager to do his bidding; many measures became law within a week of the time he proposed them, and some were enacted within a matter of hours. The labors were not quite so herculean as they appeared, for some of the more sweeping laws—including the Tennessee Valley Authority Act, the Federal Securities Act, and a new Glass-Steagall Act (creating the Federal Deposit Insurance Corporation)—resulted not from presidential initiative but from ideas that had long been bandied about in Congress. But the vast majority originated with President Roosevelt and the "brains trust" of advisers who accompanied him to Washington.[33]

32. David Burner, *Herbert Hoover,* (New York, 1979), 245–283; Martin L. Fausold, *The Presidency of Herbert Hoover* (Lawrence, KS, 1985), 125–137, 147–166; Albert U. Romasco, *The Poverty of Abundance: Hoover, the Nation, the Depression* (New York, 1965), 175–229; Harris G. Warren, *Herbert Hoover and the Great Depression* (New York, 1959), 148–167; Paul Y. Anderson, "Hoover Suffers in the House," *Nation,* March 11, 1931, 268–269; Milton Friedman and Anna Jacobson Schwartz, *A Monetary History of the United States, 1867–1960* (Princeton, NJ, 1963), 321, 331, 363, 384.

33. William E. Leuchtenburg, *Franklin D. Roosevelt and the New Deal, 1932–1940* (New York, 1963), 41–63; Frank Freidel, *Franklin D. Roosevelt: A Rendezvous with Destiny* (Boston, 1990), 92–105, 119–129; James E. Sargent, *Roosevelt and the Hundred Days: Struggle for the Early New Deal* (New York, 1981), 44–46, 142–144, 215–217, 230–232, 240–242; Sylvia Snowiss, "Presidential Leadership of Congress: An Anal-

Roosevelt was highly successful for several years. Many and perhaps most Democrats in Congress idolized him; he was open to them; he convinced them that he thought them as wonderful as they thought him. He timed his measures well and had them drafted in language that would ensure their being sent to favorably disposed committees. He kept in close touch with activities in Congress through bright young liaisons—Thomas Corcoran and Benjamin Cohen, among others. And as he consolidated power he institutionalized it by turning the Bureau of the Budget into the clearing agency for legislation. At his beckoning, the bureau sorted proposed laws into three classes: objectionable ones, those to which the president would not particularly object but would not want identified as administration measures, and those that were approved by and to be identified with the president.34

---

ysis of Roosevelt's First Hundred Days," *Publius* 1 (1971): 59–87; Schlesinger, *Age of Roosevelt,* 2:1–23; J. Frederick Essary, "The New Deal for Nearly Four Months," *Literary Digest,* July 1, 1933, 3–5, 35; William C. Murphy, Jr., "The New Deal in Action," *Commonweal,* May 5, 1933, 11–13. Roosevelt and the Seventy-third Congress were the last to take office before the adoption of the Twentieth (Lame-Duck) Amendment. Historically the president had taken office on March 4, and the first regular session of Congress began in December, thirteen months after its election. Every twentieth-century president, including Roosevelt, had called Congress into special session to avoid the long delay. The Twentieth Amendment sets the first session of each Congress to meet on January 4, and the president's inauguration is January 20. The delay to March 4 in Roosevelt's case was dangerous, for his refusal to cooperate with Hoover had grave effects, including the collapse of the banking system. In recent times the period between election and inauguration has seemed too brief to permit an adequate transition.

34. On Roosevelt's political methods, see Richard E. Neustadt, *Presidential Power and the Modern Presidency: The Politics of Leadership from Roosevelt to Reagan,* rev. ed. (New York, 1990); Burns, *Roosevelt: Lion and Fox;* Edgar E. Robinson, *The Roosevelt Leadership, 1933–1945* (Philadelphia, 1955); Jonathan Daniels, *White House Witness* (Garden City, NY, 1975); Patrick Anderson, *The President's Men* (Garden City, NY, 1968); and memoirs by persons who were close to the president, such as Raymond Moley, *After Seven Years* (New York, 1939); James A. Farley, *Jim Farley's Story: The Roosevelt Years* (New York, 1948); and Robert E. Sherwood, *Roosevelt and Hopkins: An Intimate History* (New York, 1948). On the Budget Bureau and clearances, see Neustadt, "Presidency and Legislation," *American Political Science Review* 48:647–654. H. R. Haldeman made Neustadt's *Presidential Power* required reading for Nixon staffers.

Not even Franklin Roosevelt could continue the pace forever. Having reached the pinnacle of legislative power and having taught the people to look to the president as the remedy for every problem, Roosevelt went too far and committed political blunders that made it impossible for himself and for successors to fulfill the expectations he had raised. After the failure of the court-packing plan in 1937, Roosevelt compounded his difficulties with the Democrats in Congress—more than two-fifths of whom represented the racially segregated South—by coming out with great rhetorical fervor for a federal antilynch law. The proposal was roundly defeated. In the 1938 congressional elections Roosevelt campaigned vigorously against the Democratic senators whom he regarded as responsible for the defeat, especially Walter F. George of Georgia, "Cotton Ed" Smith of South Carolina, and Millard Tydings of Maryland. They were reelected despite the president's efforts, and the Republicans gained seventy-five seats in the House. Southern Democrats, offended by what they regarded as Roosevelt's play for northern black voters (only a tiny fraction of southern blacks were allowed to vote) and by his campaigning against Democratic incumbents, ceased to be reliable supporters of presidential legislative initiatives except when they brought federal money into their states.[35]

Out of that defection grew the conservative coalition of southern Democrats and middlewestern and western Republicans that would dominate Congress until 1963. As far as Roosevelt was concerned it was of little consequence; like Wilson he had turned his attention

35. James T. Patterson, *Congressional Conservatism and the New Deal: The Growth of the Conservative Coalition in Congress, 1933–1939* (Lexington, KY, 1967); Robert H. Jackson, *The Struggle for Judicial Supremacy: A Study of a Crisis in American Power Politics* (New York, 1941); Joseph Alsop and Turner Catledge, *The 168 Days* (Garden City, NY, 1938); Alvin L. Hall, "Politics and Patronage: Virginia's Senators and the Roosevelt Purges of 1938," *Virginia Magazine of History and Biography* 82 (1974):331–350; Leuchtenburg, *Roosevelt and the New Deal*, 252–267; James T. Patterson, "A Conservative Coalition Forms in Congress, 1933–1939," *Journal of American History* 52 (1966):757–772; Caroline H. Keith, *"For Hell and a Brown Mule": The Biography of Millard E. Tydings* (Lanham, MD, 1991), 201, 205, 216–222, 223; Robert McCormick, "He's for Cotton," *Collier's: The National Weekly*, April 23, 1938, 48, 52; "Filibuster in the Senate," *Literary Digest*, Dec. 4, 1937, 5; "The Congress," *Time*, Jan. 24, 1938, 8–10; "Anti-Lynch Fight," *Newsweek*, Jan. 31, 1938, 13–14.

from domestic reform to the world arena, and Congress gave him almost unlimited power for the conduct of World War II. Harry Truman added an innovation to the legislative presidency—the submission of an annual legislative agenda, formulated for presentation in the State of the Union address and followed by detailed bills over the course of the following months—but few of his major proposals were enacted. Eisenhower offered no legislative package during his first year, but he ritualistically followed the Truman formula for the remainder of his presidency as did his successors. He got along with Congress tolerably well though Democrats controlled it during his last six years, for he won effective cooperation from Speaker Sam Rayburn and Senate Majority Leader Lyndon Johnson, and besides he did not ask for much. John F. Kennedy, whose Ivy League advisers produced an array of sweeping proposals, won a strategic victory over the House Rules Committee, through which the conservative coalition had had a stranglehold on legislation; but the contest hardened the opposition, and none of Kennedy's major initiatives became law during his lifetime.[36]

———— President Johnson was able to break the logjam for a time. Circumstances favored him: Johnson had a comfortable (and after

36. John F. Manley, "The Conservative Coalition in Congress," *American Behavioral Scientist* 17 (1973):223–247; Mack C. Shelley, *The Permanent Majority: The Conservative Coalition in the United States Congress* (Tuscaloosa, AL, 1983); Stephen J. Wayne, *The Legislative Presidency* (New York, 1978), 102–109; McCoy, *Harry Truman,* 93–95; Chester J. Pach, Jr., and Elmo Richardson, *The Presidency of Dwight D. Eisenhower* (Lawrence, KS, 1991), 49–73; James N. Giglio, *The Presidency of John F. Kennedy* (Lawrence, KS, 1991), 123–143, 173, 182–187, 284–287; Robert J. Williams and David A. Kershaw, "Kennedy and Congress: The Struggle for the New Frontier," *Political Studies* 27 (1979):390–404; Hart, *Presidential Branch,* 117–119, 172–175; Nelson W. Polsby, "Some Landmarks in Modern Presidential-Congressional Relations," in *Both Ends of the Avenue: The Presidency, the Executive Branch, and Congress in the 1980s,* ed. Anthony King (Washington, DC, 1983), 5–8; Abraham Holtzman, *Legislative Liaison: Executive Leadership in Congress* (Chicago, 1970), 239–241, 242–243, 253; Jeffrey E. Cohen, "The Impact of the Modern Presidency on Presidential Success in the U.S. Congress," *Legislative Studies Quarterly* 7 (1982):518; C. Dwight Dorough, *Mr. Sam* (New York, 1962), 450–545; Alfred Steinberg, *Sam Rayburn: A Biography* (New York, 1975), 279–295. Kennedy "never had much success in getting his programs through Congress," according to Tip O'Neill (*Man of the House,* with William Novak [New York, 1987], 165).

1964 an overwhelming) Democratic majority in Congress; he had a potent legislative agenda inherited from the Kennedy administration; he exploited the emotional shock of Kennedy's assassination for support of his proposals; he played on popular unrest and the eagerness for action that pervaded the nation. He was able to use these favorable conditions to get enacted Kennedy's tax cut, the Civil Rights Act of 1964, the Voting Rights Act of 1965, and the various "Great Society" programs, however, only because he understood congressmen and understood how Congress operated.[37]

A Lyndon Baines Johnson manual of how to manage Congress would have included the following precepts. First, recognize and use the powerful aura that surrounds the president, even among avowed enemies. Inviting congressmen and their spouses for cruises on the presidential yacht, to receptions, to bill-signing ceremonies wins friends, as does the giving of small gifts emblazoned with the presidential seal, such as pens or cuff links or charm bracelets, which Johnson passed out profusely. Second, be accessible to congressmen and maintain contact. Johnson issued a standing order to switchboard operators that calls from Lawrence F. O'Brien—who as head of the White House Office of Congressional Relations was the principal liaison with members of Congress—were to be put through immediately, any time of day or night. Third, understand and feed the members' amour propre. He gave credit to leaders, and in dealing out patronage and pork, he did not (except in special cases) tie them directly to immediate votes, lest congressmen feel threatened or bribed. Fourth, take into account the congressmen's work loads,

---

37. Wayne, *Legislative Presidency,* 41–45, 109–113; Lyndon Baines Johnson, *The Vantage Point: Perspectives of the Presidency, 1963–1969* (New York, 1971), 18–41, 69–87; Rowland Evans and Robert Novak, *Lyndon B. Johnson* (New York, 1966), 407–434; George Reedy, *Lyndon B. Johnson: A Memoir* (New York, 1982), 135–143; Alonzo L. Hamby, *Liberalism and Its Challengers,* 2d ed. (New York, 1992), 256–258; Richard M. Pious, *The American Presidency* (New York, 1979), 122–123, 135, 154, 202; Cary R. Covington, "Congressional Support for the President: The View from the Kennedy/Johnson White House," *Journal of Politics* 48 (1986):725; Cary R. Covington, "Mobilizing Congressional Support for the President: Insights from the 1960s," *Legislative Studies Quarterly* 12 (1987):77–95; after 1966, of course, Johnson's "success rate" declined (Jon R. Bond and Richard Fleisher, *The President in the Legislative Arena* [Chicago, 1990], 206–208, 211).

which includes sending bills one by one instead of in great clumps and picking times when the appropriate committee is not overburdened with other matters that it considers important. Fifth, be persistent, following the progress of legislation daily from submission to enactment. Sixth, move swiftly, for at best a president can count on a year or two of honeymoon time in which to get his program enacted. Finally, go public as a last resort; Congress considers going over its head an act of war.[38]

President Nixon never had a honeymoon period. He and his advisers regarded members of Congress as lacking the ability to govern or to set policy, and a relationship based upon mutual distrust between White House and Congress, begun in Johnson's last year, was much aggravated. Nixon was not especially interested in legislation or in the legislative process. He talked about domestic policy from time to time, usually citing a need to consolidate or to eliminate the more chaotic of Johnson's programs, but he appeared to Congress to lose interest quickly. Some observers said that trying to oppose him on domestic policy was "like pushing on a string," meaning that he offered no resistance. Instead, he sought to govern without Congress, and given the institutional ineptness of that body he might have been able to do it had not Watergate brought him down.[39]

---

38. The format and much of the information in this paragraph are derived from Charles O. Jones, "Presidential Negotiation with Congress," in King, ed., *Both Ends of the Avenue,* 107–111; but rich supplementary material has been taken from Polsby, "Presidential-Congressional Relations," ibid., 10–12; George C. Edwards III, *Presidential Influence in Congress* (San Francisco, 1980), 117–134; Nigel Bowles, *The White House and Capitol Hill: The Politics of Presidential Persuasion* (New York, 1987), 28, 34–80; David Mervin, "The President and Congress," in *Roosevelt to Reagan,* ed. Malcolm Shaw (London, 1987), 93–95; Joseph A. Califano, *Governing America* (New York, 1981); Evans and Novak, *Johnson;* Pious, *American Presidency,* 187, 188–189, 198; Harry McPherson, *A Political Education* (Boston, 1972), 245–333; Cary R. Covington, "Guess Who's Coming to Dinner," *American Politics Quarterly* 16 (1988):243–265; Doris Kearns, *Lyndon Johnson and the American Dream* (New York, 1976), 226, 227, 232–237; Barbara Kellerman, *The Political Presidency: Practice of Leadership* (New York, 1984), 116–124. See also Mark A. Peterson, *Legislating Together: The White House and Capitol Hill from Eisenhower to Reagan* (Cambridge, MA, 1990), 54 and passim; O'Neill, *Man of the House,* 180, 184, 185–186.

39. Charles O. Jones, "Congress and the Presidency," in *The New Congress,* ed.

Nor did President Carter have a honeymoon, even though president and Congress were of the same party. Carter was an engineer who had a Wilsonian faith in reason and in his own rightness. He dumped a massive number of bills on Congress and, expecting the members to share his faiths, sat back and waited for Congress to do his bidding. But the congressmen were heady after their successful confrontation with Nixon, and having tasted presidential blood, they were hungry for more. No president, in the circumstances, would have had an easy time, and Carter's amateurish, rationalist approach doomed his legislative program.[40]

The changes that Congress enacted made legislative leadership, whether by a president or from within, exceedingly difficult and made intelligent domestic policy a thing of the past. Many changes were internal. The House stripped committee chairmen of much of their

---

Thomas E. Mann and Norman J. Ornstein (Washington, DC, 1981), 229–232; Ralph K. Huitt, "White House Channels to the Hill," in *Congress against the President,* ed. Harvey C. Mansfield, Sr. (New York, 1975), 76; Jones, "Presidential Negotiations with Congress," in King, ed., *Both Ends of the Avenue,* 112–115; Rowland Evans, Jr., and Robert D. Novak, *Nixon in the White House* (New York, 1971), 103–132, 212–213, 231, 241, 375–377, 409; Kellerman, *Political Presidency,* 147–148, 152–154.

40. Jones, "Congress and the Presidency," in Mann and Ornstein, ed., *New Congress,* 237–244; Edwards, *Presidential Influence,* 173–180; Jones, "Presidential Negotiation with Congress," in King, ed., *Both Ends of the Avenue,* 118–123; Hamilton Jordan, *Crisis: The Last Year of the Carter Presidency* (New York, 1982); Burton I. Kaufman, *The Presidency of James Earl Carter, Jr.* (Lawrence, KS, 1993); Erwin C. Hargrove, *Jimmy Carter as President: Leadership and the Politics of the Public Good* (Baton Rouge, LA, 1988), 1–67; Wallace Earl Walker, "Presidential Transitions and the Entrepreneurial Presidency," *Presidential Studies Quarterly* 23 (1993):61–63; Haynes Johnson, *In the Absence of Power: Governing America* (New York, 1980); Bowles, *White House and Capitol Hill,* 212–215; James MacGregor Burns, *The Power to Lead* (New York, 1984), 25–37; Pious, *American Presidency,* 122–123; Hamby, *Liberalism and Its Challengers,* 356; Califano, *Governing America,* 24–27, 89, 118, 402–403, 405–407, 428–431; Kellerman, *Political Presidency,* 209–219. As Tip O'Neill said, "During the Carter years, congressional Democrats often had the feeling that the White House was actually working against us. . . . We had a chance to accomplish so much, but the White House people simply wouldn't cooperate" (*Man of the House,* 308–309). Carter admitted that "it would have been advisable to have introduced our legislation in much more careful phases—not in such a rush" (quoted in Carl M. Brauer, *Presidential Transitions: Eisenhower Through Reagan* [New York, 1986], 202).

power and abolished the seniority system. Committees and subcommittees multiplied until every member had at least one fiefdom. As indicated, the size of staffs exploded, until Congress (like the White House) had become a sizable bureaucracy of specialists. Groups emerged that political scientists called "iron triangles," consisting of representatives of executive agencies who dealt with a particular program, the appropriate congressional committee or subcommittee, and the lobbyists for special interest groups affected by the program. Members of each triangle accepted on faith, voting to approve without reading, the legislation drafted by other triangles—and received payment in kind. This model, though an oversimplification, described a reasonably efficient means of brokering favors for constituents that ensured the reelection of incumbents: The turnover rate in the House of Representatives before the 1992 elections was approximately on a par with that of Britain's hereditary House of Lords. And as congressmen in effect bought lifetime tenure, they loaded up privileges, ranging from exempting themselves from the laws they passed to operating a private bank in which members could cash checks without having funds to cover them.[41]

41. For the congressional resurgence in general, see *Congress Reconsidered,* ed. Lawrence C. Dodd and Bruce I. Oppenheimer, 2d ed. (Washington, DC, 1981). Regarding the iron triangles, see Roger H. Davidson, "Two Avenues of Change: House and Senate Committee Reorganization," ibid., 112, 116; Roger H. Davidson, "Breaking Up Those 'Cozy Triangles' An Impossible Dream?" in *Legislative Reform and Public Policy,* ed. Susan Welch and John G. Peters (New York, 1977), 30–53; Hedrick Smith, *The Power Game: How Washington Works* (New York, 1988); *New York Times,* Dec. 14, 1988, B, 12:6. Fisher, *Politics of Shared Power,* 190, says that the triangle "is not a fixed and permanent institution," for it can be "interrupted by outside political events" and can change shape when the courts enter a case. Hugh Heclo says, in "Issue Networks and the Executive Establishment," in *The New American Political System,* ed. Anthony King (Washington, DC, 1978), 88, that the triangle "is not so much wrong as it is disastrously incomplete." For a sustained attack upon the developments in this paragraph, see Jones and Marini, ed., *Imperial Congress.* Revelations about corruption and privilege in Congress appeared frequently in the *New York Times* between 1990 and 1992; see, for example, Martin Tolchin, "Officials Facing Loss of Privilege in Washington," *New York Times,* National, March 31, 1992, A, 8. Such revelations appeared even more frequently in conservative periodicals, which are strongly biased against Congress; see, for example, Ray Kerrison, "A Former Member Details the Shame of Congress," *Human Events,* May 23, 1992, 10, and "GOP Assails Foley for Repeated Cover-Ups," ibid., May 30, 1992, 5.

Some of the changes were aimed directly at the presidency. One was the creation of the extragovernmental office of independent counsel, which was done by the Ethics in Government Act in 1978 as a means of investigating charges of cocaine use by some of President Carter's top aides, including Hamilton Jordan. Independent counsels were set up by a complex mechanism triggered by Congress. Counsels were instructed to investigate not crimes but named members of the executive branch, and they were given almost unlimited time and money. Their capacity for harassment, reputation shattering, and bankrupting people was unbounded; their ability to bring wrongdoers to justice was virtually nonexistent. The office of independent counsel Lawrence Walsh, established in 1987 to investigate the Iran-Contra affair, had by 1992 spent at least $30 million and had yet to obtain a major conviction that stood. The long and short of it was that the employment of independent counsels amounted to an attempt to criminalize policy differences.[42]

The most serious effort to wrest power from the executive was the Congressional Budget and Impoundment Control Act of 1974. Under the old system, each house of Congress had separate appropriations and tax committees and numerous subcommittees, and though there was always scrambling for funds, appropriations generally stayed within the broad limits set by the Bureau of the Budget, and deficits were normally minimal. Indeed, between 1921 and 1961, excepting the World War II period, there was a budget surplus in sixteen of the thirty-five years. During the sixties, however, as President Johnson attempted to maintain a "guns and butter" policy—that is, to conduct the fighting in Vietnam without curtailing expenditures or rais-

---

42. *Congressional Quarterly Almanac*, 1978:10–11, 14, 835–850; L. Gordon Crovitz, *Ethics as Politics: Congress vs. the Executive Branch* (Washington, DC, 1989); L. Gordon Crovitz, "The Criminalization of Politics," in Jones and Marini, ed., *Imperial Congress*, 239–267; Leonard Garment, "The Guns of Watergate," *Commentary* 83 (1987): 15–23; "Independent Counsel Needs Fundamental Changes," *Human Events*, April 18, 1992, 6; "Walsh, Media Botch Weinberger Story," *Human Events*, June 27, 1992; Terry Eastland, *Ethics, Politics, and the Independent Counsel: Executive Power, Executive Vice, 1789–1989* (Washington, DC, 1989); Jordan, *Crisis*, 171–174, 189–190, 201, 235–239, 268–269, 291–293; and Clark R. Mollenhoff, "Ham Jordan—Blue Denim Machiavelli," in the *The President Who Failed: Carter Out of Control* (New York, 1980), 69–79.

ing taxes—whopping deficits began to appear. Nixon inherited the situation, and by 1972 total federal outlays, which before Johnson became president had never exceeded $100 billion, soared above $250 billion. Nixon asked Congress for power to impose a ceiling of $250 billion, cutting as he saw fit. Congress refused, and the impoundment debacle followed.[43]

The Budget and Impoundment Control Act had ten titles, of which impoundment control was the tenth; the first nine initiated a complex budget process that was doomed to failure. The act established budget committees in both houses and provided them technical assistance in the form of a Congressional Budget Office. The committees were charged with preparing two resolutions a year: in spring a nonbinding target to serve as a guide in working out appropriations, in fall a binding ceiling on spending and floor under revenues. Since the Office of Management and Budget continued to operate, Congress had two budgets, one congressional and the other executive, but neither had enforcement mechanisms. The budget committees could not require the appropriations committees to stay within guidelines; as Senate Finance Committee Chairman Russell Long asked rhetorically, "Is the Senate to expect a single committee [the budget committee] to tell all other committees in advance what they would do, in detail, and police them to see that they do precisely that?" The Office of Management and Budget could not impose controls for the obvious reason that the president had no vote in Congress. In short, nobody was responsible.[44]

43. Data on budget surpluses tabulated from *Historical Statistics of the United States,* 711, *Statistical Abstract,* 1962:380. Allen Schick, "The Three-Ring Budget Process: The Appropriations, Tax, and Budget Committees in Congress," in Mann and Ornstein, ed., *New Congress,* 288–328. See also chap. 11 of this book; Louis Fisher, *Presidential Spending Power* (Princeton, NJ, 1975), 9–58; *New York Times,* July 27, 1972, 1:4, Aug. 2, 1972, 14:1, and Aug. 11, 1972, 1:8.

44. *Congressional Quarterly Almanac,* 1974:145–153; Schick, "Budget Process," in Mann and Ornstein, ed., *New Congress* (quote at 323); John W. Ellwood and James A. Thurber, "The Politics of the Congressional Budget Process Re-examined," in Dodd and Oppenheimer, ed., *Congress Reconsidered,* 246–271; Fisher, "Constitution and Presidential Budget Powers," in Fausold and Shank, ed., *The Constitution and the American Presidency,* 154–160; Davis, "The Congressional Budget Mess," in Jones and Marini, ed., *Imperial Congress,* 158–182; Allen Schick, "The Budget as an Instrument

Various pressures ensured that a sequence of deficits resulted. Mandatory "entitlements"—payments the government had obligated itself by law to make, such as welfare, social security, veterans' benefits, and contractual obligations—plus interest on the public debt were regarded as "uncontrollable" parts of the budget and had become more than half the total of federal outlays by 1967, when annual figures began to be published. By the 1980s entitlements and other uncontrollables constituted three-fourths of federal expenditures and were rapidly rising. Also playing havoc with the budget, especially during the hyperinflation of the middle and late seventies, were cost of living adjustments (COLAs). Since transfer payments were generally tied to the consumer price index, as prices rose, payments automatically increased by a fraction more than the prices.[45]

For a brief period peculiar circumstances made it possible for politicians to believe they could persist in their irresponsibility without causing serious damage. In response to OPEC's jacking up the price of oil, prices began to rise worldwide, but the wages paid America's workers rose proportionately, so they were not immediately squeezed. The catch, and the hidden boon to politicians, was bracket creep: In those days of many tiers of income tax rates, getting a raise meant paying taxes at a higher rate, and thus real take-home pay, measured in buying power, was dropping even as wages were rising. Because of inflation, tax increases were coming every year without Congress'

---

of Presidential Policy," in *The Reagan Presidency,* ed. Lester M. Salamon and Michael S. Lund (Washington, DC, 1984), 91–125; Fisher, *Presidential Spending Power,* 198–201; Aaron Wildavsky, *The New Politics of the Budgetary Process* (Glenview, IL, 1988), 31, 120, 140–149.

45. Schick, "Budget as an Instrument of Presidential Policy," in Salamon and Lund, ed., *Reagan Presidency,* 99–102; Charles Murray, *Losing Ground: American Social Policy, 1950–1980* (New York, 1984), 14, 67–68; Wildavsky, *New Politics of the Budgetary Process,* 8–9, 121–122, 268–273, 295–347; Rudolph G. Penner, *Dealing with the Budget Deficit* (Washington, DC, 1989), 1–5. In 1992 retiring Republican Sen. Warren Rudman of New Hampshire said, "We're heading toward 60–65 percent entitlement programs, 13 or 14 percent defense, 17 percent interest" (*Human Events,* June 20, 1992, 1). The situation was not unique to America: On NPR's "Morning Edition," July 7, 1992, it was reported that entitlements formed 90 percent of the German budget.

having to vote them. Besides, most workers believed they paid no taxes because the withholding system was invisible to them; when they received refunds in April they counted them as bonuses. The economy seemed to be a big-spenders' paradise.[46]

By the late seventies reality began to intrude, and something happened that orthodox economics had said was impossible. The Keynesian model assumed that there was a trade-off between inflation and deficit spending on the one hand and jobs on the other. Now, suddenly, the country began to face double-digit inflation and massive deficits as well as large-scale unemployment: "stagflation." And, in a nation conditioned to believe that the government in general and the president in particular could and should make sure that the economy worked well, it became apparent that neither the government in general nor the president in particular could do a thing.[47]

Small wonder that by September of 1979 President Carter's approval rating, according to the Associated Press/NBC poll, had fallen to 19 percent, and only 13 percent expressed approval of Congress— and this was before the Iranian hostage crisis began.

————— Ronald Reagan took on the presidency with a belief, oversimplified in one of his campaign slogans, that "government cannot solve our problems, government is the problem." His domestic goals were to end the stagflation at home and to reduce governmental

46. In 1980 married taxpayers filing jointly paid zero to 28 percent on taxable incomes up to $24,600; between $24,600 and $29,900, 32 percent; between $29,900 and $35,200, 37 percent; between $35,200 and $45,800, 43 percent; and so on, up to 70 percent on taxable incomes over $215,400. See *Human Events,* May 30, 1992, 16.

47. For my analysis of how this came about, see *The Phaeton Ride* (Garden City, NY, 1974). See also Joseph Hogan, "Back to the 1970s: The context of the Reagan presidency," in *The Reagan years: The record in Presidential leadership,* ed. Joseph Hogan (Manchester, Eng., 1990), 11–13; Wildavsky, *New Politics of the Budgetary Process,* 227–228; Melville J. Ulmer, "Stagflation," *New Republic,* Oct. 29, 1977, 11–13; *The Reagan Experiment: An Examination of Economic and Social Policies under the Reagan Administration,* ed. John L. Palmer and Isabel V. Sawhill (Washington, DC, 1982), 31–57. George C. Edwards III and Stephen J. Wayne, *Presidential Leadership: Politics and Policy Making* (New York, 1985), 98–116, discuss the public's high expectations and offer various explanations for the persistence of expectations despite disappointing performances.

interference in the lives of the citizenry or, that failing, at least to prevent the enactment of any new federal regulatory programs.

President Reagan viewed stagflation as two problems, each requiring different solutions. Inflation, he believed, could be brought under control through careful application of fiscal restraints by the Federal Reserve Board, which had begun even before he took office; and in fact inflation rapidly ceased to be a problem though the monetary stringency prolonged the recession for more than a year. The centerpiece in Reagan's program to stimulate economic growth was a large cut in income taxes, amounting to a 30 percent reduction phased in over three years. The thinking behind the tax-cut proposal was dual. The tax cut proposed by Kennedy in 1963 and pushed through Congress the next year had stimulated the economy powerfully, and there was reason to expect it would work that way again in the 1980s. On the revenue side of the equation, Reagan had been convinced by the economist Arthur Laffer that tax rates beyond a certain level were counterproductive because they encouraged the wealthy to invest in tax shelters rather than in more profitable and productive enterprises. Cut the top rates, Laffer argued, and tax revenues would actually increase.[48]

Reagan did have a honeymoon period, and he exploited it. Republicans had a majority in the Senate for his first six years, and though Democrats retained control of the House the old conservative coalition was reactivated for Reagan's first two years, the southern Demo-

48. M. Stephen Weatherford and Lorraine M. McDonnell, "Ideology and Economic Policy," in *Looking Back on the Reagan Presidency*, ed. Larry Berman (Baltimore, 1990), 122–151; A. S. Blinder, "Reaganomics and Growth: The Message in the Models," in *The Legacy of Reaganomics: Prospects for Long-Term Growth*, ed. C. R. Halten and I. V. Sawhill (Washington, DC, 1984), 199–228; A. S. Blinder, "Tight Money and Loose Fiscal Policy," *Society* 24 (1987):80–83; Paul Craig Roberts, *The Supply Side Revolution: An Insider's Account of Policymaking in Washington* (Cambridge, MA, 1984); Stephen Grubaugh and Scott Sumner, "Monetary Policy and the US Trade Deficit," in Hogan, ed., *Reagan years*, 237–258; Irving Kristol, "Ideology and Supply-Side Economics," *Commentary* 71 (April 1981):48–54; George Gilder, *Wealth and Poverty* (New York, 1981), 179–181, 184–187, 190–197, 204–205. Stopping inflation may well have been as much due to the collapse of OPEC oil prices—caused by increased American production and worldwide fuel conservation measures—as to all fiscal adjusting combined.

crats being dubbed boll weevils this go-round. The tax cut was steered through Congress fairly easily, though it was reduced from 30 percent to 25, and bracket creep was ended by indexing incomes for inflation. Moreover, Reagan got a huge increase in military spending (itself a stimulus for the economy) and some reductions in spending for social programs. Neither was of the magnitude he requested, but it is probable that the defense appropriations he asked for were deliberately padded so that the compromise lower figure would be adequate.[49]

The results of the policies were mixed. The economy responded by mid-1983, and thereafter the nation experienced a period of economic growth and prosperity that lasted more than seven years. The Laffer effect worked, too: Federal revenues increased from $599 billion in 1981 to $909 billion in 1988. On the negative side, federal expenditures increased from $657 billion to $1,064 billion, and by no means just because of defense spending, since outlays for civilian programs increased considerably faster. To help cover the mounting deficit, in the summer of 1982 Reagan pushed through Congress the biggest single tax increase in American history, a $98 billion excise tax. For structural reasons, it was reckoned that this would not cancel the economic stimulus provided by the income tax cut, and it did not.[50]

49. Weatherford and McDonnell, "Ideology and Economic Policy," in Berman, ed., *Looking Back,* and Charles L. McLure, Jr., "Reagan's Tax Policy," ibid., 156–169; Bowles, *White House and Capitol Hill,* 216–241; Nigel Ashford, "The Conservative Agenda and the Reagan Presidency," in Hogan, ed., *Reagan years,* 189–213; Roberts, *Supply Side Revolution;* Edward R. Koch, "How Reagan's Tax Indexing Helped the Middle Class," in *Human Events,* May 30, 1992, 16; David Mervin, *Ronald Reagan and the American Presidency* (London, 1990), 103–118.

50. *Congressional Quarterly Almanac,* 1982:174, 175, 1989:67, 1990:119; Robert Rector and Michael Sanera, "The Reagan Presidency and Policy Change," in *Steering the Elephant,* ed. Rector and Sanera (New York, 1987), 338–341; Schick, "Budget as an Instrument of Presidential Policy," in Salamon and Lund, ed., *Reagan Presidency,* 105, places the 1982 tax increase at "almost $100 billion"; Joseph Hogan, "The Federal Budget in the Reagan Era," in Hogan, ed., *Reagan years,* 226, says "The legislation increased taxes by over $215 billion"; the *New York Times* reported a $98.3 billion excise tax on Aug. 20, 1982, 1:1. For "The Real Reagan Record," see *National Review,* Aug. 31, 1992. See also Paul Craig Roberts, "Whose Idea Was Reagonomics? 'The Best Economic Minds in the World,'" *Business Week,* May 23, 1988, 22.

But the deficit continued despite the administration's efforts to contain it. For the first two years Reagan pleaded and wheedled and threatened to veto, but except for the excise tax he made little headway with Congress. Then in the 1982 congressional elections liberal Democrats gained enough seats in the House to break the hold of the conservative coalition, and hope of getting Congress to make spending cuts was forlorn. For practical purposes, at that point Reagan essentially stopped trying and left Congress to solve the problem if and when it saw fit. The deficit rose from $128 billion in 1982 to $200-plus billion in 1983. It is entirely conceivable that some people in the executive branch viewed the deficit with ambivalent feelings. It was inherently bad, but the economy was growing so rapidly that it was less as a percentage of gross national product when Reagan left office than when he had entered it; and it had the effect of preventing Congress from enacting many new social or economic programs.[51]

In 1985 Congress attempted to bring the budget under control by passing the Gramm-Rudman-Hollings Act, requiring that Congress reduce the deficit in steps to reach a balance in five years. The legislation's principal enforcement device was automatic across-the-board spending reductions if the deficit in any year exceeded specified targets. The mechanics of the operation were that the executive Office of Management and Budget and the Congressional Budget Office jointly went over the books, calculated the deficit, and informed the Office of the Comptroller General. Comptroller General then reported to the president, who was required to issue a sequester order mandating the percentage by which the budget of every affected agency (some were exempted) was to be cut. The act was quickly challenged in the Supreme Court, which rediscovered the doctrine of the separation of powers—as it is wont to do from time to time—and

51. Norman B. Ture, "To Cut and to Please," *National Review,* Aug. 31, 1992, 37; Schick, "Budget as an Instrument of Presidential Policy," in Salamon and Lund, ed., *Reagan Presidency,* 102–113; Hogan, "Federal Budget," in Hogan, ed., *Reagan years,* 224–227; Davis, "Congressional Budget Mess," in Jones and Marini, ed., *Imperial Congress,* 167–168; *U.S. News & World Report,* Nov. 8, 1982, 24, and Nov. 15, 1982, 18–25. "Budget Deficits: The Endless River of Red Ink," *U.S. News & World Report,* Feb. 7, 1983, 24–25, sets the 1982 deficit at $110.7 billion and estimates the 1983 deficit at $208 billion.

ruled that the sequestering mechanism was unconstitutional inasmuch as it required the president to do the bidding of an officer of the Congress. In 1987 the Office of the Comptroller General was transferred to the Office of Management and Budget, thus reactivating the process. No cuts were actually made under it, however, not even of the bogus variety Washingtonians called a cut: a smaller-than-projected increase. Deficits continued at the level of $200 billion, and the public debt had long since exceeded $1 trillion.[52]

In 1988 Vice-pres. George Bush made a solemn and widely publicized campaign promise. "Read my lips," he said, "no new taxes." After nearly two years of struggling with the deficit, however, he capitulated to a joint congressional committee and agreed to support a tax increase in exchange for a promise to cut spending. Congress lived up to half the agreement, namely the tax increase.[53]

President Bush proved unable to have a legislative program enacted, and despite grave national woes, he did not appear to be particularly interested in any domestic program. Congress, ignoring real problems in favor of preferred causes that might garner votes, hit upon a way of financing its compulsion to micromanage everything despite the lack of funds; it passed laws making private businesses finance social and environmental programs.[54] President Bush wielded the veto pen, but that was his only legislative tool.

52. *Congressional Quarterly Almanac,* 1985:459–468, 1988:181; Davis, "Congressional Budget Mess," in Jones and Marini, ed., *Imperial Congress,* 168–170; Fisher, "Constitution and Presidential Budget Powers," in Fausold and Shank, ed., *The Constitution and the American Presidency,* 160–163, 168–169; Steven M. Sheffrin, "Constitutional Principles and Economic Policy," in Berman, ed., *Looking Back,* 106–118; James D. Gwartney and Richard E. Wagner, *The Federal Budget Process: Why It Is Broken and How It Can Be Fixed* (Tallahassee, FL, 1988).

53. *Congressional Quarterly Almanac,* 1990:166–173; Scott A. Hodge and Robert Rector, *What George Bush Is Not Being Told About Federal Spending* (Washington, DC, 1992); "Captain of Enterprise: Christopher C. DeMuth on the Business of Liberty," an interview by Adam Meyerson, *Policy Review* (Spring 1992):14; Terry Eastland, "Bush's Fatal Attraction," *Policy Review* (Spring 1992):22–24; and the *New York Times,* Aug. 19, 1988, A, 14:1, Dec. 7, 1988, A, 1:4, Jan. 20, 1989, A, 1:6, Oct. 3, 1990, A, 1:2, D, 28:1, Oct. 11, 1990, A, 1:6, Oct. 29, 1990, A, 1:5, Nov. 7, 1990, B, 6:2, Nov. 9, 1990, A, 1:1.

54. See, for example, the Americans with Disabilities Act, *Congressional Quarterly Almanac,* 1990:447–459; Clean Air Act, ibid., 1990:229, 248–275; Oil Pollution

By the year 1992 American citizens had become sick unto death of their government and of their president.[55] Somehow they managed to retain faith in the office of the president—if the right candidate would come along.

Prevention, Response, Liability and Compensation Act, ibid., 1990:283; reauthorization of the Magnuson Fishery Act of 1976 (PL 101-627), ibid., 1990:399. For the voluntary beginnings of this policy and the White House Office of Private Sector Initiatives, see Renée A. Berger, "The Private-Sector Initiatives in the Reagan Era: New Actors Rework an Old Theme," in Salamon and Lund, eds., *Reagan Presidency*, 181–211.

55. See, for example, *Business Week*, April 27, 1992, 80–81; Rush Limbaugh, "Why Americans Are Angry," an interview by William J. Bennett, *Policy Review* (Summer 1992):47–49; *New York Times*, March 2, 1992, A, 13:1, March 26, 1992, A, 19:1, March 29, 1992, A, 14:1, April 2, 1992, D, 21:4, April 4, 1992, A, 1:4, April 5, 1992, A, 1:1, April 8, 1992, A, 1:3, A, 20:1, April 12, 1992, F, 38:1.

President and Congress:

Foreign Affairs

In discussions and debates about the making of foreign policy in the United States, two questions have been central. The first is whether the powers of the federal government, when dealing with other sovereign states, are limited to those delegated or implied in the Constitution or whether the American government, like others, is empowered to do whatever it deems necessary to promote and protect the nation's legitimate interests. The second is whether the president is "the sole organ of the nation in its external relations, and its sole representative with foreign nations," as John Marshall maintained in Congress in 1800 and as the Senate Committee on Foreign Relations declared in 1816, or whether foreign policy is ultimately determined by Congress, and the power of the president in this regard is instrumental, not determinative, as James Madison insisted in 1794.[1]

These questions lie beyond the justiciable, and accordingly for

1. Marshall as quoted in Christopher H. Pyle and Richard M. Pious, ed., *The President, Congress, and the Constitution* (New York, 1984), 233, 238; chapter 10, note 33 of this book; Edward S. Corwin, *The President, 1789–1957* (New York, 1957), 180–181.

most of its history the Supreme Court considered them as political and refused to rule on them; but in one famous and fateful case it took a bold and unequivocal stand. Writing for the Court in 1936 in *U.S. v. Curtiss-Wright Export Corp.,* Justice George Sutherland advanced a novel doctrine. In domestic affairs, he declared, the powers of the federal government were granted by the states, and those powers not granted or reasonably implied by the "necessary and proper" clause were reserved to the states or to the people, as the Tenth Amendment specified. In foreign affairs, however, the powers could not have been delegated by the states because the states had never possessed the powers. Instead, they had been inherited by the Continental Congress from the British Crown upon the Declaration of Independence and had in turn been inherited from that Congress by the new federal government after 1787. Besides, they had not simply been inherited, they were *inherent* in sovereignty, and as such they were unlimited.[2]

Addressing the second question, Sutherland was equally unreserved, and he sided with Marshall, not Madison. "In this vast external realm," he wrote, "with its important, complicated, delicate and manifold problems, the President alone has the power to speak or listen as a representative of the nation. He *makes* treaties with the advice and consent of the Senate; but he alone negotiates. Into the field of negotiation the Senate cannot intrude; and Congress itself is powerless to invade it." In the international arena, Congress must "accord to the President a degree of discretion and freedom from statutory restriction which would not be admissible were domestic affairs alone involved."[3]

2. *U.S. v. Curtiss-Wright Export Corp.,* 299 U.S. 304 (1936); Louis Fisher, *American Constitutional Law,* (New York, 1990), 317–320. Sutherland's history was highly questionable; see David M. Levitan, "The Foreign Relations Power: An Analysis of Mr. Justice Sutherland's Theory," *Yale Law Journal* 55 (1946):467–497, and Charles A. Lofgren, "*United States v. Curtiss-Wright Export Corporation:* An Historical Reassessment," *Yale Law Journal* 83 (1973):1–32; Joel Francis Paschal, *Mr. Justice Sutherland: A Man against the State* (Princeton, NJ, 1951). Nonetheless, some of the more nationalistic of the Framers had argued for the principle of inherent powers; see, for example, Hamilton in *Federalist* 23 and in his opinion on the constitutionality of the Bank of the United States, in *The Papers of Alexander Hamilton,* ed. Harold C. Syrett et al., 26 vols. (New York, 1961–1979), 4:415 and 8:98.

3. *U.S. v. Curtiss-Wright Export Corp.,* 299 U.S. 304; Fisher, *American Constitutional*

Incumbent presidents ever after generally shared Sutherland's view. Perhaps the strongest statement of the position was made by Richard Nixon, who regarded Congress as "irrelevant" in matters of national security and foreign relations. Asked in a television interview if the president "can decide whether it's in the best interests of the nation or something, and do something illegal," the former president replied, "Well, when the President does it, that means it is not illegal. . . . If the President, for example, approves something because of the national security, . . . then the President's decision in that instance is one that enables those who carry it out, to carry it out without violating a law."[4]

But in practice the Constitution, despite the claims of advocates of judicial power, is not necessarily what the Supreme Court says it is, nor is it what the president says it is, nor, for the matter of that, is it what the Constitution says it is. E. S. Corwin was close to the mark when he wrote that the Constitution "is an invitation to struggle for the privilege of directing American foreign policy." President and Congress both have advantages in the contest, but the "verdict of

---

Law, 319. The Court had earlier advanced something like a doctrine of inherent powers in relation to domestic affairs; *In re Neagle,* 135 U.S. 1-2 (1890). For a discussion, see Corwin, *President,* 148ff. See also Arthur W. Rovine, "Separation of Powers and International Executive Agreements," *Indiana Law Journal* 52 (1977):397–447; Louis Fisher, "War Powers: A Need for Legislative Reassertion," in *The Presidency Reappraised,* ed. Rexford G. Tugwell and Thomas E. Cronin (New York, 1974), 56–73. For a persuasive argument that John Marshall "had a far more radical theory of Executive power" than is realized today and that Sutherland's "reiteration of Marshall's position" is "a more radical opinion as well," see Ruth Wedgwood, "The Revolutionary Martyrdom of Jonathan Robbins," *Yale Law Journal* 100 (1990):339–352.

4. Theodore C. Sorensen, "Political Perspective: Who Speaks for the National Interest?" in *The Tethered Presidency: Congressional Restraints on Executive Power,* ed. Thomas M. Franck (New York, 1981), 10; David Frost interview with Richard Nixon, televised May 19, 1977, *New York Times,* May 20, 1977, A, 16:5; also in Pyle and Pious, ed., *President, Congress, and Constitution,* 74. Lee H. Hamilton, "Congress and the Presidency in American Foreign Policy," *Presidential Studies Quarterly* 18 (1988):507, quotes Harry Truman's categorical statement, "I make American foreign policy." "Essentially," according to Raymond G. O'Connor, "the president can do whatever he can get away with"; *Commanders in Chief: Presidential Leadership in Modern Wars,* ed. Joseph G. Dawson III (Lawrence, KS, 1993).

history," as Corwin concluded in mid-century, "is that the power to determine the substantive content of American foreign policy is a *divided* power, with the lion's share falling usually, though by no means always, to the President."[5] That judgment continued to be accurate as the century moved toward a close.

———— The treaty-making power did not work according to the Framers' intentions, whatever they were, because the nature of treaties changed radically not long after the founding. At the time of the adoption of the Constitution treaties were a relatively insignificant instrument of international relations. They were employed under exceptional conditions or for special purposes such as alliances, the transfer of territory, reciprocal trade, or the termination of hostilities. In ordinary circumstances relations among the states of the western world were governed by the conventions of international law that Europeans had evolved over the centuries and that had been codified by the great natural law commentators. Accordingly, though the world was at war almost continuously from the establishment of the government until 1815 and though international turmoil underlay almost all the major American political struggles of the period, only thirteen treaties with foreign states were concluded during that quarter of a century. In 1804 Jefferson wrote to a friend, "On the subject of treaties, our system is to have none with any nation, as far as can be avoided," and between December of 1805 and February of 1815 not one treaty was submitted to the Senate.[6]

Limited use of treaties ceased to be the norm after 1815, perhaps in response to the efforts of the Congress of Vienna to put in writing a peacekeeping structure to replace the old order that the French Revo-

5. Corwin, *President,* 171. For a rebuttal, see John T. Rourke and Russell Farnen, "War, Presidents, and the Constitution," *Presidential Studies Quarterly* 18 (1988):513–522. For the fluctuating balance, see John Lehman, *Making War: The 200-Year-Old Battle between the President and Congress over How America Goes to War* (New York, 1992), 75–128.

6. W. Stull Holt, *Treaties Defeated by the Senate: A Study of the Struggle between President and Senate over the Conduct of Foreign Relations* (Baltimore, 1933), 15–16; Jefferson to Philip Mazzei, July 18, 1804, in *The Writings of Thomas Jefferson,* ed. Andrew A. Lipscomb and Albert E. Bergh, 20 vols. (Washington, DC, 1903–1904), 11:38–39.

lution and Napoleon had destroyed. Whatever the cause, during the course of the nineteenth century formal written treaties came to be substituted for an abstract law of nature in determining what was internationally lawful, much in the way that statutory enactments in the English-speaking world came to replace the older theory that the law was fixed and immutable and that legislative bodies could only discover and declare it, not make it. It was in this changing context that the treaty-making powers of the president and the Senate evolved.[7]

Nineteenth-century presidents sometimes sought senatorial advice or approval before undertaking negotiations, though in writing, not in person. President Jackson, for example, did so in regard to an Indian treaty in 1830; Polk sought the Senate's approval of a treaty with Britain before signing it in 1846; Johnson consulted the Senate in 1869 as to the expediency of a naturalization treaty with Britain; and Grant asked the Senate's advice on three occasions. Moreover, prior to 1815 presidents commonly but not invariably sought senatorial approval of proposed negotiators.[8]

As a rule, however, presidents after 1815 conducted negotiations through the State Department and without formally consulting or seeking the advice of the Senate, though as a matter of prudence they frequently talked privately with influential senators when negotiations were especially delicate. From time to time the Senate adopted

7. *The Great European Treaties of the Nineteenth Century,* ed. Sir Augustus Oakes and R. B. Mowat (Oxford, Eng., 1918); Sir Charles Petrie, *Diplomatic History, 1713–1933* (London, 1948), 117–128; Edward Vose Gulick, *Europe's Classical Balance of Power: A Case History of the Theory and Practice of One of the Great Concepts of European Statecraft* (Ithaca, NY, 1955); Woodrow Wilson in his December 4, 1917, address to Congress condemned "such covenants of selfishness and compromise as were entered into at the Congress of Vienna."

8. Samuel B. Crandall, *Treaties: Their Making and Enforcement,* 2d ed. (Washington, DC, 1916), 68–76; Robert V. Remini, "The Jackson Era," in *The Constitution and the American Presidency,* ed. Martin Fausold and Alan Shank (Albany, NY, 1991), 41–42; John M. Belohlavek, "'Let the Eagle Soar!': Democratic Constraints on the Foreign Policy of Andrew Jackson," *Presidential Studies Quarterly* 10 (1980):36–47; *Messages and Papers of the Presidents,* comp. James D. Richardson, 10 vols. (Washington, DC, 1889–1905), 4:456–457, 458, 459, 5:666–668, 6:696; Philip Shriver Klein, *President James Buchanan: A Biography* (University Park, PA, 1962), 181–182.

resolutions volunteering its advice regarding pending negotiations, but presidents felt no obligation to accept advice and customarily refused the Senate access to the instructions issued to negotiators.[9]

The Senate, thus frozen out of the process, relied increasingly on the practice of partial ratification. In the first international treaty it had been requested to ratify, Jay's Treaty with Britain, it had rejected outright one of the twenty-nine articles, and on Hamilton's advice Washington approved the rejection. The British did not object either, but when the Senate partially approved another treaty in 1803 Britain protested fiercely that the practice was "new, unauthorized, and not to be sanctioned." It refused to confirm the altered pact, saying that it could "never acquiesce" in the selective ratification of a convention "formally agreed upon by a minister with full powers for the purpose." For a time thereafter American ministers were careful to point out to foreigners that constitutionally the Senate had the right to negate parts of agreements the negotiators reached, and though Europeans were vexed and perplexed by this practice, they generally came to accept it. The Senate did make it a rule, until 1868, that amendments to treaties required two-thirds majorities; after 1868 a simple majority vote was sufficient.[10]

From the War of 1812 until the end of Reconstruction, with an occasional conspicuous exception, the cooperative exercise of the treaty-making power worked reasonably smoothly. One exception was the luckless Tyler, who presented the Senate with fifteen treaties of which it rejected five. Other conflicts arose when treaties violated the principle of states' rights by altering laws regulating the inheritance and disposal of real property: Between 1830 and 1860 the

---

9. Joseph E. Kallenbach, *The American Chief Executive* (New York, 1966), 488–494, 505–508; Louis Fisher, *Constitutional Conflicts between Congress and the President,* 3d ed., rev. (Lawrence, KS, 1991), 219; Thomas M. Franck and Edward Weisband, *Foreign Policy by Congress* (New York, 1979), 136; Corwin, *President,* 204ff.

10. Washington to Hamilton, July 5, 1795, Hamilton to Washington, July 9–11, 1795, in Syrett, ed., *Hamilton Papers,* 18:398–404, 404–454; Holt, *Treaties Defeated by the Senate,* 19–23, 35–36, 120; Henry Cabot Lodge, "The Treaty-Making Powers of the Senate," *Scribner's Magazine* (January 1902):33–43; *William Plumer's Memorandum, 1803–1807,* ed. Everett S. Brown (New York, 1923), 262; Crandall, *Treaties,* 79–81, 86–87; Franck and Weisband, *Foreign Policy,* 138–141.

Senate rejected or substantially changed seven such treaties. But over-all the Senate usually consented, approving (albeit with amendments) 189 of the 220 treaties it considered from 1815 to 1869; of those it rejected, few were of real consequence.[11]

Then came a period during which the Senate assumed a more active role. Its activism stemmed partly from the general revulsion against executive power that followed the Lincoln and Johnson presidencies. Partly, too, it resulted from partisanship. Nearly half the time from Grant's presidency to the end of the century a majority of the Senate belonged to the opposite party from the president. The Senate did not reject a greater percentage of treaties than it had before, but it rejected every major treaty presented to it between 1871 and 1898. Among those rejected were treaties to annex the Dominican Republic and Hawaii, a Mexican extradition treaty, a Chinese exclusion treaty, and treaties with Britain concerning extradition, the northeastern fisheries, and the Venezuelan boundaries. John Hay, the American ambassador to the Court of St. James, wrote his friend Henry Adams in 1898 that "I have told you many times that I did not believe another important treaty would ever pass the Senate."[12]

The way around the Senate was the executive agreement. Executive agreements had standing in international law, but they had rarely been used as substitutes for treaties. Vattel, who was cited approvingly by Americans as disparate as Hamilton and Roger Brooke Taney, described them (along with conventions and pactions) as compacts between sovereign states that "are accomplished by one single act,"

11. Holt, *Treaties Defeated by the Senate,* 40, 56, 61, 84–86, 101–102; Ralston Hayden, "The States' Rights Doctrine and the Treaty-Making Power," *American Historical Review* 22 (1917): 566–585; Norma L. Peterson, *The Presidencies of Harrison and Tyler* (Lawrence, KS, 1989), 201–228.

12. Holt, *Treaties Defeated by the Senate,* 122–123; John Hay to Henry Adams, May 27, 1898, in William Roscoe Thayer, *The Life and Letters of John Hay,* 2 vols. (Boston, 1915), 2:170; Arthur M. Schlesinger, Jr., *The Imperial Presidency* (Boston, 1973), 76–81; Bureau of the Census, *Historical Statistics of the United States* (Washington, DC, 1961), 691; Justus D. Doenecke, *The Presidencies of Garfield and Arthur* (Lawrence, KS, 1981), 133, 135, 161, 176–177, 178; Richard E. Welch, Jr., *The Presidency of Grover Cleveland* (Lawrence, KS, 1988), 157–199; Homer E. Socolofsky and Allan B. Spetter, *The Presidency of Benjamin Harrison* (Lawrence, KS, 1987), 125–126; Kenton J. Clymer, *John Hay: The Gentleman as Diplomat* (Ann Arbor, MI, 1975).

whereas treaties called for acts that "must continue as long as the treaty exists." Minor agreements that were legally binding had been made from the beginning, as when the postmaster general, with congressional authorization, agreed with British officials for mutual mail delivery. In 1817 a major agreement that entailed permanent commitments was made: the Rush-Bagot Agreement, wherein the United States and Great Britain agreed to the limitation of naval armaments on the Great Lakes. At first President Monroe thought it unnecessary to submit the pact to the Senate, but about a year later he requested an opinion as to whether it required ratification. The Senate offered no opinion but endorsed the arrangement by a two-thirds vote, though not in the form of a treaty ratification; ratifications were never exchanged with Britain. Such agreements became common throughout the remainder of the century, but they were not used in regard to important matters again until the advent of Theodore Roosevelt.[13]

Roosevelt was not the sort of man to countenance comfortably the Senate's frustration of his foreign policy aims, deferential though he was in domestic affairs during his first term. Shortly after being elected president in his own right, he threw down a gauntlet. In 1905 the Senate refused to ratify a treaty with the Dominican Republic whereby the United States would administer its customs collections. Roosevelt was convinced that dishonesty in the Dominican government, combined with debts it owed foreign creditors, would result in a takeover by a European power, in violation of the Monroe Doctrine. Accordingly, he did an audacious thing. He reached a new

13. Pacificus 3, July 6, 1793, in Syrett, ed., *Hamilton Papers,* 15:67; *Holmes* v. *Jennison,* 14 Peters 540, 572 (1840); Emmerich de Vattel, *The Law of Nations* (London, 1797; repr., Philadelphia, 1817), Book 2, chap. 12, para. 153, p. 192; Schlesinger, *Imperial Presidency,* 85; Crandall, *Treaties,* 102–103; Bradford Perkins, *Castlereagh and Adams: England and the United States, 1812–1823* (Berkeley, CA, 1964), 201, 216, 240–244; Richardson, comp., *Messages and Papers of the Presidents,* 2:12, 33, 36. Kallenbach, *American Chief Executive,* 504, has a table of treaties and executive agreements showing: 1789–1839, 60 treaties, 27 executive agreements; 1839–1889, 215 treaties, 238 executive agreements; 1889–1939, 524 treaties, 917 executive agreements. As of January 1, 1972, the United States was a party to 947 treaties and 4,359 executive agreements; *Congressional Quarterly Almanac,* 1972:158. See also Lawrence Margolis, *Executive Agreements and Presidential Power in Foreign Policy* (New York, 1986), 101–139; Franck and Weisband, *Foreign Policy,* 141–145.

agreement with the Dominicans, under which, in his own words, he "went ahead and administered the proposed treaty anyhow, considering it as a simple agreement on the part of the Executive which would be converted into a treaty whenever the Senate acted." Two years later the Senate approved the treaty, but Roosevelt recorded in his autobiography that "I would have continued it until the end of my term, if necessary, without any action by Congress." Other executive agreements were soon forthcoming, including agreements to approve Japan's military protectorate in Korea, to restrict Japanese immigration into the United States, to uphold the Open Door policy in China, and to recognize Japan's "special interests" in China.[14]

Woodrow Wilson was even more vigorous in arrogating control of foreign policy, yet in the end his efforts were repudiated by both the Senate and the electorate. He resorted to executive agreements in lieu of treaties, as Roosevelt had done, but that was not what brought his undoing. What doomed him was his interjection of partisan politics and personal animosities into vital concerns of war and peace. In 1918, as World War I was approaching a climax, he went on the stump to campaign passionately for a Democratic Congress to support him in the upcoming peace negotiations. Instead the voters gave Republicans a two-vote majority in the Senate. Early in 1919 he went to Europe to lead the negotiations in person—becoming the first president to leave the country and conduct negotiations directly with other heads of state—and he took just one Republican along. The

14. Theodore Roosevelt, *Autobiography,* 510, 511, as quoted in Holt, *Treaties Defeated by the Senate,* 223, and Schlesinger, *Imperial Presidency,* 88; Margolis, *Executive Agreements,* 10–12; Lewis L. Gould, *The Presidency of Theodore Roosevelt* (Lawrence, KS, 1991), 175–179; Howard C. Hill, *Roosevelt and the Caribbean* (repr., New York, 1965); James R. Reckner, *Teddy Roosevelt's Great White Fleet* (Annapolis, MD, 1988); Raymond A. Esthus, *Theodore Roosevelt and Japan* (Seattle, WA, 1967); David H. Burton, *Theodore Roosevelt: Confident Imperialist* (Philadelphia, 1968), 58–131; Richard H. Collin, *Theodore Roosevelt's Caribbean: The Panama Canal, the Monroe Doctrine, and the Latin American Context* (Baton Rouge, LA, 1990). The Monroe Doctrine had been more or less moribund until Roosevelt revived it with the Roosevelt Corollary. See the Fourth Annual Message to Congress, December 6, 1904, in *Safeguarding the Republic: Essays and Documents in American Foreign Relations, 1890–1991,* ed. Howard Jones (New York, 1992), 31–32; Dexter Perkins, *Hands Off: A History of the Monroe Doctrine* (Baltimore, 1941).

resulting Treaty of Versailles, with its provision for a League of Nations, was generally acceptable to the country and to the Senate, only thirteen senators being "irreconcilables" in opposition; but Henry Cabot Lodge, chairman of the Senate Foreign Relations Committee, led a sizable group who had reservations about particular provisions, especially those having to do with the commitment of American troops abroad. The British and the French urged Wilson to accept the reservations, but Wilson, who personally despised and was despised by Lodge, declared that he would not accept anything "with that man's name on it." Wilson took his case to the people, delivering thirty-seven major addresses in twenty-two days. Then he suffered a massive stroke that paralyzed his left side and made him an invalid the rest of his life. For nearly two months he was unable to attend his duties, and his wife and his physician shared the role of acting president. Early in 1920, after a complex series of votes, the Senate rejected the treaty. Wilson vowed to make the election of 1920 a solemn referendum on his league, but to no avail. The Republican Warren G. Harding defeated the Democrat James M. Cox by the biggest margin of popular votes to date, 16,143,000 to 9,130,000.[15]

————— In contrast to the tendency in the arena of diplomacy for power to swing back and forth between president and Senate, the power to commit American armed forces in combat abroad was usually exercised by the president alone. That may seem strange, in light of the Constitution's explicit conferral upon the Congress of the power to declare war. Moreover, it has been argued repeatedly and

15. Howard Jones, *The Course of American Diplomacy from the Revolution to the Present*, 2d ed. (Chicago, 1988), 346–364; *Historical Statistics of the United States*, 682; Arthur S. Link, *Woodrow Wilson: Revolution, War, and Peace* (Princeton, NJ, 1979), passim; Robert H. Ferrell, *Woodrow Wilson and World War I, 1917–1921* (New York, 1985); Ralph Stone, *The Irreconcilables: The Fight against the League of Nations* (Lexington, KY, 1970); William C. Widenor, *Henry Cabot Lodge and the Search for an American Foreign Policy* (Berkeley, CA, 1980), 300–348; John A. Garraty, *Henry Cabot Lodge: A Biography* (New York, 1953), 357–401; Dewey W. Grantham, Jr., "The Southern Senators and the League of Nations, 1918–1920," *North Carolina Historical Review* 26 (1949):187–205; Thomas A. Bailey, *Woodrow Wilson and the Great Betrayal* (New York, 1947), 65–71; Arthur Walworth, *Wilson and His Peacemakers: American Diplomacy at the Paris Peace Conference, 1919* (New York, 1986).

persuasively that even if the president, by virtue of being commander in chief, can send the military anyplace he pleases, the ultimate power resides in Congress because it can refuse to appropriate the necessary funds. Nonetheless, most presidents followed the precedents set by Jefferson and Madison and deployed the military in alien lands without congressional authorization and often without congressional approval before or after the fact. On five occasions Congress declared war—against Britain in 1812, Mexico in 1848, Spain in 1898, Germany and the Central Powers in 1917, and the Axis in 1941—whereas American fighting men were sent to fight in foreign climes on more than 200 occasions.[16]

Most military operations were relatively small, justifiable under some law or another, and defensible under international law. About a third involved invasion of Latin American countries to protect the lives and property of United States citizens in times of civil wars, revolutions, or other occasions of violent political instability. Nine more were incursions into Spanish America prior to the dismemberment of the Spanish empire. Eighteen were retaliatory attacks on remote Pacific peoples who essentially lacked formal governments. A

16. Library of Congress, Congressional Research Service, *Instances of the Use of United States Armed Forces Abroad, 1789–1983,* ed. Ellen C. Collier (Washington, DC, 1983); Schlesinger, *Imperial Presidency,* 90–91; Elihu Root, *The Military and Colonial Policies of the United States* (Cambridge, MA, 1916), 157–158; W. Taylor Reveley III, *War Powers of the President and Congress: Who Holds the Arrows and Olive Branch?* (Charlottesville, VA, 1981); Ann Van Wynen Thomas and A. J. Thomas, Jr., *The War-Making Powers of the President: Constitutional and International Law Aspects* (Dallas, TX, 1982); Francis D. Wormuth and Edwin B. Firmage, *To Chain the Dog of War: The War Power of Congress in History and Law,* 2d ed. (Urbana, IL, 1989); Barry M. Blechman and Stephen S. Kaplan, *Force without War: U.S. Armed Forces as a Political Instrument* (Washington, DC, 1978); David Gray Adler, "The President's War-Making Power," in *Inventing the American Presidency,* ed. Thomas E. Cronin (Lawrence, KS, 1989), 119–153. Many of the writers on the subject are opposed to presidential warmaking, but they cannot escape the historical usage. Sometimes presidents have vetoed appropriations bills because they forbade the use of troops in certain circumstances, as President Hayes did in 1879. See Michael Les Benedict, "The Lincoln Presidency and the Republican Era," in Fausold and Shank, eds., *The Constitution and the American Presidency,* 60–61. Thomas and Thomas, *War-Making Powers,* 149, n. 39, contains a bibliography of articles on the subject.

number were raids to interdict smugglers or slave traders. Several were invasions of Mexico to apprehend bandits and cattle thieves who had committed crimes in the United States; Mexico repeatedly protested, though from 1882 until 1896, in a succession of agreements, it ceded the United States the right.[17]

Some of the deployments, on the other hand, were large-scale affairs. The opening of Japan offers an early example. Shipwrecked Americans in the Far Eastern trade had occasionally been picked up by Japanese and treated "as if they were the most atrocious criminals." Ostensibly to ensure their protection but also with a view toward forcing the traditionally isolated Japanese into opening their markets to American goods, a naval vessel under James Biddle was sent to Japan in 1846. That mission failing, in 1852 President Fillmore sent Matthew C. Perry with an armada of ten ships and nearly 2,000 officers and men—about 10 percent of the American armed forces at the time—to intimidate the Japanese into submission. Perry's instructions, written by Secretary of State Daniel Webster, gave him "full and discretionary powers" to negotiate, and if he failed "after having exhausted every argument and every means of persuasion," he was to "change his tone" and inform the Japanese that if they persisted in their behavior "they will be severely chastised." For form's sake he was cautioned that "as the President has no power to declare war his mission is necessarily of a pacific character, and will not resort to force unless in self-defence," but between the lines it was clear that if the Japanese resisted, Perry was to retaliate with overpowering force. The Japanese saw fit not to commit hara-kiri, however, and the United States got what it wanted in a series of treaties beginning in 1854. American forces were dispatched to Japan six more times during the 1860s, the last three in 1868 to protect American interests during Japan's civil war that restored the mikado and abolished the shogunate.[18]

17. Tabulated from Collier, ed., *Use of Armed Forces Abroad*. The interventions can also be traced in Richardson, comp., *Messages and Papers of the Presidents;* they are summed up on an annual basis, with explanations, in the annual messages to Congress. For an argument that most of these deployments were not "minor undertakings" nor the precedent "short-lived," see J. Terry Emerson, "War Powers Legislation," *West Virginia Law Review* 74 (1971):71–73, 80–81, 114–119.

18. Herbert H. Gowen, *An Outline History of Japan* (New York, 1932), 291–301;

On a considerably larger scale was the undeclared war to suppress the rebellion that broke out in the Philippines in the wake of the Spanish-American War. A native uprising led by Emilio Aguinaldo began early in 1899 when locals learned that the United States had annexed the territory instead of granting it independence. An American army of about 70,000 men fought a Filipino army of about the same size and crushed the organized resistance by year's end. But guerrilla warfare continued for nearly three more years; 126,000 American troops were used in suppression campaigns, and about 200,000 Filipinos were killed. Sporadic fighting occurred even after Theodore Roosevelt declared the war "officially" terminated on July 4, 1902. It had never been officially started, but except for a short-lived antiimperialist movement, few people protested. Reports of atrocities committed by Americans disturbed some, but most people apparently shared the attitude of Gen. Robert P. Hughes. Asked by the Senate Foreign Relations Committee whether the killing of women and children was "within the ordinary rules of civilized warfare," the general replied, "These people are not civilized."[19]

William L. Neumann, *America Encounters Japan, From Perry to MacArthur* (Baltimore, 1963), 19–71; Samuel Eliot Morison, *"Old Bruin": Commodore Matthew C. Perry, 1794–1858* (Boston, 1967), 282–338, 357–382, 400–410; Schlesinger, *Imperial Presidency*, 54–55; *A Documentary History of U.S. Foreign Relations*, ed. David F. Long, 2 vols. (Washington, DC, 1980), 1:96; Elbert B. Smith, *The Presidencies of Taylor and Fillmore* (Lawrence, KS, 1988), 224–226; Benson Lee Grayson, *The Unknown President: The Administration of President Millard Fillmore* (Washington, DC, 1981), 87–91; Foster Rhea Dulles, *Behind the Open Door: The Story of American Far Eastern Relations*, ed. Marguerite Ann Stewart (St. Louis, 1944), 19–30; Frederic Austin Ogg, *Daniel Webster* (Philadelphia, 1914), 286–395; Claude Moore Fuess, *Daniel Webster*, vol. 2, *1830–1852* (Boston, 1930), 247–266; Richardson, comp., *Messages and Papers of the Presidents*, 5:211, 236, 279, makes it clear that the shipwrecked seamen were a pretext and that the mission actually was "for the purpose of opening trade with Japan" (Pierce to Senate, March 31, 1854).

19. William J. Pomeroy, *American Neo-Colonialism: Its Emergence in the Philippines and Asia* (New York, 1970), 84–98 (quotations at 90); Lewis L. Gould, *The Spanish-American War and President McKinley* (Lawrence, KS, 1982), 114–119, 123–126; John Morgan Gates, *Schoolbooks and Krags: The United States Army in the Philippines, 1898–1902* (Westport, CT, 1973); Richard E. Welch, Jr., *Response to Imperialism: The United States and the Philippine-American War, 1899–1902* (Chapel Hill, NC, 1979); Stuart C.

While the Filipino rebellion was running its course, the United States was beginning a long-term military commitment in China. In 1900 President McKinley ordered 2,500 American troops to China, nominally to protect American lives and property, actually to join a multinational force to suppress the Boxer Rebellion and to support the Open Door policy, whereby China was to remain open to trade instead of being carved into spheres of influence by various European powers. China declared war against the United States, but the United States did not reciprocate. Congress was not consulted, and it did not object. The force remained at varying strength until 1912, when it began to be enlarged in response to the Kuomintang Rebellion. The American presence continued through the years: In 1927 the United States had 5,670 troops on shore in China and forty-four naval vessels in its waters. American forces were still there in 1941. The presence of these troops was authorized by China through agreements for China's "protection"; it was never authorized by Congress.[20]

Theodore Roosevelt expanded McKinley's practice of deploying armed forces to implement broad policy aims and, sometimes, simply to demonstrate to European governments that the United States had emerged as a world power with which they must reckon. His best known venture was in Panama, which until 1904 was part of Colombia. A French company headed by Ferdinand de Lesseps had started building a canal across Panama, gone bankrupt, and sold out to a group called the New Panama Canal Company. In 1902 Congress appropriated funds to buy the company, to complete the canal, and to compensate Colombia, but the Colombian Senate wanted more money for itself. Roosevelt was enraged, and he dispatched a cruiser

---

Miller, *"Benevolent Assimilation": The American Conquest of the Philippines, 1899–1903* (New Haven, CT, 1982); Oscar M. Alfonso, *Theodore Roosevelt and the Philippines, 1897–1909* (New York, 1974); Peter W. Stanley, *A Nation in the Making: The Philippines and the United States, 1899–1921* (Cambridge, MA, 1974).

20. Collier, ed., *Use of Armed Forces Abroad*, 9–11; Gould, *Spanish-American War and McKinley*, 132–135; Schlesinger, *Imperial Presidency*, 88–89; A. Whitney Griswold, *The Far Eastern Policy of the United States* (New Haven, CT, 1938), 36–86; Jones, *Course of American Diplomacy*, 270–272, 294ff., 371–372, 400–403; Michael H. Hunt, *The Making of a Special Relationship: The United States and China to 1914* (New York, 1983).

and troops to fend off the Colombian army while an assortment of Americans in Panama rose in "revolution," declared independence, and agreed to sell the United States the rights of the canal company and full sovereignty over a ten-mile-wide strip across Panama. But that was not the sole episode: Roosevelt sent troops into Honduras, the Dominican Republic, Syria, Abyssinia, Morocco, Korea, and Cuba. President Taft continued interventionist policies, sending troops into half-a-dozen countries; forces he sent to Nicaragua established a presence that lasted, with a brief interruption, until 1933.[21]

At the turn of the century, interventionism and imperialism were policies espoused by most Republicans and rejected by most Democrats. At one point in the second of Grover Cleveland's terms, for instance, a congressional delegation called upon him and announced, "We have about decided to declare war against Spain over the Cuban question." Cleveland replied, "There will be no war with Spain over Cuba while I am President"; if Congress declared war, he would refuse to mobilize the army. In a similar spirit, Woodrow Wilson rejected activism at first. His secretary of state, William Jennings Bryan, negotiated "cooling off" treaties with some thirty countries in the Americas, aimed at preventing armed clashes, and elicited outrage by negotiating a treaty (rejected by the Senate) that would have given Colombia $25 million as compensation for the loss of Panama. Wilson himself refused to extend diplomatic recognition to the brutal Mexican regime of Victoriano Huerta, declaring that "I will not recognize a government of butchers"—thereby at once reversing a traditional American policy of granting de jure recognition to de facto regimes and laying the foundation for a human rights policy to replace the traditional policy of protecting and extending national interests.[22]

21. Gould, *Theodore Roosevelt*, 91–99 and passim; David G. McCullough, *The Path between the Seas: The Creation of the Panama Canal, 1870–1914* (New York, 1977); Richard L. Lael, *Arrogant Diplomacy: U.S. Policy toward Colombia, 1903–1922* (Wilmington, DE, 1987); Perkins, *Hands Off*; Dana G. Munro, *Intervention and Dollar Diplomacy in the Caribbean, 1900–1921* (Princeton, NJ, 1964); Collier, ed., *Use of Armed Forces Abroad*, 10–11; Holt, *Treaties Defeated by the Senate*, 238–239. For William Howard Taft's attitudes about presidential power in regard to treaties and making war, see *Our Chief Magistrate and His Powers* (New York, 1916), 94–99, 105–117.

22. Robert McElroy, *Grover Cleveland, The Man and the Statesman; An Autho-*

But despite the democratic rhetoric, Wilson proved to be as active an interventionist as his predecessors. His emphasis changed from dollar diplomacy to an insistence that America's southern neighbors govern themselves as stable democracies; whenever they did not, he governed them with American troops. After a year of fruitless negotiations with Haiti, during which time the country had three regimes, Wilson sent in the marines and essentially adopted the place as an American protectorate. Relations with the Dominican Republic followed a similar course. In 1914 the navy and marines occupied Veracruz, Mexico, for seven months, and through most of 1916 Gen. John J. Pershing commanded an army of 15,000 in northern Mexico in a vain effort to subdue the revolutionary/bandit Pancho Villa. United States forces entered Mexico three more times in 1918 and six times in 1919. Meanwhile, Wilson had sent more than 12,000 soldiers into the Soviet Union as part of a joint allied force. In none of these instances did Wilson ask Congress to declare war.[23]

rized Biography, 2 vols. (New York, 1923), 2:249–250; Arthur S. Link, *Woodrow Wilson: The New Freedom* (Princeton, NJ, 1956), 277–286, 320–327, 349–350; Holt, *Treaties Defeated by the Senate,* 243–247; Paolo E. Coletta, *William Jennings Bryan III: Political Puritan, 1915–1925* (Lincoln, NE, 1969), 83–102; Louis W. Koenig, *Bryan: A Political Biography of William Jennings Bryan* (New York, 1971), 502–552. The president's power to grant or withhold diplomatic recognition to a regime is derived from Article 2, Section 3, of the Constitution: "He shall receive Ambassadors and other public Ministers." This was originally regarded as merely ceremonial, but it rapidly became substantive. For a discussion, see Corwin, *President,* 184–193.

23. Link, *Wilson: New Freedom,* 107–110, 327–377; P. Edward Haley, *Revolution and Intervention: The Diplomacy of Taft and Wilson with Mexico, 1910–1917* (Cambridge, MA, 1970), 83–224; Thomas and Thomas, *War-Making Powers,* 14–17; Frederick S. Calhoun, *Power and Principle: Armed Intervention in Wilsonian Foreign Policy* (Kent, OH, 1986); Robert E. Quirk, *An Affair of Honor: Woodrow Wilson and the Occupation of Veracruz* (Lexington, KY, 1962); Mark T. Gilderhus, *Diplomacy and Revolution: U.S.–Mexican Relations under Wilson and Carranza* (Tucson, AZ, 1977); David F. Healy, *Gunboat Diplomacy in the Wilson Era: The U.S. Navy in Haiti, 1915–1916* (Madison, WI, 1976); Hans Schmidt, *The United States Occupation of Haiti, 1915–1934* (New Brunswick, NJ, 1971); Mark T. Gilderhus, *Pan American Visions: Woodrow Wilson in the Western Hemisphere, 1913–1921* (Tucson, AZ, 1986).

———— As the power of the president to wage war without a congressional declaration was growing and gathering the sanction of usage, a different set of powers known as war powers had likewise been established. The Constitution is inexplicit on the subject of the conduct of wars, and except for the commander-in-chief clause, its provisions suggest that Congress was expected to supervise the waging of war, as the pre-Constitution Congress had done during the Revolution. During the first seventy-one years under the Constitution that expectation was generally prevalent, along with the expectation that a state of war created no extraordinary powers in either Congress or the president. Jefferson's invocation of a Lockean emergency prerogative was outside the mainstream of constitutional thought, and so was John Quincy Adams's opinion that "the *peace power*" was limited by the Constitution but that "the *war power* is limited only by the laws and usages of nations" and "breaks down every barrier so anxiously erected for the protection of liberty, of property and of life."[24]

The issue first became serious during the Civil War, for that was the country's first war that could be called a genuine national emergency requiring the drafting of civilians and the mobilization of the civilian economy. As indicated, Lincoln took a number of unconstitutional and extralegal actions, including, in addition to those mentioned earlier, spending public funds without appropriations. As the war progressed he declared martial law in various areas, ordered people arrested without warrant, tried civilians in military courts, closed the use of the post office for "treasonable" correspondence, seized property, and emancipated slaves.[25]

In regard to two of his courses of action, the federal courts were asked to intervene, but the president's hand was in nowise stayed.

24. Adams as quoted in Schlesinger, *Imperial Presidency*, 60.

25. James G. Randall, *Constitutional Problems under Lincoln* (New York, 1926), is the standard source. A good balanced appraisal is Michael Les Benedict's "The Constitution of the Lincoln Presidency and the Republican Era," in Fausold and Shank, ed., *The Constitution and the American Presidency*, 45–61. For Lincoln's own account of what he did and why he did it, see Richardson, comp., *Messages and Papers of the Presidents*, 6:20–31. See also Arthur Schlesinger, Jr., "War and the Constitution: Abraham Lincoln and Franklin D. Roosevelt," *Gettysburg Review* 2 (1989):7–24.

One case concerned the legality of the blockade that Lincoln had imposed upon the South, which the Supreme Court upheld in 1863 through somewhat tortured reasoning and a bare five-to-four vote over the argument of the opposition counsel and the dissenters that the president was being made "the impersonation of the country," like a medieval king, and that "all constitutional government [is] at an end whenever he should think that 'the life of the nation' is in danger." It is scarcely conceivable, however, that had the Court ruled against the blockade Lincoln would have lifted it.[26]

That supposition is lent credit by the fate of the court challenge to Lincoln's authority that concerned the suspension of the writ of habeas corpus. The Constitution provides that the privilege of the writ, which in Anglo-American jurisprudence was the firmest legal bulwark against arbitrary arrest and imprisonment, could not be suspended "unless when in Cases of Rebellion or Invasion the public Safety may require it." Few people in the North believed the Civil War was anything other than a rebellion, but the provision is in Article 1, Section 9, suggesting that it is for Congress to decide when the public safety requires suspension and to provide by law the rules governing the exercise of suspension. Lincoln judged otherwise, and instructed the army to suspend the writ and to imprison without evidence, charges, or trial any persons thought to be dangerous to the public safety. As was observed earlier, Lincoln flatly defied the courts on the matter, and realizing that their marshals were no match for the United States Army, the courts had no option but to let the president do as he pleased.[27]

26. *The Prize Cases,* 2 Black 635 (1863); quotation from Corwin, *President,* 232. See also Charles Warren, *The Supreme Court,* 2 vols. (Boston, 1922, 1926), 2:380–385; Fisher, *American Constitutional Law,* 305–306, 327–332; Wormuth and Firmage, *To Chain the Dog of War,* 25–26, 70–72, 74–75, 246, 307; Ludwell H. Johnson III, "Abraham Lincoln and the Development of Presidential War-Making Powers: *Prize Cases* (1863) Revisited," *Civil War History* 35 (1989):208–224.

27. The case in which Taney issued a writ of habeas corpus that Lincoln refused to obey was *Ex parte Merryman,* 17 *Federal Cases,* No. 9,487 (1861):144–153; Wormuth and Firmage, *To Chain the Dog of War,* 120–122; Benedict, "Lincoln Presidency," in Fausold and Shank, ed., *The Constitution and the American Presidency,* 50–52. For discussion and bibliography of contemporary commentary, see Warren, *Supreme Court,* 2:368–374 and notes.

Many people, then and later, criticized Lincoln's conduct as excessive. The abolitionist Wendell Phillips called Lincoln an "unlimited despot," and Justice Benjamin R. Curtis wrote that he had established "a military despotism." When William Whiting, solicitor of the War Department, published a book called *War Powers under the Constitution* in which he maintained that in wartime the president's actions are subject to no constitutional restraints whatever, Sen. Charles Sumner thundered that that doctrine (and Lincoln's behavior under it) was "a pretension so irrational and unconstitutional, so absurd and tyrannical" as to deserve no respect. The doctrine when followed changed the federal authority "from a government of law to that of a military dictator." Twentieth-century historians and political scientists routinely characterized Lincoln's presidency as a "dictatorship" or as a "constitutional dictatorship"—sometimes using the word in the benign Roman sense, sometimes in a sinister modern sense.[28]

The matter is not entirely clear-cut. Lincoln was far more modest in his claims to power—at least at first, though he grew bolder in his claims as the war dragged on—than either his defenders or his detractors maintained. He took the steps he did, he explained to Congress in 1861, because he was bound by the Constitution to take care that the laws be faithfully executed, and in the insurrection the "whole of the laws which were required to be faithfully executed were being resisted and failing of execution in nearly one-third of the States." He

28. For characterization of Lincoln's conduct as dictatorial, see, for example, W. E. Binkley, *The Powers of the President: Problems of American Democracy* (Garden City, NY, 1937), 116–117, 133; George Fort Milton, *The Use of Presidential Power, 1789–1943* (Boston, 1944), 107; William A. Dunning, *Essays on the Civil War and Reconstruction and Related Topics* (New York, 1898), 19–21; Clinton L. Rossiter, *Constitutional Dictatorship: Crisis Government in the Modern Democracies* (Princeton, NJ, 1948), 223–239; Richard M. Pious, *The American Presidency* (New York, 1979), 57; Corwin, *President*, 20, 23–24, 449–456 (Sumner quote at 452); Phillips and Curtis quotes in Schlesinger, *Imperial Presidency*, 59. Arguments rebutting this view include Herman Belz, *Lincoln and the Constitution: The Dictatorship Question Reconsidered* (Fort Wayne, IN, 1984); David Donald, *Lincoln Reconsidered: Essays on the Civil War Era*, 2d ed. (New York, 1966), 187–208; and Don E. Fehrenbacher, *Lincoln in Text and Context: Collected Essays* (Stanford, CA, 1987), 113–142; Daniel P. Franklin, *Extraordinary Measures* (Pittsburgh, PA, 1991), 125–126, 136–137.

justified his actions on the ground that he had taken the constitutionally mandated oath to "preserve, protect and defend the Constitution of the United States." The first purpose for which the Constitution was established, according to its preamble, was "to form a more perfect Union," and if the president was to preserve and defend the Constitution he must necessarily preserve and defend the Union. As for the suspension of habeas corpus, Lincoln claimed that he had exercised the authority "but very sparingly," and if he had exercised it in violation of the law—which he denied—nonetheless, he asked rhetorically, "Are all the laws *but one* to go unexecuted, and the Government itself go to pieces lest that one be violated?"[29]

In the emergency Lincoln did exert greater powers than his predecessors, and he exceeded the bounds that had previously been regarded as the limits of the Constitution; but it is scarcely accurate to describe his presidency as a dictatorship, for dictatorship means absolute rule by one man or a junto, and Lincoln generally treated his "war powers" as being shared with Congress. Moreover, he did not stint in reminding Congress that its was the ultimate authority, since if it found his conduct unacceptable it could impeach and remove him from office. He went so far as to allow Congress, through its Joint Congressional Committee on the Conduct of the War, to participate in the actual direction of military operations. As for habeas corpus, in 1861 he invited Congress to act on the subject if it chose, and when Congress passed the Habeas Corpus Act of 1863 he followed its dictates in suspending the writ thereafter.[30]

In the same spirit, he believed that the confiscation of the slaves of

29. Richardson, comp., *Messages and Papers of the Presidents*, 6:25.

30. Benedict, "Lincoln Presidency," in Fausold and Shank, ed., *The Constitution and the American Presidency*, 56; William S. Church, *A Treatise on the Writ of Habeas Corpus*, 2d ed. (San Francisco, 1893), 44–47; Hans L. Trefousee, "The Joint Committee on the Conduct of the War: A Reassessment," *Civil War History* 10 (1964):5–19; T. Harry Williams, "Lincoln (1861–1865)," in *The Ultimate Decision: The President as Commander in Chief*, ed. Ernest R. May (New York, 1960), 79–89; Benjamin P. Thomas and Harold M. Hyman, *Stanton: The Life and Times of Lincoln's Secretary of War* (New York, 1962), 147–149; Richardson, comp., *Messages and Papers of the Presidents*, 6:25, 170–171; Jacob K. Javits, *Who Makes War: The President Versus Congress* (New York, 1973), 129–135. See also the studies by Belz, Donald, and Fehrenbacher cited in note 28 of this chapter.

rebels—though not the abolition of slavery as an institution, which was beyond the scope of federal authority—was a concurrent power shared by president and Congress. When Lincoln did issue his emancipation proclamation, he justified it as a war measure under his power as commander in chief, for the slaves were contributing materially to keeping the South functioning and thus to keeping the rebellion alive, but he also grounded it on congressional legislation.[31]

In sum, the Civil War experience established a potent precedent for the existence of war powers beyond the boundaries of the Constitution but not for the exclusive authority of the president to exercise those powers. Thereafter, it was generally conceded that "powers limited only by the laws and usages of nations," as John Quincy Adams had maintained, entered into play in wartime and broke down the constitutional barriers "for the protection of liberty, of property, and of life." But those powers were to be jointly employed by president and Congress.

The conferral of near-dictatorial powers on Woodrow Wilson during World War I and of truly dictatorial powers on Franklin Roosevelt during World War II reflected that understanding. Under the war-powers doctrine, Congress first assumed authority to regulate the minutest activities of the citizenry in areas that in peacetime were still reserved to the people or to the states, and then it delegated those powers to the president. The president, in turn, delegated them to subordinates in or out of government, who exercised them on his orders with minimal interference by the courts. The Bill of Rights, for practical purposes, was suspended for the duration.[32]

Under Roosevelt another dimension appeared: He assumed the

31. Benedict, "Lincoln Presidency," in Fausold and Shank, ed., *The Constitution and the American Presidency*, 57–58; Richardson, comp., *Messages and Papers of the Presidents*, 6:96–98, 158–159, 213–215, 223; John Hope Franklin, *The Emancipation Proclamation* (Garden City, NY, 1963).

32. The emergency powers assumed by Congress and granted to Wilson and Roosevelt are recounted in some detail in Corwin, *President*, 234–250. For Wilson's leadership during World War I, see Robert Ferrell's chapter in Dawson, ed., *Commanders in Chief*. For an interesting approach to "FDR: Commander in Chief of Our Generation," see Javits, *Who Makes War*, 210–238. See also note 39 of this chapter, and Charles F. Croog, "FBI Political Surveillance and the Isolationist-Interventionist Debate, 1939–1941," *Historian* 54 (1992):441–458.

authority to act not only beyond his congressional mandate but directly in opposition to Congress if need be. In a remarkable message delivered on September 7, 1942, Roosevelt peremptorily demanded the repeal of certain legislation and said that if "Congress should fail to act, and act adequately, I shall accept the responsibility, and I will act." Claiming a presidential power under the Constitution and unspecified statutes "to take measures necessary to avert a disaster," he assured the American people "that I will use my powers with a full sense of responsibility to the Constitution and to my country. . . . I shall not hesitate to use every power vested in me to accomplish the defeat of our enemies in any part of the world where our own safety demands such defeat. When the war is won, the powers under which I act automatically revert to the people—to whom they belong."[33]

Executive power had come full circle, back to what Bracton had called *gubernaculum* and Fortescue had called *dominium regale*.

———— Roosevelt could strike that audacious, almost contemptuous stance because of his extreme self-confidence, his sense of responsibility in the face of mortal peril to the nation, and his belief that he represented the will of the people; but his position was also grounded upon recent changes in the rules governing the conduct of foreign policy. These changes were neither the work of presidents nor that of Congress. The interwar Republican presidents, as indicated, continued the practice of intervening in Latin America and the Far East, and they involved the United States more thoroughly in European affairs than ever before, but they confined themselves largely to the methods of their predecessors. Roosevelt turned his back on the world as he set out to combat the depression as a domestic problem, and in the virtually total isolationism of his first term there was no place for innovation in the techniques of foreign policy. As for Congress, it was more isolationist than the president, and it continued to

33. Corwin, *President*, 250–251; *New York Times*, Sept. 8, 1942. Notice Roosevelt's careful use of "shall" and "will"—a distinction that has all but disappeared from the language. Roosevelt "seemed at times to believe that the most patriotic thing Congress could do was to adjourn for the duration" (David Brinkley, *Washington Goes to War* [New York, 1988], 201).

be into his second term. It even came close to passing a constitutional amendment preventing war without a popular referendum—at the very time when Roosevelt was beginning to cast a worried eye toward the prospect of renewed war in Europe.[34]

Rather, the innovations, revolutionary in their bestowal of power on the president, had been the doing of an otherwise conservative Supreme Court. The beginnings had been seemingly innocuous. In 1913 Congress passed a law regulating the killing of migratory game birds. On the ground that regulating the hunting of game was properly an exercise of the police powers of the states and of no constitutional concern to the federal government, a federal district court struck down the statute. In 1916, however, the Wilson administration announced the conclusion of a treaty between the United States and Canada, providing for the establishment of limited seasons and other restrictions on killing the birds. Under the authority of the treaty, Congress in 1918 substantially reenacted the disallowed 1913 act. The state of Missouri brought suit, requesting the Supreme Court to declare the act an unconstitutional violation of the Tenth Amendment.[35]

The Supreme Court upheld the act, and in so doing pronounced a sweeping new constitutional doctrine. Justice Holmes, speaking for the majority, said that "acts of Congress are the supreme law of the land only when made in pursuance of the Constitution, while treaties are declared to be so when made under the authority of the United States." There might or might not be limitations upon the treaty-making power, but "it is obvious that there may be matters of the sharpest exigency for the national well being that an act of Congress could not deal with but that a treaty followed by such an act could,

34. Jones, *Course of American Diplomacy*, 366–399, 402; Selig Adler, *The Uncertain Giant: 1921–1941, American Foreign Policy between the Wars* (New York, 1965); Frank Costigliola, *Awkward Dominion: American Political, Economic, and Cultural Relations with Europe, 1919–1933* (Ithaca, NY, 1984); Wayne S. Cole, *Roosevelt and The Isolationists, 1932–1945* (Lincoln, NE, 1983); Manfred Jonas, *Isolationism in America, 1935–1941* (Ithaca, NY, 1966); Richard Dean Burns and W. Addams Dixon, "Foreign Policy and the 'Democratic Myth': The Debate on the Ludlow Amendment," *Mid-America* 47 (1965):288–306; Justus Doenecke, *Anti-intervention: A Bibliographical Introduction to Isolationism and Pacifism from World War I to the Early Cold War* (New York, 1987).

35. *Missouri* v. *Holland*, 252 U.S. 416–435 (1920).

and it is not lightly to be assumed that, in matters requiring national action, 'a power which must belong to and somewhere reside in every civilized government' is not to be found." In other words, a treaty did not have to be consonant with the Constitution, it needed only to be made under its authority, which is to say by the president with the advice and consent of two-thirds of the Senate; it could vest the Congress or the president with powers that neither derived directly from the Constitution itself.[36]

The next step toward giving the president "dictatorial" powers was taken in 1937 in *U.S.* v. *Belmont,* handed down five months after the Court had announced the doctrine of inherent powers in the *Curtiss-Wright* case. The *Belmont* decision involved executive agreements negotiated with the Soviet Union after Roosevelt accorded it diplomatic recognition in 1933. Upon coming to power, the Soviet regime had confiscated a great deal of private property, including that of Russian corporations abroad. One corporation had money deposited in the Belmont bank in New York, which continued to hold it for its owners. The "Litvinov Assignment" of 1933 promised to turn over that property to the United States government in exchange for the federal government's payment of claims of Americans against the Soviet Union. In *Belmont* the Court extended the supremacy-of-treaties ruling of *Missouri* v. *Holland,* declaring that the same rule applied "in the case of all international compacts and agreements from the very fact that complete power over international affairs is in the National Government and is not and cannot be subject to any curtailment or interference on the part of the several states," whose property-rights laws would otherwise govern. Five years later, in a related case, the Supreme Court held that the president's authority "included the power, without the consent of the Senate, to determine the public policy of the United States with respect to the Russian nationalization decrees" even though the pol-

---

36. Ibid. Holmes was being disingenuous. The Supreme Law clause reads "Treaties made . . . under the Authority of the United States" instead of "in Pursuance thereof" because the Framers wanted to include the treaties made by the United States before 1787. For an angry attack on the decision, see Forrest Black, "*Missouri* v. *Holland*—A Judicial Milepost on the Road to Absolutism," *Illinois Law Review* 25 (1937):911–928.

icy meant the confiscation of property without concern for Fifth Amendment protections.[37]

Armed with these decisions (though much of what they said was obiter dicta) and with opinions of Attorney General Robert Jackson, Roosevelt believed he had constitutional authority to do anything he saw fit in matters of foreign affairs. The one limitation was public opinion. In keeping with that belief he began to exercise war powers before the United States entered World War II. For example, after the fall of France he turned over fifty American destroyers to Great Britain in exchange for naval bases in the British West Indies, though the deal was in direct violation "of at least two statutes" and contrary to the letter of the Constitution. In 1941 he ordered the navy to harass and attack German submarines in the Atlantic, in the vain hope that the Germans would strike back and thereby help Roosevelt mobilize public opinion in favor of declaring war.[38]

In directing the war effort Roosevelt was ruthless, but he was careful to woo popular support and to avoid making political enemies unnecessarily. Politically he did not repeat Wilson's partisan

37. *U.S. v. Belmont,* 301 U.S. 324 (1937); *U.S. v. Pink,* 315 U.S. 203 (1942); Corwin, *President,* 214; Fisher, *Constitutional Conflicts,* 238–239; editors' note, "United States v. Pink—A Reappraisal," *Columbia Law Review* 48 (1948):895–900; Stefan A. Riesenfeld, "The Power of the Congress and the President in International Relations; Three Recent Supreme Court Decisions," *California Law Review* 25 (1937):643–675; Levitan, "Justice Sutherland's Theory," *Yale Law Journal* 55:493; Raoul Berger, "The Presidential Monopoly of Foreign Relations," *Michigan Law Review* 71 (1972):1–58; Raoul Berger, *Executive Privilege* (New York, 1975), 152–153, 157–162. In *U.S. v. Pink,* the Court said that "aliens as well as citizens are entitled to the protection of the Fifth Amendment" but that the amendment "does not stand in the way of giving full force and effect to the Litvinov Agreement" (quotes at 228).

38. Corwin, *President,* 238–239; Wormuth and Firmage, *To Chain the Dog of War,* 64–65; *The Public Papers and Addresses of Franklin D. Roosevelt,* 13 vols. (New York, 1938–1950), 10:391; Jones, *Course of American Diplomacy,* 414–417, 424–425; Waldo Heinrichs, "President Franklin D. Roosevelt's Intervention in the Battle of the Atlantic, 1941," *Diplomatic History* 10 (1986):311–332; Louis William Koenig, *The Presidency and the Crisis: Powers of the Office from the Invasion of Poland to Pearl Harbor* (New York, 1944), 11, 46, 55–57, 120; Edward S. Corwin, *Total War and the Constitution: Five Lectures* (New York, 1947), 10–11, 29–31, 33; Eugene C. Gerhart, *America's Advocate: Robert H. Jackson* (Indianapolis, IN, 1958), 210–229; Walter LaFeber, "The Creation of the Republican King," *Constitution* (Fall 1991):46.

mistake and instead made bipartisanship integral to the conduct of his policy. In June of 1940, for instance, he appointed Republicans to two key posts in his cabinet, Henry L. Stimson as secretary of war and Frank Knox as secretary of the navy. On the popular front, he created the Office of War Information to direct a steady stream of propaganda toward maintaining high morale, he instituted censorship, and he won the unquestioning support of newspaper and radio journalists. As a consequence, the nation was solidly unified throughout the war.[39]

When the war was over, however, the emergency powers of the president did not "automatically revert to the people—to whom they belong," as Roosevelt had promised they would, and for that and other reasons a political and popular reaction against executive excess set in. One result was that in 1946 the Republicans won control of both houses of Congress for the first time in almost twenty years. Another was the proposal in 1947 and the adoption in 1951 of the Twenty-second Amendment, limiting presidents to two terms—a posthumous slap at Roosevelt for having been elected four times.[40]

39. Jones, *Course of American Diplomacy,* 413; Richard N. Current, *Secretary Stimson, A Study in Statecraft* (New Brunswick, NJ, 1954); Jack Goodman, ed., *While You Were Gone: A Report on Wartime Life in the United States* (New York, 1946); Elmer Davis and Bryon Price, *War Information and Censorship* (Washington, DC, 1943); Betty Houchin Winfield, *FDR and the News Media* (Urbana, IL, 1990); Brinkley, *Washington Goes to War;* Richard W. Steele, "The Great Debate: Roosevelt, the Media and the Coming of the War, 1940–41," *Journal of American History* 71 (1984):69–92. Remembering the persecutions of German-Americans during World War I, Roosevelt had the European side of the war billed as being not against nations but against systems, namely fascism. Efforts to do the same with regard to the Japanese were unavailing and half-hearted, and some 117,000 of them were incarcerated in camps for the duration. That was the only significant exception to the wartime consensus. The Supreme Court upheld the internments under the war-powers doctrine (*Korematsu v. U.S.,* 323 U.S. 214 [1944]). One Japanese-American female did manage to get out on a writ of habeas corpus (*Ex parte Endo,* 323 U.S. 283 [1944]).

40. *Historical Statistics of the United States,* 691; Twenty-second Amendment. Truman was exempted from the terms of the amendment. Lyndon Johnson was eligible for reelection in 1968 because he had served less than half of the term for which John F. Kennedy had been elected. For a reappraisal of the amendment and its impact, see *Restoring the Presidency: Reconsidering the Twenty-Second Amendment* (Washington, DC, 1990).

Still another manifestation of the reaction against executive power was the Bricker amendment, proposed by Sen. John Bricker of Ohio in response to a recommendation by the American Bar Association. The amendment would have provided that no treaty that conflicted with the Constitution could be valid, that no treaty could become effective as internal law without an act of Congress that would have been valid in the absence of the treaty, that Congress be empowered to regulate executive agreements, and that executive agreements violative of the Constitution be invalid. After vigorous debate in and out of the Senate, Bricker announced early in 1953 that the constitutionally required two-thirds of the senators had promised to support the proposal. But the strongest backers had been Republicans who had feared a continuing Democratic monopoly of the White House, and Republican Dwight Eisenhower had just become president. Eisenhower strongly opposed the Bricker amendment, and many people, trusting him absolutely, found it difficult to believe that he would ever betray the Constitution. Despite a general cooling of enthusiasm, however, when the amendment was at last acted upon in January of 1954 it fell just one vote short of the needed two-thirds majority.[41]

The controversy did not, of course, end there, for both the Supreme Court and the Congress had more to say on the subject. The Court, for its part, retreated somewhat from the extreme implica-

41. Stephen Ambrose, *Eisenhower* (New York, 1984), 151–152; Robert J. Donovan, *Eisenhower: The Inside Story* (New York, 1956), 238–242; Schlesinger, *Imperial Presidency*, 151–152; Frank Ezekiel Holman, *Story of the "Bricker" Amendment (The First Phase)* (Seattle, WA, 1954); Duane Tananbaum, *The Bricker Amendment Controversy: A Test of Eisenhower's Political Leadership* (Ithaca, NY, 1988); Cathal J. Nolan, "The Last Hurrah of Conservative Isolationism: Eisenhower, Congress, and the Bricker Amendment," *Presidential Studies Quarterly* 22 (1992):337–349; Alfred H. Kelly and Winfred A. Harbison, *The American Constitution,* 4th ed. (New York, 1970), 867–869; Pyle and Pious, ed., *President, Congress, and the Constitution,* 246–248. The Bricker amendment would have nullified *Missouri* v. *Holland* (Jean Edward Smith, *The Constitution and American Foreign Policy* [St. Paul, MN, 1989], 114); but in one sense the question had become moot, for since *Missouri* v. *Holland* the powers of Congress had expanded to cover almost any conceivable subject. See Louis Henkin, *Foreign Affairs and the Constitution* (New York, 1972), 147. Supporters of the resolution were also upset, however, over the wartime Yalta and Potsdam agreements and the prospect that the United Nations might use human rights as an excuse for meddling in American internal affairs.

tions of the earlier decisions. In 1953 it invalidated an executive agreement contravening an existing statute regulating international trade, and in 1957 it ruled that an executive agreement allowing American military courts in Britain to try American military personnel and their dependents in courts-martial violated their right to trial by jury and was therefore unconstitutional.[42]

Congress, in the hostility toward the White House rekindled by the Vietnamese war, attempted to check the practice of making secret executive agreements. A subcommittee of the Senate Foreign Relations Committee found in 1969 and 1970 that the United States had reached significant covert agreements with South Korea, Laos, Thailand, Ethiopia, and Spain, as well as with other countries, and in response Congress passed the Case-Zablocki Act of 1972, requiring the secretary of state to send to Congress within sixty days the text of all international agreements other than treaties; if the president decided that publication would compromise national security, he was to send copies to the foreign relations committees of each house under injunction of secrecy. Presidents Nixon and Ford ignored or circumvented the 1972 act, whereupon Congress stiffened it in 1974. The Carter administration found a way around it: Before SALT 1 was to expire in September of 1977, the United States and the Soviet Union issued "parallel policy statements" saying each would adhere to the limits. Inasmuch as the statements were unilateral and separate, the State Department could claim that they did not constitute an agreement and were thus exempt from the revised Case-Zablocki Act. In 1987 Congress voted to cut off funding for agreements not complying with the act, but that method also had limited effectiveness. The conduct of international relations through nontreaty agreements had become too entrenched a practice to be curtailed, and besides, there lingered in both presidency and Congress the belief announced by George Washington two centuries earlier that sometimes foreign relations simply must be kept secret and that in the last analysis the president was the one who must decide.[43]

---

42. *United States v. Guy W. Capps, Inc.,* 348 U.S. 296 (1955, confirming a 1953 circuit decision); *Reid v. Covert,* 354 U.S. 1, 16 (1957); Fisher, *Constitutional Conflicts,* 239–241.

43. Case-Zablocki Act (PL 92–403), *Congressional Quarterly Almanac,* 1972:158–

————— The president's extraordinary powers did not automatically revert to the people after the end of World War II because a protracted cold war with the Soviet Union had begun. To understand the impact of the cold war on the presidency, it is necessary to review its origins and early development. At the end of World War II the American economy was booming, whereas Europe and the Far East lay in ruins both materially and politically. The Soviet Union had suffered unspeakable losses, some 20 million of its people having been killed and the entire area west of Leningrad, Moscow, and Stalingrad having been devastated—by Communists as well as by Nazis. But the Soviet Union was still inordinately powerful in comparison with its neighbors. The Red Army was 10 million strong and well equipped, in large measure because of American lend-lease, and the Soviets were providing for future industrial strength by stripping eastern Germany of factory equipment and by removing German scientists and engineers as well.[44]

The postwar aims of the United States and the Soviet Union were different but not necessarily incompatible. Americans wanted to forge a just and lasting peace. In regard to the means of securing the peace, most Americans were as clear and certain as they were naive. Determined not to repeat the mistakes that had led to worldwide depres-

---

160, 619–621; Margolis, *Executive Agreement,* 86–88; Fisher, *Constitutional Conflicts,* 239–243; Louis W. Koenig, "The Modern Presidency and the Constitution: Foreign Policy," in Fausold and Shank, ed., *The Constitution and the American Presidency,* 179; *Newsweek,* June 27, 1977, 13; James M. McCormick, "The Changing Role of the House Foreign Affairs Committee in the 1970s and 1980s," *Congress and the Presidency* 12 (1985):1–20; Cecil V. Crabb, Jr., and Pat M. Holt, *Invitation to Struggle: Congress, the President and Foreign Policy,* 2d ed. (Washington, DC, 1984), 17, 163–177; *New York Times,* Sept. 3, 1977, 3:3, and Sept. 27, 1977, 6:4; *Newsweek,* Oct. 3, 1977, 44; *Congressional Quarterly Almanac,* 1987:80. On the question of secrecy, see the devastating attack in Berger, *Executive Privilege;* Stuart Symington, "Congress Right to Know," *New York Times Magazine,* Aug. 9, 1970; R. A. Paul, *American Military Commitments Abroad* (New Brunswick, NJ, 1973).

44. The bibliography on the origins of the cold war is large and diverse. For a good balanced account, see Randall B. Woods and Howard Jones, *Dawning of the Cold War: The United States' Quest for Order* (Athens, GA, 1991). The authors' bibliography, 309–320, covers the important literature. For a cold war retrospective, see William G. Hyland, *The Cold War Is Over* (New York, 1990).

sion and renewed warfare after World War I, Americans generally agreed that this time they should see to the establishment of an international peacekeeping organization, an improved League of Nations with the United States as a leading participant. They also supported the economic and political rehabilitation of Europe.[45]

The Soviets, for their part, had broad territorial aims. They wanted to regain territory that had been lost in earlier wars: those parts of northeastern Europe that had been ruled by the tsars but had become independent as a result of World War I, namely Poland, part of Finland, and Latvia, Estonia, and Lithuania, as well as the Oriental possessions lost to Japan in 1905. They wanted to retain control of the territory in Europe that the Red Army had occupied on V-E Day, or as much of it as possible. This would provide a buffer zone between the Soviet Union and the West, would make possible continued milking of the area for economic advantage, and would fulfill the hopes embodied in the romantic nineteenth-century movement called Pan-Slavism. They also wanted to control as much of the Near East as possible, thus acquiring an all-season outlet to the sea, adding access to rich oil resources, and realizing an ancient ambition of the tsars.[46]

Out of a Wilsonian belief in national self-determination, many Americans were made uneasy and distrustful as the Soviets set up puppet Communist regimes in Eastern Europe in 1945 and 1946 and engaged in various obstructionist tactics in the United Nations. A few Americans talked loosely of having it out with the Red Army

45. On the new internationalism and American attitudes at war's end, see Robert A. Divine, *Second Chance: The Triumph of Internationalism in America during World War II* (New York, 1967).

46. Vojtech Mastny, *Russia's Road to the Cold War: Diplomacy, Warfare, and the Politics of Communism, 1941–1945* (New York, 1979); Adam B. Ulam, *Expansion and Coexistence: Soviet Foreign Policy, 1917–1973*, 2d ed. (New York, 1974); William L. Neumann, *After Victory: Churchill, Roosevelt, Stalin and the Making of the Peace* (New York, 1967); Coit D. Blacker, "The Collapse of Soviet Power in Europe," *Foreign Affairs* 70 (1990/91):89. For revisionist views, holding essentially that capitalist America was unilaterally to blame for the cold war, see Gabriel Kolko, *The Politics of War: The World and United States Foreign Policy, 1943–1945* (New York, 1968), and Lloyd C. Gardner, *Architects of Illusion: Men and Ideas in American Foreign Policy, 1941–1949* (Chicago, 1970).

while American forces were still in Europe, but most were anxious to demobilize the armed forces and get on with their lives, secure in the belief that the Soviet Union would not pose a serious threat because the United States had the atomic bomb and no one else did.

President Truman, however, feared that the Soviet Union might render the victory in Europe a nullity by overrunning the entire continent. Communist guerrillas were fighting fiercely in the Balkans, it seemed possible that Communists would be elected to power in Italy and France, and quite as ominously Russian troops were massed on the Turkish border. But Truman's efforts to slow American demobilization and to arouse public opinion against the Soviet threat were of little avail. He brought Winston Churchill over to give his celebrated Iron Curtain speech at Fulton, Missouri, in the spring of 1946, and the speech was widely discussed, but the American people did not rally behind Truman to halt the Soviets. Britain alone was making the effort.[47]

Early in 1947, however, Truman decided that the United States had no option but to intervene. In January the British government notified the State Department that it could defend the Balkans no longer and that without American help the collapse of Greece and Turkey was imminent. Truman decided to meet the challenge, to take the lead and seek public support afterward. He called Congress into special session and requested $400 million in emergency aid to Greece and Turkey. On March 12 he announced to Congress what became known as the Truman Doctrine or policy of containment: "I believe that it should be the policy of the United States to support free peoples that are resisting attempted subjugation by armed minorities or by outside pressures." Congress voted the funds. That was an awesome commitment, amounting to nothing less than declaring the United States policeman to the world and the president chief of police.[48]

47. Woods and Jones, *Dawning of the Cold War,* 98–117. See also Fraser J. Harbutt, *The Iron Curtain: Churchill, America, and the Origins of the Cold War* (New York, 1986), 159–216; George M. Alexander, *The Prelude to the Truman Doctrine: British Policy in Greece, 1944–1947* (Oxford, Eng., 1982); Dean Rusk, *As I Saw It* (New York, 1990), 129; and, for example, *Newsweek,* March 18, 1946, 29–31.

48. Howard Jones, *"A New Kind of War": America's Global Strategy and the Truman*

Congress and the president began forthwith to create the apparatus necessary to carry out the mission. The military was reorganized, the several branches being consolidated under a new Department of Defense (though they retained their separate identities and department heads). Each branch was enlarged, the draft was reinstituted, and research and development of new weaponry received priority status. The Strategic Air Command was assigned the job of patroling the skies on a continuous basis. The go-ahead was given for developing the hydrogen bomb. The Joint Chiefs of Staff was instituted as was the National Security Council. A purge of government employees suspected of being Communists or Communist sympathizers was begun. The Central Intelligence Agency, charged with worldwide espionage and covert operations, was organized on a basis so secret that Congress voted it funds without being allowed to ask what it was doing. Soon, the United States negotiated collective security arrangements—the North Atlantic Treaty Organization (NATO) and later the Southeast Asia Treaty Organization (SEATO)—that created permanent alliances in opposition to the Soviet Union and its satellites. These steps were departures from American tradition, and as a whole they redefined the president's role in directing foreign relations.[49]

Doctrine in Greece (New York, 1989), 36–62; Woods and Jones, *Dawning of the Cold War,* 133–152; *United States News,* March 21, 1947, 5, 6, 12, 24–25, 57–58, and full text of the speech at 69–70; and, for example, *New York Times,* March 13, 1947, 1:8 and 2:2.

49. *Congressional Quarterly Almanac,* 1947:457–463; Daniel H. Yergin, *Shattered Peace: The Origins of the Cold War and the National Security State* (Boston, 1977); Schlesinger, *Imperial Presidency,* 167, 316–319; *The Central Intelligence Agency: History and Documents,* ed. William M. Leary (Tuscaloosa, AL, 1984); Arthur B. Darling, *The Central Intelligence Agency: An Instrument of Government, to 1950* (University Park, PA, 1990), 166–192; Timothy P. Ireland, *Creating the Entangling Alliance: The Origins of the North Atlantic Treaty Organization* (Westport, CT, 1981); Lawrence F. Kaplan, *The United States and NATO: The Formative Years* (Lexington, KY, 1984); Anna Kasten Nelson, "President Truman and the Evolution of the National Security Council," *Journal of American History* 72 (1985):360–378; John Ranelagh, *The Agency: The Rise and Decline of the CIA* (London, 1986), 112–142; Donald R. McCoy, *The Presidency of Harry S. Truman* (Lawrence, KS, 1984), 115–142; Harry R. Borowski, *A Hollow Threat: Strategic Air Power and Containment Before Korea* (Westport, CT, 1982).

Almost as momentous was the ideological rationale underlying the shift. The theory, as formulated by George Frost Kennan and adopted by the State Department, held that there was an "innate antagonism between capitalism and socialism," that "peaceful coexistence" was impossible, and that Communist leaders would press for worldwide domination. The Soviet leaders were in no hurry and would retreat in the face of serious obstacles, but they were engaged in a never-resting conspiracy with agents in every country in the world. The policy of the United States "must be that of a long-term, patient, but firm and vigilant containment of Russian expansive tendencies," which would put pressure on the Kremlin and eventually result "in either the break-up or the mellowing of Soviet power." Acceptance of the theory as the guide for presidential policy meant that for the next four decades international relations would be viewed through the prism of cold war ideology.[50]

———— At first and throughout the 1950s cold war policy was bipartisan and a joint venture of president and Congress. Indeed, Republicans became generally more hawkish than Truman, and Congress tended to be more hawkish than either Truman or Eisenhower. President Truman sent troops to fight in a fruitless war in Korea, billed as a United Nations police action, and instead of criticizing him Republican senators led by Joseph McCarthy of Wisconsin attacked him for being "soft on Communism"—especially after 1951, when Truman removed Douglas MacArthur from command in Korea for insubordination. Liberal Democrats in the Senate, led by Hubert Humphrey of Minnesota, attempted to outdo the McCarthyites, proposing to declare American Communists criminals and to put them in concentration camps. And congressional spending on the military became so lavish that President Eisenhower, in his last address to Congress,

50. Kennan's article was first published in *Foreign Affairs* 25 (July 1947):566–582 and was subsequently published separately by the State Department. For an analytical biography of Kennan, see Walter L. Hixson, *George F. Kennan: Cold War Iconoclast* (New York, 1989). Later Kennan changed his mind about many positions he had advocated in 1947; see, for example, Edward N. Luttwak, "The Strange Case of George F. Kennan," *Commentary* (Nov. 1977):30–35.

felt compelled to warn the nation of the dangers of a "military-industrial complex" that threatened to dominate government.[51]

Congress continued to give presidents at least as much money and power as they requested, even as the United States became increasingly involved in the Vietnamese conflict. To be sure, the Gulf of Tonkin Resolution of August, 1964, under which the war in Vietnam was fought, had been obtained from Congress by President Johnson on the basis of false information, and the resolution authorized not war but taking "all necessary measures to repel any armed attacks against the forces of the United States and to prevent further aggression." But almost no one in Congress complained as Johnson increased the number of American troops in Vietnam from 17,000 to more than 500,000 and along the way built a credibility gap by issuing contradictory statements about his policies, objectives, prospects, and progress.[52]

In the summer of 1967, however, protests started to mount and soon reached major proportions. A few senators began to speak in opposition, and toward the end of the year, Sen. Eugene McCarthy announced that he would be a candidate for the Democratic presi-

51. *Bipartisanship and the Making of Foreign Policy: A Historical Survey,* ed. Ellen C. Collier (Boulder, CO, 1991); McCoy, *Harry Truman,* 221–280; David R. Kepley, *The Collapse of the Middle Way: Senate Republicans and the Bipartisan Foreign Policy, 1948–1952* (New York, 1988); Lewis McCarroll Purifoy, *Harry Truman's China Policy: McCarthyism and the Diplomacy of Hysteria, 1947–1951* (New York, 1976); John W. Spanier, *The Truman-MacArthur Controversy and the Korean War* (Cambridge, MA, 1959); C. David Tompkins, *Senator Arthur H. Vandenberg: The Evolution of a Modern Republican, 1884–1945* (Lansing, MI, 1970); Carl Solberg, *Hubert Humphrey: A Biography* (New York, 1984), 156–159; Nelson W. Polsby, "Down Memory Lane with Joe McCarthy," *Commentary* (Feb. 1983): 55–59, a review of the studies of McCarthyism; Eisenhower's "Farewell Radio and Television Address to the American People," Jan. 17, 1961, in *Public Papers of the Presidents of the United States: Dwight D. Eisenhower, 1960–61* (Washington, DC, 1961), 1038; Charles J. G. Griffin, "New Light on Eisenhower's Farewell Address," *Presidential Studies Quarterly* 22 (1992): 469–479.

52. Jones, *Course of American Diplomacy,* 594–618; *The Pentagon Papers as Published by the New York Times* (New York, 1971); Schlesinger, *Imperial Presidency,* 179–181; *Congressional Quarterly Almanac,* 1964: 331–332; *Time,* Aug. 14, 1964, 11–19; Edward Keynes, *Undeclared War: Twilight Zone of Constitutional Power* (University Park, PA, 1982), 112–114. The Tonkin Gulf Resolution of August 7, 1964, is reproduced in Long, ed., *Documentary History of U.S. Foreign Relations,* 2:139 and Jones, ed., *Safeguarding the Republic,* 262.

dential nomination in 1968, using as his "troops" the large number of college students who were increasingly becoming involved in antiwar demonstrations. When McCarthy ran well in the New Hampshire primary, President Johnson withdrew from the race. Throughout the remainder of the term, Johnson was pilloried unmercifully by students, politicians, and the news media.[53]

And it was not Lyndon Johnson alone who was being repudiated. On the part of the Congress, much of the news media, and a sizable segment of the population the repudiation extended to the presidency itself. Thenceforth, Congress would write no more blank checks for the president to carry on the cold war. At best, it would give its grudging cooperation, and more commonly than not it put obstacles in the way.

Richard Nixon assumed the presidency unaware of this profound change. Given the war he inherited, given Congress' suspicion and hostility, and given the president's naive belief that he still had as free a hand in the conduct of foreign affairs as Roosevelt, Truman, and Eisenhower had had, it is surprising that he managed to achieve anything. In fact he achieved a great deal. During the eight years between his defeat by Kennedy and his election in 1968 he had devoted himself to the study of international relations, current and historical, and he built on his understanding by making Henry Kissinger his national security adviser. Their most important accomplishment was detente, including the Strategic Arms Limitation Talks and the resulting agreements and the creation of a "new structure for peace" by opening relations with Communist China. The transformation of the world order from bipolar to multipolar would in time bring the cold war to an end.[54]

---

53. McCarthy received 42 percent of the vote in the New Hampshire primary; see *New York Times*, March 14, 1968, 31:2. See also Eugene J. McCarthy, *The Year of the People* (Garden City, NY, 1969); Doris Kearns, *Lyndon Johnson and the American Dream* (New York, 1976), 335–352; Irwin Unger and Debi Unger, *Turning Point: 1968* (New York, 1988); Joseph A. Califano, Jr., *The Triumph and Tragedy of Lyndon Johnson: The White House Years* (New York, 1991), 253–272; Herbert Y. Schandler, *The Unmaking of a President: Lyndon Johnson and Vietnam* (Princeton, NJ, 1977); "A Call to Resist Illegitimate Authority," *New York Review*, Oct. 12, 1967, as reproduced in Jones, ed., *Safeguarding the Republic*, 267–269.

54. A thorough study of Nixon's foreign policy achievements is Herbert S. Parmet,

But the immediate response to Nixon's foreign policy was to discredit and weaken the president's power over foreign relations. Once a cease-fire ending the war was reached in January, 1973, Congress adopted the pretense that it had never acquiesced in the war. In summer it began to cut off funds for further military activity in Southeast Asia, thus ensuring the subsequent slaughter of millions. Then in November Congress passed, over the president's veto, the War Powers Resolution, aimed at making future armed ventures by the United States the joint responsibility of Congress and the White House. The resolution required that "in every possible instance" the president "consult with Congress" before sending American forces "into hostilities or into situations where imminent involvement in hostilities is clearly indicated." If, in the absence of a declaration of war, the president should send troops into hostile situations or enlarge combat forces where they were already stationed, he was required to notify Congress within forty-eight hours, and if Congress did not vote to approve the deployment the forces must be withdrawn within sixty days.[55]

Judgments on the merits of the War Powers Resolution were mixed.

Richard Nixon and His America (Boston, 1990). See also Richard M. Nixon's *Memoirs* (New York, 1978); Henry Kissinger, *White House Years* (Boston, 1979); Rowland Evans, Jr., and Robert D. Novack, *Nixon in the White House* (New York, 1971), 383–410; Franz Schurmann, *The Foreign Politics of Richard Nixon: The Grand Design* (Berkeley, CA, 1987); Paul Johnson, "In Praise of Richard Nixon," *Commentary* (Oct. 1988):50–53; Jones, *Course of American Diplomacy,* 620–639.

55. Alton Frye and Jack Sullivan, "Congress and Vietnam: The Fruits of Anguish," in *The Vietnam Legacy: The War, American Society and the Future of American Foreign Policy,* ed. Anthony Lake (New York, 1976), 194–215; Thomas and Thomas, *War-Making Powers,* 126–138; Reveley, *War Powers of the President and Congress,* 226, 287–297 (contains the resolution and Nixon's veto message; quotes at 288); Bradley Larschan, "The War Powers Resolution: Conflicting Constitutional Powers, the War Powers and U.S. Foreign Policy," *Denver Journal of International Law and Policy* 16 (1987):33–78; Marc E. Smyrl, *Conflict or Codetermination? Congress, the President, and the Power to Make War* (Cambridge, MA, 1988), 19–29; Wormuth and Firmage, *To Chain the Dog of War,* 190–193, 234. For an interesting article that shows public and media perceptions of the war—based on false but widely repeated allegations—and the mood that led to the War Powers Resolution, see Guenter Lewy, "Vietnam: New Light on the Question of American Guilt," *Commentary* (Feb. 1978):29–49.

As a gesture, it was a wholesome corrective to the abuses of presidential power, and its enactment may have caused subsequent presidents to act somewhat less precipitously in committing the armed forces. Whether it was constitutional was moot. If one was guided by the letter of the Constitution, it was obviously constitutional; if one was guided by constitutional usage, it was clearly unconstitutional. Every president from Ford through Bush took the latter position. When Ford sent armed forces to rescue the crew of *Mayaguez* in 1975, he phrased his notification, "In accordance with my desire that the Congress be informed on this matter and taking note of . . . the War Powers Resolution"—"taking note" of it, not in obedience to it—and his successors followed the same formula.[56]

The decline in the prestige of the presidency that began in 1967 and came close to totality in 1974 did not begin to pass until 1981. In the meantime, amid frustration and steadily declining popular morale in the aftermath of Vietnam, the United States met one foreign policy reversal after another. Terrorist activities abounded. A Communist regime came to power in Nicaragua, and Marxist rebels threatened to overthrow the government in El Salvador. President Carter, committed to a policy of human rights, sent "humanitarian" aid to both countries in an attempt to buy peace. Attributing unrest in Central America to hostility toward the United States, an attitude with which he sympathized, he negotiated treaties turning over the Panama Canal to the Republic of Panama and tried to minimize the American presence in Latin America. From the point of view of veteran cold warriors, Carter's administration was a catastrophe in which the United States government gave up trying to retain nuclear

56. *Congressional Quarterly Almanac,* 1975:310–311, 19-A; Wormuth and Firmage, *To Chain the Dog of War,* 219–223; Robert F. Turner, *Repealing the War Powers Resolution: Restoring the Rule of Law in U.S. Foreign Policy* (New York, 1991); Thomas and Thomas, *War-Making Powers,* 138–144; Smyrl, *Conflict or Codetermination?* 63–152; quote in Reveley, *War Powers of the President and Congress,* 302 (the text of Ford's report, May 15, 1975); Fisher, *Constitutional Conflicts,* 255–261, 268–277, 279–280; Michael J. Glennon, "The Gulf War and the Constitution," *Foreign Affairs* (Spring 1991):84–101; J. Gregory Sidak, "To Declare War," *Duke Law Journal* 41 (1991):29–121; Martha Liebler Gibson, *Weapons of Influence: The Legislative Veto, American Foreign Policy, and the Irony of Reform* (Boulder, CO, 1992), 142–152.

superiority and settled for parity under the doctrine of Mutually Assured Destruction: that if each side knew the other could destroy it in case of an attack, neither would attack. The nadir came in November, 1979, when "students" seized the American embassy in Teheran and held its personnel hostage for 444 days.[57]

Into this dreary and defeatist atmosphere Ronald Reagan brought a buoyant optimism and a simple faith in America, capitalism, and freedom, and a conviction that the Soviet Union was an "evil empire." He resurrected the Truman Doctrine, supporting anti-Communist forces in Africa and Central America. In 1983 he sent forces into Grenada to overthrow a Marxist regime, and in 1986 he ordered the bombing of Tripoli to retaliate against the terrorist activities supported by Libyan dictator Muammar al-Qaddafi. When the Solidarity Movement began Poland's break from Soviet control, he worked secretly and effectively with the pope to support the Polish workers.[58]

57. Donald S. Spencer, *The Carter Implosion: Jimmy Carter and the Amateur Style of Diplomacy* (New York, 1988); Walter Laqueur, "The World and President Carter," *Commentary* (Feb. 1978):56–63; Theodor Meron, "The Treaty Power: The International Legal Effect of Changes in Obligations Initiated by Congress," in Franck, ed., *Tethered Presidency,* 111–123; John Prados, *Presidents' Secret Wars: CIA and Pentagon Covert Operations from World War II through Iranscam* (New York, 1986), 349–356; Crabb and Holt, *Invitation to Struggle,* 75–97, 199–201; Phil Williams, "The President and Foreign Relations," in *Roosevelt to Reagan,* ed. Malcolm Shaw (London, 1987), 206–243; Thomas and Thomas, *War-Making Powers,* 144–145; *New York Times,* Jan. 21, 1981, 1:1, 1:3, 7:4; "444 Strikes and You're Out," *National Review,* Feb. 6, 1981, 75–76; Jones, *Course of American Diplomacy,* 656–685. Carl M. Brauer, *Presidential Transitions* (New York, 1986), 170–171, 220, notes that a poll of historians in 1982 placed Carter near the bottom of "average" presidents, just behind Ford and just ahead of Harrison; Carter's 21 percent approval rating in July 1980 was a record low for any president; Brauer finds it hard "to imagine his ever being seen as an inspirational leader or as a masterful politician."

58. Jones, *Course of American Diplomacy,* 702–709; Edwin Meese III, "The Man Who Won the Cold War: Ronald Reagan's Strategy for Freedom," *Policy Review* (Summer 1992):36–39; Edwin Meese III, *With Reagan* (Washington, DC, 1992), 163–173; *Newsweek,* Nov. 7, 1983, 52–58, 66–72, 83; "Letter from Washington," *National Review,* May 9, 1986, 15; Wormuth and Firmage, *To Chain the Dog of War,* 219–220 (a hostile account of the Grenada invasion); Ramsay Clark, "Libya, Grenada, and Reagan," *Nation,* May 3, 1986, 604–605 (another hostile view); Carl Bernstein, "The Holy Alliance," *Time,* Feb. 24, 1992, 28–35; "U.S.–Vatican Plot," *Christian*

Most tellingly, he set out to push the already faltering, inefficient Soviet economy into bankruptcy by pitting the vastly more productive American economic system against it. To that end, he cut American trade and credit to the Soviets, which had helped prop up the regime, and he banned the export of advanced technology to them. At the same time, he modernized the American military and resumed the arms race, now giving it a stunningly expensive dimension, that of Strategic Defense Initiative (SDI). Skeptics referred to it as "Star Wars" and said the technology would not work, but the Soviet Union did not dare to act on that assumption. As Reagan's Chief of Staff Donald Regan put it, "To stay in the arms race, the Russians had to spend a lot more money because President Reagan had committed the United States, with all its wealth and all its technical capacity, to developing . . . a defensive system that might make the entire Soviet missile force useless." The Soviets, tottering on bankruptcy, did not have the means to continue the race. Mikhail Gorbachev, representing a new generation of leadership that had come to power in the Soviet Union, sought an arms-reduction agreement in exchange for canceling SDI. That failing, in December of 1988 he took a bold step and announced a unilateral reduction of 500,000 troops from the Soviet armed forces and the withdrawal of some tank divisions from Eastern Europe. The next year the "evil empire" began to crumble, and by 1991 the Soviet Union itself had ceased to exist. The cold war was over.[59]

Century, April 1, 1992, 328–329; National Review, March 16, 1992, 16; Prados, Presidents' Secret Wars, 379–395 (a very hostile account); Robert A. Pastor, "The Centrality of Central America," in Looking Back on the Reagan Presidency, ed. Larry Berman (Baltimore, 1990), 33–49; Joseph Hogan, "The Reagan presidency: an assessment," in The Reagan years, ed. Hogan (Manchester, Eng., 1990), 304–306. Lech Walesa said that "Reagan was the only good candidate in your presidential campaign, and I knew he would win." He also thought that Reagan "will make the U.S. strong and make it stand up" to the Soviets; quoted in Roland Evans and Robert Novak, The Reagan Revolution (New York, 1981), 11, 12.

59. Francis P. Sempa, "Considerations on the Cold War," Presidential Studies Quarterly 22 (1992):611–612; Fareed Zakaria, "The Reagan Strategy of Containment," Political Science Quarterly 105 (1990):373–395; John Lewis Gaddis, "The Reagan Administration and Soviet-American Relations," in Reagan and the World, ed. David E.

This triumph might have restored to the presidency the prestige it had lost in the 1960s and 1970s but for the implacable hostility of the news media and the Iran-Contra affair, which they sought to use as another Watergate. Terrorists held several Americans hostage in Lebanon, and in mysterious ways the government was informed that if it supplied Iran with certain military spare parts, a "moderate" faction in that revolutionary theocracy would gain strength, thus softening Iran's hostility toward the United States and incidentally leading the moderates to use their influence to induce the Lebanese terrorists to release the hostages. The offer was sufficiently indirect so that it did not quite amount to a violation of the Reagan administration's pledge not to make deals with terrorists for hostages, and it was agreed to. Meanwhile, the administration's assistance to the anti-

---

Kyvig (New York, 1990), 17–38; Condoleezza Rice, "U.S.–Soviet Relations," in Berman, ed., *Looking Back,* 71–89 (a sound analysis of the policy written before the collapse of the Soviet empire); Donald T. Regan, *For the Record: From Wall Street to Washington* (New York, 1988), 328–355, 376–396 (quote at 331); Edwin Meese III, "The Man Who Won the Cold War," *Policy Review* 1992:38–39; David Mervin, *Ronald Reagan and the American Presidency* (London, 1990), 150–172. The disintegration of the Soviet bloc and of the Soviet Union itself is abundantly reported (not always accurately) from 1989 through 1991. But except for such journals as *National Review* and *Policy Review* there was little recognition at the time that the collapse was related to Reagan's policy. Reagan's own description of his policy is revealing: "Gorbachev must have realized it could no longer support or control Stalin's totalitarian colonial empire. . . . He must have looked at the economic disaster his country was facing and concluded that it couldn't continue spending so much of its wealth on weapons and on an arms race that—as I told him at Geneva—we would never let his country win" (*An American Life* [New York, 1990], 708). Some of Reagan's critics in the mid-1980s recognized clearly his intention to "deal from strength," gain "military superiority," and "bankrupt" the Soviets, but they were at great pains to deride the plan as naive and unworkable; see, for example, Russell J. Leng, "Reagan and the Russians: Crisis Bargaining Beliefs and the Historical Record," *American Political Science Review* 78 (1984):338–355, and Samuel P. Huntington, "The Defense Policy of the Reagan Administration, 1981–1982," in *The Reagan Presidency: An Early Assessment,* ed. Fred I. Greenstein (Baltimore, 1983), 88–101. Other critics still maintain that Reagan's policy was not successful; see Lou Cannon, *President Reagan: The Role of a Lifetime* (New York, 1991), 296–297, 314–315, 318–319, 321–322, 332–333, 492, 739ff., 791. For a full explication of the policy, see George P. Shultz, *Turmoil and Triumph: My Years as Secretary of State* (New York, 1993).

Communist rebels (contras) in Nicaragua had met with on-again, off-again support in Congress. In 1984 Congress adopted the Boland amendment, prohibiting the use of any public funds for the contras, whereupon the administration began soliciting private funds and money from foreign governments to continue the aid. That was not strictly illegal, but it was obviously in violation of the intent of Congress. Then somebody—probably Robert C. McFarlane, the national security adviser, and Col. Oliver North—hatched the idea of selling the spare parts to Iran at a profit and using the proceeds to supply the contras.[60]

These doings began to come to light two days after the 1986 congressional elections, and for several months it appeared that Iran-Contra would become a destructive scandal. The president and other high officials admitted knowledge of both the spare-parts deal with Iran and the private supplying of the contras but denied that they had known about the linkage. Most Democrats were convinced they were lying and cried "cover-up"; even people disposed to believe Reagan were upset by the notion that such things could go on without the president's knowing. Some observers pointed out that it had been standard procedure to engage in covert activities that assistants knew the boss wanted to happen but to keep him uninformed about such actions so that he could retain "deniability." Whatever the truth—and the subject was probed by a special commission headed by former senator John Tower, by a joint committee of Congress, and by an independent counsel—the scandal petered out, no effective new restrictions were imposed on the presidency, Ronald Reagan left office a popular man, and George Bush won the presidential election of 1988 handily. (The Nicaraguan Communists were voted out of power in free elections held in 1990, and the last of the American hostages

60. *Congressional Quarterly Almanac,* 1984:86–93. For Iran-Contra, see ibid., 1987: 57–111; Oliver North, *Under Fire: An American Story* (New York, 1991); United States Congress, Select Committee on Secret Military Assistance to Iran and the Nicaraguan Opposition, *Taking the Stand: The Testimony of Lieutenant Colonel Oliver L. North* (New York, 1987); John Prados, *Presidents' Secret Wars,* 396–463, puts CIA director William Casey at the center of the Iran-Contra exchange.

came home from Lebanon in 1991.) At most, the lingering odor of
the Iran-Contra affair neutralized some of the trust in the presidency
that Reagan had won.[61]

But President Reagan's legacy in foreign affairs was a troublesome
one. President Bush inherited magnificent machinery for fighting a
cold war that ended not long after he took office. He had popular
support in the form of a new patriotism and a sense of pride; he had
electronic espionage wizardry that could keep every foot of the earth
under surveillance; he had well-trained combat forces equipped with
awesomely smart weaponry. The effectiveness of it was spectacularly
demonstrated in the Persian Gulf War in 1991, as was Bush's ability to
hold together a coalition five

Something quite different, however, was demonstrated by what
followed. The president declared at the time that the war represented
the emergence of a "new world order," but what had emerged was
chaos, not order. Moreover, the justification of the Gulf War as the
execution of a United Nations mandate had grave implications for
American sovereignty: It suggested that the president's federative
powers might in future be under the control neither of the president

---

61. *The Tower Commission Report: The Full Text of the President's Special Review
Board* (New York, 1987); "Special Report: The Iran Contra Affair," *Congressional
Quarterly Almanac,* 1986:415–447. I find Regan's *For the Record,* 3–109, a convincing
account of what happened and of who knew what and when; others may find it less
so. See also the account in Meese, *With Reagan;* Wormuth and Firmage, *To Chain the
Dog of War,* 26, quote Adm. John Poindexter's testimony that he "made a very
deliberate decision" to keep President Reagan uninformed so as to "provide some
future deniability for the President if it ever leaked out." George C. Edwards III,
Presidential Approval: A Sourcebook (Baltimore, 1990), 169, has a graph of Reagan's
approval ratings: in 1981 and 1986 he hit his highest level of 68 percent; at the end of
1988 he had a 63 percent approval rating. *Commentary* (Sept. 1990) ran a symposium,
"The American 80's: Disaster or Triumph?" and views of Reagan's impact varied
widely; see especially Jeane J. Kirkpatrick, 14–16, Joseph Epstein, 25–27, Michael
Novak, 34–37, and Hilton Kramer, 50–52. See also Arturo J. Cruz, Jr., and Mark
Falcoff, "Who Won Nicaragua?" *Commentary* (May 1990):31–38, and *U.S. News &
World Report,* Dec. 16, 1991, 28–29. For the hostility of media and academia and the
continued attacks on Reagan, see Martin Anderson, "When The Losers Write The
History," *National Review,* Aug. 31, 1992, 58–62.

nor of the Congress but of the international body. In any event, Bush's approval rating plunged from a record high at the end of the war to a negative figure in less than a year, in no small measure because his skills in diplomacy and foreign affairs had somehow come to seem irrelevant.[62]

62. Richard Rose, *The Postmodern President: George Bush Meets the World,* 2d ed. (Chatham, NJ, 1991), 332–336; Jean Edward Smith, *George Bush's War* (New York, 1992); James Nathan, "Salvaging the War Powers Resolution," *Presidential Studies Quarterly* 23 (1993):235–268. *Gallup Poll Monthly* (Feb. 1991) notes in the February 24 poll that 86 percent approved of Bush's handling of the Gulf Crisis; in the February 24 poll 75 percent called the war "just" (in ranking American wars 89 percent regarded World War II as a just war; 25 percent characterized Vietnam as a just war). The March 1991 *Gallup Poll Monthly,* 2, headline read "Bush Approval at 89%, Highest in Polling History"; Bush's approval rating in March 1992, ibid., 27, was 42 percent. See also L. Gordon Crovitz, "How Bush Outflanked Iraq and Liberated the Constitution," *Wall Street Journal,* March 6, 1991, A, 9; Bruce Russett and James S. Sutterlin, "The U.N. in a New World Order," *Foreign Affairs* (Spring 1991):69–83; "A Tale of Two Bushes," *Time,* Jan. 7, 1991, 18–26. *Gallup Poll Monthly* (April 1992):2, presented a table of the importance of campaign issues; 93 percent said that the economy was very important as an issue; 67 percent thought AIDS very important; 38 percent regarded abortion as very important; 37 percent regarded foreign affairs as very important.

Images and Elections,

Myths and Symbols

That the policies of George Bush could seem irrelevant in 1992 was a function not of their content but of what that president, in his patented fashion, might have described as "the image thing." For in addition to the powers and responsibilities vested in the presidential office by the Constitution and those acquired over the years, the office inherently had the ceremonial, ritualistic, and symbolic duties of a king-surrogate. Whether as warrior-leader, father of his people, or protector, the president is during his tenure the living embodiment of the nation. Hence it is not enough merely to govern well; the president must also seem presidential. He must inspire confidence in his integrity, compassion, competence, and capacity to take charge in any conceivable situation. Indeed, it is scarcely possible to govern well in the absence of such confidence because the president's job is to persuade other people to implement his decisions, and his persuasiveness rests largely on what those others perceive his public perception to be. The image thus determines the reality.[1]

1. George Reedy, *The Twilight of the Presidency* (New York, 1970), chaps. 2, 3;

In part, a president's image is shaped (or distorted) spontaneously as a reflection of his personality, his physical appearance, his voice, or the act he has to follow. William Howard Taft, an extremely obese man, was a gifted and energetic political and administrative operator, but after the histrionics of the youthful Theodore Roosevelt, he was seen as a bloated and lethargic plutocrat. (Roosevelt said that Taft "means well feebly.") Gerald Ford, possibly the most athletic president since Washington, was nonetheless widely regarded as a clumsy oaf. Lyndon Johnson was more skillful in running the federal government than John Kennedy had been, but he was heartily disliked withal—even before the war in Vietnam took its toll—because he was a homely man with a cornball manner who followed a glamorous, polished predecessor.[2]

Emmet John Hughes, *The Living Presidency: The Resources and Dilemmas of the American Presidential Office* (New York, 1973), 55–58, 159–166, 218–219; Harold M. Barger, "The Prominence of the Chief of State Role in the American Presidency," *Presidential Studies Quarterly* 8 (1978):127–139; Barbara Hinckley, *The Symbolic Presidency* (New York, 1990), 133–143; Elmer E. Cornwell, Jr., *Presidential Leadership of Public Opinion* (Bloomington, IN, 1965); *The President and the Public,* ed. Doris A. Graber (Philadelphia, 1982); Mary E. Stuckey, *The President as Interpreter-in-Chief* (Chatham, NJ, 1991); Daniel J. Boorstin, *The Image: A Guide to Pseudo-Events in America* (New York, 1973); the 1984 issue (vol. 14) of *Presidential Studies Quarterly.* Hedley Donovan, "Job Specs for the Oval Office: A Memorial Essay," *Presidential Studies Quarterly* 21 (1991): 141–146, lists thirty-one necessary attributes, plus luck, most of which have to do with image. Tip O'Neill, *Man of the House,* with William Novak (New York, 1987), 314, said, "What Carter failed to understand is that the American people love kings and queens and royal families. They *want* a magisterial air in the White House, which explains why the Kennedys and the Reagans were far more popular than the four first families who came in between."

2. Roosevelt's quotation on Taft is from George Will's column, *Tuscaloosa News,* July 30, 1992, A, 6; on Johnson, see Eric Goldman, *The Tragedy of LBJ* (New York, 1969), 418–475, esp. 437; Richard H. Rovere, *Waist Deep in the Big Muddy: Personal Reflections on 1968* (Boston, 1968), 6–7; O'Neill, *Man of the House,* 182; Tom Wicker, *JFK and LBJ: The Influence of Personality Upon Politics* (New York, 1968); on Ford, see Ron Nessen, *It Sure Looks Different from the Inside* (Chicago, 1978), 170–178; see also Joseph C. Spear, *Presidents and the Press: The Nixon Legacy* (Cambridge, MA, 1984), 280; John Tebbel and Sarah Miles Watts, *The Press and the Presidency: From George Washington to Ronald Reagan* (New York, 1985), 519. Taft was concerned about his image; in 1910, for example, he sought to identify himself with the national pastime

In general, however, the president's image is the product of craft, deception, legerdemain, the calculated manipulation of words and pictures that begins when the candidate first decides to seek the office. Nor does it stop when the president leaves the White House; friends and admirers raise enormous sums of money to build palatial monuments in the form of presidential libraries, and former presidents customarily seek to establish their place in history by writing memoirs that put the best face on their brief reigns. Those players who stage the best show win the power and—usually but not invariably—win star billing in the history books as well.[3]

It would be easy to suppose that the cynical approach to presidential image making was a function of the television age and that in some pristine past things were otherwise. In truth, the system emerged in the 1820s and 1830s, and though a succession of techno-

of baseball by throwing out the first ball in the Washington Senators' opening game—a practice that became a tradition; Lawrence S. Ritter, *Lost Ballparks: A Celebration of Baseball's Legendary Fields* (New York, 1992), 85. For Ford's image as created by the press, see Mark J. Rozell, *The Press and the Ford Presidency* (Ann Arbor, MI, 1992), 10, 129–130, 146–148, 156–157, 214–216, and passim. As Peter Lisagor said, "I honestly believe that we, the press, created the imperial presidency. . . . In the American personality somewhere there must be a royal itch, a kind of an imperial itch [that] we feed on" (quoted in Lou Cannon, *Reporting: An Inside View* [Sacramento, CA, 1977], 237).

3. Reedy, *Twilight of the Presidency,* 22–23; Kathleen Hall Jamieson, *Packaging the Presidency: A History and Criticism of Presidential Campaign Advertising,* 2d ed. (New York, 1992); Homer F. Cunningham, *The Presidents' Last Years: George Washington to Lyndon B. Johnson* (Jefferson, NC, 1989), 299–301; Doris Kearns, *Lyndon Johnson and the American Dream* (New York, 1976), 355–357; Thomas Brown, *JFK: History of an Image* (Bloomington, IN, 1988), 6–8, 41–45, 80–83; *New York Times,* May 23, 1971, 1:1, Oct. 13, 1985, B, 30:1; Robert F. Burk, "New Perspectives for Presidential Libraries," *Presidential Studies Quarterly* 11 (1981):399–410. The main exceptions were Lincoln and Truman, who had bad presses while president but came to be regarded as great, and Harding and Coolidge, who were popular while president but came to be judged harshly. As part of the shaping process, see among others, Lyndon Baines Johnson, *The Vantage Point: Perspectives of the Presidency 1963–1969* (New York, 1971); Gerald R. Ford, *A Time To Heal: The Autobiography of Gerald R. Ford* (New York, 1979); and Rosalynn Carter, *First Lady from Plains* (Boston, 1989). See also James Reston, "What Was Killed Was Not Only The President But The Promise," *New York Times Magazine,* Nov. 15, 1964, 24.

logical changes necessitated and facilitated new techniques, the rules and the game remained essentially the same in 1992 as they had been for more than a century and a half.

———— During the era of the Jeffersonian presidents, partisan newspapers on both sides attempted to portray their candidates as larger than life, but for electioneering purposes there was not much to be gained since presidential politics was an insider's game. The suffrage was confined to white male adults, in several states to propertied white males. Moreover, as late as 1816 nearly half the presidential electors were still elected by the state legislatures. As a practical matter, presidents were the creatures of Congress, for the two parties decided upon their candidates in caucuses held at the end of the last session before each presidential contest. In practice, too, a regular order of succession was established, for the Republicans always opted to support the secretary of state, and he always won over his Federalist rival.[4]

The caucus system broke down in 1824 under the weight of numbers. By that time nearly everybody had become a Republican—Federalists held roughly a tenth of the seats in Congress—and when there is only one party it tends to break into factions. In any event, the Republican caucus could not agree on a single candidate for 1824, with the result that no candidate won a majority of the electoral

4. William N. Chambers, *Political Parties in a New Nation* (New York, 1963); Stuart Gerry Brown, *The First Republicans: Political Philosophy and Public Policy in the Party of Jefferson and Madison* (Syracuse, NY, 1954); M. Ostrogorski, *Democracy and the Party System in the United States: A Study in Extra-Constitutional Government* (New York, 1912), 7–12; Noble E. Cunningham, Jr., *The Jeffersonian Republicans in Power* (Chapel Hill, NC, 1963). In hotly contested state elections there were often large turnouts, but as the Federalist party declined, participation dropped precipitously. In New Hampshire, 80 percent of the eligible voters cast ballots in the gubernatorial election of 1814, but the percentage fell to 44 in 1822; in Connecticut voter participation dropped from 45 percent in 1819 to 22 percent in 1822; in Rhode Island the decline was from 50 percent in 1818 to 15 percent in 1819. Richard P. McCormick, "Political Development and the Second Party System," in *The American Party Systems: Stages of Political Development,* ed. William Nisbet Chambers and Walter Dean Burnham, 2d ed. (New York, 1975), 95–96, 107n; Chilton Williamson, *American Suffrage from Property to Democracy, 1760–1860* (Princeton, NJ, 1960).

votes, and the choice was made by the House of Representatives. Allegedly after a "corrupt bargain" between Speaker Henry Clay and second-runner John Quincy Adams, Adams was elected instead of the front-runner Andrew Jackson.[5]

Jackson thought that he had been robbed and "the people" defrauded. His desire to be president, moderate before 1824, became a consuming passion, and from that passion a new Democratic party was born. Various other politicians, for their own reasons, agreed to support Jackson in 1828. John C. Calhoun, for instance, had a large following in his native South Carolina and among the Scotch-Irish in Pennsylvania, and he endorsed Jackson's bid in the expectation that the Jacksonians would back him for vice-president (which they did) and as Jackson's successor in 1832 (which they did not). The whole enterprise was orchestrated by the wily Martin Van Buren of New York, who saw future opportunities for himself but who, like many another political operative, was driven mainly by a love of the manipulative game.[6]

5. Henry Jones Ford, *The Rise and Growth of American Politics: A Sketch of Constitutional Development* (New York, 1989), 157–158; Eugene H. Roseboom and Alfred E. Eckes, Jr., *A History of Presidential Elections: From George Washington to Jimmy Carter,* 4th ed. (New York, 1979), 36–42; Ostrogorski, *Democracy and the Party System,* 12–17; Joseph E. Kallenbach, *The American Chief Executive* (New York, 1966), 94–95. Federalists in 1824 held 4 of the 48 Senate seats and 26 of 213 in the House; Bureau of the Census, *Historical Statistics of the United States* (Washington, DC, 1961), 691. Robert V. Remini, *Henry Clay* (New York, 1991), 234–250; Mary W. M. Hargreaves, *The Presidency of John Quincy Adams* (Lawrence, KS, 1985), 19–40; Samuel Flagg Bemis, *John Quincy Adams and the Union* (New York, 1956), 11–53; Philip Jackson Green, *The Life of William Harris Crawford* (Charlotte, NC, 1965), 199–225; Chase C. Mooney, *William H. Crawford, 1772–1834* (Lexington, KY, 1974), 269–301.

6. Chambers, *Political Parties,* 206–207; Theodore J. Lowi, "Party, Policy, and Constitution in America," in Chambers and Burnham, eds., *American Party Systems,* 243–244; Roseboom and Eckes, *Presidential Elections,* 42–44; Robert V. Remini, *The Election of Andrew Jackson* (Philadelphia, 1963); Florence Weston, *The Presidential Election of 1828* (Washington, DC, 1938); *The Essential Calhoun: Selections from Writings, Speeches, and Letters,* ed. Clyde N. Wilson (New Brunswick, NJ, 1992), xxi–xxii, 333–334, 351. Davy Crockett wrote of Van Buren that "he is an artful, cunning, intriguing, selfish, speculating lawyer" whose fame was as "a most adroit political manager" (Tebbel and Watts, *Press and Presidency,* 93). See also Douglas W. Jaenicke, "The Jacksonian Integration of Parties into the Constitutional System," *Political Science Quarterly* 101 (1986):85–107.

The election of 1828 was entirely personal. Though Adams had a superb record as a diplomat and though his presidency was marked by prosperity, his supporters chose to conduct a negative campaign. They characterized Jackson as an uncouth frontier ruffian, a murderer, and an adulterer. They slandered his wife. They charged that his mother had been the concubine of a black man and thus that he was a bastard mulatto. The Jackson men responded in kind, charging Adams with corruption, with using public funds for private advantage, for having had premarital sex with the woman he later married, and for being involved, while minister to Russia, in facilitating the seduction of an American girl by the tsar. But they also ran a positive campaign, playing upon Jackson's heroism in winning the Battle of New Orleans and depicting him as the champion of the common man against the "interests."[7]

The striking fact about the 1828 election, and the quality that distinguished it dramatically from the election of 1800, is that nothing at all was said about what the candidates would do if elected. Nobody knew, possibly not even the candidates themselves, and nobody seemed to care. Adams and Jackson wanted to be president, not to do anything as president. The thousands of volunteers who campaigned for them did so partly because they were attracted to their man but more commonly because they sought the patronage—in the broad sense of the term, including public lands, construction contracts, printing contracts, roads, and harbor improvements as well as jobs—that the winner could dispense to the faithful. Because the sole purpose of the organization of the Democratic party was to elect Jackson and because the party represented a cross-section of people with different and sometimes mutually exclusive views on public policy, there was no way to campaign except by manufacturing artificial images of the candidate.[8]

7. Remini, *Election of Jackson*, 151–163; Weston, *Election of 1828;* James E. Pollard, *The Presidents and the Press* (New York, 1947), 149–153; Tebbel and Watts, *Press and Presidency*, 70–75.

8. Tebbel and Watts, *Press and Presidency*, 78–81. A good brief analysis of patronage in the broad sense used here is Theodore J. Lowi, *The Personal President: Power Invested, Promise Unfulfilled* (Ithaca, NY, 1985), 25–28. John C. Calhoun's description of the party system is precisely to the point: "The sole object of strife is to elect a

Two developments, the adoption of the convention system of nominating candidates and the rise of the Whigs as a full-fledged opposition party, were soon forthcoming. The nominating convention had been evolving as a means of choosing local and state candidates, and in 1831 a splinter group called the Antimasonic party held the first national convention. Democrats adopted the innovation, as did the rival Whigs. Delegates to the national conventions were selected by state conventions whose members had been picked by local conventions at the county, town, city, or ward level. The convention system became an immense and elaborate pyramid involving participation by tens of thousands—and then hundreds of thousands and ultimately millions of people. The party organizations thus established became semipermanent.[9]

The Whig party tried a number of variations on the general approach pioneered by the Democrats. In 1836, in a foolhardy experiment, they ran regional candidates, hoping to prevent Van Buren's getting a majority and seeking to throw the election into the House. In that campaign and again in 1840 William Henry Harrison traveled around giving speeches in behalf of his own candidacy. (Though he won in 1840, subsequent candidates maintained the polite eighteenth-century pretense that the office seeks the man—until 1896, when

---

President, in order to obtain the control through him of the powers of the government. The only material difference between the two parties is, that the Democraticks look more exclusively to plundering through the finances & the treasury, while the Whigs look more to plundering by whole sale, through partial legislation, Banks, Protection and other means of monopoly. . . . Both have entirely forgot the principles, which originally gave rise to their existence; and are equally proscriptive & devoted to party machinery. To preserve party machinery & to keep up party union are paramount to all other considerations" (Wilson, ed., *Essential Calhoun*, 341).

9. McCormick, "Second Party System," in Chambers and Burnham, ed., *American Party Systems*, 101, 104–107; Lowi, *Personal President*, 36–37; V. O. Key, Jr., *Politics, Parties & Pressure Groups*, 5th ed. (New York, 1964), 399–433; James W. Davis, *The President as Party Leader* (New York, 1992), 23; James S. Chase, *Emergence of the Presidential Nominating Convention, 1789–1832* (Urbana, IL, 1973); James S. Chase, *The National Party Convention: Retrospect and Prospect* (St. Charles, MO, 1974); Congressional Quarterly, *National Party Conventions 1831–1972* (Washington, DC, 1976), 21–99; William Preston Vaughn, *The Antimasonic Party in the United States, 1826–1843* (Lexington, KY, 1983), 25–26.

William Jennings Bryan toured the nation, giving the same rousing campaign speech hundreds of times.) In the hard-cider and log-cabin campaign of 1840 the Whigs created a carnival atmosphere, holding torchlight parades, featuring floats and effigies, and staging mass rallies at which portable log cabins were stocked with coonskin caps, barrels of cider, and campaign hats for distribution to prospective voters. They had not yet adopted the Democratic practice of drafting and publishing campaign platforms, but they stole a page from the Jacksonians' original book by choosing former generals as candidates. In the years between 1840 and 1888, the United States elected as president six former generals and five lifetime civilians; of the six, all were Whigs or the Whigs' successors, the Republicans, and all the civilians except Lincoln were Democrats.[10]

To supplement the showmanship, the parties developed various devices for lending the illusion of substance and seriousness to their campaigns. One was the creation of images for the parties as well as for their candidates. In a vague sort of way, the Whigs depicted themselves as the party of respectability, loose construction of the Constitution, federal promotion of economic growth, congressional dominance, and energetic national government; the Democrats posed as the party of the common man, strict construction, economy in government, the farmer, relatively strong presidents, and states' rights. Again, the parties invented the campaign "issue." An ideal issue, from the politicians' point of view, had little substance and was ethically neutral but could inflame voters as if it were a primal moral cause. Good issues at the time included protective tariffs and the recharter of the Bank of the United States; emphatically not good issues, because they were genuinely moral and potentially explosive, were slavery and Indian policy.[11]

10. Davis, *President as Party Leader,* 23; Roseboom and Eckes, *Presidential Elections,* 50–52; Robert Gray Gunderson, *The Log-Cabin Campaign* (Lexington, KY, 1957); Tebbel and Watts, *Press and Presidency,* 93–94, 98–104. In 1836 Richard M. Johnson, Democratic candidate for vice-president, fell one vote short of a majority, and for the only time in American history the Senate chose the vice-president. Data on generals are my tabulations from standard biographical sources.

11. Lawrence Frederick Kohl, *The Politics of Individualism: Parties and the American Character in the Jacksonian Era* (New York, 1989); Ostrogorski, *Democracy and the*

Presidential campaigns (notice the military metaphor) came by these means to be ritual substitutes for war, battles between the forces of good and the forces of evil. It was a poor way to choose a king, but it was an excellent way to release tensions among economic classes, ethnic groups, and sections. To be sure, the system came apart upon the disintegration of the Whig coalition in the 1850s, but the Republican coalition emerged as a replacement almost immediately. Moreover, the ritual contributed powerfully to bringing on the Civil War, for when its function of concentrating and then dissipating hostilities failed in the face of a real issue—slavery—mock warfare was replaced by real warfare. Even so, the party system was such an effective instrument of social control, appealing to something deep in the American psyche, that it slipped easily into operation, fundamentally unchanged, as soon as the Civil War and Reconstruction passed.[12]

And, despite continuing technological revolutions and widespread discontent with the system, it was in operation and fundamentally unchanged in 1992. (There is no point in asking why Americans get caught up in the presidential election ritual even when the campaigns are obviously manipulative and the candidates are far from the best the country has to offer—just as it is pointless to inquire why ancient

---

Party System, 36–50; Wilfred E. Binkley, *American Political Parties: Their Natural History,* 4th ed. (New York, 1962), 152–205; Robert A. Rutland, *The Democrats From Jefferson to Carter* (Baton Rouge, LA, 1979), 82–105; Michael Novak, *Choosing Presidents: Symbols of Political Leadership,* 2d ed. (New Brunswick, NJ, 1992), 16–18, 24–26, 41, 43–47, 63–68.

12. See, for example, Ollinger Crenshaw, *The Slave States in the Presidential Election of 1860* (Baltimore, 1945); Emerson David Fite, *The Presidential Campaign of 1860* (New York, 1911); Paul Leland Haworth, *The Hayes-Tilden Disputed Presidential Election of 1876* (Cleveland, OH, 1906); Reinhard Luthin, *The First Lincoln Campaign* (Cambridge, MA, 1944); Keith Ian Polakoff, *The Politics of Inertia: The Election of 1876 and the End of Reconstruction* (Baton Rouge, LA, 1973). For a perceptive brief analysis of ritual elections as mock warfare, see George E. Reedy, "The Presidency in the Era of Mass Communications," in *Modern Presidents and the Presidency,* ed. Marc Landy (Lexington, MA, 1985), 35–37. Michael Novak, *Choosing Presidents,* 49, says Ray Price advised Nixon that "the response is to the image, not to the man, since 99 percent of the voters have no contact with the man. It's not what's there that counts, it's what is projected."

Romans accepted unquestioningly the divinations of soothsayers, or why tribal peoples believe in their totems, or why pentecostals have confidence in their healers. All rituals rest upon faith, not logic; all involve suspension of disbelief; and all seem as reasonable to the faithful as they seem absurd to unbelievers.)

————— The Civil War did repolarize American politics. In the 1840s and 1850s practically every state had a functioning two-party system, and either party could win state and local as well as presidential elections. After the war New England and the trans-Mississippi Middle West were Republican, and the South was solidly Democratic. The remaining eight or ten states had two-party systems and could go either way in presidential elections. Consequently, the parties directed their presidential campaigns toward winning the swing states, taking the others for granted. It should be added that not even the swing states swung often: In the half century after 1860, Democrats won the presidency only in 1884 and 1892.[13]

That half century saw the development of a number of tools for sharpening the images of presidents and presidential candidates. Given the limitations on travel and communication prior to the Civil War, a minuscule portion of the voters saw or heard a candidate or a president. Images, therefore, had to be fabricated by the printed word, and each voter could conjure his own vision. Then, along with the technology that made mass-circulation newspapers and magazines possible, came photography and the capacity to reproduce photographs in the print media. In addition, increased productivity resulting from technological innovation—the linotype machine, high-speed rotary presses, cheap pulp paper, and the like—created an enormous demand for news, gathered by practitioners of the new craft, reporters, and circulated nationally by the wire services provided by the Associated Press. Demand far exceeded supply, and reporters early on learned to file stories about nonevents such as speeches, ceremonies, and rumors. In those circumstances, trivial doings became marketable products, for presidents and candidates were among the few

13. These observations are based upon the table in *Historical Statistics of the United States,* 682–693.

people whose names newspapers readers everywhere could recognize. Beginning around 1885 Americans were fed information (or misinformation or disinformation) about their president on a daily basis.[14]

Theodore Roosevelt was the first president to take full advantage of the mass media by becoming his own press agent. To be sure, President McKinley had paved the way, as he did with other innovations attributed to Roosevelt. McKinley had space and a large table and chairs provided for reporters in the outer reception room of the White House, and there, according to the journalist Ida Tarbell, "representatives of half a dozen or more papers [were] always to be found." Every evening about ten o'clock they were briefed at length by McKinley's secretary, John Addison Porter. Most White House press correspondents, however, were allowed only to hang around outside, where they interviewed callers leaving the building after presidential appointments; it was an unwritten rule that the president himself was not to be bothered with questions as he passed "newspaper row" unless he stopped to talk with the reporters. The story is told that Roosevelt saw them one day in unusually inclement weather and invited them inside, and later in his administration, when an executive office wing was added to the White House, he saw to it that the wing included a sizable and well-equipped press room.[15]

Roosevelt's relations with the press were unprecedentedly casual and candid. The contrast of his style to McKinley's was striking. McKinley, in his 1896 "front porch" campaign, had received large numbers of reporters at his Canton, Ohio, home, but he saw none in his reelection noncampaign in 1900, saying that "the proprieties demand that the President should refrain from making a political can-

14. Frank Luther Mott, *American Journalism, A History of Newspapers in the United States Through 260 Years: 1690 to 1950,* rev. ed. (New York, 1950), 388–406, 495–513, 591–592; Cornwell, *Presidential Leadership of Public Opinion,* 10–13; Elmer E. Cornwell, Jr., "Presidential News: The Expanding Public Image," *Journalism Quarterly* 36 (1959):275–283; Pollard, *Presidents and the Press,* 499–566; Boorstin, *Image,* 14–16. United Press was formed in 1907, International News Service in 1909.

15. Lewis L. Gould, *The Presidency of William McKinley* (Lawrence, KS, 1980), 2, 38, 92–93; Cornwell, *Presidential Leadership of Public Opinion,* 16–20; Pollard, *Presidents and the Press,* 557–558, 574; Ida M. Tarbell, "President McKinley in War Times," *McClure's Magazine,* July 1898, 209–224 (quotation at 214).

vass in his own behalf." Roosevelt talked with reporters endlessly. He used them to float trial balloons and to leak information for political purposes, he held informal press conferences, and he regularly invited a handful of reporters to chat while he had his daily shave, just after noon. Furthermore, his personal secretary, William Loeb, Jr., was "in all but name the President's press secretary," feeding the reporters colorful anecdotes about Roosevelt's family as well as serious information. By such means the people could feel for the first time that they really knew their president. He increased that feeling by traveling for speech-making purposes far more than any predecessor.[16]

These doings were part of a shrewdly calculated agenda to win the presidency for Roosevelt "in his own right" in 1904—no vice-president succeeding to the presidency on the death of the incumbent had ever been nominated for another term—but they also reflected Roosevelt's deeper understanding of the office. He called the presidency a bully pulpit, and he chose his words carefully, recognizing that the people expected the president in his monarchical capacity to be a moral leader. Congress symbolically endorsed that function when, in 1906, it voted him a generous fund for railroad travel, thus putting his pulpit on wheels.[17]

Roosevelt was a vigorous performer in another arena, that of the newly instituted presidential primary. A movement for presidential primaries had been afoot for some time prior to 1912, supported by

16. Edward N. Saveth, "Theodore Roosevelt: Image and Ideology," *New York History* 72 (1991):66, remarks that "Roosevelt *was* his imagery." Pollard, *Presidents and the Press,* 569–598; Cornwell, *Presidential Leadership of Public Opinion,* 13–26; Louis W. Koenig, *The Invisible Presidency* (New York, 1960), 136–189 (quote at 172); Mark Sullivan, *Our Times, 1900–1925,* 3 vols. (repr., New York, 1971), 3:71–75; Tebbel and Watts, *Press and Presidency,* 330–343; Lincoln Steffens, *The Autobiography of Lincoln Steffens* (New York, 1931), 508, 509–511; George Juergens, *News from the White House: The Presidential-Press Relationship in the Progressive Era* (Chicago, 1981); Erwin C. Hargrove, *Presidential Leadership* (New York, 1966), 19–22.

17. Roosevelt's concern with the image of the president as moral leader is illustrated by several libel suits he brought against publishers who had slurred his reputation—as, for instance, a Michigan newspaper that said "Roosevelt lies and curses in a most disgusting way; he gets drunk, too, and that not infrequently." He won that suit and was awarded minimal damages—six cents (Pollard, *Presidents and the Press,* 587–590). The travel fund was $25,000; *New York Times,* June 24, 1906, 4:5.

the same kind of elitists who supported civil service reform and for much the same reason—to cast off the rule of political bosses who dominated the party and its convention machinery. In 1912 a dozen states, mainly in the Middle West, adopted the primary system. Roosevelt, in his bid for a third term, entered them all, as did the Progressive hopeful Robert M. La Follette and President Taft. Roosevelt mopped up, carrying states with a total of 278 delegates as opposed to 48 for Taft and 36 for La Follette. But because most of the primaries were preferential, not binding, and because the incumbent controlled much of the party machinery, Taft won the Republican nomination. Failing to secure the nomination, Roosevelt defected from the party, and the Democratic candidate, Woodrow Wilson, won the election. (The primary system spread gradually, but more than half a century passed before primary elections became the determining factor in choosing candidates.)[18]

Wilson's relations with the press were strained, even though it was he who introduced the regularly scheduled press conference open to all reporters. As far as was possible, Wilson tried to get his speeches— which were masterful products—published in their entirety, out of an ideological conviction that he must, as his daughter put it, "take the people of the country into his confidence." Often, however, Wilson defeated his purpose by failing to produce advance copies. His secretary, Joseph P. Tumulty, had a genuine flair for public relations and a good rapport with the press, but he could not fully compensate for Wilson's deficiencies. Wilson made it clear that he was appalled by what he considered the reporters' impertinence, lack of respect, and prying ways. The reporters, for their part, regarded Wilson as cold and aloof, prone to lecture as if he were still a professor, and somewhat dictatorial in his efforts to control the news. Accordingly, despite great legislative successes, Wilson failed to capture the popular imagination during his first term.[19]

18. James W. Davis, *Presidential Primaries: Road to the White House* (New York, 1967), 24–37; Howard P. Nash, Jr., *Third Parties in American Politics* (Washington, DC, 1959), 217–264; Roseboom and Eckes, *Presidential Elections,* 136. As late as 1964 only sixteen states held primaries (F. Clifton White, *Suite 3505: The Story of the Draft Goldwater Movement* [New Rochelle, NY, 1967], 100).

19. Cornwell, *Presidential Leadership of Public Opinion,* 31ff.; Pollard, *Presidents and*

That changed during the war, when Wilson proved to be a skillful, ruthless, and frightening propagandist. His speech asking Congress to declare war was powerfully inspiring. "It is a fearful thing," he concluded, "to lead this great peaceful people into war, into the most terrible and disastrous of all wars, civilization itself seeming to be in the balance." But after itemizing the ideals for which the United States would fight, he ringingly declared that "the day has come when America is privileged to spend her blood and her might for the principles that gave her birth and happiness and the peace which she has treasured. God helping her, she can do no other."[20]

To conduct the war properly, he believed, the people must become infected by a "spirit of ruthless brutality," and to infect them Wilson established the Committee on Public Information, headed by a former newspaperman, George Creel. Creel enlisted ministers, college professors, and hordes of wordsmiths to write and distribute anti-German hate literature, distort history and current events, harangue audiences, and maintain a steady barrage of propaganda. High schools and colleges quit teaching German, orchestras stopped playing Wagner and Beethoven, teachers scoured high school and college history texts and literally cut out all favorable references to Germany. A subsidiary organization known as the Four-Minute Men gathered a team of 75,000 speakers who regularly delivered, simultaneously, identical four-minute speeches in motion-picture theaters, school auditoriums, and other public places across the country.[21]

---

the Press, 632–646; Eleanor Wilson McAdoo, *The Woodrow Wilsons* (New York, 1937), 274; Joseph P. Tumulty, *Woodrow Wilson as I Know Him* (New York, 1921); Hughes, *Living Presidency,* 165n.; Hargrove, *Presidential Leadership,* 42–44; George Juergens, "Woodrow Wilson and the Press," in *The Media,* ed. Kenneth Thompson (Lanham, MD, 1985), 185–193.

20. *Documents of American History,* ed. Henry Steele Commager, 7th ed. (New York, 1963), 2:128–132 (quotes at 132). For the background to the war message, see Arthur S. Link, *Woodrow Wilson: Campaigns for Progressivism and Peace* (Princeton, NJ, 1965), 419–426.

21. Cornwell, *Presidential Leadership of Public Opinion,* 48–57; George Creel, *How We Advertised America* (New York, 1920); George Creel, *Complete Report of the Chairman of the Committee on Public Information 1917: 1918: 1919* (Washington, DC, 1920); Harold D. Lasswell, *Propaganda Technique in the World War* (New York, 1927);

The message of hatred at home was counterbalanced by the promise of peace and brotherhood abroad. As fresh American troops by the hundreds of thousands landed in France in 1918, betokening a rapid end to the carnage, Wilson issued a series of proclamations calling for open diplomacy, freedom of the seas, freedom of trade, national self-determination of peoples, reduction of arms, and a league of nations to preserve a just and lasting peace. Europeans believed him and thought of him as their deliverer. When Wilson went to Europe after the war tens of millions of people cheered him, and women and children strewed flowers in his path as if he represented the Second Coming.[22]

Thus was created yet another persona for the president: the leader of the free world. It mattered not that no one could play the role successfully for long. The poet Robert Frost, a lifelong Democrat, captured the essence of Wilson's awesome legacy to future presidents when he wrote in 1928 that Wilson "saw as vastly as anyone that ever lived. He was a great something, if it was only a great mistake. And he wasn't merely his own mistake. He was the whole world's mistake." Then Frost added a penetrating judgment: "Some might think his failure was in missing a mark that someone to come after him will hit, but I suspect it was worse than that: he missed a mark that wasn't there in nature or in human nature."[23]

———— As Emmet John Hughes and others have pointed out, presidents at all times perform for "two constituencies: the living citizens

Frederick L. Allen, "The State Councils of Defense," *Century Magazine,* Dec. 1917; Illinois State Council of Defense, *Final Report of the State Council of Defense of Illinois, 1917–1918–1919* (Springfield, IL, ca. 1919); Cedric Larson and James R. Mock, "The Lost Files of the Creel Committee of 1917–19," *Public Opinion Quarterly* (Jan. 1939): 5–29; Elmer E. Cornwell, Jr., "Wilson, Creel and the Presidency," *Public Opinion Quarterly* (Summer 1959):189–202.

22. Arthur S. Link, *Woodrow Wilson the Diplomatist: A Look at his Major Foreign Policies* (Baltimore, 1957), 91–125; Frederick Lewis Allen, *Only Yesterday: An Informal History of the Nineteen-Twenties* (New York, 1931), 23–24; Kendrick A. Clements, *Woodrow Wilson: World Statesman* (Boston, 1987), 197–199.

23. Quoted in Peter J. Stanlis, "Robert Frost: Social and Political Conservative," *Chronicles* (August 1992):21.

and the future historians." The Republicans who served between Wilson and the second Roosevelt came to be judged by historians as mediocrities, if not disasters, but they did not fail in the cardinal function of image management in their own times. Harding, as a former newspaper editor, was especially skillful in working with the press; he understood and respected their needs. He reinstituted the regular press conferences that Wilson had dropped during the war, scheduling them twice weekly at different hours so that the timing favored neither morning nor afternoon papers. Harding controlled the content of the conferences by requiring that questions be submitted in advance, and he allowed no attribution of direct quotations (the phrase "according to a White House spokesman" came into vogue at this time), but he treated the reporters well, and they responded in kind. Specialists in political communication rate Harding as the equal or even the superior of that communications wizard, Franklin Roosevelt, in the management of the news. (Harding, incidentally, was the first to employ a full-time speechwriter to promote his image.) A measure of his effectiveness was the outpouring of grief when he died. The *New York Times* called it "the most remarkable demonstration in American history of affection, respect, and reverence for the dead."[24]

Herbert Hoover was so adept at image management that it can be said that he engineered his own demise. Hoover was world-renowned, for his wartime relief work in Belgium and for his monumental organization of the distribution of food in postwar Europe. As secretary of commerce under Harding and Coolidge he was extremely effective. He cultivated an image as a retiring, publicity-shy man, but he quietly and effectively managed to have his every accomplishment be attended with enormous publicity. Hoover entered the White House as the Great Engineer, the man who could perform miracles. When

24. Hughes, *Living Presidency*, 26, 96; Allen, *Only Yesterday*, 134; *New York Times*, Aug. 8, 1923, 1:5; Pollard, *Presidents and the Press*, 776–777; Cornwell, *Presidential Leadership of Public Opinion*, 70. Among the articles mourning Harding was a *New York Times* column, Aug. 4, 1923, 7:5, headed "Harding Is Mourned By Newspaper Men, Came Into Closer Contact With Them Than His Predecessors In Office Did." Indeed his dues as a member of the National Press Club were paid up to March 4, 1925.

he failed to perform the miracle of stopping the worldwide depression, he was renounced as a charlatan and an unfeeling one at that. Years of media hyperbole exaggerating both his qualities and the inherent mystique and power of the office contributed to the vehemence of the rejection. No previous president had been so openly blamed or reviled for economic difficulties. The difference between the election results of 1928 and 1932 attested the disappointment: Hoover carried the popular vote by roughly 21 million to 15 million in 1928 and lost it by 22 million to 15 million in 1932. (On the other hand, the results showed the stability of the ritual system, for though this was the most thoroughgoing reversal in American history and a time of severe dislocation, the net change of votes was six million—one voter in six.)[25]

Perhaps the most wily and gifted presidential image makers were Franklin Roosevelt and his cohorts. They also had one of the most difficult tasks. Roosevelt's polio attack, despite his determined efforts at rehabilitation, had left his legs almost totally paralyzed, and to a public that had seen two recent presidents incapacitated by the rigors of office—or, more properly, by the rigors of extended speech-making tours—the question of Roosevelt's health might have posed an insurmountable obstacle. He and his team removed the obstacle by pretending that it was not there. As governor and as president Roosevelt imposed a ban on photographs or newsreels showing his braces or showing him in a wheelchair, being lifted in or out of a car, or dragging himself along on his crutch and cane. To dramatize the illusion that he was in vigorous health, Roosevelt went to Chicago in 1932 to accept the Democratic nomination in person, and he flew

25. Cornwell, *Presidential Leadership of Public Opinion,* 99–109; *Dateline: Washington,* ed. Cabell Phillips et al. (Garden City, NY, 1949), 164–165; Drew Pearson and Robert Allen, *Washington Merry-Go-Round* (New York, 1931), 51–77; Charles Michelson, *The Ghost Talks* (New York, 1944), 27–33; Harris G. Warren, *Herbert Hoover and the Great Depression* (New York, 1959), 3, 19–38, 237–268; Pollard, *Presidents and the Press,* 737ff.; election figures from *Historical Statistics of the United States,* 682. David Burner, *Herbert Hoover* (New York, 1979), 91–92, 160ff, says that "Hoover was honestly uncomfortable with personal publicity" (91) but was a master at publicizing his enterprises. See also Patrick G. O'Brien and Philip T. Rosen, "Hoover and the Historians: The Resurrection of a President, Part II," *Annals of Iowa* (Fall 1981): 83–99.

there in a small airplane. The action was calculatedly reminiscent of the derring-do that people associated with his distant cousin Theodore.[26]

The press went along with the blackout on mentioning his infirmity; indeed, at the Democratic convention in 1936 Roosevelt fell full-length on his face while approaching the speakers' platform, and though hundreds of reporters saw the mishap, no photograph, cartoon, or mention of it appeared in print. *Time* magazine, whose publisher Henry Luce hated Roosevelt and his policies, did make references to his "shriveled legs" at first but discontinued the practice after readers protested. A handful of journals published pictures of him on crutches, but just a handful. The public was acutely aware that he had had polio, for it was publicized by the annual March of Dimes commemorating his birthday through raising money for polio research; but as David Brinkley wrote, "most Americans were unaware that Franklin Roosevelt had no use of his legs."[27]

The news media collaborated in the deception because Roosevelt thoroughly seduced the White House press corps. He reinstituted most of Harding's rules for press conferences but abolished the requirement of written questions. Any subject could be discussed. (When he feared that reporters might not ask about something he wanted to discuss, he would have press secretary Stephen Early plant a question with an especially friendly reporter.) Roosevelt could be extremely candid and lucid; at the first press conference in 1933 he explained the banking crisis and the measures he was taking to cope with it so clearly that, when the conference ended, the reporters burst into spontaneous applause—a response that had never before happened. He could also be charmingly evasive. The journalist John Gunther said of one interview that in twenty minutes the president's face had expressed "amazement, curiosity, mock alarm, genuine inter-

26. Betty Houchin Winfield, *FDR and the News Media* (Urbana, IL, 1990), 10–23; Frank Freidel, *Franklin D. Roosevelt: The Triumph* (Boston, 1956), 312–316; Hugh Gregory Gallagher, *FDR's Splendid Deception* (New York, 1985), 93–94; James MacGregor Burns, *Roosevelt: The Lion and The Fox* (New York, 1956), 139.

27. Brinkley, *Washington Goes to War,* 105; Winfield, *FDR and the News Media,* 114–115; Burns, *Roosevelt: Lion and Fox,* 273; *Time,* Jan. 2, 1933, 2, 4; Gallagher, *FDR's Splendid Deception,* 94–98, 100–102, 145–152.

est, worry, rhetorical playing for suspense, sympathy, decision, play-fulness, dignity, and surpassing charm. Yet he *said* almost nothing. Questions were deflected, diverted, diluted." He heaped favors on the reporters and intuitively knew that small kindnesses from a presi-dent could go a long way. One reporter said that "being called 'Bill' by the president left a glow that lingered while the news was being written."[28]

Roosevelt used press conferences for a variety of purposes. One was to cultivate the impression that he was fully in command of the country's situation and busy with a program that would end the de-pression. That was indeed a self-fulfilling public service, for the crisis of 1933 was a crisis of confidence as well as of institutions. Another purpose was what came to be called "putting a spin on the news," making policies seem other than they were. In support of his social security legislation, for instance, he induced the reporters to treat it not as a radical departure but as a "return to values lost in the course of our economic development and expansion." Perhaps the most im-portant function of the conferences was educational. To quote Gun-ther again, at the meetings Roosevelt "was like a friendly, informal schoolmaster conducting a free-for-all seminar." In addition to an-swering questions directly and for attribution, he discussed "off the record" matters that were to be held in strictest confidence (on pen-alty of ostracism were the confidence violated), and he instituted a "background" category of discussion consisting of "material which can be used by all of you on your own authority and responsibility, not to be attributed to the White House."[29]

Yet Roosevelt had a problem with the news media, one that to a lesser man or in different times might have been fatal: The reporters

28. Winfield, *FDR and the News Media,* 29–43 (quote at 33); Cornwell, *Presidential Leadership of Public Opinion,* 142–161; John Gunther, *Roosevelt in Retrospect: A Profile in History* (New York, 1950), 22–23; Raymond Clappe, "Why Reporters Like Roose-velt," *Review of Reviews* (June 1934):14–17.

29. Cornwell, *Presidential Leadership of Public Opinion,* 129 (first quotation), 147–148; Gunther, *Roosevelt in Retrospect,* 135 (second quotation); Winfield, *FDR and the News Media,* 38–42; Pollard, *Presidents and the Press,* 773–783; Graham J. White, *FDR and the Press* (Chicago, 1979), passim; Chalmers Roberts, "Franklin Delano Roosevelt and the Press," in Thompson, ed., *Media,* 185–193.

loved him but their editors and publishers did not. When he was first elected he won 57 percent of the popular vote but had the editorial support of 41 percent of the nation's daily newspapers, and the gap steadily widened. In 1936 he and his press advisers tried to appear above politics, and to some extent they succeeded. He took many "look-see" trips to inspect areas affected by droughts or floods, giving brief speeches and handing out "press releases," and since these activities were covered by wire services, on which most newspapers depended, the stories were generally printed. Too, his press people had taught the employees of the executive departments the ways of publicity so that a barrage of proadministration information was unleashed upon the press. But the *Chicago Tribune,* the *New York Daily News,* the *New York Sun,* the *New York Times,* the *Detroit Free Press,* the *Los Angeles Times,* and the powerful Hearst chain were vehemently antiadministration. Reporters from the Hearst papers and the *Chicago Tribune* were ordered not to write "anything that even suggested the possibility of Roosevelt's reelection." Roosevelt had the editorial support of just 37 percent of the daily papers in the year in which he won 60 percent of the popular vote. Running for his third term in 1940, he was supported by only 25 percent of the dailies while capturing 55 percent of the popular vote.[30]

Roosevelt outran the print media by taking his messages directly to the people through the medium of radio. Radio was not new; the first broadcast had been in 1920. Harding had spoken on the radio a few times, Coolidge did so about once a month, and Hoover as often as twice a month. But those presidents were uncomfortable before the microphones, had poor radio voices, and did not appreciate ra-

---

30. Winfield, *FDR and the News Media,* 86–87, 90, 127–147; Leo C. Rosten, "President Roosevelt and the Washington Correspondents," *Public Opinion Quarterly* (Jan. 1937):36–52; George Wolfskill and John A. Hudson, *All but the People: Franklin D. Roosevelt and His Critics, 1933–1939* (Toronto, 1969); Pollard, *Presidents and the Press,* 797–802, 809–814; Frank Luther Mott, "Newspapers in Presidential Campaigns," *Public Opinion Quarterly* (Fall 1944):348–367; Frederick Lewis Allen, *Since Yesterday: The 1930s in America* (New York, reissue 1986), 271–275; White, *FDR and the Press,* 49–66. For an updating of this situation, see Robert Locander, "Modern Presidential In-Office Communications: The National, Direct, Local, and Latent Strategies," *Presidential Studies Quarterly* 13 (1983):243–253.

dio's possibilities as an instrument for mass persuasion. By the time Roosevelt became president nearly two-thirds of the households in America had radio sets (more than four-fifths by 1940), and most families listened to those sets every night. Roosevelt recognized radio's potential and was an absolute natural at radio speaking.[31]

He did not, however, leave it to nature: He carefully scripted, diligently rehearsed, and beautifully executed the performances. Usually he formulated the main ideas he wanted to discuss and explained them in general terms to scriptwriters—Raymond Moley, Harry Hopkins, Samuel Rosenman, and others—who put them in logical sequence, whereupon the playwright Robert Sherwood polished the script and infused it with drama. Roosevelt then applied the final touches to adapt the script to his voice and sense of rhythm. He had a cultivated, upper-class accent and a voice that inspired confidence, but he spoke in a folksy way, eschewing oratory, using simple language and homey examples; it has been calculated that 75 to 80 percent of the words he used were among the 1,000 most commonly used words in the American tongue. He even made grammatical errors if correct speech would have sounded stilted or pretentious. He spoke quite slowly, around 100 words a minute. He often departed from the script to make a point more clearly, and he never sounded as if he was reading. He registered precisely the appropriate tone for everything he said. Sherwood, who had seen the greatest actors of Broadway, said, "I never saw a better actor than F.D.R."[32]

31. Joe S. Foote, *Television Access and Political Power: The Networks, the Presidency, and the "Loyal Opposition"* (New York, 1990), chap. 1, "Radio: Setting the Precedent"; Edward W. Chester, *Radio, Television, and American Politics* (New York, 1969), 23, 27; Samuel L. Becker, "Presidential Power: The Influence of Broadcasting," *Quarterly Journal of Speech* 47 (1961):11–14; Cornwell, *Presidential Leadership of Public Opinion*, 71–72, 89–94, 111–113, 253–265; Francis Chase, Jr., *Sound and Fury: An Informal History of Broadcasting* (New York, 1942), 287–303; Jamieson, *Packaging the Presidency*, 18–29; Allen, *Since Yesterday*, 103–106, 110.

32. Winfield, *FDR and the News Media*, 104–109; Richard Lee Strout, "The President and the Press," *The Making of the New Deal: The Insiders Speak*, ed. Katie Louchheim (Cambridge, MA, 1983), 12–15; Robert E. Sherwood, *Roosevelt and Hopkins: An Intimate History* (New York, 1948), 213–219; Samuel I. Rosenman, *Working with Roosevelt* (New York, 1952), 2–15, 124–127, 226–235, 297–302, 492–496; Cornwell, *Presidential Leadership of Public Opinion*, 284–289; Chester, *Radio, Television, and Politics*, 31.

Roosevelt's memorable performances included the first inaugural ("The only thing we have to fear is fear itself"), the war message to Congress ("Yesterday, December 7, 1941—a date which will live in infamy"), and his fireside chats. The chats were conversational, intimate broadcasts designed to explain, to educate, to uplift, or to persuade. He rationed the chats carefully to avoid diluting their impact by overexposure; during 1933 he broadcast twenty addresses but only four fireside chats. There were about twenty of the chats in twelve years; twice they failed to accomplish what he sought, but both times sensational real news—heavy bombing of London and the shelling of California, allegedly by a Japanese submarine—upstaged him. Normally, he established close rapport with the audience, and when he used personal words, "you and I know" or "together we cannot fail" or "my friends," the millions listening in their living rooms—a talk in May of 1941 drew an estimated 53,800,000 listeners—believed he was speaking directly to them.[33]

The airways were almost always available to him. Because he attracted audiences, the networks were usually eager to accommodate requests for air time; and besides, William Paley and David Sarnoff, heads of CBS and the Red and Blue NBC networks, which together had 86 percent of the station outlets, were close friends of the president. Whenever any network or stations threatened to balk, Roosevelt was not above using the Federal Communications Commission to whip them into line. The federal government had life or death power over radio if stations did not offer enough public service broadcasts, whereas it had no control over the press. When newspapers started buying into network radio in the late 1930s, the FCC conducted an investigation that resulted in separating the Red and Blue

33. Commager, ed., *Documents*, 2:240, 451; Sherwood, *Roosevelt and Hopkins*, 42–43, 225–228, 504, 548–599; Winfield, *FDR and the News Media*, 106–111; Cornwell, *Presidential Leadership of Public Opinion*, 253–254, 257–265; Frank Freidel, *Franklin D. Roosevelt: A Rendezvous with Destiny* (Boston, 1990), 99, 162, 195, 198, 322–323, 360, 406, 433, 499–500, 598; Waldo W. Braden and Earnest Brandenburg, "Roosevelt's Fireside Chats," *Speech Monographs* (Nov. 1955):290–302; Hinckley, *Symbolic Presidency*, 121–126; Chester, *Radio, Television, and Politics*, 32–50; Helen Sioussat, *Mikes Don't Bite* (New York, 1943), 160–165; Orrin E. Dunlap, Jr., *Talking on the Radio* (New York, 1936), 64–68, 75–82, 87–89, 95, 120–122.

NBC networks and reducing the network's control over affiliates, thereby preventing the press from gaining control of the medium. As for the "equal time" requirement of the Communications Act of 1934, providing that broadcasters offer time to opposing candidates during election years, Roosevelt got around it in 1936 and 1940 by maintaining that he was making "presidential," not "candidate" talks.[34]

———— After twelve years of listening to Franklin Roosevelt, American voters were hooked on hearing the presidential voice. In the words of a distinguished student of political communications, they were "led to believe that if a president can speak in public he can lead in private *and* that he is unable to do the latter unless he can do the former." The advent of television accentuated this perception, and accordingly presidents in the television era engaged not only scriptwriters but drama coaches and elocutionists and makeup artists and lighting experts—"a full-time rhetorical manufacturing plant."[35]

The television age for the presidency began in earnest in 1960. Television was in its infancy as Truman left office, and though Eisenhower used it to some extent (and engaged the movie actor Robert Montgomery as a coach), it was not much more significant to his presidency than radio had been to Coolidge's. The real beginning was

34. Sioussat, *Mikes Don't Bite,* 34; Foote, *Television Access and Political Power,* 20–21; Winfield, *FDR and the News Media,* 108–110; James M. Herring and Gerald C. Gross, *Telecommunications: Economics and Regulations* (New York, 1936), 376ff.; Newton N. Minow, *Equal Time: The Private Broadcaster and the Public Interest* (New York, 1964), 25–26, 74–84, 116–117, 176–184, 220–221.

35. Roderick P. Hart, *The Sound of Leadership: Presidential Communication in the Modern Age* (Chicago, 1987), 47 (the quotation), 158; Foote, *Television Access and Political Power,* 62; Douglas Kellner, *Television and the Crisis of Democracy* (Boulder, CO, 1990), 150–160; John Osborne, *White House Watch: The Ford Years* (Washington, DC, 1977), 259–267, 348–353, 418–426; Gregory W. Bush, "Edward Kennedy and the Televised Personality in the 1980 Presidential Campaign," in *American History, American Television: Interpreting the Video Past,* ed. John E. O'Connor (New York, 1983), 328–362; Haynes Johnson, *In the Absence of Power* (New York, 1980), 95–100; Peter Meyer, *James Earl Carter: The Man and the Myth* (Kansas City, MO, 1978), 107–108, 115–118, 127, 131, 134, 150–153; Herbert G. Klein, *Making It Perfectly Clear* (New York, 1980), 438–439; Robert J. Donovan and Ray Scherer, "Politics Transformed," *Wilson Quarterly* (Spring 1992):19–33.

the televised debates between candidates Richard Nixon and John F. Kennedy. That Vice-president Nixon consented to take part in the debates showed that he did not yet understand the impact of television. He could easily have begged off, saying that the dignity of his office precluded his taking part in meaningless exercises, but he had prided himself on his talents as a debater since high school, and he accepted Kennedy's challenge. Unless Nixon could have handled Kennedy the way Daniel Webster might have handled a schoolboy, however, he could not possibly have gained by the encounter. Although opinions differed as to who won, Kennedy came across as having far the more attractive personality, and television is a personality medium. Thus Nixon dissipated in one hour the advantage he had had as the experienced statesman running against the inexperienced youth.[36]

During Kennedy's short incumbency the presidency and television discovered one another. He allowed the cameras to come into the White House to film it and his photogenic wife and children, he sat for a long interview to introduce a half-hour format for "CBS Evening News," he opened the traditional press conferences to live telecast. At these Kennedy was cool, crisp, incisive, authoritative, and witty. Every presidential event or pseudoevent, whether showing him in a bad light (the Bay of Pigs fiasco, the encounter with Krushchev in Berlin) or in a favorable light (the Cuban missile crisis, the space shots) sent his popularity ratings soaring. Along the way, the networks built a large, permanent infrastructure of technicians, camera crews, correspondents, and producers solely for the purpose of covering the president's day-to-day activities. The White House responded

36. Foote, *Television Access and Political Power,* 62; Jamieson, *Packaging the President,* 139–161; Theodore H. White, *The Making of the President, 1960* (New York, 1967), 279–296; Sherman Adams, *Firsthand Report: The Story of the Eisenhower Administration* (New York, 1961), 296–298; Richard Gehman, "He 'Produces' the President," *Good Housekeeping* (Nov. 1955):64–67; Boorstin, *Image,* 41–44; Spear, *Presidents and the Press,* 50–51; Stephen Hess, "Only the Style Was Important," *Washington Post,* Sept. 1, 1972, A, 24; Kurt Lang and Gladys Engel Lang, "Ordeal by Debate: Viewer Reactions," *Public Opinion Quarterly* (Summer 1961):277–288. Pierre Salinger, *With Kennedy* (Garden City, NY, 1966), 47, said that Kennedy's "election would have been impossible without the debates"; Theodore C. Sorensen, *Kennedy* (New York, 1965), 201, concluded that "even a draw, if it was a draw, was a Kennedy victory."

by building its own television infrastructures. Being president had become full-time show business.[37]

The determinants of the relationship were numerous and varied. One constant was that the White House and the network news departments became interdependent, though the mutual dependence was as often parasitical as symbiotic. At an earlier time, the president had had the upper hand simply because he was president, and the reporters and commentators, even the best known of them, were relative nobodies; with the rise of the news anchors as celebrities, the balance became more nearly equal. Indeed, when the prestige of the presidency hit its nadir in the 1970s, polls revealed that CBS anchor Walter Cronkite was "the most trusted man in America." ("I can't compete with Walter Cronkite," Lyndon Johnson complained. "He knows television and he's a star.") Sometimes the relationship was adversarial, as when in 1969 Vice-president Agnew was sent on the hustings to lambaste the media elite as an "effete corps of impudent snobs" and "nattering nabobs of negativism," and as when, after both Agnew and Nixon had fallen, the networks danced gleefully on their corpses. Conservatives generally complained that television and the other media had a liberal bias—they obviously had a stake in big government, and most people in the television news industry did prefer Democratic candidates from 1964 to 1992. Radicals argued that they served the interests of corporate capitalism.[38]

37. David Halberstam, *The Powers That Be* (New York, 1979), 316–390; Mary Ann Watson, *Expanding Vista: American Television in the Kennedy Years* (New York, 1990); Foote, *Television Access and Political Power,* 30–35, 143–144; Joseph P. Berry, Jr., *John F. Kennedy and the Media: The First Television President* (Lanham, MD, 1987); James N. Giglio, *The Presidency of John F. Kennedy* (Lawrence, KS, 1991), 255, 260–263, 272–273, 287; Tebbel and Watts, *Press and Presidency,* 476–489; George C. Edwards III, *Presidential Approval: A Sourcebook* (Baltimore, 1990), 143–152; Lyn Ragsdale, "The Politics of Presidential Speechmaking," *American Political Science Review* 78 (1984): 971–984; *Ten Presidents and the Press,* ed. Kenneth W. Thompson (Washington, DC, 1983).

38. Foote, *Television Access and Political Power,* 136–137; Tebbel and Watts, *Press and Presidency,* 502–515; Spear, *Presidents and Press,* 111–176; Halberstam, *Powers That Be,* 434 (quoting Lyndon Johnson), 415, for Cronkite as "simply the most trusted man in America"; Erik Barnouw, *Tube of Plenty: The Evolution of American Television* (New York, 1975), 443–467; *Readings in Mass Communication,* ed. Michael C. Emery and

More important were the structural limitations imposed by the nature of television and the presidency as institutions. The need for short visual segments defined the news and how it occurred. For example, for the most part the network staffs had to decide in the mornings, before the day's news happened, which events would be the evening news so that camera crews could shoot film in time for selection and editing. Presidents scheduled ceremonial activities, such as bill signings, dedications, speeches, and the welcoming of dignitaries, to give the networks a suitable shopping bag of "news" to choose from. (One scholar has calculated that in 1976 President Ford, if it be assumed that he worked twelve hours a day during every day in the year, made a "newsworthy" appearance, on average, every six hours.)[39]

Similarly, because television deals in two-dimensional pictures accompanied by sounds, it often distorts reality even when every effort is made to be faithful to the truth. The *Washington Post* reporter Meg Greenfield wrote in 1984 of a campaign tour through Alabama with Sen. Gary Hart, then a candidate for the Democratic presidential nomination, at which the "crowds" were "miniscule—mostly little knots of people." Yet "given all the agitation and disruption and noisy *thronginess* the traveling party itself created in a series of fairly small settings," the tour "took on the aspect of a crush. That's what it

---

Ted Curtis Smythe (Dubuque, IA, 1972), Spiro T. Agnew, "The Des Moines Speech," Nov. 13, 1969, 309–318, and "The Montgomery Speech," Nov. 20, 1969, 347–353; Jody Powell, *The Other Side of the Story* (New York, 1984), 38–42; Edith Efron, *The News Twisters* (Los Angeles, 1971); Kellner, *Television and the Crisis of Democracy,* 163ff.; Donald T. Regan, *For the Record* (New York, 1988), 57–58; Hart, *Sound of Leadership,* 115–116. Stephen Hess, "All the President's Reporters: A New Survey of the White House Press Corps," *Presidential Studies Quarterly* 22 (1992):311–321, reported that in 1978, 42 percent of the corps considered itself liberal, 39 percent middle-of-the-road, and 19 percent conservative; in 1991 the figures were 42.4 percent, 24.2 percent, and 33.3 percent.

39. Edward Jay Epstein, *News from Nowhere: Television and the News* (New York, 1973), 133–199; Hart, *Sound of Leadership,* 7, 17–18, 40, 59–60; Hinckley, *Symbolic Presidency,* 89–98; Av Westin, *Newswatch: How TV Decides the News* (New York, 1982), 53–120; Fred Smoller, "The Six O'Clock Presidency: Patterns of Network News Coverage of the President," *Presidential Studies Quarterly* 16 (1986):31–49, and his *The Six O'Clock Presidency* (New York, 1990).

looked like on the screen. That's what people think happened." The networks' opportunities for deliberately distorting a president's or a candidate's speechifying were abundant, should the news people choose to do so, simply by selecting what they showed or by panning the live audience for favorable or hostile reactions—all the while maintaining the illusion of objectivity.[40]

Presidents had two main devices for taking control of what the public saw and heard of them, the press conference and "nonpolitical" speeches in the public interest. The effectiveness of the press conference for boosting a president's image depended on his ability to perform in that particular format, but there were general perils as well. If the conference was held during the day it reached a minimal audience; most people saw only edited excerpts on the evening news. If it was held in prime time, it often alienated viewers by disrupting regular programming, though the networks generally resorted to "sliding" or delaying programs rather than preempting them.[41]

The advantages to a president of directly televised speeches were described bluntly by John F. Kennedy: "I always said that when we don't have to go through you bastards, we can really get our story to the American people." To get free air time, the White House usually pretended it was offering a speech, not asking or demanding coverage, but through much of the sixties and into the seventies obtaining time was almost a matter of seizing it by force. The networks were terrified of Lyndon Johnson at first, and he commonly telephoned the

40. Hart, *Sound of Leadership,* 130; Robert E. Denton, Jr., *The Primetime Presidency of Ronald Reagan: The Era of the Television Presidency* (New York, 1988), 41–61; Stephen J. Wayne, *The Road to the White House 1992: The Politics of Presidential Elections* (New York, 1992), 232–233, 236, 237–238; David L. Altheide and Robert P. Snow, *Media Logic* (Beverly Hills, CA, 1979), 97–102; John Anthony Maltese, *Spin Control: The White House Office of Communications and the Management of Presidential News* (Chapel Hill, NC, 1992).

41. Foote, *Television Access and Political Power,* 143–144, 154–156; Westin, *Newswatch,* 204–215; Douglass Cater, "How a President Helps Form Public Opinion," *New York Times Magazine,* Feb. 26, 1961, 32, 27; Jarol B. Manheim and William W. Lammers, "The News Conference and Presidential Leadership of Public Opinion: Does The Tail Wag The Dog?" *Presidential Studies Quarterly* 11 (1981):177–188, and Jill McMillan and Sandra Ragan, "The Presidential Press Conference: A Study in Escalating Institutionalization," ibid., 13 (1983):231–241.

networks on a moment's notice, informing them he was on his way to the studios, even in the middle of a prime-time show. In 1964 he carried his high-handed ways to extremes in regard to the Democratic National Convention. A black female spokeswoman for the racially integrated Mississippi Freedom Democratic party, contesting the state's segregationist regular delegation, was testifying before the credentials committee; she broke down in tears before the national television audience as she described the beatings and other abuses she had suffered for being active in the civil rights movement. Johnson, furious at the prospect of a dissident group's shattering his dream of a unified, harmonious convention, had aides telephone the networks and say a news conference would begin immediately. The Mississippian's testimony was cut off, and the networks switched instantly to the White House, where Johnson calmly predicted a quiet convention.[42]

President Nixon likewise got television time whenever he wanted it: on thirty-two occasions in five-and-a-half years, during which he reached audiences as large as 70 million people. After each, despite a rising tide of antiwar sentiment, support for his Vietnam policy soared. But Nixon made a grave mistake in dealing with television and the other news media. Convinced that they were hostile to his administration, he went on the attack (mainly through Agnew), and the attack inspired counterattack. The attitude in some media quarters was that they had brought down Johnson, and the time had come to bring down another president.[43]

The networks had already begun to stiffen their policies by instituting "instant analysis," in which immediately after a presidential speech commentators discussed and dissected what had been said.

42. Berry, *Kennedy and the Media,* 66 (the quotation); Juan Williams, *Eyes on the Prize: America's Civil Rights Years, 1954–1965* (New York, 1987), 241–242; Foote, *Television Access and Political Power,* 34–39. Johnson tried to cope with the Mississippi Freedom Democratic party problem well before the convention; he and his aides began to consider it on May 14, 1964 (Harold F. Bass, Jr., "Presidential Party Leadership and Party Reform: Lyndon B. Johnson and the MFDP Controversy," *Presidential Studies Quarterly* 21 [1991]:88, 94).

43. Foote, *Television Access and Political Power,* 39–40; Barnouw, *Tube of Plenty,* 443ff. As for the fact that some in the media were determined to bring Nixon down, the then-president of CBS, Arthur Taylor, so informed me in a telephone conversation in December, 1972.

Usually these post orationems were rather insipid, but no matter how good or bad, fair or unfair, they undermined the effectiveness of the president's performance. As one of President Carter's aides complained, "If they say it was monstrous, many people think it was. If they say it was good, then it becomes good."[44]

In addition to that interference, networks became less generous in granting presidents air time. On two occasions, once with Ford and once with Carter, they flatly refused proffered speeches. After negotiations ABC agreed to carry Ford's; in Carter's case, the offer was changed into a demand, and the networks capitulated. Confrontations threatened at other times during the Carter administration, however, and the president's staff learned that automatic acquiescence was a thing of the past.[45]

Ronald Reagan restored equilibrium to the process, and he exploited television skillfully. A seasoned professional actor who understood television's needs at least as well as Harding had understood those of print journalists, he saw to it that aides arranged for air time through careful, mutually respectful, and usually indirect negotiations. As for the way he used televised speeches, he saw the main task in his role as head of state (as distinguished from head of government) as restoring the nation's confidence and self-respect after the traumas of Vietnam and Watergate. President Carter had perceived the same need but had exacerbated the problem by giving a television speech in 1979 in which he almost whiningly complained about a "crisis in confidence." Reagan, by contrast, exuded faith in himself and in his country, and the confidence was contagious.[46]

44. Foote, *Television Access and Political Power,* 141–143; Haynes Johnson, "Just How Will An Energy Program Affect Fred Doxsee?" *Washington Post,* April 21, 1977, A, 1; Johnson, *In the Absence of Power,* 110–115, 184–193; Harvey G. Zeidenstein, "News Media Perceptions of White House News Management," *Presidential Studies Quarterly* 14 (1984):391–398.

45. Robert Locander, "Carter and the Press: The First Two Years," *Presidential Studies Quarterly* 10 (1980):113; Foote, *Television Access and Political Power,* 59–68. In part the networks' policies reflected audience interest. Carter's third energy speech, for example, drew 80 million viewers, but his fourth drew only 30 million. His 1979 "crisis of confidence" speech, however, drew 100 million viewers (Mark J. Rozell, *The Press and the Carter Presidency* [Boulder, CO, 1989], 128, 131).

46. Foote, *Television Access and Political Power,* 79–84, 103–104. Rozell, *Press and*

Critics of the president scorned the "show" as just show, and there was an element of truth in the criticism. Press Secretary Larry Speakes had on his desk a sign that read, "You don't tell us how to stage the news, and we don't tell you how to cover it." Donald Regan remarked that "no government in history can have been more sensitive to the media, or more driven by the printed word and the television image." Yet, although Reagan's performances were acts, they were not merely acts. He was of a generation of type-cast movie stars (others included Gary Cooper, Cary Grant, and James Stewart) who always played essentially the same part. Reagan was the "nice guy"—honest, sincere, decent, enthusiastic, patriotic—and, like an eighteenth-century gentleman living up to his "character," he grew into the part until it was second nature to him, whether it had been his first nature or not. He was what he pretended to be. Similarly, understanding that posturing needed the reinforcement of action, he ordered the liberation of Grenada and the bombing of Libya, both because they had symbolic value and because he believed they were of practical utility.[47]

Carter, 131–140, 211, says that Carter's crisis-of-confidence speech was initially well received but that it came to be a political liability when, two days later, thirty-four top officials resigned and a cabinet shake-up occurred. Carter appeared to be "bleeding from a thousand self-inflicted wounds" (Joseph Kraft, "Self-Inflicted Wounds," *Washington Post,* July 29, 1979, D, 7), and he seemed to be a "trapped leader striking out in panic" (*U.S. News & World Report,* July 31, 1979, 14). "If they agree on little else, friends and critics share the view that Ronald Reagan is a 'skilled communicator,' probably the best to occupy the White House since Franklin D. Roosevelt" (Dom Bonafide, "Executive Report," *National Journal,* June 27, 1981, 1153). Mark Shields, *On the Campaign Trail* (Chapel Hill, NC, 1985), 97, captured the Reagan spirit: "Reagan is probably the best-liked American president in at least twenty years. One reason for this is that Ronald Reagan is a man publicly free of self-pity; he doesn't spend time telling us what a tough, thankless job he has and how lonely and burdensome are the duties of the chief executive." Peter Goldman, Tony Fuller et al., *The Quest for the Presidency 1984* (New York, 1985), 29, reported that Reagan's "command of the medium [TV] was instinctive and sure; no one since John Kennedy had played the *role* of president nearly so well." Bruce Buchanan, *The Citizen's Presidency: Standards of Choice and Judgment* (Washington, DC, 1987), 166, said Reagan "could do the one thing that had to be done—win the confidence and support of the electorate. And he could do it better than anybody else on the scene. This fact made experience and expertise secondary."

47. Mary E. Stuckey, *Playing the Game: The Presidential Rhetoric of Ronald Reagan*

As for press conferences, Reagan used them sparingly but effectively. He was as glib, articulate, witty, and charming in fielding questions as Kennedy had been, and if he did not always seem as well informed, he turned that to his advantage. By deflecting questions, by saying that the subject was under study, and by answering different questions from those asked, he capitalized on a generally prevailing uneasiness about the media by making a persistent interrogator appear hostile toward the president and disrespectful toward the presidency. ABC White House correspondent Sam Donaldson, for instance, won the admiration of Reagan-haters but the anger of everyone else by his bulldog tenacity in trying to pin Reagan down when Reagan refused to be pinned.⁴⁸

There were lessons to be learned from Reagan's relations with the media. Candidates from both parties realized that innovation was necessary if one wished to grab and hold the attention of a fickle viewing public. The use of the thirty-second sound bite was not a Reagan innovation, but he used it to great effect. It had been used dramatically in the 1964 campaign; with a daisy and a mushroom cloud Democrats created the fear that Barry Goldwater would bring about a nuclear holocaust. If novel enough the sound bite could be powerful: One clever bumper sticker, as it were, could be more persuasive than a thousand reasoned arguments.⁴⁹

(New York, 1990), 22; Regan, *For the Record,* 6, 276–277 (Regan uses the term "second nature"); David Mervin, *Ronald Reagan and the American Presidency* (London, 1990), 181–182; Mark A. Peterson, "The Presidency and Organized Interests: White House Patterns of Interest Group Liaison," *American Political Science Review* 86 (1992):612–625. Reagan "restored the idea that America can whip anybody (Grenada, the Olympics) and persuaded the public that he had retrieved American defense policy from one of 'weakness,' even 'unilateral disarmament,'" and Reagan "not only says that America is 'standing tall' but he stands tall as well" (Elizabeth Drew, "A Political Journal," *New Yorker,* Dec. 3, 1989, 107, 110).

48. Stuckey, *Playing the Game,* 18–19; Foote, *Television Access and Political Power,* 87–89; "Reagan Meets the Press," *USA Today,* Nov. 19, 1986, 1; Sam Donaldson, *Hold On, Mr. President!* (New York, 1987), 10.

49. Jamieson, *Packaging the Presidency,* 198–204; Daniel C. Hallin, "Sound Bite Democracy," *Wilson Quarterly* (Spring 1992):34–37. Stephen C. Wood, "Television's First Political Spot Ad Campaign: Eisenhower Answers America," *Presidential Studies*

George Bush learned enough as Reagan's vice-president to engineer a winning campaign for the presidency in 1988. He learned enough to win popularity for a time through foreign-policy theater in Panama and during the Gulf War. He did not, however, learn what for his presidency was a crucial lesson. He was, in the parlance of people inside the beltway, a pragmatist, meaning a person who had no guiding philosophy or ideology but who tried to manage the machinery of government well. But, to shift the metaphor, merely being competent at steering the ship of state became meaningless, for the passengers felt that the skipper knew not his destination.[50]

The Democratic party also learned. For years Democratic presidents and candidates were maladroit in the use of the media, but as a party the Democrats finally learned how to exploit television. The contrasts between the disastrous 1968 national convention and the perfectly staged 1992 convention tell the story. In 1968 Democratic mayor Richard J. Daley, the last of the old-time bosses, took especial pains to spruce up Chicago for the occasion, but he simply could not accommodate the reality that the convention was a television event. Tens of thousands of radical young whites converged on Chicago, where they provoked the constabulary into a bloody "police riot" in which young skulls were cracked on live television. In 1992 nothing "live" outside the convention hall was allowed to happen, and inside the convention every line, every action, every gesture was carefully choreographed and orchestrated. Bill Clinton, the candidate, was introduced as a new persona by a video biography made by one of television's most successful sitcom producers. The "new" Democratic party returned to the smiling hokum of yesteryear, of change and

---

Quarterly 20 (1990):265–283, details the importance of this first use on television of a spot-ad campaign. Jimmy Carter pioneered an innovative use of radio by having a presidential call-in program; on March 5, 1977, with Walter Cronkite as moderator, Carter answered the questions of forty-two callers out of 9.5 million calls nationwide (Locander, "Carter and the Press," *Presidential Studies Quarterly* 10:115; see also Rozell, *Carter and the Press,* 33, 38–40).

50. A good summary analysis of Bush's presidency, complete with many citations to the media coverage of it, is chapter 15 of Richard Rose, *The Postmodern President,* 2d ed. (Chatham, NJ, 1991). See also Novak, *Choosing Presidents,* 334–335.

unity, of the moderation of politicians of diverse views and aims coming together with masses of delegates—just everyday people—and convincing themselves and their candidates that they were at one in a righteous cause.[51]

The whole campaign had become an expanded media event. It started when the Dallas tycoon H. Ross Perot temporarily became the front-runner as a prospective third-party candidate by appearing on popular talk shows and using call-in telephone formats. He lost many supporters when he dropped out of the race in July, but his workers got him on the ballot in all fifty states anyway. He reentered at the eleventh hour and spent huge sums buying prime time on the major networks ("Infomercials," his folksy appearances were dubbed). By such means, he drew 19 percent of the popular vote—the largest percentage of any third-party candidate except Theodore Roosevelt.[52]

Bill Clinton, inspired by Perot's ingenuity, emulated his example, going so far as to play the saxophone on a late-night talk show. His efforts were abetted by the rise of television outlets other than the three major networks. The broadcast networks, facing budget cutbacks, reduced their coverage, but the cable channels did not. C-Span, for example, devoted a whopping 1,200 hours to the campaign. Most telling, perhaps even decisive, was the participation by MTV, whose audience was mainly young people. Voters between the ages of eighteen and twenty-nine, traditionally apathetic voters, were bombarded by a "Choose or Lose" MTV campaign, and 17 million of them—an all-time high—showed up at the polls. As a result, total voter turnout increased from about 50 percent in 1988 to 55 percent in 1992.[53]

51. Observations regarding the 1992 convention are drawn from viewing the joint PBS-NBC coverage and reading daily newspapers during July 1992. For 1968, see Norman Mailer, *Miami and the Siege of Chicago: An Informal History of the Republican and Democratic Conventions of 1968* (New York, 1968); *History of American Presidential Elections 1789–1968*, volume 4, ed. Arthur M. Schlesinger, Jr., Fred L. Israel, and William P. Hansen (New York, 1971), 3731–3739; Mike Royko, *Boss: Richard J. Daley of Chicago* (New York, 1971), 167–189; Bill Gleason, *Daley of Chicago: The Man, the Mayor, and the Limits of Conventional Politics* (New York, 1970), 289–351.

52. Howard Fineman, "People's Politics," *Newsweek,* April 20, 1992, 32–33; *New York Times,* Nov. 5, 1992, B, 4:4.

53. *New York Times,* Nov. 5, 1992, A, 16, and B, 4:1; Sharon D. Moshavi, "Elections Enter New Television Age," *Broadcasting* (Nov. 2, 1992):12–13.

As a result, too, Clinton won the election.[54] He could scarcely be said to have been given a mandate, for he received just 43 percent of the popular vote (less than a quarter of the registered voters), but he won handily in the electoral college. And he won because he was skillful at projecting an image.

54. After his inauguration, a lavish media-oriented occasion, Clinton continued to use television. On February 11, he held an electronic town meeting in Detroit to "build a constituency" for his economic program; journalists complained that the device was designed to circumvent them by avoiding news conferences (see R. W. Apple, Jr., "Clinton as Salesman: A Vox Populi Approach," *New York Times,* Feb. 11, 1993, A, 1:2, 15:6).

CHAPTER **16**

Afterthoughts

Any large and complex institution that involves the thinking and acting of thousands of people—and affects the lives of millions—necessarily houses internal tensions, frictions, and contradictions. The presidency is no exception. Some of the inner tensions and contradictions have been described in the foregoing chapters, but others, particularly characterizing the modern presidency, require a bit of elaboration.

The image-making presidency, for instance, together with the image-manipulating campaign for the office, contains self-defeating properties. The projection of appealing images is crucial to the process of getting elected, it is important if a president is to play the role of king-surrogate, and it is necessary if he is to have the credibility to persuade the myriad other players to implement his decisions. It may be said to be an indispensable tool of the presidential trade. And yet it consumes an inordinate amount of time and energy. More troubling, it tends (like a bureaucracy) to take on a life of its own. When that happens, it (again like a bureaucracy) ceases to be a useful means to effect desired ends and becomes a self-sustaining end unto itself.

Related to the problems arising from image making are those that arise from campaigning. Campaigns have become progressively longer, more grueling, and increasingly demeaning. Jimmy Carter announced his candidacy for the Democratic presidential nomination in December of 1974, almost two years before the election, and he campaigned nearly full-time until he was elected. When Carter announced, his chief rival for the nomination, Walter Mondale, had already logged 200,000 miles of travel, delivered hundreds of speeches, appeared on scores of radio and television shows, and slept night after night in motels. During that campaign and in each that followed, the dynamics of the contest required candidates to make promises they could not keep, curry favor with groups and individuals they disliked, and pander to all and sundry.

Nor is there time to rest (or leisure to take off the mask) between election day and inauguration day. The adoption of the Twentieth (Lame-Duck) Amendment in 1933 cut the time between election and inauguration from four months to about ten-and-a-half weeks—during which "transition" period the president-elect has to select appointees for approximately 3,000 important offices, or forty a day. President-elect Bill Clinton found it expedient to spend much of his time during that period in public-relations activity in an effort to build support for his proposed legislative agenda. In such circumstances, it is almost inevitable that many appointees are people the president does not know well, if at all, and that some of them will be incompetents or scoundrels for whose discreditable deeds the president will be held responsible.[1]

1. Thomas E. Cronin, *The State of the Presidency*, 2d ed. (Boston, 1980), 21, 164; Richard Rose, *The Postmodern President*, 2d ed. (Chatham, NJ, 1991), 146–147; *Chief of Staff: Twenty-Five Years of Managing the Presidency*, ed. Samuel Kernell and Samuel L. Popkin (Berkeley, CA, 1986), 183–189; Richard A. Watson and Norman C. Thomas, *The Politics of the Presidency*, 2d ed. (Washington, DC, 1988), 35–39; Jules Wilcover, *Marathon: The Pursuit of the Presidency, 1972–1976* (New York, 1977); Edwin Meese III, *With Reagan* (Washington, DC, 1992), 56–70; Stephen J. Wayne, *The Road to the White House 1992* (New York, 1992), 112–113, 117, 122; David Chagall, *The New Kingmakers* (New York, 1981), 71–72, 74, 77, 80–81, 98–99, 121; Martin Schram, *Running for President 1976: The Carter Campaign* (New York, 1977); Rosalynn Carter, *First Lady from Plains* (Boston, 1989), 112–135, 140, 152. Harry S Truman, *Memoirs by Harry S. Truman*, 2 vols. (Garden City, NY, 1956), 2:508, wrote, as did other presidents, "It is a terrible handicap for a new President to step into office . . . without adequate briefing. I thought it was an omission in our political tradition that a

Inasmuch as it can be assumed that aspirants to the presidency have a fairly good idea of what they are letting themselves in for, it seems legitimate to ask why they do it. What kind of people are willing to enter the race? And what kind of people have the colossal effrontery to suppose that they deserve the honor or have the ability to be president of the United States?

These questions have been investigated by several political scientists, but before considering what they have to say, it may be helpful to take a general view of the subject and to begin with an eighteenth-century model of human behavior. John Adams, who was far more gifted as a scholar and a political theorist than as a president, built upon the philosophical writings of David Hume and Adam Smith to formulate a system of ideas that is highly indicative. Because men are social animals, Adams wrote, nature has endowed them "with passions, appetites, and propensities, . . . calculated both for their individual enjoyment, and to render them useful to each other in their social connections." Among these the most potent was "the *passion for distinction*. A desire to be observed, considered, esteemed, praised, beloved, and admired by his fellows, is one of the earliest, as well as keenest dispositions discovered in the heart of man." All other cravings, whether for "riches, honors, every thing," derive not from the pleasure those things afford of themselves but from "the attention they command." Moreover, the desire moves people of all ranks and walks of life and in every arena: "In a city or a village, little employments and trifling distinctions are contended for with equal eagerness, as honors and offices in commonwealths and kingdoms."[2]

Professional politicians—or those individuals euphemistically referred to as "public servants"—are driven by Adams's "passion for

retiring President did not make it his business to facilitate the transfer of government." Regarding the lack of time to make good appointments, John F. Kennedy said, "I must make the appointments now [though] a year hence I will know who I really want to appoint" (quoted by R. Gordon Hoxie, "Democracy in Transition," *Presidential Studies Quarterly* 23 [1993]:32).

2. "Discourses on Davila," in *The Works of John Adams,* ed. Charles Francis Adams, 10 vols. (Freeport, NY, 1969), 6:232, 235, 241. I am indebted to Bradley Thompson for calling my attention to Adams's views; in 1993 he completed a Ph.D. dissertation on Adams at Brown University.

distinction" to make careers out of running for and holding public office. The pool of prospective presidential aspirants is confined largely, though not quite exclusively, to such professionals. Of the twentieth-century presidents, only Wilson, Hoover, Eisenhower, and Reagan had attained any kind of distinction before entering politics, and only Eisenhower moved to the presidency without also attaining distinction in the political arena.

The pool, even among professional politicians, is limited by a number of considerations. One must hold a position that attracts national attention, which means mainly that of governor of a state, member of the House of Representatives or the Senate, or cabinet officer. Normally governors of large states are more visible than governors of small states, and senators are more visible than members of the House. Many politicians in these positions, whether because they know their limitations or simply because their passion for distinction has been sated (which Adams thought impossible), are content to remain where they are. Among others, seeking the presidency is undesirable because of what political scientists call the risk factor—unwillingness to jeopardize a comfortable position by aiming for a higher one. In 1960 Lyndon Johnson was permitted by a special act of the Texas legislature to run for the Senate and the vice-presidency at the same time so that if he lost the vice-presidency he could retain his seat in the Senate. Most senators, lacking that option, would not choose to run for the presidency in a year in which they are up for reelection to the Senate; Barry Goldwater did in 1964, turning down an offer by Arizona to accord him the favor that Texas had given Johnson, and he lost his Senate seat. Another consideration is the matter of age. Apart from Ronald Reagan, who was an exceptional case, it is generally believed that the upper limit for a candidate is around sixty or sixty-five and that the lower limit (though the Constitution sets it at age thirty-five) is around forty-five. That gives politicians perhaps three or four elections in which to make a bid—fewer if the incumbent president is of one's own party and is up for reelection.[3]

3. Paul R. Abramson, John H. Aldrich, and David W. Rohde, "Progressive Ambition among United States Senators: 1972–1988," *Journal of Politics* 49 (1987):3–35; Joseph A. Schlesinger, *Ambition and Politics: Political Careers in the United States*

Political scientists have conducted fairly thorough studies of just which people actually have made the run. In an article published in 1987, three scholars found that in the presidential campaigns of 1972, 1976, 1980, and 1984 a total of thirty-five major Democratic candidates and thirteen major Republican candidates sought their party's nomination. Of these, seven were incumbents in the House of Representatives (only one such incumbent, Garfield, has ever been elected president). Seventeen senators sought nomination, along with five state governors and twelve former congressmen or governors. (Senators not facing reelection were twice as likely to run as those who were up for reelection.) In one respect, a historic trend has been reversed in recent years. Between 1840 and 1956, no sitting vice president received a major-party nomination; in the eight elections beginning in 1960, three vice-presidents received nominations though only one was elected. Meanwhile, four governors or former governors were nominated, and three were elected.[4]

Overwhelmingly, those who have sought the office in modern times have, like Andrew Jackson, craved merely to be president, not to do anything in particular if they became president. Conspicuous exceptions were Barry Goldwater, Hubert Humphrey, George McGovern, and Ronald Reagan. Some political scientists regard such exceptions as dangerous; in the cases of three of the four, the voters apparently agreed.

———— No matter how extensive an incoming president's experiences in government have been, he is always surprised to learn what holding the office is really like. His whole existence is transformed, and the new circumstances tend to make him feel like a king—or a god. He no longer has a name: Friends of a lifetime address him

---

(Chicago, 1966), 1–21. In his pioneering work, Schlesinger insists that ambition motivates all politicians but distinguishes three types: *discrete,* in which a politician seeks a specific office on a one-time basis; *static,* in which a politician seeks to make a career in a single office; and *progressive,* in which a politician is continuously seeking a higher office.

4. Abramson, Aldrich, and Rohde, "Progressive Ambition among United States Senators," *Journal of Politics* 49:4–5, 7–10, 31–32.

deferentially as "Mr. President." He is surrounded night and day by sycophants whose function is to satisfy his every physical need and cater to his whims. He finds himself using the royal we instead of the mortal I. He has at his disposal an awesome array of technological gadgetry. All these circumstances, together with having command of the most potent implements of individual and mass destruction the world has known, work to give the president an exaggerated sense of power. (Lyndon Johnson once gave a speech at an air force base, after which he started toward the presidential plane for the flight back to Washington. A soldier in the official escort, noting that Johnson had made a wrong turn, said hesitantly, "Sir . . . Mr. President . . . *your* plane is over there on the *other* side, sir." Johnson replied slowly, for emphasis, "Son, I want to tell you something—just so you never forget. . . . *All* of them—those over here *and* those over there—are *my* planes.")[5]

The exalted sense of self intensifies the utter loneliness of the job. It is lonely because of its responsibilities. A president can surround himself with countless advisers, wise or foolish, but it is the president alone who must decide what to do and who must live with the consequences. Living with the consequences is not always comfortable, and when it is not, the president must lie to himself through a process of sublimation. For example, every modern president sends young men and women to their deaths on foreign soil. To look at military action in that naked light is unbearable, so the president tells himself that they died in noble sacrifice for their country or the cause of freedom. And yet, heavy as the burden is, no president wants to share the decision-making authority. It has been suggested from time to time that the president could reduce the load and possibly avoid mistakes by keeping a nay-sayer on the premises. When a staff member so suggested to Harry Truman, saying that it might be a good

5. Hamilton Jordan, *Crisis* (New York, 1982), 371–372; Emmet John Hughes, *The Living Presidency* (New York, 1973), 17; Robert E. Denton, Jr., "On 'Becoming' President of the United States: The Interaction of the Office with the Office Holder," *Presidential Studies Quarterly* 13 (1983): 367–382. George Reedy's description of what becoming president is like, *The Twilight of the Presidency* (New York, 1970), chaps. 2 and 3, is excellent. By and large, works by former White House aides are good sources of information on the subject. Presidents, in their memoirs, are less helpful.

idea even if the person lasted only six months, the president snorted, "Six *months?* I wouldn't have him around six *minutes.*"[6]

The conduct of foreign relations is an especially heavy burden. The psychological costs of the Vietnamese war to Johnson and Nixon and of the Iranian hostage crisis to Carter were incalculable, and there is a heavier responsibility that presidents must bear—that of the possible use of nuclear weapons. The effects of the threat of nuclear holocaust upon ordinary people have doubtless been greatly overrated, but the effect on presidents is powerful, for the bomb is literally ever with them. In 1961 President Kennedy obtained an estimate of the minimum number of American lives that would be lost in an atomic war, and he was horrified to learn that, even if the United States launched a successful preemptive first strike, it would sustain 2–15 million casualties. Since the deployment of ICBMs, every president has had in his possession what is known in White House circles as "the football"—the codes to confirm that the president is ordering the launching of nuclear weapons. As President Reagan recalled, "when he was inaugurated, he took on the largest responsibility of his life—'of any human being's life': 'The plastic-coated card, which I carried in a small pocket of my coat,'" that would unleash nuclear weapons.[7]

Not long after the swearing-in, the president also realizes, with a

6. Reedy, *Twilight of the Presidency,* 20–21; George E. Reedy, "On the Isolation of Presidents," in *The Presidency Reappraised,* ed. Rexford G. Tugwell and Thomas E. Cronin (New York, 1974), 119–132; Hughes, *Living Presidency,* 143; Joseph E. Kallenbach, *The American Chief Executive* (New York, 1966), 444–445; Kernell and Popkin, eds., *Chief of Staff,* 27–30, 43. Harding told William Allen White, "This is a hell of a job. I have no trouble with my enemies. . . . But my damn friends, my God-damn friends, White, they're the ones that keep me walking the floor nights" (*The Autobiography of William Allen White* [New York, 1946], 619).

7. In 1961 the Joint Chiefs estimated that worldwide a nuclear war would cause 360 to 525 million deaths; John Prados, *The Soviet Estimate: U.S. Intelligence Analysis and Russian Military Strength* (New York, 1982), 120. The estimate of American loss is in Michael R. Beschloss, *The Crisis Years: Kennedy and Khrushchev, 1960–1963* (New York, 1991), 310, and for the cost to Kennedy, see 11, 468–469, and passim. Donald T. Regan, *For the Record* (New York, 1988), 11, 184; Meese, *With Reagan,* 187. For the cost of the hostage crisis, see Carter, *First Lady from Plains,* 319–352, and Jordan, *Crisis,* 365ff. See also Alonzo L. Hamby, "An American Democrat: A Reevaluation of the Personality of Harry S. Truman," *Political Science Quarterly* 106 (1991):49–51.

sinking feeling, that the monarchical perquisites available mask a harsh reality: the vast gap between expectations and the capacity to deliver. For instance, the president is expected to "handle" the economy, which includes restraining inflation, providing full employment, and ensuring economic growth, and since the passage of the Employment Act of 1946, he has been charged by law to do those things. He is supplied with a council of economic advisers to tell him how, but he is given none of the tools to implement policy, if indeed policy is capable of altering economic reality in desired directions. The president cannot raise or lower taxes, cannot hire or fire people, cannot reward productivity or punish inefficiency, and has but an indirect voice in setting interest rates and expanding or contracting the money supply. Moreover, the emergence of a global economy has made the American economy subject to gusts and squalls from the world over, quite beyond anyone's control. The frustrations that arise from being held totally responsible for situations that one is helpless to manage are scarcely calculated to strengthen the presidential psyche.[8]

Beyond such constraints, what presidents do in office, or try to do, is powerfully influenced by a unique conception of history. The president lives in a museum of the history of the presidency. When walking along the halls of the White House, the president is constantly reminded that Jefferson walked the same halls as he waited for news of negotiations with Napoleon, that Lincoln walked them when waiting for news from Antietam. When dining, the president never en-

8. Cronin, *State of the Presidency,* 91–92, 150–151, 180; Richard Rose, *Managing Presidential Objectives* (New York, 1976), 147, 151, 153–154, 167; Watson and Thomas, *Politics of the Presidency,* 405, 416–426; Theodore J. Lowi, *The Personal President* (Ithaca, NY, 1985), 51–58, 67; Jeffrey Leigh Sedgwick, "Tenure in Office and the President's Role as Chief Executive," in *Restoring the Presidency: Reconsidering the Twenty-Second Amendment* (Washington, DC, 1990), 86, 87–89; Mel Elfin, "Shrinking the Oval Office," *U.S. News & World Report,* Dec. 7, 1987, 26, 29; Peter Goldman, "The Presidency: Can Anyone Do the Job?" *Newsweek,* Feb. 26, 1981, 37. Presidents Truman and Nixon drew on assorted emergency powers to institute price controls, but those are effective only in warping the forces of market pressures. In 1992 none of the presidential candidates showed much awareness that the relatively moderate economic recession in the United States was part of a worldwide phenomenon that was considerably more severe than the problems at home.

tirely escapes the realization that he is using the same silver that Madison and both Roosevelts used. The president understands that he is a member of a mystical fraternity, representing an unbroken chain of history and mythology, and knows that far into the future presidents will be aware that he was a link in that chain, and cannot avoid wondering what his place will be in their memory and in the nation's memory. (When Richard Nixon was about to leave the White House, he was reported to have wandered around, talking to portraits of presidents past. Detractors heralded that as evidence that he had lost his mind, but as George Reedy remarked, "To anyone who has had the opportunity to observe a president at close range, it is perfectly normal conduct." One imagines that Nixon received special solace from talking to Lincoln and Truman, whom contemporaries judged harshly but who fared rather well in the judgment of history.)[9]

Passing judgment on past presidents is a pursuit that provides fascination for many Americans. Ranking the presidents was pioneered by Arthur Schlesinger, Sr., who in 1948 solicited the opinions of fifty-five "experts" (mostly professional historians) and published the results in *Life* magazine. In 1962 he repeated the survey, broadening the group of experts to seventy-five and publishing the results in the *New York Times Magazine*. The Schlesinger polls were popularly accepted as representing the common verdict of historians though quite a number of historians themselves questioned their validity. In 1966 Thomas A. Bailey criticized the polls in a book, and subsequent surveys were published by other persons and groups in 1977, 1981, 1982, and 1983—the last being a lengthy questionnaire to which 846

9. Alexander Haig, who "served seven presidents, four at very close range," described "their overall concern about their place in history" (Kernell and Popkin, eds., *Chief of Staff*, 63). See also Reedy, *Twilight of the Presidency*, 21; Hughes, *Living Presidency*, 107–115; Richard Nixon, *In The Arena: A Memoir of Victory, Defeat, and Renewal* (New York, 1990), 15–18, 26–27. For Truman and history, see Herbert Lee Williams, *The Newspaperman's President: Harry S Truman* (Chicago, 1984), 11–13, 100–102; Merle Miller, *Plain Speaking: An Oral Biography of Harry S. Truman* (New York, 1974), 24–31, 35–36, 63–64, 347–356. LBJ once said, "I walk through the White House and I think about Lincoln walking through the same corridors. . . . I may not be so bad off after all" (Hugh Sidey, "The Presidency: Some pages not in L.B.J.'s book," *Life*, Nov. 5, 1971, 4).

professional historians responded. None of the surveys reveals much about the criteria for deeming presidents "great" or a "failure," but the results have been fairly consistent. Lincoln, Washington, and Franklin Roosevelt head all the lists; Jefferson, Wilson, Jackson, Truman, and Theodore Roosevelt are in the next rank; and Andrew Johnson, Buchanan, Nixon, Grant, and Harding bring up the rear.[10]

——— Among other recent developments in the presidency has been the severing of contact with ordinary humans; as the responsibilities of the president have grown, the isolation from the people has grown in lockstep. Until the major parties declined into being little more than the means of perpetuating the ritual system of elections, the old-fashioned political bosses had the ear of the president. The likes of Chicago's Richard Daley, Ohio's Mike DiSalle, and New Jersey's Frank Hague knew their constituents' hopes and dreams and fears, and until the early sixties they could and did see to it, directly or indirectly, that the president remained in touch with what they knew. Similarly, until approximately the same time, presidents actually saw and talked with real people. In November of 1946, as was his wont, Harry Truman went home to Independence, Missouri, to vote in the congressional elections. Two days later he boarded a train alone to return to Washington. When he arrived in Washington, the only person waiting at the station to meet him was Undersecretary of State Dean Acheson; having nothing else to do, the two men caught a taxicab to the empty White House for a nightcap. By the mid-sixties, assassination, mass demonstrations, riots, and violent crime had made casual contact too perilous to tolerate. Subsequent presidents, when they traveled through a city, were driven in what amounted to army tanks disguised as limousines. When the first such vehicle was completed, the builders learned that it cut off all sounds from outside, and they added electronic equipment to pipe in the crowd

10. See Robert K. Murray and Tim H. Blessing, "The Presidential Performance Study," *Journal of American History* 70 (1983):535–555. President Nixon's stock has risen sharply during the past few years, and it is my personal belief that some day he will be reckoned among the "great" or "near great" presidents—depending upon the course history takes in the future.

sounds; metaphorically, the same thing happened to the presidency in its relations with ordinary human beings.[11]

Cut off from direct communication with the world outside Washington, the president depends for information on data received through personal or technological filters. In one area, foreign affairs, the quantity and scope of information available is stupefying. Through electronic satellite surveillance, for instance, the president can know how many people ate at a given picnic table in Moscow yesterday or what is happening in a terrorist training camp in Libya. The dangers in the sources are mainly two: information overload, which can obscure larger trends and bury significant matters under a mountain of trivia, and excessive reliance on computerized wizardry, which can result in a failure to take into account what the satellites cannot see. Both dangers led to serious policy miscalculations during the Carter and Bush administrations.[12]

11. Reedy, *Twilight of the Presidency,* 14–15, 89–91; Roy Jenkins, *Truman* (London, 1986), 92–93; Dayton David McKean, *The Boss: The Hague Machine in Action* (Boston, 1940), 101–103; Thomas F. X. Smith, *The Powerticians* (Secaucus, NJ, 1982), 11–12, 114–115, 184, 210–211; Bruce M. Stave, "The New Deal, No Last Hurrah," in *Urban Bosses, Machines, and Progressive Reformers,* ed. Bruce M. Stave and Sondra Astor Stave (Malabar, FL, 1984), 205–211; John M. Allswang, "The Best of Machines? The Last of Machines?" ibid., 216–231; Lyle W. Dorsett, *Franklin D. Roosevelt and the City Bosses* (Port Washington, NY, 1977); Michael Dorman, *The Secret Service Story* (New York, 1967), 252–256; Frederick M. Kaiser, "Presidential Assassinations and Assaults: Characteristics and Impact on Protective Procedures," *Presidential Studies Quarterly* 11 (1981):545–558. The severing of contact is vividly illustrated by LBJ's plaintive question, "How could these people be so ungrateful to me after I have given them so much?" (Doris Kearns, *Lyndon Johnson and the American Dream* [New York, 1976], 356). Hughes, *Living Presidency,* 121, reports a conversation in which Johnson complained to a friend that he had done many great things but heard only complaints about Vietnam. His friend replied, "What do you think would be the place in history of Abraham Lincoln if he had been right and wise about everything— *except* the Civil War?" President Clinton tried to maintain one-to-one contact with ordinary Americans; he presented his four-city electronic forum as "an effort to keep in touch with the voters, saying that after only three weeks in office he realized 'how easy it is for a President to get out of touch'" (*New York Times,* Feb. 11, 1993, A, 15:1).

12. Kernell and Popkin, eds., *Chief of Staff,* 58–60 (comments of H. R. Haldeman and Alexander Haig on the technology available to presidents). Presidents find it more or less necessary to act upon their intelligence even if in their hearts they do not

In regard to what is going on in the United States, everything the president learns is warped by passage through the sources with which he is in contact—the principal ones being public opinion polls, the mass media, congressmen and administrators, and his staff. Public opinion polls have come a long way since 1936, when a *Literary Digest* poll predicted that Gov. Alfred Landon of Kansas would defeat Franklin Roosevelt in the presidential election, but they are close to worthless for learning what people are thinking. The American people are, according to the polls, notoriously fickle, and they have short attention spans; they hold few opinions for very long and are concerned with few issues throughout an extended period. They also contradict themselves, as in 1959, eight years after the adoption of the Twenty-second Amendment—which limited presidents to two terms—when almost two-thirds of those polled said that they approved the amendment, yet 58 percent of the same people said they wanted to elect Eisenhower for a third term. Polls taken by the American Institute of Public Opinion since the 1930s have reflected two unchanging popular attitudes toward the presidency, namely that the people want strong, activist presidents and that they distrust and fear strong, activist presidents. Some presidents, notoriously Lyndon Johnson, followed approval ratings feverishly, but the only certainty about the ratings is that they normally rise when the president makes an unmistakable blunder in his handling of foreign relations. And whatever the polls signify, they cannot adequately guide a president.[13]

---

believe it. Harry Truman did not believe the Soviet Union had either the atomic bomb or the hydrogen bomb, for instance. He said, "After all, they're Russians. They're basically peasants. They're not Americans. They can't hope to achieve the technology we've achieved." But he admitted that the United States had to assume that the Soviets did have the bomb (Richard E. Neustadt, "Truman in Action: A Retrospect," in *Modern Presidents and the Presidency,* ed. Marc Landy [Lexington, MA, 1985], 4).

13. Hughes, *Living Presidency,* 70, 72; Betty Houchin Winfield, *FDR and the News Media* (Urbana, IL, 1990), 216–218; *The President and The Public,* ed. Doris A. Graber (Philadelphia, 1982), 1–14; Lowi, *Personal President,* 15–16; George C. Edwards III, *The Public Presidency: The Pursuit of Popular Support* (New York, 1983), 247; Elmer E. Cornwell, Jr., *Presidential Leadership of Public Opinion* (Bloomington, IN, 1965), 247–250; Charles W. Smith, Jr., "Measurement of Voter Attitude," in *The Annals of the*

Then there are the mass news media, which means particularly print journalism, for the president and the staff watch television newscasts primarily to see how the news they have manufactured that day is playing. Most presidents read newspapers and newsmagazines avidly—Eisenhower was an exception, deliberately giving them a miss—but their reading is usually confined to the establishment publications, the *Washington Post,* the *New York Times, Time* magazine, *Newsweek,* and *U.S. News & World Report.* A shortcoming in relying on these sources is that the writers for them tend to be inbred and to see matters from the same limited perspectives. (A well-known establishment film critic still maintained twenty years after the fact that George McGovern could not have lost the 1972 election, "Nixon must have stolen it, because everybody I know voted for McGovern.") Another drawback is that journalists, herd-like, seize upon one issue or another as vital, and to the extent that presidents accept their judgments, they forfeit a valuable asset, that of setting the agenda for public debate and legislation.[14]

Yet another weakness in relying on the print media is that, despite

American Academy of Political and Social Science, ed. Thorsten Sellin and James C. Charlesworth (Philadelphia, 1952), 148–155; George F. Will, *Restoration: Congress, Term Limits and the Recovery of Deliberative Democracy* (New York, 1992), 116, 120, 124–127, 133, 181; Bruce E. Altschuler, *LBJ and the Polls* (Gainesville, FL, 1990), xi–xvii, 75–109.

14. Hughes, *Living Presidency,* 157; James W. Ceaser, "The Rhetorical Presidency Revisited," in Landy, ed., *Modern Presidents and the Presidency,* 27–31; Reedy, *Twilight of the Presidency,* 107–125; Mark J. Rozell, *The Press and the Carter Presidency* (Boulder, CO, 1989), passim; Graber, ed., *President and Public,* 11–12; Joseph C. Spear, *Presidents and the Press* (Cambridge, MA, 1984), passim; William C. Spragens, *The Presidency and the Mass Media in the Age of Television* (Washington, DC, 1979), 1–36, 246–337; Daniel P. Moynihan, "The Presidency and the Press," *Commentary* (March 1971):41–52; Nixon, *In the Arena,* 136–139; Jody Powell, *The Other Side of the Story* (New York, 1984), passim; Michael Baruch Grossman and Martha Joynt Kumar, *Portraying the President: The White House and the News Media* (Baltimore, 1981), 19–130; John Herbers, "The Press and the Press Corps," *New York Times Magazine,* May 9, 1982, 45–46, 74–75, 96–98; Mark J. Rozell, *The Press and the Ford Presidency* (Ann Arbor, MI, 1992), 217–233; J. Anthony Lukas, "The White House Press 'Club'," *New York Times Magazine,* May 15, 1977, 22, 64–68, 70–72; Midge Decter, "Ronald Reagan and the Culture War," *Commentary* (March 1991):28.

the time and energy presidents invest in manipulating news and despite their awareness of the frequency with which events are misreported, they tend to believe what they read unless they know for a certainty it is false. As Bill Moyers said, "The real problem with Lyndon Johnson is that *he* probably believes about ninety percent of what he reads or *hears*. So he finds it perfectly natural to expect the *people* to believe about 90% of what he *says*."[15]

That leaves people in government as a main source of information for the president. Since the president is, after all, supposed to be running the government, the people in it should know more about it than the people outside it and should function as a good conduit. With due allowance for the reality that nearly everyone who sees the president has an axe to grind, governmental sources can usually supply the president more or less candidly with necessary information. The quality of the information varies according to the way it is presented, small groups communicating most effectively. Maximizing the president's time by getting the right groups into the Oval Office is one of the jobs of the chief of staff. Cabinet meetings, once an arena of give-and-take in which the president could learn from different perspectives, have grown too unwieldy to be of use and have degenerated into ceremonial photo-ops.[16]

15. Hughes, *Living Presidency,* 119; William L. Rivers, *The Opinion-Makers* (Boston, 1965), 15–19, 191, 192; Martin Linsky, *Impact: How the Press Affects Federal Policymaking* (New York, 1986), 87–118; Grossman and Kumar, *Portraying the President,* 311–322; Kernell and Popkin, eds., *Chief of Staff,* 84, 87. Williams, *Newspaperman's President: Truman,* 182, 193–194, 198, underscores the paradox; Truman advised Chester Bowles when he was running for reelection in 1950 to ignore the press because "the press has lost its influence due to the fact that it pays lying columnists to write editorials and slant the news in the headlines. . . . People just didn't put their trust in the press." And yet he was an avid newspaper reader. Williams says that his reading did not influence him (193) and calls to task Robert Allen and William Shannon, who charged that Truman responded in a "ready manner" to "forceful suggestions from the press." One finds it difficult, however, to believe that extensive reading produces no effect. Donald Regan said that Ronald Reagan was "an old-fashioned, small-town American who believes what he reads in the papers" (Regan, *For the Record,* 64).

16. Rose, *Postmodern President,* 175; Hughes, *Living Presidency,* 340, 344–345, 349, 366–367; R. Gordon Hoxie, "The Cabinet in the American Presidency, 1789–1984,"

The quality of the president's information depends on other variables as well. One negative is that the people who are allowed to talk to him tend to be trapped in the beltway mentality, to let the needs of government obscure or refract perceptions of the needs of the country being governed. Then, too, presidents differ in how much they want to know. Some, notably Roosevelt, Kennedy, and Johnson, wanted to know everything of consequence that was happening in government, and heads were likely to roll when they learned that something had been kept from them. In contrast, the Nixon White House strictly limited access to the president. Eisenhower took another approach; he wanted no datum until it had been thrashed out ("staffed out," in the White House jargon) and reduced to its essence, on the basis of which he made a decision.[17]

Since Eisenhower's time, the pattern of staff access to the president—and through the staff, the president's access to information—has been fairly constant. Six to ten staffers have regular access, and three or four (typically, the chief of staff, the national security ad-

---

Presidential Studies Quarterly 14 (1984):209–230; Cronin, *State of the Presidency,* 253–293; Rozell, *Press and Carter,* 216–219; Theodore C. Sorensen, "Presidential Advisers," in *The Presidential Advisory System,* ed. Thomas E. Cronin and Sanford D. Greenberg (New York, 1969), 3–10; Richard F. Fenno, "Presidential Cabinet and Advisory Politics," ibid., 25–28; Watson and Thomas, *Politics of the Presidency,* 288–293; Roger B. Porter, "Economic Advice to the President: From Eisenhower to Reagan," *Political Science Quarterly* 98 (1983):403–426. President-elect Kennedy said in 1961, "Just what the hell good does a cabinet *do,* anyway?" (Hughes, *Living Presidency,* 149). For access during the Bush administration, see James P. Pfiffner, "The President's Chief of Staff," *Presidential Studies Quarterly* 23(1993):92–94.

17. Kernell and Popkin, eds., *Chief of Staff,* 21–22, 39–40, 76, 78–80; Spragens, *Presidency and Mass Media,* 145–156; Erwin C. Hargrove, *Presidential Leadership* (New York, 1966), 70–73, 136–140, 149; James J. Best, "Who Talked to the President When? A Study of Lyndon B. Johnson," *Political Science Quarterly* 103 (1988):531–545; David M. Barrett, "Secrecy and Openness in Lyndon Johnson's White House: Political Style, Pluralism, and the Presidency," *Review of Politics* 54 (1992):72–111; Robert E. Denton, Jr., and Dan F. Hahn, *Presidential Communication: Description and Analysis* (New York, 1986), 105–124; Patrick Anderson, *The President's Men: White House Assistants of Franklin D. Roosevelt, Harry S Truman, Dwight D. Eisenhower, John F. Kennedy, and Lyndon B. Johnson* (New York, 1968); Raymond J. Saulnier, "On Advising the President," *Presidential Studies Quarterly* 15 (1988):583–588.

viser, and the counselor to the president) have the inside track. Like courtiers at Versailles under the reign of the Bourbons, some staffers serve their master faithfully, but most also conspire continuously to be nearest the throne. To that end, many staffers are willing to plant disinformation directly in the president's ear or indirectly by way of leaks to the news media.[18]

The problems attendant upon White House court politics are illustrated by the course of the Reagan presidency. The initial troika of advisers closest to the president did not include the national security adviser (Reagan had six during his eight years, and though they had ready access, none was of the inner circle). Instead, the three were counselor Edwin Meese, media manager Mike Deaver, and chief of staff James Baker. It soon became evident that these men and other top staffers were divided into two camps that Meese described as "Reaganauts," who shared the president's conservatism and his vision, and "pragmatists," who had little interest in policy but every interest in the power and perquisites of the established Washington order. Among those in the first group were Meese, national security adviser Richard Allen, and economic advisers Martin Anderson and William Niskanen. The second group included Baker, Deaver, Richard Darman, and David Stockman. Without the Reaganauts, the president, despite the strength of his convictions, might have lost

18. Rose, *Postmodern President,* 153–159; Kernell and Popkin, eds., *Chief of Staff,* viii–ix, 142–158; R. Gordon Hoxie, "Staffing the Ford and Carter Presidencies," *Presidential Studies Quarterly* 10 (1980):386–401; James P. Pfiffner, "White House Staff Versus the Cabinet: Contripetal and Contrifugal Roles," ibid., 16 (1986):666–690. On the reason for deliberate leaks, see Meese, *With Reagan,* 105–116, and Regan, *For the Record,* 103–104, 280–286. Spear, *Presidents and the Press,* 25–26, outlines Carter's extreme difficulty in controlling cabinet leaks; see also Joseph A. Califano, *Governing America* (New York, 1981), 417, and Jack Anderson, "Cabinet News Leaks Baffle Carter," *Washington Post,* April 13, 1978, E, 23:4. The problem of presidential information calls to mind Thomas Paine's attack on monarchy in *Common Sense:* "There is something exceedingly ridiculous in the composition of Monarchy; it first excludes a man from the means of information, yet empowers him to act in cases where the highest judgment is required. The state of a King shuts him from the World, yet the business of a king requires him to know it thoroughly." According to Richard Nixon, the problem of "information" is most serious and probably insoluble (conversation, Oct. 30, 1992, with the author).

sight of his goals, which in fact the pragmatists devoutly wished he would. To that end, the pragmatists tried to limit his contact with conservatives and went so far as to pilfer the president's copies of the conservative weekly, *Human Events.* The Reaganauts tried to offset the efforts of the pragmatists with equal vigor. And yet, even the Reaganauts recognized that the mix and the balance were needed; the pragmatists were necessary for implementation. As Ed Meese said, the "President was well served by such differences, since the mixture . . . melded together to form a highly functional team."[19]

———— Finally, we may consider the physical and psychological costs of the presidency to the incumbents. Woodrow Wilson, who was destroyed by the pressures of the office, once said, "Men of ordinary physique and discretion cannot be Presidents and live, if the strain be not somehow relieved. We shall be obliged to be picking our chief magistrate from among wise and prudent athletes—a small class." The observation is confirmed by reference to mortality rates. One of every five presidents has died in office, the average age at the time of death being fifty-seven. Almost as many died less than three years after they left office, their average age being sixty. Not counting the five former presidents who were still alive in 1993 (an unprecedentedly large number), the average longevity of presidents in the preceding century was sixty-four years, considerably less than the norm for white American males who survived to adulthood. The increased stress of the office is indicated by comparative figures: The presidents who served before the Civil War lived to an average age of seventy-three, those after the war to an average age of sixty-three, despite the enormous improvement in medical care.[20]

19. Meese, *With Reagan,* 81, 84, 102–105, quotation at 81. See also Michael K. Deaver with Mickey Herskowitz, *Behind the Scenes* (New York, 1987), 123–137; Laurence I. Barrett, "The Triumvirate," *Esquire* (July 1983):51–61; Hugh Sidey, "The Troika that Worked," *Time,* June 3, 1985, 22; Morton Kondracke, "Second-Term Shuffle," *New Republic,* Feb. 4, 1985, 10–12; Walter Shapiro, "The President's New Men," *Time,* April 6, 1987, 24; Daniel Seligman, "Look Out for the Ideolog!" *Fortune,* Dec. 21, 1987, 169–170.

20. Wilson as quoted by Hughes, *Living Presidency,* 168. Mortality data are my tabulations from conventional biographical sources. See also Homer F. Cunningham,

The costs are compounded by what has been called the lame-duck syndrome, which has affected almost all two-term presidents. Historically, presidents have tended in their first terms to concentrate on domestic affairs, and their legislative successes came in that term, usually during the honeymoon period. The reason was institutional. The president and the members of his party needed one another, for each could help in the other's reelection. But once the president was reelected, the relationship abruptly changed; neither was of any future political use to the other. The mutual estrangement was normally exacerbated by a peculiarity of American political history, namely, that when a president was reelected he almost always won by a bigger majority than he did the first time around. A considerable measure of arrogance began to mark his behavior, and he tended to indulge in overseas adventuring, in which his hands were less tied and he no longer had to deal with the members of Congress.[21]

The decline of the party system brought a virtual end to the president's "coattail" effect in his reelection, but the lame-duck syndrome persisted. And in the second term, the president became fair prey for every manner of vilification. Once the reality of lame-duck status penetrated the popular consciousness, press and politicians moved in

---

The Presidents' Last Years (Jefferson, NC, 1989); "A Man-Killing Job," *New York Times,* Aug. 5, 1923, E, 4:1 ("The phrase is President Harding's own"); Robert K. Murray, *The Politics of Normalcy: Governmental Theory and Practice in the Harding-Coolidge Era* (New York, 1973), 92–93, 95–96, 99–101; Robert E. Gilbert, *The Mortal Presidency: Illness and Anguish in the White House* (New York, 1992); Robert E. Gilbert, "Personality, Stress and Achievement: Keys to Presidential Longevity," *Presidential Studies Quarterly* 15 (1985):33–50; Milton Plesur, "The Health of Presidents," in Tugwell and Cronin, ed., *Presidency Reappraised,* 187–204.

21. Bill Moyers, *A World of Ideas* (New York, 1989), 111–118; Forrest McDonald, "A Mirror for Presidents," *Commentary* (Dec. 1976):34–41; George C. Edwards III, *Presidential Approval* (Baltimore, 1990), 117–130; Karen S. Johnson, "The Portrayal of Lame-duck Presidents by the National Print Media," *Presidential Studies Quarterly* 16 (1986):50–65. On the honeymoon effect, see Rose, *Postmodern President,* 137, 148–149. LBJ's assessment was "you've only got one year. No matter what your mandate is and vote, you've only got a year because in the second year, you will have done a lot of things that will make even people in your own party want to put distance between themselves and you" (Kernell and Popkin, eds., *Chief of Staff,* 96). In a second term the president does not even have the one-year honeymoon.

like hyenas gathering to devour a wounded lion. The troubles that presidents Lyndon Johnson, Nixon, and Reagan had during their last years in office were not exceptional; they were normal. The vicious attacks on Washington and Jefferson were mentioned in earlier chapters. During the last years of Andrew Jackson's and Theodore Roosevelt's presidencies the Senate refused to accept any communications from the White House. Abraham Lincoln, had he not been assassinated, might have suffered the fate of Andrew Johnson. Woodrow Wilson was destroyed at the end. Harry Truman's last years were plagued by scandals and by McCarthyism. Lyndon Johnson also suffered greatly; he would lie "in bed early in the morning in the darkened room with the covers pulled almost up to his chin, and the window shades pulled down, reluctant to get out of bed. He would say, 'I can't read the *Washington Post* this morning,' or 'I read the bulldog edition last night, and it kept me awake all night.' He suffered deep depression because of what was written about him."[22]

Franklin Roosevelt avoided the syndrome by continuing to run for office and by never being a lame duck, but he illustrates dramatically the effects of the presidency on a person. In 1943 David Brinkley attended his first presidential press conference and was appalled at what he saw. Instead of the president he had seen in pictures a thousand times, he saw a man whose "face was more gray than pink, his hands shook, his eyes were hazy and wandering, his neck drooped in stringy, sagging folds accentuated by a shirt collar that must have fit at one time but now was two or three sizes too large." He was dying, and by early 1944 he knew it. He was diagnosed as having gallstones,

22. Moyers, *World of Ideas,* 115–116. On Wilson's illness, see Kenneth R. Crispell and Carlos F. Gomez, *Hidden Illness in the White House* (Durham, NC, 1988), 13–74. For the vilification of Lincoln, see David Cushman Coyle, *Ordeal of the Presidency* (Washington, DC, 1960), 155–208, and for other presidents through FDR, passim; Cunningham, *Presidents' Last Years,* 111–122, 198–209; Williams, *Newspaperman's President: Truman,* 184–185; Lewis L. Gould, *The Presidency of Theodore Roosevelt* (Lawrence, KS, 1991), 144, 276–277. Reagan was an exception to the pattern, for although he was strongly attacked during his second term and lost his congressional links, he left office with a higher approval rating than he had had when he entered office; such was the force of his personality. David Morgan, "The peeling of Teflon: Ronald Reagan and the mass media," in *The Reagan years,* ed. Joseph Hogan (Manchester, Eng., 1990), 76–91; Edwards, *Presidential Approval,* 169, 175–179.

a badly enlarged heart, hypertension, "cardiac failure in the left ventricle," and acute bronchitis. He was growing deaf, he suffered lapses in memory and concentration, and his mind was failing. Such was the toll taken by twelve years in the White House; yet the hold of presidential power so gripped Roosevelt that he had his physician announce that he was "in as good condition as a man of 62 could be. . . . The canards about the President's health are below the belt." He ran for and won a fourth term, dying three months after it began.[23]

Other presidents have attested abundantly to the high personal cost of the office. Herbert Hoover called the office "a compound hell." Harry Truman referred to the White House as his prison and wrote in his *Memoirs* that "the pressures and the complexities of the presidency have grown to a state where they are almost too much for one man to endure." John F. Kennedy said, "If they want this job, they can have it—it's no great joy to me." Jimmy Carter said to Hamilton Jordan, "1980 was pure hell—the Kennedy challenge, Afghanistan, having to put the SALT Treaty on the shelf, the recession, Ronald Reagan, and the hostages . . . always the hostages! It was one crisis after another." Jordan described what the office had done to Carter's physical appearance: "The boyish look of his early forties had disappeared. The formerly sandy hair was gray, and wrinkles were creeping across his face." Modern presidents, as they neared the end of their terms, could well appreciate the view expressed by Thomas Jefferson in 1809: "Five more weeks will relieve me from a drudgery to which I am no longer equal."[24]

23. David Brinkley, *Washington Goes to War* (New York, 1988), 252, 260–261; Crispell and Gomez, *Hidden Illness,* 121–159; Winfield, *FDR and the Media,* 204; Cunningham, *Presidents' Last Years,* 241–251; Robert H. Ferrell, *Ill-Advised: Presidential Health and Public Trust* (Columbia, MO, 1992).

24. Shortly after he was elected president, Grover Cleveland wrote to a friend, "I look upon the four years next to come as a dreadful self-inflicted penance for the good of my country" (*Letters of Grover Cleveland, 1850–1908,* ed. Allan Nevins [Boston, 1933], 48). Hughes, *Living Presidency,* 167–168; Truman, *Memoirs,* 2:508; Sorensen, *Kennedy,* 702–703; James N. Giglio, *The Presidency of John F. Kennedy* (Lawrence, KS, 1991), 258–260, 263–265; Jordan, *Crisis,* 7, 417; Jefferson to Monroe, Jan. 28, 1809, in *Thomas Jefferson: Writings,* ed. Merrill D. Peterson (New York, 1984), 1198; Kallenbach, *American Chief Executive,* 266; Coyle, *Ordeal of the Presidency,* pas-

In 1937 Louis Brownlow began the report on reform of the federal administrative machinery with a once-famous statement: "The president needs help." By 1992 what the president needed was not help but relief—relief from the pressures of the office, relief from the demands on his time, relief from the impossible tasks that people expected and required. On February 1, 1993, a political cartoon suggested a solution to the new president. The first panel has a voice speaking from the White House saying, "Americans have high expectations of us. . . ." The next reads, "So we need to get right to work!" It continues, "Our first order of business: lowering expectations." But no lowering of expectations or demands appeared to be on the horizon.[25]

———— Clearly the presidency has become a troubled and somewhat troublesome institution. That judgment, however, is one-dimensional; it leaves out of account the historical and international perspectives. The office was created at a specific historical moment out of materials and in circumstances that cannot be replicated, and it has evolved along lines that are peculiarly American. Unlike other institutions of American devising—the system of divided sovereignty and federalism, for example—it is not suitable for export. Scores of republics have come into existence during the last two centuries, and no small number of them adopted constitutions that more or less copied the American Constitution, but none successfully adopted the American presidency.

The institution is unique, or nearly so. The norm among the governments of the Western world is some variant of the British system, in which the executive and legislative branches are effectively merged. Such parliamentary systems are usually far more efficient than the American government, and from time to time political scientists have advocated that the Constitution be revised in a European direction. (The most persistent and eloquent advocate has been James MacGregor Burns.) But the American system was designed to be

————

sim; Donald L. Horowitz, "Is the Presidency Failing?" *Public Interest* (Summer 1987): 3–27.

25. *Saint Petersburg Times'* syndicated cartoonist "Bennett," appeared in the *Tuscaloosa News,* Feb. 1, 1993, 10A.

inefficient, in the interest of the preservation of liberty, and for all its shortcomings, the system has done what it was designed to do. The pundit who coined the saying, "Thank goodness we don't get nearly as much government as we pay for," was showing wisdom as well as wit. Besides, there are reasons to believe that a parliamentary system would not work in America, for the efficacy of that form of government depends on party discipline, and party discipline has been a rarity on the national level.

The presidency is unique in another way than in being separated from the legislative branch, namely, in combining in one office the functions of head of state and chief executive magistrate. Some other nations have tried to combine the functions, but the norm among free governments has been to assign the head-of-state role to a generally powerless monarch or to a surrogate monarch in the form of an elected president and to place the executive power in a ministry whose members are at least nominally chosen by the head of state. The American combination has not always been a happy one. As we have seen, several presidents have been able to play one of the roles well but not the other, a few have been inept in both capacities, and fewer yet have been virtuosos in both. But presidential heroics once every generation or two are quite enough to satisfy the periodical popular itch for derring-do as well as to give government renewed impetus. And when presidents do not satisfy, it is always possible to turn them out. Three of the four presidents who served between Nixon and Clinton were rejected in their quests to be reelected; of the presidents who have been elected since 1836 only five have served two full consecutive terms.

Despite the frequency with which presidents have been rejected, the institution of the presidency has proved to be unparalleled in its stability. The United States has changed presidents according to the Constitution's rules for more than two centuries; on twenty-one occasions the change was accompanied by a change of parties, and though campaigns have aroused intense feelings and fears, every transition but one—that of 1860–1861—has been peaceful. Compared with the changes in regimes in other countries since 1789, the peaceful transfers of power from president to president in America have been models of order and sanity.

In sum, the presidency has been and remains a powerful force for ensuring domestic tranquillity among a diverse and sometimes bellicose people, and it has served well to protect the nation in a dangerous and often hostile world. Accordingly, I return to the assertion I made at the outset of this lengthy inquiry: Though the powers of the office have sometimes been grossly abused, though the presidency has become almost impossible to manage, and though the caliber of the people who have served as chief executive has declined erratically but persistently from the day George Washington left office, the presidency has been responsible for less harm and more good, in the nation and in the world, than perhaps any other secular institution in history.

Index